The Psychobiology of Aging:
Problems and Perspectives

The Psychobiology of Aging: Problems and Perspectives

Proceedings of the First Luxembourg Conference on the Psychobiology of Aging held in Walferdange, Luxembourg on May 24-25, 1979

Editor:

Donald G. Stein

Professor of Neurology and Psychology
Clark University and University of Massachusetts Medical Center
Worcester, Massachusetts, U.S.A.

ELSEVIER/NORTH-HOLLAND
New York • Oxford • Amsterdam

Published by:

Elsevier North Holland, Inc.
52 Vanderbilt Avenue, New York, New York 10017

Sole distributors outside U.S.A. and Canada:

Elsevier/North-Holland Biomedical Press
335 Jan van Galenstraat, P.O. Box 211
Amsterdam, The Netherlands

Library of Congress Cataloging in Publication Data

Luxembourg Conference on the Psychobiology of Aging,
1st, Walferdange, Luxembourg, 1979.
The psychobiology of aging.

Bibliography: p.
Includes index.
1. Aging—Congresses. 2. Aging—Psychological aspects—Congresses.
3. Psychobiology—Congresses. I. Stein, Donald G. II. Title. [DNLM:
1. Aging—Congresses. 2. Psychophysiology—In old age—Congresses.
W3 LU975 1st 1979p / WT104 L977 1979p]
QP86.L88 1979 155.67 80-17351
ISBN 0-444-00391-6

Manufactured in the United States of America

Contents

Preface

In May, 1979, an International conference on the Psychobiology of Aging was held at the Institute Pedagogique, Walferdange, Luxembourg. The conference was designed to bring together a relatively small number of American and European investigators who shared a common interest in brain functions, behavior and aging. The country setting of the Institute provided an ideal environment for informal exchange of ideas and plentiful discussion of the current issues. The participants were invited to present a description of his or her ongoing research or a critical review of the literature pertinent to the psychobiology of aging and these presentations are now represented in the present volume.

This book is divided into six sections that reflect the research interests of the conference participants, as well as my attempts to organize the material in a hierarchical fashion that represents both the molecular and molar approaches to the study of aging, behavior and brain functions. Thus, in accordance with the schema, the first section of the book presents several papers reviewing the behavioral genetics of aging as well as discussion of how one might consider and manipulate genetic variables in research on the psychobiology of aging.

The second section describes some of the structural and functional aspects of the aging Central Nervous System that have been studied with animal models. Of particular interest, perhaps, are the findings that early environmental manipulations can have long-term consequences for neuronal morphology and that the effects of brain lesions on behavior and neuronal organization are not necessarily the same for young and old subjects.

The third section of the book explores some of the nutritional and pharmacological factors that can affect aging and behavior in laboratory animals. Here, the participants describe their efforts to determine whether deficits in behavioral performance typically seen in aged subjects, can be attenuated by pharmacological manipulations or by dietary restrictions early in life. Current research concerning the relationship between aging, behavioral performance and neurotransmitter levels in the brain is also presented.

Section four provides a state-of-the-art look and some of the sensory and electrophysiological correlates of brain function in aging laboratory animals. Apparently, subtle changes in neuronal activity can be measured with unit recording techniques and these changes are reflected in altered patterns of learning as well as in response to sensory stimulation. Of particular interest is the research describing limbic system alterations in aging animals because some of the behavioral and morphological characteristics of the rats may reflect aspects of the dementias observed in aging humans.

The final two sections of the book reflect current approaches to the study of human aging and its pathology. The initial chapters describe some of the anatomical alterations seen in certain areas of the aging human brain. It is worth noting that both neuronal hypertrophy as well as atrophy may be characteristics of changing organization in the aging brain. The biochemistry of CNS aging has also received considerable attention, especially as it relates to the problem of senile dementia and related disorders. This area of research may be the most controversial since there seems to be little overall agreement as to the nature of the specific changes that occur in the brains of normal, aged, and demented individuals. The last chapter of section five provides a review of the literature on attempts to facilitate cognitive and mnemonic performance in demented individuals and there is a description of the problems one faces in attempting research in this area.

Finally, section six of this volume will describe some of the sensory and perceptual changes related to CNS activity in aging humans. Here, sensory reaction time and sensory evoked potentials are the dependent variables used to evaluate information-processing capacities in aged human subjects. Some of the methodological and theoretical problems associated with this type of research are also discussed.

Unfortunately, we were not able to end the 3-day conference by discovering a "cure" for aging or even how one might attenuate some of the more debilitating, age related alterations that the flesh is sometimes heir to. We did, however, learn a great deal from each other and did attempt to come to grips with some of the difficult problems that one faces in attempting to study aging *per se*. The role of the individual's past experience, nutritional history, health factors and social conditions can all play a determining role in biological aging; these points were emphasized throughout the conference whether or not the approach to the study of aging was at the molecular or molar level of analysis.

Perhaps the main advantage of the Luxembourg Conference was that it gave a small group of Americans and Europeans a chance to share their ideas in an open and relaxed manner. Indeed, one of the most important aspects of the meeting was that several individuals on both sides of the ocean joined forces for collaborative research projects. For this reason alone, I think, the conference could be considered worthwhile.

One of the most enjoyable aspects of our meetings was the quality of the facilities and the hospitality provided by the Government of Luxembourg and the Director of the Institute Pedagogique, Dr. Gaston Schaber. His kindness and that of his excellent staff will long be remembered by all of us who had the pleasure of spending those few days in the spring, in Walferdange. The conference itself would not have been possible but for a generous grant from Mr. Henry J. Leir who is interested in fostering international cooperation along a number of different educational and scientific dimensions. His kind support was supplemented by a grant from the National Institute on Aging, #1 R13 AG 01493-01 NSS, which provided travel funds for many of the American participants.

As editor and organizer of the conference, I was very fortunate in having an enthusiastic and productive group of colleagues and I believe that some of their enthusiasm is expressed in the quality of their final manuscripts. I am grateful to all of them for providing me with the opportunity to learn more about aging from their perspectives. Finally, I express my deep appreciation to Mrs. A. Bassett who once again provided the much needed secretarial support and understanding required for this meeting. And most of all, to Darel for her unswerving patience.

Worcester, Massachusetts
1980

Conference Participants

Dr. Gilbert S. Omenn
Associate Director for Human Resources, Veterans and Labor, Office of Management and Budget, Washington, D. C. 20503

Dr. Richard L. Sprott, Ph.D.
Staff Scientist, The Jackson Laboratory, Bar Harbor, Maine 04609

Dr. Alberto Oliverio
Consiglio Maxionale delle Ricerche, Laboratorio Di Psicobiologia e Psicofarmacologia, 00198 Roma, Italy

Dr. Sergio Algeri
Istituto Di Ricerche Farmacologiche, Mario Negri, 20157 Milano, Italy

Pr. A. Calas
Institut de Neurophysiologie, C.N.R.S., 31 chemin Joseph-Aiguier, 13274 Marseille Cedex 2, France

Dr. Albert William Klein
Department of Anatomy, Eastern Virginia Medical School, Norfolk, Virginia.

Dr. Elliott J. Mufson
Neurological Unit, Beth Israel Hospital, 330 Brookline Avenue, Boston, Massachusetts 02215

Dr. Wail A. Bengelloun
Maitre des Conferences, Departement de Biologie, Faculté des Sciences, Université Mohammed V, Rabat, Morocco

Dr. William B. Forbes
Staff Scientist, The Worcester Foundation for Experimental Biology, Shrewsbury, Massachusetts 01545

Dr. Henk Rigter
CNS Pharmacology R&D Labs, Organon International B.V., Scientific Development Group, P.O. Box 20, 5340 BHOSS, The Netherlands

Dr. Ingrid F. de Koning-Verest
Medical Biological Laboratory TNO, 139, Lange Kleiweg, Rijswijk Z.H., The Netherlands

Dr. Byron Campbell
Department of Psychology, Princeton University, Green Hall, Princeton, New Jersey 08540

Dr. Philip W. Landfield
Department of Physiology and Pharmacology, Bowman Gray School of Medicine, Winston-Salem, North Carolina 27103

Dr. Carol Barnes
Department of Psychology, Dalhousie University, Halifax, N.S., Canada, B3H 4J1

Dr. Arnold B. Scheibel
Professor of Anatomy and Psychiatry, School of Medicine, The Center for the Health Sciences, Los Angeles, California 90024

Dr. Paul Coleman
Department of Anatomy, University of Rochester, Rochester, New York 14642

Doz. Dr. Med. William Meier-Ruge
Institute of Basic Medical Research, Lichtstrasse 35, Basel, Switzerland

Pr. W. J. Dekoninck
Geriatric Clinique, Le Rayon de Soleil, 6110 Montignies-le-Tilleul, Belgium

Dr. David Bowen
33, John's Mews, London, WICIN, 2NS, England

Dr. David A. Drachman
Department of Neurology, University of Massachusetts Medical Center, Worcester, Massachusetts 01605

Dr. Merrill F. Elias
Professor of Psychology, Little Hall, University of Maine, Orono, Maine 04473

Prof. John E. Desmedt
Brain Research Unit, University of Brussels, Boulevard de Waterloo 115, B1000 Brussels, Belgium

Dr. Gail R. Marsh
Associate Professor of Medical Psychology, Center for the Study of Aging and Human Development, Box 3003, Duke University Medical Center, Durham, North Carolina 27710

Prof. Dr. Med. L. Deecke
Facharzt fur Neurologie, Abteilung Neurologie der Universität, 79 Ulm, Steinhövelstr., 9, West Germany

Dr. Patrick Rabbitt
Department of Experimental Psychology, University of Oxford, South Parks Road, Oxford, OClm 3UD, England

The Psychobiology of Aging:
Problems and Perspectives

Stein, ed. The Psychobiology of Aging: Problems and Perspectives

Behavior Genetics of Aging

Gilbert S. Omenn, M.D., Ph.D.

Associate Director, Office of Science and Technology Policy, Executive Office of the President, Washington, D.C.; on leave: Professor of Medicine (Medical Genetics), University of Washington, Seattle, Washington.

Introduction

The great variation of ability and interests among the elderly is well known to every layman. Some octogenarians are intensely active and productive, apparently still healthy of body, as well as mind. Five years ago, I participated in a program at Stanford University heralded as "The Majesty of Man". Against a background of neurophysiological and biochemical studies of mammalian and human brain, that program celebrated the remarkable prowess of pianist Arthur Rubinstein (then age 88) and chemist Linus Pauling (then age 74). Many less famous old persons delight their families and friends with their alertness, wisdom, and memory.

However, as average life expectancy continues to increase and the proportions of the general population over age 65, over 75, and over 85 grow rapidly, all statistics indicate an increasing prevalence of diseases, disability, and depression. Our social institutions seem swamped with the numbers of older people requiring stimulation, support or basic care. There is no question that the need for better understanding of the processes of aging and for appropriate, humane, and effective public programs is great and still growing.

It is necessary to define the domain of "aging" and the phenomena or phenotypes suitable for analysis by the methods of behavior genetics. One definition might encompass the many diseases or disorders that befall people as they grow older. Essentially all of these disorders have a significant genetic predisposition, including heart disease, high blood pressure, cancers, diabetes, stroke, osteoporosis with fractures, depression and senile dementia. These diseases likewise have marked effects on intellectual and emotional behaviors. Given the realization that some very old persons have remarkably intact cognitive function, one might postulate that any decline is due to recognizable or more subtle effects of cerebrovascular disease or other diseases like those just mentioned. *The Handbook on the Psychology of Aging* (Birren and Schaie, 1977) used the following definition: "Aging is any time-dependent change which occurs after maturity of size, form or function is reached and which is distinct from daily, seasonal, and other biological rhythms." The gerund form of the term *aging* emphasizes the time-dimension of the phenomenon and the need to assess phenotypes of processes involved in aging over time. Clearly, different individuals bring different genetic make-up and different phenotypes to the stage of life referred to as "maturity." Thus, many researchers interested in aging consider developmental changes early in life to be highly relevant.

The interaction between biological and pathological orientations of these investigating aging is illustrated in Figure 1 (Bowden, 1979, personal comm.). Those whose orientation focuses on the biology of aging tend to regard aging as part of a normal life process. Their studies include assessment of characteristics that seem to correlate with, and perhaps account for, species differences in longevity and characteristics that undergo measurable change in close correlation with chronological age. Those whose orientation is to the pathology of aging tend to consider any deviations from the optimal state of the mature adult as pathological. Most of this type of research is aimed at understanding, preventing, reversing, or coping with human needs that have their peak incidence in

Figure 1. Approaches to the study of aging.
SOURCE: *Bowden, 1979, personal communication.*

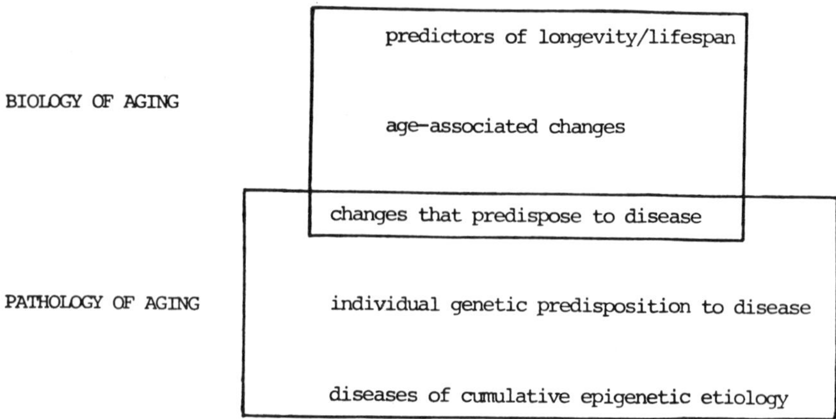

old age. This approach leads to a strategy of selecting animal models in which pathological conditions seem to resemble the human diseases.

Behavior Genetics

Geneticists share with poets a consuming interest in the uniqueness of the individual. Of course, most of the differences among people are differences intuitively perceived in various aspects of their behavior. At the molecular and biochemical level, one can demonstrate quite readily that no two persons, except for identical twins, are identical genetically. With a battery of tests for some 23 blood enzyme and antigen markers such as those used in population genetic studies or paternity testing (Omenn and Motulsky, 1972, Table 6), the probability of identical profiles for two randomly selected persons is one in three to four billion, which is approximately the world's population. These twenty-three gene markers are only a minor sampling of the estimated 20,000 genes having variant forms potentially suitable for such testing. Genetically determined variation at the biochemical level occurs not only in the blood cells but in all tissues and can be presumed to underlie anatomical, physiological, and behavioral differences in man and in animals. Recent studies have shown such genetically-determined variation not only in the protein products (enzymes and antigens) but also in the DNA itself (Kan and Dozy, 1978).

Behavior genetics has become identified as a significant field of study only over the past fifteen years or so. Several texts, workshops, and journals have appeared (see Omenn, 1977). However, the founder of Behavior Genetics is acknowledged universally to be Sir Francis Galton. Galton was a first cousin of Charles Darwin and had made contributions as a geographer, explorer, and inventor (Forrest, 1974). Greatly influenced by his cousin's book on the *Origin of Species,* Galton turned his efforts to biological phenomena and the inheritance of mental characteristics. He pioneered the study of families, the notion of a normal curve of distribution of quantitative measures, and the twin-study method for analysis of genetic and environmental influences on behavior.

There are two major aims of modern behavior genetics: first, to define the degree to which genetic factors determine or predispose to specific behavioral phenotypes; and, second, to describe the mechanisms through which environmental variables interact with genetically programmed variation in cellular and metabolic functions to produce such behavioral phenotypes.

The interaction of genetic and environmental factors cannot be emphasized too strongly. For far too long, polemics about nature versus nurture dominated studies of behavior, particularly of human behavior. The interaction and co-variance of genetic and environmental factors greatly complicate statistical or biometrical analyses which try to retain these important elements of variation, but the interactions become far more understandable as metabolic processes are elucidated.

Search for Mechanisms

Autoimmune

An important potential mechanism for deterioration of tissue function involves immunological damage to the cells. When the antibodies or cytotoxic lymphocytes are produced by the same individual, the mechanism is termed autoimmunity. The phenomenon involves some of the basic questions of recognition of "self" and "non-self." Burnet (1977) has argued for a central role of autoimmunity in the decreasing efficiency of the body's organ systems with age and noted the high frequency of lymphomatous tumors and deposition of amyloid. To account for deterioration in the self-monitoring or controlling mechanisms of the immune system, he postulated Orgel-type genetic errors. The potential roles of autoimmunity in aging are still speculative, but genetic factors are definitely implicated in autoimmunity—both from familial aggregation and from HLA associations. According to Greenberg and Yunis (1978), the HLA-A1-B8-DW3 linkage group (specifying histocompatibility antigens on the surface of cells) may be associated with earlier decline of some immune (T cell) functions and with decreased survival.

Effects of Identifiable Exogenous Agents

Genetically-determined differences in the metabolism of the host may explain the marked individual variation in susceptibility to adverse effects from such agents as ionizing radiation, behavior-modifying and other drugs, food additives and pollutants (Omenn and Motulsky, 1978). In some cases, these differences are due to differences in the metabolism of the exogenous agent. Aged humans and animals with declining organ functions are often more susceptible than younger subjects.

Biological Rhythms

Most physical and biological phenomena are tied to certain rhythmical cycles, including the rotation of the earth and numerous circadian (daily) rhythms in our behavior and physiology. The adrenal gland secretion of cortisol, for example, has an early morning peak and a late afternoon and evening nadir. Deviation from this rhythmical cycle is an early sign of disease of the adrenal cortex. The levels of other circulating hormones and many other constituents of the blood vary according to time and in conjunction with eating and sleeping patterns. On a longer scale, there may be important built-in rhythms in the hypertrophy and involution of tissues and in the migration and death of cells. These rhythms surely have a genetic basis, and they are likely to have genetically-determined individual variation, which may change with age.

Molecular

One of the most dramatic findings of overall gene action in the nervous system has come from studies of DNA/RNA hybridization. In such tissues as liver, kidney, and spleen, only 3–6% of the unique-sequence DNA is transcribed into extractable RNA (Hahn and Laird, 1971; Grouse, Chilton, and McCarthy, 1972). In brain tissue, a remarkably higher proportion is transcribed: 10–13% in the mouse brain and up to 20% in human brain (Grouse, Omenn, and McCarthy, 1973). The limited results suggest that the values for complexity of RNA messengers are substantially higher in the cortex than in the brain stem. Cross-hybridization with heterogeneous nuclear RNA from macaque, chimpanzee, and human brain showed considerable conservation of expressed sequences (Omenn and Farquhar, 1976). No significant differences with age were observed when brain RNA from 4, 10, and 20 year-old *Macaca nemestrina* were compared (Farquhar, Kosky, and Omenn, 1979). A value of 20% hybridization means that 40% of the genome is expressed (transcribing from one DNA strand or the other). The amount of DNA per cell (about 6 picograms) is the same in the mouse and in man, so these data indicate that evolution has been associated with an increasing assignment of the genome to functions of the central nervous system, particularly the cortex. Such a biochemical finding is certainly consistent with anatomical and psychological characterizations of the development of higher corical functions.

Brain proteins also can be compared as a function of age and abilities. Studies of the proteins of different tissues are of essentially two kinds. First, there are comparisons of the physical properties of proteins of unknown function, simply identified as separable "bands" on polyacrylamide electrophoretic gel systems, for example. Second, there are studies of particular enzymes or other proteins whose functions are known, preferably involving key metabolic steps.

Electrophoretic profiles of proteins of the brain appear significantly different from similar preparations from other tissues (Caplan, Cheung, and Omenn, 1974). Two proteins highly specific for the brain have been found: the S-100 protein (named for its solubility in 100% saturated ammonium sulfate) in glial cells (Moore, Perez, and Gehring, 1968) and the 14-3-2 protein (named for its position on three successive chromatographic elutions) in neuronal cells (Cicero, Cowan, Moore, and Suntzeff, 1970). Unfortunately, the functional role of the S-100 protein remains unknown, despite much research, but 14-3-2 has been shown to be a brain isozyme of the glycotic enzyme enolase (Marangos et al, 1976; Chen and Omenn, unpublished).

The electrophoretic method has revealed developmental changes in brain proteins (see Omenn, 1977). Grossfield and Shooter (1971) and Cain, Ball, and Dekaban (1972) have reported changes during development in the profiles of aqueous-soluble and aqueous-insoluble proteins in whole brain extracts of the mouse and the rabbit, respectively. Similar techniques have shown differences among the regions of the auditory pathway in the guinea pig (Davies, 1970) and between neuronal membrane fractions of DBA and C57 mice (Gurd, Mahler, and Moore, 1972). In our laboratory, Caplan, Cheung, and Omenn (1974) have reported some differences in the electrophoretic profile of aqueous-soluble cortical human proteins between adults and fetuses or infants. In addition, affinity chromatography for glycoproteins revealed another fetal/adult difference. No age-related differences were found in profiles for 100 adults ranging in age from 20 to 88 years.

Another important strategy for research on metabolism of key pathways and processes in brain is to identify analogous functions in more accessible tissues and to determine whether they represent the same gene product and are under similar genetic control. Thus, dopamine-β-hydroxylase can be measured in plasma, catechol-O-methyl transferase in red blood cells, monoamine oxidase in platelets, and serotonin uptake in platelets (see Weinshilboum, 1978 and Omenn, 1978). Platelet uptake of serotonin is an excellent mimic of reuptake of serotonin into presynaptic neurons, but dopamine uptake is entirely different between platelets and brain (Omenn and Smith, 1978a). Studies of the kinetics of serotonin uptake into platelets and of competitive inhibition of uptake by tricyclic antidepressants showed no significant differences as a function of age, either in humans (Omenn and Smith, 1978b) or in monkeys *(Macaca nemestrina)* (Omenn, Smith, and Hanson, 1979).

Metabolic and Physiological

There are many ways in which the metabolism of brain and of other tissues may change with age. Disease, alterations in cerebral blood flow, or re-distribution of regional brain perfusion may trigger physiological changes and activate or inhibit certain enzymes. Accumulated mutations, affecting the structural genes for the proteins themselves or, as in the error catastrophe hypothesis, affecting the transfer RNAs or other components of the protein synthesizing system, may have detectable effects on the protein products in tissues from aged individuals.

Alternatively, repair of abnormalities in the DNA (mutations) or clearance of abnormal proteins may be impaired with age. Some of these theoretical possibilities are under intensive investigation, as will be illustrated later in the case of Werner syndrome (see below).

In a series of 7 species from shrew and mouse to elephant and man, Hart and Setlow (1974) found a linear relationship between the logarithm of species life span and the amount of DNA repair of UV-induced thymine dimers. Sacher and Hart (1978) interpret that finding as support for "longevity-assuring" mechanisms—positive, genetically controlled mechanisms, rather than an aging process which the organism endures passively.

Normal aging might be accompanied by changes in the expression of genes for key enzymes in metabolism. The models in man for such developmental transition include the change from fetal hemoglobin to adult hemoglobin at the time of birth (Motulsky, 1969) and the change in fetal skeletal muscle from "brain-type" isozymes of creatine phosphokinase (Eppenberger, Richterick, and Aebi, 1964) and phosphoglycerate mutase (Omenn and Cheung, 1974) to adult muscle-type isozymes of these key enzymes of energy metabolism. The transformation of normal cells to malignant brain tumors may be accompanied by changes in gene expression for certain iso-enzymes (Omenn and Cheung, 1974). However, in an electrophoretic study of all eleven steps of glycolysis and of more than a dozen other enzymes intimately involved in energy metabolism in brain, we found no examples of changes in the properties of these enzymes between ages 20 and 88 years (Cohen, et al., 1973).

The genetic aspects of such studies include both the search for programmed developmental changes and the search for differences across individuals in the nature or timing of any such changes. Analogous questions may be asked about neurophysiological properties of the brain, including EEGs and evoked cortical responses, and of cultured neural cells.

Behavior Genetics of Aging: Animal Studies

Mouse. A bibliography of behavioral studies using genetically defined mice has been published (Sprott and Staats, 1975). Included among the 1,222 entries were only 11 primarily identified under "age: early development" and 16 under "age: maturity and senescence." I shall leave discussion of this literature to Dr. Sprott.

Rat. The Norway rat has been the favored animal of laboratory research in psychology, but less is known about its genetics and fewer established strains exist (FASEB 1979). Two important pairs of rat lines derived by selective breeding are available: the "maze-bright" and "maze-dull" rats of Tryon (1940) and the Maudsley reactive and non-reactive set (see Broadhurst, 1969). There is growing literature on rodents as model systems to study aging (Gibson, Adelman and Finch, 1979; Bergsma and Harrison, 1978). Since the rat has been studied intensively by neurophysiologists, detailed biobehavioral analysis of regional function with age is feasible. For example, Barnes (1979) has correlated hippocampus granule cell synaptic responses with performance on specific memory tasks.

The rat serves as a convenient animal in which to test certain metabolic or pharmacologic effects deduced from studies of abnormal behavior in man. For examples, fetal and infant rats have been exposed to excess phenylalanine and excess galactose to mimic the interference by these substances with normal brain development in man in the diseases phenylketonuria and galactosemia, respectively (Chase and O'Brien, 1970; Haworth, Ford, and Younoszai, 1969).

Dog. Dogs are the oldest domestic animal (about 12,000 years) adapted to as wide a range of environments as is man, and dogs are highly variable by many criteria. Unlike all the other animals described in this section, dogs are commonly kept to "old age" and monitored and treated for diseases. Among common breeds, Great Danes usually live only 6 years, while others survive 12 to 20 years. Terriers and shepherd dogs tend to be longest-lived. The book *Genetics and the Social Behavior of the Dog* (Scott and Fuller, 1965) is based on a 13-year breeding project at The Jackson Laboratory, using Central African basenjis, beagles, American cocker spaniels, Shetland sheep dogs (shelties), and wire-haired fox terriers. Emotional reactivity, trainability for a variety of obedience tests, motor skills, problem-solving behavior, and social behavior underlying mother-offspring, littermate, and dog-human relationship have been studied (Stewart and Scott, 1975).

Monkeys and Chimps. The Regional Primate Centers in eight locations around the United States emphasize behavioral research, because of the obvious closer relationship of nonhuman primates to man. At the University of Washington, for example, large projects on early infancy experiences and post-maturity changes (aging) have been initiated. The projects include breeding schemes and intensive neurophysiological and biochemical analyses, the beginnings of behavior genetics in these species. A major reference work, *Aging in Nonhuman Primates* (Bowden, 1979), has emerged from these collaborative studies. My colleagues and I contributed two studies to that project. One analyzed the complexity of RNA as a measure of gene expression (Farquhar, Kosky, and Omenn, 1979), and the other compared serotonin uptake into blood platelets and into brain synaptosomes as a function of age (Omenn, Smith, and Hanson, 1979).

Behavior Genetics of Aging: Studies in Man

Longevity. Genetic and familial influences on life-expectancy are well-recognized by the layman and were studied by Pearl (1922) and others, who showed that the mean life-expectancy was greater if one's parents had lived to an older age. Pearl estimated the "total immediate ancestral longevity" (TIAL), which is the sum of the ages attained by an individual's two parents and four grandparents; in one pedigree, a proband of age 100 had a TIAL of 599 years! Twin studies support the conclusion that genetic factors are important in longevity, as MZ twin pairs had smaller within-pair differences in life span than did DZ twins, 48.7 vs. 66.5 months (Kallmann and Jarvik, 1959). Somehow there is a well-set maximum longevity for each species, even without supervening illnesses; perhaps this phenomenon was described best by Oliver Wendell Holmes in his "One Hoss Shay," which unaccountably just disintegrated during one day of old age!

Phylogenetic comparisons have led to such generalizations as a rough correlation between body size and longevity, with monkeys longer-lived than cats, rats, and mice (in that order); however, cats, horses, and elephants have shorter life spans than does man. Other correlations exist between length of gestation and longevity, and between rate of metabolism, heart rate and longevity. In the case of the mouse and the elephant, heart rates of 520–789/minute $\times$ 3.25 years and 25–28/minute $\times$ 70 years gave lifetime total heart beat estimates of 1×10^9 for each species (Heilbrunn, 1943). In addition of course, other factors must be important variables, particularly nutrition (McCay, 1952; see Forbes, this volume).

Intelligence. Extensive reviews of cognitive abilities (Botwinick, 1967; Arenberg, 1973) deal with measures of registering, storing, and retrieving information, and solving problems, usually with response-time as a critical dependent variable. In general, aged groups are less capable than younger groups on these parameters, but the pace of stimulus presentation and the state of autonomic arousal, which can be manipulated by certain drugs, have been identified as crucial technical and clinical variables (Eisdorfer and Wilkie, 1977; Marsh, this volume). Most studies compare means of groups, with little attention to the individual differences within age groups; these individual differences usually are quite substantial.

One of the most remarkable family studies of intellectual achievement is the classic book of Galton (1869), *Hereditary Genius*. Galton classified men and women according to their reputation, using historical accounts and published biographical data on eminent persons. It is relevant to this discussion that very many of the cases were over 50 years of age, reflecting both time for achievement and time for recognition of achievement.

Cunningham, Clayton, and Overton (1975) tested the theory of fluid and crystallized intelligence (Horn and Cattell, 1966) for its developmental implications in an aged population. Fluid intelligence, purported to reflect functioning of neurological structures, increases until the cessation of neural maturation during adolescence and declines thereafter. Crystallized intelligence, said to reflect cultural assimilation, is highly influenced by formal and informal education factors throughout the life span. Crystallized intelligence tends to increase, but it is limited by the capacity of the fluid intelligence system so that increments become smaller with age. A reasonable test of this hypothesis was applied: the correlation between measures of these constructs should be lower in an elderly sample than in a sample of young adults. The Raven Progressive Matrices were used as an index of fluid intelligence, and the vocabulary subtest of the WAIS as an index of crystallized intelligence. The Pearson product moment correlation between these indices fell from .67 in the young to .39 in the elderly group; among the 40 subjects in the elderly group, the correlation was lower for those in their seventies than for those in their sixties. Both of these indices have been analyzed to have substantial heritability, .68 for the vocabulary subtest (Block, 1968) and .44 to .85 for the Raven Matrices (see Guttman, 1974).

Spatial Abilities. The tests of space and form perception and spatial manipulation on various test batteries seem to draw upon distinguishable components of spatial abilities. With the Raven Progressive Matrices, for example, Guttman (1974) has found different familial correlations and heritabilities for the different matrices. Extensive comparisons of young and elderly persons for a variety of spatial tasks have been carried out by Cohen, Schaie and Gribbon (1977).

Temperament and Related Behavior. Kallman and his associates reported observations on many aspects of behavior in twin pairs reaching senescence, with a registry of 2,500 senescent twin index cases and a sample of 240 index cases over age 60 years, followed for more than 6 years (Kallmann, Feingold, and Bondy, 1951). Severe maladjustment to aging, resulting in symptoms of an involutional or senile psychosis, coexisted more frequently in MZ than in DZ twin pairs, presumably due to genetic influences on a mixture of contributing factors, such as age-related personality factors, declining adaptational plasticity, and increasing emotional and socioeconomic insecurity. However, discordance was the rule in the extreme maladaptation of suicide (Kallmann, Deporte, and Feingold, 1949). A battery of tests designed to demonstrate declining intellectual function gave smaller intra-pair differences in MZ pairs than in DZ pairs for tests measuring abstract intellectual functions (vocabulary, digits backward, digit symbol, block designs, similarities), suggesting that genetic factors are involved in the decrements. Jarvik and Blum (1971) have followed these twin pairs another 20 years (see below).

Psychophysiological Studies. Marsh and Thompson (1977) have summarized much information about changes in the EEG, sleep patterns, evoked responses and autonomic nervous system responses from young adulthood to senescence and their relationships to behavioral impairment in the elderly. Associated behavioral changes are slowing in performance, deficiency in registration of raw stimuli, and decreased ability to handle inputs (Jarvik and Cohen, 1973). Wide differences among individuals characterize most studies.

One of the most consistent findings is a slowing with age in the normal alpha rhythm of the EEG, usually by about 1 cycle per second. There is also a decrease in percent time alpha, with an increase of fast or beta waves. Early atherosclerotic changes may be the determining factor, since "superhealthy" elderly subjects have cerebral blood flow equal to that of young controls and alpha frequencies nearly equal to those of the controls.

Any changes in the EEG associated with aging are superimposed upon an EEG pattern highly determined by heredity. MZ twins share not only identical EEG patterns, but closely-timed maturational transitions in the EEGs in adolescence and in later life. Analysis of pedigrees points to a polygenic mode of inheritance, not surprising for the complex electrical activity recorded from the scalp. However, there are several specific variant EEG patterns inherited as Mendelian autosomal dominant traits (Vogel, 1970). Four % of the population (normal German and Japanese subjects) had the monotonous tall alpha pattern, determined by a single gene. Another 5–10 % had a beta wave pattern, with multifactorial determination; this pattern increases in prevalence in middle age, especially among females. These different baseline EEG patterns are now being analyzed for possible correlations with psychometric measures and personality tests (Vogel et al, 1979). Further studies could include photic, auditory, sleep, or other physiological stimuli and pharmacological agents that might reveal different susceptibilities to sedative or behavior-modifying actions.

Cytogenetic Studies. Court-Brown et al. (1966) have reported that abnormal chromosome content of cells increases with age, indicating abnormalities in the process of mitosis (cell division); both hypomodal cells (45 or fewer chromosomes) and hypermodal cells (47 or more chromosomes) were increased in frequency. Increased frequency of chromosome loss has been correlated with memory impairment and cognitive impairment on various tests of both institutionalized and noninstitutionalized older persons (Jarvik and Cohen, 1973). Furthermore, precipitous decline in cognitive performance has served as a predictor of approaching death (Jarvik and Blum, 1971).

Mutant Approach

Effects of Single Abnormal Genes on Aging

There should be no simplistic assumptions that single-gene disorders represent good models for human beings. In fact, Martin (1978) listed many aspects in which each of these conditions differs from "normal aging" and has suggested "segmental progeroid syndromes" to indicate that the mimicking of aspects of aging is partial at best.

Werner Syndrome. These individuals have an autosomal recessive disorder which provides an interesting caricature of some features associated with aging. More than 125 cases have been reported. These persons have no adolescent growth spurt and reach their final height (mean 61 inches for men, 57 inches for women) at around 13 years of age. Gray hair is developed by age 20, cataracts by age 25, appearance of old age by 30 to 40 years of age, with mean survival 47 years. Calcification occurs in atheromatous blood vessels and in thick subcutaneous tissues, muscles become wasted with fibrous replacement, teeth are lost, 44 percent have mild diabetes, and a minority have mild neurological defects (primarily loss of distal deep tendon reflexes) (Epstein et al., 1966).

Progeria. This exceedingly rare autosomal recessive disorder (McKusick, 1978) consists of alopecia (loss of scalp hair), near-absence of subcutaneous fat, skeletal hypoplasia and dysplasia, onset of generalized atherosclerosis as early as age five years, elevated serum cholesterol, hearing loss, cataracts, and death from what appears to be "old age." It is extremely impressive that brain development and intelligence do not appear to be impaired.

Cockayne Syndrome. This rare autosomal recessive disorder is characterized by dwarfism, precociously senile appearance, pigmentary degeneration of the retina, optic atrophy, deafness, bone changes, sensitivity to sunlight, mental retardation, and abnormal regulation of glucose and cholesterol metabolism (McKusick, 1978). Growth and development proceed fairly normally in early infancy, and the pattern of defects becomes evident only at age two to four years.

Xeroderma Pigmentosum (Several Subtypes). These rare recessive disorders merit inclusion because of the peculiar type of metabolic errors involved. Clinically, benign and malignant skin lesions appear on exposed parts of the body, due to sensitivity to ultraviolet radiation. Carcinomas are recognized usually in the first few years of life. One subtype, inherited within particular families, has central nervous system involvement, as well. Several different mutations are responsible, all acting to interfere with the normal repair of DNA damaged by ultraviolet radiation. The importance of this disease is its demonstration that the body's cells have the means normally to overcome environmentally-induced mutagenesis and that loss of that capacity leads to cancers and death. DNA repair mechanisms should be high on the list of metabolic pathways to be examined closely as a function of aging; as noted above, DNA repair capacity has been correlated with life span across seven species (Hart and Setlow, 1974).

In none of these four single-gene-determined disorders has there been any useful psychological or neurophysiological characterization of the patients. As criteria are agreed upon and test protocols developed for features of "normal" aging, the same criteria and tests should be applied to these rare, but potentially very interesting, subjects with just one primary abnormality. One may be confident that no single gene determines all the varied features of the usual aging process; yet the genes which produce the dramatic effects of these four syndromes may have less severely altered genetic forms (alleles) which contribute to the normal variation in the process of aging. Furthermore, even though the patients are rare, their cells may be studied in tissue culture *in vitro,* so that the biochemical basis of the particular defective gene action might yet be elucidated.

The limited replicative capacity of cultured human fibroblasts has provided a model for aging in the laboratory (Epstein et al., 1966; Goldstein, 1971). Normal human fibroblasts are capable of 75 mean population doublings under conditions in which fibroblasts from a patient with Werner syndrome and from a patient with progeria were capable of only 15 and 36 doublings, respectively (Goldstein, Stotland, and Cordero, 1976). However, glial-like cells from cerebellum and cerebrum of a Werner syndrome patient who died at age 57 years grew normally (Martin, 1978).

Some studies indicate that toward the end of their replicative life span, normal fibroblasts accumulate a significant proportion of defective enzymes and incorporate increased amounts of amino acid analogues, which may make inactive proteins. Werner syndrome skin fibroblasts had 14–24 % heat-labile G6PD (glucose-6-phosphate dehydrogenase), compared with 1 % heat-labile G6PD in normal controls (Goldstein and Singal, 1974). Similar results were obtained with fibroblasts from patients with progeria, and fibroblasts from patients with diabetes gave suggestive results in the same direction. However, there is no proof that defective proteins cause rather than result from cellular aging.

Single-gene Mendelian Disorders with Effects Apparently Limited to the Brain

Alzheimer Disease and Pick Disease

Although these two conditions are distinct, their clinical appearances during life are so similar that they may be discussed together here. Slowly progressive dementia begins with insidious onset usually in the fifth or sixth decade, at least 10 years before the onset of senile dementia. Thus, these diseases are termed "presenile dementias." Disturbances of speech also are prominent. Focal neurological abnormalities appear, with parietal lobe signs and disturbance of gait in Alzheimer disease and with frontal lobe signs and no gait disturbance in Pick disease. Pathologically, they are entirely different. In Alzheimer disease there is atrophy of all areas of the brain, loss of cells, and formation of plaques and characteristic neurofibrillary loops and tangles. Such histological changes do occur in other degenerative disorders of the brain. Pick disease is characterized by severe atrophy and cell loss in the outer layers of the frontal and temporal regions of the cerebral cortex, glial proliferation, but no senile plaques or neurofibrillary tangles. Alzheimer is 20 times more common than Pick disease, with autosomal dominant inheritance, at least in some families. Heston and White (1978) have shown defective organization of microfilaments and microtubules in Alzheimer brain material.

Huntington disease

This relatively common neurological disease of middle life produces involuntary movements and progressive mental deterioration, usually over about 15 years. The primary abnormality is a loss of neurons in the putamen and caudate of the basal ganglia, as well as in certain layers of the cerebral cortex. Lipofuscin pigment accumulates in the brain. Change in personality, irresponsibility, frank psychosis, and dementia occur. If involuntary movements have not yet become apparent, the patient commonly is mis-diagnosed as having schizophrenia or manic-depressive illness. Although the disease thus far appears to be limited to the central nervous system, it is striking that families and friends often exaggerate the age of affected individuals, as though they had appeared much older than their chronological ages. The disease is determined by an autosomal dominant gene, but its biochemical basis is not known. Attempts to show abnormalities in accessible peripheral tissues, such as platelets (Omenn and Smith, 1978b) and cultured fibroblasts (Goetz, Roberts and Comings, 1975) have not yet yielded a useful biochemical test.

Senile Dementia

The main clinical features are a progressive disorganization of all aspects of the mind, personality being as early and as much affected as memory, intelligence, judgment, and conceptual powers. Progression is unremitting and usually fairly even, though accompanying somatic illnesses can precipitate worsening. Pathologically, there is universal loss of neurons, accumulation of lipofuscin, neurofibrillary changes identical with the plaques and tangles of Alzheimer disease, and increase of astrocytic cells. These changes are readily distinguished from those due to cerebral vascular disease. The major genetic study of this phenotype (Larsson, Sjogren, and Jacobson, 1963) examined 377 probands and their families in Sweden. First-degree relatives had a 4.3 times risk of this disorder.

It must be emphasized that a very substantial proportion of patients are mislabeled as having senile dementia. These patients include many with eminently treatable and reversible conditions, such as over-medication, depression, systemic illnesses, and certain hormonal imbalances.

The lipofuscin pigment accumulated in brains of patients with senile dementias, including Huntington disease, is of great interest. It is a yellow autofluorescent lipid "wear and tear pigment" somehow related to the aging process (Nandy, 1978). It can be produced experimentally by dietary deficiency of vitamin E; a rather similar, though distinguishable, pigment is accumulated in children with an autosomal recessive, degenerative neurological disorder called neuronal ceroid storage disease (Zeman, 1974).

Autosomal Trisomy 21, Down Syndrome

If children with Down syndrome (formerly called mongolism) survive the first few years (as more than 70 % do now), the prospect for survival to middle age is quite good. Sexual development may be delayed or incomplete, or both. However, there is an adolescent growth spurt, and menstruation usually begins at the average age and follows a normal course. The aging process in these individuals tends to occur early, including dryness and coarsening of the skin and recession of the gums with loss of teeth. As in other individuals of the same IQ level, the relative mortality is high after age 40; the causes of death tend to be the same as those which affect the normal aging population. An interesting histopathological sign of early aging has been noted in the brains of adults with Down syndrome. The typical changes associated with Alzheimer disease or presenile dementia—senile plaques, neurofibrillary tangles, and granulovacuolar changes in cortical and other brain cells—have been present in all brains so examined from Down syndrome patients over age 35 (Olson and Shaw, 1969). Patients with other types of mental retardation lack such early changes in the brain.

Disorders Affecting the Sensory Apparatus

Without going into any detail here, it should be noted that numerous inherited conditions affect vision, hearing, inner ear function, taste, and other sensory input systems (McKusick, 1978). Visual problems and hearing loss are among the most common complaints of older people, and often reversible. As we develop sophisticated measures of neurophysiology in the central nervous system, peripheral sensory apparatus should not be neglected as behavioral changes of aging are examined for mechanisms.

Concluding Remarks

The methods and observations of behavior genetics have many applications in studies of aging in both animals and humans. Greater attention to individual differences may provide clues to underlying mechanisms of biological and pathological aspects of aging. The principle of genetic heterogeneity should be stressed. Just as there are many, many causes of anemia or of mental retardation, there are probably many specific differences among individuals contributing to the processes of aging. No unitary answer to the question "what is aging" should be expected, and no single intervention, either behavioral or psychopharmacological, should be expected to be effective in all types of subjects.

ACKNOWLEDGMENT

I wish to acknowledge the roles in some of the studies mentioned of my colleagues R. Caplan, S.H. Chen, S. Cheung, P.T.W. Cohen, M.N. Farquhar, D.R. Hanson, K. Kosky, A.G. Motulsky, and L.T. Smith.

References

Arenberg D: Cognition and aging: verbal learning, memory, problem solving, and aging. In Eisdorfer C, Lawton MP, (eds.) *The Psychology of Adult Development and Aging*. Washington, DC, American Psychological Association, 1973, pp. 74–97.

Barnes CA: Memory deficits associated with senescence: a neuro-physiological and behavioral study in the rat. *J Compar Physiol Psychol* 93:74–104, 1979.

Bergsma D, Harrison DE: *Genetic Effects on Aging*. New York, AR Liss Inc, 1978.

Birren JE, Schaie KW, (eds.) *Handbook on the Psychology of Aging*. New York, Van Nostrand Reinhold Co, 1977.

Block JB: Hereditary components in the performance of twins on the WAIS. In Vandenberg SG, (ed.) *Progress in Human Behavior Genetics*. Baltimore, Johns Hopkins University Press, 1968, pp. 221–228.

Botwinick J: *Cognitive Processes in Maturity and Old Age*. New York, Springer-Verlag, 1967.

Bowden DM, ed.: *Aging in Non-Human Primates*. New York, Raven Press, 1979.

Broadhurst PL: Psychogenetics of emotionality in the rat. *Ann NY Acad Sci* 159:806–824, 1969.

Burnet FM: Autoimmunity and aging. In Talal N, (ed.) *Autoimmunity, Genetic, Immunologic, Virologic and Clinical Aspects*. New York, Academic Press, 1977, pp. 513–530.

Cain DF, Ball ED, Dekaban AS: Brain proteins: qualitative and quantitative changes, synthesis and degradation during fetal development of the rabbit. *J Neurochem* 19:2031–2042, 1972.

Caplan R, Cheung SCY, Omenn GS: Electrophoretic profiles of aqueous soluble proteins of human cerebral cortex: population and developmental characteristics. *J Neurochem* 22:517–520, 1974.

Chase HP, O'Brien D: Effect of excess phenylalanine and of other amino acids on brain development in the infant rat. *Pediat Research* 4:96–102, 1970.

Cicero TJ, Cowan WM, Moore BW, Suntzeff V: The cellular localization of the two brain specific proteins S-100 and 14-3-2. *Brain Res* 18:25–34, 1970.

Cohen D, Schaie KW, Gribbon K: Organization of spatial abilities in older men and women. *J Gerontology* 32:578–585, 1977.

Cohen PTW, Omenn GS, Motulsky AG, Chen SH, Giblett ER: Restricted variation in the glycolytic enzymes of human brain and erythrocytes. *Nature New Biol* 241:229–233, 1973.

Court Brown WM, Jacobs PA, Buckton KE, Tough IM, Kuenssberge EV, Know JDE: Chromosome studies on adults. Eugenics Laboratory Memoirs XLII, London, 1966.

Cunningham WR, Clayton V, Overton W: Fluid and crystallized intelligence in young adulthood and old age. *J Gerontology* 30:53–55, 1975.

Davies WE: The disc electrophoretic separation of proteins from various parts of the guinea pig brain. *J Neurochem* 17:297–303, 1970.

Eisdorfer C, Wilkie F: Stress, disease, aging and behavior. In Birren JE, Schaie KW, (eds.) *Handbook on the Psychology of Aging*. New York, Van Nostrand Reinhold Co., 1977, pp. 251–275.

Eppenberger HM, Eppenberger M, Richterick R, Aebi H: The ontogeny of creatine kinase isoenzymes. *Develop Biol* 10:1–16, 1964.

Epstein CJ, Martin GM, Schultz AL, Motulsky AG: Werner's syndrome: a review of its symptomatology, natural history, pathologic features, genetics and relationship to the natural aging process. *Medicine* 45:177–222, 1966.

Farquhar MN, Kosky KJ, Omenn GS: Gene expression in brain as a function of age in *Macaca nemestrina*. In Bowden DM, (ed.) *Aging in Non-Human Primates*. New York, Raven Press, 1979, pp. 71–79.

FASEB 1979: Biological Handbooks III. Inbred and Genetically Defined Strains of Laboratory Animals. Part 1, Mouse and Rat. Federation of American Societies of Experimental Biology, Bethesda, Md.

Forrest DW: Francis Galton: The Life and Work of a Victorian Genius. New York, Taplinger Publ Co, 1974.

Galton F: Hereditary Genius, 1869. New York, Meridian Books, World Publishing, Reprinted 1962.

Gibson DC, Adelman RC, Finch C, (eds.): *Development of the Rodent as a Model System of Aging. Vol. II.* DHEW Publ No 79-161, Rockville, Md.

Goetz I, Roberts E, Comings DE: Fibroblasts in Huntingtons disease. *New Engl J Med* 293:1225–1227, 1975.

Goldstein S: The biology of aging. *New Engl J Med* 285:1120–1129, 1971.

Goldstein S, Singal DP: Alteration of fibroblast gene products *in vitro* from a subject with Werner's syndrome. *Nature* 251:719, 1974.

Goldstein S, Stotland D, Cordero RAJ: Decreased proteolysis and increased amino acid efflux in aging human fibroblasts. *Mechanisms of Aging and Development* 5:221–233, 1976.

Greenberg LJ, Yunis EJ: Histocompatibility determinants, immune responsiveness, and aging in man. *Fed Proc* 37:1258–1262, 1978.

Grossfeld RM, Shooter EM: A study of the changes in protein composition of mouse brain during ontogenetic development. *J Neurochem* 18:2265–2277, 1971.

Grouse L, Omenn GS, McCarthy BJ: Study by DNA/RNA hybridization of the transcriptional diversity of human brain. *J Neurochem* 20:1063–1073, 1973.

Gurd RS, Mahler HR, Moore WJ: Differences in protein patterns on polyacrylamide gel-electrophoresis of neuronal membranes from mice of different strains. *J Neurochem* 19:553–556, 1972.

Guttman R: Genetic analysis of analytical spatial ability: Raven's progressive matrices. *Behavior Genetics* 4:273–284, 1974.

Hahn WR, Laird CD: Transcription of nonrepeated DNA in mouse brain. *Science* 1973:158–161, 1971.

Hart RW, Setlow RB: Correlation between deoxyribonucleic acid excision-repair and life-span in a number of mammalian species. *Proc Nat Acad Sci* 71:2169–2173, 1974.

Haworth JC, Ford JD, Younoszai MK: Effect of galactose toxicity on growth of the rat fetus and brain. *Pediat Research* 3:441–447, 1969.

Heilbrunn LV: *An Outline of General Physiology,* 2nd Edition. Philadelphia, WB Saunders, 1943.

Heston LL, White J: Pedigrees of 30 families with Alzheimer disease: associations with defective organization of micro-filaments and microtubules. *Behavior Genetics* 8:315–331, 1978.

Horn JL, Cattell RB: Refinement and test of the theory of fluid and crystallized intelligence. *J Educ Psych* 57:252–270, 1966.

Jarvik LF, Blum JE: Cognitive declines as predictors of mortality in twin pairs: a twenty-year longitudinal study of aging. In Palmore E, Jeffers F, (eds.) *Prediction of Lifespan.* Massachusetts, Heath-Lexington, 1971.

Jarvik LF, Cohen D: A biobehavioral approach to intellectual changes with aging. In Eisdorfer C, Lawton MP, (eds.) *The Psychology of Adult Development and Aging.* Washington, DC, American Psychological Association, 1973, pp. 220–280.

Kallmann FJ, Deporte J, Deporte E, Feingold L: Suicide in twins and only children. *Amer J Hum Genet* 1:113–126, 1949.

Kallmann FJ, Feingold L, Bondy E: Comparative adaptational, social, and psychometric data on the life histories of senescent twin pairs. *Amer J Hum Genet* 3:65–73, 1951.

Kallmann FJ, Jarvik LF: Individual differences in constitution and genetic background. In Birren JE, (ed.) *Handbook of Aging and the Individual.* Chicago, University of Chicago Press, 1959, pp. 216–263.

Kan YW, Dozy AM: Polymorphism of DNA sequence adjacent to the human beta globin structural gene, its relation to the sickle mutation. *Proc Natl Acad Sci* 75:5631–5635, 1978.

Larsson T, Sjogren T, Jacobson G: Senile dementia: a clinical, sociomedical, and genetic study. *Acta Psychiat Scand.,* Suppl 167, 1963.

Marangos PJ, Zomzely-Neurath C, York C: Determination and characterization of neuron specific protein (NSP)-associated enolase activity. *Biochem Biophys Res Commun* 68:1309–1316, 1976.

Marsh GR, Thompson LW: Psychophysiology of aging. In Birren JE, Schaie KW, (ed.) *Handbook of the Psychology of Aging.* New York, Van Nostrand Reinhold Co., 1977, pp. 219–248.

Martin GM: Genetic syndromes in man with potential relevance to the pathobiology of aging. In Bergsma D, Harrison DE, (eds.) *Genetic Effects on Aging.* New York, AR Liss, Inc., 1978, pp. 5–39.

McCay CM: Chemical aspects of aging and the effect of diet upon aging. In Lansing AI, (ed.) *Cowdry's Problems of Aging, 3rd Edition.* Baltimore, Williams and Wilkins, 1952, pp. 139–220.

McKusick VA: *Mendelian Inheritance in Man: Catalogs of Autosomal Dominant, Autosomal Recessive, and Linked Phenotypes* 5th Edition. Baltimore, Johns Hopkins University Press, 1978.

Moore BW, Perez VJ, Gehring M: Wallerian degeneration in rabbit tibial nerve: changes in amounts of the S-100 protein. *J Neurochem* 15:971–977, 1968.

Motulsky AG: Biochemical genetics of hemoglobins and enzymes as a model for birth defects research. *Proc 3rd Inter Congr Congenital Malformations, Hague, Excerpta Medica* 433–446, 1969.

Nandy K: Morphological changes in the aging brain. In Nandy K, (ed.) *Senile Dementia: A Biomedical Approach.* New York, Elsevier/North Holland Biomedical Press, 1978, pp. 19–32.

Olson MI, Shaw CM: Presenile dementia and Alzheimer's disease in Mongolism. *Brain* 92:147–156, 1969.

Omenn GS: Behavior Genetics. In Birren JE, Schaie KW, (eds.) *Handbook of the Psychology of Aging.* New York, Van Nostrand Reinhold Co., pp. 190–218, 1977.

Omenn GS: Psychopharmacogenetics: an overview and new approaches. *Human Genetics,* Suppl 1, 1978:83–90.

Omenn GS, Cheung SCY: Phosphoglycerate mutase isozyme marker for tissue differentiation in man. *Amer J Hum Genet* 26:393–399, 1974.

Omenn GS, Farquhar MN: Gene expression in human brain: DNA/RNA hybridization studies. *Abst. V Inter Congress of Human Genetics, Mexico City,* Oct 10–15, 1976.

Omenn GS, Motulsky AG: Biochemical genetics and the evolution of human behavior. In Ehrman L, Omenn GS, Caspari E, (eds.) *Genetics, Environment, and Behavior: Implications for Educational Policy.* New York, Academic Press, 1972, pp. 129–172.

Omenn GS, Motulsky AG: Ecogenetics: genetic variation in the susceptibility to environmental agents. In Cohen BH, Lilienfeld AM, Huang PC, (eds.) *Genetic Issues in Public Health.* CC Thomas, Springfield, Illinois, 1978, pp. 83–111.

Omenn GS, Smith LT: A common uptake system for serotonin and dopamine in human platelets. *J Clin Invest* 62:235–240, 1978a.

Omenn GS, Smith LT: Platelet uptake of serotonin and dopamine in Huntingtons disease. *Neurology* 28:300–303, 1978b.

Omenn GS, Smith LT, Hanson DR: Pharmacogenetic investigations of platelet uptake of serotonin III. Serotonin uptake in platelets and in brain synaptosomes from young and aged *Macaca nemestrina*. In Bowden D, (ed.) *Aging in Non-Human Primates*. New York, Raven Press, 1979.

Pearl R: *The Biology of Death*. Philadelphia, JB Lippincott, 1922.

Sacher GA, Hart RW: Longevity, aging and comparative cellular and molecular biology of the mouse, Mus musculus, and the white-footed mouse, Peromyscus leucopus. In Bergsma D, Harrison DE, (eds.) *Genetic Effects on Aging*. New York, AR Liss, Inc., 1978, pp. 71–96

Scott JP, Fuller JL: *Genetics and the Social Behavior of the Dog*. Chicago, University Chicago Press, 1965.

Sprott RL, Staats J: Behavioral studies using genetically defined mice—a bibliography. *Behavior Genetics* 5:27–82, 1975.

Stewart JM, Scott JP: Genetics of the Dog. In King R, (ed.) *Handbook of Genetics*. New York, Plenum Press, 1975.

Tryon RC: Genetic differences in maze-learning ability in rats. *Yearbook Nat Soc Study Educ* 39:111-119, 1940.

Vogel F: The genetic basis of the normal human electroencephalogram (EEG). *Humangenetik* 10:91–114, 1970.

Vogel F, Schalt E, Kruger J, Propping P, Lehnert KF: The electroencephalogram (EEG) as a research tool in human behavior genetics: psychological examinations in healthy males with various inherited EEG variants. I. Rationale of the study, material, methods, heritability of test parameters. II. Results. III. Interpretation of the results. *Human Genetics,* 1979.

Weinshilboum RM: Human biochemical genetics of plasma dopamine-β-hydroxylase and erythrocyte catechol-0-methyltransferase. *Human Genetics* Suppl 1:101–112, 1978.

Zeman W: Neuronal ceroid storage disease. *J Neuropath, Exp Neurol* 33:1–12, 1974.

Stein, ed. The Psychobiology of Aging: Problems and Perspectives

An Appraisal of the Utility of Genetic Techniques for the Study of Neurobiology and Aging in Mice[a]

Richard L. Sprott

The Jackson Laboratory, Bar Harbor, Maine.

Introduction

While there is genuine, and hopefully justified, enthusiasm for the potential contribution to be made by the application of behavior genetic techniques to gerontological research, the enthusiasm must be for promise rather than performance. The major aging contribution of animal behavior genetic models so far has been to the study of learning and memory changes with advancing age, primarily in the laboratories of Dr. Charles Goodrick, Dr. Alberto Oliverio, and myself. Some of these studies (Oliverio et al., 1973; Sprott, 1978) bear on the topic of the paper and will be discussed below, but most have little direct bearing on neurobiology. I have included a supplemental bibliology at the end of the paper which includes most aging studies using genetically defined mice. Most of this literature is also summarized in reviews by Elias and Elias (1975), Sprott and Stavnes (1975), and Sprott (1976). Elias (1979) has provided an excellent review of similar studies in aging inbred rats.

There are, to my knowledge, only two recent reviews of nervous system *function* in aging, genetically defined subjects, one by Finch (1979) and one by Russell and Sprott (1974). The Finch review is based primarily upon work with male C57BL/6J, and DBA/2J mice. The evidence Finch reports suggests that there are few generalized changes in mouse brain other than increases in lipofuscin levels and spontaneous

[a]Preparation of this manuscript was supported by NIH research grant AG 00250 from the National Institute on Aging. The Jackson Laboratory is fully accredited by the American Association for Accreditation of Laboratory Animal Care.

brain-reactive antibodies. There are no reports of major losses of neuron populations in strains which have so far been studied, although such losses do occur as a consequence of specific mutations (Russell and Sprott, 1974). Cerebrovascular disease has been observed in rats, but not in mice, and is in fact a highly unlikely occurrence in mice where arteriosclerosis is virtually unknown.

The Russell and Sprott review (1974) deals primarily with neurological mutations which might be useful for aging research. So far, little actual aging research has been conducted with such mice. However, some of these mutations have problems which seem particularly pertinent to gerontology, such as: jimpy *(jp)* which has a myelin synthesis defect; tottering *(tg)* and learner (tg^{la}) which have Purkinje and granule cell deficits; shambling *(shm)* with age correlated neural plaques in spinal cord and brain stem; and beige *(bg)* with accelerated deposition of lipofuscin granules. The beige mutation and a similar lipofuscin mutation reported by O'Steen (1970) are possible models for Chediak-Higashi syndrome and human progeria respectively. Mice bearing the beige mutation show coat-color dilution and abnormal leukocyte granules which are also seen in Chediak-Higashi syndrome. O'Steen's mutants accumulate lipofuscin in the nerve tissue, particularly Purkinje cells, at an accelerated rate, and die prematurely at around 50 days. The development and pattern of change in these mice resembles that seen in human progeria (O'Steen, 1970). There are some 65 neurological mutations in mice, most of which lead to early death, but a few live long enough to be of interest to gerontologists. A current listing of these mutations appears annually in *Mouse News Letter.*

A variety of genetic techniques is available for application to behavioral and neurological problems, in an aging context. Since these techniques have been the subject of two recent reviews (Roderick, 1979; Russell and Sprott, 1974), I will try to keep the genetic discussion as brief as possible and present examples of potential aging studies with the discussion of each technique.

There are two major reasons for the use of genetically defined animals in aging research: to reduce genetic variance as an experimental variable or to investigate directly the influence of genotype upon a parameter of interest. In the first situation, a genetically homogeneous population, such as a single strain or F_1 hybrid population, could be used and would usually be preferable to so called "random bred" populations which are seldom if ever truly random bred. The discussion which follows will describe the genetic materials which are available to the investigator who wishes to investigate the influence or importance of genetic variables or to take advantage of the particular characteristics of a genetic model for a particular problem.

Of the many types of genetically defined material which have been developed, five are especially relevant to aging research: 1. Inbred strains and F_1 hybrids; 2. Single gene mutations; 3. Congenic lines; 4. Recombinant inbred strains; and 5. Genetically selected strains and stocks.

Inbred Strains and F_1 Hybrid Mice

Inbred strains of mice are, by definition, the product of at least twenty generations of brother-sister mating. The individual members of an inbred strain are as alike as identical twins. Once the characteristics of a strain are known they can be reproduced repeatedly. Mice of several strains live to ages of 24 to 28 months and a few to beyond 36 months. The influence of genotype upon a particular characteristic can be investigated by placing mice from several inbred strains in a common environment. Observed differences must then be, within limits, the consequence of genetic factors. By reversing this strategy, and placing mice from a single inbred strain in a variety of environments, it is possible to estimate the importance of environmental influences upon a parameter of interest. Thus, inbred mice can be used to determine whether genetic variation in the expression of a characteristic exists and the environmental malleability of the characteristic. However, the use of strain comparisons has a major limitation. While strain differences are easily demonstrated, it is often very difficult to attach much meaning to these differences, since the genes and gene products involved are usually unknown.

Since comparisons of mice from two or more strains do not usually provide any information about the nature of the genetic differences, crosses between genotypes must be used to analyze patterns of genetic influence. The first stage in any such analysis is typically a cross between two phenotypically different inbred strains in order to produce the genetically uniform but highly heterozygous F_1 hybrid. In addition to their use in breeding tests, these mice have other advantages for aging research. Each of the parental strains is homozygous for certain recessive genes which may be age-limiting. Many of the deleterious alleles carried in one parental strain will not be found in the other strain. Therefore, the F_1 hybrid mouse usually has many more positive genetic factors and increased longevity. Figure 1 shows a typical example of C57BL/6, DBA/2J, and B6D2F_1 mice maintained in a clean conventional colony (Myers, unpublished). Survival of mice of these three genotypes has been assessed in several environments (Sprott, unpublished), and the genotype relationship (F_1 longest lived, DBA/2J shortest lived) remains constant across all environments, some of which are very deleterious and some of which are quite supportive.

Figure 2 shows the performance of these three types of mice (C57BL/6J, DBA/2J, and B6D2F_1) in a passive avoidance learning situation at ages ranging from six weeks to thirty months. Data from these experiments have been published previously (Sprott, 1978) and the avoidance

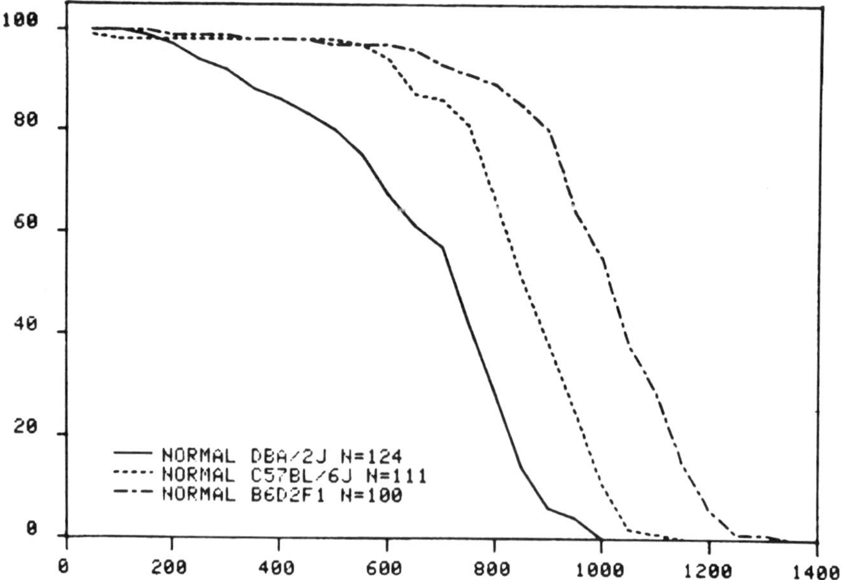

Figure 1. Longevity of DBA/2J, C57BL/6J, and B6D2F$_1$ mice in clean conventional colony conditions. Mice were housed four per cage with food and water available *ad libitum*.

SOURCE: *Myers, unpublished.*

procedure has been described in detail (Sprott, 1978, 1974, 1972). The important point for this discussion is that while the performance of mice of the two strains is different, no senescence effect on learning is observed. Thus, in a simple task such as this one, genotype and environment are both important determinants of performance, but age, post maturity, has very little influence. There is a senescence effect upon survival in this situation, which might be of interest to investigators interested in genotype-age interaction in responses to stress.

Single Gene Mutations and Other Single Locus Effects

The study of inbred strains and F$_1$ hybrids usually provides very little information about mechanisms of gene action. The analysis of single normal versus mutant genes, or a series of normal alternative alleles is often a more useful approach. Many mutant alleles limit lifespan, and comparisons between homozygous mutant mice and their "normal" homozygous wild-type and heterozygous littermates may provide specific information, especially when the mutation is of interest to behaviorists, physiologists, and biochemists. The mutations in mice which may be of most interest to psychobiologists of aging are the "neurological" mutants. In excess of 65 such mutations have been described which have

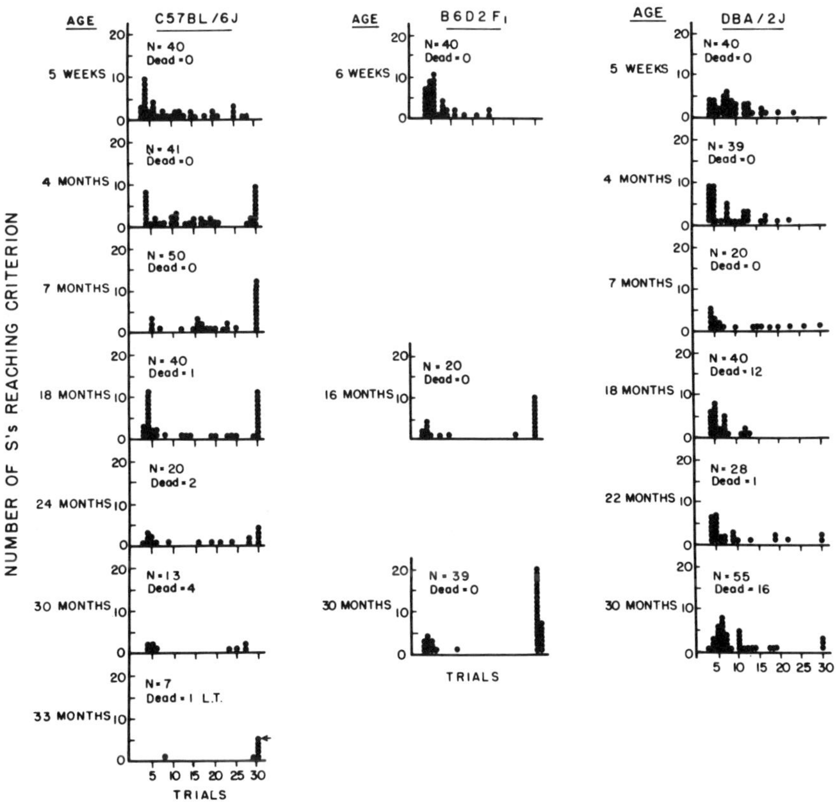

Figure 2. Performance of DBA/2J, C57BL/6J, and B6D2F$_1$ mice in a passive avoidance situation at ages ranging from eight weeks to thirty-three months.

demonstrable effects upon behavior and lifespan (Sprott, 1979). However, only a few of these mutations permit survival to maturity. In the case of very short-lived types it may be possible to analyze the effects of a "single dose" of the mutation in the heterozygous carriers.

Among the mutations which appear to be most likely to be useful for aging research are: dystonia musculorum *(dt)*, which shows smaller than normal nerve trunks and increased collagen between nerve fibers; jimpy *(jp)* and quaking *(qk)*, which have disturbances of myelination; tottering *(tg)* and leaner (tg^{la}), which have Purkinje and granule cell deficits; shambling *(shm)*, which develop neural plaques; ataxia (*ax* and ad^{j}), which have abnormalities in a variety of sites including the corpus callosum, Purkinje cells, brain stem nuclei, and spinal nerves; and beige *(bg)*, which may be a model for Chediak-Higashi syndrome. The utility of these mutations, and a few others, for aging research has been discussed by Russell and Sprott (1974).

Another potential source of material for the analysis of gene action throughout the lifespan is the single-locus behavioral effect of normal alternative alleles. The advantages of analysis of "normal" alleles are that, unlike the mutations described above, they do not involve "abnormal" or disruptive modifications of metabolic pathways or CNS structures. Further, it should be possible to follow a well studied effect throughout the lifespan of the subjects without the complications which are always present with more complex (polygenic) behaviors. Behaviors which are influenced by many genes (e.g., aggression, learning, memory, sexuality) are also likely to be influenced by *different* genes at different developmental stages. Genetic analysis, in an aging context, becomes enormously more complex under such conditions. The avoidance behavior described earlier in this paper has been shown to be influenced by alternative alleles at a single locus (Passive performance, *Pp,* Sprott, 1974). Dr. Oliverio has shown a similar effect in active avoidance (Active avoidance learning, *Aal,* Oliverio et al., 1973). These single-locus effects offer the best hope for correlation of behavior and physiology since they can be genetically manipulated in ways which can almost completely eliminate the possibility of spurious correlation. For example, if a behavioral effect and a physiological correlate stay together through a series of genetic crosses and in a battery of recombinant inbred strains (described below), then they must be causally related or very tightly genetically linked. Table 1 lists ten single-locus behavioral effects which are potentially useful for analysis of this type.

Congenic Lines

Mutations and identified allelic alternatives are particularly useful when they constitute the only genetic difference between the affected individual and other individuals of the same strain. This will naturally be the case when the mutation arises in the strain of interest. When this is not the case, the mutation or allele can be transferred to the strain of interest by a repeated back-cross strategy, where mutant bearing animals are mated with non-mutant animals of the strain of interest generation after generation. When this process is continued long enough (7 or 8 generations), brother-sister matings of mutant bearing animals are begun. Eventually (after 16 to 20 generations) a new inbred strain is created which differs from the original only at the mutant locus (Green, 1966). For mutations with major effects, such as many of the neurological mutants, this may not be necessary, but for more subtle effects it may be very important to eliminate background effects, that is the effects of interactions between other genes, characteristic of a strain, and the mutation of interest. An added advantage is the fact that transfer is usually made to a commonly studied strain (e.g., C57BL/6J) so that the behavioral and physiological characteristics of the strain are well known. The best known example of

Table 1. Mouse Behavioral Gene Effects: Single Locus Behaviors[a]

Gene Symbol	Gene Name	Chromosome	Test Situation	Reference[b]
Aal	Active avoidance learning	9	Shuttle box	(7)
Aap	Active avoidance performance	–	Jump box	(9)
asp	Audiogenic seizure prone	4	Bell jar	(2,3)
Bfo	Bell-flash ovulation	4	Home cage	(4)
Cpz	Chlorpromazine avoidance	9	Shuttle box	(1)
Exa	Exploratory activity	4	Open-field	(6)
Pp	Passive avoidance	–	Jump box	(8)
Sac	Saccharin preference	–	Home cage	(5)
Sco	Scopolamine modification of exploratory activity	17	Open-field	(6)
Sip	Schedule induced polydipsia	–	Operant chamber	(10)

[a] Reprinted from *Inbred and Genetically Defined Strains of Laboratory Animals.* Altman PL, Katz DD (eds.). F.A.S.E.B., Bethesda, 1979.

[b] References: (1.) Castellano, C., et al. 1974. *Psychopharmacologia* 34:309-316; (2.) Collins, R. L., and J. L. Fuller. 1968. *Science* 162:1137-1139; (3.) Collins, R. L. 1970. *Behav. Genet.* 1:99-209; (4.) Eleftheriou, B. E., and M. B. Kristal. 1974. *J. Reprod. Fertil.* 38:41-47; (5.) Fuller, J. L. 1974. *J. Hered.* 65:33-36; (6.) Oliverio, A., et al. 1973. *Physiol. and Behav.* 10:893-899; (7.) Oliverio, A., et al. 1973. *Physiol. and Behav.* 11:497-501; (8.) Sprott, R. L. 1974. *Behav. Biol.* 11:231-237; (9.) Stavnes, K., and R. L. Sprott. 1975. *Psych. Rep.* 36:515-521; (10.) Symons, J. P., and R. L. Sprott. 1976. *Physiol. and Behav.* 17:837-839.

this strategy is the series of studies by D. L. Coleman and his collaborators (Coleman and Hummel, 1973; Hummel, Coleman, and Lane, 1972) on the interaction with strain background of genes producing obesity and diabetes. Dr. David Harrison at the Jackson Laboratory is conducting a series of lifespan studies with the same genetic materials. Coleman's studies and one by Sprott (1972) have shown that the life-shortening effects of the obese *(ob)* and *(db)* mutations are dependent upon environment and upon strain background. For example, both mutations have severe life-shortening effects when they are expressed in C57BL/KsJ mice, but do not have such effects on C57BL/6J mice.

Recombinant Inbred (RI) Strains

Since aging and behavioral changes are influenced by environmental and genetic differences, genetic analysis of late-life behavior is particularly difficult. The most promising genetic approach to this problem is by use of the recently developed recombinant inbred (RI) strain technique developed by D. W. Bailey (1971). Crosses are made between two inbred strains known to show genetic difference in some characteristic of interest. Following the production of an F_2 generation from this interstrain cross, 20 or more different brother-sister pairs of F_2 individuals are mated, and offspring from each such pair are used to start a new recombinant inbred strain.

In these new strains the allele carried at each of the genetic loci by which the original parent lines differed, must be identical with that in one or another of those lines. Thus, a new homozygous combination of the genes carried by the two strains has been produced and can be replicated indefinitely, simply by continuing brother-sister inbreeding. If expression of a certain phenotype, (say a particular behavior or brain structure), were controlled by alleles at one specific genetic locus, then, in any given family of recombinant inbred strains, developed following a cross between two specific inbred strains, the phenotype of interest in about half of the RI strains would resemble closely that seen in one parental line, and in the other half would resemble the other original parent. Finding exact copies of a parental characteristic in several of the RI strains is very good evidence that the characteristic is controlled by alleles at a single genetic locus.

The use of RI strains may allow detection of the effects of single genes even in cases where there are strong environmental influences. Since each RI strain is homozygous, all variations observed within a strain must be environmental; one might observe for each strain a reliable mean and characteristic variation around that mean, or a fairly constant incidence of a particular lesion. If for a particular quantitative character two distinct mean levels are seen in a family of RI strains, with half of the lines resembling one original parent and half the other parent, then there is probably one major gene responsible for the difference between these levels.

If interaction of recessive alleles at two loci were required to produce the distinguishing characteristic, then the proportion of RI strains with a phenotype resembling closely the parent strain showing that phenotype would be much smaller, not differing significantly from one-fourth. If the phenotype of interest were determined by combined action of many different genes, the probability of achieving that unique gene combination in even one of the RI strains would be vanishingly small, and thus none would show the characteristic.

One advantage of the RI strain technique, especially pertinent for analysis of behavior differences, is the opportunity it affords for reduction in apparent complexity of genetic factors. As already stated, the effects of a single gene may vary in different genetic environments. Recombinant inbred strains represent a variety of different genetic backgrounds drawn from a limited gene pool. The amount of variation in the effects of one single known gene substitution as observed in a family of recombinant inbred strains can therefore be used to provide an estimate of the lower limit of the extent to which expression of that specific gene is affected by other portions of the genome. This step should make it increasingly possible to measure relative genetic, environmental, and interaction contributions to total variance.

In addition, this RI strain technique can be used to advantage in attempts to locate genes within the mouse genome. Since linked genes will tend to appear together in particular recombinant inbred strains, an array of characteristics can be typed for each line within an RI group; and observed association of any one of these characteristics, with presence in the same line of particular alleles at genetic loci known to be assorting among this family of RI strains, may be used to establish and measure genetic linkage. As knowledge of segregating and assorting genetic loci increases, the recognition and location of single genes affecting behavior should proceed more rapidly than is possible using conventional techniques.

The application of this technique to aging research could provide a new approach to difficult research problems. For example, when a particular behavior, such as passive-avoidance performance (Sprott, 1972) shows different age patterns in two inbred strains, the RI strain technique can first be used to estimate the number of genes involved. Subsequent RI strain analysis could lead to the identification of a small number of physiological correlates of the behavioral trait. These physiological correlates could then be followed throughout the lifespan of individual subjects to ascertain whether or not they show parallel lifespan development. We have begun an analysis of this type for passive-avoidance in my laboratory, using RI strains derived from C57BL/6J and DBA/2J inbred parental strains. While this analysis has not yet resulted in the identification of the physiological substrate of the Passive-performance locus described earlier, it has allowed us to eliminate several possible correlates (e.g., adrenal lipid levels, which decrease with advancing age in DBA/2J mice). This analysis has also helped us to improve our characterization of the behavioral effect. We now know that the effects of the genes involved are upon the subjects' response to the test environment, not upon learning ability, foot shock thresholds, or activity levels. This may help explain why we do not observe any change in the behavior in the last third of the subjects' lifespans, when activity levels, sensory thresholds, and, perhaps, learning abilities are declining.

Genetically Selected Strains and Stocks

Genetic selection is usually accomplished by repeated matings of population extremes for the characteristic of interest. Roderick (1979) provides an excellent review of the uses of genetic selection in studies of brain-behavior interaction, and Elias (Elias and Elias, 1975) has described the advantages and disadvantages of genetic selection in aging research.The technique is primarily useful for exaggerating traits or characteristics which are polygenically controlled. Roderick and the Wimers have used selection to produce variations in brain size which are then used to study behavior (Roderick et al., 1976). Their studies have provided examples of causal linkage between morphology and behavior and are the best examples of the strengths of the technique. What is needed now is a lifespan study of the Roderick and Wimer mice to assess the effects of variations in various brain areas upon longevity, terminal pathology, and behavior.

While each of the techniques described above is particularly useful for certain types of questions, they differ greatly in terms of the resources needed for their use and the time and expense needed to complete an analysis. When a lifespan dimension is added to these differences, it should be obvious that the choice of technique should be made with great care. While simple paradigms using inbred strains and F_1 hybrids provide little genetic information, they are also the least time consuming and expensive. Mice are readily available commercially which obviates the necessity for maintaining an expensive breeding colony. Even so, I find that the cost of producing a single 36 month-old mouse of a long-lived strain (C57BL/6J) in an efficient colony is approximately $350. This figure includes maintenance ($0.07/day) for this mouse and the other nine mice needed to insure one live mouse at 36 months, and the cost of technician time to monitor these mice as they age.

When a much larger number of mice must be bred and maintained in order to produce a limited number of mice for study, as in genetic analysis, using genetic crosses, and in selection studies, this cost is multiplied enormously, and can only be justified when the information can be obtained in no other way. Finally, the RI strain technique is the most cumbersome and expensive in the short-term, since it requires the establishment of 20 to 30 inbred lines and may take 7 to 10 years to complete. However, once the lines are established (or if they are already available by collaboration), they can be used for analysis of any characteristic for which the parental strains differed. Clearly, no investigator should consider creating an RI strain battery for aging research unless he is committed to a 10 to 20 year research program. In spite of this limitation, the technique will become increasingly important as these mice become more generally available, and perhaps even commercially, available.

In summary, I hope it is apparent that the use of genetically defined subjects offers the opportunity for precise formulation of research questions and is worth the trouble and expense as long as the investigator understands the technique he chooses and it is appropriate to the problem of interest. The primary advantage of genetically defined mouse models is the control of genetic variance and the increase in the specificity of hypotheses which can result. Aggression can be studied throughout the lifespan in long-lived aggressive (BALB/cJ) and non-aggressive (C57BL/6J) mice. The effects of lipofuscin accumulation on behavior can be studied in one or more lipofuscin accumulating mutant mouse models (e.g., *beige*). The importance of activity level in late-life performance in learning situations could be studied in highly active and less active mouse strains, in the absence of the confounding influences of varying levels of motivation, health status, and motor coordination. Studies of each of these types are currently in progress, but they have not yet reached a point where results are available. However, many more investigators are using genetically defined materials in aging research. This will inevitably result in wider dissemination of information about models for particular age conditions and greater understanding of the advantages and disadvantages of each.

References

Bailey DW: Recombinant inbred strains; an aid in finding identity, linkage, and function of histocompatibility and other genes. *Transplant* 11:325–327, 1971.

Coleman DL, Hummel KP: The influence of genetic background on the expression of the obese *(ob)* gene in the mouse. *Diabetologia* 9:287–293, 1973.

Elias ME, and Elias PK: 1975. Hormones, aging and behavior in infrahuman mammals. In Eleftheriou BE, Sprott RL (eds.), *Hormonal Correlates of Behavior.* Plenum Press, New York, 1975, pp. 395–439.

Elias MF: Aging studies of behavior with Fischer 344, Sprague-Dawley, and Long Evans rats. In Gibson D (ed.) *Development of the Rodent as a Model System of Aging.* USPHS-DHEW Publication No. (NIH) 79–161, 1979, pp. 255–297.

Finch CE: Endocrine, reproductive, neural functions, and drug responses in aging mice. In Gibson D (ed.) *Development of the Rodent as a Model System of Aging.* USPHS-DEW Publication No. (NIH) 79–161, 1979, pp. 45–55.

Green EL: 1966. Breeding Systems. In Green EL (ed.) *Biology of the Laboratory Mouse.* McGraw-Hill, New York, 1966, pp. 11–12.

Hummel KP, Coleman DL, Lane PW: The influence of genetic background on expression of mutations at the diabetes locus in the mouse I. C57BL/KsJ and C57BL/6J strains. *Biochemical Genetics* 7:1–13, 1972.

Oliverio A, Eleftheriou BE, Bailey DW: A gene influencing active avoidance performance in mice. *Physiology and Behavior* 11:497–501, 1973.

O'Steen WK, Nady K: Lipofuscin pigment in neurons of young mice with hereditary central nervous system defect. *Amer J Anatomy* 128:359–565, 1970.

Roderick TH: Genetic techniques as tools for analysis of brain-behavior relationships. In Hahn MT (ed.) *Development and Evolution of Brain Size: Behavioral Implications.* Academic Press, New York, 1979, (in press).

Roderick TH, Wimer RE, Wimer CC: 1976. Genetic manipulation of neuroanatomical traits. In Petrinovich L, McGaugh JL (eds.) *Knowing, Thinking, and Believing.* Plenum Press, New York, 1976, pp. 143–178.

Russell ES, Sprott RL: Genetics and the aging nervous system, In Maletta GJ (ed.) *Survey on the Aging Nervous System.* USPHS-DHEW, Publication No. (NIH) 74–296, 1974, pp. 23–46.

Sprott RL: Long term studies of feeding behavior of obese, diabetic, and viable yellow mice under *ad lib.* and operant conditions. *Psych Rep* 30:991–1003, 1972.

Sprott RL: Passive-avoidance conditioning in inbred mice: effects of shock intensity, age, and genotype. *J Comp Physiol Psychol* 80:327–334, 1972.

Sprott RL: Passive-avoidance performance in mice: Evidence for single-locus inheritance. *Behav Biol* 11:231–237, 1974.

Sprott RL: Behavior characteristics of C57BL/6J, DBA/2J, and B6D2Fl mice which are potentially useful for gerontologic research. *Exper Aging Research* 1:313–323, 1975.

Sprott RL: Behavior genetics in aging rodents. In Elias MF, Elias PK, Eleftheriou BE (eds.) *Special Review of Experimental Aging Research: Progress in Biology.* E.A.R., Bar Harbor, 1976.

Sprott RL: The interaction of genotype and environment in the determination of avoidance behavior of aging inbred mice. In Harrison DE, Bergsma D (eds.) *Birth Defects: Vol. XIV, 1.* National Foundation, 1978, pp. 109–120.

Sprott RL: Behavioral gene effects: Mouse. In Altman PL, Katz DD (eds.) *Inbred and Genetically Defined Strains of Laboratory Animals.* FASEB Bethesda, 1979, pp. 154–157.

Sprott RL, Stavnes K: Avoidance learning, behavior genetics, and aging: a critical review and comment on methodology. *Exp Aging Res* 1:145–168, 1975.

Sprott RL, Symons JP: The effects of age and genotype upon the jaw-jerk reflex in inbred mice. *J Gerontol* 31:660–662, 1976.

Symons JP, Sprott RL: Genetic analysis of schedule induced polydipsia. *Physiol and Behav* 17:837–839, 1976.

Additional References of Interest

Collins RL: Longevity, aging, and environmental stress: a multivariate study. *Anat Rec* 151:337–338 (abst), 1965.

Eleftheriou BE: Changes with age in pituitary-adrenal responsiveness and reactivity in mild stress in mice. *Gerontologia* 20:224–230, 1974.

Elias MF, Eleftheriou BE: Separating measures of learning and incentive in water maze experiments with aging inbred strains of mice. *Psychol Rep* 36:343–351, 1975.

Elias PK, Elias MF: Effects of age on learning ability: Contributions from the animal literature. *Exp Aging Res* 2:165–186, 1976.

Elias PK, Elias MF, Eleftheriou BE: Emotionality, exploratory behavior, and locomotion in aging inbred strains of mice. *Gerontologia* 21:46–55, 1975.

Elias PK, Redgate E: Effects of immobilization stress on open field behavior and plasma corticosterone levels of aging C57BL/6J mice. *Exp Aging Res* 1:127–135, 1975.

Elias MF, Zolovick AJ, Elias PK, Eleftheriou BD: Some methodological problems in age comparisons of EEG sleep patterns for C57BL/6J mice. *Exp Aging Res* 1:107–119, 1975.

Freund G, Walker DW: The effect of aging on acquisition and retention of shuttle box avoidance in mice. *Life Sci* 10:1343–1349, 1971.

Goodrick CL: Behavioral characteristics of young and senescent inbred female mice of the C57BL/6J strain. *J Gerontol* 22:459–464, 1967.

Goodrick CL: The effects of exercise on longevity and behavior of hybrid mice which differ in coat color. *J Gerontol* 29:129–133, 1974.

Goodrick CL: Behavioral differences in young and aged mice: Strain differences for activity measures, operant learning, sensory discrimination, and alcohol preference. *Exp Aging Res* 1:191–207, 1975.

Lindop P, Rotblat J: Aging effects of ionizing radiations. *Proc 2nd Internat Conf Peaceful Uses Atomic Energy* 22:46–52, 1958.

Lindop P, Rotblat J: Aging effects of ionizing radiations. *Progr Nuclear Energy Biol Sci* 2:58–68, 1959.

Meier GW: Irradiation, genetics and aging: Behavioral implications. In *Effects of Ionizing Radiation on the Nervous System*. International Atomic Energy Agency, Vienna, 1962, pp. 97–196.

Meier GW: Differences in maze performances as a function of age and strain of house mice. *J Comp Physiol Psychol* 58:418–422, 1964.

Meier GW, Foshee DP: Genetics, age and the variability of learning performances. *J Genet Psychol* 102:267–275, 1963.

Oliverio A, Bovet D: Effects of age on maze learning and avoidance conditioning of mice. *Life Sci* 5:1317–1324, 1966.

Samorajski T, Rolsten C: Nerve fiber hypertrophy in posterior tibial nerves of mice in response to voluntary running activity during aging. *J Comp Neurol* 159:553–558, 1975.

Samorajski T, Rolsten C, Collins, RL: Environmental stress and biological aging. *Anat Rec* 148:330 (abst), 1964.

Samorajski T, Rolsten C, Ordy JM: Changes in behavior, brain, and neuroendocrine chemistry with age and stress in C57BL/10 male mice. *J Gerontol* 26:168–175, 1971.

Samorajski T, Strong JR, Sun A: Dihydroergotoxine (Hydergine) and alcohol-induced variations in young and old mice. *J Gerontol* 32:145–152, 1977.

Spalding JF, Brooks MR: The possible influence of a single gene locus on life span and its relationship to radiation resistance and activity. *Proc Soc Exptl Biol Med* 136:1091–1093, 1971.

Spalding JF, Brooks MR, Archuleta RF: A possible single gene locus effect on life span, radiation resistance and activity. *Radiat Res* 47:287–288 (abst), 1971.

Spalding JF, Freyman RW, Holland LM: Effects of 800-M Hz electromagnetic radiation on body weight, activity, hematopoiesis and life span in mice. *Health Phys* 20:421–424, 1971.

Sprott RL, Eleftheriou BE: Open-field behavior in aging inbred mice. *Gerontologia* 20:155–162, 1974.

Sprott RL, Stavnes K: Avoidance learning, behavior genetics, and aging: a critical review and comment on methodology. *Exp Aging Res* 1:145–168, 1975.

Wax TM: Runwheel activity patterns of mature-young and senescent mice: The effect of constant lighting conditions. *J Gerontol* 30:22–27, 1975.

Wax TM: Effects of age, strain, and illumination intensity on activity and self-selection of light-dark schedules in mice. *J Comp Physiol Psychol* 91:51–62, 1977.

Wright WE, Werboff J, Haggett BN: Aging and water submersion in C57BL/6J mice: Initial performance and retest as a function of recovery and water temperature. *Develop Psychobiol* 4:363–373, 1971.

Stein, ed. The Psychobiology of Aging: Problems and Perspectives

A Genetic Approach to Behavioral Ontogeny and Aging in the Mouse

Alberto Oliverio, Enrico Alleva and Claudio Castellano

Istituto di Fisiologia Generale, University of Rome and Laboratorio Psicobiologia e Psicofarmacologia via Reno, 1 - 00198 Rome, Italy.

Introduction

The increasing concern about aging processes has led to the expression of a variety of theories on the nature and causes of aging in animals and man (Comfort, 1974; Rockstein, 1974). Genetic mechanisms, in addition to environmental agents, may be responsible for different aging patterns and longevity, and a number of reviews presenting a genetic approach to aging, notably those of Meier and Foshee (1963), Goodrick (1967), Elias and Elias (1975), Russell (1976) and Sprott (1976) have recently appeared. Though the genetic approach has had little impact on behavioral gerontology until very recently, findings indicate that in mice from different inbred strains, there is an outstanding variability in mean life span and incidence of diverse age-related pathological conditions. As indicated by Russell and Sprott (1975) these facts have led to the theory that "there may be a variety of aging patterns, and genetically different individuals within a species may have different weak spots (page 297)." The genetic approach permits one to assess the role of a number of complex behavioral factors, such as learning ability, motor skills, activity level and sensory threshold, which result in age-dependent changes in performance (Doty, 1966; Oliverio & Bovet, 1966; Freund & Walker, 1971).

Most of the studies within this area are devoted to an analysis limited to the later part of life span. A number of findings also indicate that there are clear, behavioral genetic differences not only in relation to aging, but also in early developmental patterns of behavior. In other words, there are strains which are more precocious at birth and strains which are less mature; a fact which may result in important strain differences which characterize the behavioral pattern of individuals during their entire life spans. The evolutionary significance of aging was analyzed by Wilson (1974) who discussed the "between-species" (or within species) genetic differences in development and aging. In this chapter we present some findings describing some of the behavioral differences observed during the life span of different strains of mice.

A Genetic Approach to Developmental Differences

What is the evolutionary meaning of brain and behavioral maturity at birth? In the precocial species (such as guinea pigs or ruminants), sensory and motor maturation at birth allows for immediate identification with the mother and the establishment of social and mother-offspring relationships which resemble imprinting in birds (Scott, 1958; Sluckin, 1965). In contrast, in nonprecocial (altricial) mammals, which form a heterogeneous group ranging from rodents to carnivores, primates and man, the immediate postnatal period is characterized by great maternal dependency, by a later onset of primary and social relationships, and by immaturity or sensory and motor abilities.

From an evolutionary point of view, precocity at birth may be regarded as characteristic of behavioral plasticity and generalization. The precocial species have the advantage that the ontogeny of the CNS is realized during the fetal period and that the newborn organism is practically ready for independent life soon after birth. The behavioral adaptation of a precocial species is set, in large part, through innate mechanisms (Sedlacek, 1974). The immaturity of behavioral functions in the altricial neonate at birth and during the first days, months or even years, of postnatal life, is compensated for by parental care. The immature brain passes through critical developmental periods under different influences of the external environment which may have positive or negative effects on brain and behavioral maturation. In other words, while precocial species have the advantage of the "specialist" and rely to a greater extent on innate patterns, altricial species have the advantages of the "generalist", and are more flexible and open to the effects of the environment. At one extreme the nervous system and the behavior which it mediates, confine the *specialist* animal to a relatively narrow niche. At the other end of the continuum, the nervous system and behavior are more flexible and versatile, and allow the animal to exploit a greater array of environmental situations. These broad niched animals are known as *generalists* (Parker, 1974).

These different points are summarized in a tentative model in Figure 1 where the various mechanisms leading to behavioral rigidity or plasticity are considered in relation to infancy and adulthood. Different maturational and behavioral patterns during infancy lead to specific interactions

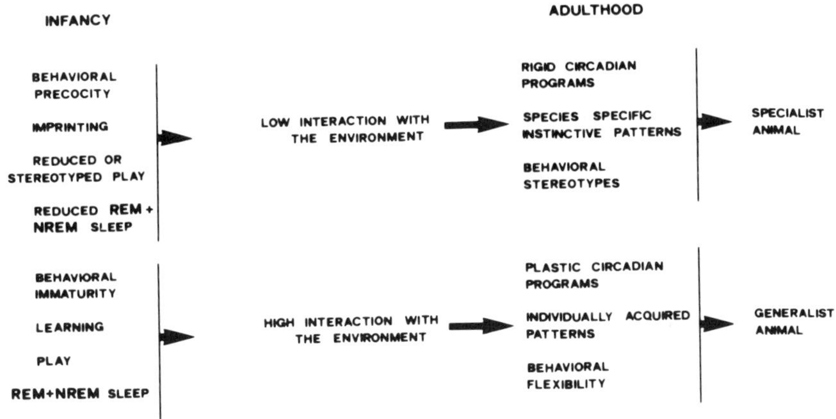

Figure 1. Behavioral rigidity (specialization) or plasticity (generalization) in relation to a number of factors acting during infancy or adulthood.

SOURCE: *Oliverio et al., 1979.*

with the environment; and the stimulating or detrimental effects of the environment have a more pronounced effect on those species which reach their maturity at a later age. Whether an adult animal is a "specialist" or a "generalist" depends upon these early mechanisms and behavioral categories, upon the type of interaction with the environment, and finally, upon the evolutionary genetic mechanisms which set the types of species-specific or individual, cerebral and behavioral organization.

A number of findings can be taken to indicate that there are strains of mice which are differentiated according to their behaviors (Oliverio et al., 1975; Oliverio and Malorni, 1979; Oliverio et al., 1979), and which also differ in their patterns of postnatal neurological development. If we consider electrocorticographic activity, which was shown to parallel different stages of maturation of the cortex (Kobayashi et al., 1963), there are strains (such as C57BL/6J–C57 mice) which are more mature at birth and strains (like SEC 1/ReJ–SEC mice) which are less mature. For example, at eight days of age, electrical activity of the cortex of SEC mice was similar to the C57 strain on the first day of postnatal life (Oliverio et al., 1975a). The recordings of the two strains were almost identical at 32 days of age and substantially similar in one year old mice (Figure 2). Similar developmental differences are also evident for a number of reflexes, such as cliff aversion, righting, placing, grasping, or the startle response which appeared at an earlier age (also 3-4 days in advance) in the C57 strain (Oliverio et al., 1975b) (Figure 3). These findings indicate that there are clear genetic differences in the intraspecific patterns of postnatal maturation, a fact which was supported by a

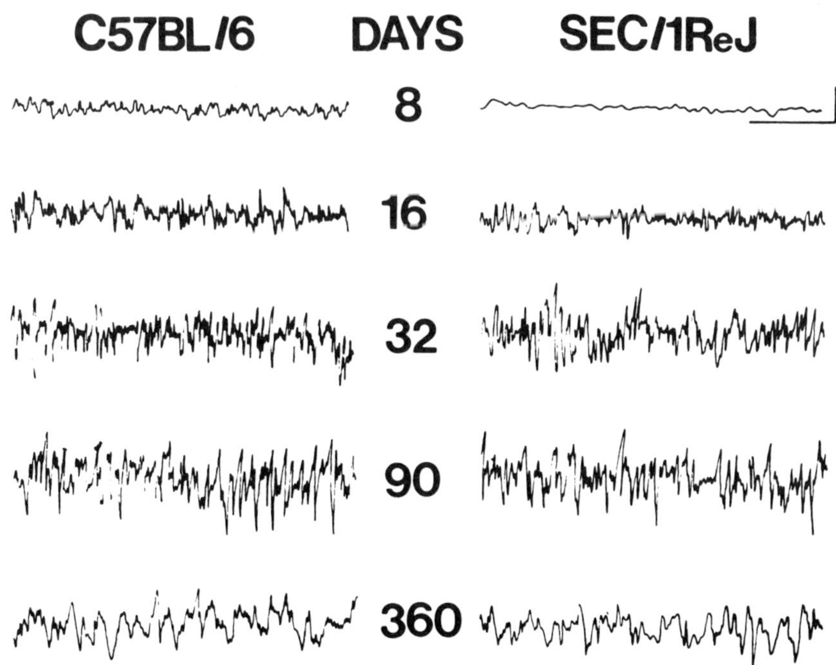

Figure 2. Electrocorticograms at each chronological age of C57BL/6 and SEC/1ReJ mice.
SOURCE: *Alleva et al., 1979.*

number of findings on amphetamine-induced locomotor and stereotyped behavior (SB) in C57 and SEC mice aged from 8 to 360 days of age (Alleva et al. 1979).

CNS Sensitivity to Drugs Through Age

Postnatal behavioral development involves maturation of several systems and excitatory and inhibitory mechanisms which appear to control behavioral maturation and arousal in mammals. Evidence suggests that these mechanisms are modulated by various components of the reticular system and by forebrain structures such as the frontal cortex and hippocampus (Campbell and Mabry, 1972). At the neurochemical level, it has been shown that among neuronal pathways there exist major differences in the time of their appearance and the rate of their differentiation and that the availability of neurotransmitters at the synaptic cleft exhibit different rates of development within a particular neuronal group (Coyle, 1977). In this regard, the ontogeny of stereotyped behavior represents a reliable indication of the development of cerebral catecholaminergic processes (Coyle, 1977). The rationale for a pharmacological

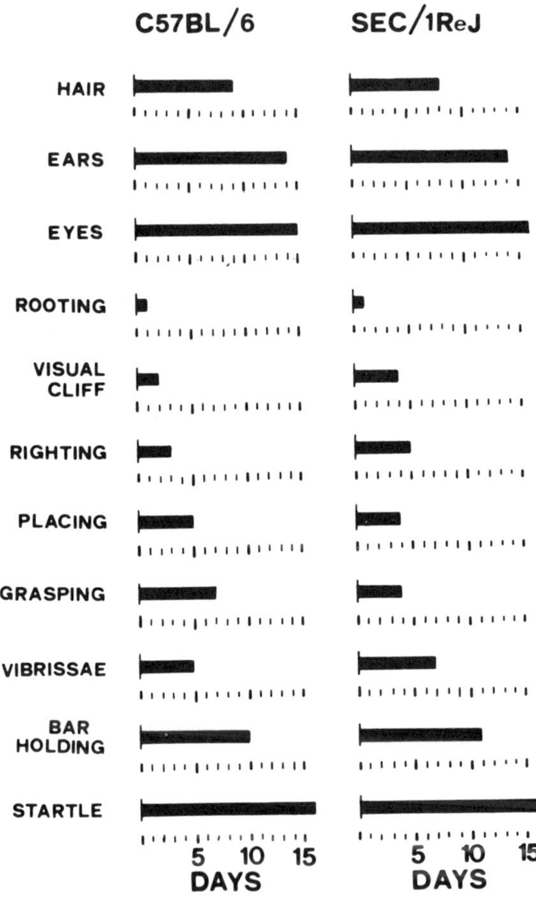

Figure 3. Reflex and behavioral measures. Mean scores on each behavioral test at each chronological age.

SOURCE: *Oliverio et al., 1975b.*

approach to behavioral ontogeny relies on the clear brain biochemical differences evident between these two strains (Oliverio, 1977; Oliverio et al., 1979), and on a number of psychopharmacogenetic findings which indicate a different reactivity of C57 and SEC adult mice to adrenergic or cholinergic agents (Oliverio et al., 1979).

When the effects of amphetamine on locomotor activity and stereotyped behavior were considered, it was evident that different patterns of behavioral development characterize C57 and SEC mice. The SB observed were: rearing (when the mouse leaned with both forepaws on the wall of the cylinder), sniffing and gnawing. Also amphetamine-induced SB indicates that C57 mice are more mature at birth since sniffing and rearing appear at eight days of age while these behaviors are not evident in eight days old SEC mice (Figure 4). This indicates that the dopaminergic mechanisms which are responsible for the outcome of SB (Lal and Sourkes, 1973; Kellog and Lundborg, 1971; Reinstein et al., 1978) undergo different developmental patterns in these strains. However different regions and receptor sites must be involved in different units of SB since gnawing was evident in the SEC strain and completely absent in C57 mice. This indicates that we are dealing with qualitative strain differences rather than with quantitative differences, as one might suggest by assuming that SEC mice are less sensitive to a dose of amphetamine which instead is effective in the C57 strain.

When spontaneous locomotor activity is considered, strain differences are also evident but in terms of magnitude of behavioral arousal rather than on differences in developmental times (Figure 5). In fact, the overall activity of both control and amphetamine-injected C57 mice was higher than that evident in the SEC strain. In control and amphetamine-injected mice of both strains, a sharp rise of activity between days 8 and 16 and a subsequent fall between day 16 and day 32 was evident; a fact which has been previously related to the time course for maturation of excitatory and inhibitory structures in the CNS of altricial mammals (Fox, 1965; Sedlacek et al., 1961; Campbell and Mabry, 1972; Oakley and Plotkin, 1975). Our findings indicate that after this decline in behavioral arousal during the juvenile period, an increase in activity was evident in adult mice (90 days old) while a subsequent decrease paralleled the aging

Figure 4. Percent stereotypes of C57BL/6 and SEC/1ReJ mice at each chronological age following the administration of amphetamine (4 mg/kg). S: sniffing; R: rearing; G: gnawing.

SOURCE: *Alleva et al., 1979.*

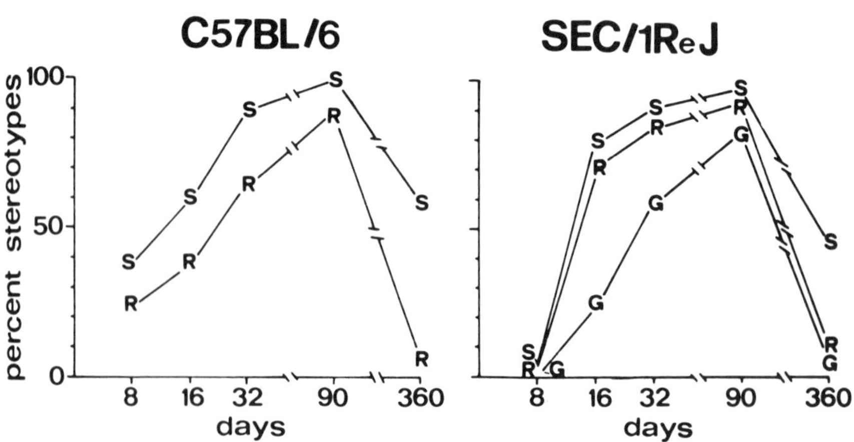

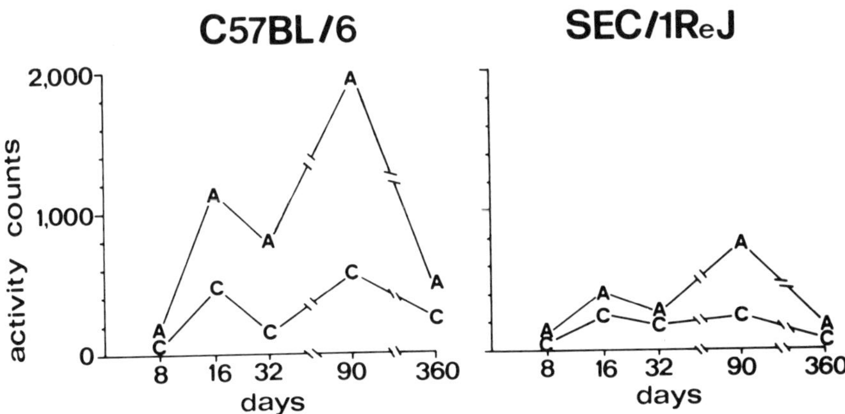

Figure 5. Mean number of movements of saline (C) and amphetamine (4 mg/kg) (A) injected C57BL/6 and SEC/1ReJ mice at each chronological age.
SOURCE: *Alleva et al., 1979.*

process. Though it is possible that the fall of activity evident after the second week of postnatal life, is related to the maturation of inhibitory (serotonergic) structures in the CNS (Mabry and Campbell, 1974), our findings suggest that other mechanisms may be involved in the regulation of the "arousal motivational systems."

It appears that there are clear intraspecies differences in postnatal neurological and behavioral maturity. In fact, C57 mice are more precocial when we consider the development of the cortex, brain myelination processes and the development of specific dopaminergic mechanisms involved in SB.

For other measures of behavioral arousal, such as locomotor activity which is probably modulated by the reticular formation (Fibiger et al., 1970) and by noradrenergic mechanisms, the developmental patterns of the strains are rather similar, though C57 mice are characterized by higher levels of arousal. Since amphetamine exerts both noradrenergic (arousal) or dopaminergic (SB) effects it is possible to use this drug in order to assess the ontogeny of the different catecholaminergic processes and to indicate that different receptor sites do not develop at similar ages (Coyle, 1977).

A general decrease in the level of arousal is evident in 360 day-old mice belonging to both strains. In fact, both the level of locomotor activity of controls and amphetamine-injected mice, and the ECoG pattern reflect a fall of brain excitatory mechanisms (Elias et al., 1975; Sprott, 1976). It is possible that this decrease in arousal mechanisms is also responsible for the sharp decrement of SB evident in 360 day-old mice. In other words it is possible that the fall of SB evident in the aging mice does not only reflect a possible specific decrease of dopaminergic function, but is also related to a decrease in arousal noradrenergic mechanisms.

Circadian Rhythms and Age

In general, the data reported here indicate that there are strains such as C57, which are more precocious and strains such as SEC which are less mature at birth. This fact suggests that there are genetic programs which lead to different rates of brain and behavioral development throughout life. As previously indicated, precocity at birth and more precocious rates of development are characteristic of behavioral specialization, or, in other words, of a more "rigid" genetic program which results in more rigid adaptation mechanism to the environment. The following findings on wheel running behavior and on its modifications throughout life indicate: 1. that genetic mechanisms are important in the modulation of behavioral rigidity (e.g., a reduced behavioral repertoire and specialized mechanisms of adaptation) and plasticity (e.g., the ability to generalize or cope with the environment with plastic, adaptive behavior); and 2. that with aging these mechanisms may deteriorate.

It was shown that C57 mice are characterized by significant differences with respect to the circadian patterns of sleep evident during the day or the night, while no sharp differences are evident in the SEC strain (Valatx et al., 1974). Furthermore, recent experiments have shown that free-running rhythms of sleep and activity may be plastic or rigid depending on genetic factors involved in the expression of circadian rhythmicity (Oliverio and Malorni, 1979). Under 12 hours light-12 hours dark (L/D) schedules, it was shown that the shift from darkness to brightness induces well defined activity phases at night and lower activity levels during the hours of light in C57 and SEC mice. However when the running activity of the strains was assessed under constant light or darkness it was shown that C57 mice (and other strains) conserve a pronounced circadian rhythm while SEC mice (and other strains as BALB/c) do not (Malorni et al., 1975; Oliverio, 1977).

A better demonstration of the importance of genetic factors in modulating the plasticity or rigidity of behavior in these two (and other) strains was evident by studying wheel running and sleep under L/D schedules shorter than 12 hours-12 hours. The effect of 12-12 h, 6-6 h, 3-3 h and 1-1 h L/D cycles, and of constant light (L/L) were studied in C57 and SEC mice (Oliverio and Malorni, 1979). Wheel running activity and sleep were inhibited by light and enhanced by darkness; however, in the C57 strain the L/D induced changes were less pronounced and superimposed on a clear circadian rhythm. Under the subsequent L/L schedule clear patterns of daily rhythmicity were evident in the C57 strain but not in the SEC strain (Figure 6).

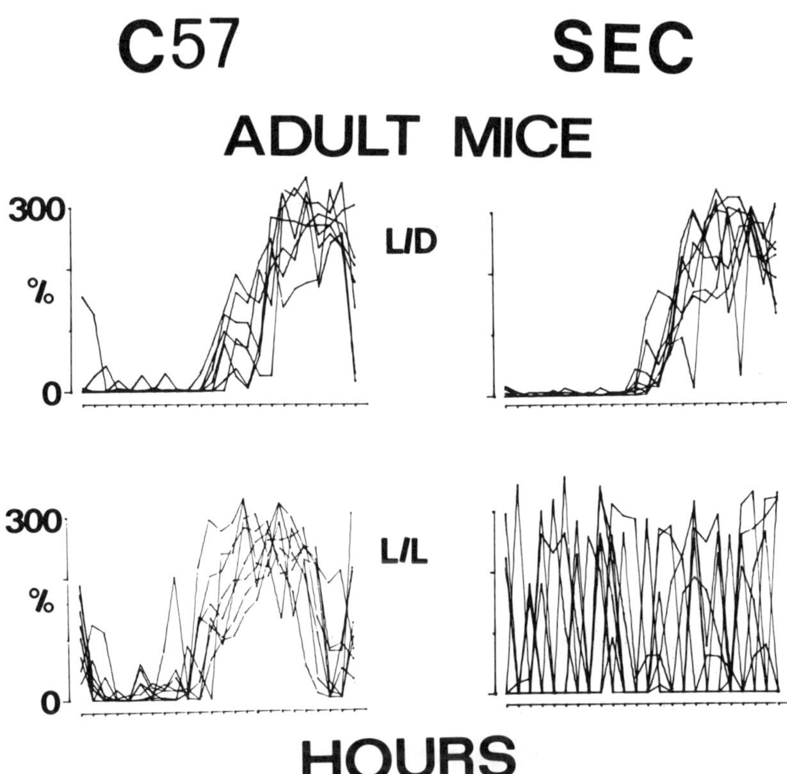

Figure 6. Wheel running activity in 90 day-old mice (Adult) subjected to a 12-12 h light-dark schedule (L/D) or to continuous light (L/L). Each curve represents the performance of a single mouse. Each group consisted of 8 C57BL/6 or 8 SEC/1ReJ male mice.

When two year-old mice were compared to young adults, the SEC strain did not show any pattern of circadian rhythmicity under continuous light. In the C57 strain, the synchronizing effects of the light were still evident in the old animals subjected to a L/D rhythm while no circadian activity was evident in the animals subjected to a schedule of constant light (Figure 7). This finding seems to suggest that the rigid genetic programs which regulate the circadian behavior of C57 mice decay in aged animals. Thus, mouse strains such as the C57, which are characterized by behavioral precocity and by a number of inborn "rigid" mechanisms of adaptation may represent a useful model in the study of aging. In fact, their precocity and their dependence on a number of inborn behavioral patterns represent the expression of a genetic program which deteriorates with advancing age. The data discussed in this chapter

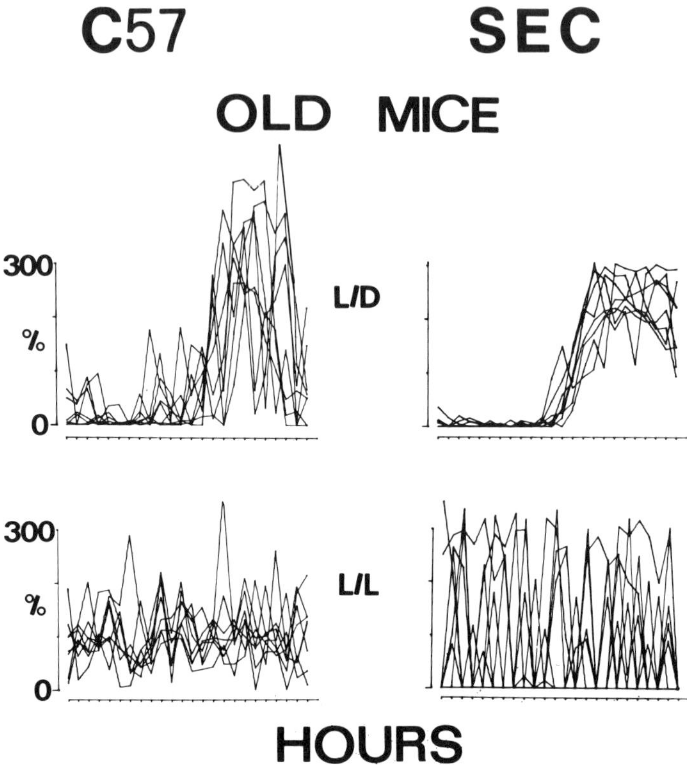

Figure 7. Wheel running activity in two years-old mice (Old) subjected to a 12-12 h light-dark schedule (L/D) or to continuous light (L/L). Each curve represents the performance of a single mouse. Each group consisted of 8 C57BL/6 or 8 SEC/1ReJ male mice.

also can be taken to indicate, as suggested by Parker (1974), that the existence of rigid inborn mechanisms in precocious species (or strains) may represent an advantage in terms of adaptability early in life but also a disadvantage as evidenced by more rapid decline in old age.

In summary, behavior genetics may help us to understand some aspects of brain mechanisms and aging through an analysis of a number of behavioral differences during the entire life span: the initiation and decay of a number of inborn or acquired behavioral patterns are related to neurophysiological and neurochemical processes which seem to be largely dependent on a genetic program, whose influences can be demonstrated through behavioral, neurophysiological and psychopharmacogenetic analyses.

References

Alleva E, Castellano C, Oliverio A: Ontogeny of behavioral development, arousal and stereotypes in two strains of mice. *Experimental Aging Research* 5:335–350, 1979.

Campbell BA, Mabry PD: Ontogeny of behavioral arousal: a comparative study. *J Comp Physiological Psychology* 81:371–379, 1972.

Coyle JT: Biochemical aspects of neurotransmission in the developing brain. *Internat Rev Neurobiology* 20:65–107, 1977.

Comfort A: The position of aging studies. *Mechanisms of Aging Development* 3:1, 1974.

Doty BA: Age and avoidance conditioning in rats. *J Gerontology* 21:287, 1966.

Elias MF, Elias PK: Hormones, aging and behavior in infrahuman mammals. In Eleftheriou BE, Sprott RL (eds.) *Hormonal Correlates of Behavior.* New York, Plenum Press, 1975.

Elias PK, Elias MK, Eleftheriou BE: Emotionality, exploratory behavior and locomotion in aging inbred strains of mice. *Gerontology* 21:46, 1975.

Fibiger HC, Lytle LD, Campbell BA: Cholinergic modulation of adrenergic arousal in the developing rat. *J Comparative Physiological Psychology* 72:384–389, 1970.

Fox MW: Reflex ontogeny and behavioral development of the mouse. *Animal Behavior* 13:234–241, 1965.

Freund G, Walker DW: The effect of aging on acquisition and retention of shuttle box avoidance in mice. *Life Sciences* 10:1343, 1971.

Goodrick CL: Behavioral characteristics of young and senescent inbred female mice of the C57BL/6J strain. *J Gerontology* 22:459, 1967.

Kellog C, Lundborg P: Ontogenic variations in responses to L-Dopa and MA receptor-stimulating agents. *Psychopharmacologia* 23:187–200, 1972.

Kobayashi T, Inman P, Buno W, Himwich HE: A multidisciplinary study of changes in mouse brain with age. *Recent Advances in Biological Psychiatry* 5:293–308, 1963.

Lal S, Sourkes T: Ontogeny of stereotyped behavior induced by apomorphine and amphetamine in the rat. *Archives Internationaux de Pharmacodynamie* 202:171–182, 1973.

Mabry PD, Campbell BA: Serotonergic inhibition of catecholamine-induced behavioral arousal. *Brain Research* 49:381–391, 1973.

Malorni W, Oliverio A, Bovet D: Analyse génétique d'activité circadienne chez la souris. *Comptes Rendus des Séances de l'Académie des Sciences, Paris,* 281 (Série D):1479–1484, 1975.

Meier GW, Foshee DP: Genetics, age and the variability of learning performances. *J Genetic Psychology* 102:267, 1963.

Oakley DA, Plotkin HC: Ontogeny of spontaneous locomotor activity in rabbit, rat and guinea pig. *J Comparative Physiological Psychology* 89(3):267–273, 1975.

Oliverio A: La maturation de l'E.E.G. et du sommeil: Facteurs génétiques et du milieu. *Revue de Electroencéphalographie et Neurophysiologie* 7:263–268, 1977.

Oliverio A, Bovet D: Effects of age on maze learning and avoidance conditioning of mice. *Life Sciences* 5:317, 1966.

Oliverio A, Castellano C, Renzi P: Genotype or prenatal drug experience affect brain maturation in the mouse. *Brain Research* 90:357–360, 1975a.

Oliverio A, Castellano C, Puglisi-Allegra S: Effects of genetic and nutritional factors on post-natal reflex and behavioral development in the mouse. *Experimental Aging Research* 1:41–56, 1975b.

Oliverio A, Castellano C, Puglisi-Allegra S: A genetic approach to behavioral plasticity and rigidity. In Royce JR (ed.) *Theoretical Advances in Behavioral Genetics*. NATO Advanced Study Institute, Sijthoff and Noordhoff, Alphen aan den Rijn, The Netherlands, Germantown, Maryland, USA, 139–165, 1979.

Oliverio A, Malorni W: Wheel running and sleep in two strains of mice: plasticity and rigidity in the expression of circadian rhythmicity. *Brain Research* 163:121–133, 1979.

Parker CR: Behavioral diversity in ten species of non human primates. *J Comparative Physiological Psychology* 87.930–937, 1974.

Reinstein DK, McClearn D, Isaacson RL: The development of responsiveness to dopaminergic agonists. *Brain Research* 150:216–233, 1978.

Rockstein M: The genetic basis for longevity. In Rockstein M (ed.) *Theoretical Aspects of Aging*. New York, Academic Press, 1974.

Russell ES: Genetic bases of aging in animals. In Elias MF, Eleftheriou BE, Elias PK (eds.) *Special Review of Experimental Aging Research, Progress in Biology*. Bar Harbor, Maine, EAR Inc., 1976.

Russell ES: Genetic considerations in the selection of rodent species and strains for research in aging. In *Development of the Rodent as a Model System of Aging*. Bethesda, DHEW Publ. 72-121, 1972.

Russell ES, Sprott RL: Genetics and the aging nervous system. In *Survey Report on the Aging Nervous System*. Bethesda, DHEW Publ. No. NIH 74:296, 1975.

Scott JP: *Animal Behavior*. Chicago, University of Chicago Press, 1958.

Sedlacek J: The significance of the perinatal period in the neural and behavioral development of precocial mammals. In Gottlieb G (ed.) *Aspects of Neurogenesis*. New York, Academic Press, 1974.

Sedlaceck J, Svehlova, Sedlackova M, Marsala J, Kapras J: New results in the ontogenesis of reflex activity. *Plzensky lekarsky Sbornik* Suppl. 3:167–173, 1961.

Sluckin W: *Imprinting and Early Learning*. Chicago, Aldine, 1965.

Sprott RL: Behavior genetics in aging rodents. In Elias MF, Eleftheriou BE, Elias PK (eds.) *Special Review of Experimental Aging Research*. Bar Harbor, Maine, EAR Inc., 1976.

Valatx JL, Bugat R: Facteurs génétiques dans le déterminisme du cycle veille-sommeil chez la souris. *Brain Research* 69:315–330, 1974.

Wilson DL: The programmed theory of aging. In Rockstein M (ed.) *Theoretical Aspects of Aging*. New York, Academic Press, 1974.

Stein, ed. The Psychobiology of Aging: Problems and Perspectives

Neurobiological Aspects of Aging: Biochemical Changes in Central Catecholaminergic Systems[a]

Sergio Algeri

Istituto di Ricerche Farmacologiche ''Mario Negri'', Via Eritrea, 62 20157 Milano, Italy.

Introduction

Breakdown of the functions controlled by the nervous system is unquestionably one of the most distressing aspects of aging in the animal organism. In fact, the threat of aging would seem much less dramatic if it were not for the image we all have of old people with the shakes, with memory and movement problems and other neurovegetative disturbances.

These considerations apart, aging of the nervous system is of fundamental biological importance because it underlies the whole general process of senescence. The organism can only maintain its integrity as long as it is able to activate hemeostatic mechanisms to oppose all the external factors that would otherwise harm it. These defense mechansims are all regulated—some directly, some less so—by the nervous and endocrine systems, which are in turn closely linked, and govern interactions between an organism and its environment. Clearly, therefore, any decay in nervous function has repercussions on other organs, so the nervous system acts as a sort of ''pace maker'' in the whole process of aging.

In examining aging of the nervous system, we focussed our attention on synaptic transmission, because most of the regulatory mechanisms of neuronal transmission are found at the synapse. Therefore faults in any of them, arising through senescence, may impair normal nerve function.

[a]Supported by a Grant from Ministero della Sanità, Rome, Italy, contract no. 79.0235565

The following are some synaptic mechanisms that may be altered by processes associated with senescence:

1. Degeneration of nerve terminals because of loss of neurons.
2. Changes in neurotransmitter release due to alternation of the enzymes which regulate their synthesis, or to alteration of the pre-or post-synaptic mechanism regulating release from the nerve terminal.
3. Greater inactivation of the released neurotransmitter, caused by increased activity of some of the metabolizing enzymes or by increased reuptake of the transmitter into the nerve terminal.
4. Alteration of the neurotransmitter-receptor interaction because of changes in the affinity of the receptors or modifications in some of the biochemical steps necessary for translating receptor stimulation into depolarization of the transynaptic membrane.

Modifications in any one of these events are sufficient to affect the functions of a neuronal population. Add to this the fact that the various neuronal systems are all linked in a complicated network of interactions (Garattini et al., 1978), and it becomes clear why, in tackling the biological question of aging, we have chosen to focus on age-related changes in neurotransmitters.

To date, there are believed to be about a dozen substances with neurotransmitting activity (Table 1) (Cooper et al., 1978).

Of these, the catecholamines are probably the best characterized to date. Catecholaminergic neurons are involved in many functions such as motility, neuro-endocrine regulation, central regulation of arterial pressure, of body temperature, and of mental behavior. Because many of these functions show decay over time, it appeared interesting to review present-day knowledge of what changes occur in brain catecholamines during senescence.

Table 1. Substances Believed to Be Chemical Mediators of Intersynaptic Transmission

Amines	Aminoacids	Peptides
Acetylcholine	Gamma-aminobutyric acid (GABA)	Substance P
Dopamine	Glycine	Endorphin
Norepinephrine	Glutamate (putative)	
Epinephrine	Aspartate (putative)	
Serotonin (putative)		
Histamine (putative)		

Catecholamines in Senescence

The concentration of a neurotransmitter in any given brain region is the result of a balance between its synthesis and its catabolism, i.e., its consumption in neuronal function. This concentration normally remains constant, and is affected only by drastic alterations such as neuronal degeneration or major changes in the activity of the enzymes which regulate synthesis and catabolism. Consequently, a fall in neurotransmitter concentrations in any one brain region may herald degeneration of the neurons present or projecting to that region.

A classic example is the drop in dopamine levels in basal nuclei of patients with parkinsonism; a symptom taken to indicate degeneration of the dopaminergic neurons in these areas (Hornykiewicz, 1966). As dopamine levels seem low in elderly, non-neuropathic subjects (Carlsson and Winblad, 1976), and as parkinsonism appears to affect mainly elderly people, it is logical to ask whether this disease is not merely an exacerbation of a general state typical of aging. Such findings, obtained from studies on autopsy specimens, are extremely interesting but it is obvious that because of the difficulty of investigation in man, if we are to extend our knowledge of the effects of aging on the nervous system, we must have appropriate animal models. Research on the functions of the catecholaminergic system in senescent animals is scant, very probably because of the difficulty of establishing an adequate model. For example, in mice, diminished dopamine levels have been observed in the striatum, a region rich in dopaminergic terminals. In the rat, however, no such decrease is seen (Table 2).

Slightly diminished norepinephrine levels were seen in the hypothalamus of monkeys (Macacus rhesus) aged between 12 and 16 years (Table 3). In rodents, however, this neurotransmitter showed no change, except for a lower level in the brain stem (Table 3). This region is known to contain the cell bodies of neurons which project their terminals into various noradrenergic regions. Does the lowered norepinephrine level indicate degeneration of these neurons? This would be out of line with the finding that there is no reduction in norepinephrine concentrations in

Table 2. Dopamine Concentrations in the Brain of Some Rodents at Different Ages

Species	Age	Tissue	Change in Level	Authors
C5BI/6J mouse	12 vs 28 mo	Striatum	–20%	Finch, 1973
Sprague Dawly rats	3 vs 36 mo	Striatum	0	Ponzio et al., 1978

Table 3. Norepinephrine Concentrations in the Brain of Some Animals Species at Different Ages

Species	Age	Tissue	Change in Level	Authors
C5BI/6J mouse	12 vs 20 mo	Brain	0	Finch, 1973
C5BI/6J mouse	12 vs 20 mo	Cerebellum	0	Finch, 1973
C5BI/6J mouse	12 vs 20 mo	Hypothalamus	0	Finch, 1973
C5BI/6J mouse	12 vs 20 mo	Brainstem	0	Finch, 1973
C5BI/10 mouse	8 vs 12 mo	Brain	0	Samorajski et al., 1971
Macacus rhesus	6-10 vs 12-18 yr	Hypothalamus	−10%	Samorajski and Rolsten, 1973
Macacus rhesus	6-10 vs 12-18 yr	Brainstem	−37%	Samorajski and Rolsten, 1973
Sprague Dawley rats	3 vs 36 mo	Hypothalamus	0	Ponzio et al., 1978
Sprague Dawley rats	3 vs 36 mo	Brainstem	−35%	Ponzio et al., 1978

the areas where the terminals themselves are found. However, since only a limited number of such areas has been examined, it cannot be excluded that degeneration may occur in other areas.

Catecholamine Turnover in Old Animals

As discussed above, it may be useful to determine the levels of a transmitter in the brain, in order to obtain information on possible severe neuronal alterations. As a means of establishing the functional state of the neurons, though, this parameter suffers considerable limitations, as only the fraction of the neurotransmitter that interacts with receptors is functionally important. As the system tends to keep its neurotransmitter levels constant by balancing changes in the rate of use with changes in the rate of synthesis, a better way of investigating functional changes is to measure transmitter turnover. For this reason, but also because there are many motives for suspecting that decay occurs in at least some nervous functions during aging, we thought it would be interesting to review the studies which describe the effects of aging on brain catecholamine turnover. For example, Finch (1973) reported diminished dopamine and norepinephrine synthesis in the brain of aging rats and our group made similar observations in 36 month-old rats, close to the end of their life span. Tritiated-1-tyrosine (50 Ci/mmol—14 uCi/rat) was injected through two permanently implanted cannulas, into the lateral ventricles of senescent and 3 month-old rats. Twenty minutes after the injection, the formation of dopamine (DA) and norepinephrine (NE) was determined in striata, hypothalamus and lower brain stem by calculating the ratio between the concentration of labelled monoamine and the specific activity of the precursor (C.I.) (Ponzio et al., 1978). Tyrosine (Ty), DA, NE and the methylated catabolites were separated and determined fluorimetrically and/or radiometrically (Di Giulio et al., 1979). A synthesis value for each catecholamine was evaluated by calculating an index of conversion (C.I.) of the injected ^{3}H L-tyrosine into DA or NE according to the formula proposed by Sedvall et al. (1968):

$$\text{C.I.} = \frac{\text{dpm/g catecholamine}}{\text{Ty specific activity}}.$$

This formula, which corrects the radioactivity accumulated as monoamine for the specific activity of the amino acid precursor present in the brain area considered, does not take into account the neurotransmitter released from the nerve terminal. Nevertheless, during a short interval, such as that used in our experiments, most of the newly formed catecholamines are retained and their accumulation will in fact reflect the rate of synthesis. The C.I.s of the old and young rats were compared and the results are summarized in Figure 1.

Synthesis of both DA and NE was significantly lower in the older rats in all areas considered. These findings indicate that in the old rat's brain, there is fairly widespread diminution of catecholaminergic tone.

It is too early as yet to try and relate this diminution with any functional or behavioral change, but it is interesting to note the findings in the hypothalamus. In view of the relation between catecholaminergic systems in this area and the systems that release hormonal releasing factors, the drop might be related with the slowing of neuro-endocrine functions typical of old animals. It is also worth noting the decrease in striatal dopamine, synthesis which confirms findings in man.

Modifications of Catecholamine Synthesizing Enzymes During Senescence

Catecholamine synthesis is regulated by the activity of the enzyme tyrosine hydroxylase (TH) which catalyzes hydroxylation of L-tyrosine to L-3,4-dihydroxy-phenylalanine (DOPA), through a three-substrate reaction involving L-tyrosine oxygen and a reduced pterine cofactor (Pt. H_2) (Cooper et al., 1978). Regeneration of reduced pterine is accomplished by means of a pyridine nucleotide-dependent enzyme, dihydropteridine reductase (DHPR). TH activity has been found to be low in several brain areas of mammals including man (Mc Geer et al., 1971; McGeer and Mc Geer, 1976), suggesting that decreased catecholamine synthesis may be the consequence of this reduction. Similarly, we have found a decrease in TH activity measured *in vitro* in preparation of striata from brains of old rats (Table 4) (Algeri et al., 1977). This suggests that the decrease of CA synthesis observed *in vivo* may be due at least

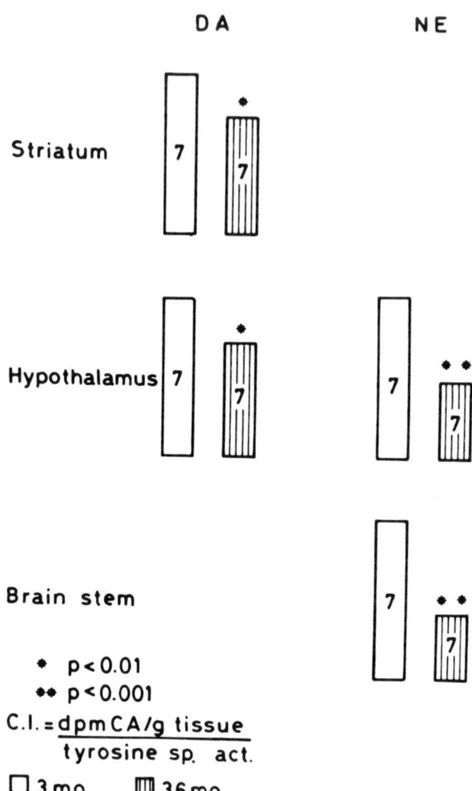

Figure 1. Conversion of L-^{3}H tyrosine into DA and NE in some brain areas of young adult and senescent rats. Data are expressed as percent of controls.
SOURCE: *Ponzio F, Brunello N, Algeri S: J. Neurochem 30:1617, 1978.*

in part to decreased TH activity. The K_m of this enzyme for L-tyrosine and for $DMPH_4$, the synthetic substitute of PtH_2, is not changed (Table 4). These results indicate that the decrease in enzyme activity is probably the consequence of a lower enzyme concentration and not of a change in TH affinity for substrate or cofactor. However, it should be borne in mind that in these experiments, we did not determine the K_m for O_2 so we do not know whether the affinity for this substrate is changed. An increased K_mO_2 could be important if, as is often the case in aging, the brain's blood supply is abnormal because of atherosclerosis.

Unlike TH, DHPR activity was enhanced in all brain areas tested (Algeri et al., 1978) (Table 5). The biological meaning of this finding remains to be clarified. Some authors have demonstrated that a higher concentration of pterine cofactor stimulates an *in vivo* TH activity

Table 4. Age dependent modifications of Tyrosine Hydroxylase (TH) from Homogenates of Different Brain Region of Senescent Rats

	Activity[a]	Km($DMPH_4$) x 10^{-4} M	Km tyr x 10^{-4} M
Young Adults:			
Striatum	0.450 ± 0.071(4)	3.7 ± 0.4(4)	3.3 ± 1.1(4)
Cortex	0.287 ± 0.010(3)		
Diencephalon	0.109 ± 0.006(4)		
Brainstem	0.055 ± 0.010(4)		
Cerebellum	0.023 ± 0.003(3)		
Senescent:			
Striatum	0.306 ± 0.031[b](4)	3.6 ± 0.2(4)	3.4 ± 0.1(4)
Cortex	0.199 ± 0.035(3)		
Diencephalon	0.074 ± 0.0010[c](4)		
Brainstem	0.039 ± 0.005(4)		
Cerebellum	0.024 ± 0.002(4)		

In vitro TH activity was measured coupling TH with DOPA decarboxylase and measuring the $^{14}CO_2$ released by ^{14}C-DOPA synthesized by TH.

[a] Activity is expressed as pmol $^{14}CO_2$/min/mg protein ± S.E. – In parenthesis, the number of determination.

[b] Different from young adult $p < 0.01$ by two tailed Student's t test.

[c] Different from young adult $p < 0.05$ by two tailed Student's t test.

(Kettler et al., 1974). If enhanced DHPR activity is followed, as might be expected, by a rise in the cofactor concentration in the neurons, this could constitute a compensatory mechanism put into action by the organism to counteract the decrease in tyrosine hydroxylase.

Increases in Some Catecholamine Metabolizing Enzymes During Senescence

Catecholaminergic neuronal function may also be reduced by increasing the inactivation of neurotransmitters. For catecholamines there are two enzymatic metabolic pathways: oxidative deamination accomplished by monoamineoxidase (MAO) and o-methylation catalyzed by catechol-o-methyl transferase (COMT) (Cooper et al., 1978). Increased MAO activity with aging has been reported in the human brain (Robinson et al., 1972), and in our colony of aged rats, we observed an increase in COMT activity (Stramentinoli et al., 1972) (Table 6). As this enzyme is located extraneuronally, it is thought to metabolize the neurotransmitter released from the nerve terminal. Consequently enhancement of this enzyme's activity could have important functional implications.

Table 5. Modification of DHPR in Some Brain Areas of Senescent Rats

	Young Adult	Senescent
Striatum	62 ± 5 (10)	132 ± 25[a] (7)
Cortex	43 ± 1 (8)	61 ± 7[b] (7)
Diencephalon	95 ± 13 (10)	144 ± 12[c] (7)
Brainstem	145 ± 4 (10)	226 ± 13[d] (7)
Cerebellum	65 ± 9 (8)	95 ± 8[a] (8)

DHPR acivity is measured as described in Ref. (2) and it is expressed as nmol NADH/min/mg protein ± S.E.

[a] Different from young adult $p < 0.01$ by two tailed Student's t test.

[b] Different from young adult $p < 0.005$ by two tailed Student's t test.

[c] Different from young adult $p < 0.001$ by two tailed Student's t test.

Modification of Catecholamine Receptor Systems in the CNS of Senescent Rats

As mentioned in the introduction, interaction between receptors and neurotransmitters is one of the fundamental steps in the regulation of synaptic transmission. Dopaminergic and β adrenergic receptors are composed of sub-units: membrane-bound protein which specifically binds the neurotransmitter or related agonists, and adenylate cyclase; this enzyme, coupled to the receptor, indirectly controls some biochemical events leading to changes in membrane permeability when stimulated by the agonist to synthesize cAMP. Many experimental conditions have been reported in which there is change in the number of receptors or in their affinity for agonists, or changes in the activity of adenylate cyclase or its sensitivity to stimulation by the agonists.

If aging has any effects on receptor mechanisms, these would obviously also affect the normal operation of the CNS. Some studies of this aspect of the question have been published fairly recently. Greenberg and Weiss

Table 6. COMT Activity in Brain and Liver of Senescent Rats

	Young Adult	Senescent
Brain	20.6 ± 0.6	27.4 ± 0.8[b]
Liver	1639 ± 57	1945 ± 65[a]

Enzyme activity is expressed as nmol ^{14}C metanephrine/30 min/g tissue and measured according to the method of Axelrod and Tomchick (14).

[a] Different from young adult $p < 0.005$ by Student's t test.

[b] Different from young adult $p < 0.001$ by Student's t test.

(1978) reported a decreased number of adrenergic receptors in the rat cerebellum and striatum as the animal aged. Other authors found lower numbers of dopaminergic receptors in the striatum of rats (Govoni et al., 1978). Adenylate cyclase activity is also reported as markedly diminished in the brain of old rats (Walker and Walker, 1973; Govoni et al., 1977).

Finally I would like to mention here the recent work from Axelrod's laboratory (Hirata et al., 1979), indicating that the coupling of adenylate cyclase with the β receptor seems to be related to changes in membrane viscosity determined by transmethylation of membrane phospholipids. In the light of these findings, the fact that we found (Stramentinoli et al., 1977) S-adenosylmethionine, the cofactor of the transmethylatic reactions, is particularly reduced in many tissues including the brain, seems of particular interest.

Conclusions

The findings discussed here represent the extent of our knowledge on the effects of aging on central monoaminergic systems function. The findings are rather scanty, but, there is agreement among the results obtained by different investigators which indicate that there is a drop in catecholaminergic tonus during aging. This phenomenon seems to be rather generalized among different species, i.e., decreased dopamine synthesis has been found both in rat (Ponzio et al., 1978) and in mouse (Finch, 1973). Tyrosine hydroxylase activity has been reported to be decreased in rat (McGeer et al., 1971; Algeri et al., 1978) and in man (McGeer and McGeer, 1976). Finally, an inverse relationship between β receptor number and age holds both for rat (Greenberg and Weiss, 1978) and man (Schocken and Roth, 1977). The fact that this drop involves presynaptic as well as as post-synaptic receptor mechanisms suggests that the various effects combined may amplify the overall physiological effect.

The information available today is too limited and fragmentary to serve as a basis for establishing any clear correlation between these findings and the breakdown in nervous function seen in man and higher mammals as they age. However, the probable involvement of catecholamines in many neuronal functions known to decline with age, make this information of particular interest from both a theoretical and practical point of view. Recent evidence suggests that catecholaminergic malfunction is associated with affective disorders (Garattini, 1978). In the light of this hypothesis and in the fact that depression is one of the most common features of geriatric patients (Busse and Pfeiffer, 1973), the findings that in old age there are several impairments in catecholaminergic function, acquires particular interest. Senile dementia also seems to involve a catecholamine deficit, particularly in dopamine (Gottfries et al., 1969), and the importance of dopamine in parkinsonians has been already discussed here.

The finding of a decrease synthesis of dopamine and norepinephrine in hypothalamus is of particular interest because of the integration between neurotransmitters and hormonal activity that take place in this area (Müller et al., 1977). Due to this close correlation the hypothalamus normally regulates various physiological activities throughout the body, and a derangement of its normal function may increase the possibility of pathological processes resulting in illness and ultimately death. Some hints for a strategy of psychopharmacological treatment in the elderly may perhaps be derived. On the basis of the experimental results, it may be inferred that drugs, that stimulate catecholamine receptors or that inhibit catecholamine catabolizing enzymes, should be useful in senescence when the former are decreased and/or the latter are enhanced.

Several drugs of this kind already exist, but more efforts should be directed to discovering new compounds with a higher selectivity of action and with less side effects, particularly when used in prolonged treatment.

Moreover, in general, it is clear that there is a need for a better knowledge of the action of psychodrugs on the aged organism. In fact, while elderly patients account for a high proportion of the psychopharmaceutical market (Prien, 1975) they have been relatively neglected in the area of drug research which is mainly based on results obtained in adult organisms. The experimental findings discussed here show that in the aged brain profound differences in the basal activity of some neuronal systems exist. Therefore, the possibility that response to psychodrugs may be different in the elderly should be considered and investigated thoroughly.

References

Algeri S, Bonati M, Brunello N, Ponzio F: Dihydropteridine reductase and tyrosine hydroxylase activities in rat brain during development and senescence: a comparative study. *Brain Research* 132:569–574, 1977.

Busse EW, Pfeiffer E (eds.): *Mental Illness in Later Life*. Washington, D.C., American Psychiatric Association, 1973.

Carlsson A, Winblad B: Influence of age and time interval between death and autopsy on dopamine and 3-methoxytyramine levels in human basal ganglia. *J Neural Transmission* 38:271–276, 1976.

Cooper JR, Bloom FE, Roth RH: *The Biochemical Basis of Neuropharmacology*, 3rd. Ed. New York, Oxford University Press, 1978.

Di Giulio AM, Groppetti A, Algeri S, Ponzio F, Cattabeni F, Galli CL: Measurement of 3,4-dihydroxyphenylacetic acid and 3-methoxytyramine specific activity in rat striatum. *Analytical Biochemistry* 92:82–90, 1979.

Finch CE: Catecholamine metabolism in the brains of aging male mice. *Brain Research* 52:261–276, 1973.

Garattini S: Concluding Remarks. In *Depressive Disorders*. Stuttgart, Schattauer, 1978, pp. 477–481.

Garattini S, Pujol JF, Samantin R (eds.): *Interaction Between Putative Neurotransmitters in the Brain*. New York, Raven Press, 1978.

Gottfries CG, Gottfries I, Ross BE: The investigation of homovanillic acid in the human brain and its correlation to senile dementia. *Brit J Psychiatry* 115: 563–574, 1969.

Govoni S, Loddo P, Spano PF, Trabucchi M: Dopamine receptor sensitivity in brain and retina of rats during aging, *Brain Research* 138:565–570, 1977.

Govoni S, Spano PF, Trabucchi M: [^{3}H] Haloperidol and [^{3}H] spiroperidol binding in rat striatum during aging. *J Pharmacy and Pharmacology* 30:448–449, 1978.

Greenberg LH, Weiss B: β-adrenergic receptors in aged rat brain: reduced number and capacity of pineal gland to develop supersensitivity. *Science* 201:61–63, 1978.

Hirata F, Axelrod J, Strittmatter WJ: Methylation of membranes phospholipids. In Usdin E, Borchardt RT, Creveling C (eds.) *Transmethylation*. Amsterdam, Elsevier/North Holland, 1979, pp. 233–240.

Hornykiewicz O: Dopamine (3-hydroxytyramine) and brain function. *Pharmacological Review* 18:925–964, 1966.

Kettler R, Bartholini G, Pletscher A: *In vivo* enhancement of tyrosine hydroxylation in rat striatum by tetrahydrobiopterin. *Nature* (London) 249:476–478, 1974.

McGeer EG, Fibiger HC, McGeer PL, Wickson V: Aging and brain enzymes. *Experimental Gerontology* 6:391–396, 1971.

McGeer PL, McGeer EG: Enzymes associated with the metabolism of catecholamines, acetylcholine and GABA in human controls and patients with Parkinson's disease and Huntington's Chorea. *J Neurochemistry 26:65–76, 1976.*

Müller EE, Nistico' G, Scapagnini U: *Neurotransmitters and Anterior Pituitary Function*. New York, Academic Press, 1977.

Ponzio F, Brunello N, Algeri S: Catecholamine synthesis in brain of aging rat. *J Neurochemistry* 30:1617–1620, 1978.

Prien RF: A survey of psychoactive drug use in the aged at Veterans Administration Hospitals. In Gershon S, Raskin A (eds.) *Aging*, Vol. 2. New York, Raven Press, 1975, pp. 143–154.

Robinson DS, Nies A, Davis JN, Bunney WE, Davis JM, Colburn RW, Bourne HR, Shaw DM, Coppen AJ: Aging, monamines, and monoamine-oxidase levels. *Lancet* 1:290–291, 1972.

Samorajski T, Rolsten C: Age and regional differences in the chemical composition of brains of mice, monkeys and humans. *Progress in Brain Research* 40:253–265, 1973.

Samorajski T, Rolsten C, Ordy JM: Changes in behavior, brain, and neuroendocrine chemistry with age and stress in C57BL-10 male mice. *J Gerontology* 26:168–175, 1971.

Schocken DD, Roth GS: Reduced β-adrenergic receptor concentrations in aging man. *Nature* (London) 267:856–858, 1977.

Sedvall GC, Weise VK, Kopin IJ: The rate of norepinephrine synthesis measured *in vivo* during short intervals; influence of adrenergic nerve impulse activity. *J Pharmacology and Experimental Therapeutics* 159:274–282, 1968.

Stramentinoli G, Gualano M, Catto E, Algeri S: Tissue levels of S-adenosylmethionine in aging rats. *J Gerontology* 32:392–394, 1977.

Walker JB, Walker JP: Properties of adenylate cyclase from senescent rat brain. *Brain Research* 54:391–396, 1973.

Stein, ed. The Psychobiology of Aging: Problems and Perspectives

Comparative Radioautographic Study of Serotonergic Neurons in Young and Senescent Rats[a]

A. Calas and P. Van Den Bosch de Aguilar

Départment de Neurobiologie cellulaire, Institut de Neurophysiologie et Psychophysiologie, CNRS, 31 chemin J.-Aiguier, 13274 Marseille Cedex 2, France and Unité de Morphologie animale, Université Catholique de Louvain, Place Croix du Sud, B-1348-Louvain-La-Neuve, Belgium.

Introduction

Senescence is roughly defined as the increase of mortality with time; the probability that an organism will die during a certain interval of time increases with the age of the organism. As Rosen (1978) pointed out, this concept contains a multitude of obscurities which must be solved before the mechanisms of senescence can be understood. Among these mechanisms the interrelationships between the cells within the organism are particularly fascinating. Is the senescence of a multicellular organism only determinated by the senescence of its cells? If so, what deficiencies in cellular properties produce senescence? If not, are there cells in the organism which act as "pace-makers" to determine the rate and the amplitude of senescence (Finch, 1973)?

The question whether proliferating cells age is not yet solved. On the contrary, it is generally recognized that the post-mitotic cells, which do not proliferate, do senesce (Rosen, 1978; Martin, 1977). In the organism we can study old neurons as unique models of the morphological and functional impairments elicited by aging at the cellular level as well as in the neuronal network itself.

Cytological alterations in the neurons of senescent animals have been known for a long time, but their characteristics can vary according to

[a] This study was supported by Grants # 77 41786 of the INSERM and 78 72772 of the DGRST (A.C.) and by the "Fondation interuniversitaire pour l'Etude des Processus du Vieillissement", Montignies-le-Tilleul (P. V.d.B.).

the animal species, the individuals and the regions of the nervous system studied (Dayan, 1971; Samorajski and Rolstein, 1973).

From a more functional point of view, two contrasting theoretical views influence research on brain aging (Ordy and Kaack, 1975). For the first, the cellular connection hypothesis, the basic units in neuronal functions are individual cells and specific synaptic connections among cells in pathways and centers of the brain. From this perspective, aging corresponds to a dysfunction of the neurons themselves (or neuronal clusters) and/or their relationships with glial cells. The second theory, the aggregate field hypothesis, emphasizes alterations of the whole neural network and/or its relationships to the organism.

The maintenance of the neural network is due, to a large part, to the integrity of synaptic connections and to neurotransmitter functional capacity, including the transport systems which convey substances along the neuronal processes in order to integrate the metabolism of the processes with that of the perikaryon.

To approach aging of the nervous system, we have chosen not an anatomically defined region but instead, neurons which are defined by their neurotransmitter. The choice of one, well defined category of neurons allows us to study alterations related to aging at both the individual neuronal level as well as in the entire neuronal network. We chose the serotonergic neurons as an experimental model for the following reasons:

1. These neurons, whose metabolism is well known, are widely distributed across species and throughout the central (Dahlström and Fuxe, 1964) and peripheral nervous system (Calas et al., 1978).
2. Their capacity to take up and selectively retain their neurotransmitter, allows them to be easily recognized by radioautography after administration of ^{3}H serotonin (Calas et al., 1974; Calas and Segu, 1976; Chan-Palay, 1976; Descarries et al., 1979).
3. Their functions are very numerous and are closely related to physiological regulations and behaviors which are particularly altered during senescence (Samorajksi, 1977); for example, sleep, mood, motor activity, neuroendocrine regulations (mainly gonadotropic function: Meites et al., 1977; Finch, 1979).

Our experiments examined young and old rats given tritiated serotonin (^{3}H-5 HT) sometime before fixation and histological radioautographic study of the brain. Moreover, we used a high resolution radioautographic approach to study selected areas implicated in physiological regulation (spinal cord, brain stem, cortex, basal hypothalamus, median eminence and spinal ganglia) to define the cytological features of some ^{3}H-5 HT labelled structures in old rats.

Material and Methods

The male Wistar rats used in our experiments were bred in our colony over a span of 40 generations. They were kept under constant conditions of temperature and humidity, and artificial lighting from 7 A.M. to 7 P.M. The animals were placed 3 to a cage beginning at the age of 1–5 months and observed until death which occurred at about 2.5 years. The rats were allowed to feed and drink at will with a diet consisting of 20.8% of digestible proteins, 5% fat, 55% carbohydrates, 3% cellulose, 6% minerals and 10.2% moisture. They were weighed at regular intervals. They reached their maximum weight at about 20 months with an average of 350 g, and a range from 250 to 500 g. The aged animals, 24 months or more, showed a weight decrease: at the moment of experimentation they weighed about 300 g. They were devoid of any apparent pathological symptoms. Ten rats were 24 months old (referred to as old rats) and eight were 3-6 months old (referred to as young rats).

All animals were pretreated with a monoamine oxidase (MAO) inhibitor: nialamide or pargyline (200 or 75 mg/kg 3 hrs before ^{3}H-5 HT administration). For *in vitro* experiments, Nembutal anesthetized rats were decapitated. Brains were rapidly exposed and pieces of nervous tissue (brain or spinal thoracic ganglia) of both young and old rats were removed, then incubated in 5.10^{-7}M ^{3}H-5 HT (Amersham, S.A. 10 Ci/mMole) with 5.10^{-6}M cold Noradrenaline (NA) dissolved in an artificial cerebro-spinal fluid (CSF), (Merlis, 1940), for 20 min at 37°C under constant stirring and oxygenation by air bubbling. Pieces were then rinsed in CSF for 5 min, fixed in the Karnovksy paraformaldehyde-glutaraldehyde-phosphate buffer mixture for 60 min, post-fixed in 2% osmium tetroxide in the same buffer, dehydrated in ethanol and embedded in epon.

For *in vivo* experiments, 10^{-4} or 10^{-5}M ^{3}H-5 HT in 200 μl of CSF was stereotaxically infused into the fourth cerebral ventricle for 1 hr or intravenously 20 min before sacrifice, animals being under nembutal anesthesia. The rats were fixed by intra-aortic perfusion of 200 ml of the same fixative. Some entire brains were histologically processed for paraffin embedding. For other animals, small brain pieces were post-fixed in osmium-tetroxide and further epon-embedded.

For histological radioautography, 10 μm paraffin or 1 μm epon thick sections were coated by dipping with K5-Ilford Nuclear Emulsion diluted 1:1 in water. Following 9–15 days of exposure, radioautographs (RAG) were developed in D 19 B Kodak, stained with Cresyl Violet or Azur Blue and mounted in Entellan. Histological RAG were subsequently observed with photonic microscope in light or dark field.

For high resolution radioautography, thin sections were deposited on glass slides bearing a celloidin pellicle, stained with uranyl acetate and lead citrate, lightly vaporized with carbon and coated by dipping in Ilford L4 Emulsion diluted 1:4. Following 12 days of exposure, these RAG were developed with D 19, Microdol-X Kodak or a Phenidon developer (Lettre and Paweletz, 1966), collected on grids, and examined with a Siemens Elmiskop 102 electron microscope after thinning the celloidin film by immersion of the grids in amyl acetate (Larra and Droz, 1970; Boyenval and Fischer, 1976).

Results

Our radioautographic techniques showed the general topographical distribution of labelled neurons, particularly cell bodies observed in coronal paraffin sections of the entire brain. We also examined the regional patterns of labelled structures (namely of fibers) in epon thick sections and finally, the cytological aspect of labeled varicosities and perikarya from electron microscope-observed thin sections.

General Pattern of Cellular Radioactivity

We shall limit the description to the topography of labelled cell bodies in the whole brain. The distribution of labelled fibers and varicosities appears more clearly in epon thick section radioautographs and will be described later.

In old rats intraventricularly injected with ^{3}H-5 HT, a noticeable diffuse reaction constituted by randomly distributed silver grains was observed with a decreasing gradient from the ventricle or the lower surface of the mesencephalon. Within the labelled mesencephalic area, nuclear accumulations of cell bodies distinguished by a RAG reaction clearly more intense than the diffuse one were observed in several locations: raphe (*dorsalis, magnus, pontis and pallidus*), *nucleus paragigantocellularis, nucleus reticularis interfasciularis hypoglossi, interpeduncular nucleus and its lateral edges, lemniscus medianus* (Figures 1,2,3). Similar localizations were found in young animals and apparently there was no striking difference in the number, histological aspect and relative intensity of radioautographic reactions for labelled neurons in the two kinds of animals.

Outside of the central nervous system an intense radioautographic reaction was observed on some cell bodies of thoracic spinal ganglia following *in vitro* incubation. Labelled cells had a small size (20 μm). They were scattered in the whole structure and their number did not exceed 20–30 in one ganglion in young as well as in old rats (Figure 4).

Regional Distribution of Fiber Radioactivity

There were no significant differences in the distribution of uptake between old and young rats. Following *in vitro* incubation with ^{3}H-5 HT the same general pattern of radioactivity was observed in these regions of old rat brain: fronto-parietal cortex, mesencephalic raphe area (Figures 5–6) and median eminence (ME)—ventral hypothalamic complex (Figures 7–8): a gradient of diffuse reaction decreasing from the edges of incubated tissue was accompanied by a similar gradient of the density of intense reactions constituted by dense accumulations of silver grains. The density of these clusters seemed to be nearly homogenous in the four edges of the sectioned cortex. In the frontally sectioned raphe region, the density of intensely labelled structures was also nearly the same in the lower and lateral edges. However, in the ventricular region rows of silver grain clusters were observed above all the ependymal cells (Figure 6). In the basal hypothalamic region, the density of intense reactions was very high in the lateral and upper edges of frontal sections but in the ME itself clusters of silver grains appeared sparse in the external and in the internal layers.

Finally in spinal ganglia very few dense reactions were detected. They were exclusively localized within blood vessels.

After *in vivo* administration of ^{3}H-5 HT, the diffuse reaction and the density of intense reactions appeared to decrease from the site of tracer penetration, i.e., the ventricular lumen and the surface of the brain. After intraventricular injection intense reactions were noticed, for example, in the intraventricular supraependymal fibers and in the suprachiasmatic area. In the upper spinal cord, intense radioautographic reactions were particularly abundant in the whole grey matter and much more scarce in the white matter. After intravenous injection of ^{3}H-5 HT, significant radioautographic reactions were noticed in the ME itself with respect to the surrounding hypothalamic regions which were completely devoid of silver grains. In the ME, densely packed silver grains occurred throughout the structure and were more frequent in the external zone.

Radioautographic Ultrastructural Data

The high resolution radioautographic study in old rats was confined to areas previously analyzed at light microscope level in the median eminence and spinal cord (*in vivo* experiments) and in the raphe, cortex and spinal ganglia (*in vitro* experiments). The cytological features of the tissues were easier to appreciate in the former, since for the latter, the incubation produced an appreciable extraction of the cytoplasm and membrane disruptions leading to a poor preservation of the tissues. However, in the raphe as well as in the cortex, densely labelled structures might be defined as nerve fibers longitudinally or transversally sectioned or more generally as varicosities. They were always amyelinic but very frequently appeared to be in close contact with myelinated axons. They contained mitochondria, neurotubules and profiles of endoplasmic reticulum (ER) and, for the varicosities numerous clear vesicles (40–60 nm) and some round or elongated large granular vesicles (LGV: 80–100 nm)

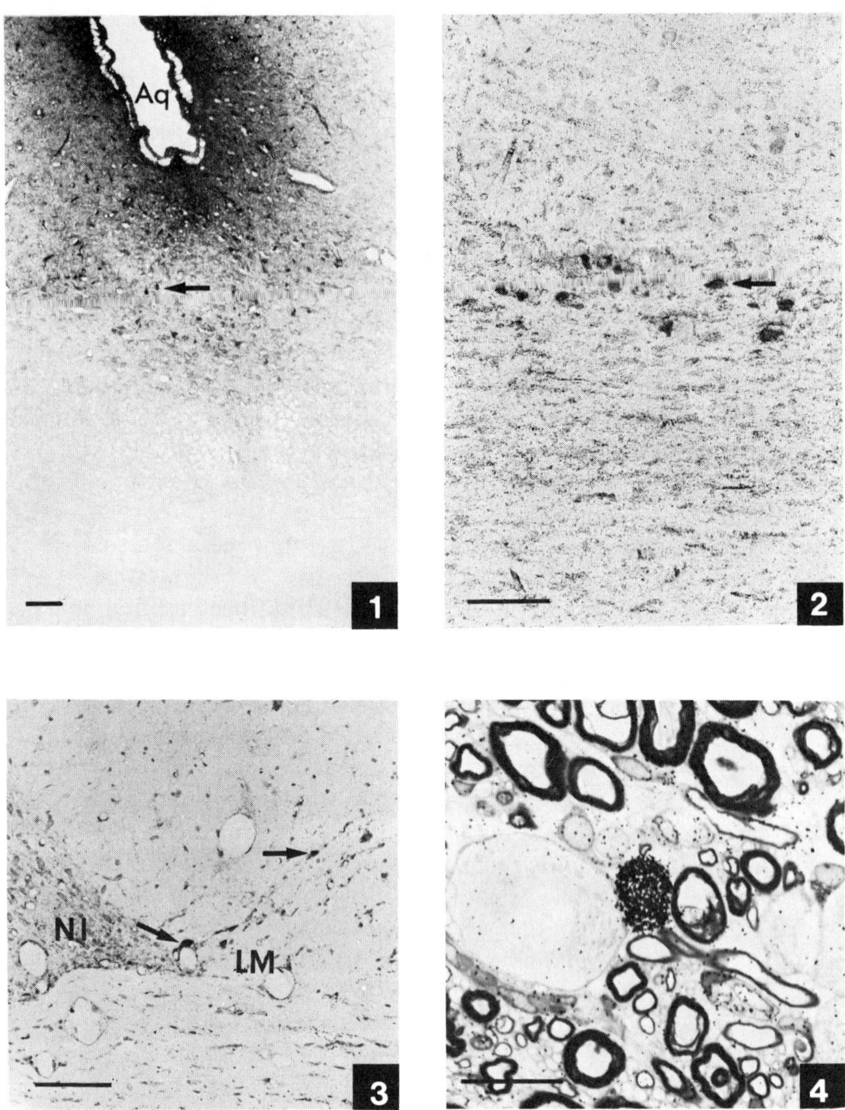

Plate I. (Figures 1-4). Serotonergic cell bodies (arrows). Radioautographs of paraffin (2 - 3 - 4) or epon (5) thick sections of old rat nervous tissues following intraventricular (2 - 3 - 4) or *in vitro* (5) administration of ^{3}H-5 HT.

Figure 1. Raphe dorsalis. Aq: Aqueduct.

Figure 2. Raphe magnus (sagittal section).

Figure 3. Nucleus Interpeduncularis (NI) and Lemniscus Medianus (LM).

Figure 4. Spinal thoracic ganglion.

II. Bar = 100 μm (1,2,3) or 20 μm (4).

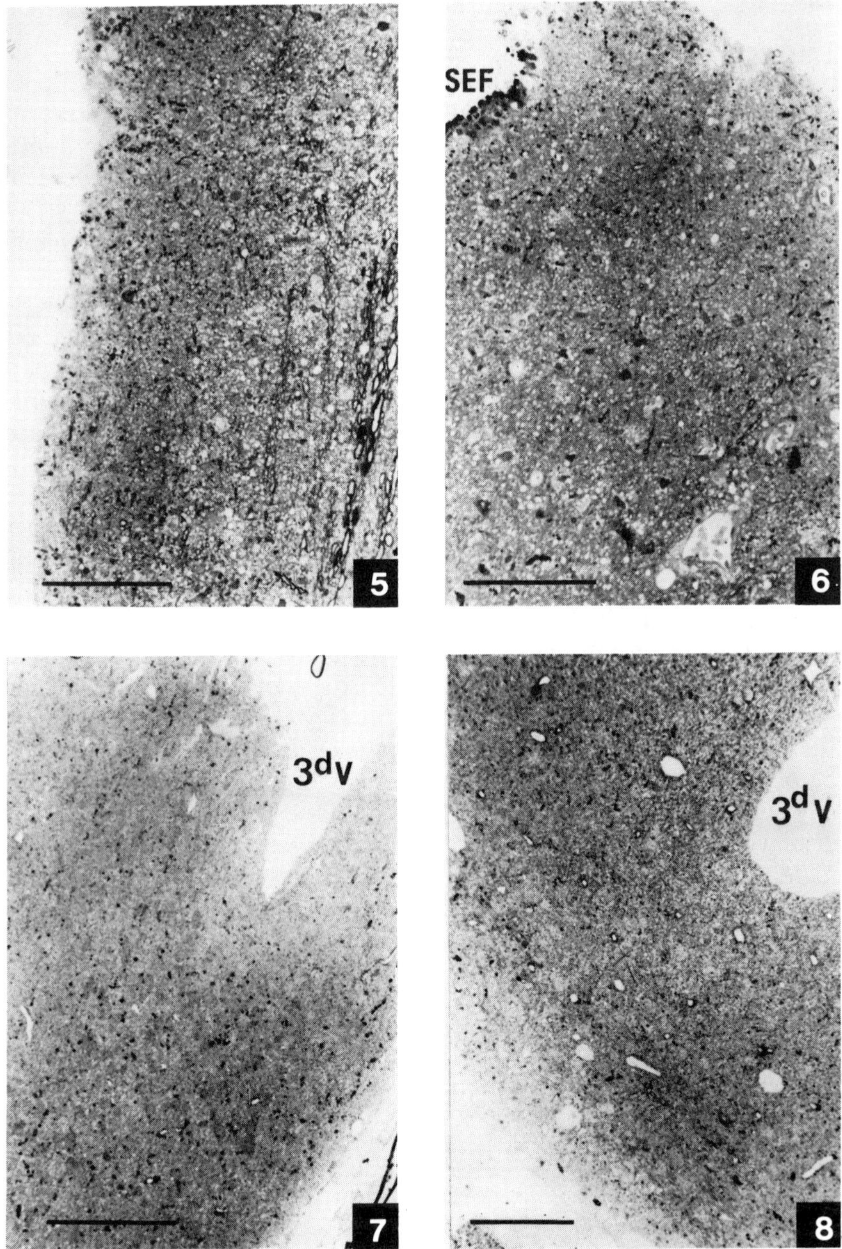

Plate II. (Figures 5-8). Serotonergic terminals. Histological radioautographs of epon thick sections of the brains of young (5 & 7) and old (6 & 8) rats following *in vitro* (5 & 6) or intraventricular (7 & 8) administration of ^{3}H - 5 HT.

Figures 5-6. Raphe region. The density of labelled terminals is similar in the incubated lateral edges. SEF: intensely labelled supraependymal fibers.

Figures 7-8. Rostral part of the floor of the third ventricle (3d V). The beginning of the median eminence (ME) and its lateral edges display a similar labelling on both animals.

III. Bar = 100 μm.

(Figures 9,11). They occasionally displayed synaptic differentiation upon unlabelled structures mainly of dendritic nature. The cytological preservation was particularly convenient in the intraventricular supra-ependymal fibers at the level of the raphe dorsalis which were all intensely labelled and contained clear vesicles together with LGV, mitochondria and profiles of ER but never displayed any synaptic differentiation (Figure 10). In spinal ganglia, intense reactions observed within the blood vessels at photonic microscope level were always observed superimposed to platelets (Figure 15). Upon labelled cell bodies, radioautographic reaction invariably arose from the same perikaryon when observed on successive sections. These labelled neurons were ensheathed by a satellite cell. They displayed a clear cytoplasm with occasional LGV and lipofuscin sometimes associated with mitochondria or ER cisternae (Figure 16).

However, our best cytological results were obtained in *in vivo* experiments in the ME and the spinal cord (Figure 12). In the spinal cord grey matter, intensely labelled structures were mainly varicosities which displayed the ultrastructural features described above and some asymmetrical synaptic differentiations upon contacted elements probably of dendritic nature. When labelled varicosities and entire intervaricose segments could be observed, silver grains were more numerous over vesicles containing varicose parts. Sometimes a labelled varicosity could be observed in close contiguity with unlabelled perikaryon but without any synaptic differentiation. The cell bodies observed in the spinal cord displayed numerous residual bodies and lipofuscin (Figure 12). These features were very rare in young rats. By contrast, labelled fibers did not display any peculiar ultrastructural difference in old and young rats respectively, except in rare cases a myelin-like figure around the LGV in old rats.

In the ME-basal hypothalamic region, important alterations were observed in the cytoplasm of arcuate neurons which could present either a nearly normal appearance with numerous parallel ergostoplasmic cisternae or were completely filled with lipofuscin and residual bodies with all intermediary stages (Figures 18 to 20). Moreover frequent giant Herring bodies containing numerous autophagic figures were observed (Figure 17) but labelled fibers detected in the vicinity of the external basement membrane or in the different layers of the organ did not display any particular feature.

In the raphe region a cytological analysis performed without radioautography showed in the old rat general modifications of all the neurons in this area involving: numerous lipofuscin pigments sometimes associated with ER cisternae, granulo-vacuolar degenerations (Figures 13,14), and occasionally neurofibrillary tangles and nuclear inclusions. These features were also found in young rats but at a much lesser frequency.

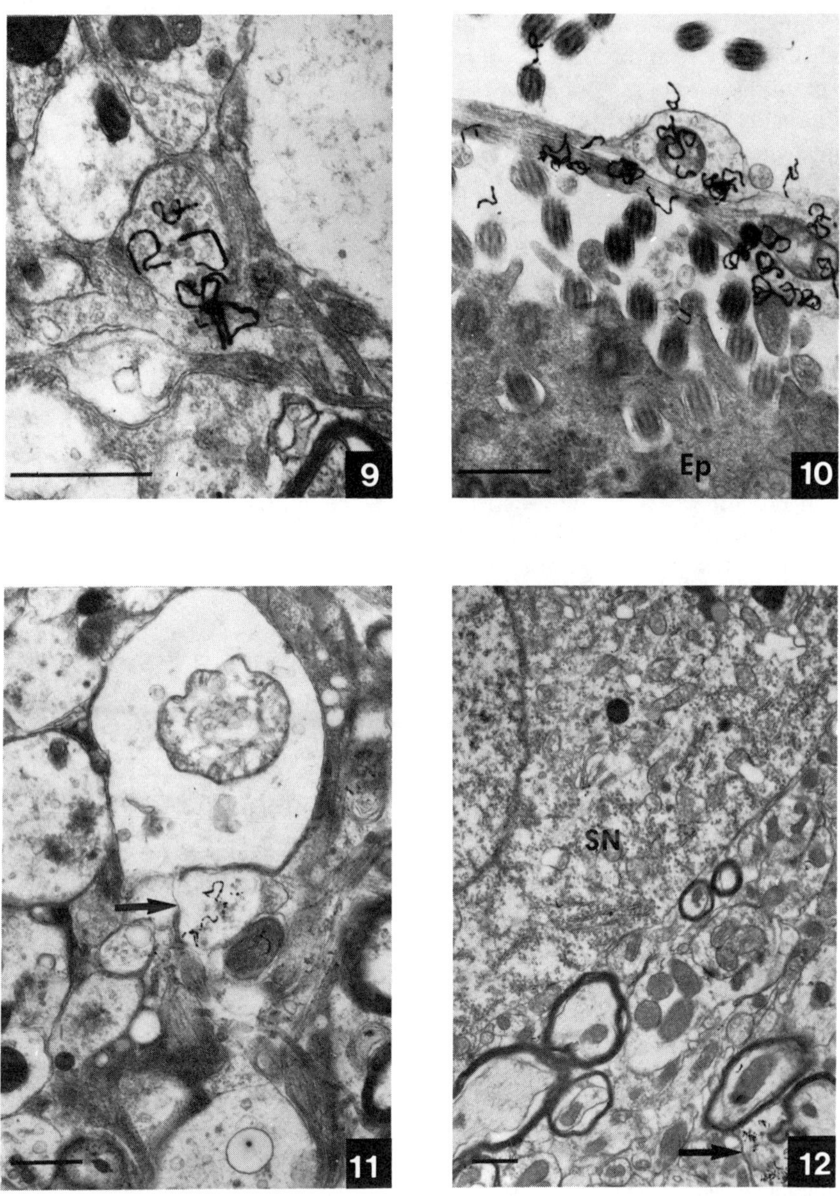

Plate III. (Figures 9-12). Serotonergic terminals. High resolution radioautographs following *in vitro* (9 - 10 - 11) or intraventricular (12) administration of ^{3}H-5 HT in old rats. The labelling and ultrastructural content of 5 HT fibers with small clear and large granular vesicles seem to be normal in the raphe (9), the supraependymal fibers (10), the cortex (11) and the spinal cord grey matter (12).

EP: Ependymocyte. SN: Spinal neuron with lipofuscin inclusions. Bar = 1 μm.

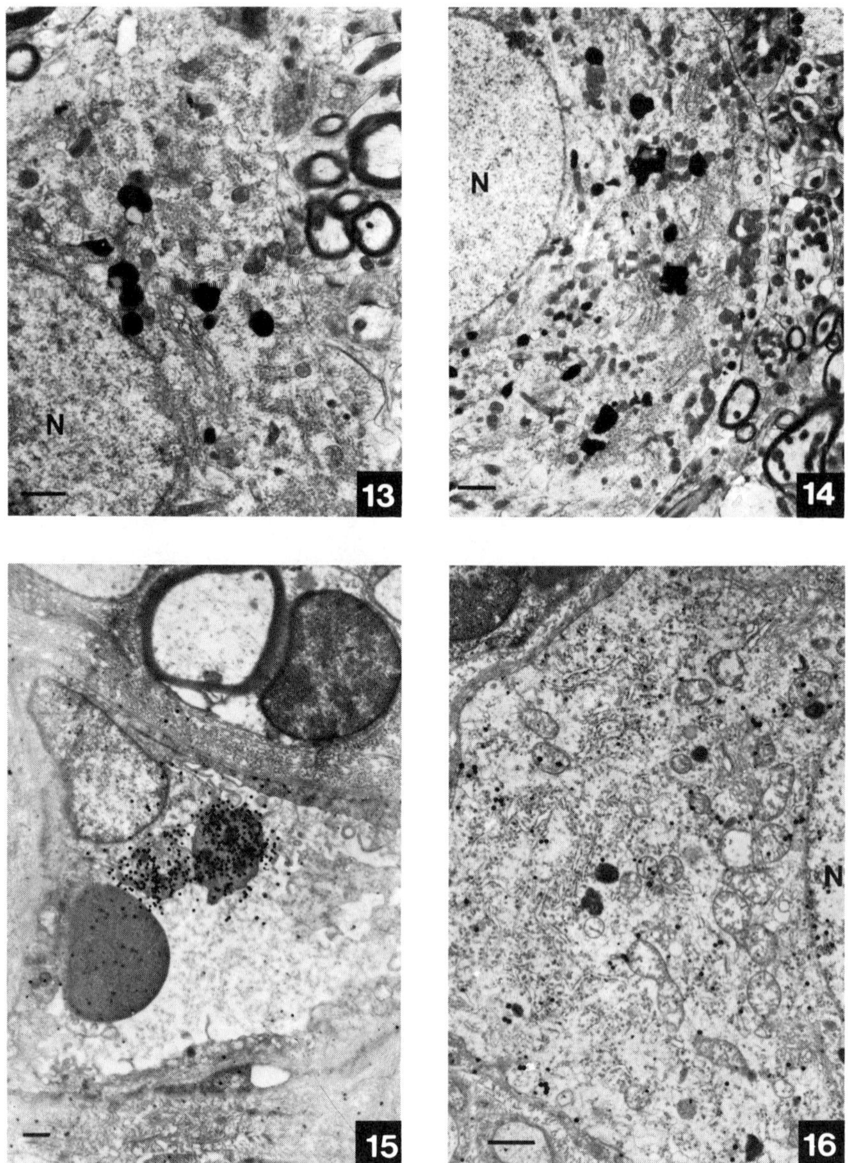

Plate IV. (Figures 13-16). Cell bodies in the raphe dorsalis (13 - 14) and a spinal thoracic ganglion (15 - 16) of old rats.

Figure 13-14: Lipofuscin are abundant in these raphe neurons. N: nucleus.

Figure 15. Intravascular platelets are intensely labelled.

Figure 16. This serotonergic cell body shows some lipofuscin inclusions and a rather well preserved ultrastructural content.

(15 and 16: High resolution radioautographs after *in vitro* ^{3}H-5 HT; phenidon developer.

Bar = 1 μm.

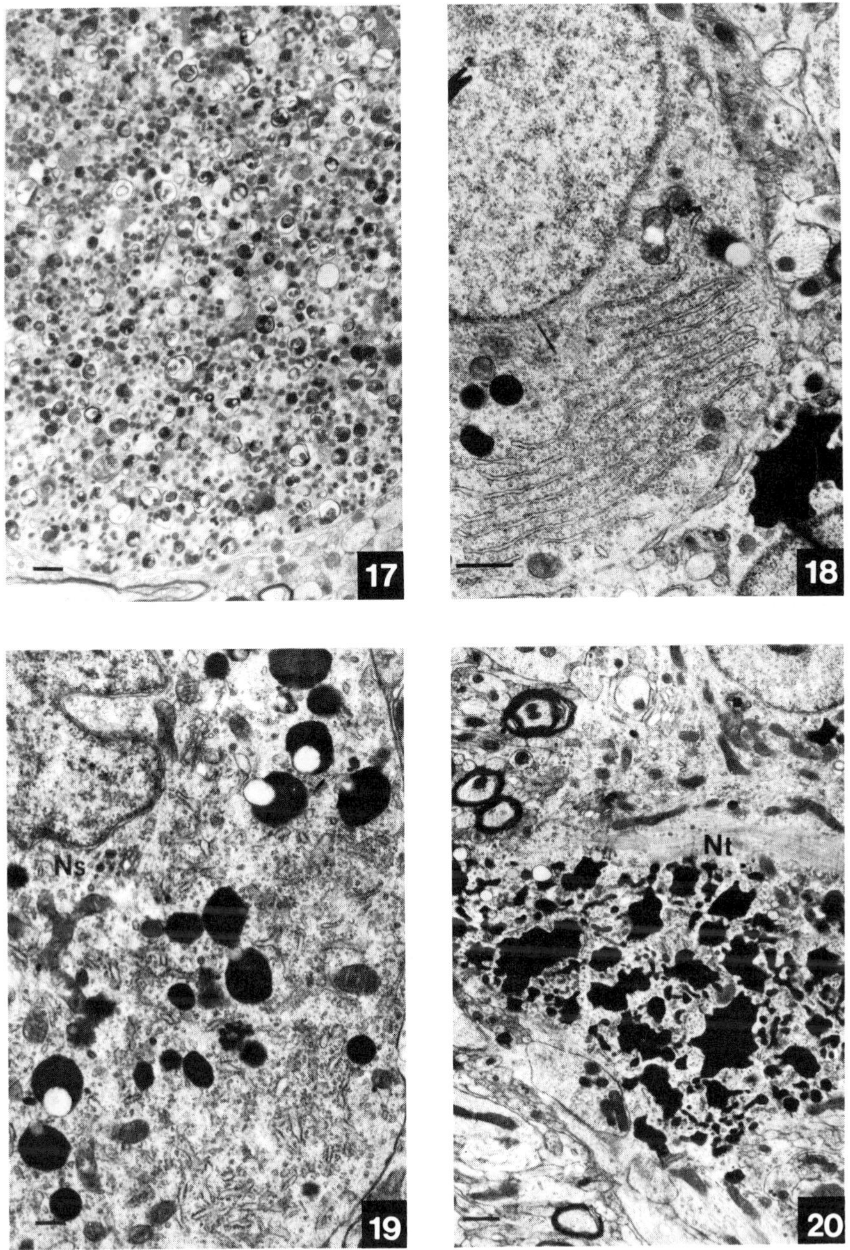

Plate V (Figures 17-20). Basal hypothalamus of old rats.

Figure 17. Herring body.

Figures 18 - 20. Various features of pigment accumulations and ultrastructural alterations in hypothalamic neurosecretory neurons.

NS: Neurosecretory granulation. Nt: Neurofibrillary tangles. Bar = 1 μm.

Discussion

Our results clearly show that following *in vivo* or *in vitro* administration of ^{3}H-5 HT, the pattern and intensity of radioautographic reactions either on cell bodies or on fibers are not qualitatively different in young and old rats. The significance of radioautographic reactions has to be determined before discussing the implications of their similarity in both types of animals.[1]

Since we did not perform a quantitative analysis, it is impossible to assume a difference in the number or uptake capacity of these neurons. Moreover, the 5 HT uptake in blood platelets seems to be normal as well as the properties of the Blood-Brain-Barrier (BBB) which prevents the access of systemically injected 5 HT to brain tissues but which is lowered at the level of circumventricular organs like ME. In fact, following intravenous injection of ^{3}H-5 HT, we have observed an important labelling of the ME with respect to surrounding hypothalamic tissues. Similarly Rapoport (1979) recently observed no differences in the BBB properties between young and old rats.

---

[1]METHODOLOGY. Since MAO which is the main pathway of 5 HT catabolism was inhibited in our experiments, we can assume that the radioactivity observed in the sections is due to ^{3}H-5 HT itself and, at a lesser extent, to its metabolites. The diffuse radioautographic reaction corresponds to free radioactive molecules which have been retained *in situ* by the fixative action of the glutaraldehyde (Descarries et al., 1975). This reaction constitutes a good index for measuring the tracer penetration which limited our study to periventricular or superficial cerebral structures after intraventricular injections or to the edges of incubated regions following incubation procedures. The diffuse reactions also allow us to appreciate the relative value of other radioautographic reactions and mainly of intense ones. These latter clusters of silver grains correspond to a specific uptake and retention of ^{3}H-5 HT by serotonergic neurons. The arguments for such an assumption are the following: the range of concentration used for *in vitro* experiments corresponds mainly to a high affinity uptake attributable to serotonergic neurons (Shaskan and Snyder, 1970). It is the same for *in vivo* experiments despite the higher initial concentration of the tracer which is further diluted in CSF and interstitial medium (Descarries et al., 1975). Moreover, an unselective uptake by catecholaminergic neurons was prevented in both cases by the addition of a higher concentration of Na. Finally, ^{3}H-5 HT labelled structures correspond to neurons previously demonstrated by several techniques (Dahlström and Fuxe, 1964; Calas et al., 1974; Segu and Calas, 1978; Descarries et al., 1975; Chan-Palay, 1976, 1977) or postulated (for spinal ganglia, Calas and Van Den Bosch, in prep.) as serotonergic. Thus, we can conclude that neurons labelled in our experiments are serotonergic and we can study comparatively their distribution and organization.

Concerning the distribution of serotonergic neurons in young and senescent rats, it appears from our results that the localization of 5 HT cell bodies, either in the raphe nuclei, in other mesencephalic areas (Chan-Palay, 1977; Dupuy and Calas, 1979) or in spinal ganglia, are apparently the same in young and old rats.

The absence of qualitative differences in the distribution of serotonergic cell bodies and terminals does not exclude the following possibilities.

1. More important variations in other areas than those particularly studied in the central and in the peripheral nervous system (although regions studied were crucial for the most of the important serotonergic regulations).
2. Modifications occurring in the terminal steps of the life of the animal. However, 24 months of age constitutes a late senescent state for our strain of rats (Ordy, 1975).
3. Modifications of other parameters than the uptake capacity in the physiology of 5 HT neurons.
4. Variations in the number of 5 HT receptors and/or the mechanisms of response of target cells. Recently a 30% decrease in high affinity binding of 5 HT has been described in human frontal cortex between the ages of 65 and 95 (Goodhardt, 1979).
5. Quantitative alterations in the number of serotonergic cell bodies or terminals as well as in the uptake processes which could not be detected in our experimental conditions. However, only slight differences in the kinetic parameters of 5 HT uptake into brain synaptosomes and blood platelets have been found in young and aged monkey (Omenn, Smith and Hanson, 1979).

As shown in our tables, aging can impair several processes involved in the metabolism of serotonin (Tables 1 and 2) as well as of catecholamines (Tables 2 and 3). The enzyme systems have been more thoroughly studied than the neurotransmitters themselves because the enzymes are more stable, less likely to diffuse and more easily estimated. Generally, the activity of the enzymes necessary for transmitter synthesis is reduced or remains unchanged (Table 2), while the activity of those involved in catabolism and namely MAO tends to increase (Tables 2 and 3; see also Algeri, this book). The age-related MAO changes are not restricted to specific areas in the brain with high amine content or specialized functions. The similar age linked MAO alterations observed in plasma and blood platelets support the view that the increasing enzyme activity is a general aging process (Robinson, 1975) although this fact has not been confirmed by Sandler et al. (1975).

The reduction of monoamine synthesis capacity has been noted by many authors. The dopaminergic system seems to be the most highly vulnerable (Adolfsson et al., 1979; Finch, 1973; 1976; McGeer and McGeer, 1975; Ponzio et al., 1978). The decreased capacity to synthesize catecholamines is questioned (Robinson et al., 1977) but it is clear that the capacity to destroy them increases. Thus aging involves a progressive imbalance between dopaminergic and other transmitter systems (McGeer

Table 1. Aging and Serotonin Level

Subjects	Ages	Nervous Tissues	Changes	References
Human	15 vs 70 yr	Caudate nucleus, hindbrain	0.23 vs 0.20 μg/g	Robinson et al. (1972). Nies et al. (1971)
	43-60 vs 73-87 yr	Caudate nucleus Putamen Hypothalamus	0.25 vs 0.29 μg/g 0.22 vs 0.23 μg/g 0.44 vs 0.31 μg/g	Bertler (1961)
	25 vs 70 yr	Hindbrain and various discrete nuclei	No change	Robinson (1975)
Rat	35-45 d vs 24 mo	Raphe nucleus, hippocampus, septum	Decrease 20 to 50%; tryptophane hydroxylase decreases or does not change	Meek et al. (1977) Meek et al. (1977) Reis et al. (1977)
	Young vs old	Hypothalamus	Decrease	Benetato et al. (1967)
	3-4 vs 21 mo	Whole brain, hypothalamus	No change (after inhibition of MAO with pargyline, hypothalamic serotonin increases more in old than in young males)	Simpkins et al. (1977) and Algeri (pers. comm.)
Mouse	3 vs 21 mo 12 vs 28 mo	Forebrain Whole brain	0.91 vs 1.08 μg/g No change	Samorajski and Rolstein (1973) Finch (1973)
Rhesus monkey	3 vs 18 yr	Hypothalamus	5.30 vs 4.33 μg/g	Samorajski and Rolstein (1973)
Chicken	3 vs 36 mo	Cerebral hemispheres	Slight decrease	Vernadakis (1975)

Table 2. Aging and Monoamine Oxidase Activity

Subjects	Ages	Nervous Tissues	Changes	References
Human	15 vs 70 yr	Hindbrain	Increase	Nies et al. (1973)
	14 vs 90 yr	Frontal cortex Caudate nucleus	98.9 vs 156.6 190.2 vs 238.4 nmoles tyramine/min/g protein	Samorajski and Rolstein (1973)
	25 vs 70 yr	Hindbrain	Slight increase	Robinson (1975)
	30-40 vs 60-70 yr	Various areas of the brain	Increase 34% Increase	Grote et al. (1974) Robinson et al. (1977)
	Young vs old	Brain	Increase	Cote and Kremzner (1974); Tryding et al. (1972)
Rat	2 vs 4 mo	Whole brain	17.3 vs 23.3 nmoles Ty2/mg protein/hr	Shih (1975)
Mouse	3 vs 21 mo	Forebrain Cerebellum Brain stem	97.4 vs 89.1 95.8 vs 167.1 166 vs 150.1 nmoles tyramine/min/g protein	Samorajski and Rolstein (1973)
Rhesus monkey	3 vs 18 yr	Frontal cortex Caudate nucleus	56.8 vs 141.4 142.7 vs 191.7 nmoles tyramine/min/g protein	Samorajski and Rolstein (1973)

Table 3. Aging, Neurotransmitters and Associated Enzymes Activity[a]

Tyrosine ⟶ DOPA ⟶ Dopamine ⟶ Norepinephrine ⟶ MAO deaminated and COMT O-methylated **metabolites (see MAO** Table 2)

Tyrosine hydroxylase	**Dopa decarboxylase**	Dopamine	**Dopamine β hydroxylase**	Norepinephrine	MAO deaminated and COMT O-methylated metabolites
human (1, 2, 3)[b] ↘ putamen (1, 2, 3) ↘ globus pallidus (1, 2) ↘ amygdala (1, 2) ↘ caudate (3) = (18) rat (4, 5, 6) = whole brain (4, 5) except striatum and cerebellum ↘ striatum (4, 5, 6) ↘ caudate (4, 5, 20) ↘ putamen (4, 5) ↘ **hypothalamus (6),↗ (20)** ↘ brain stem (6)	human (1, 2, 7, 3) ↘ extrapyramidal structures (3, 7) ↘ putamen (1, 2) ↘ globus pallidus (1, 2) ↘ amygdala (1, 2) mouse (8) = hypothalamus (8) = striatum (8)	human (9, 10, 17, 18, 19) ↘ caudate (9, 10, 17, 18, 19) ↘ putamen (9, 10, 19) ↘ various areas (17) mouse (8, 21) ↘ striatum (8, 21) rat (8, 21) ↘ brain (8) ↘ hypothalamus (21)	Rat (20) ↘ hypothalamus (20) = locus coeruleus (20) Mouse (20) = various areas (20)	human (12, 13, 14) ↘ hindbrain (12, 13, 14) mouse (8, 15, 21) = whole brain (8, 15) = hypothalamus (8, 21) = brain stem (8) = cerebellum (8) rat (11, 21) ↘ hypothalamus (11, 21) ↘ brain stem (Algeri, ibid)	human (15, 16, 18) = various areas mouse (15) = forebrain = cerebellum = brain stem Rhesus monkey (15) = frontal cortex = caudate = cerebellum = brain stem = rat ↗ brain (Algeri, ibid)

[a] See chapter by Algeri.

[b] References: (1) Mc Geer and McGeer (1975); (2) McGeer and McGeer (1976); (3) Cote and Kremzner (1974); (4) McGeer, McGeer and Wada (1971); (5) McGeer, Fibiger, McGeer and Wickson (1971); (6) Ponzio, Brunello and Algeri (1978); (7) Lloyd and Hornykiewicz (1972); (8) Finch (1973); (9) Bertler (1961); (10) Carlsson and Winblad (1976); (11) Austin, Connole, Kett and Collins (1978); (12) Robinson et al. (1972); (13) Robinson (1975); (14) Nies et al. (1973); (15) Samorajski and Rolstein (1973); (16) Grote et al. (1974); (17) Adolfsson, Gottfries, Roos and Winblad (1979); (18) Robinson et al. (1977); (19) Riederer and Wuketich (1976); (20) Reis et al. (1977); (21) Finch (1979).

and McGeer, 1975). The mechanism of reuptake, by which the released monoamines are inactivated, is reduced in the case of DA (Jonec and Finch, 1975) as well as the number of neurotransmitter storage vesicles for Na (Sun, 1976).

The rate of axonal transport (measured by labelled glycoproteins in the rat, Geinisman et al., 1977) is about 25% slower in senescent animals and the amount of transported material is significantly smaller. More generally a defect in the ability of the neurons to synthesize and transport material might impair the maintenance of synaptic connections and the reactive synaptogenesis which is reduced in senescent brain, resulting for example, in a decreased sprouting of NA axons (Scheff et al., 1978). With aging, the metabolism of the processes of the neurons seems to be less integrated with that of the perikaryon. All these factors may impair the plasticity of the aging brain.

On the post-synaptic side, the density, but not the affinity, of beta-adrenergic receptors is reduced in rat pineal gland, corpus striatum and cerebellum (Greenberg and Weiss, 1978). DA and histamine receptor systems selectively decrease with age in some areas of the rabbit brain (Makman et al., 1979) or in striatum and substantia nigra of rat but increase in this aging animal within the retina (Govoni et al., 1977).

The consequences of these impairments in each step of the metabolism or action of neurotransmitters are important in determining the physiology and the pathology of the nervous system. For instance, the increased MAO activity may be a predisposing factor of the multiple affective disorders which arise with age (Nies et al., 1973) while the illness itself might be induced by other influences. The most apparent manifestation of the vulnerability of the dopaminergic system to aging may be the slowness of movement and shuffling gait of the elderly. These Parkinson-like symptoms are accompanied by a severe striatal dopamine deficiency (Hornykiewicz, 1974).

The studies performed on serotonin are not so advanced. However our results emphasize the cytological alterations occurring mainly in cell bodies of central nervous tissue, in the raphe as well as in the basal hypothalamus. Indeed, there is a general agreement about cytological alterations observed in neurons with aging, as for instance (Andrew and Winston-Salem, 1956; Brizzee et al., 1975a; Brizzee et al., 1975b; Hasan and Glees, 1972, 1973; Hinds and McNelly, 1977; Johnson and Miquel, 1974; Lin et al., 1976; Samorajski, 1976; Samorajski, 1977; Vaughan and Vincent, 1979; Wisniewski and Terry, 1976): inconstant decrease of cellular and nuclear diameter; decrease of ribosomes and Nissl material; alteration of internal membrane system (Golgi complex and endoplasmic reticulum); abnormal mitochondria, sometimes containing inclusions; deposition of pigment bodies like lipofuscin or eosinophilic bodies; areas of degeneration consisting of granules surrounded by vacuoles; tangles or neurofibrils.

The typical raphe neuron is marked, although to a slight extent, by these cytological alterations while, at the level of 5 HT terminals, the ultrastructural content and the synaptic differentiations are practically normal. Autophagic processes observed within the Herring bodies normally occur in these large swellings of neurosecretory axons (Dellmann and Rodriguez, 1970) but they seem to be exacerbated in old animals.

Summarizing our results it appears that for serotonergic neurons, cell and terminal loss in aged rats is difficult to determine in any 5 HT area without a quantitative study. Uptake capacity is not altered and cytological alterations are discrete. If uptake is coupled with the release of transmitter (Chan-Palay, 1976), the continuity of this essential function of the neuron could explain the preservation of the pattern of interconnections and the maintenance of the serotonergic pathways in the brain of an aging animal.

As serotonergic neuron network is apparently normal, we might suppose that it is less sensitive to aging than the other networks but it would be best to perform a quantitative study of its synaptic connections to confirm this assumption.

There is a growing evidence from varous studies that aging of the nervous system is a heterogeneous phenomenon, differently affecting the areas of the brain. The more evident manifestation of this conception is for instance the selectivity in the nerve cell loss (Monagle and Brody, 1974; Brody, 1976).

Aging could affect neurons in two ways. First is a diffuse and progressive form of neuronal degradation affecting more or less all the neurons. Its manifestations would be lipofuscin accumulation, neurofibrillary tangles, etc. It increases the vulnerability of the brain and may be exacerbated in pathological cases. Sudden impairments specifically affecting a center or a pathway in the brain, and mainly correlated with transmitter metabolism and synaptic connections, would constitute the second mode of senescence.

The aging clock of the neuron would have two different rhythms, a progressive one increasing its vulnerability and a sporadic one which provokes heavy damage.

Apparently the most vulnerable system to aging is constituted by dopaminergic neurons whose alterations seem to be sudden (Hornykiewicz, 1974). By contrast, the serotonergic neurons seem to be less sensitive and the 5 HT network apparently maintains its stability throughout the life. The different sensitivities of DA and 5 HT neurons to aging support the first hypothesis that we have previously described and which emphasizes the importance of individual neurons or of particular networks. But in this view, 5 HT network could hardly be qualified as a pacemaker of aging.

ACKNOWLEDGMENT
The authors thank Dr. J.J. Dupuy for his appreciated advice in neuroanatomy and Miss A. Christolomme and Mr. M. Moya for their technical assistance.

References

Adolfsson R, Gottfries CG, Roos BE, Winblad B: Post-mortem distribution of dopamine and homovanillic acid in human brain, variations related to age, and a review of the literature. *J Neural Transmission* 45:81–105, 1979.

Andrew, W. and Winston-Salem, N.C. Structural alterations with aging in the nervous system. *J Chronical Diseases* (3), 575–596, 1956.

Austin JH, Connole E, Kett D, and Collins J: Studies in aging of the brain V. Reduced norepinephrine, dopamine and cyclic AMP in rat brain with advancing age. *Age* 1:121–124, 1978.

Benetato G., Uluitiu M, Suhaciu G, Iordache S: *Fiziologia normala i patologica* 13:245, 1967.

Bertler A: Occurrence and localization of catecholamines in the human brain. *Acta Physiologica Scandinavica* 51:97–107, 1961.

Boyenval J, Fischer J: Dipping technique. *J Microscopie et Biologie Cellulaire* 27:115–120, 1976.

Brizzee K R, Kaack B and Klara P : Lipofuscin: intra- and extraneuronal accumulation and regional distribution. In Ordy, J.M. & Brizzee, K.R. (eds.), *Neurobiology of Aging*. Plenum Press, 1975a; pp. 463–484.

Brizzee K R, Klara P and Johnson J E : Changes in microanatomy, neurocytology and fine structure with aging. In Ordy, J M & Brizzee, K R (eds.), *Neurobiology of Aging*. Plenum Press. 1975b; pp. 425–461

Brody H: An examination of cerebral cortex and brain stem aging. In Terry RD, Gershon S (eds.) *Aging 3, Neurobiology of Aging*. Raven Press, 1976, pp. 177–181.

Calas A, Segu L: Radioautographic localization and identification of monoaminergic neurons in the central nervous system. *J Microscopie et Biologie Cellulaire* 27:249–252, 1976.

Calas A, Alonso G, Arnauld E, Vincent JD: Demonstration of indolaminergic fibers in the median eminence of the duck, rat and monkey. *Nature* 250:241–243, 1974.

Calas A, Bessone R, Bosler O, Christolomme A, Dupuy JJ, Fons R, Gamrani H, Puizillout JJ, Segu L: The serotonergic neuron. New cytofunctional data. *Neuroscience Letters* (supp. l), S 268, 1978.

Carlsson A, Winblad B: Influence of age and time interval between death and autopsy on dopamine and 3-methoxytryptamine levels in human basal ganglia. *J Neural Transmission* 38:271, 1976.

Chan-Palay V: Serotonin axons in the supra- and subependymal plexuses and in the leptomeninges; their roles in local alterations of cerebrospinal fluid and vasomotor activity. *Brain Research* 102:103–130, 1976.

Chan-Palay V: Indolamine neurons and their processes in the normal rat brain and in chronic diet-induced thiamine deficiency demonstrated by uptake of ^{3}H-serotonin. *J Comparative Neurology* 176:467–494, 1977.

Cote LJ, and Kremzner LT: Changes in neurotransmitter systems with increasing age in human brain. *Transactions of American Society for Neurochemistry* 5:83, 1974.

Dahlström A, Fuxe K: Evidence for the existence of monoamine neurons in the central nervous system. 1. Demonstration of monoamines in the cell bodies of brain stem neurons. *Acta Physiologica Scandinavica* 62 (supp. 232): 1–55, 1964.

Dayan AD: Comparative neuropathology of aging. *Brain* 94:31–42, 1971.

Dellmann HD, Rodriguez EM: Herring bodies: an electron microscopic study of local degeneration and regeneration of neurosecretory axons. *Zeitschrift für Zellforschung* 111:293–315, 1970.

Descarries L, Beaudet A, Watkins KC: Serotonin nerve terminals in adult rat neocortex. *Brain Research* 100:563–588, 1975.

Descarries L, Beaudet A, Watkins KC, Garcia S: The serotonin neurons in nucleus raphe dorsalis of adult rat. *Anatomical Record* 193:520, 1979.

Dupuy JJ, Calas A: Detection radioautographique des corps cellulaires sérotonergiques dans le système nerveux central du rat. *J Physiologie,* Paris, 1979, 75:52A.

Finch CE: Monoamine metabolism in the aging male mouse. In Rockstein and Sussman (eds.) *Development and Aging in the Nervous System.* New York, Academic Press, 1973, pp. 199–218.

Finch CE: Endocrine and neural factors of reproductive aging. A speculation. In Terry RD, Gershon S. (eds) *Neurobiology of Aging.* Raven Press, 1976, pp. 335–338.

Finch CE: Neuroendocrine mechanisms and aging. *Federation Proceedings* 38:178–183, 1979.

Geinisman Y, Bondareff W, Telser A: Diminished axonal transport of glycoproteins in the senescent rat brain. *Mechanisms of Aging and Development* 6:363–378, 1977.

Goodhardt MJ: Neurotransmitter uptake and binding in ischaemia and senile dementia. Ph. D. Thesis, London, 1979.

Govoni S, Loddo P, Spano PF, Trabucchi M: Dopamine receptor sensitivity in brain in retina of rats during aging. *Brain Research* 138:565–570, 1977.

Greenberg LH, Weiss B: Beta-adrenergic receptors in aged rat brain: reduced number and capacity of pineal gland to develop supersensitivity. *Science* 201:61–63, 1978.

Grote SS, Moses SG, Robins E, Hudgens RW, Croninger AB: A study of selected catecholamine metabolizing enzymes: a comparison of depressive suicides and alcoholic suicides with controls. *J Neurochemistry,* 23:791–802, 1974.

Hasan M. and Glees P: Genesis and possible dissolution of neuronal lipofuscin. *Gerontologia* 18:217–236, 1972.

Hasan M, Glees P: Ultrastructural age changes in hippocampal neurons, synapses and neuroglia. *Experimental Gerontology* 8:75–83, 1973.

Hinds J W and McNelly N A: Aging of the rat olfactory bulb: growth and atrophy of constituent layers and changes in size and number of mitral cells. *ComparativeNeurology* 171: 345–368 1977.

Hornykiewicz O: Abnormalities of nigrostriatal dopamine metabolism: neurochemical, morphological and clinical correlations. *J Pharmacology* 5 (suppl):64, 1974.

Johnson J E and Miquel J Fine structural changes in the lateral vestibular nucleus of aging rats. *Mechanisms of Ageing and Development*, 1974, (3), 203–224.

Jonec V and Finch C E Aging and dopamine uptake by subcellular fractions of the C5713L/6J male mouse brain. *Brain Research*, 1975, (91), 197–215.

Larra F, Droz B: Techniques radioautographiques et leur application à l'étude du renouvellement des constituants cellulaires. *J Microscopie* 9:845–880, 1970.

Lettre H, Paweletz N: Probleme des elektronen mikroskopischen autoradiographie *Naturwissenschaften* 53:268–271, 1966.

Lin K H , Peng Y M , Peng M T and Tseng T M Changes in the nuclear volume of Rat hypothalamus neurons in old age. *Neuroendocrinology*, 1976, (21), 247–254.

Lloyd KG, Hornykiewicz O: Occurrence and distribution of aromatic L-amino acid (L-DOPA) decarboxylase in the human brain. *J Neurochemistry* 19:1549–1559, 1972.

McGeer EG, McGeer PL: Age changes in the human for some enzymes associated with metabolism of catecholamines, Gaba and acetycholine. In Ordy JM, Brizzee KR (eds.) *Neurobiology of Aging*. Plenum Press, 1975, pp. 287–305.

McGeer EG McGeer PL: Neurotransmitter metabolism in the aging brain. In Terry RD, Gershon S (eds.) *Neurobiology of Aging*. Raven Press, 1976, pp. 389–403.

McGeer, EG, Fibiger HC, McGeer PL, Wickson V: Aging and brain enzymes. *Experimental Gerontology* 6:391–396, 1971.

McGeer EG, McGeer PL, Wada JA: Distribution of tyrosine hydroxylase in human and animal brain. *J Neurochemistry* 18:1647–1658, 1971.

Makman MA, Ahn HS, Thal LJ, Sharpless NS, Dvorkin D, Horowitz SG, Rosenfeld M: Aging and monoamine receptors in brain. *Federation Proceedings* 38:1922–1926, 1979.

Martin GM: Cellular aging-postreplicative cells. *Amer J Pathology* 89:513–530, 1977.

Meek JL, Bertilsson L, Cheney DL, Zsilla G, Costa E: Aging-induced changes in acetylcholine and serotonin content of discrete brain nuclei. *J Gerontology* 32:129–131, 1977.

Meites J, Simpkins JN, Mueller GP, Huang HH:. Relation of brain catecholamines and serotonin to secretion of LH, FSH, prolactin and TSH in old and young rats. *Proc International Union of Physiological Sciences* 12:547, 1977.

Merlis JK: The effect of changes in the calcium content of the cerebrospinal fluid on spinal reflex activity in the dog. *Amer J Physiology* 131:67–72, 1940.

Monagle RD, Brody H: The effects of age upon the main nucleus of the inferior olive in the human. *J Comparative Neurology* 155:61–66, 1974.

Nies A, Robinson DS, Davis JM, Ravaris CL: Changes in monoamine oxidase with aging. In Eisdorfer C, Fann WE (eds.) *Psychopharmacology and Aging*. Plenum Press, 1973, pp. 41–54.

Nies A, Robinson DS, Ravaris CL: Amines and monoamine oxidase in relation to aging and depression in man. *Psychosomatic Medicine* 33:470, 1971.

Omenn, GS, Smith LT, Hanson DR: Pharmacogenetic investigations of platelet uptake of serotonin. III Serotonin uptake in platelets and in brain synaptosomes from young and aged Macaca Nemestrina. In Rowden DM (ed.) *Aging in Non Human Primates*. New York, Raven Press, 1979 (in press).

Ordy JM: Principles of mammalian aging. In Ordy JM, Brizzee KR (eds.) *Neurobiology of Aging*. New York, Plenum Press, 1975, pp. 1–22.

Ordy JM, Kaack B: Neurochemical changes in composition metabolism and neurotransmitters in the human brain with age. In Ordy JM, Brizzee KR (eds.) *Neurobiology of Aging*. New York, Plenum Press, 1975, pp. 253–285.

Ponzio F, Brunello N, Algeri S: Catecholamine synthesis in brain of aging rat. *J Neurochemistry* 30:1617–1620, 1978.

Rapoport SI: Blood-brain-barrier permeability in senescent rats. *J Gerontology* 34:162, 1979.

Reis DJ, Ross RA, Joh TH: Changes in the activity and amounts of enzymes synthetizing catecholamines and acetylcholine in brain, adrenal medulla and sympathetic ganglia of aged rat and mouse. *Brain Research* 136:465–474, 1977.

Riederer P, Wuketich S: Time course of nigrostriatal degeneration in Parkinson's disease. *J Neural Transmission* 38:277–301, 1976.

Robinson DS: Changes in monoamine oxidase and monoamines with human development and aging. *Federation Proc* 34:103–107, 1975.

Robinson DK, Sourkes TL, Nies A, Harris LS, Spector S, Bartlett DK, Kaye IS: Monoamine metabolism in human brain. *Archives of General Psychiatry* 34:89–92, 1977.

Rosen R: Cells and senescence. *International Review of Cytology* 54:161–191, 1978.

Samorajski T How the human brain responds to aging. *American Geriatrical Society*, 1976, 24 , 4–11.

Samorajski T Central neurotransmitter substanccs and aging : a review. *American Geriatrical Society*, 25 , 337–348, 1977,

Samorajski T, Rolstein C: Age and regional differences in the chemical composition of brains of mice, monkeys and humans. *Progress in Brain Research* 40:253–265, 1973.

Sandler M, Carter S, Cuthbert MT, Pare CMB: Is there an increase in monoamine oxidase activity in depressive illness? *Lancet* 1:1045–1047, 1975.

Scheff SW, Bernerdo LS, Cotman CW: Decrease in adrenergic axon sprouting in the senescent rat. *Science* 202:775–778, 1978.

Segu L, Calas A: The topographical distribution of serotoninergic terminals in the spinal cord of the cat: quantitative radioautographic studies. *Brain Research* 153:449–464, 1978.

Shaskan E G and Snyder S H Kinetics of serotonin accumulation into slices from rat brain : relationship to catecholamine uptake. *Journal of Pharmacology and Experimental Therapeutics*, 1970, (175), 404–418.

Shih JC: Multiple forms of monoamine oxidase and aging. In Brody H, Harman D, Ordy JM (eds.) *Aging 1, Clinical, Morphologic, and Neurochemical Aspects in the Aging Central Nervous System*. Raven Press, 1975, pp. 191–198.

Simpkins JW, Mueller GP, Huang HH, Meites J: Evidence for depressed catecholamines and enhanced serotonin metabolism in aging male rats: possible relation to gonadotropin secretion. *Endocrinology* 100:1672, 1977.

Sun A Y Aging and in vivo norepinephrine uptake in mammalian brain. *Experimental Aging Research*, 1976, (2), 207–220.

Tryding N, Tufvesson G, Ilsson S: Aging, monoamines and monoamine oxidase levels, *Lancet* 1:489, 1972.

Vaughan D W and Vincent J M Ultrastructure of neurons in the auditory cortex of ageing rats : a morphometric study. *Neurocytology*, 1979, (8), 215–228.

Vernadakis A: Neuronal-glial interactions during development and aging. *Federation Proc* 34:89–95, 1975.

Wisniewski H M and Terry R D Neuropathology of the aging brain. In Terry R D & Gershon S (eds.), *Aging 3, Neurobiology of Aging*. Raven Press, 1976, pp. 265–280.

Stein, ed. The Psychobiology of Aging: Problems and Perspectives

A Rat Model for the Neuroanatomical Basis of Performance Decline with Aging

Albert William Klein

Department of Anatomy, Eastern Virginia Medical School, Norfolk, Virginia.

Introduction

Scientific observations of aging changes in the human brain have dated back more than 100 years. Over that entire time span, gross observable alterations such as cortical atrophy and dural calcification have long been noted to occur in a consistent number of old brains. More recently, intranuclear inclusions have been seen at the fine structural level (Feldman and Peters, 1976). Between these extremes of morphologic resolution, Yakovlev (1962) reported loss of the massa intermedia and Brody (1955) reported the loss of specific regional neuron populations. These and other investigators recognized the value of integrating function with morphologic studies for greater understanding of the aging brain. One of the earliest integrative studies was that of Alzheimer (1907) and his classic description of the occurrence of senile plaques in the brains of former patients who had suffered from presenile dementia. Simchowicz in 1911 causally related the patient's psychological condition with the subsequent numbers of plaques seen in brain cortical regions after autopsy.

Numerous investigators have studied both function and structure in CNS material and have attempted to correlate the two in an explanatory manner. One example is the finding of cell loss that occurs in specific regions of aging human brains, such as the loss of granular cells from aged temporal cortex, coincidental with a hearing deficit frequently exhibited by the elderly (Brody, 1955 and 1978). Causal evidence for this loss is lacking. In another approach to structure-function relationships,

Diamond et al. (1966) demonstrated changing numbers of glial cells in the brains of rats of different ages exposed to different environments. Similarly, Brizzee et al. (1968) compared cell populations in the cerebral cortex of young and aged rats showing an increased glial/neuronal ratio in aged rats. A fine structural study documenting structural differences between functionally divergent cognitive groups has suggested that mentally defective individuals may show a compensatory increase in the number of synapses per unit area (Cragg, 1975). Cragg's work did not document a neuronal *density* loss in those areas that he studied. Weisnewski (1978) and Terry (1978) have shown an association between dementia, increases in neurofibrillary tangles and increases in amyloid deposits in older brain tissue observed after autopsy.

Animal models for functional loss or changes in performance ability with age have been difficult to develop. Botwinick et al. (1962) employed a four-choice maze in an unsuccessful effort to distinguish performance differences between young and aged rats. Goodrick at the Gerontology Research Center in Baltimore, Maryland has repeatedly been able to demonstrate maze-performance differences between young and old rats (1972 and 1973). Goodrick, in effect, duplicated the earlier report of Verzear-McDougall (1975), who employed a 14 choice "T" maze first devised by Stone (1929). This maze was not only able to differentiate the performance of young rats from old, but also divided the old rat category into two additional groups, an old maze-bright group and an old maze-dull group. Using this maze program to produce functionally different old animals, it was the aim of this study to discover possible morphological differences between the young and old animals, and more importantly between the old maze-bright and the old maze-dull animals.

Methods

Female Wistar rats from the Gerontology Research Center (GRC), Animal Care Laboratory, in Baltimore, Maryland, USA, were used in this study. The study began with five young adult (six months old) animals and 25 old rats (aged 25 months at the start). At the conclusion of this study all animals were two months older. The mean life expectancy of rats in the G.R.C. animal colony is 24 months and it was expected that approximately one-half of our old animals would be dead at the conclusion of the behavioral differentiation study. Each rat was housed separately and weighed daily. The first three days the rats were fed *ad libitum* diets and their weights were considered to be baseline for each animal. All animals were then put on a reduced diet of six to ten grams of Purina Rat Chow in order to reduce their weight to 80% and 75% (young and old respectfully) of their baseline in order to motivate them to perform in the maze (Goodrick, 1972).

Maze Performance

After five days of food reduction the animals were introduced to the reward solution in their home cages. The solution was 10% sucrose in canned milk, 1 ml placed in the depression of a heavy glass slide. Within another three days the animals were trained to run in a straight runway similar to construction to that of the maze. Following five days of such pre-training at three trials per day, the animals were introduced to the training in the 14 choice Stone maze (Michel and Klein, 1978). Training followed Goodrick's (1972) methods with one trial per day given for 20 days. All errors were scored as was the time required for each rat to go from the start box to the reward. Animals that died during the training were eliminated from the data bank of this study. In actuality, the animals that did die represented both good learners and poor learners. On the day following the twentieth day of maze training all animals were sacrificed.

Preparation of Brain Tissue for Microscopy

Animals were anesthetized and perfused with Karnovsky's fluid via the left ventricle. The flesh was removed and the skulls and brains were placed in fresh fixative overnight. The next morning the brains were removed and placed in fresh fixative. The left hemisphere was embedded for light microscope observation and wedge-shaped samples of the frontal and occipital cortex were removed for transmission electron microscopy. Parasagittal sections for light microscopy were cut from the left hemisphere starting at the midline and progressing laterally for one millimeter. Consecutive sections lateral to the first one millimeter were saved and numbered. Sections were stained with Windle's thionin stain, numbered, and those numbered 1, 25 and 50 were subjected to extensive mensuration. Because the rat cortex is lisenecephalic, the length of it was divided into eight segments and segments 2 and 7 were those sampled for both light and electron microscopy (See Figure 1). The thickness of each cortical layer was measured using the light microscope and random Chalkley counts were proportionally used to sample the neural components in each layer. The method has been described elsewhere in detail (Klein and Michel, 1977). Thirty-five hundred (3500) counts were made in each cortical area for 7000 counts per animal and those components that were distinguished were: astrocytes, oligodendrocytes, pyramidal neurons, non-pyramidal neurons, blood vessels and neuropil. Slides were coded by a naive colleague prior to observation and counting.

Small specimens from corresponding cortical regions of the right hemisphere were prepared for transmission electron microscopy. These were osmicated (1% osmium in caccodylate buffer) and routinely processed for embedding and polymerization in plastic. Sections were cut

RIGHT TELENCEPHALIC CORTEX OF THE RAT

MEDIAL

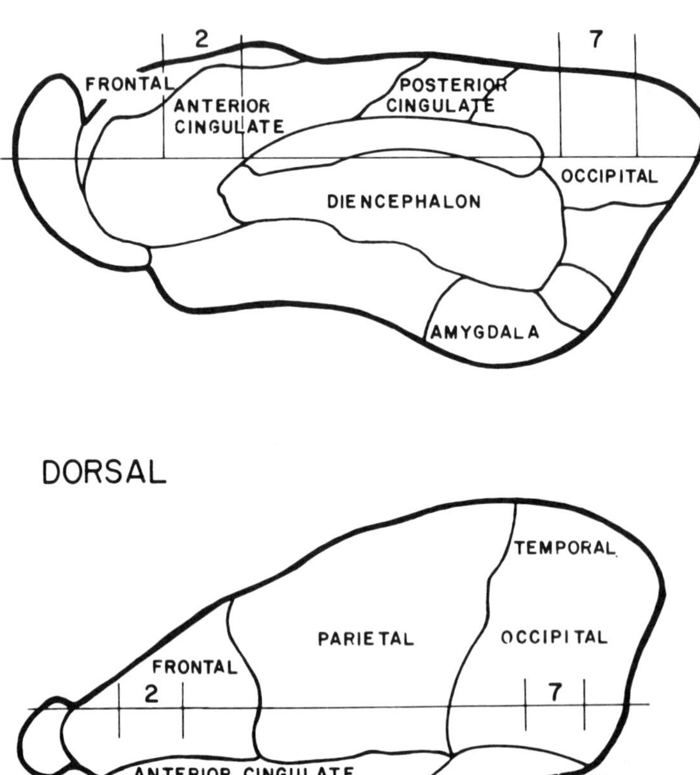

Figure 1. Medial and dorsal views of the rat lissencephalic cortex are shown. From the dorsal view, tissue sectioning advanced inward from the median plane through the anterior cingulate gyrus to the section line shown.

with a diamond knife and trimmed so that layer III of the cortex could be observed on a Philips 301 electron microscope. Three animals were processed for study from each of the three performance groups. Two blocks were sectioned from each frontal cortex specimen and two from each occipital cortex specimen. Examinations of the pyramidal cell layer (III) were performed in detail on two sections per block and four photos per section were subjected to synapse counts per unit area (scaled) of photo. Synapse counts per area were pooled within functional groups and compared using Student's t test.

Results

Maze Performance Studies

Restrictions in available rat chow caused the expected reductions in animal weight. Six to ten grams of chow per day per rat reduced the weights of the young and old groups to 76% and 75% of their respective baseline weights. All rats readily accepted the reward solution. Figure 2 shows the mean number of errors committed per day during the 20 days of learning undergone by both the young rats and the old rats. The average times that were required by these rats to negotiate the maze from start to reward are similarly plotted in Figure 3. Both of these two measures, maze errors and maze negotiation times, indicate that progress was rapid until about the 14th trial day when the older animals failed to exhibit the same rate of improvement that was seen in the progress of the younger rats.

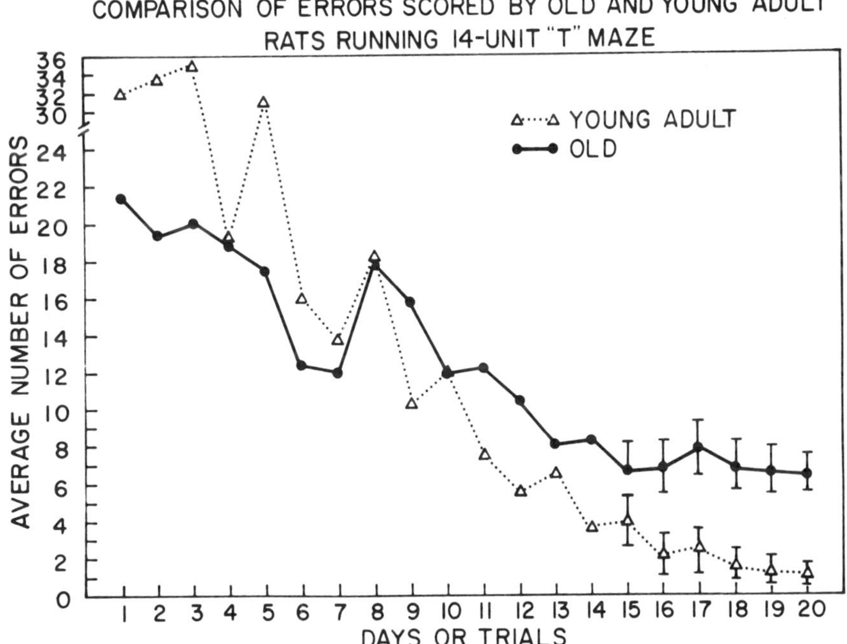

Figure 2. The mean number of errors scored by the young adult and the old rats.

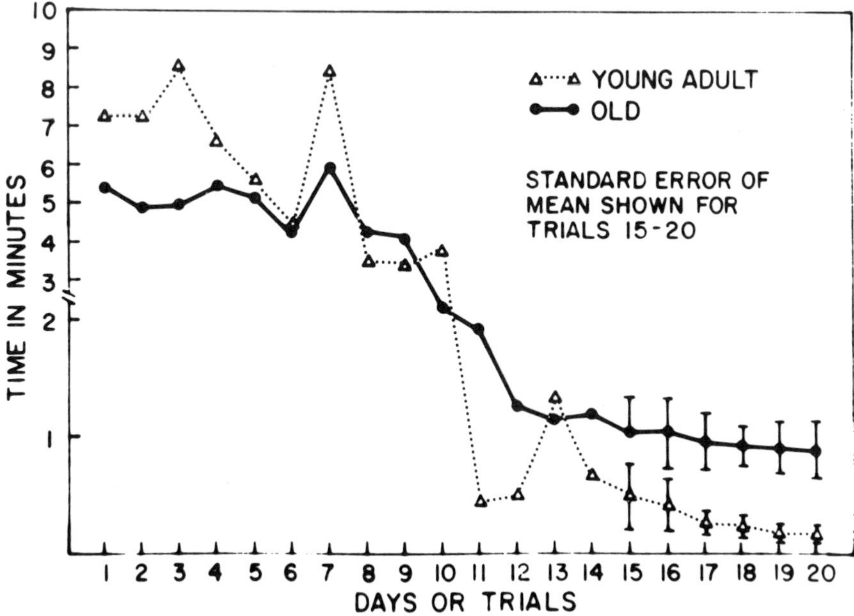

Figure 3. The average times that were required for the rats to negotiate the maze from start to finish is shown.

On close examination of the data, it was observed that several of the older rats performed as well as did the younger rats (two errors or less on day 20). When the maximum number of errors committed by the younger rats was used as a criterion for separation, the older group could be divided into two functional groups, approximately equal in number, termed old maze-bright and old maze-dull. This division into groups was previously done by Goodrick (1973) and he showed that even with longer training, the old maze-dull group failed to perform as well as the young animals or the old maze-bright animals. He demonstrated that the old maze-dull rats continued to commit repetitive errors.

Table 1 lists the mean number of errors committed by the three functional groups. It shows the errors for days 15 through 20 for the young group, the old group and for the functionally divided old animals, i.e., the old maze-bright and the old maze-dull. Table 2 indicates the level of significance for possible difference in the error scores for these groups. A morphologic correlate of functional differences such as those described above, has not been generally accepted.

Brain Weight Differences

The dissected brains of the animals were each weighed after the completion of the microscopic study and after decoding they were compared within their functional groups. Table 3 data show that the older rats appear to have heavier brains than do the younger rats. The relationship was surprising however because the old maze-dull animals had the heaviest mean brain weight. Student's t test indicated that differences existed between the young and the old maze-dull only ($P < .05$). The old maze-bright animals were not significantly different from either the young maze-bright rats or the old maze-dull rats.

Light Microscopic Study

Rats, like most other mammals, have a six-layered neocortex with cytoarchitechtonics similar to that of a human. Each of the six layers

Table 1. Daily Errors Scored by the Various Rat Groups in a 14-Unit "T" Maze

Day	Young Adult	Total Old	Old Group I Maze-bright	Old Group II Maze-dull
1	32[a] 11[b]	21 3	20 2	21 3
5	32 3	24 3	23 2	25 3
10	12 4	12 2	14 6	12 2
15	4 2	7 1	3 0	11 3
16	2 1	7 2	4 1	11 3
17	3 1	8 1	3 1	11 2
18	2 1	7 1	2 1	11 2
19	1 0	7 2	2 1	11 2
20	1 0	7 1	2 1	10 1

[a] The first number in each day-group cell represents the mean errors for that group.

[b] The second number in each day-group represents the standard error of the mean for that group.

Table 2. Significance of Different Error Scores of 3 Groups of Rats Running a 14-Unit "T" Maze

Trials (days)	Total Errors			Significance
	Young	Old Maze-bright	Old Maze-dull	
1-5	152.3	104.2	121.2	N.S.[a]
6-10	70.0	94.4	85.8	N.S.
11-15	27.0	32.6	57.2	N.S.
16-20	10.67	13.0	52.7	$P < .01$
Total Errors	260.0	244.2	216.8	N.S.

[a] Not significant

were measured and the proportion that each layer represented of the total was calculated. Sampling was done by the random point counting method of Chalkey (1943) and has previously been described in detail (Klein and Michel, 1977). Sample counts were proportionally derived from the various layers as represented in Figure 4. The component structures that were counted included: astrocytes, oliogodendroglia, pyramidal neurons, non-pyramidal neurons, vascular elements and neuropil. Table 4 tabulated these elements for the three functionally differentiated groups. There were *no clear* statistical differences for these brain components between the maze differentiated groups. Results of an analysis of variance did suggest a difference at the $P < .1$ level for vascular elements.

Morphological observations of 1 nm plastic sections revealed a striking difference between the young rat cortex and the old rat cortex. Specifically the appearance of some large neurons differed conspicuously among samples of the three groups. Many nuclei within the old animal specimens appeared crenated and shrunken. Their nuclear chromophilia was also enhanced while the perikarya exhibited the opposite appearance, i.e., that of being washed out and watery (Figure 5). Interspersed with crenated neurons were normally appearing neurons that contained those

Table 3. Brain Weights of Maze-differentiated Wistar Rats

	Young Adult Maze-bright	Old Maze-bright	Old Maze-dull
Mean	2.075 gm	2.150	2.275
S.D.	±.025	±.109	±.050
Percent Δ	100%	104%	110%

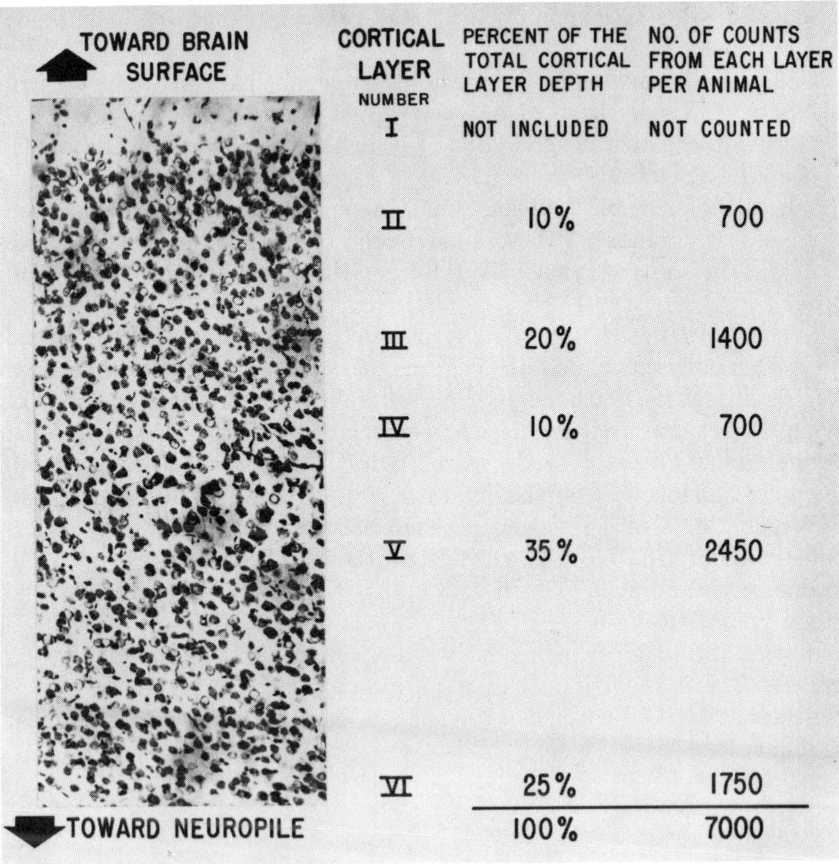

CORTICAL LAYER NUMBER	PERCENT OF THE TOTAL CORTICAL LAYER DEPTH	NO. OF COUNTS FROM EACH LAYER PER ANIMAL
I	NOT INCLUDED	NOT COUNTED
II	10%	700
III	20%	1400
IV	10%	700
V	35%	2450
VI	25%	1750
	100%	7000

Figure 4. Rat neocortex demonstrating layers I and VI, in low magnification, is shown. To the right are shown the percentages of neocortex and the counts that came from each layer.

cellular organelles thought of as necessary for a functional existence. These sections also revealed an abundance of lipofuscin pigment within neurons.

Electron Microscopic Study

At the higher resolution of the transmission electron microscope (TEM), it was clear that a certain amount of lipofuscin pigment was also present in neurons of the eight-month-old, young, animals. However, it was also the case that *both* functional groups of older rat neurons contained more intracellular pigment than did the younger rat brains. Magnifications sufficient to discern membranes indicated that the pigments were often associated with lysosomal bodies and generally appeared membrane bound (Figure 6).

Neurons that exhibited the same crenated nuclear and watery cytoplasm appearance were also observed at the TEM level. Figure 7 illustrates these two observations at a higher magnification. The nuclei appeared atypical with a suggestion of extra condensed chromatin material. Vacuoles, both large and small, appeared in the perikarya which was void of organelles. The crenated cells comprised an obvious group that was in some ways vastly different from those in the young rat brains.

Synapse profiles were counted on coded micrographs (Figure 8) and their frequency calculated as synapses per square millimeter of section. The results of these calculations are on Table 5 as the mean number of synapses per unit area and as a percentage of the number present in the young animal cortex. The decreased number of observable synapses in the older animals was significant at the $P < .01$ level, by Student's t test. This same level of significance existed between the functionally differentiated older rats, i.e., the maze-bright rats and the maze-dull rats. The old maze-dull animals yielded counts that were only 53% of that found in the young rat brains.

Several intranuclear inclusions were observed and photographed (Figure 9). These inclusions had a periodicity of about 90Å and were considered to be either disc or rod shaped, because when they did appear in thin sections, they were as rods.

Discussion

The Stone 14-choice maze has been established by a number of investigators as a tool to differentiate old rats into efficient maze learners and poor maze learners (Verzar-McDougall, 1977; Goodrick, 1973; and Mich-

Table 4. Combined Chalkley Counts for Frontal and Occipital Rat Cortex

Astrocytes	Oligodendrocytes	Pyramidal cells	Other neurons	Blood vessels	Neuropil
Young Adult (N=5)					
64	107	3593	357	523	15787
0.3%	0.5%	17.1%	1.7%	2.5%	75.2%
Old Maze-bright (N=5)					
130	173	3440	527	347	16383
0.6%	0.8%	16.4%	2.5%	1.7%	78.0%
Old Maze-dull (N=5)					
147	157	3685	385	277	16546
0.7%	0.7%	17.5%	1.8%	1.3%	78.0%

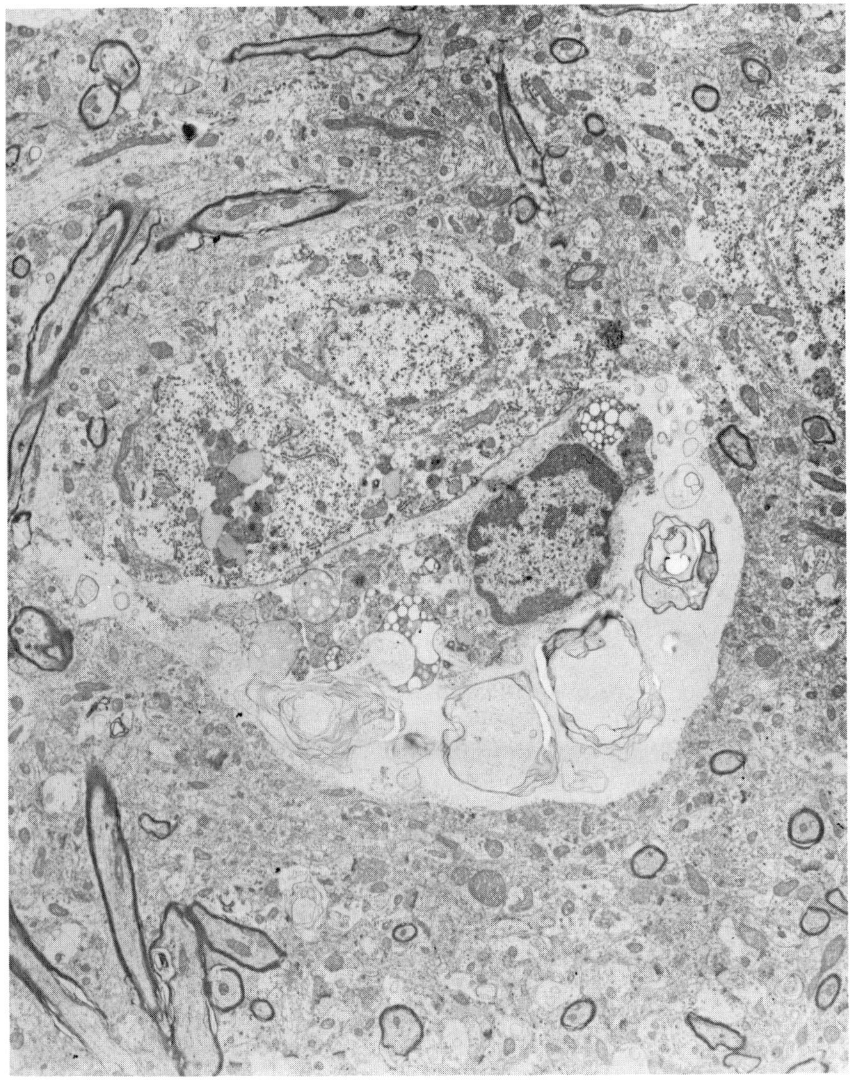

Figure 5. An old neuron showing vacuolated cytoplasm and photographed at 9,000 ×.

el and Klein, 1978). There has been presumed importance to this distinction, but exactly what might be reflected in terms of morphology or physiology is questionable. This separation of learning has a human correlate in the work of Arenberg (1974) and Friedman (1974). Their studies seem to indicate that if certain intellectual tasks are selected for testing in young and elderly subjects, the young subjects can uniformly perform adequately, but that some older subjects can, and some cannot,

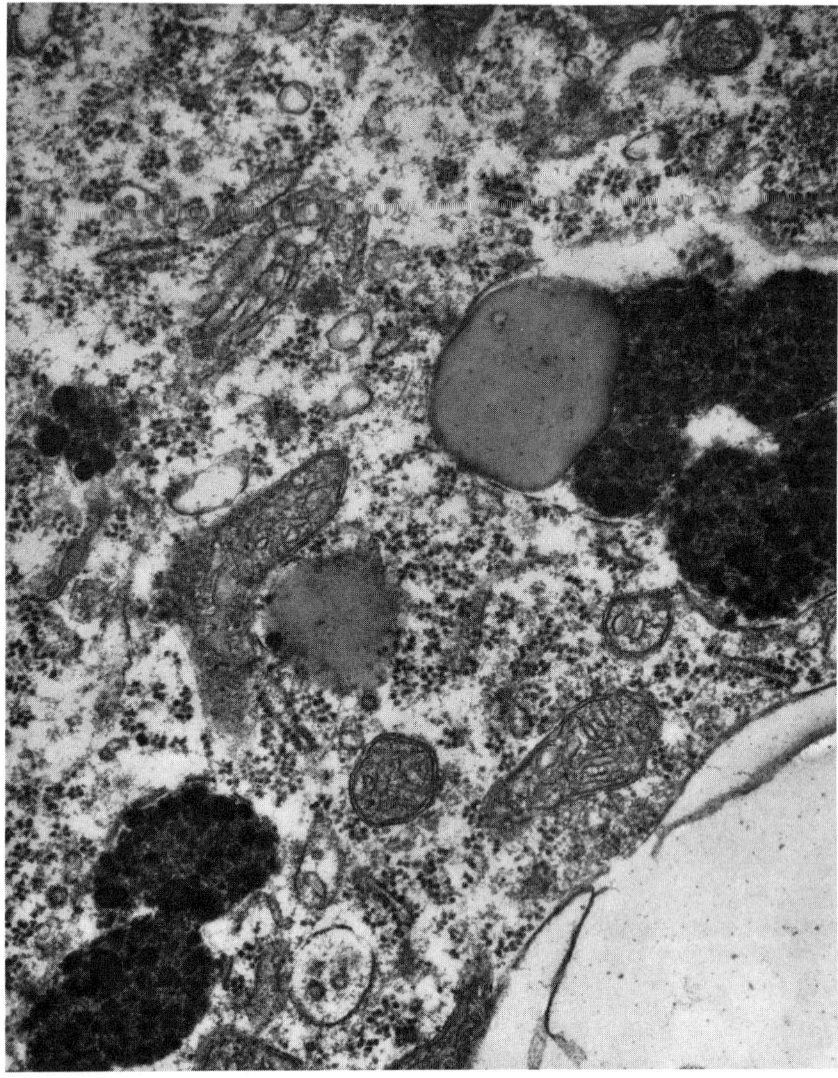

Figure 6. Here are illustrated membrane bound lysosomal bodies and lipofuscin pigments photographed and printed at 80,000 ×.

adequately handle these intellectual efforts. Data from this study pointed directly to the concept that the mammalian C.N.S. undergoes morphological changes that may be responsible for the decline of neural function with aging.

The present light microscopic results differ slightly from the literature. Published measurements of neural components state that the glial/neu-

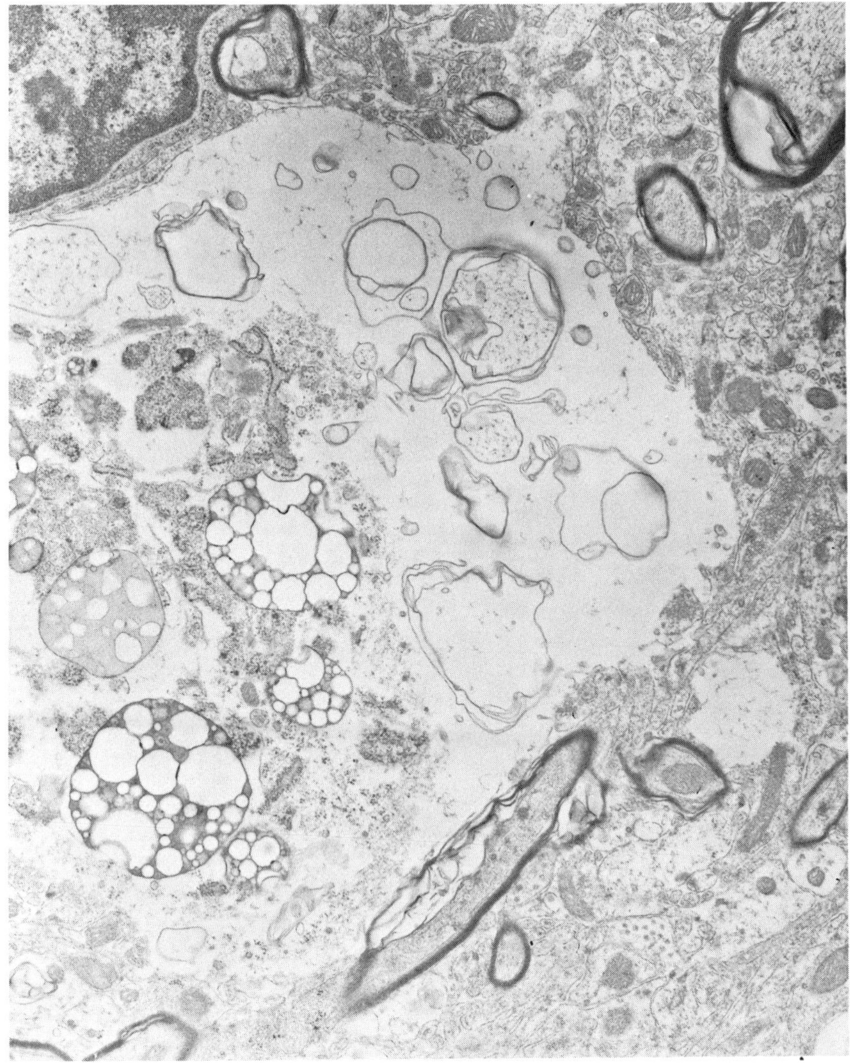

Figure 7. The cytoplasm of this cell is undergoing dissolution, print magnification is 21,000 ×.

ronal ratio goes up with age (Brizzee, 1964). This finding differs from the data presented here, but so did the ages of the rat specimens. Brizzee's young rats were three-months-old and the young rats of my study were six-months-old at the beginning of maze training and eight-months-old at the time of sacrifice and brain examination. Significant glial proliferation could have occurred between the third and the eighth month resulting in

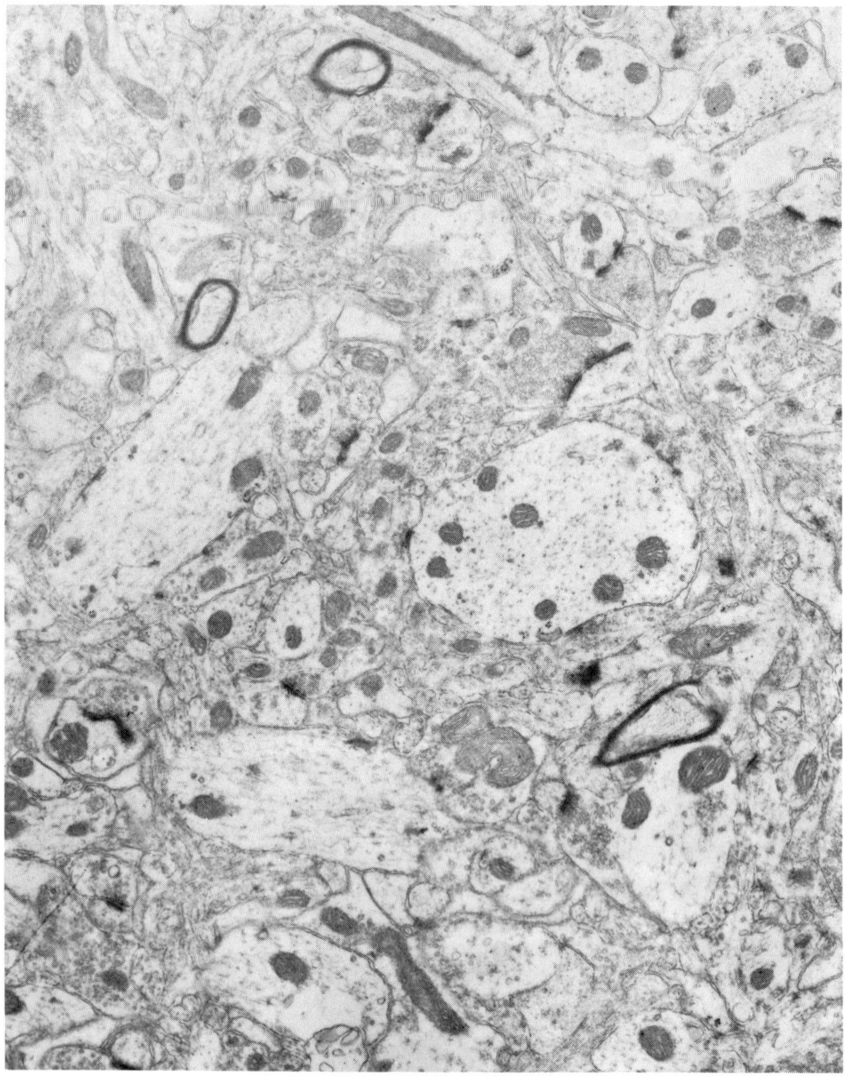

Figure 8. The synapse profiles seen here were counted and expressed per square millimeter, 21,000 ×.

Table 5. Section Exposed Synapses per Square Millimeter

	Young Adult Maze-bright	Old Maze-bright	Old Maze-dull
Mean	395.7	338.8	215.6
± S.D.	± 31.	± 58.	+ 53.
Percent Δ	100%	85.6%	54.5%

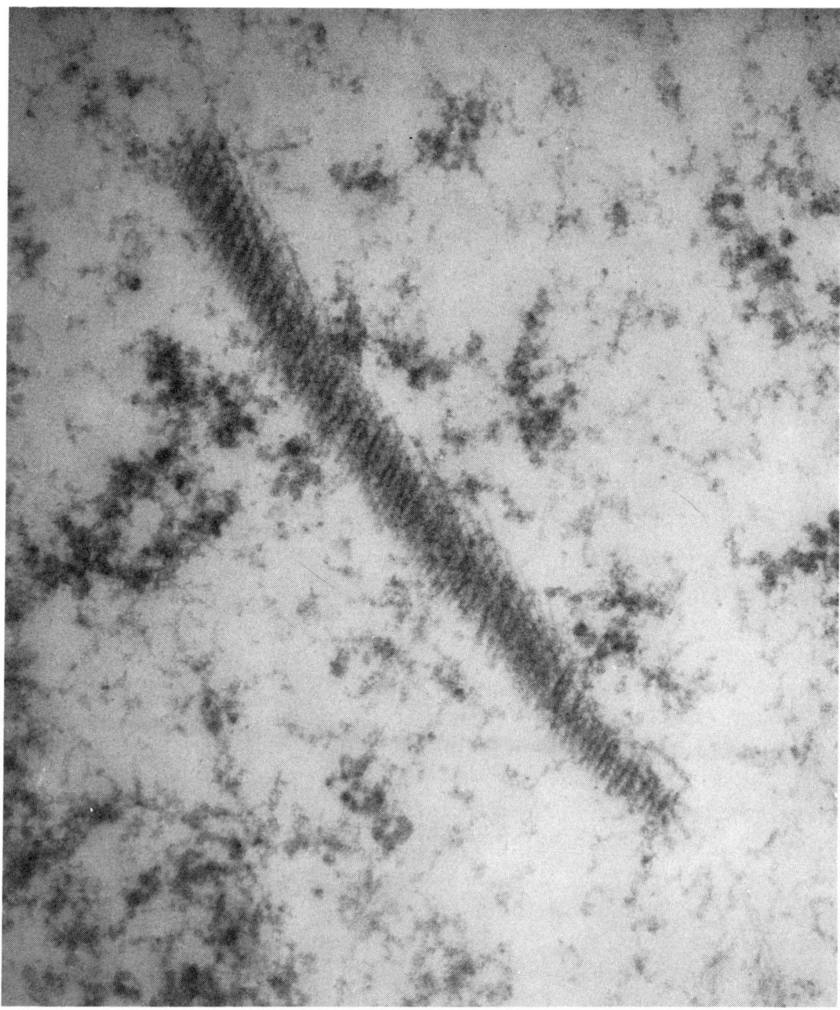

Figure 9. A rod or disc shaped intranuclear inclusion is printed here at a magnification of 112,500 ×.

no differences between this study's eight-month-olds and the 27-month-old rats.

The appearance of the young versus old rat neocortex, as seen in the 1 nm light microscopic sections, and as seen in thin sections with the TEM, suggests that there is an important difference in their neuronal reaction to fixation. The younger neurons reacted routinely to Karnovsky's fixative but a large number of neurons from the aged rats did not appear to have reacted to fixation in a uniform mannner. Zs-Nagy (1979) has discussed the theoretical basis for different function regarding membrane permeability between young and old animals. He proposed that older neuronal membranes were less permeable to specific elements and compounds. This thesis is a possible explanation for selected neuronal adequate fixation and non-adequate fixation. Whatever the discriminating factor has been, it was conspicuous that different aged neurons, treated in similar ways, did not appear the same in thin sections. Older cortex contained neurons that appeared swollen and vacuolated with a loss of apparent organelles. This observation may have some relation to the differences in the gross weights of the brains of the different groups. The heavier brains of the older animals, most heavy were the old maze-dull animals, could have been caused by fluid accumulation or perivascular edema. This possibility may or may not have a causal relationship, but the relationship should be quantified and investigated.

The quantification of synapses in different aged rats has been done by numerous investigators (Schiebel et al., 1975; Feldman and Dowd, 1975; Mervis, 1978). Their work involved the counting of dendritic spines per unit length of dendrite in Golgi preparations. Invariably, these investigators have shown a loss of spines and while their work did show the regions from where the spines were lost, it did so only for those dendrites that were selectively stained with the Golgi technique. This investigation quantified in a systematic manner, the synapses present in a given level of neocortex (layer III). Moreover, it quantified these synaptic frequencies (profiles to sectional area, an index of frequency or density) in young animals and more importantly in old animals that had been separated functionally on the basis of their maze learning abilities. These data showing old maze-dull animals to have had a significant decline in numbers of intercellular communication sites are an important addition to the aging literature. While a causal relationship between maze performance and synaptic abundance is not a certainty, these data are suggestive that anatomical alterations, as well as other possible factors, play an important role in determining the range of abilities and ineptitudes exhibited by aged animals.

References

Feldman M, Peters A: Intranuclear rods and sheets in rat cochlear nucleus. *J Neurocytology* 5:63–84, 1976.

Yakovlev PL: Limbic nuclei of thalamus and connections of limbic cortex in monkey. *Archives of Neurology* 5:364, 1961.

Brody H: Organization of the cerebral cortex. *J Comparative Neurology* 102:511–556, 1955.

Alzheimer A: Uber einen eigenartigen schweren Erkrankungsforogress de Hernrinde (Zu Kurzem refect nicht geeignet). *Allg Z Psychiatr* 64:146, 1907.

Simchowicz T: Histologische studien uber die senilen demeng, Nissls arbeiten. *Histol histopath Arb Grosshirnrinde IV,* 1911, 267–444.

Brody H: Personal Communication. 1978.

Diamond MC, Law H, Rhodes H, Lindner B, Rosenweig M, Bennett E: Increases in cortical depth and glial numbers in rats subjected to enriched environment. *J Comparative Neurology* 128:117–126, 1966.

Brizzee KR, Sherwood N, Timiras P: Comparison of cell populations at various levels in cerebral cortex of young-adult and aged Long-Evans rats. *J Gerontology* 23:289–297, 1968.

Cragg BG: The density of synapses and neurons in normal, mentally defective and aging human brains. *Brain* 98:81–91, 1975.

Weisniewski H, Johnson A, Raine C, Kay W, Terry R: Senile plaques and amygloidosis in aged dogs. *Laboratory Investigation* 23:287–296, 1970.

Terry R: Senile Dementia, *Federation Proceedings* 37:2837–2840, 1978.

Botwinick J, Brinley J, Robbin J: Learning a position discrimination and position reversals by Sprague-Dawley rats of different ages. *J Gerontology* 17:315–319, 1962.

Goodrick C: Error goal-gradients of mature young and aged rats during training in a 14-unit spatial maze. *Psychological Rep* 32:359–362, 1973.

Verzear-McDougall E: Studies in learning and memory in aging rats. *Gerontologia* 1:65–85, 1957.

Stone C: The age factor in animal learning: rats in the problem box and the maze. *Genet Psychol Monograph* 5:1–130, 1929.

Michel M, Klein AW: Performance differences in a complex maze between young and aged rats. *Age* 1:13–16, 1978.

Klein AW, Michel M: A morphometric study of the neocortex of young adult and old maze-differentiated rats. *Mech of Aging and Development* 6:441–452, 1977.

Chalkley H, Cornfield J, Park H: A method for estimating volume-surface ratios, *Science* 110:295–297, 1949.

Arenberg D: A longitudinal study of problem solving in adults. *J Gerontology* 29:650–659, 1974.

Friedman D: Interrelations of two types of immediate memory in the aged. *J Psychology* 87:177–183, 1974.

Zs-Nagg I: The role of membrane structure and function in cellular aging: a review. *Mech of Aging and Development* 9:237–246, 1979.

Schiebel M, Lindsey R, Tomizasu U, Scheibel A: Progressive dendritic changes in aging human cortex. *Experimental Neurology* 47:392–403, 1975.

Feldman M, Dowd C: Loss of dendritic spines in aging cerebral cortex. *Anatomic Embryology* 148:279–301, 1975.

Mervis R: Structural alterations in neurons of aged canine neocortex: A Golgi study. *Experimental Neurology* 62:417–432, 1978.

Stein, ed. The Psychobiology of Aging: Problems and Perspectives

Behavioral and Morphological Aspects of Aging: An Analysis of Rat Frontal Cortex[a]

Elliott J. Mufson[b] and Donald G. Stein

Department of Psychology, Clark University, Worcester, Massachusetts; and Department of Neurology, University of Massachusetts Medical Center.

Structure-Function Relationships in the Aging Brain

The behavioral consequences of damage to the central nervous system (CNS) depend upon many different factors and not just the site of the initial injury. For example, it is generally thought that early onset of brain injury results in less severe impairment of behavioral function than when the same kind of damage is inflicted in later life. The explanation usually offered for the sparing of behavior that occurs after brain lesions early in development is that specific, anatomically defined structures have not yet become committed to mediating specific behavior; that is, the behavioral functions have not yet been "localized" in the appropriate CNS regions. Whether or not this notion is correct, the implication is that there are age-related factors that influence the severity of symptoms following CNS injury.

As a specific test of this hypothesis, Patricia Goldman (1974) sought to determine how development and experience can alter a subject's response to brain damage by performing surgery on monkeys immediately after they were born and then comparing their performance to monkeys that received surgery as older animals. In one study, 50 day-old monkeys sustained bilateral dorsal frontal cortex ablations. Normally, such frontal cortex lesions in juvenile or adult rhesus monkeys produce long-standing

[a]This reseach was conducted at Clark University and the University of Massachusetts Medical Center, supported by a Mellon Foundation Grant to Elliott Mufson and a grant from the National Institute of Aging, #RO1-AG-00295 to Donald G. Stein.

[b]Present address: Neurological Unit, Beth Israel Hospital, Boston, Massachusetts

deficits in performance of spatial tasks. In contrast, those animals given neonatal operations and then tested at 12-months of age, were unimpaired in comparison to intact animals. However, as these early-operated monkeys reached juvenile and mature ages, their performance deteriorated. These data led Goldman to suggest that the onset of the behavioral deficits appeared as the need for a mature frontal cortex committed to specific functions became manifest. To test further the possibility of alterations in structure-function relationships with advancing age, Goldman performed a second experiment in which she first ablated the orbitofrontal cortex of infant monkeys and then tested the animals as juveniles and again later, as young adults. Initially, the "orbitofrontal" group was very impaired on a series of spatial problems. In contrast to the performance of animals with dorsolateral frontal cortex lesions (which deteriorated behaviorally with age), the monkeys with orbitofrontal damage grew out of their deficits as they aged. These findings suggested to Goldman and her colleagues that the orbital region was initially committed to the mediation of spatial behaviors, but as other brain structures matured, they replaced the capacity of the orbital cortex to mediate spatial behavior. In another demonstration of how age at time of insult to the nervous system influences behavioral outcomes, Goldman and Galkin (1978) removed the frontal cortex of a fetal rhesus monkey (i.e., at embryonic day E106) and then returned the animal to the womb where it was allowed to develop to term. At 12 months of age, the monkey was tested on a battery of spatial alternation tasks and its performance compared to other animals which had sustained similar surgery either on post-natal (P) days 50 or 540. All of the operated monkeys were compared to unoperated, age-matched controls. The monkeys operated at E106 and P50 attained criterion on delayed response in the same number of trials as unoperated controls. In contrast, the monkeys that received bilateral removals of frontal cortex at 540 days of age were severely debilitated and did not evidence any recovery. On delayed alternation, acquisition and retention, the differences in performance resulting from age at time of surgery were even more dramatic. The animal receiving surgery in the fetal stage was normal; those operated 50 days after birth were impaired but still significantly better than monkeys given the lesions as juveniles.

Histological evaluation revealed that monkeys given surgery during the fetal period of development did not show the typical pattern of retrograde cellular degeneration in the mediodorsal thalamic nucleus that normally occurs after frontal ablations. Moreover, Goldman and Galkin found evidence of ectopic sulci and gyri in the intact regions of the frontal cortex, as well as in regions of the brain far removed from the site of injury. Thus, it would appear that structure-function relationships are dynamic—at least, it is thought until the organism reaches maturity at which time genetically determined cellular and biochemical mechanisms begin to specify the relationship between anatomical structures and behavior.

As an organism grows old, its capacity to recover from trauma is said to diminish. Thus, for the most part, it has been a well accepted principle that once an organism has reached sexual maturity, the adaptability to injury often seen in young animals is extremely limited, if it appears at all (see Goldberger and Murray, 1978). There is considerable evidence to support this contention, and most of these data are derived from lesion studies or clinical reports which demonstrate that focal, bilateral brain injury almost always produces permanent impairments in behavioral functions, especially in older subjects.

In the adult, one way to minimize the effects of CNS trauma is to inflict the damage slowly or in successive stages. In this experimental situation, bilateral lesions are given to adult subjects in two or more stages, with a fixed interval between the first and second operations (for details, see Finger, Walbran and Stein, 1973; Finger 1978). The most consistent finding associated with the serial lesion experiments has been that the placement of successive lesions in different brain areas often results in complete sparing of function while the same damage inflicted simultaneously, produces permanent impairments in adult animals.

Previous experiments in our laboratory show that the frontal cortex of the adult rat is well suited to the study of serial lesion phenomena. Young adult rats receiving bilateral, two-stage lesions of the frontal cortex are able to perform spatial alternation tasks as well as age-mates without lesions, while groups of adult rats receiving the lesion in a single, bilateral operation remain seriously impaired (Patrissi and Stein, 1975). Since it is important to realize that the functional effects of bilateral brain injury are also age-dependent, behavioral evaluation of brain-damaged animals should begin as soon as the subjects are able to perform the task under investigation. Recently, experiments related to this problem have shown that rats given single-stage lesions early in life and then tested at maturity, perform a spatial alternation learning task as well as mature unoperated, age-matched controls (Nonneman and Kolb, 1978). The investigations of Nonneman and Kolb demonstrated that the effects of the brain damage on this behavior were not merely a function of the site of damage, but rather that the age of the subject was a crucial factor in determining the outcome of traumatic brain injury.

In continuing this line of analysis, the question arises as to whether the same extent of recovery or sparing of function that follows serial brain damage in fully mature, but relatively young, rats also occurs in aged animals. To examine this question, Walbran (1976) created serial lesions in the sensorimotor cortex of young (30 days of age) or senescent (570 days of age) rats and compared the performance of the brain-damaged groups to intact, age-matched controls on acquisition and retention of a tactile discrimination task. Walbran reported that rats given serial lesions when immature (30 days) or as young adults and tested while still young, were able to perform as well as intact, young adult animals. Those rats given single-stage lesions were very impaired on learning and retention of the sensory task. When Walbran tested the performance of the senescent rats given serial or single-stage somatosensory cortex ablations, no sparing of acquisition or retention of the previously learned tasks was seen in either of the aged, brain-damaged groups. In contrast, both groups with lesions were severely impaired with respect to intact, aged controls. These findings were taken by us to indicate that whatever reorganization of function that may have followed the serial lesions in young subjects, was not evident in the aged animals. Although Walbran advanced several hypotheses to explain her failure to find a serial lesion effect, she did not attempt an anatomical or neurophysiological analysis of different aged brains. Perhaps such an evaluation could have provided some insight into changes in the aging CNS that may have prevented functional recovery after brain injury in the old animals.

In our laboratory at Clark University, we were interested in whether aged rats given serial, bilateral lesions of the frontal cortex late in life would show the same extent of behavioral sparing that we had observed when similar damage was inflicted in young animals (Stein, 1974; Patrissi and Stein, 1975). Accordingly, experiments were performed using 575-day-old male, Sprague-Dawley rats which were subjected to bilateral frontal cortex removal in one or two stages. The animals had been raised in our own colony and throughout their development they were handled several times per week. The rats were housed in individual cages and they remained in a general colony room until testing began and all surgery was completed. We performed all surgery by gently aspirating all of the rat's frontal cortex 2.0 mm anterior to bregma until we could visualize the dorsal surfaces of the olfactory tracts with aid of a dissecting microscope. The specific experimental methods have been described in detail elsewhere (Stein, 1974; Stein and Lewis, 1975; Stein and Firl, 1976). In the case of those animals given two operations, the rats were permitted a 30-day interoperative "rest" period in their home cages. At the end of this period, these rats received a second lesion contralateral to the first and were then permitted a two week recovery period prior to initiation of testing. One half of the rats given bilateral one-stage lesions underwent surgery at the time the first operations were made in the two-stage group. The remaining aged rats underwent surgery at the time of the second operation. This procedure enabled us to determine whether testing at different times after surgery might be a factor in facilitating functional recovery (Dawson, 1973). In our experiments, however, this variable appeared to have negligible effects (Patrissi and Stein, 1975).

Once the rats began to eat dry laboratory pellets, we placed them on a water deprivation schedule (Stein and Firl, 1976) and then began training them on a delayed spatial alternation task. The rats were permitted to go either to the left or to the right in the arms of a T maze on the first of 16 successive trials, and then were required to alternate their response on the subsequent trials in order to obtain water reinforcement. Between each trial, we introduced a 5-second delay and the animals had to attain 15 out of 16 successively correct responses before we terminated their training.

After the rats had reached criterion on the spatial alternation task, we gave them *ad libitum* access to food and water in their home cage and then measured their activity levels for 5 minutes in an open field marked off in squares. Next, all of the rats were rested for approximately 4 weeks and then trained to avoid footshock by running into a safe compartment indicated by an open door. The position of this door was alternated from left to right in a random sequence. If an incorrect response was made, the animal was prevented from entering into the safe compartment by a locked gray door. Each rat was given a total of 100 trials before training was terminated.

When all behavioral training was complete, the aged rats were killed by an overdose of anesthetic, perfused intracardially with 10% Formol-saline, and their brains prepared for histological evaluation. Planimetric measurement of lesion size was made by tracing the perimeter of the lesion from 30 micron thick, cresyl violet stained coronal sections mounted on glass slides. Furthermore, light microscopic analysis was performed to determine the extent of retrograde neuronal degeneration in the thalamic dorsomedial nucleus of intact and brain-damaged young and aged rats. We did this by counting only those neurons having a clearly visible nucleolus in the plane of focus at ×320 magnification.

Our behavioral analysis provided data paralleling those of Walbran (1976). We found that the serial lesion phenomenon seen in young adult rats was completely absent in aged rats that had been subjected to bilateral serial removals of the frontal cortex at about 1½ years of age. However, what is particularly interesting, is the fact that on the spatial alternation task and the open-field activity levels, the aged rats with one- or two-stage lesions were not significantly different in their performance from aged animals that had not received surgery (Figure 1). Thus, on measures of trials to criterion, total percentage of errors and percentage of perseverative errors as well as general activity, aged brain-damaged and aged intact rats did not differ from one another. In contrast, when old, sham-operated controls were compared to young adult controls, the former group was markedly impaired on the spatial alternation performance. Again, these data can be visualized by comparing the histograms in the left part of the graph (Figure 1) with those on the extreme right, where it can be seen that the young adult shams learn the task significantly faster than their older counterparts. Note also that the young adult

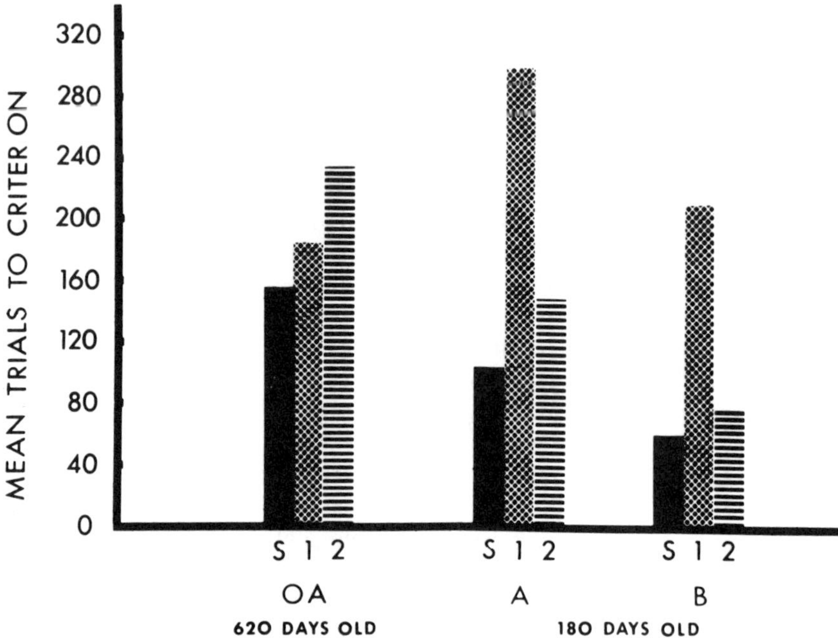

Figure 1. Spatial alternation performance in young adults or old rats with either lesions of frontal cortex or sham operations. The animals were tested to a criterion of 15/16 correct responses. Groups A and B were tested at different times and were therefore kept separate for the analyses.

rats receiving serial lesions are significantly better than their one-stage counterparts who are markedly impaired in learning the task. The serial lesion phenomenon is clearly demonstrated in the case of young rats.

As can be seen in Figure 2, performance on the shock avoidance task was equivalent for the aged one- and two-stage operated rats and the aged controls. Taken together, we think these data indicate that lesions inflicted upon old rats may not have the same behavioral consequences as similar damage created in younger conspecifics. Spatial alternation performance has been shown to be repeatedly sensitive to bilateral frontal cortex lesions in young adult rats (Kolb and Nonneman, 1978) and monkeys (Goldman, 1974). In our studies, brain-damaged, aged rats with bilateral lesions perform as well as aged controls who are significantly impaired when their performance is compared to intact younger rats. In addition, no sparing of shock avoidance performance was observed following serial lesions in the aged rats.

What might account for this age-dependent effect of the lesions? Our histological evaluations of cell counts in the dorsomedial nucleus of the thalamus revealed some interesting and thought provoking data. Table 1 shows comparisons of neuronal cell counts between young and aged intact and brain-damaged rats. The results summarized in the table show a dramatic difference in the number of neurons found in the thalamus of aged and young rats as well as between brain-damaged and intact animals. First, we observed a significant decrease in the number of neurons in aged rats without brain lesions, as well as for all of those that had received surgery, regardless of whether it was inflicted in one or two operations. We also noted that more glial cells were present in the non-operated as well as the brain-damaged, senescent rats. Figure 3 presents photomicrographs of neurons in the mediodorsal nucleus (× 240) in a 180-day old non-operated rat (A), a 575-day-old non-operated rat (B), and a 620-day-old rat with an ablation of the frontal cortex (C). It seems apparent to us from these observations that brain damage and aging (whatever the factors that might contribute to aging) apparently leave the animal in much the same morphological condition. It may be for this reason that the intact and the brain-damaged aged rats showed basically the same impaired performance with respect to younger controls. Perhaps deterioration of the thalamo-cortical system had effectively been performed by the aging process; thus, frontal cortex lesions might have had a reduced impact on the animal's already altered nervous system. These

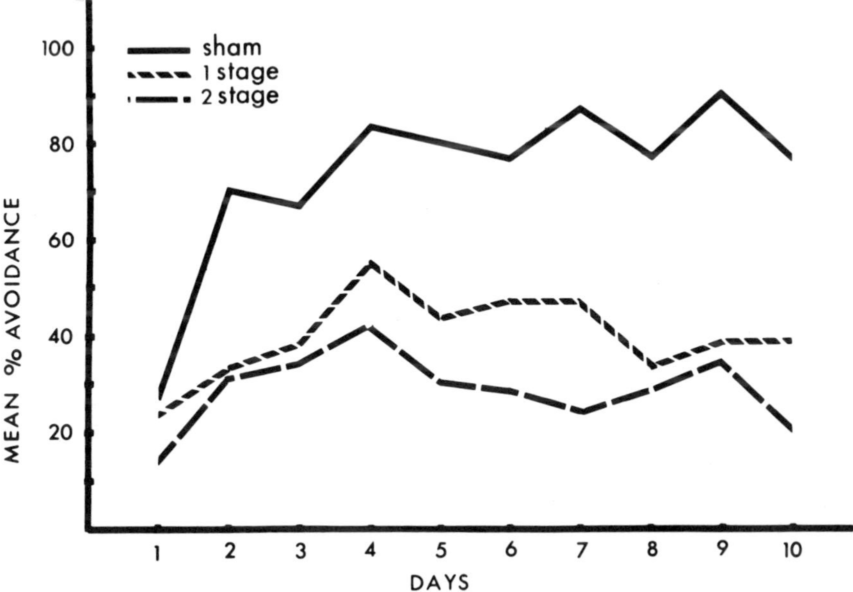

Figure 2. Percentage of avoidance for old rats given ten trials per day for 10 days. One-stage refers to rats given simultaneous, bilateral operations. Two-stage refers to those rats given two unilateral operations spaced 30 days apart.

Table 1. Mean Number of Normal Neurons Counted in the Medial and Lateral Divisions of the Mediodorsal Thalamic Nucleus

	Sections Taken Through Nucleus Medialis Dorsalis		
Anterior-Posterior Stereotaxic Coordinates:	A4890	A4380	A4110
180 day-old standard	40.0	40.0	34.5
180 day-old standard with frontal lesions	2.0	3.5	5.5
575 day-old standard	8.5	2.5	7.0
775 day-old rats with one-stage frontal lesions(n = 6)	5.0	3.6	3.3
775 day-old rats with two-stage frontal lesions (n = 4)	1.9	3.2	3.4

particular findings do imply that the structural components of the brain are constantly changing and it is reasonable to assume that such changes may underlie some of the altered behaviors so often observed in senescent organisms.

At this point, the overall picture concerning the relationship between brain-damage, aging and behavior seems rather pessimistic. For example, in the old rat, there is dramatic neuronal loss (which we will document more fully in the anatomical section of this chapter); there is a loss of the adaptability that seems to accompany serial lesions of the young nervous system and there is a loss of the capacity to learn and remember a discrimination task in comparison to younger animals (as described by Barnes and McNaughton—see this volume).

In order to provide a more complete analysis of the effects of lesions on aging, we decided to extend our investigations by employing a method often used in developmental psychobiology, namely an analysis of the consequences of brain injury inflicted early in life with measures taken repeatedly at different points along the developmental continuum. As we mentioned in our introduction, Patricia Goldman has successfully used this technique with monkeys to demonstrate that the consequences of early-inflicted brain injury varies as a function of the age of the subject at the time of testing (Goldman, 1974; Goldman and Galkin, 1978).

In the earlier experiments (Stein and Firl, 1976; Walbran, 1976), we had compared young, adult rats given one- or two-stage lesions with conspecifics given the same type of surgery in old age. In the experiments to be described below, we created single-stage or serial lesions of the frontal cortex in mature (5-month-old) Fischer (344) male rats and tested their performance on delayed spatial alternation and spatial reversal learning at 6-month intervals up to 2 years of age.

The operative procedures for the production of one- or two-stage frontal lesions were essentially the same as we had employed in our earlier experiments (Stein and Firl, 1976), although in this series we attempted to limit the extent of damage to the frontal pole and in particular, to the medial surface of this region. As a result, the lesions were smaller and more discrete than those we had created previously. This new procedure was followed in order to avoid the possibility of damaging sensorimotor cortex as defined by Hall and Lindholm (1974) and to limit fatalities due to excessive bleeding that we sometimes encountered with the more extensive damage.

The behavioral tests for delayed spatial alternations (DSA) were identical to those already described. At approximately 6-months of age, the rats began initial training. Following a 6-month inter-test interval, the rats were then retested until they attained the same performance criterion originally employed. Once again, after reaching criterion on the retention test, the rats were given another 6-month "break" and retested a final time prior to being killed for histological examination.

We decided to assess the generality of the one- or two-stage frontal

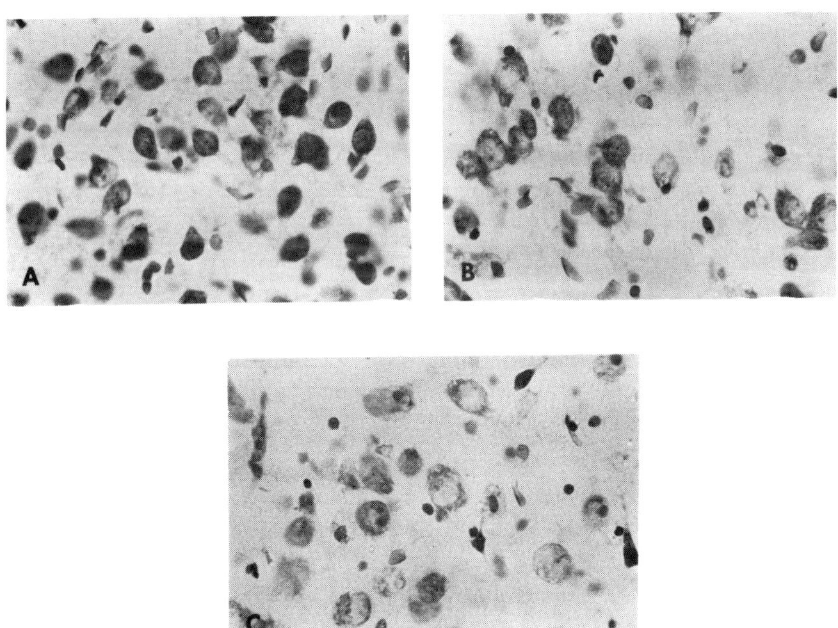

Figure 3. Photomicrographs of cresyl violet stained sections of the mediodorsal thalamic nucleus (× 240) in a 180-day-old non-operated rat (A), a 575-day-old non-operated rat (B), and a 620-day-old rat with frontal cortex ablated (C). Note the paucity of Nissl material, the central chromatolysis, poor definitions of limiting membranes, and the presence of glia cells in B and C.

lesion effects by giving our subjects another learning task beginning two weeks after they had reached criterion on the DSA problem. Thus, the rats were taught to inhibit a previously learned response that was required to obtain water reinforcement. For example, in this new problem, the rats were taught to go repeatedly to the left for water. After ten perfect trials, they had to reverse their previous response and choose the right arm to obtain the reward. This test measured perseverative responding and was considered to be sensitive to bilateral, single-stage, frontal cortex lesions.

An analysis of variance and individual comparisons among animals with sham operations and serial or one-stage frontal ablations provided some unexpected results in the initial phases of testing. We were surprised to find that on initial *acquisition* of delayed spatial alternation and reversal learning, the brain-damaged animals given either serial or simultaneous lesions, performed as well as intact young adult controls. When the animals were tested for a second time, between 12 and 13 months of age, the results of the retention tests were the same; the brain-damaged rats were not significantly impaired with respect to the intact controls. At this point, we became concerned that our lesions might have been somehow misplaced or far too small to produce any sign of deficits, despite the fact that the literature (Kolb and Nonneman, 1978) provides many examples of behavioral impairments following damage limited only to the medial wall of the frontal pole. We cannot explain the absence of a lesion effect in the initial phase of testing; however, almost 18 months later, impaired performance did emerge in some of the rats at 24 months of age.

Figure 4 shows the retention performance of aged intact rats on delayed spatial alternation was significantly better than the aged rats with frontal lesions. Note that in the brain-damaged groups, those rats given serial lesions as mature, but relatively young adults, were impaired, but despite the deficit they manifested significantly more savings than their one-stage counterparts who were completely debilitated on the test-retest at 24 months of age. The reversal learning task showed essentially the same unusual findings; no impairments in the brain-damaged animals up to 23 months of age but a significant lesion-induced deficit in performance toward the end of life (Figure 5). Once again, there was also a long-delayed serial lesion effect; the rats with two-stage damage of the frontal cortex showed much greater retention than one-stage operates. These behavioral findings are puzzling but similar to other data reported in the literature. For example, Finger and his students (1976) demonstrated that young rats given serial lesions of somatosensory cortex, and tested on a series of tactile discrimination tasks followed by a total decortication much later in life, showed greater savings after the decortication than animals given the initial surgery in a single stage.

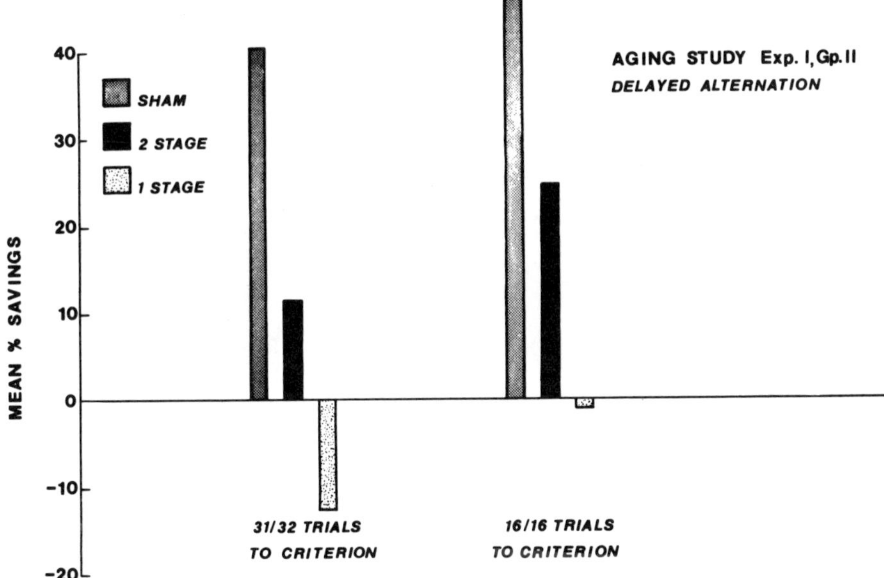

Figure 4. Histogram showing retention scores on delayed alternation in brain-damaged and intact rats operated upon at approximately 6 months of age and retested at 24 months of age.

Thus, a long-delayed effect of serial lesions was demonstrated although Finger was unable to account for the mechanisms that might underlie these findings.

At the present time, we can only speculate as to what might account for the extended and initially "hidden" serial lesion effect we observed in our aged rats. It is probably the case though, that the limited behavioral sparing was mediated by change in the CNS that occurred while the rats were still fairly young. Serial lesions inflicted upon older rats have not, at present, shown any recovery of function, at least in the systems studied so far. There are some tempting clues to consider that can be derived from our anatomical analyses. In the first place, we found that planometric tracing of the lesion boundaries did not differentiate between one- and two-stage rats although the lesions were, in fact, smaller than those created in earlier investigations. We did observe some interesting differences in the brain morphology of rats given one- or two-stage lesions when compared to intact controls. Figure 6 presents some representative data from four animals per group showing the relative differences in glial and neuronal counts in the dorsomedial nucleus of the thalamus. It can be seen that sham and serial operated rats have similar neuron counts, while rats with one-stage lesions are consistently lower. Although the differences in number of neurons were not statistically

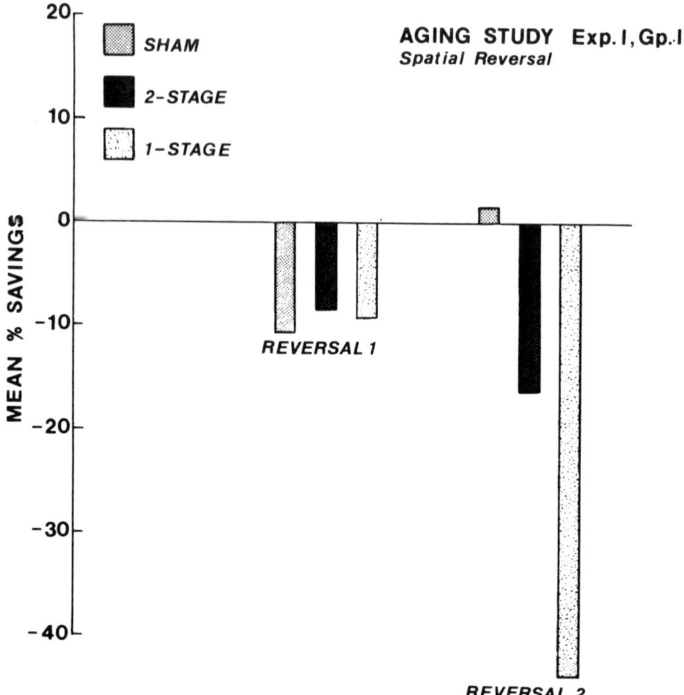

Figure 5. Retention scores of spatial reversal tasks in rats operated upon as young adults and retested at 24 months of age.

significant, it should be noted that *all* of the animals with single-stage lesions of the frontal cortex had lower neuron counts in the thalamus than their two-stage counterparts, possibly reflecting more cortical damage due to bleeding when the lesions were first inflicted. It is also interesting that the glial counts were consistently higher in the two-stage operated rats. We cannot say for certain that glia are necessary for behavioral recovery, because our studies were not designed to manipulate this factor. Although the notion is far fetched at present, there is some limited evidence which does tend to indicate that glial cells may play an important role in behavioral recovery after brain damage. In a recent paper, Eccles (1977) suggested that glial cells mediate collateral axonal sprouting after nerve injury although Cotman and Scheff (1979) argue that astrocytic activity may suppress collateral growth, espceially in aged animals. Raisman (1969) has also proposed that glial response to injury may be the critical stimulus necessary to trigger axonal sprouting or regeneration of new terminals. In fact, recent findings have shown that under certain circumstances, glial cells secrete Nerve Growth Factor, a hormone-like peptide with trophic influence on central and peripheral nerve tissue (Smith and Kreutzberg, 1976; Varon and Somjen, 1979). Why serial lesions of frontal cortex appear to provoke a greater glial response (that may be very long-lasting) and less neuronal loss comparable to one-stage lesions is not known. Here the rather hackneyed expression that "more research is needed" may be the best reply that we can presently offer.

Experiments on brain damage and aging, especially those concerned with what is spared rather than what is lost, are so few that it would be foolhardy at this point to paint broad generalizations concerning the implications of our findings. In addition to age, many factors such as a subject's health status, nutritional experience, environment during development, sex and strain, as well as many other variables, most certainly will influence and determine the outcome of traumatic brain injuries. We are just beginning to understand that brain-behavior relationships may not remain constant over time and that anatomical specificity may be the exception rather than the rule (see recent review by Greenough, 1976). Nonetheless, anatomical inquiry is of critical value in determining what specific parameters in the CNS might change as a function of age. We

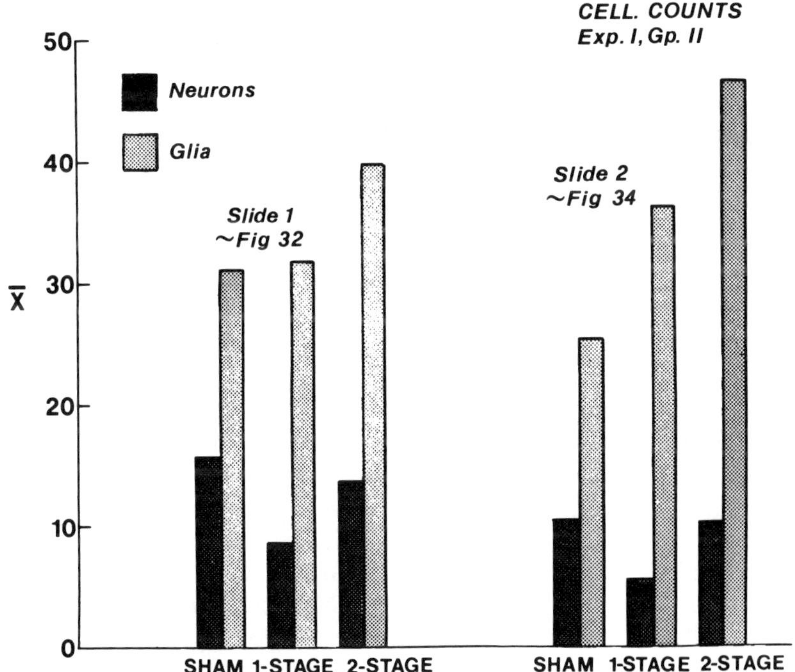

Figure 6. Representative data from four animals per group showing relative differences in glial and neuronal counts in the dorsomedial nucleus of the thalamus. (See text for details.)

are now systematically evaluating changes in neuronal morphology in animals of different ages that have been subjected to "standard" laboratory nutritional and housing regimes, and our findings provide clear evidence that with aging there is significant neuronal loss in subcortical areas of the brain involved with emotion and arousal (septum and reticular formation) and motivation (lateral and ventromedial hypothalamic nuclei), to name a few of the brain regions we have examined (Sabel and Stein, in preparation). In the second part of this chapter, we will present morphological findings associated with the frontal cortex which were derived from rats of different ages raised on *ad libitum* feeding schedules and kept in individual rack-mounted cages for the duration of their lives.

Age-Related Histopathologic Differences in Rat Frontal Cortex

The fact that progressive neuropathologies have been widely studied in human aged subjects emphasizes the concern for understanding age-related changes in the structural and functional organization of the central nervous system (CNS). Despite a rapidly increasing interest in the neuronal alterations correlated with aging, little attention has been directed toward systematic evaluation and manipulation of the psychological changes that may parallel the anatomical degradation of the aging brain. The central nervous system in particular is said to show numerous age-related alterations in its structural integrity including cell loss (Brody, 1955), senile plaque formation (Simchowitz, 1911), neurofibullary tangle formation (Terry and Wisniewski, 1975), dendritic deterioration (Scheibel and Scheibel, 1975; Machado-Salas, Scheibel and Scheibel, 1977a, b), lipofuscin accumulation (Brizzee, Carcilla, Sherwood, and Timiras, 1969; Sekhon and Maxwell, 1968; Brizzee, Harkin, Ordy and Keach, 1975) and axonal fiber degeneration (Johnson, Mehler and Mequel, 1975; Naranjo and Greene, 1977; Mufson and Stein, 1979). The cerebral cortex of humans exhibits many, if not all, of the histopathologic changes described above. For example, Brody (1955) performed cell counts on brain tissue obtained from patients who did not show CNS pathology prior to histological evaluation. A comparison of neuron counts between young and old patients showed a pattern of cortical cell loss between 20 and 90 years of age. Cell depletion appeared most prominent in the prefrontal and superior temporal cortical regions. More recently, Scheibel and Tomiyasu (1978) using the golgi silver impregnation method showed that the aged, human prefrontal cortex exhibits alterations in dendritic and neuronal configuration and eventual cell death. Mervis (1978) has reported similar age-related changes in the frontal cortex of dogs while others describe the thinning of apical (Feldman, 1976) and basilar dendrites (Vaughan, 1977) in the aged cortex of rats. Interestingly, however, there have been reports indicating that there is no diminution in neuronal cell populations in certain selected areas of rat cortex (Brizzee, Sherwood and Timiras, 1968). In general, the data support the contention that the morphology of the brain alters with age and that such changes may affect an organism's behavioral capabilities. For example, various investigators have speculated that progressive neuronal histopathologies may be the underlying biological substrates correlated with decreasing motor strength, deteriorating cognitive performance, problems in retrieval and recall (Scheibel and Scheibel, 1975) as well as senile dementia (Tomilson, 1977).

While much attention has been paid to neuroanatomical and biochemical alterations in the aging brain, there are only a few reports in the literature which have systematically investigated age as a variable in determining brain-behavior relationships. In one recent study, no differences in numbers of neocortical neurons or glial cells were found between rats classified either as young adult maze-bright, old maze-bright or dull, based on performance scores on a complex T-maze (Klein and Michel, 1977). In another study, Stein and Firl (1976) ablated the frontal cortex of senescent rats in one or two stages and the effects of these ablations were measured by the animals' performance on spatial alternation and avoidance tasks. As mentioned in the previous section of this chapter, Stein and Firl (1976) proposed that the behavioral ineffectiveness of these lesions might be due to the fact that the frontal cortex had altered its structural and functional capacities. As support for this contention, these authors stated that a comparison of three rats showed a 42% reduction in the numbers of frontal cortical neurons between young and old rats. Stein and Firl, however, did not extensively investigate age-dependent morphological changes in the rat frontal cortex. Thus, the purpose of the present investigation was to extend the anatomical analysis of the earlier study in order to determine what age-related alterations occur in the frontal cortex of rats of different ages.

In this study, groups of three male Fischer (344) rats aged 90, 365, and 720 days obtained from the National Institute of Aging were examined. All the rats were individually housed in standard laboratory stainless steel cages, maintained on a 12:12 hr light-dark cycle at 72°F and given *ad libitum* access to food and water.

The animals were anesthesized with Nembutal (sodium pentobarbital) and placed in a stereotaxoc head holder. We opened the skull from the bregma to the anterior tip of the frontal pole and then we cut and retracted the dura overlying the cortex. For each group of rats, the frontal cortex 2 mm anterior to bregma was aspirated unilaterally until the white matter was exposed, and cortical tissue was then removed down to the dorsal surface of the olfactory bulb, and this included the medial and lateral cortices. Unilateral frontal cortex ablations were performed in order to determine whether there are differences in the pattern of anterograde fiber degeneration in rats of different ages. These animals served as controls for the effect of frontal cortex damage on cortical morphology and anterograde degeneration.

The rats which had received frontal cortex damage were allowed to survive for 1–14 days after the surgery. We killed each brain-damaged and unoperated animal with an overdose of sodium pentobarbital and perfused the rats intracardially with physiological saline followed by 10% formol-saline. We removed the brains from the skull, embedded them in gelatin albumin and then cut them in the coronal plane at 25 microns. Every seventh section was processed by either the Fink and Heimer I or II procedures (Fink and Heimer, 1967) for the demonstration of anterograde fiber degeneration. Adjacent sections were stained with cresyl violet and the intact, contralateral, frontal cortex was used for an analysis of changes in neuronal morphology, neuronal cell numbers and determination of neuronal lipofuscin accumulation. We performed all of our morphological and morphometric analyses using light microscopy, whereas lipofuscin determinations were analyzed by the epi-fluorescence technique of West (West, 1979).[1]

We took our neuronal counts according to procedures described by Konigsmark (1969). Briefly, a 1 mm^2, 25 grid eyepiece reticule was placed in the upper left hand corner of the intact, contralateral frontal cortex. Only neurons with a well defined nucleolus which fell within the four corners and center grids of the reticule were counted. Upon completion of a grid count, we moved the slide vertically using any well-defined landmark on the lower line of the reticule line and this procedure was repeated for each frontal cortex section until we could evaluate the dorsoventral extent of the medial wall of the frontal cortex throughout its rostral-caudal axis. For each age we summed individual neuron counts and calculated a grand mean. All neuron cell counts were performed at 180 × magnification under light field microscopy.

Our histological analysis revealed that the unilateral extent of the frontal cortex lesions were similar to those described by Stein and Firl (1976). In all cases, the most anterior portions of the frontal pole were completely removed, whereas lateral cortex damage was less extensive than damage to the medial dorsal frontal cortex. Figure 7 shows a coronal

[1]A slide was placed on the stage of a Zeiss microscope which was simultaneously illuminated from above by a Zeiss Epi-fluorescence Ultraviolet Illuminator (BP-440-490, barrier filter 520) and from below by the visible light source. Illumination by the visible light source obscured lipofuscin fluorescence. A Zeiss 40X (1.5 mm corr.), long working distance, oil immersion objective was focussed until neuron cell bodies with clearly visible nucleoli appeared. At this point, visible light was terminated revealing the fluorescence lipofuscin. Epi-fluorescence microscopy was used to photograph lipofuscin material, whereas light field microscopy was used for all other photography.

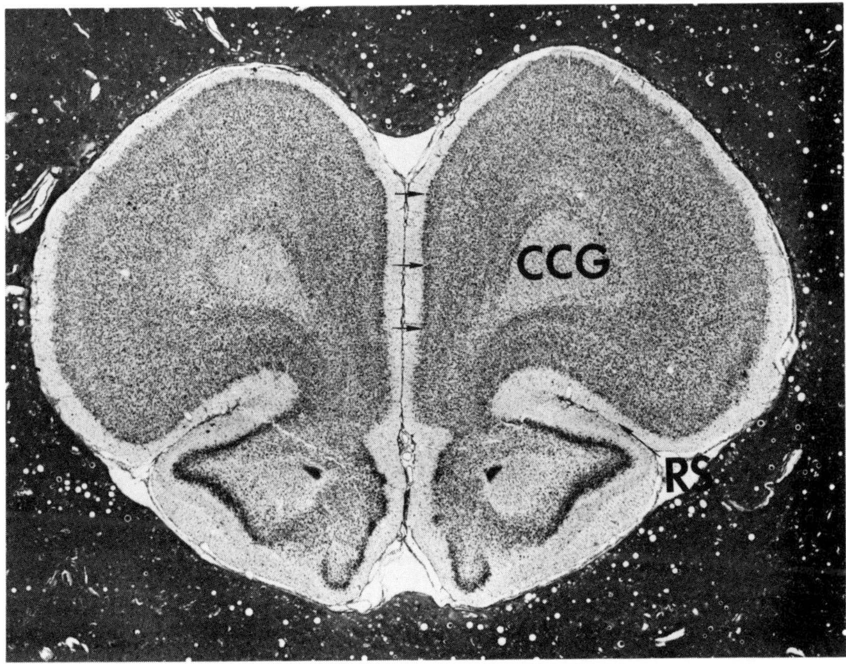

Figure 7. Photomicrograph of Nissl stained coronal section of frontal pole from a control animal. Arrows indicate approximate region of medial frontal cortex from which cell counts were performed. Abbreviations: CCG = genu of corpus callosum, RS = rhinal sulcus.

representative section of the frontal cortex from which our neuron counts were taken. The counts were restricted to the medial of the frontal pole. As can be seen in Figure 8, there is a consistent reduction in the number of cortical neurons across ages. Our statistical evaluation of the cell counts revealed a significant depletion in neurons between the 90 and 720-day-old rats ($P < .05$) whereas no significant difference was found between the 90 and 365 nor the 365 and 720-day-old rats.

Reexamination of the Nissl stained, frontal cortex sections from each age group showed several age-dependent differences in neuronal morphology. We observed that neurons of the medial frontal cortex undergo dramatic structural alterations. In young rats, 90 days of age, the staining characteristics of cortical neurons included impregnation of Nissl granules which were distributed throughout the perikaryon, layer three neurons appeared pyramidal in shape and the neurons had darkly stained centrally located nucleoli (Figure 9A).

Our examination of medial frontal cortex in 12-month-old animals revealed the initial phases of changes in cellular morphology that are

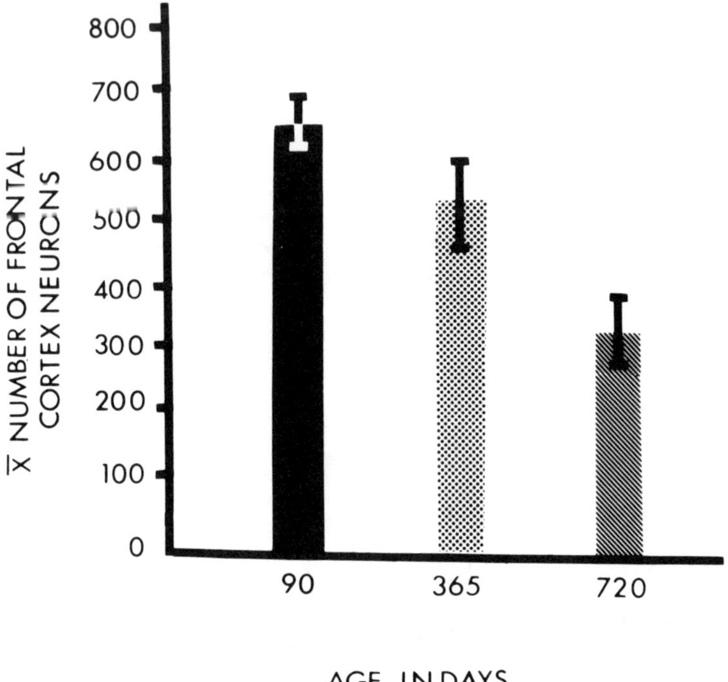

Figure 8. Histogram showing mean number of frontal cortex neurons counted in rats 90, 365, and 720 days of age.

suggestive of deterioration in those older cortical cells. In contrast to cortical neurons of 3-month-old rats, many, though not all cells, appear to be ovoid in shape and had laterally displaced nucleoli and dispersion of Nissl material to the periphery of the cells. Further analysis of frontal cortex taken from 24-month-old animals demonstrates this apparent age-related reaction in a more advanced stage (Figure 9B). At 24 months, almost all neurons in the medial frontal cortex exhibited the characteristics seen at 12 months, including cellular swelling, ovoid shape, enlarged nucleus and an eccentrically placed nucleolus, as well as a dense rim of peripherally dispersed Nissl material (Figure 9B). The structural alterations observed in senescent frontal cortex neurons, it is believed, are indicative of an age-associated reaction similar to chromatolysis of perikarya often observed in diseased or brain-damaged animals.

Similar deterioration was also seen in those 24-month-old rats which had not sustained unilateral frontal cortex damage (Figure 9C). The evidence derived from "intact" rats argues against the possibility that the age-related differences observed were artifacts resulting from lesion-induced trauma. It is important to note that the structural alterations seen in the aged frontal cortex were not observed in more posterior neocortical regions, although the entorhinal and hippocampal regions showed similar age-dependent changes in morphology.

Reexamination of brain tissue with fluorescence microscopy revealed a progressive age-dependent accumulation of lipofuscin pigments. Neurons of young animals exhibited only a few lipofuscin granules as seen under the fluorescent microscope (Figure 9A). In contrast, older frontal cortex neurons, exhibit very large aggregations of lipofuscin (Figure 9D) which were, in many cases, peripherally situated in the perikaryon and appeared as clusters of small granules or as larger clumps (Figure 9D), possibly formed by the accumulation of the smaller lipofuscin granules.

Light microscopic evaluation of tissue processed by the Fink and Heimer procedure for degenerating axons and terminals did *not* demonstrate any age-dependent alteration in the degeneration pattern associated with frontal cortex lesions. Although there is extensive neuronal loss in the aged rat, the distribution of fiber systems seen in the present study at all ages corresponds to that observed in previous investigations using younger rats (Leonard, 1969; Gentile et al., 1978; Mufson and Stein, 1978).

In summary then, the rat frontal cortex appears to undergo important morphological changes as the animals age to senescence. Observations of the medial frontal cortex in senescent, as compared to young, rats indicates a sequence of events which involve distortion of the neuronal somata, lateral displacement of the nucleolus, a reduction in neuron numbers as well as an accumulation of lipofuscin material. However, at this point in time, it is not clear if any of these age-associated histopathologies are correlated with behavioral dysfunction often seen in the aged organism. Neurons of aged prefrontal cortex in humans (Scheibel and Scheibel, 1975) and canines (Mervis, 1978) are known to exhibit progressive degenerative alterations which eventually lead to cell loss. Such pathologies have been said to result in cognitive, mnemonic and motor dysfunctions (Scheibel and Scheibel, 1975) as well as senile dementia (Tomilson, 1977). Other morphological age-associated brain changes have also been ascribed to psychological alterations in old subjects. For example, Alzheimer (1907) reported the appearance of neurofibrillary bundles or senile plaque in brains of patients suffering from senile dementia. Four years later, these morphological findings were related to the psychological profile of patients (Simchowitz, 1911).

Unlike the clinical reports, many experiments dealing with differences in brain morphology between aged and young animals have *not* correlated behavioral differences with morphological alterations. Although Brizzee et al. (1968), in one experiment with rats found no neuronal loss in older subjects, no functional investigation of the animal's behavior was performed. Some differences in the learning ability between young adult

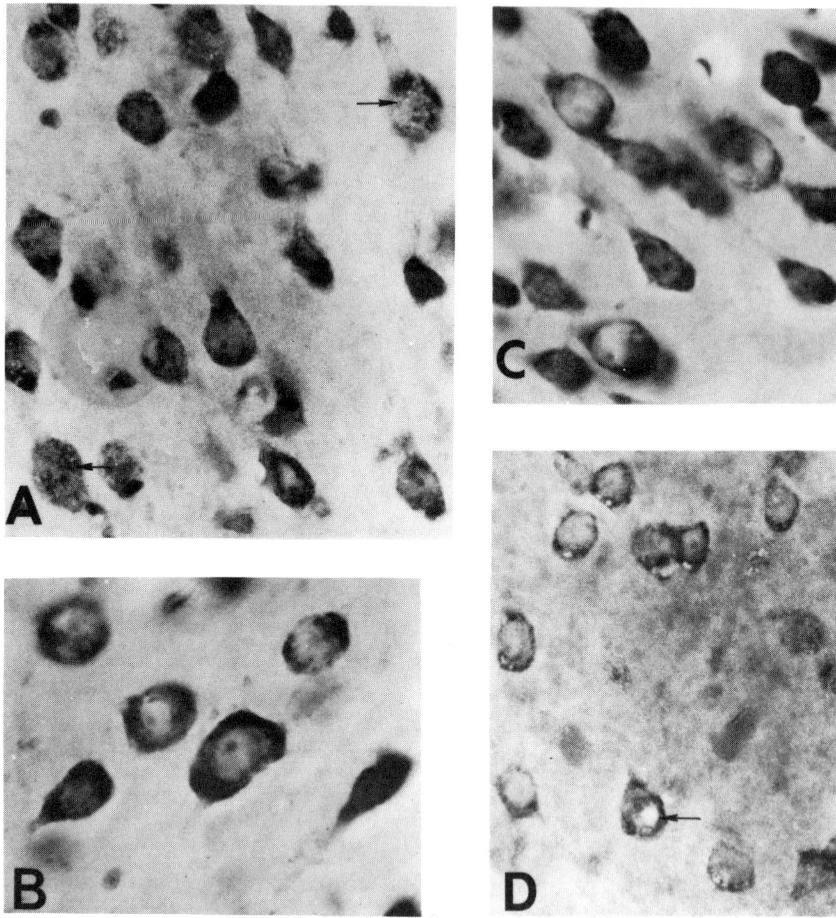

Figure 9. Photomicrographs of young and old frontal cortex neurons.

A. Epi-fluorescent photomicrographs of 90-day-old rat. Note pyramidal shape of neurons, centrally located nucleoli as well as sparse granules of lipofuscin pigment.

B. High power photomicrographs of Nissl stained frontal cortical neurons of 24-month-old rat.
Note the eccentric nucleoli, cellular swelling, ovoid shape, and hollow appearance of the neurons.

C. Photomicrograph of frontal cortex neurons from a non-damaged 24-month-old rat. Morphological changes are similar to those described in Figure 9B.

D. Lipofuscin granules in frontal cortex neurons of a 24-month-old rat. Note the aggregation of lipofuscin pigment as well as the peripheral location of the deposits. Compare the heavy lipofuscin accumulation at 24 months of age (arrow) with the sparse accumulation (arrow) seen at 90 days of age in Figure 9A.

and aged rats have been demonstrated in the laboratory (Goodrick, 1962) although there is not complete agreement on this issue. On the one hand, Klein and Michel (1977) have reported no difference in relative volume of cortex occupied by pyramidal cells, astrocytes, oligodendrocytes or other neural elements between young and old Wistar rats which were classified as maze-bright or dull. On the other hand, the present data are taken to indicate that the aged Fischer 344 rat shows neuronal profiles not seen in younger animals. The area of frontal cortex we analyzed has been postulated to be structurally and functionally different in young and old rats (Stein and Firl, 1976). A direct comparison between our findings and those of Stein and Firl (1976) is not, however, possible because of several discrepancies between the studies. Stein and Firl (1976) used Sprague Dawley rats; the age of these animals was approximately 3 months younger than our subjects, and a less detailed histological analysis of the frontal cortex of aged rats was performed. We can speculate, at least, that the failure of frontal cortex ablations in the senescent rat to produce performance impairments on a spatial alternation task (Stein and Firl, 1976) may be related to the age-dependent brain changes described here. The profiles of the aged frontal neurons seen in our rats are similar to those attributed to central nervous system neurons which are undergoing chromotolysis caused by mechanical insult (Carmel and Stein, 1969). An additional sign of cellular deterioration may be the heavy lipofuscin deposits observed in the aged neurons. Brizzee et al. (1969) have also reported a ten-fold increase in lipofuscin pigment in aging rat cortex while others (Reichel, Hollander, Clark, and Strehler, 1968) describe lipofuscin pigments in the aged rat hippocampus. The significance of lipofuscin accumulation, both physiologically and behaviorally, remains to be investigated, but various hypotheses concerned with the action of this substance at the cellular level suggest that its accumulation is detrimental to the function of cell bodies. Several such hypotheses include: 1. that the chromidal substance extruded from the nucleus during depressed function is transferred into lipofuscin (Dolley and Guthrie, 1918), 2. that highly active cells tend to accumulate less lipofuscin than less active ones (Wilcox, 1959), and 3. that in disease states (e.g., neuronal ceroid-lipofuscin) lipofuscin pigments form at the expense of a neuron's cytoplasm. This accumulation might damage the perikaryon by distorting and disturbing the cellular shape and also block diffusion pathways (Zeman, 1974). Thus, neurons may become metabolically inefficient, and the replacement of crucial biosynthetic substances would be reduced. Brizzee et al. (1975) suggest that such alterations in cellular functions might interfere with axonal transport. In fact, a decrease in axonal transport of glycoprotein has been demonstrated in the aged rat brain (Geinisman, Bondareff and Telstar, 1977). Furthermore, the increased accumulation of lipofuscin pigment, as well as other variables associated with aging, might lead to a loss of neurons (Brody, 1955; Mufson and Stein, 1978), a loss of dendritic spines (Feldman, 1976) or a loss of dendrites as shown in the aged human cerebral cortex (Scheibel and Scheibel, 1975). There is, however, no evidence, to our knowledge, to suggest that frontal cortex neurons which show prominent fluorescence granules differ functionally from non-fluorescing cells.

In contrast to the many theories suggesting that lipofuscin is detrimental to cellular function in the aged animal, there are those who believe that this pigment may be a harmless product of normal cell activity (Nandy, 1968; Kromendy and Bender, 1971). For example, Karnaukhov and co-workers (Karnaukhov, 1973; Karnaukhov, Tutaryunas and Petrunyaka, 1973) have indicated that lipofuscin granules contain cartinoids, myoglobin and respiratory enzymes, form the "intracellular oxygen stock," and that these granules under conditions of low rates of oxygen uptake into tissues provide energy. Large lipofuscin accumulations under these circumstances may be beneficial to the aged neuron, although this is not clear. Thus, the relevance of lipofuscin deposits as emphasized by Toth (1968) requires more attention.

Concerning neuronal loss, we are aware that there is some controversy in this area. In fact, although we have described a significant decrease in frontal cortex neuron numbers across ages, others have not. For example, Brizzee et al. (1968) and Klein and Mitchel (1977) did not demonstrate an age-dependent loss of neurons in cortical area 2 in Long-Evans rats or cortical frontal and occipital areas in the Wistar rat, respectively. The discrepancies between our findings and others may indicate that the phenomenon of neuron loss may not be a prominent characteristic of all strains of rat. However, it is possible that various strains of rat age differently and that cortical neuron loss may occur at older ages than previously studied.

There was no attempt in the present series of experiments to determine whether or not neurogenesis occurs throughout the life span of the Fischer rat, (which may offset neuronal loss) although recent evidence indicates that adult *rat* brain is capable of forming new neurons (Kaplan and Hinds, 1977). While there is no evidence which indicates that neurogenesis takes place in the aged rat frontal cortex, we do know that unilateral, prenatal, frontal pole resection in the rhesus monkey results in the sprouting of aberrant axonal connections (Goldman, 1978). It should be noted that a similar "rewiring" phenomenon has not been reported for the rodent frontal cortex at any age although young (Cotman and Nadler, 1979; Raisman, 1969) and old (Cotman and Scheff, 1979; Scheff, Bernardo and Cotman, 1978) rats are capable of developing anomalous fiber pathways after brain injury.

There is now some data suggesting that the senescent human brain exhibits a form of anomalous neural plasticity. Golgi staining of human cortex obtained at autopsy from apparently normal subjects (Buell and Coleman, 1979) as well as patients afflicted with Alzheimer's presenile dementia (Scheibel and Tomiyasu, 1978), revealed the presence of dendritic expansion in conjunction with a series of progressive deteriorative neuronal changes. Despite the concern with age-related anatomical and biochemical changes in the CNS, there is still much to be learned about the behavioral correlates of these alterations.

Although we observed significant neuronal loss in the frontal cortex, we were unable to detect any differences in the pattern of axonal and terminal degeneration between young and senescent rats given unilateral frontal pole lesions. Perhaps, a quantitive evaluation or the use of labelled amino acid tracer procedures would have revealed a difference in the projections to those areas receiving efferents from the frontal cortex.

In closing, it is important to emphasize that many unanswered questions remain in the area of gerontological research. Both aging animals and humans are continually subjected to adverse conditions throughout their development and it will be a long and arduous task to determine which particular factors contribute directly to the behavioral and morphological differences described in this chapter. Environmental experiences (e.g., complex versus isolated or impoverished environments), nutritional history, disease, as well as hormonal and genetic variables might all contribute to "aging." Indeed, the differences observed in the laboratory situation may not even be due to the passage of time *per se* nor to experimental manipulations; we must recognize the limitations on the numbers of variables that can be investigated in the laboratory at any one time. Thus, the findings obtained from experiments may only produce partial answers to the question of what constitutes aging, if any answers at all. Our data in conjunction with the other results described in this book, suggest that the aging brain like the developing nervous system, is always changing; however, the principles of organization that guide and determine the neuronal changes during the latter years of life are not well understood. In fact, the principles underlying aging may differ somewhat from those associated with the early years of development. The developmental analysis of brain-behavior relationships may be one research strategy that can provide the clues needed to understand some of the many conditions that influence aging as well as those factors which lead to neuromorphological deterioration in senescence so that those factors may eventually be modified and controlled.

ACKNOWLEDGMENT

We wish to thank Ms. Carol Craig for assistance in behavioral testing and preparation of the histological materials, and Mrs. A. Bassett for typing the manuscript.

References

Alzheimer A: Ueberune eigenartige Erkankung der Hirnrinde, Cbl. Nervenheik Psychiatry, 18:177–179. In Torack R, Wells C (eds). *Dementia.* F. A. Davis Company, Philadelphia, 1971.

Brizzee KR, Cancilla PA, Sherwood N, Timiras PS: The amount and distribution of pigments in neurons and glia of the cerebral cortex. *J Gerontology* 24:127–135, 1969.

Brizzee KR, Harkin JC, Ordy JM, Keach B: Accumulation and distribution of lipofuscin, amyloid, and senile plaque in the aging nervous systems. In Brady H, Hartman D, Ordy JM (eds). *Aging,* Volume I. Raven Press, New York, 1975.

Brizzee KR, Sherwood N, Timiras PS: A comparison of cell populations at various depth levels in cerebral cortex of young adult and aged Long-Evans rats. *J Gerontology* 23:289–197, 1968.

Brody H: Organization of the cerebral cortex III. A study of aging in the human cerebral cortex. *J Comparative Neurology* 102:511–556, 1955.

Buell SJ, Coleman PD: Dendritic growth in aged, human brain and failure of growth in senile dementia. *Science* 206:854–856, 1979.

Carmel PW, Stein BM: Cell changes in sensory ganglia following proximal and distal nerve section in the monkey. *J Comparative Neurology* 135:145–166, 1969.

Cotman CW, Nadler JV: Reactive synaptogenesis in the hippocampus. In Cotman CW (ed) *Neuronal Plasticity.* 1978, pp. 227–271.

Cotman CW, Scheff W: Compensatory synapse growth in aged animals after neuronal death. *Mechanisms of Aging and Development* 9:103–117, 1979.

Cotman CW, Scheff S: Synaptic growth in aged animals. In Cherkin A, Finch C, Kharasch T, et al. (eds.) *Physiology and Cell Biology of Aging* (Vol. 8). Raven Press, New York, 1979, pp. 109–120.

Dawson, RG: Recovery of function: implications for theories of brain function. *Behavioral Biology* 8:439–460, 1973.

Dolley DH, Guthrie FV: The pigmentation of nerve cells. *J Medical Research* 34:123–142, 1918.

Eccles J: The plasticity of the mammalian central nervous system with special reference to new growths in response to lesions. *Naturwissenschaften* 63:8–15, 1976.

Feldman, ML: Aging changes in the morphology of cortical dendrites. In Terry RD, Gershon S. (eds.) *Aging, Neurobiology of Aging,* Vol. 3. Raven Press, 1976, pp. 211–227.

Finger, SW: *Recovery from Brain damage: Research and Theory.* Plenum Press, New York, 1978.

Finger SW, Simonds D: Effects of serial lesions of somatosensory cortex and further neodecortication on retention of a rough-smooth discrimination in rats. *Experimental Brain Research* 25:183–197, 1976.

Finger S, Walbran B, Stein DG: Brain damage and behavioral recovery: serial lesion phenomena. *Brain Research* 63:1–18, 1973.

Fink RP, Heimer L: Two methods for selective impregnation of degenerating axons and their synaptic endings in the central nervous system. *Brain Research* 4:369–374, 1967.

Geinisman Y, Bondareff W, Telstar A: Transport of [^{3}H] frucose labelled glycoproteins in the septo-hippocampal pathway of young adult and senescent rats. *Brain Research* 125:182–186, 1977.

Gentile AM, Green S, Nieburgs A, Schmelzer W, Stein DG: Disruption and recovery of locomotor and manipulatory behavior following cortical lesions in rats. *Behavioral Biology* 22:417–455, 1978.

Goldberger M, Murray M: Recovery of movement and axonal sprouting may obey some of the same laws. In Cotman C (ed.) *Neuronal Plasticity.* Raven Press, New York, 1978, pp. 73–96.

Goldman P: An alternative to developmental plasticity: heterology of CNS structures in infants and adults. In Stein DG, Rosen JJ, Butters N (eds.) *Plasticity and Recovery of Function in the Central Nervous System.* Academic Press, 1974, pp. 149–174.

Goldman P: Neuronal plasticity in primate telencophalon: anomalous crossed cortico-caudate projections induced by pre-natal removal of frontal association cortex. *Science* 202:768–770, 1978.

Goldman P, Glakin T: Pre-natal removal of frontal association cortex in the fetal rhesus monkey: anatomical and functional consequences in post-natal life. *Brain Res* 152:451–485, 1978.

Goodrick CL: Learning by mature-young and aged Wistar Albino Rats as a function of test complexity. *J Gerontology* 27:353–357, 1972.

Greenough W: Enduring effects of differential experience and training. In Rosenzweig MR, Bennett EL (eds.) *Neural Mechanisms of Learning and Memory.* M.I.T. Press, 1976, pp. 255–278.

Hall RF, Lindholm EP: Organization of motor and somatosensory neocortex in the albino rat. *Brain Research* 66:23–28, 1974.

Johnson JE, Mehler WR, Miquel J: A fine structural study of degenerative changes in the dorsal column nucli, of aging mice. Lack of protection by vitamin E. *J Gerontology* 30:395–411, 1975.

Kaplan MS, Hinds JW: Neurogenesis in the adult rat: electron microscopic analysis of light radioautographs. *Science* 197:1092–1094, 1977.

Karnoukhov VN: The role of carotenoids in the formation of lipofuscin and the adaptation of animal cells to oxygen insufficiency. *Tsitologiia* 15:538–542, 1973.

Karnaukhov VN, Tutaryunas TG, Petrunyaka VV: Accumulation of carotenoids in brain and heart of animals of aging: the role of carotenoids in lipofuscin formation. *Mechanisms of Aging and Development* 2:201–210, 1973.

Klein AW, Michel ME: A morphometric study of the neocortex of young adult and old maze-differentiated rats. *Mechanisms of Aging and Development* 6:441–452, 1977.

Kolb B, Nonneman AJ: Sparing of function in rats with early prefrontal cortex lesions. *Brain Research* 151:135–148, 1978.

Konigsmark BW: Methods for the counting of neurons. In Nauta WJH, Ebbesson SOE (eds.) *Contemporary Research Methods in Neuroanatomy.* Springer-Verlag, N.Y., 1970, pp. 315–340.

Kormendy CG, Bender AD: Chemical interference with aging. *Gerontolgia* 17:52–64, 1971.

Leonard CM: The prefrontal cortex of the rat. I. Cortical projection of the mediodorsal nucleus. II. Efferent connections. *Brain Research* 12:321–343, 1969.

Machado-Salas J, Scheibel ME, Scheibel AB: Neuronal changes in the aging mouse: spinal cord and lower brain stem. *Experimental Neurology* 54:504–512, 1977.

Machado-Salas J, Scheibel MR, Scheibel AB: Morphologic changes in the hypothalamus of the mouse. *Experimental Neurology* 57:102–111, 1977.

Mervis R: Structural alterations in neurons of aged canine neocortex: a golgi study. *Experimental Neurology* 62:417–432, 1978.

Mufson EJ, Stein DG: Age-related changes in axonal and terminal degeneration after frontal cortex (FC) lesions in rats. *Neuroscience Abstracts* 4:121, 1978.

Mufson EJ, and Stein DG: Histopathological changes in the aging rat: frontal cortex and spinal cord. *First International Conference on the Psychobiology of Aging,* Abstracts, Luxembourg, 1979.

Nandy K: Further studies on the effects of centrophenoxine on the lipofuscin pigment in the neurons of senile guinea pigs. *J Gerontology* 23:82–92, 1968.

Naranjo N, Greene E: Use of reduced silver staining to show loss of connections in aged rat brain. *Brain Research Bulletin* 2:71–74, 1977.

Nonneman AJ, Kolb B: Functional recovery after serial ablation of prefrontal cortex in the rat. *Physiology and Behavior* 22:895–901, 1978.

Patrissi G, Stein DG: Temporal factors in recovery of function after brain damage. *Experimental Neurology* 47:470–480, 1975.

Raisman G: Neuronal plasticity in the septal nuclei of the adult rat. *Brain Research* 14:25–48, 1969.

Reichel W, Hollander J, Clark JH, Strehler BL: Lipofuscin pigment accumulation as a function of age and distribution in rodent brain. *J Gerontology* 23:71–78, 1968.

Scheff SE, Bernardo LS, Cotman CW: Decrease in adrenergic axon sprouting in the senescent rat. *Science* 202:775–778, 1978.

Scheibel ME, Scheibel AB: Structural changes in the aging brain. In Brody H, Harman D, Ordy JM (eds.) *Aging, Vol. I.* Raven Press, New York, 1976.

Scheibel AB, Tomiyasu U: Dendritic sprouting in Alzheimer's presenile dementia. *Experimental Neurology* 60:1–8, 1978.

Sekhon SS, Maxwell DS: Ultrastructural changes in neurons of the spiral anterior horn of aging mice with particular reference to the accumulation of lipofuscin pigment. *J Neurocytology* 3:59–72, 1974.

Simchowitz T: *Histologische Studien ueber die Senildemenz.* Nissl-Alzheimer Arbeiten, 1911, 3, 268.

Smith BH, Kretuzberg GW: Neuron target cell interactions. *Neurosciences Research Program Bulletin* 14:211–453, 1976.

Stein DG: Some variables influencing recovery of function after central nervous system lesions in the rat. In Stein DG, Rosen JJ, Butters N (eds.) *Plasticity and Recovery of Function, in the Central Nervous System.* Academic Press, New York, 1974, pp. 373–427.

Stein DG, Firl AC: Brain damage and reorganization of function in old age. *Experimental Neurology* 52:157–167, 1976.

Stein DG, Lewis ME: Functional recovery after brain damage in adult organisms. In Vital-Durand F, Jeannerod M. (eds.) *Aspects of Neural Plasticity.* Les Colloques D'INSERM 43, 1975.

Terry RD, Wisniewski H: Structural and chemical changes of the aged human brain. In Gershon MS, Raskin A (eds.) *Aging,* Vol. 2. 1975, pp. 127–141.

Tomlinson BE: Morphological changes and dementia in old age. In Smith WL, Kinsbourne M (eds.) *Aging and Dementia.* New York, Spectrum Publications, Inc. 1977.

Toth SE: The origin of lipofuscin age pigments. *Experimental Gerontology* 3:19–30, 1968.

Varon S, Somjen G: Neuron glia interactions. *Neurosciences Research Program Bulletin 17,* 1979, No. 1, 3–186.

Vaughan DW: Age-related deterioration of pyramidal cell basal dendrites in rat auditory cortex. *J Comparative Neurology* 3:405–429, 1977.

Walbran B: Age and serial ablations of somatosensory cortex in the rat. *Physiology and Behavior* 17:13–17, 1976.

West CD: A quantitative study of lipofuscin accumulation with age in normals and individuals with Down's Syndrome, phenylkitonuria, progeria and transneuronal atrophy. *J Comparative Neurology* 186:109–116, 1979.

Wilcox HH: Structural changes in the nervous system related to the process of aging. Present status of knowledge. In Birren JE, Imus H, Windle W (eds.) Charles C Thomas, Springfield, Illinois, 1959, pp. 16–23.

Zeman W: Studies in the neuronal ceroid-lipofusciminoses. *J Neuropathology and Experimental Neurology* 33:1–42, 1974.

Stein, ed. The Psychobiology of Aging: Problems and Perspectives

Brain Damage in Mature and Aged Rats:

Behavioral Effects of Septal Lesions

Wail A. Bengelloun, Mohammed El Hilali, Zhor Bouizzar and Jean-Pierre Veillat

Département de Biologie, Faculté des Sciences, Université Mohammed V, Rabat, Morocco.

Introduction

The wide-ranging behavioral effects of septal lesions in the adult rat have been repeatedly reviewed during the past few years (e.g., Caplan, 1973; Dickinson, 1974; Fried, 1972; Grossman, 1976; Isaacson, 1974). Perhaps the most striking of these effects is the transient postsurgical hyperreactivity to handling ("septal rage syndrome") first described by Brady and Nauta (1953, 1955). Hyperreactivity to stimulation along several sensory dimensions has also been demonstrated; light (Bengelloun, Nelson, Zent and Beatty, 1976; Donovick, 1968; Schwartzbaum, Green, Beatty and Thompson, 1967), sudden tactile or auditory cues (Gotsick, 1969), maintenance in a cold environment (Wakeman, Donovick and Burright, 1970), electric footshock (Lints and Harvey, 1969), and extremely palatable or unpalatable drinking solutions (Beatty and Schwartzbaum, 1967) have typically all been reported to lead to enhanced reactivity by rats with septal lesions long after dissipation of the rage syndrome.

Possibly related to this generalized hyperreactivity to stimulation, several reports indicate an increase in intra-species aggression following lesions of the septum (e.g., Ahmad and Harvey, 1968). It is becoming clear, however, that septal lesions in fact decrease the intensity of many of the components of normal attack behavior (piloerection, biting, lateral attack), and only increase reflexive defense behaviors (Blanchard, Blanchard, Takahashi and Takahashi, 1977; Miczek and Grossman, 1972).

Apparently paradoxical effects of septal lesions on the performance of rats in seemingly related learning paradigms have prompted an extensive literature in this area. Briefly, rats with septal lesions exhibit improved acquisition of shock-motivated 2-way active avoidance (King, 1958; Schwartzbaum et al., 1967), but are impaired in the acquisition of one-way active (McNew and Thompson, 1966; Thomas and McCleary, 1974) and passive avoidance responses (Fox, Kimble and Lickey, 1964; Fried, 1971). Rats with septal lesions are also deficient in the acquisition of DRL tasks (Ellen and Aitken, 1971), but are faster than controls in the acquisition of a Sidman avoidance (Sodetz, 1970). Both these latter tasks require the temporal spacing of responses. Finally, in discrimination problems reversal of the response in a kinesthetic, but not a visual task, is disrupted (Fried, 1972; Isaacson, 1974).

For the past several years our research interests have focussed on the reversibility of septal lesion-induced changes in behavior. In particular, we have been concerned with the role of non-surgical factors. We have found that the genetic constitution and experiential history of the subject, as well as the situational specifics surrounding the task to be acquired, are all critical determinants as to the severity of the lesion syndrome (Donovick, Burright and Bengelloun, 1979). To cite a few examples, the intensity and the duration of septal rage depend upon pre-operative experience (Nielson, McIver and Boswell, 1965), time of day at testing (Seggie, 1970), the distribution of handling during the post-operative period (Gotsick and Marshall, 1972), and the capture procedures employed (Max, Cohen and Lieblich, 1974). Additionally, castration of prepuberal male rats at 23 to 30 days of age results in a failure to exhibit hyperemotionality following septal lesions in adulthood (Bengelloun et al., 1976; Lieblich, Isseroff and Phillips, 1974).

The level of activity of rats with septal lesions in the open field may also be influenced by the manipulation of specific aspects of the stimulus complex (e.g., Donovick and Wakeman, 1969; Mattingly, Osborne and Gotsick, 1979). Moreover, a presurgical history of handling (Bengelloun, Finklestein, Burright and Donovick, 1977), enriched rearing conditions (Donovick, Burright and Swidler, 1973), or variety-enriched diet (Donovick, Burright and Bentsen, 1975) results in more vigorous exploration of a novel environment by rats with septal lesions. In the latter two studies, it was also demonstrated that presurgical social history and presurgical dietary regimen influence fluid consumption by rats with septal lesions, as do environmental conditions (Sanes, Donovick and Burright, 1975).

We also have found situational and experiential variables to be critical determinants of learning performance by rats with septal lesions. The septal deficit in one-way active avoidance may be significantly ameliorated by the elimination of intertrial handling while maintaining the traditional task characteristics of distinct safe and shock areas (Bengelloun, 1979). Likewise, the septal passive avoidance deficit may be eliminated by the provision of cues as to the impending commission of the punished response (Bengelloun, Burright and Donovick, 1977), or by manipulating either nutritional experience or the distribution of shock opportunities (Bengelloun, Burright and Donovick, 1976).

Once we became interested in experiential modulation of the behavioral effects of septal lesions, it was only a matter of time before our attention turned to an intimately related factor, the age of the animal at the time of surgery. Although work from several laboratories has addressed the effects of early septal lesions, little or no work has been directed toward the consequences of such lesions in the aged rat.

Reports on the effects of septal lesions in neonatal or juvenile animals suggest that there is little behaviorally manifested recovery of function when these animals are tested in adulthood. Thus, juvenile lesions facilitated active avoidance responding in the shuttle box to a degree comparable to that of adult lesions in the rat (Johnson, 1972; Johnson, Poplawski, Bieliauskas and Liebert, 1972; Molino, 1975; Schoenfeld, Hamilton and Gandelman, 1974) and in the guinea pig (Lown, 1975). Septal lesions in the juvenile rat, as in the adult, led to an increase in fixed-ratio responding and social contact (Johnson, 1972), and to an impairment in the acquisition of a passive avoidance response as well as in the reversal of a position habit (Gittis and Gordon, 1977). Several reports (Gittis and Gordon, 1977; Gittis and Hothersall, 1974; Johnson, Bieliauskas and Lancaster, 1973; Stahl and Ellen, 1977) indicate a deficit in the acquisition of a DRL task following neonatal or juvenile lesions, such deficit being analogous to that produced by septal lesions in the adult rat. This general lack of behavioral "recovery of function" following early septal lesions was all the more remarkable in view of the extensive neuronal plasticity observed following experimentally-induced injury to the septum and related limbic structures early in life (Goldman, 1976).

The question for us thus became whether septal lesions in the aged rat would have behavioral consequences similar to those observed in juvenile and young adult counterparts and if so, whether such consequences would also be subject to experiential and situational influences. Our first effort in this domain (Bengelloun, Burright and Donovick, 1977) showed that aged septal rats, unlike young adults, appeared not to benefit from the provision of "warning" cues in a passive avoidance paradigm. That is, whereas young septal rats acquired the passive avoidance response at rates comparable to those of brain-intact controls in the presence of cues, older septal rats continued to exhibit the classic deficit irrespective of cue availability.

We then undertook a series of studies to determine whether such differential "behavioral rigidity" following septal lesions in the aged rat may also be observed in other behavioral paradigms. In the present paper, we report on some aspects of the activity and reactivity of aged rats with septal lesions.

Method

Animals

Animals used in the present study were 36 male albino rats of Wistar origin, born and raised at our breeding facilities. Eighteen rats which served as aged subjects were between 500 and 530 days of age at surgery. The remaining 18 rats, serving as young adults, were 60 days of age at surgery. All animals were experimentally naive and had been group-housed since birth. One week prior to surgery, animals were housed in individual plastic cages (30 × 45 × 15 cm high) with metal grill tops. Laboratory chow and water were available *ad libitum* unless otherwise specified. Rats in each age group were assigned randomly without replacement to receive lesions of the septum or sham operations. This resulted in 4 treatment groups (n = 9 each): Aged/Lesion, Aged/Control, Young Adult/Lesion, Young Adult/Control.

Surgery and Histology

Rats in the two lesion groups received bilateral electrolytic lesions of the septum, performed under sodium pentobarbital (40 mg/kg) anesthesia, using procedures we have previously described in detail (Bengelloun, 1979). In brief, a No. 1 stainless steel insect pin insulated with Epoxylite except for a 0.5 mm tip was placed using the following stereotaxic coordinates: 1.0 mm anterior to bregma, 1.0 lateral, and 5.5 mm below the surface of the dura at an angle of 11° toward the midline. DC current (2.0 ma) was then passed between this electrode and a rectal cathode for 20 sec. Following current passage, the electrode was withdrawn and the same procedure performed on the other side of the brain. Control surgery consisted of a scalp incision followed by drilling of the skull, without electrode penetration. Theraplix (SMARIP, Casablanca) was administered topically, as we have found routine antibiotic treatment effective in reducing infection risk in aged rats.

At the conclusion of behavioral testing, rats with septal lesions were heavily anesthetized with ethyl urethane (ip) and intracardially perfused with isotonic saline followed by 10% formalin. After several days in 10% formalin, the brains were frozen and sectioned at 50 micra. Sections through the lesion area were saved, metachromatically stained (Donovick, 1974) and microscopically examined for extent of brain damage.

Apparatus and Procedure

Emotionality

Emotionality was assessed during 4 test sessions (1 day prior to surgery, and on days 1, 5 and 10 postsurgery). The technique used was essentially that described in a previous paper (Bengelloun et al., 1976), with slight modifications. Each rat was rated by two independent observers (only one of whom manipulated the animal) on each of 5 behavioral criteria during each test session. The behavioral criteria were: 1. resistance to capture in the home cage, 2. biting or attacking the observer's glove or a proferred pencil, 3. vocalization, 4. defecation and 5. urination. A rating of zero was recorded by an observer if the animal did not exhibit the behavior, and a rating of 1 was recorded if it did exhibit the response. Scores of both observers were summed across the 5 measures, and the maximum emotionality score for each animal was thus 10. Test sessions typically lasted 3 to 5 min, and were started by the observer's hand slowly approaching the animal head-on in an attempt to pick it up.

Aggression

Intra-specific aggression was examined one week following the last emotionality rating session. Each subject was tested during two encounters, separated by 24 hours. The animals were paired for these tests according to surgical treatment, one session with an animal of the same age group that had like-surgery (e.g., control-control or septal-septal), and one session with a same-age subject of different surgical treatment (control-septal). The order of these pairings was balanced such that half the animals in each surgical group had their first session with an animal of the same surgical treatment, while the other half had their fist session with an animal of differing surgical condition. Because of the odd number (9) of animals in each of our groups, one subject was chosen at random from each group to undergo a third encounter with a like-surgery counterpart. In this manner, for each age group there were 5 septal-septal encounters, 9 control-septal encounters, and 5 control-control encounters.

The aggression test encounters took place in a neutral animal cage, into diagonal corners of which were placed the two rats under study. Durations to contact and attack, as well as the animal initiating contact and attack were noted. For this purpose, the animals' backs were marked with ink. Because these rats were to be subsequently tested on other behavioral tasks, the session was terminated upon attack or, in the absence of attack behavior, after 10 min.

24-hour Activity

Home cage activity during a single 24-hour period was examined for each animal between 7 and 17 days after the last aggression encounter. The test apparatus consisted of two identical Model 31406x Electronic Activity Monitors (Stoelting Co., Chicago, IL), each of which was calibrated so as to filter out low amplitude activities such as grooming and twitching. Output from these units was fed to a 2-channel Varian A-

25 recorder. We thus had measures of both total activity count and 24-hour activity distribution for animals housed in their home cages.

Open Field

Three weeks following testing on the activity monitors, each rat was exposed to 3 daily 5-min sessions in an open field. The open field was constructed of wood, with a 75 × 45 cm floor divided into 15 equal squares. The entire field was painted flat black, and illumination in the middle of the field was 22.5 ft candles. Centrally placed along one wall, a small triangular hole was drilled into the floor of the field, allowing the nose but not the entire head of the rat to poke through. Wooden supports maintained the floor of the open field 2 cm above the surface on which it was placed.

At the beginning of each of the three daily sessions, the animal was placed in the middle square of the field. Activity (number of squares entered with all four feet) and stand-ups (both supported and unsupported) were recorded. We also recorded time spent in the square containing the triangular hole, but not nose pokes *per se*. At the end of the 5-min session the animal was returned to its home cage.

Quinine-adulterated Fluid Consumption

The last behavioral test to which animals were exposed was a quinine consumption test one week after the last open field session. Rats were deprived of water for 23.5 hours, then presented a single tube containing a solution of 0.025% quinine hydrochloride. The volume of this solution consumed over a 0.5-hour period was recorded.

Results

Histology

Microscopic evaluation revealed extensive neural damage to the precommissural septum similar to that we have described earlier using the same techniques (Bengelloun, 1979). Whereas the medial septum was bilaterally destroyed in all cases, the more lateral aspects of the lateral septal nuclei were occasionally spared. In antero-posterior extent, lesions extended from the hippocampus pars anterior to the crossing of the anterior commissure. Occasional minor damage was seen to the nucleus accumbens, caudate-putamen complex and corpus callosum. There were no readily apparent systematic differences in lesion extent between young adult and aged subjects.

Behavior

Emotionality

Data from the emotionality tests were evaluated using analyses of variance (Anova). All 4 groups exhibited statistically comparable levels of emotionality during the rating session which preceded surgery by 24 hours (Figure 1). Comparison by Anova of presurgical (−1) scores with scores during the first postsurgical session (+1) yielded significant main effects of Lesion ($F=5.80$, df 1/32, $p < 0.025$) and Session ($F=6.02$,

Figure 1. Mean emotionality rating scores for the 4 groups one day preceding surgery and on days 1, 5 and 10 postsurgery.

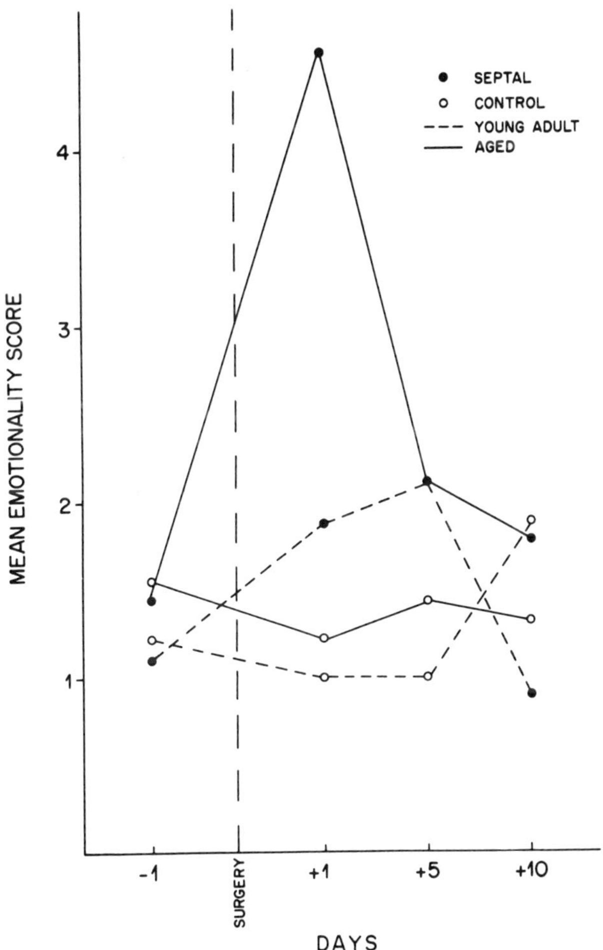

df 1/32, $p < 0.025$). Interpretation of these main effects must however take into consideration the significant Lesion × Session interaction ($F=9.80$, df 1/32, $p < 0.01$): septal lesions resulted in an important increase in emotionality when rats were tested 24 hours following surgery. Interestingly, although the lesion effect appeared to be more potent in aged animals, the Age × Lesion and Age × Lesion × Session interactions fell short of statistical significance ($F=$ 1.68 and 3.78, respectively). A specific comparison between the scores of aged and young adult animals with lesions on the first postsurgical session was nevertheless conducted since it was felt justified by the design. Aged subjects with septal lesions were significantly more emotional ($p < 0.05$) during this session (+1) than young adults with septal lesions.

Anova of emotionality scores for the three postsurgical rating sessions (+1, +5, +10) resulted in a significant Lesion × Session interaction ($F=5.05$, df 2/64, $p < 0.01$). Subsequent t tests (using the overall error term from the Anova with its assoicated df value) revealed that the lesion-induced hyperemotionality decreased over time to attain essentially control levels on the last two rating sessions (+5 and +10).

Aggression

Table 1 presents the median latencies to attack for the three encounter conditions under which aggressive behavior was assessed for each age group. A rank order test for small samples (White, 1952) was used to evaluate differences on this measure between encounter conditions. Septal-septal encounters were found to lead to shorter latencies (faster attack) than control-control encounters in both young adult ($p < 0.01$) and aged ($p < 0.05$) rats. Latencies to attack for septal-control encounters in each age group were intermediate, and did not statistically differ from those for control-control or septal-septal encounters. The performance of animals in each type of encounter did not statistically differ as a function of age insofar as this measure was concerned. It is of further interest to note that in control-septal encounters, all attacks were initiated by septal rats following initiation of contact by the control rat.

Table 1. Median Latencies to Attack (Range in Parentheses) Under the Three Encounter Conditions for the 2 Age Groups During the Aggression Test

	Type of Encounter		
	Septal-Septal (n = 5)	**Septal-Control (n = 9)**	**Control-Control (n = 5)**
Young Adult	185 (120-263)	268 (142-600)	525 (385-600)
Aged	105 (005-209)	300 (010-600)	560 (109-600)

24-hour Activity

Anova of the total activity counts on the electronic activity monitors (Figure 2) indicated that aged animals were significantly more active than younger animals ($F=9.56$, df 1/32, $p < 0.01$) and septal rats were more active than controls ($F=5.46$, df 1/32, $p < 0.05$). The Age × Lesion interaction, however, did not attain statistical significance.

Distribution of activity over the 24-hour period is presented in Figure 3. In accord with the total activity count data, aged animals spent a greater portion of the 24-hour period in activity ($F=6.29$, df 1/32, $p < 0.025$) than young adults, and rats with septal lesions spent more of the 24-hour period in activity ($F=11.55$, df 1/32, $p < 0.01$) than brain-intact controls. The Age × Lesion × Light Period (Light: 6-18 hrs, Dark: 18-

Figure 2. Mean total activity count registered during 24 hours on the electronic activity monitors. Multiplication of means in this figure by 10^3 yields the real values obtained.

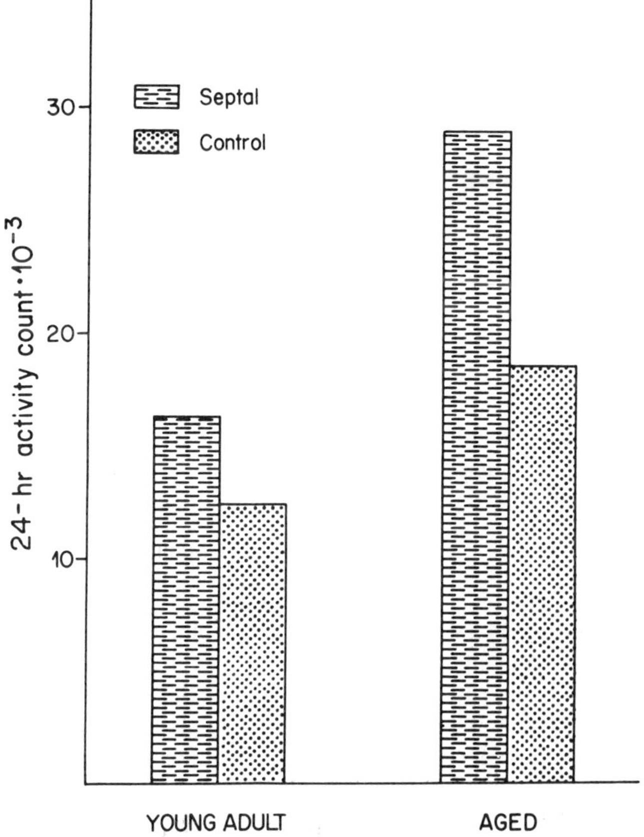

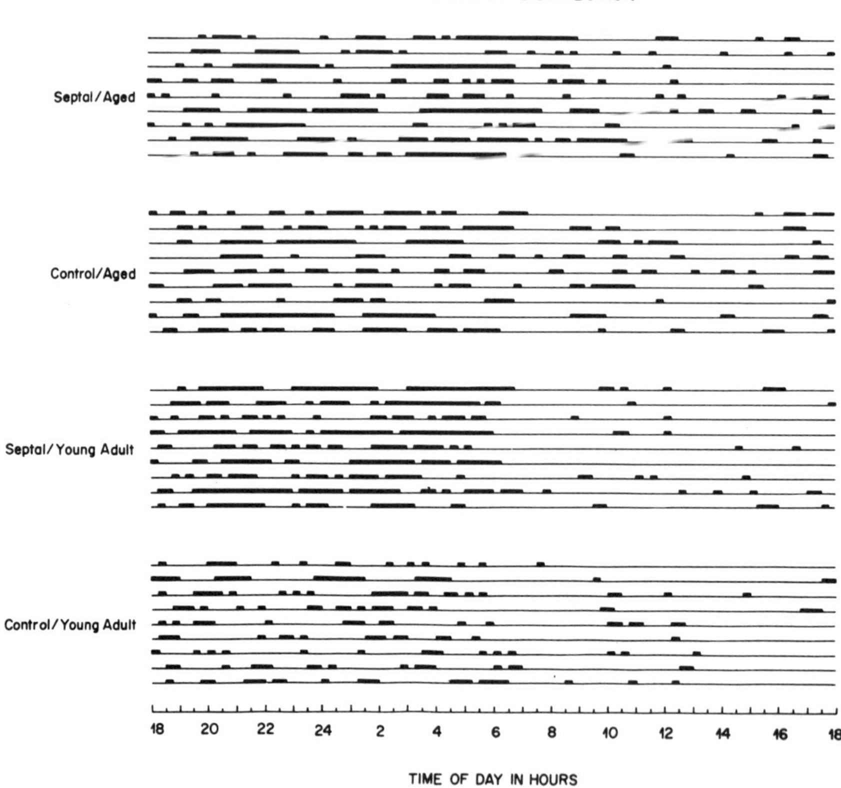

Figure 3. Distribution of activity periods for individual animals in each of the four groups.

6 hrs) interaction was also significant ($F=9.39$, df 1/32, $p < 0.01$). Septal lesions increased activity time relative to controls during the dark ($p < 0.001$), but not during the light period; aged animals exhibited more activity relative to young adults during the light period ($p < 0.001$), but did not differ from young adults on this measure during the dark period.

Open Field

The top panel of Figure 4 presents the means of open field activity for all 4 groups. The only statistically significant effect by Anova was that of days ($F=6.43$, df 2/64, $p < 0.025$), with number of squares entered being significantly less ($p < 0.05$) in general on day 3 than on day 2. Neither age nor lesion appeared to influence open field activity under the conditions of the present experiment. There was however a marked tendency (top panel, Figure 4) for aged septal rats to be less active than

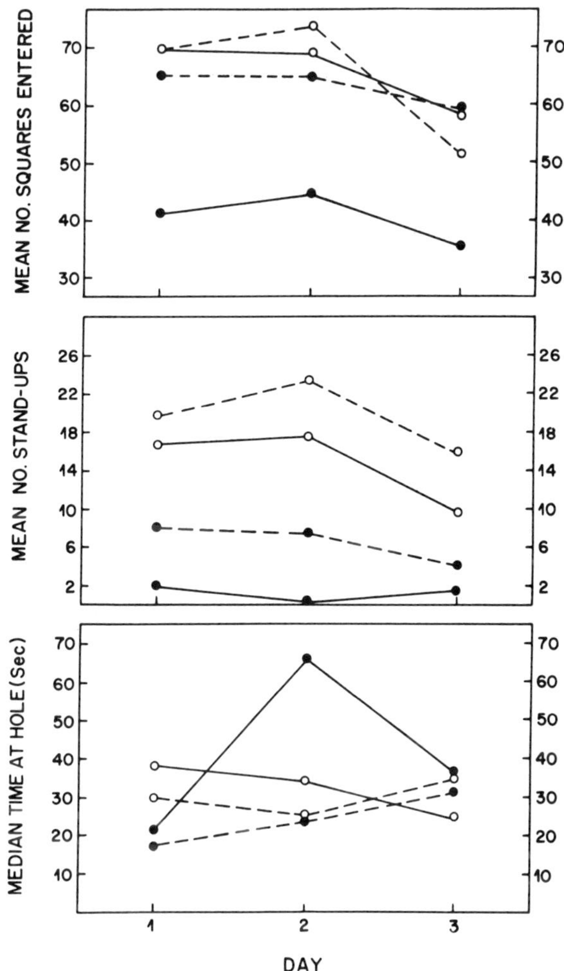

Figure 4. Open Field behavior. Key: septal lesions = black circles; brain-intact controls = open circles; aged rats = solid lines; young adults = broken lines.

the other three groups. This difference was statistically significant by specific comparison ($p < 0.05$) in all 3 cases, on all three days.

Anova of the number of stand-ups in the open field yielded significant main effects for Lesion ($F=21.43$, df 1/32, $p < 0.001$) and Days ($F=13.88$, df 2/64, $p < 0.001$), as well as a significant Lesion × Days interaction ($F=6.11$, df 2/64, $p < 0.025$). Rats with septal lesions stood-up significantly less than controls, maintaining essentially the same level of performance on this measure throughout the three days of testing. Controls, on the other hand, decreased their number of stand-ups significantly ($p < 0.05$) from day 2 to day 3 (middle panel, Figure 4).

The bottom panel of Figure 4 presents the number of seconds spent in the square containing the triangular hole. Kruskal-Wallis H test for independent samples was used to evaluate the time spent in this square on each of the three days. No significant effects were found, indicating that this particular measure was not influenced by either age of the animal or brain surgery.

Quinine-adulterated Fluid Consumption

Aged animals consumed significantly less quinine-adulterated solution (see Figure 5) following a 23.5-hr water deprivation period ($F=10.56$, df 1/32, $p < 0.01$). Interestingly, neither the Lesion main effect nor the Lesion × Age interaction was statistically significant.

Discussion

Septal lesions were found to increase emotionality, in keeping with previous reports (Brady and Nauta, 1953; Gotsick and Marshall, 1972). This increase in emotionality was found to be particularly striking in aged animals (Figure 1). Our present values were nevertheless lower than emotionality scores we have previously reported for septal rats (Bengelloun et al., 1976), and this discrepancy may be related to differences in handling technique between the two studies. In the present investigation, the experimeter approached the animal from the front to pick it up, and not from the rear as in the earlier study. Max et al. (1974) have reported that such a procedure markedly reduces the intensity of the septal rage syndrome.

The differentially more powerful manifestation of septal lesion-induced hyperemotionality in aged subjects is interesting, and may reflect a generalized hyperreactivity in aged animals. It may be noted in Figure 1, for example, that aged controls obtained slightly higher (though not significantly different) emotionality scores than young adult controls. Increased reactivity in aged subjects may also be seen upon examination of the data from the quinine-adulterated fluid consumption test (Figure 5), where aged animals drank less of this unpalatable solution than young adults, in spite of their greater body weights.

Our failure to observe the classic lesion effect on quinine-adulterated fluid consumption (e.g., Beatty and Schwartzbaum, 1967) may be related to the short presentation period utilized (0.5 hr). On the other hand, the failure of septal rats to exhibit both the rage syndrome and enhanced reactivity to quinine has been reported previously by some authors (for a discussion see Donovick, Burright and Bengelloun, 1979).

We tend to interpret the results from the present aggression tests within a reactivity framework, based both on our own subjective observations during testing and on results reported by other investigators

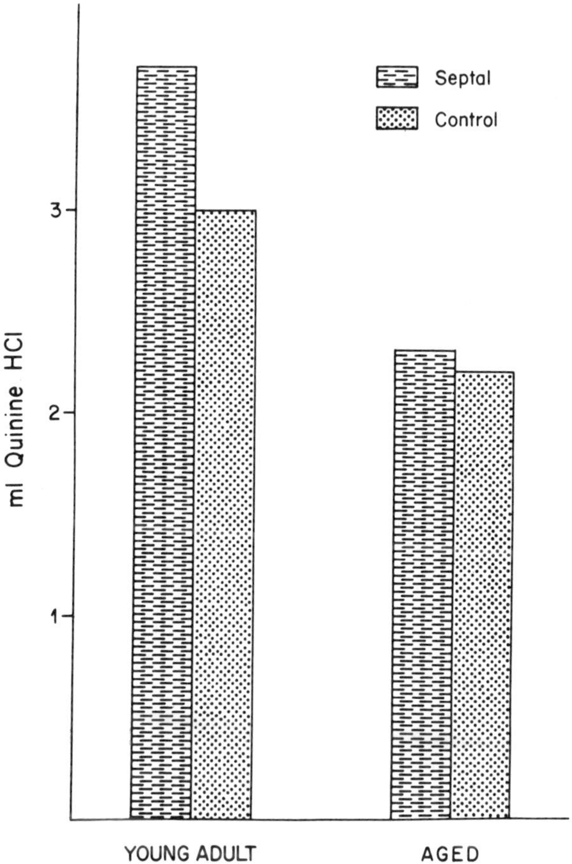

Figure 5. Mean number of ml of 0.025 Quinine hydrochloride solution consumed by each of the 4 groups.

(Blanchard et al., 1977). Septal rats tended to show gross signs of emotional disturbance (e.g., hyperventilation, vocalization) as soon as they were placed in the encounter situation, and their attacks tended to be reflexive rather than directed. This was particularly evident in our septal-control encounters, where attacks were invariably initiated by the septal rat following initiation of contact by the control counterpart. The most effective attack-eliciting stimuli appeared to be contact to the back or the neck of the septal rat. Both Blanchard et al. (1977) and Miczek and Grossman (1972) have reported essentially similar results. Our data extend these findings to aged animals; septal lesions did not differentially influence latency to attack in young adult and aged animals.

The reactivity tests used in the present study reflect widely differing facets of the animal's behavioral repertoire and, as such, may be expected to be differentially susceptible to the effects of brain damage and aging. Septal hyperemotionality, for example, is considerably more transient than the effects of septal lesions on social interaction (e.g., aggressive behavior) or reactivity to other sensory stimuli (Fried, 1972). It is thus perhaps not surprising to find differential lesion effects in young adult and aged septal rats on one form of reactivity (hyperemotionality) but not on others. This finding does suggest, however, that a more systematic examination of the interactive effects of septal lesions and age on sensory and social reactivity is desirable.

Our activity data were especially useful, in that they permitted the comparison between behavior in a novel environment (open field) with that in familiar (home cage) surroundings. In the open field (Figure 4), the activity of aged septal rats was markedly reduced when compared to young adult septal rats or either group of brain-intact controls. The relatively dim lighting conditions were meant to minimize a differential reactivity to light in septal and control rats (Donovick and Wakeman, 1969) and, indeed, young adult septals did not differ from controls in open field activity. We also observed the classic (e.g., Bengelloun et al., 1976) septal lesion-induced depression of stand-ups in both age groups. There were, however, no differences in terms of time spent in the square with the triangular hole, a measure we had intended to use as an index of exploratory behavior.

Although brain damage and aging exerted apparently non-interactive effects on total activity count (Figure 2) in the home cage as measured on the electronic activity monitors, they did interact in the determination of activity distribution (spread) over a 24-hr period (Figure 3). Whereas active time of aged control and aged septal rats was equivalent in the dark period (18 hr–6 hr), young adult septals spent significantly more time in activity during the dark period than young adult controls. During the light period (6 hr–18 hr), aged animals spent more time in activity than young adults. It thus seems clear that the presence or absence, as well as the direction, of interactive effects between brain damage and aging in the determination of activity, as was the case for reactivity, depend upon the specific methods used to assess behavior.

The present results are particularly important from a developmental viewpoint. Most previous data (Johnson, 1972; Johnson et al., 1972, 1973; Gittis and Gordon, 1977; Gittis and Hothersall, 1974; Lown, 1975; Molino, 1975; Schoenfeld et al., 1974; Stahl and Ellen, 1977) had indicated that the age of the animal at surgery does not influence the characteristics of septal lesion-induced behavioral changes. All of these studies utilized neonatal or juvenile animals. In the present study, using aged rats, we have clearly shown that in several behavioral test situations the effects of septal lesions in the aged rat do differ from the effects of septal lesions in young adults. These findings strongly suggest that more attention should be paid to the effects of brain damage in the aged organism. They also suggest a reconsideration of current concepts of a differential capacity for organizational plasticity in the nervous system of young organisms (Goldman, 1976).

ACKNOWLEDGMENTS
We thank Dr. Richard G. Burright for a critical reading of this manuscript.

References

Ahmad SS, Harvey JA: Long-term effects of septal lesions and social experience on shock-elicited fighting in rats. *J Comparative and Physiological Psychology* 66:596–602, 1968.

Beatty WW, Schwartzbaum JS: Enhanced reactivity to quinine and saccharin following septal lesions in the rat. *Psychonomic Science* 8:483–484, 1967.

Bengelloun WA: Elimination of the septal deficit in one-way active avoidance. *Physiology and Behavior* 22:615–619, 1979.

Bengelloun WA, Burright RG, Donovick PJ: Nutritional experience and spacing of shock opportunities alter the effects of septal lesions on passive avoidance acquisition by male rats. *Physiology and Behavior* 16:583–587, 1976.

Bengelloun WA, Burright RG, Donovick PJ: Septal lesions, cue availability, and passive avoidance acquisition by hooded male rats of two ages. *Physiology and Behavior* 18:1033–1037, 1977.

Bengelloun WA, Finklestein J, Burright RG, Donovick PJ: Presurgical handling and exploratory behavior of rats with septal lesions. *Bull Psychonomic Society* 10:503–505, 1977.

Bengelloun WA, Nelson DJ, Zent HM, Beatty WW: Behavior of male and female rats with septal lesions: influence of prior gonadectomy. *Physiology and Behavior* 16:317–330, 1976.

Blanchard DC, Blanchard RJ, Takahashi LK, Takahashi T: Septal lesions and aggressive behavior. *Behavioral Biology* 21:157–161, 1977.

Brady, JV, Nauta WJH: Subcortical mechanisms in emotional behavior: affective changes following septal forebrain lesions in the albino rat. *J Comparative and Physiological Psychology* 46:339–346, 1953.

Brady, JV, Nauta, WJH: Subcortical mechanisms in emotional behavior: the duration of affective changes following septal and habenular lesions in the albino rat. *J Comparative and Physiological Psychology* 48:412–420, 1955.

Caplan M: An analysis of the effects of septal lesions on negatively reinforced behavior. *Behavioral Biology* 9:129–167, 1973.

Dickinson A: Response suppression and facilitation by aversive stimuli following septal lesions in rats: a review and model. *Physiological Psychology* 2:444–456, 1974.

Donovick, PJ: Effects of localized septal lesions on hippocampal EEG activity and behavior in rats. *J Comparative and Physiological Psychology* 66:569–578, 1968.

Donovick PJ: A metachromatic stain for neural tissue. *Stain Technology* 49:49–51, 1974.

Donovick PJ, Burright RG, Bengelloun WA: The septal region and behavior: an example of the importance of genetic and experiential factors in determining effects of brain damage. *Neuroscience and Biobehavioral Reviews* 3:83–96, 1979.

Donovick PJ, Burright RG, Bentsen EO: Presurgical dietary history differentially alters the behavior of control and septal lesioned rats. *Developmental Psychobiology* 8:13–25, 1975.

Donovick PJ, Burright RG, Swidler MA: Presurgical rearing environment alters exploration, fluid consumption, and learning of septal lesioned and control rats. *Physiology and Behavior* 11:543–553, 1973.

Donovick PJ, Wakeman KA: Open-field luminance and "septal hyperemotionality." *Animal Behavior* 17:186–190, 1969.

Ellen P, Aitken WC: Absence of temporal discrimination following septal lesions. *Psychonomic Science* 22:129–131, 1971.

Fox SS, Kimble DP, Lickey ME: Comparison of caudate nucleus and septal-area lesions on two types of avoidance behavior. *J Comparative and Physiological Psychology* 58:380–386, 1964.

Fried, PA: Limbic system lesions in rats: differential effects in an approach-avoidance task. *J Comparative and Physiological Psychology* 74:349–353, 1971.

Fried, PA: Septum and behavior: a review. *Psychological Bulletin* 78:292–310, 1972.

Gittis AG, Gordon M: Developmental analysis of behavioral dysfunction in rats with septal lesions. *J Comparative and Physiological Psychology* 91:94–106, 1977.

Gittis A, Hothersall D: DRL performance of juvenile rats with septal lesions. *Physiological Psychology* 2:38–42, 1974.

Goldman PS: Maturation of the mammalian nervous system and the ontogeny of behavior. *Advances in the Study of Behavior* 7:1–90, 1976.

Gotsick JE: Factors affecting spontaneous activity in rats with limbic system lesions. *Physiology and Behavior* 4:587–593, 1969.

Gotsick JE, Marshall RC: Time course of the septal rage syndrome. *Physiology and Behavior* 9:685–687, 1972.

Grossman SP: Behavioral functions of the septum: a re-analysis. In DeFrance JF (ed.) *The Septal Nuclei*. New York, Plenum Press, 1976.

Isaacson RL: *The Limbic System*. New York, Plenum Press, 1974.

Johnson DA: Developmental aspects of recovery of function following septal lesions in the infant rat. *J Comparative and Physiological Psychology* 78:331–348, 1972.

Johnson DA, Bieliauskas LA, Lancaster J: DRL training and performance following anterior, posterior, or complete septal lesions in infant and adult rats. *Physiology and Behavior* 11:661–669, 1973.

Johnson DA, Poplawski A, Bieliauskas L, Liebert D: Recovery of function on a two-way conditioned avoidance task following septal lesions in infancy: effects of early handling. *Brain Research* 45:282–287, 1972.

King FA: Effects of septal and amygdaloid lesions on emotional behavior and conditioned avoidance response in the rat. *J Nervous and Mental Disease* 126:57–63, 1958.

Lieblich I, Isseroff, A, Phillips AG: Developmental and hormonal aspects of increased emotionality produced by septal lesions in male rats: a parametric study of the effects of early castration. *Physiology and Behavior* 12:45–53, 1974.

Lints CE, Harvey JA: Altered sensitivity to footshock and decreased brain content of serotonin following brain lesions in the rat. *J Comparative and Physiological Psychology* 67:23–32, 1969.

Lown, BA: Alterations in active avoidance acquisition in the guinea pig following septal lesions at three ages. *Physiological Psychology* 3:374–378, 1975.

Mattingly BA, Osborne FH, Gotsick JE: Activity changes during a conditioned aversive stimulus in rats with septal lesions. *Physiology and Behavior* 22:521–525, 1979.

Max DM, Cohen E, Lieblich I: Effects of capture procedures on emotionality scores in rats with septal lesions. *Physiology and Behavior* 13:617–620, 1974.

McNew J, Thompson R: Role of the limbic system in active and passive avoidance conditioning in the rat. *J Comparative and Physiological Psychology* 61:173–180, 1966.

Miczek KA, Grossman SP: Effects of septal lesions on inter- and intra-species aggression in rats. *J Comparative and Physiological Psychology* 79:37–45, 1972.

Molino A: Sparing of function after infant lesions of selected limbic structures in the rat. *J Comparative and Physiological Psychology* 89:868–881, 1975.

Nielson H, McIver H, Boswell R: Effect of septal lesions on learning, emotionality, activity, and exploratory behavior in rats. *Experimental Neurology* 11:147–157, 1965.

Sanes J, Donovick PJ, Burright RG: Consummatory behavior as a function of ambient temperature in septal-lesioned and control rats. *J Neuroscience Research* 1:333–341, 1975.

Schoenfeld TA, Hamilton LW, Gandelman R: Septal damage during the maturation of inhibitory responding: effects in juvenile and adult rats. *Developmental Psychobiology* 7:195–205, 1974.

Schwartzbaum JS, Green RH, Beatty WW, Thompson JB: Acquisition of avoidance behavior following septal lesions in the rat. *J Comparative and Physiological Psychology* 63:95–104, 1967.

Seggie J: Endocrine and circadian variables in manifestation of affective behavior following septal ablation in rats. *Proc 78th Annual Convention, APA* 5:199–200, 1970.

Sodetz, FJ: Septal ablation and free-operant avoidance behavior in the rat. *Physiology and Behavior* 5:773–777, 1970.

Stahl JM, Ellen P: Influence of neonatal septal lesions on DRL performance in adulthood. *J Comparative and Physiological Psychology* 91:87–93, 1977.

Thomas JB, McCleary RA: One-way avoidance behavior and septal lesions in the rat. *J Comparative and Physiological Psychology* 86:751–759, 1974.

Wakeman KA, Donovick PJ, Burright RG: Septal lesions increase bar pressing for heat in animals maintained in the cold. *Physiology and Behavior* 5:1193–1195, 1970.

White C: The use of ranks in a test of significance for comparing two treatments. *Biometrics* 8:33–41, 1952.

Stein, ed. The Psychobiology of Aging: Problems and Perspectives

Dietary Restriction, Longevity, and CNS Aging

William B. Forbes

Worcester Foundation for Experimental Biology, Shrewsbury, Massachusetts.

Introduction

Various regimens of dietary restriction have been shown to produce substantial increases in the mean life span of laboratory animals. This observation is extremely robust, having been reported in a variety of species using any of several methods of dietary restriction. Moreover, the degree of life span extension can be quite large—up to 50% in rodents. On the face of it, one might infer that restriction-induced increases in longevity were associated with a decrease in the rate of senescent changes in various tissues, including nervous tissue. Unfortunately, there currently is very little experimental evidence to either support or refute that inference. This chapter will provide a review of the literature pertaining to restriction-induced enhancement of life span and discuss some of the issues raised by the available data. It will also describe preliminary results of an experimental attempt to correlate a restriction-induced increase in longevity and the rate of lipofuscin accumulation in nervous tissue.

Dietary Effects on Life Span

The earliest experimental demonstrations of enhanced longevity associated with dietary restriction in rodents were conducted by McKay and co-workers over 40 years ago (McKay et al., 1935, 1939, 1943). They reported that rats fed restricted amounts of a complete diet throughout post-weaning life exhibited a mean life span 50% greater than control animals fed *ad libitum*. Similar results have been reported by others in various infra-mammalian species (e.g., Comfort, 1963; Fanestil and Barrows, 1965; Ingle, Wood, and Banta, 1937; Loeb and Northrup, 1917) and in rodents that were subjected to a (*op. cit.* below) wide variety of methods of diet restriction. In general, it has been found that dietary manipulations which chronically limit growth also prolong life and *vice versa*. The efficacy of a particular dietary regimen in restricting growth and prolonging life appears to be dependent on several factors, among which are the timing and severity of the restriction and the classes of nutrients to which access is limited.

The most effective methods of limiting growth and promoting longevity in rodents are those in which the dietary restriction is initiated at an early age and is maintained throughout life. Widdowson and McCance (1963) reported that finite periods of undernutrition were of decreasing effectiveness in limiting growth the later in life they occurred. They found that even severe restriction or disease occurring over a period of several weeks in the post-weaning rat did not result in completely inhibited growth and that under these circumstances complete catch-up growth would occur following the restitution of an adequate diet. Nolen (1972) reported that mild limitations in caloric intake, sufficient to inhibit growth for a circumscribed period, which were imposed only for the first 12 weeks following weaning did not increase life span in the rat despite a small, persistent deficit in the weight of certain organs. He also reported that only those regimens in which access to food was restricted throughout the later part of life (*viz.* 12 weeks to 3 years) were effective in enhancing longevity. This was the case whether or not diet was restricted in early life as well.

Ross (1972) described a comprehensive series of experiments testing the relationship between timing and severity of dietary restriction, growth and longevity in rats. His results confirmed earlier findings that chronic restriction beginning early in life was most effective in promoting longevity. He also found that dietary restriction confined to the first 50 days following weaning resulted in a modest (10%) permanent growth deficit and a slight increase in mean life span. Restriction imposed chronically beginning 50 days after weaning, which produced a much more pronounced growth deficit, resulted in a substantial increase in longevity. However, in this case, the increase in life span was not as great as would have been achieved had the restriction begun at weaning. Rats for which chronic, restricted regimens were imposed only after 300–365 days of age were found to benefit, only if the restriction was moderate in comparison with degrees of restriction which effectively increased the life span of young rats. In these older rats, degrees of restriction which were greatly effective in younger rats actually decreased life expectancy, though less drastic restriction was capable of causing moderate increases in life span. Thus, the efficacy of post-weaning restriction in rats is an interactive function of the age at onset of the treatment, the severity and the duration of restriction.

Undernutrition during the suckling period followed by *ad libitum* feeding for up to 12 months reportedly results in a permanent slowing of growth rate (Chow and Lee, 1964; Winick and Nobel, 1966). Williams and Hughes (1975) showed that dietary restriction lasting only to post-natal day 8 was not effective in permanently retarding growth, but that restriction lasting to day 15 was. Widdowson and McCance (1975) have speculated that the long-term effect on growth restriction during suckling is due to the establishment of a life-long behavioral pattern of reduced food intake which is subsequently the cause of the reduction in growth rate. Indeed, on the one hand, Ross and Bras (1975) have shown that individual differences in feeding patterns within a homogeneous population of normally reared rats are correlated with life expectancy, lower levels of food intake throughout later life (over 49 days of age) being associated with greater longevity. On the other hand, the possibility remains that the apparently permanent retardation in growth following severe dietary restriction during the suckling period results from alterations in fundamental metabolic mechanisms of growth rather than from purely behavioral factors. For example, Stephan et al. (1971) have shown that dietary restriction during the suckling period results in reduced pituitary weights and lower pituitary concentrations of growth hormone. Whatever the reason, it is clear that dietary restriction prior to weaning may produce life-long growth deficits in rats. The reported growth deficits are generally not large—on the order of 10–20%—and are not clearly accompanied by increases in life expectancy. Roeder (1972) reported an unpublished observation that perinatal undernutrition was not associated with increased life span in rats. Widdowson and Kennedy (1962) reported that the life expectancy at weaning of rats suckled in large litters was somewhat less than that of well-fed control animals in spite of the fact that they exhibited a persistent growth deficit. In my experience (see below), rats suckled in litters of 16 exhibit a small growth deficit in comparison with rats suckled in litters of 8. The deficit persists to at least 750 days of age but does not appear to increase life expectancy. These data can be taken to imply that dietary regimens are not the crucial factor in the promotion of longevity.

There is some evidence that restricting access to a nutritionally balanced diet or limiting caloric intake by any other means is more effective in promoting longevity than restricting the availability of dietary protein. Nakagawa and co-workers (1974) found no effect of chronic *ad libitum* feeding of diets varying in protein content over a range of 10–36% on growth or longevity of female rats. Ross (1961) claimed that groups of rats fed restricted amounts of two isocaloric purified diets which differed in casein content, did not significantly differ in life expectancy. In fact, his data show a trend to longer life span in the group fed the high casein diet. In this same study, Ross reports that rats fed a low protein diet *ad libitum* lived longer than rats fed a high protein diet *ad libitum*. However, he points out, that the low-protein group grew more slowly and consumed fewer calories than the high protein group. Thus, the greater longevity of the *ad libitum* fed low-protein group may be attributed to this decrease in caloric intake. Barrows and Kokkonen (1975) reported that rats fed a 12% casein diet *ad libitum* beginning at 16 months of age lived 25% longer than rats fed a 24% casein diet. Rats fed 8% or 4% casein diets did not differ in longevity from the 25% casein group. The authors did not provide detailed information concerning caloric intake in the four dietary treatment groups. They did point out that only the 4% casein group suffered a decrement in body weight following introduction of the low-casein diet when the rats were 16 months of age. Taking all these reports into consideration, I would have to conclude that chronic dietary protein restriction begun early in life probably does not affect longevity, except in that it results in restricted growth and subsequent reduction of caloric intake.

The relationship between diet and longevity has been studied by retrospective analysis of feeding behavior by Ross and Bras (1975). They gave 121 individually housed male rats free access to three isocaloric diets differing only in the ratio of protein to carbohydrate. By measuring intake of each diet daily throughout the life span of the animals, they were able to analyze individual differences in total food intake, and the relative and absolute amounts of protein and carbohydrate consumed. These data were then correlated with individual differences in longevity. They found that those animals which ate the least food lived the longest. Based upon average daily food consumption, they divided their animals into 6 groups. Group mean food consumption varied between 18.3 and 24.1 gm/day. Mean group life span was monotonically related to food intake ranging from 733 days, for the group that ate least, to 556 days for the group that ate most. In addition, they found by comparing the behavior of the longest-lived and shortest-lived rats, that long life was correlated with a relatively stable dietary protein/calorie ratio throughout life. The shortest-lived rats ate relatively less protein early in life and relatively more after 100–200 days of age. Finally, they performed simple, partial and multiple correlations between life span and dietary behavior at several ages. They found that longevity correlated most highly with dietary behavior prior to 400 days of age. It is particularly noteworthy that at ages of 300 days and more, dietary protein level became as important as, or more important than, dietary carbohydrate in predicting life span. This partially supports the observations of Barrows and Kokkonen (1975) cited above.

Another example of retrospective analysis is found in the report of Goodrick (1977) who studied growth and longevity of mutant mouse strains which differ in maximal body weight. His subjects were C57BL/6J mice and the mutant strains beige (*bg*), albino (c^J), yellow (A^y) and obese (*ob*). In general, he found that mutant strains exhibited shorter life spans than the control mice. Comparing mutant groups, he observed that obese mutants attained the highest peak body weight and exhibited the shortest life spans. However, the yellow mutants did not differ significantly from the obese mice in peak body weight and exhibited a mean life span similar to the beige and albino mutants. The best correlations observed were between growth rate and longevity, the fastest growing mice dying youngest. This was true across mutant strains and between individuals within strains as well. Goodrick did not measure food intake in any of his animals and thus, it is impossible to know, from the reported data, whether the individual and strain differences in growth were highly correlated with caloric intake.

Conceptual Implications

Taken together, the studies I cited present the clear impression that reduction of nutrient intake, either through experimental means or due to individual variation, results in increased life expectancy in laboratory animals but several important questions remain unanswered. Why does dietary restriction enhance longevity? Is the onset of senescence retarded in restricted animals or do they "age" at a normal pace? What are the implications of these data for the various theories of aging?

It is clear that animals chronically maintained on restricted dietary regimens have lower incidences of many pathologies. There have been numerous reports of decreased incidence of both benign and malignant neoplastic lesions in animals fed restricted or low-protein diets (Berg and Simms, 1960; Nakagawa et al., 1974; Ross and Bras, 1971; Saxton et al., 1944; Tannenbaum and Silverstone, 1953; Vischer et al., 1942). There have also been several reports of decreased incidence of kidney disease in rats chronically underfed (Berg and Simms, 1960; Bras, 1969; Fernances et al., 1976). Other pathologies reported to be reduced in undernourished rats include myocardial degeneration (Berg and Simms, 1960; Nolen, 1972) and hepatic degeneration (Nolen, 1972). Interestingly, Nolen (1972) reports an increased incidence of hind limb paralysis associated with chronic dietary restriction. Although total incidence of this condition is very low, I have observed three such cases in rats maintained chronically on a restricted diet and none in rats fed *ad libitum* though my underfed rats exhibit much lower mortality (see below). In general, it is clearly the case that undernutrition inhibits or retards the onset of many pathological states in rodents.

Though it is certainly reasonable to assert that undernourished animals live longer because of decreased incidences of specific pathologies, several attempts have been made to link increased longevity with other physiological factors. Fernandes et al. (1976) demonstrated that caloric restriction more than doubled the life span of a hybrid mouse strain, (NZB x NZW)F_1, which is highly susceptible to autoimmune hemolytic anemia. They proposed that their data support the autoimmune theory of aging (Walford, 1974). That theory states that over the course of life the organism's immune system loses the capacity to recognize its own cells and tissues, forming increasingly non-specific antibodies. Along the same lines, Gerbase-DeLima and co-workers (1975) showed that retarded aging in a long-lived mouse strain by dietary restriction was associated with alterations of the immune systems of those animals. Immunocompetence was suppressed early in life but was higher than that of control animals late in life. This would also be consistent with a delayed autoimmunity or could imply higher resistance to pathogens in later life.

Barrows (1971, 1972) proposed that dietary restriction promotes longevity by decreasing the rate of transfer of genetic information in the form of RNA and protein synthesis. Such a decrease would be predicted to slow aging on the basis of Orgel's (1963) error accumulation theory. That theory states that the basis of aging lies in the random occurrence of errors in transcription which result in erroneous amino acid sequences in proteins. If such errors occur in synthetases or other enzymes, the error may be compounded by the production of faulty reaction products. Leto et al. (1976) reported that the activity of several hepatic and renal enzymes were depressed throughout the adult life of mice fed a 4% casein diet chronically. Enzymatic activities in the hearts of malnourished mice did not differ from control values. Ross (1969) reported that hepatic catylase activity was lower throughout life in undernourished rats. These data may be interpreted as indicative of a lower rate of usage of genetic information in diet restricted rodents. An alternative possibility has been raised by Barrows (1972) who suggested that underfeeding delays the expression of a genetic program for aging. Fanestil and Barrows (1965), studying rotifers, and Ross (1959), studying rats, found that age-related changes in enzyme activity were delayed by underfeeding. If aging is programmed, these data suggest that the timing of the program may be affected by underfeeding.

Finally, it is possible that restriction of food intake promotes longevity by reducing the rate of accumulation of toxic metabolites. Harmon (1956) has proposed a theory of aging based on the random deleterious effects of free radical reactions in all tissues. Free radicals are intermediate by-products of nutrient catalysis. Feeding animals diets containing moderate levels of anti-oxidants such as butylhydroxytoluene (BHT), thus inhibiting oxidative metabolism to some degree and limiting the formation of free radicals, has been reported to increase life span in rodents up to 30% (Bun-Hoi and Ratsimamanga, 1959; Harman, 1968). Furthermore, feeding diets rich in easily oxidized amino acids shortens life span while diets low in these amino acids increases longevity by 16% (Harman, 1969). This raises the possibility that foods, or perhaps the metabolites of certain nutrients, act as slow poisons. By restricting food intake, life span may be prolonged by virtue of a lower rate of build-up of these naturally occurring toxic products.

Based upon the evidence cited, it is possible to formulate two distinct hypotheses regarding the basis for restriction-induced increases in longevity. On the one hand, one might propose that animals subjected to long-term dietary restriction enjoy lower susceptibility to various pathologies than animals fed *ad libitum*. In this case, senescent changes which were not secondary to pathological conditions would occur at the same rate in restricted and *ad libitum* fed animals. On the other hand, one might propose that dietary restriction produces a retardation in fundamental aspects of the aging process. If this were so, the incidence of many pathologies might be expected to be lower at any given age in diet-restricted animals since resistence to pathogenic factors declines in senescence. These two hypotheses are illustrated schematically in Figure 1.

Naturally, it is possible that there is some validity to both hypotheses. Thus, for any given senescent change the question becomes: "Does dietary restriction retard the appearance of this change or does it occur at a normal pace in restricted animals?" To the degree that dietary restriction retards senescent changes, it may be asserted that restriction serves as a key to understanding the mutability of the aging process. To the degree that senescent changes occur on schedule in restricted animals, it may be argued that animals fed *ad libitum* are inadequate models for the study of aging, since much greater degrees of senescent change would be seen in older, restricted animals.

Dietary Restriction and Lipofuscin Accumulation

Following this rationale, a study is being conducted to evaluate the rate of neuronal lipofuscin accumulation in several groups of rats exposed to various dietary regimens. Lipofuscin accumulation is used as an index of neuronal senescence. Age-related increases in neuronal lipofuscin have been reported in man (Samorajski, 1964), dogs, pigs (Whiteford and Getty, 1966), and rodents (e.g., Reichel, Hollander, Clark, and Strehler, 1968). Although the etiology of lipofuscin is not proven, several reports link its appearance to lysosomal autophagotic activity (Freide, 1962; Gopinath and Glees, 1974). Whatever the basis for lipofuscin accumulation, there is good agreement that it correlates well with aging (*op. cit.*).

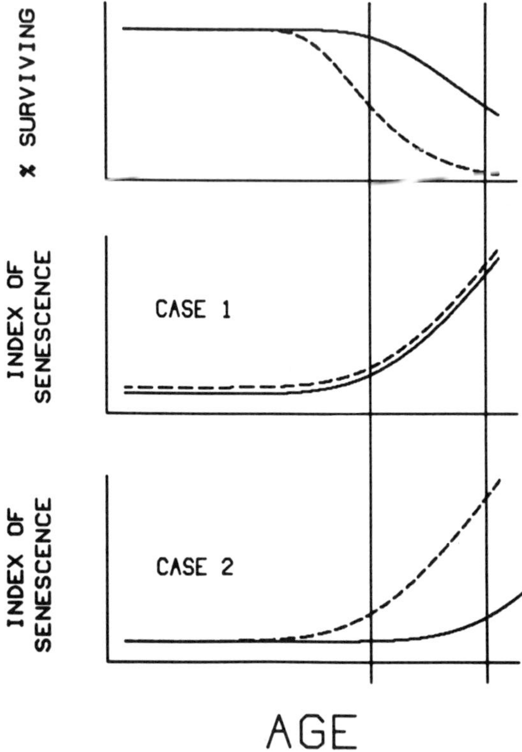

Figure 1. Diagramatic representation of two hypotheses regarding the relationship between restriction-induced increases in longevity and the rate of physiological aging. In case 1, increased longevity is not associated with a change in the rate of aging. The value of an index of senescence is greater at the mortality age of restricted animals (solid line) than at the mortality age of unrestricted animals (dashed line). In case 2, the value of an index of senescence is the same in the two groups of animals at their respective mortality ages. The validity of the first case would imply that restricted animals are superior experimental subjects for the study of aging. Case 2 would imply that dietary restriction alters the physiological processes of aging.

Furthermore, its rate of accumulation is increased by vitamin E deficiency (Lal, Pogacar, Daly, and Puri, 1973) and decreased by centrophenoxine administration (Nandy, 1978), treatments which have been reported to aggravate and ameliorate, respectively, other signs of aging. In the present study, two dietary treatments are compared to the unrestricted condition: chronic post-weaning restriction and restriction limited to the suckling period. The former follows a method reported by Ross (1972) to produce a pronounced increase in life span and the latter tests the capacity of early undernutrition to effect aging variables.

Male Sprague-Dawley rats (Charles River COBS CD strain) subjected to one of three dietary treatments were studied. Group HH rats were reared in litters of 8 pups and given free access to standard laboratory chow (Charles River RMH 3000) following weaning at 21 days of age. Group HL rats were reared in litters of 8 and fed restricted amounts of chow following weaning. The amount of chow fed was 2 gm/day immediately following weaning, raised in steps to 7.5 gm/day over the course of 120 days. Group LH animals were reared in litters of 16 pups and fed *ad libitum* following weaning. All rats were given free access to water and were individually housed following weaning. At weaning, there were 60 rats in each group. By 660 days of age, 20 rats had been taken from each group for study. An effort was made to characterize the major pathologies affecting any rat which died of natural causes during the course of the study by post-mortem dissection and, in many cases, histological evaluation of various tissues.

Group mean body weights to 750 days of age are shown in Figure 2. Group LH exhibited a mean body weight deficit in comparison with HH animals of about 35% at weaning. This deficit has persisted to 750 days of age though at this time the deficit is on the order of 16%. Group HL achieved a maximal body weight of about 200 gm at 350 days of age

Figure 2.

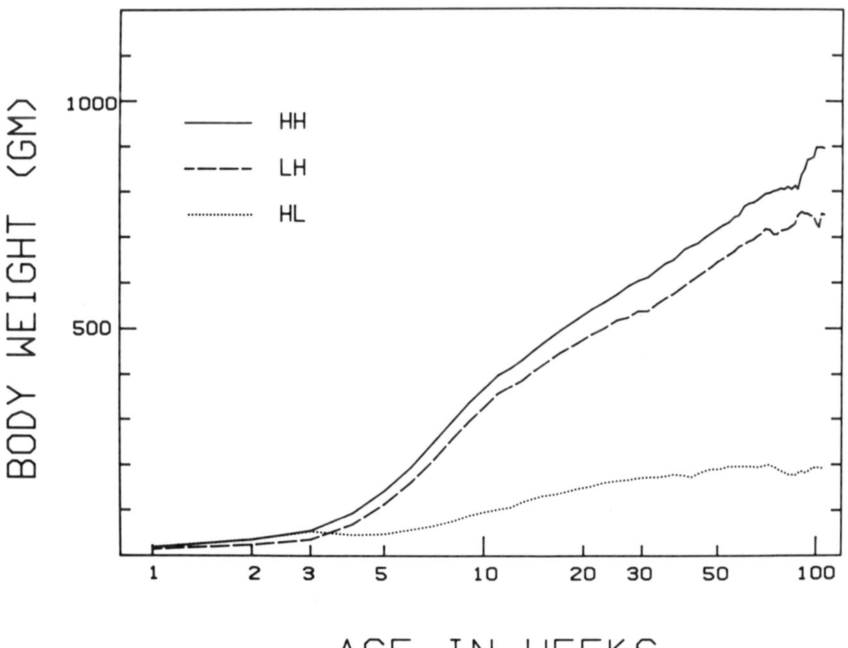

following which no major changes in group mean body weight have been observed.

Life table analysis has been performed using modifications of the methods described by Dublin, Lotka, and Spiegelman (1949). As anticipated, group HL has exhibited a much lower mortality rate than the *ad libitum* fed control group. At present (750 days of age), percent mortality for groups HH, LH, and HL stands at 52.4%, 55.4%, and 9.2%, respectively. Of the 4 HL animals dying of natural causes, 1 suffered an apparent inborn error of metabolism resulting in extreme renal calcification and kidney failure, while 3 exhibited hind limb paralysis. No signs of neoplastic lesions were seen in these animals. In groups HH and LH, 18 and 22 rats have died of natural causes, respectively. Of these, 13 HH and 7 LH animals have exhibited neoplastic lesions. Other major pathologies seen in these two groups include adrenal pheochromocytoma, proliferative periarteritis nodosa, glomerulonephritis, arterial sclerosis, and right side failure of the heart.

At 220 days of age, 10 animals from each group were sacrificed for analysis of lipofuscin accumulation. Each rat was anesthetized with pentobarbital and perfused intracardially first with saline and then with 20% neutral buffered formalin. The brains were removed, infiltrated with paraffin, embedded and sectioned at 6 microns. Unstained sections were mounted in a low-fluorescence medium and examined, using a Zeiss universal microscope equipped with mercury vapor and tungsten light sources, epifluorescence unit, phase contrast condenser, and 100X neofluar oil immersion phase objective. In the epifluorescence unit, a BP 390-440 transmitting filter and an LP 475 barrier filter were employed. In the eyepiece was mounted a 21 × 21 grid reticle which, at a total magnification of 1562×, had an apparent distance of 3.9 microns between adjacent grid intersections. A point counting technique similar to that employed by Riga and Riga (1974) was employed to quantify perikaryal and lipofuscin volume in 20 cerebellar purkinje cells from each brain. The procedure for making these determinations was as follows: using phase contrast elements, the most dorsal portion of the vermian purkinje cell layer was centered in the field of view. The purkinje cell layer was tracked in one direction until a purkinje cell with a nucleolus in the plane of section and clearly discriminable cell boundary was encountered. The first 20 cells encountered which met these criteria were studied. For each cell, the number of grid intersections lying over the perikaryon was determined. The light beam through the phase condenser was then interrupted to enable visualization of autofluorescent lipofuscin granules. Focus was adjusted to maximize the amount of pigment in sharp focus within the cell and the number of grid intersections overlying sharply focussed pigment granules was determined. Subsequently, the lipofuscin/

cell ratio was computed to yield an estimate of the proportion of cell perikaryal volume occupied by pigment granules.

There were no significant differences in group mean values of the cell volume index (Figure 3), although group LH animals tended to have smaller purkinje cell perikaryal volumes than either of the other two dietary treatment groups. Lipofuscin indicates for the three groups are shown in Figure 4, expressed as group mean counts per cell. Both groups HL and LH exhibited values of this index slightly lower than group HH but the difference was statistically significant only in the LH group (one-tailed t test; $p < .05$). However, if the data are expressed in terms of lipofuscin counts per cell volume (Figure 5), none of the group differences are statistically reliable.

This indicates that the proportion of purkinje cell perikaryal volume occupied by pigment granules is not affected by dietary treatment.

These data may be interpreted as a preliminary indication that lipofuscin accumulation occurs at a normal or near normal rate in animals

Figure 3. Average number (± s.e.m.) of grid intersections overlying cerebellar purkinje cell perikarya in the three dietary treatment groups.

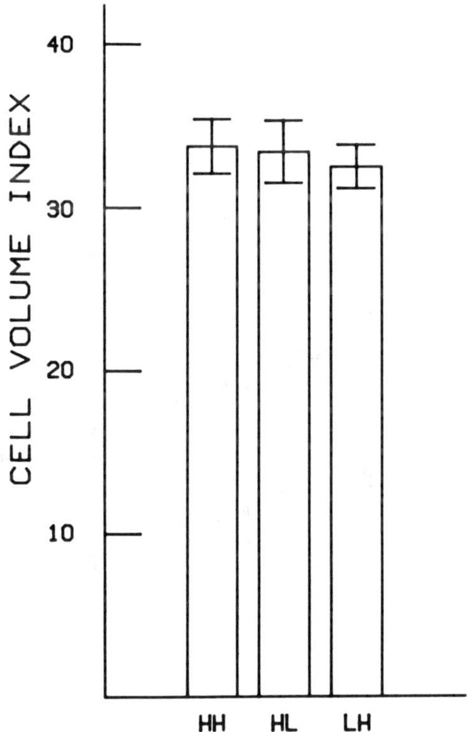

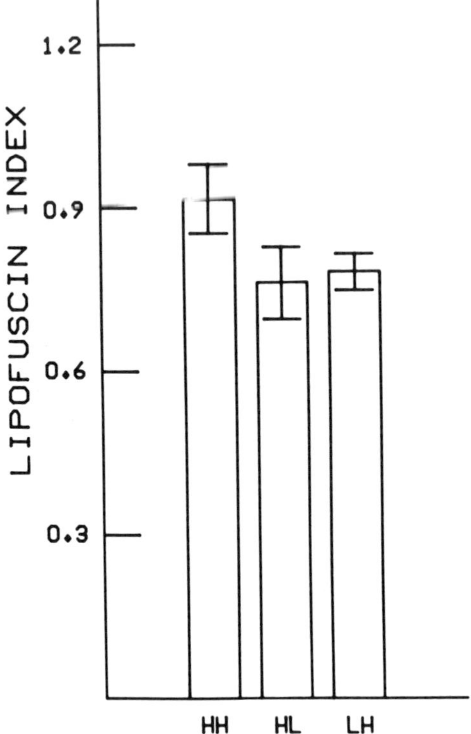

Figure 4. Average number (± s.e.m.) of grid intersections overlying intracellular lipofuscin granules in a single purkinje cell for the three dietary treatment groups.

subjected to a longevity-promoting restricted dietary regimen. Sharma and Manocha (1977; Manocha and Sharma, 1978) have reported that maternal protein malnutrition results in an increase in neuronal lipofuscin in fetal and neonatal squirrel monkeys. They also report (Manocha and Sharma, 1977) that lipofuscin accumulation resulting from pre-natal malnutrition is partially reversible by feeding an adequate diet post-natally. As cited above, the dietary treatments imposed in these studies would be expected to produce minimal effects on life expectancy. In contrast, Sohal and Donato (1978) reported that a longevity promoting treatment (restriction of flight activity) produced a decrease in lipofuscin accumulation in the housefly. However, the present results suggest that enhanced longevity due to dietary restriction may not be associated with any change in the rate of lipofuscin accumulation. Taken together, these data suggest that the effect of any given treatment on lipofuscin accumulation is not dependent upon the effect of that treatment on life span.

In material from older animals currently being studied, it may be found

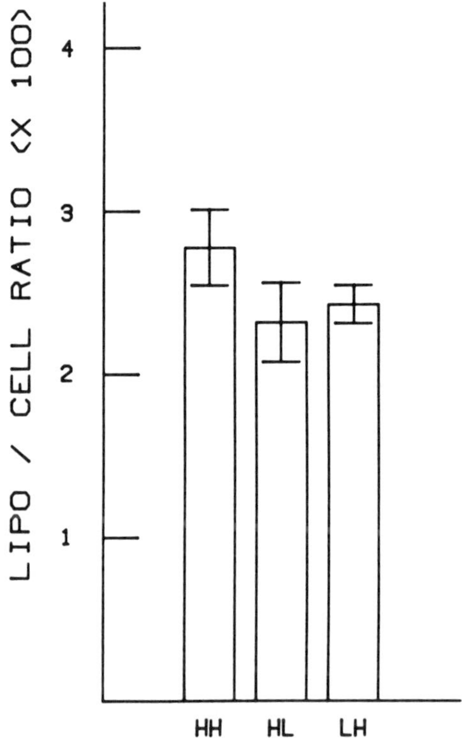

Figure 5. Average (± s.e.m.) percentage of purkinje cell volume occupied by lipofuscin granules in the three dietary treatment groups.

that the slight, statistically insignificant reductions in lipofuscin content associated with dietary restriction are greater in older animals by virtue of the cumulative nature of the process. However, if lipofuscin accumulation is a roughly linear function of age, as has been suggested, the present data indicate that the degree of reduction is not proportional to the anticipated increase in life span—about 150%. If it were, one would expect a 33% reduction in lipofuscin levels in HL rats compared to HH animals at any age. Should it prove to be the case that lipofuscin accumulates at a normal rate in chronically restricted rats, restricted rats would be expected to exhibit 50% higher levels of lipofuscin in cerebellar purkinje cells at the end of their (average) lives than *ad libitum* fed rats by virtue of their greater life span. In that case, significant functional consequences of neuronal lipofuscin accumulation might be observed which do not appear in *ad libitum* fed animals dying at younger ages. Thus, as illustrated diagramatically in Figure 1, the restricted rat may be a superior model for the study of senescent change, at least with respect to lipofuscin accumulation.

Summary and Conclusions

There is clear evidence that dietary restriction can produce pronounced increases in the longevity of laboratory animals. The efficacy of a particular restricted regimen in increasing life span is dependent on several factors, among which are the degree and duration of the restriction, period of development in which the restriction is imposed and the classes of nutrients to which access is limited. Based upon currently available data, it is unclear whether increased longevity associated with dietary restriction is synonymous with, or accompanied by, a decrease in the rate of physiological aging. Preliminary results of an experiment designed to evaluate the rate of neural lipofuscin accumulation under three dietary treatment conditions are described. Based upon the results obtained to date, it appears that the rate of lipofuscin accumulation is not affected by dietary restriction proportionally to the anticipated effect of the restriction on life span. It is concluded that the restricted rat may serve as a superior model for the study of senescent changes by virtue of its greater longevity.

References

Barrows CH: Nutrition, aging and senetic program. *Am J Clin Nutr* 25:829–833, 1972.

Barrows CH: The challenge—mechanisms of biological aging. *Gerontologist* 11:5–11, 1971.

Barrows CH, Kokkonen G: Protein synthesis, development, growth and life span. *Growth* 39:525–533, 1975.

Barrows CH, Kokkonen GC: Diet and life extension in animal model systems. *Age* 1:131–143, 1978.

Berg BN, Simms HS: Nutrition and longevity in the rat. II. Longevity and onset of disease with different levels of food intake. *J Nutr* 71:255–263, 1960.

Bras G: Age-associated kidney lesions in the rat. *J Infect Dis* 120:131–135, 1969.

Bun-Hoi NP, Ratsimamanga AR: Age retardation in the rat by nordihydroguaiaretic acid. *C r Seanc Soc Biol* 153:1180–1182, 1959.

Chow BF, Lee CJ: Effect of dietary restriction of pregnant rats on body weight gain of the offspring. *J Nutr* 82:10–18, 1964.

Comfort, A: Effect of delayed and resumed growth on the longevity of a fish (*Lebistes Reticulatus, Peters*) in captivity. *Gerontologia* 8:150–155, 1963.

Dublin LI, Lotka AJ, Spiegelman M: *Length of Life*. New York, Ronald, 1949.

Fanestil DD, Barrows CH: Aging in the rotifer. *J Gerontol* 20:462–469, 1965.

Fernandes G, Yunis EJ, Good RA: Influence of diet on survival of mice. *Proc Nat Acad Sci* 73:1279–1283, 1976.

Freide RL: The relation of the formation of lipofuscin to the distribution of oxidative enzymes in the human brain. *Acta Neuropathol* 2:113–125, 1962.

Gerbase-DeLima M, Liu R, Cheney K, Mickey R, Walford R: Immune function and survival in a long-lived mouse strain subjected to undernutrition. *Gerontol* 21:184–202, 1975.

Goodrick CL: Body weight change over the life span and longevity for C57B1 6J mice and mutations which differ in maximal body weight. *Gerontology* 23:405–413, 1977.

Goodrick CL: Body weight increment and length of life: the effect of genetic constitution and dietary protein. *J Gerontol* 33:184–190, 1978.

Goodrick CL: The effects of dietary protein upon growth of inbred and hybrid mice. *Growth* 37:355–367, 1973.

Gopinath G, Glees P: Mitochondrial genesis of lipofuscin in the mesencephalic nucleus of the V nerve of aged rats. *Acta Anat* 89:14–20, 1974.

Harman D: Aging: a theory based on free radical and radiation chemistry. *J Gerontol* 11:298–300, 1956.

Harman D: Free radical theory of aging: effect of dietary protein on mortality rate. *Proc 8th Intern Congr Gerontol* 2:11, 1969.

Harman D: Free radical theory of aging: effect of free radical reaction inhibitors on the mortality rate of male LAF1 mice. *J Gerontol* 23:476–482, 1968.

Ingle E, Wood TR, Banta AM: A study of longevity, growth, reproduction and heart rate in *Daphnia longispina* as influenced by limitations in quantity of food. *J Exp Zool* 32:5–352, 1937 (76).

Lal H, Pogacar S, Daly P, Puri S: Behavioral and neuropathological manifestations of nutritionally induced central nervous system "aging" in the rat. *Prog Brain Res* 40:129–140, 1973.

Leto S, Kokkonen GC, Barrows CH: Dietary protein, life span, and biochemical variables in female mice. *J Gerontol* 31:144–148, 1976.

Loeb J, Northrop JH: On the influence of food and temperature upon the duration of life. *J Biol Chem* 32:103–121, 1917.

Manocha SL, Sharma SP: Lipofuscin accumulation in squirrel monkey spinal cord consequent to protein malnutrition during gestation. *Experientia* 34:377–378, 1978.

Manocha SL, Sharma SP: Reversibility of lipofuscin accumulation caused by protein malnutrition in the motor cortex of squirrel monkeys, *Saimiri scireus. Acta Histochem* 58:219–231, 1977.

McCay CM, Crowell MF, Maynard LA: The effect of retarded growth upon the length of life span and upon the ultimate body size. *J Nutr* 10:63–79, 1935.

McCay CM, Maynard LA, Sperling G, Barnes LL: Retarded growth, life span, ultimate body size and age changes in the albino rat after feeding diets restricted in calories. *J Nutr* 18:1–13, 1939.

McCay CM, Sperling G, Barnes LL: Growth, aging, chronic diseases, and life span in rats. *Arch Biochem* 2:469–479, 1943.

Nakagawa I, Sasaki A, Kajimoto M, Fukuyama T, Suzuki T, Yamada E: Effect of protein nutrition on growth, longevity and incidence of lesions in the rat. *J Nutr* 104:1576–1583, 1974.

Nandy K: Lipofuscinogenesis in mice early treated with centrophenoxine. *Mech Age Devel* 8:131–138, 1978.

Nolen G: Effect of various restricted regimens on the growth, health and longevity of albino rats. *J Nutr* 102:1477–1494, 1972.

Reichel W, Hollander J, Clark JH, Strehler BL: Lipofuscin pigment accumulation as a function of age and distribution in rodent brain. *J Gerontol* 23:71–78, 1968.

Riga S, Riga D: Effects of centrophenoxine on the lipofuscin pigments in the nervous system of old rats. *Brain Res* 72:265–275, 1974.

Roeder LM, Chow BF: Maternal undernutrition and its long-term effects on the offspring. *Am J Clin Nutr* 25:812–821, 1972.

Ross MH: Aging, nutrition and hepatic enzyme patterns in the rat. *J Nutr* 97:563–602, 1969.

Ross MH: Length of life and caloric intake. *Am J Clin Nutr* 25:834–838, 1972.

Ross MH: Length of life and nutrition in the rat. *J Nutr* 75:197–210, 1961

Ross MH, Bras G: Food preference and length of life. *Science* 190:165–167, 1975.

Samorajski T, Keith JR, Ordy JM: Intracellular localization of lipofuscin age pigments in the nervous system. *J Gerontol* 19:262–276, 1964.

Saxton JA, Boon MC, Furth J: Observations on the inhibition of spontaneous leukemia in mice by underfeeding. *Cancer Res* 4:401–409, 1944.

Sharma SP, Manocha SL: Lipofuscin formation in the developing nervous system of squirrel monkeys consequent to maternal dietary protein deficiency during gestation. *Mech Age Devel* 6:1–14, 1977.

Sohal RS, Donato H: Effects of experimentally altered life spans on the accumulation of fluorescent age pigment in the housefly, *Musca domestica*. *Exp Gerontol* 13:335–341, 1978.

Stephan J, Chow B, Frohman L, Chow BF: Relationship of growth hormone to the growth retardation associated with maternal dietary restriction. *J Nutr* 101:1453–1458, 1971.

Stoltzner G: Effects of life-long dietary protein restriction on mortality, growth, organ weights, blood counts, liver aldolase and kidney catalase in BALB/c mice. *Growth* 41:337–348, 1977.

Tannenbaum A, Silverstone H: Nutrition in relation to cancer. *Adv Canc Res* 1:451–501, 1953. Visscher MB, Ball ZB, Barnes RH, Silversten I: The influence of caloric restriction upon the incidence of spontaneous mammary carcinoma in mice. *Surgery* 11:48–55, 1942.

Walford RL: Immunologic theory of aging: current status. *Fed Proc* 33:2020–2027, 1974.

Whiteford R, Getty R: Distribution of lipofuscin in the canine and porcine brain as related to aging. *J Gerontol* 21:31–44, 1966.

Widdowson EM, Kennedy GC: Rate of growth, mature weight and life span. *Proc Roy Soc Lond Ser B* 156:96–108, 1962.

Widdowson EM, McCance RA: A review: new thoughts on growth. *Pediat Res* 9:154–156, 1975.

Widdowson EM, McCance RA: The effect of finite periods of undernutrition at different ages on the composition and subsequent development of the rat. *Proc Roy Soc Lond Ser B* 158:329–342, 1963.

Williams JPG, Hughes PCR: Catch-up growth in rats undernourished for different periods during the suckling period. *Growth* 39:179–193, 1975.

Winick M, Noble A: Cellular responses in rats during malnutrition at various ages. *J Nutr* 89:300-306, 1966.

Stein, ed. The Psychobiology of Aging: Problems and Perspectives

Forgetting and Other Behavioral Manifestations of Aging

Henk Rigter, Joe L. Martinez, Jr.,[a] and John C. Crabbe, Jr.[b]

CNS Pharmacology Department, Scientific Development Group, Organon, Oss, The Netherlands.

Introduction

It is hoped that animal research will provide relevant models for the study of human aging. One type of deficit commonly associated with human aging is impairment of memory (Arenberg and Robertson-Tchabo, 1977; Botwinick, 1973; Craik, 1977; Drachman and Leavitt, 1972). If animal studies are to provide insight as to the nature of human age-related changes in memory, then an obvious place to start is with an accurate description of those human memory functions that decline with age. A distinction should be made between memory loss due to normal aging and age-related psychopathology of memory that may be associated with clinical conditions such as presenile and senile dementia and cerebrovascular accidents (Cronholm and Schalling, 1973). In practice, this dichotomy is difficult to make; however, most citations given in the present chapter are drawn from studies whose subjects did not have any diagnosed psychopathologies.

Old people often complain of increasing forgetfulness. Contrary to popular belief, laboratory data are taken to indicate that the magnitude of age-related impairments of memory are small under most testing conditions (Arenberg, 1973; Ford and Roth, 1977). Nevertheless, anecdotal reports of accelerated forgetting in the aged have been frequently

[a]Present address: Department of Psychology, University of California, Irvine, CA.
[b]Present address: Research Service, V.A. Medical Center, Portland, Oregon.

confirmed in experimental settings. This accelerated forgetting may be related to impaired mechanisms of consolidation (Drachman and Leavitt, 1972; Harkins et al., 1979) and/or retrieval (Arenberg, 1973; Craik, 1977; Waugh et al., 1978). In addition, aged subjects may also exhibit other memory deficits. For example, speed of retrieval declines with age (Waugh et al., 1978) and recall from short-term memory is somewhat affected in the elderly under most experimental conditions. Impairment of recall most clearly occurs when the information to be remembered exceeds the memory span and more elaborate processing, such as reorganization of the information, is required. Also, when the task requires division of attention between two or more mental operations, performance of aged subjects decreases disproportionately (Craik, 1977; Panek et al., 1978). Long-term memory appears to be somewhat more impaired in the aged than short-term memory. Results from a number of studies show that marked age decrements in long-term memory are observed under conditions of free recall (Craik, 1977; Harkins et al., 1979) and to a lesser extent when retention is assessed in tests of recognition (Harkins et al., 1979; Warrington and Sanders, 1971). The age-related decrement in long-term memory appears to be the result of accelerated forgetting but it may also arise in part from less efficient acquisition. When task difficulty is high and when elaborate encoding strategies and mnemonic mediators are called for, the elderly person is at a disadvantage (Craik, 1977).

Overall, these data led us to the conclusion that accelerated forgetting is one of the most salient features of the decline in memory functions in the elderly. Therefore, we decided to test aged rats in several tasks to determine if one or more of the tests could be used to develop a model of accelerated forgetting. The tasks we chose to employ were a multitrial maze, a swim escape, a step-up active avoidance, an acquired immobility, and an inhibitory avoidance task. Each of these will be described in more detail but, it seems that only one task, the inhibitory avoidance, serves the model of accelerated forgetting. Further, we encountered a number of performance anomalies in the aged rats, that complicate interpretations of learning abilities and/or memory processes of aged rats. The age-related performance differences that we observed seem to relate to differences in either response capacities or response repertoires which we will describe later, but first we will discuss the importance of acquisition strength in studies of memory processes.

Results from human studies have been interpreted to indicate that impaired retention scores of aged subjects may reflect either acquisition deficits or true forgetting or both. Campbell and his students have criticized earlier studies of accelerated forgetting in senescent animals for not stringently controlling for age-related differences in acquisition. This is a difficult issue; acquisition strength and degree of retention are both inferred from performance during retention tests. Therefore, acquisition deficits are not easily distinguished from retention losses. In order to explore this issue thoroughly, it would be necessary to examine the relationship between acquisition and retention strengths, both within and between several independent groups that received different degrees of training during acquisition. The cost of this strategy makes it unattractive. Alternatively, one could attempt to minimize differences in acquisition strength by training animals until a criterion of acquisition has been attained. In general, this means that animals receive training for a variable number of trials. However, the assumption that acquisition strength is identical for animals trained with different degrees of success until the same criterion has been reached, can be questioned. Measures of rate and strength of acquisition may be confounded if old and young animals respond differently to the stress of the training situation. For example, motivational levels may differ, or the training situation may be differentially stressful for old and young animals. It is well known that stress hormones, such as epinephrine and norephinephrine modulate memory consolidation (Gold and Van Bushirk, 1976). Recent evidence also suggests that peripheral catecholamine systems are significantly altered in aged rodents (Martinez et al., submitted; a). Thus, differences in the stress response of young and old animals that result from different durations of training may well produce equivalent levels of acquisition performance but have long-term consequences for post-registrational memory processes that ensue following training.

Another way to approach the problem of acquisition deficits is to use simple behavioral tasks that both old and young rats learn with equal facility. This strategy is developed from previous experiments showing that task complexity is an important determinant of acquisition impairments in both man and animals (Goodrick, 1972). There is research showing that old and young rats trained in simple one-trial tests do not exhibit performance deficits immediately afterwards and this finding is taken to suggest that the initial level of acquisition strength between old and young animals was the same (Gold and McGaugh, 1975).

Methods and Results

We will now proceed with a discussion of a few examples of possible sources of acquisition deficits in old rats. Some of these deficits are immediately apparent; others may only be detected on closer analysis.

One of our first experiments was to investigate acquisition and retention of an acquired immobility task in old and young rats. In this experimental situation, rats are placed in a water bath from which they cannot escape. In a single training session the rats learn to adopt a characteristic immobile posture (Porsolt et al., 1977). In this and all studies to be reported in the following sections we used young (2.5–5 months) and old (24–26 months) male "random" bred, barrier reared Wistar (TNO Zeist, the Netherlands) rats.

Acquired Immobility

The design of this study was as follows. Groups of young (4 months) and old (25 months) rats were given a single 5 min training session on day 1. Performance was measured by the time in seconds that the rats remained immobile during the training session. The groups were divided in half and given a 5 min retention test on either day 3 or day 7. Figure 1 shows that both old and young rats significantly improved their performance on

Figure 1. Young rats had superior performance scores in comparison to the old rats in the acquired immobility test on all of the testing days. However, both young and old rats significantly improved their performance on day 3 and day 7.

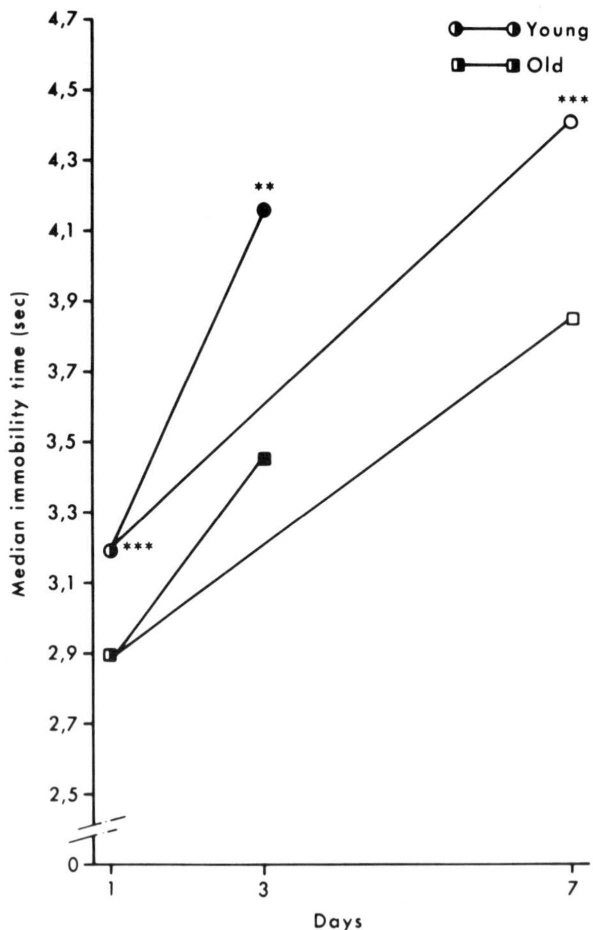

day 3 (old, $p < 0.002$; young, $p < 0.002$) and day 7 (old, $p < 0.002$; young, $p < 0.002$). In addition, the young rats had superior performance in comparison to the old rats on day 1 ($p < 0.001$), day 3 ($p < 0.01$) and day 7 ($p < 0.001$).

Our data lead us to suggest it is more difficult for old than young rats to remain immobile in a tank of water. Nevertheless, the old rats did not evidence any forgetting on day 7 and in fact significantly improved their performance over day 1. At longer acquisition-retention intervals, it is possible that forgetting might have been observed but the highly reliable differences in acquisition performance between old and young rats would complicate the interpretation of age-related changes in forgetting.

Swim Escape Task

This section presents an example of what may be a less conspicuous age-related change in acquisition strength. We found that the impaired swimming ability of old rats only manifested itself after several training trials in a swimming escape task. Thus, the use of the swim escape task as a single-trial procedure could lead to interpretative difficulties. The details of the apparatus and procedure have been described elsewhere (Martinez et al., submitted; b.). Briefly described, rats were placed in a large tub of 20°C water facing one corner. The time taken by each rat to find a vertically positioned grid in the center of the tub was recorded. Both young (5 months) and old (26 months) male Wistar rats were trained on day 1. Following this, the groups were randomly divided and half of the rats were given a retention test on day 3 and the remaining animals were tested on day 7.

Figure 2 shows that all the animals found the grid on day 1 in less than 100 sec. There were no significant differences between old and young rats in the time taken to find the grid. However, old rats took significantly longer than young animals to find the grid on day 3 ($p < 0.025$) and day 7 ($p < 0.01$). Young animals significantly improved their performance over acquisition day on day 3 ($p < 0.01$) and day 7 ($p < 0.02$). In contrast, the performance of old animals did not improve on day 3 ($p < 0.73$) and even tended to deteriorate on day 7 ($p < 0.11$). It is not clear from these data whether day 3 and day 7 performances of old rats represent forgetting or an inability to learn the task.

The following study was designed to assess the learning ability of old rats in this task. Old (26 months) and young (5 months) rats were trained as before in the swim escape task except that all rats were given a single-trial every day for 5 consecutive days. Figure 3 shows that, as before, there were no differences between old and young rats in their initial latencies to find the grid on day 1. On days 2–5, the performance of old rats was significantly poorer than that of young rats. As in the previous experiment, the old rats did not evidence any learning in only two trials.

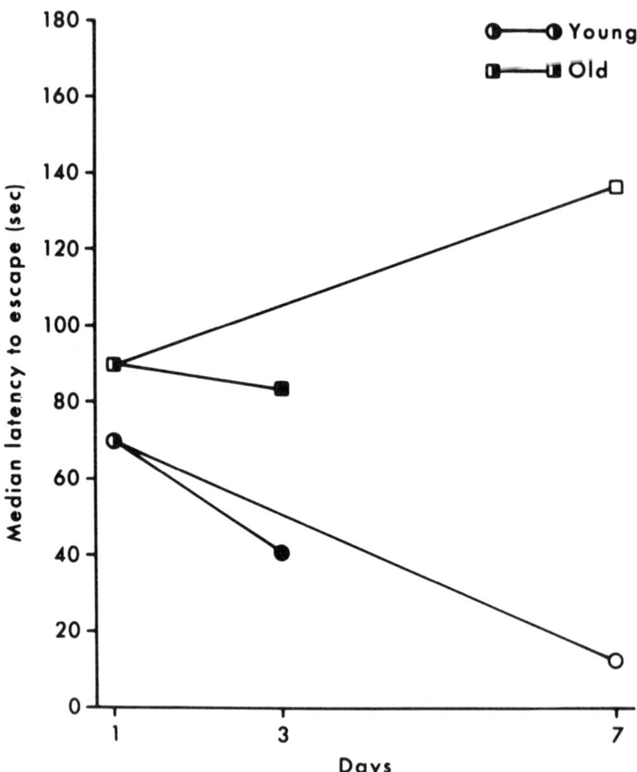

Figure 2. Old and young rats do not differ on the number of seconds taken to escape from the water tank on day 1. Young rats significantly improve their performance on day 3 and day 7. In contrast old rats do not improve on day 3 and their performance tends to deteriorate on day 7.

On the third trial, however, the old rats showed learning to a degree comparable to that of young rats on the second trial. Apparently, the old rats did not experience a general impairment of retention capacities. The results of the first swim escape experiment may suggest that the lack of improvement on day 3 and day 7 (Figure 2) was due to rapid forgetting. However, an equally likely interpretation suggested by the second experiment is that the old animals were deficient in their level of initial acquisition strength. We attempted to answer these questions in additional experiments, using massed trials on the acquisition day, but the old rats were physically incapable of performing two consecutive trials.

Another behavioral determinant of performance differences between

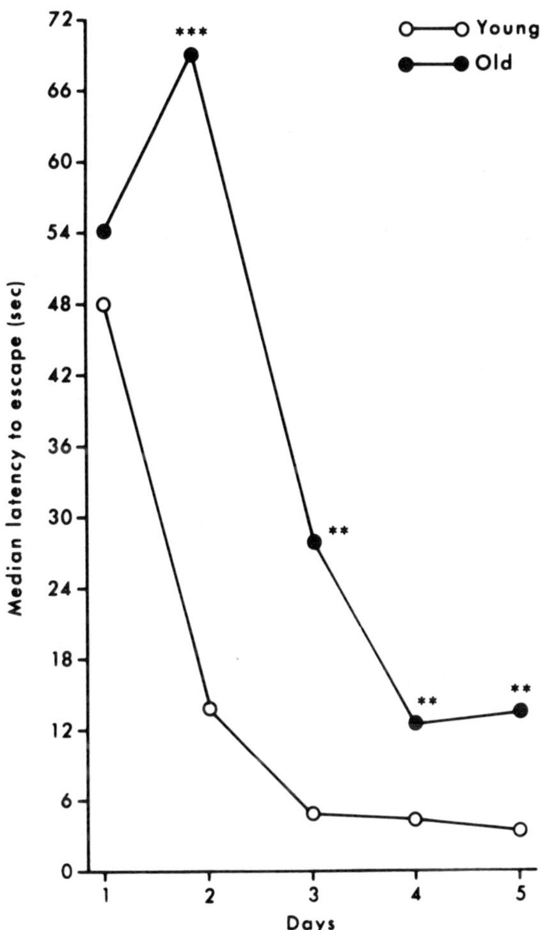

Figure 3. Old and young rats do not differ on the number of seconds taken to escape from the water tank on day 1 (see also Figure 2). However, the performance of young rats is significantly better than old rats on days 2–5. Note that old rats do not evidence any learning until day 3.

old and young rats are changes in their response repertoires. For example, the concept of perseveration has been frequently used to describe performance deficits following limbic system injury (McCleary, 1966). This term is still used to describe the tendency of subjects to persist in a dominant behavioral response. A weakness of the concept is that it often fails to specify which behavior is dominant, and therefore, which will be perseverated. However, our purpose is to emphasize that there are age-related performance differences between young and old rats in a repeated behavior that is not clearly related to a memory function. Within this context, the term perseveration is used in a descriptive sense.

Step-up Active Avoidance

The details of the step-up active avoidance apparatus and procedures have been described in detail by Rigter et al. (submitted). Briefly, rats are placed in a large open box and given 10 sec to either escape or avoid a footshock by finding and climbing onto a small platform.

In our initial experiment, the platform was placed in the middle of the open box and both old and young rats were given ten acquisition trials. This procedure yields highly reliable differences between old (25 months) and young (4 months) rats in the number of avoidances that they make during the training session (old $\overline{X}$ =0.38, SEM ± 0.38; young $\overline{X}$ = 2.88, SEM ± 0.87, $p < 0.01$). In fact, only one old rat avoided at all.

We were puzzled by this finding since others reported that old F344 rats were not impaired in their acquisition of a one way active avoidance task or were even superior to young rats in some instances (Jensen et al., in press). It seemed likely that the different results observed in our study and that of Jensen et al. were due to our use of a large open box. In our study, the old rats hugged the walls of the apparatus and did not readily venture out to the middle as did young rats. Therefore, this perseverative behavior interfered with rapid acquisition of the step-up response.

In the next study we placed the platform in either of two corners and again measured the acquisition rate of old and young rats. In all other respects this study was exactly like the previous one, except that the animals were trained to a criterion of two consecutive avoidances or to a maximum of 10 trials whichever occurred first. Rats not reaching criterion performance in 10 trials were assigned a score of 11. Table 1 shows that under these experimental conditions there are no differences in the number of trials needed by old and young rats to attain criterion performance.

Table 1. Number of Trials Needed by Old and Young Wistar Rats to Achieve Criterion Performance in a Step-up Active Avoidance Task

	Old	Young
Corner 1	8.86 ± 1.03[a]	7.10 ± 0.96
Corner 2	6.00 ± 0.76	7.00 ± 0.82

[a] $\overline{X}$ ± SEM; n = at least 7 per group.

The results of these two studies indicate that old (25 months) rats learn the step-up active avoidance task as readily as young (4 months) rats, if the platform is placed in a corner rather than the middle of the box. The perseverative tendency of old rats to stay close to the walls of the apparatus greatly influences the nature of acquisition performance. Therefore, if the behavioral strategy of the old rat fits well with the behavioral requirements of the task, then the old rat will not show an acquisition deficit. Should the opposite be true, then the old rat may show an acquisition deficit and may even appear incapable of learning the task.

Appetitive Maze Task

The previous experiments using a step-up active avoidance response demonstrated that a persistent behavioral response may influence acquisition performance in old rats. In this experiment we will show that confounding performance factors may also be operational during retention testing. In addition, we will show that this age-related performance deficit in old subjects may be reversed by treatment with an ACTH-like peptide.

ACTH-like peptides are known to improve performance of rats at retention tests, possibly by influencing attention or motivational functions (Rigter and Crabbe, 1979; De Wied, 1976; Sandman and Kastin, 1977). We examined the efficacy of one such peptide to ameliorate long-term retention of a maze problem in old rats. The peptide used was an ACTH-4-9 analog (Org 2766) that has a profile of behavioral activity similar to the parent hormone but enhanced potency (Greven and De Wied, 1973; Rigter et al., 1976).

Food-deprived young (2.5 months old) and old (24 months old) male Wistar rats were trained to traverse a maze with 5 choice points in order to obtain 5 food pellets at the end of the maze (goal section). There was only one correct route from start to goal section. Entries in cul-de-sacs were recorded as errors. Animals were trained on 2 trials each day until the criterion was attained which was a maximum of 1 error during 2 subsequent trials. One week after reaching criterion, retention was tested on 4 trials at 10-minute intertrial intervals. Rats were matched in pairs within age groups on the basis of performance during acquisition. One rat of each pair was given 0.1 μg/rat Org 2766, and the other placebo. Treatments were administered subcutaneously 1 hour before the first retention trial. All rats were food deprived for 23¼ hours each day for the duration of the experiment.

Table 2 shows that old rats did not differ from young rats on either acquisition performance or retention performance on the first retention trial. Old placebo-treated animals made most of their errors during the remaining retention trials, and it is on these later trials that the ameliorative effect of Org 2766 emerges. Thus, the inferior retention performance of old rats on later retention trials is not easily explained by either acquisition, memory or retrieval failures, since acquisition performance and retention on the first trial were the same for old and young rats. In a general way the tendency of old rats to enter cul-de-sacs on later retention trials may be described as perseverative behavior. However, as noted earlier, this is at best a *post hoc* descriptive analysis, because if old rats had persevered during their first trial it would have been expected that fewer errors would have been seen on later trials. The important point is that what seems to be a loss of retention in old subjects may in fact be something else on closer analysis. The data indicate that this particular behavioral deficit observed in aged rats may be reversed by pharmacological treatment.

Overall, we feel that the step-up active avoidance, acquired immobility, swim escape and the appetitively motivated maze tasks do not lend themselves to an analysis of forgetting in aged rodents because of confounding by various performance problems. However, the inhibitory avoidance task seems ideally suited for this purpose and we will now describe data demonstrating accelerated forgetting of this task in old rats.

Inhibitory Avoidance

Several investigators have reported that old rats forget an inhibitory avoidance response faster than young rats. Gold and McGaugh (1975), Ordy et al. (1972) and Brizzee and Ordy (1979) all reported that old F344 rats (2 years or older) exhibit impaired retention of an inhibitory avoidance response as soon as 6 hours following training. Importantly, in

Table 2. Retention of a Maze Habit in Old and Young Wistar Rats Treated with Placebo or an ACTH 4-9 Analog (Org 2766)

	Acquisition Scores		Retention Scores	
	Trials to Criterion[a]	Errors to Criterion[a]	First Trial Errors	Total Errors[b]
Old rats, placebo	15.3 ± 1.7	46.8 ± 7.5	1.0 ± 0.4	6.8 ± 0.9
Old rats, Org 2766	15.0 ± 1.2	42.2 ± 7.8	0.7 ± 0.2	3.8 ± 0.6
Young rats, placebo	13.1 ± 1.9	36.4 ± 7.3	0.9 ± 0.3	3.9 ± 1.2
Young rats, Org 2766	12.6 ± 1.5	32.7 ± 6.5	0.6 ± 0.2	2.1 ± 0.6

Values given are $\bar{X}$ ± SEM. Six rats in each old group; seven rats in each young group.

[a] Pooled old versus pooled young rats: no significant difference.

[b] Difference between placebo-treated young and old groups: $p < 0.05$ (Mann-Whitney U test). Difference between the placebo- and peptide-treated old groups: $p < 0.05$ (Wilcoxon Matched-Pairs Signed-Ranks Test).

these studies young and old rats did not seem to differ in their initial levels of acquisition strength measured by retention tests given 0–2 hours following training. In contrast to these findings McNamara et al. (1977) reported that aged Sprague-Dagley rats exhibited inferior retention of an inhibitory avoidance response in comparison to young rats both 2 min and 30 days following training. However, these Sprague-Dawley rats were not barrier-reared and the contribution of disease processes to the results is unknown. Strain differences could also be important. Nevertheless, it is clear that significant retention deficits are manifest within hours following training.

The present study was undertaken to determine if a "random" bred strain of barrier-reared old male Wistar rats would show the same accelerated forgetting as the inbred F344 strain. The inhibitory avoidance apparatus (Rigter et al., 1974) and procedure (Martinez et al., submitted; b) have been described in detail elsewhere. Briefly stated, naive rats 3 and 24 months of age were trained in a one-trial inhibitory avoidance step-through task. Each animal was placed on a pedestal facing away from a large darkened shock chamber. Upon turning around, the animal was allowed to step through, the door was closed and the animal received an inescapable 600 μA, 3 sec footshock. The latency to step through on the training trial was recorded for each animal. For the retention test, rats were placed on the pedestal either 1, 7 or 22 days following training. The latency of the animal to step-through on the testing day was taken as a measure of retention.

The results of this experiment may be found in Figure 4. A comparison of retention latencies of young and old rats 1 day following training shows that they did not differ and that their initial levels of acquisition strength were roughly equivalent. Retention performance for both young and old rats was still high 3 days following training. That young and old rats did not differ either 1 or 3 days after training supports the interpretation that there were no differences in acquisition strength.

Figure 4 also shows that aged rats exhibit accelerated forgetting. Retention performance of old rats at the 22 day interval was significantly ($p < 0.01$) poorer than that of the group of old rats tested 1 day after training. Also, old rats were inferior in their performance to young rats ($p < 0.05$, one-tailed) at this long training-testing interval. Even though the retention performance of young rats decreased at the 22 day interval, it was not significantly reduced over retention measured at 1 day.

Finally, we do not believe that our observation of accelerated forgetting in aged rats is related to age-related differences in either locomotor activity or shock sensitivity. First, there were no differences in the initial step-through entrance latencies of young and old rats, and second, flinch and jump thresholds for old and young Wister rats do not differ (Rigter, unpublished observations).

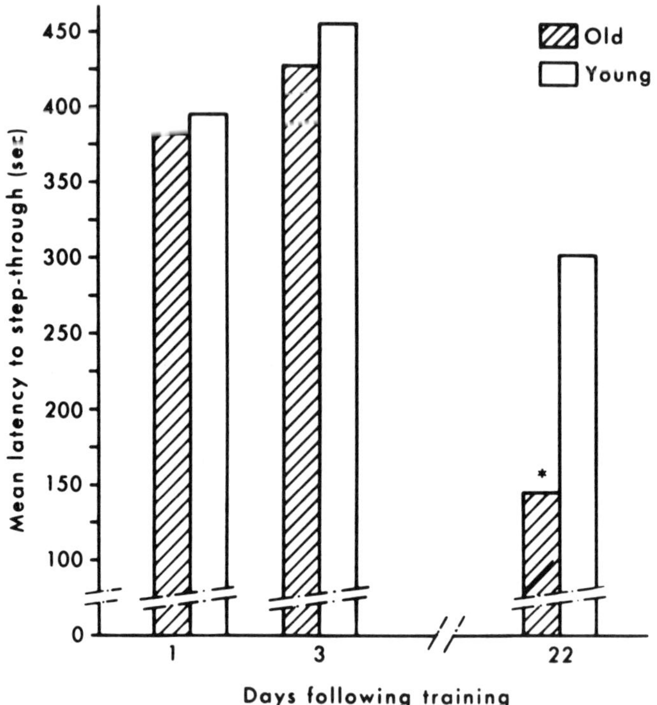

Figure 4. Retention latencies of old and young rats do not differ 1 or 3 days following training in an inhibitory avoidance task. However, 22 days following training the old rats exhibit significant forgetting. The group of old rats tested at the 22-day interval have significantly lower retention latencies than both the old rats tested 1 day and young rats tested 22 days following training.

These findings replicate and extend the earlier work of Gold and McGaugh (1975) and McNamara et al. (1977) showing that aged rats exhibit accelerated forgetting of an inhibitory avoidance response. The present results were obtained in a "random" bred Wistar strain which suggests that this phenomenon of accelerated forgetting is not limited to a particular strain.

Discussion and Conclusions

In general, the learning and memory processes of aged rats seem relatively normal if one compares the performance of young and old rats in a variety of learning situations. Nevertheless, old rats, like humans, exhibit accelerated forgetting under appropriate testing conditions. In spite of the methodological difficulties inherent in this kind of research, it appears worthwhile to explore further the retention capacities of old rats in order to develop animal models for the study of age-related alterations of memory in man. Lest our terminology should cause confusion, it should be noted that the retention deficits we have assessed in old rats may be either due to forgetting that starts sooner after training, yet proceeds at a rate similar to forgetting by young rats, or to a more rapid rate of forgetting in old rats.

We would also like to comment on two additional methodological issues that specifically relate to the data reported in this chapter. One point of concern is the question of how old the 24–26 month Wistar rats are in terms of brain aging. Although, in absolute terms, their age is comparable with that of senescent F344 rats used in many behavioral studies (Brizzee and Ordy, 1979; Campbell et al., this volume; Jensen et al., 1980), they may be relatively younger. According to data on the life span of male F344 rats, the median or 50% mortality point occurs at 22 months (Chesky and Rockstein, 1975). Median mortality for our male or female Wistar rats is 28 months (Rigter, unpublished data).

A second methodological issue concerns the use of more than two age groups. We agree that studies of aging should not only use "young" and "old" animals, but should also include groups of intermediate age, so that a more accurate assessment of progressive developmental changes is possible. However, the costs of such studies led us to adopt the strategy of comparing young and old rats in a variety of tests before repeating crucial tests with more age groups.

Finally, we would conclude by stressing the importance of determining the generality of accelerated forgetting phenomenon in aged rats in a number of different behavioral situations. It has been proposed that old rats exhibit rapid forgetting for one-time only events, such as those studied in the inhibitory avoidance task (Jensen et al., in press). Indeed, there are data which indicate that, in old rats, multitrial learning experiences are more resistant to memory loss than one-trial experiences (Jensen et al., in press; Campbell et al., this volume). However, whether or not accelerated forgetting is observed in aged rats is most likely related to the initial level of acquisition strength. If a one-trial experience is very salient, it may be very difficult to find evidence of accelerated forgetting. Accordingly, we found that retention of a conditioned taste aversion, a one-trial learning experience, was not impaired in old rats 6 weeks after initial training (Martinez et al., submitted; b). In summary, there is no *a priori* reason to expect old rats to be more forgetful than young rats at any given acquisition-retention interval. Finally, whether or not accelerated forgetting will be observed is dependent on the behavioral requirements of the task and is most likely related to the initial level of acquisition strength.

References

Arenberg D: Cognition and Aging: Verbal learning, memory, and problem solving. In Eisdorfer C, Lawton MP (eds.) *The Psychology of Adult Development and Aging*. Washington, American Psychological Association, 1973.

Arenberg D, Robertson-Tchabo EA: Learning and aging. In Birren JE, Schaie KW (eds.) *Handbook of the Psychology of Aging*. New York, Van Nostrand Reinhold Co., 1977.

Botwinick J: *Aging and Behavior*. New York, Springer, 1973.

Brizzee KR, Ordy JM: Age pigments, cell loss and hippocampal function. *Mechanisms of Aging and Development* 9:143–162, 1979.

Chesky J, Rockstein M: Survival data for a colony of male Fischer rats. *Gerontologist* 15:29, 1975.

Craik FIM: Age differences in human memory. In Birren JE, Schaie KW (eds.) *Handbook of the Psychology of Aging*. New York, Van Nostrand Reinhold Co., 1977.

Cronholm B, Schalling D: A study of memory in aged people. In Zippel HH (ed.) *Memory and Transfer of Information*. New York-London, Plenum Press, 1973.

De Wied D: Hormonal influences on motivation, learning, and memory processes. *Hospital Practice* January:123–131, 1976.

Drachman DA, Leavitt J: Memory impairment in the aged: storage versus retrieval deficit. *J Experimental Psychology* 93:302–308, 1972.

Ford JM, Roth WT: Do cognitive abilities decline with age? *Geriatrics* September:59–62, 1977.

Gold PE, McGaugh JL: Changes in learning and memory during aging. In Ordy JM, Brizzee KR (eds.) *Neurology of Aging*. New York, Plenum Publishing Corporation, 1975.

Gold PE, Van Buskirk RB: Effects of posttrial hormone injections on memory processes. *Hormones and Behavior* 7:509–517, 1976.

Goodrick CL: Learning by mature-young and aged Wistar rats as a function of test complexity. *J Gerontology* 27:353–357, 1972.

Goodrick CL: Behavioral rigidity as a mechanism for facilitation of problem solving for aged rats. *J Gerontology* 30:181–184, 1975.

Greven HM, De Wied D: The influence of peptides derived from corticotrophin (ACTH) on performance. Structure activity studies. In Zimmermann E, Gispen WH, Marks BH, De Wied D (eds.) *Drug Effects on Neuroendocrine Regulation, Progress in Brain Research Vol. 39*. Amsterdam, Elsevier, 1973.

Harkins SW, Chapman CR, Eisdorfer C: Memory loss and response bias in senescence. *J Gerontology* 34:66–72, 1979.

Jensen RA, Martinez Jr JL, McGaugh JL, Messing RB, Vasquez BJ: Psychobiology of aging. In Maletta GJ, Pirozzolo FJ (eds.) *The Aging Nervous System*. Praeger Publ., in press.

Martinez Jr JL, Vasquez BJ, Messing RB, Jensen RA, Liang KC, McGaugh JL: Catecholamine concentrations and levels in peripheral organs of aged male and female F344 rats. Submitted; a.

Martinez Jr JL, Rigter H, Crabbe JC: Assessment of retention capacities in old rats. Submitted; b.

McCleary RA: Response-modulating functions of the limbic system: initiation and suppression. In Stellar E, Sprague JM (eds.) *Progress in Physiological Psychology*, Vol. 1. New York, Academic Press, 1966.

McNamara MC, Benignus G, Benignus VA, Miller AT: Active and passive avoidance learning in rats as a function of age. *Experimental Aging Research* 3:3–16, 1977.

Ordy JM, Brizzee KR, Kaack B, Hansche J: Age differences in short-term memory and cell loss in the cortex of the rat. *Gerontology* 24:276–285, 1978.

Panek PE, Barrett GV, Sterns HL, Alexander RA: Age differences in perceptual style, selective attention, and perceptual-motor reaction time. *Experimental Aging Research* 4:377–387, 1978.

Porsolt RD, LePichon M, Jalfre M: Depression: a new animal model sensitive to antidepressant treatments. *Nature* 266:730–732, 1977.

Rigter H, Crabbe JC: Modulation of memory by pituitary hormones and related peptides. *Vitamins and Hormones* 37:153–241, 1979.

Rigter H, Martinez Jr J, Dekker I: Behavioral comparison of Met- and Leu-enkephalin. Submitted.

Rigter H, Popping A: Hormonal influences on the extinction of conditioned taste aversion. *Psychopharmacologia (Berl.)* 46:255–261, 1976.

Rigter H, Van Riezen H, De Wied D: The effects of ACTH- and vasopressin-analogues on CO_2-induced retrograde amnesia in rats. *Physiology and Behavior* 13:381–388, 1974.

Sandman CA, Kastin AJ: Pituitary peptide influences on attention and memory. In Drucker-Colin RR, McGaugh JL (eds.) *Neurobiology of Sleep and Memory.* New York, Academic Press, 1977.

Warrington EK, Sanders HI: The fate of old memories. *Experimental Psychology* 23:432–442, 1971.

Waugh NC, Thomas JC, Fozard JL: Retrieval time from different memory stores. *J Gerontology* 33:718–724, 1978.

Copyright 1980 by Elsevier North Holland, Inc.
Stein, ed. The Psychobiology of Aging: Problems and Perspectives

Behavioral and Biochemical Correlates of Aging in Rats[a]

Ingrid F. de Koning-Verest, Dick L. Knook, and Otto L. Wolthuis

The Medical Biological Laboratory TNO, 139, Lange Kleiweg, Rijswijk Z.H., The Netherlands; and the Institute for Experimental Gerontology TNO, 151, Lange Kleiweg, Rijswijk Z.H., The Netherlands.

Introduction

Conflicting observations have been reported with regard to age-related changes of learning and memory in rats. Some authors (Birren, 1962; Botwinick et al., 1962; Botwinick et al., 1963; Kay and Sime, 1962) did not observe age differences in learning, whereas others, who used more complex tasks (Doty, 1966; Goodrick, 1972; McNamara et al., 1977; Michel and Klein, 1978) provided evidence for the decline of learning capacity with age. In the selection of a method for studying possible deficits in old animals, it has to be taken into account that aged animals are more susceptible to interference (Dye, 1969), have a lower response speed (Birren et al., 1962) and in general, show reduced motor activity (Verzar, 1965).

The first objective was to investigate whether the small Wistar (WAG) strain we use would demonstrate acquisition deficits with aging. We attempted to select a task in which the above mentioned factors, i.e., interference, response speed and motor activity would not affect the results.

Behavioral Assays

The discrimination test chosen, the "drinktest," was based on conditioned suppression of drinking behavior, i.e., rats were trained to avoid licking a water tube when a set of signals indicated that no water would

[a]This work was supported by the Foundation for Medical Research FUNGO which is subsidized by the Netherlands organization for the advancement of Pure Research (ZWO).

be delivered. The mechanical simplicity of this task made it unlikely that age differences in motor skill or susceptibility to interference would affect the results. The training was completely automated and the animals remained in the test chamber for the entire experiment. Humans entered the rooms only twice weekly, for maintenance work.

It can be seen in Figure 1 that positively or negatively reinforced

Figure 1. Acquisition curves of small Wistar (WAG) rats of 3 age groups trained in the "drinktest."

Figure 1a. Curves of 3-month (n = 42), 12-month (n = 28) and 30-month (n = 30) old rats trained with punishment and reward.

Figure 1b. Curves of 3-month (n = 16), 12-month (n = 16), and 30-month (n = 16) old rats trained with reward only. The performance deficits of the 30-month-old rats are obvious. The results are expressed as % correct responses (correct/total). Means ± S.E.M.

NOTE: The results of these experiments and those presented in the next figures and tables were statistically analyzed by the Bonferoni Multiple t-test (Miller, 1966) modified according to Welch (1947). All testing was two-tailed as indicated by p_2.

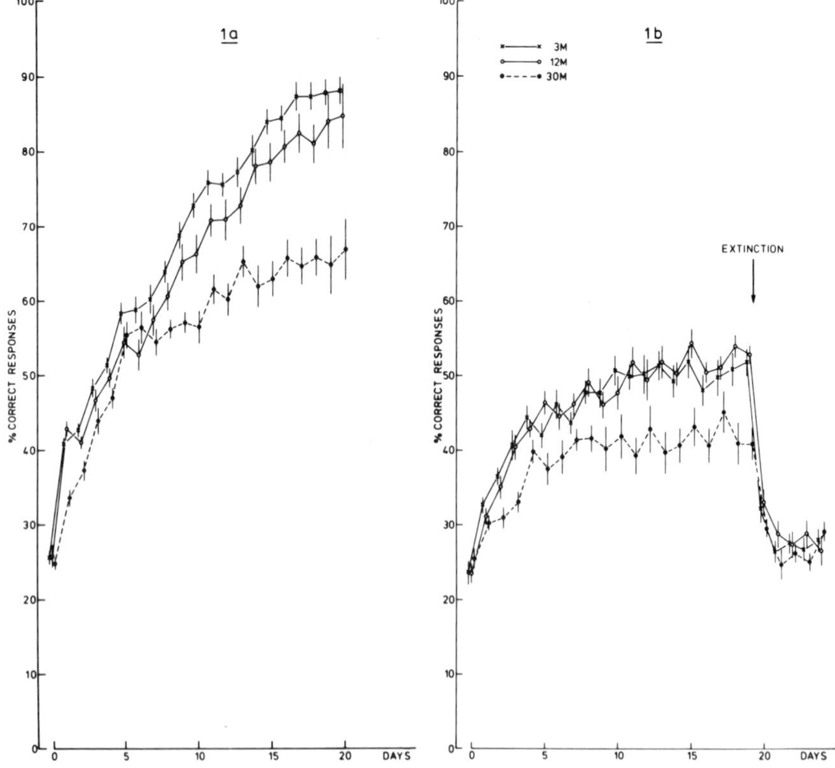

acquisition in 30-month-old female, small Wistar rats appeared to be deficient when compared with that of 3 and 12-month-old rats (Wolthuis et al., 1976). Since a simple test was used, and the deficits found were rather large, the present findings are not in accord with suggestions in the literature (Doty, 1966; Goodrick, 1972) that acquisition deficits in aged animals can best be demonstrated by using complex tasks. To see whether the acquisition deficits develop suddenly or gradually, four groups of female small Wistar rats of 12, 18, 24 or 30 months respectively were trained in the "drinktest" apparatus. Figure 2 shows that the deficits in acquisition develop gradually.

At this stage we felt it necessary to determine whether these deficits are limited to only one, perhaps peculiar, strain of rats or whether these deficits can also be found in a quite different strain. Pigmented female BN/BI rats of 3 and 30 months were trained in the "drinktest" apparatus, following a procedure that was identical to that used for the albino small Wistar rats.

When compared with the small Wistar rats, the BN/BI rats acquired the task much more slowly (Figure 3), but ultimately reached the same levels of performance. Clearly, the performance of the 30-month-old BN/BI rats also reached a plateau at a level of 65–70% correct responses, very much like the 30-month-old small Wistar rats. Independent of the speed of acquisition therefore, the acquisition deficits found in rats are obviously not limited to one strain.

When two cages, one with BN/BI and the other with small Wistar rats are placed side by side, only brief observation is required to note that the BN/BI rats are livelier and more active than the small Wistars. However, when the spontaneous motor behavior of each animal was measured individually in an automated device (Wolthuis, 1971), the activity of both the 3 and 30-month-old BN/BI rats was equivalent to that of small Wistar rats of the same age. This was in agreement with findings taken from individual animals in the "drinktest" apparatus, where the scores of the pigmented and the albino rats were approximately the same in a test situation, where the animals were not trained and were simply left to themselves. Possibly, the visually observed higher activity of the BN/BI rats does not represent a higher level of spontaneous activity *per se,* but a higher stimulus induced *re*-activity, when an observer is watching them. It is conceivable that the new environment as well as the stimuli used, such as light and sound are factors which, in view of the higher reactivity of the BN/BI rats, initially affect the acquisition rates of the BN/BI rats more than those of the small Wistar rats. In a later stage, adaptation sets in and acquisition curves start to run parallel.

To examine whether the acquisition deficits were due to differences in retention, rats of 3, 12 and 30 months of age were submitted to a passive

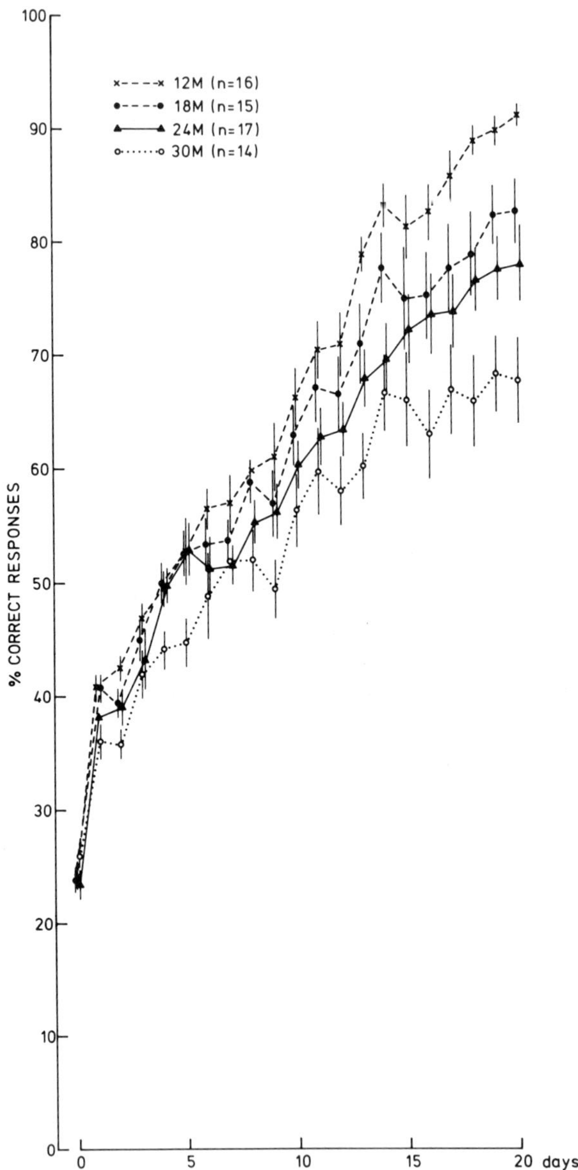

Figure 2. A comparison of acquisition of 12, 18, 24 and 30-month-old rats trained in the "drinktest." The deficits in acquisition develop gradually. The results are expressed as in Figure 1.

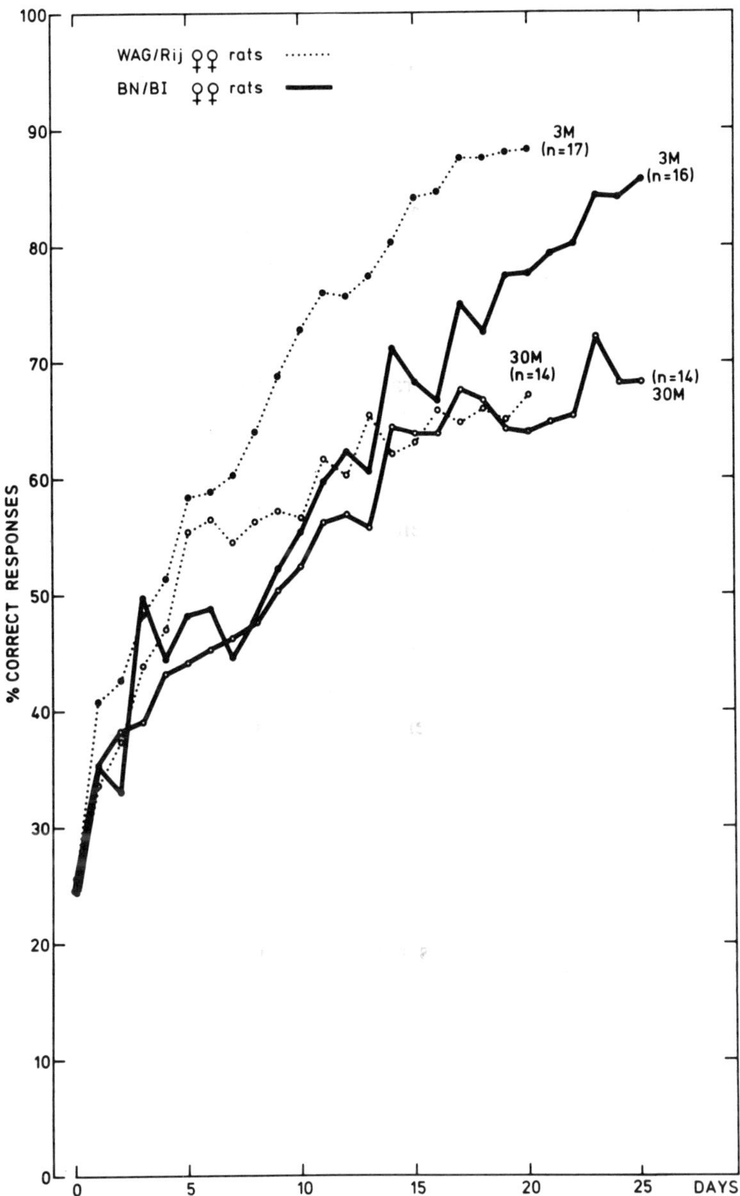

Figure 3. A comparison of acquisition of 3 and 30-month-old small Wistar (WAG) rats and 3 and 30-month-old female BN/BI rats trained in the "drinktest." The acquisition rate of the BN/BI rats appeared to be lower than that of the Wistar rats, but ultimately the BN/BI rats reached the same levels of performance. The results are expressed as mean % correct responses. For the sake of clarity the S.E.M. has been omitted in this figure.

avoidance one trial light-dark discrimination task in a two compartment apparatus consisting of a light and a dark box connected by a guillotine door. The latency time to entry of the dark compartment in which the rats had received a footshock 24 hours before, was longest in the 12-month-old rats (median latency time: 1800 sec), 1200 sec for the 30-month-old rats and 276 sec for the 3-month-old rats. After the first entry, however, the 3-month-old rats made the highest number of crossings, followed by the 12 and 30-month-old rats respectively. These differences in motor activity among the age groups confound the data and make an interpretation of the findings impossible. McNamara et al. (1977) obtained the same kind of results in a similar passive avoidance learning task: 2 min acquisition and 30 days retention were impaired in both very young (30-day) and old (547-day) rats, compared to young (180-day) and adult (365-day) rats. They suggested that incomplete brain maturation as well as senescent brain changes may be responsible for these effects. Unfortunately these authors did not take the age-related differences in motor activity into account.

The normal drinking activity of the rat is known to be maximum during the night and minimum during the day (Siegel and Stuckey, 1947). Since this basic rhythm is profoundly affected by changes in illumination schedule (Bunning, 1967), it was decided to investigate whether the speed whereby adaptation of drinking patterns occurs in reaction to reversed light-dark cycles is age-dependent. It was thought that the aged animals would adapt slower to the changed environmental stimuli and would show their "behavioral rigidity."

Three groups of 8 female Wistar rats of 3, 12 and 30 months of age respectively, were investigated. The animals were placed individually in the cages of the "drinktest" apparatus and their drinking responses were accumulated for 3 hours, 24 hours per day, during 6 days. No reinforcement was used, each lick at the water tube was recorded and resulted in the delivery of 0.25 ml of water during the following 5 seconds. During these 5 seconds, registration of further licks was blocked, thereby avoiding registration of mere licking frequencies. After these 6 days of a 12/12 hour lighting schedule switched at 7 A.M. and 7 P.M., light-dark cycles were reversed for 18 days, starting with two light periods of 12 hours in succession. At the end of these 18 days, i.e., on day 24 of the experiment, the normal 12/12 cycle (light "on" during day time) was reinstalled. At the beginning of this return to the normal rhythm, two dark periods of 12 hours followed one another. After the last reversal, the drinking activity was followed for another 10 days.

After the light-dark reversal the old (30-month) animals lagged only slightly behind the adult and the young (12 and 3-month) rats in adapting their drinking pattern (Figure 4). Similarly, return to normal lighting conditions did not result in appreciable differences between the age

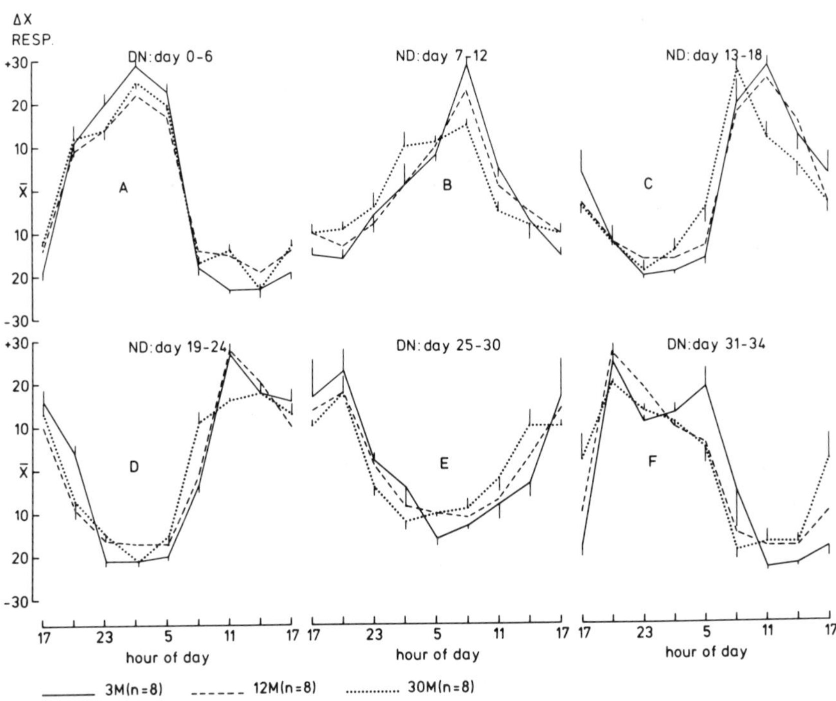

Figure 4. The shifts in the number of drink responses during the hours of the days as affected by reversed day-night illumination. The first 6 days of standard day-night (DN) lighting (curves A) were followed by 18 days of reversed (ND) lighting (curves B, C and D) and subsequently standard lighting (DN) was restored for 10 days (curves E and F). The results are expressed as the mean (± S.E.M.) differences between the actual number of responses per 3 hours and the number of responses per 3 hours when the total number of responses are averaged over 24 hours. First the mean daily changes per group were calculated and thereafter the results of 6 days were averaged. It is shown that although the cyclic curves of the old (30-month) rats tend to lag slightly during days 7–18, differences with the curves of the young and adult (3 and 12-month) rats are small. For the sake of clarity the S.E.M. of the adult rats have been omitted.

groups. The absence of a clear-cut age-difference in adapting of drinking patterns to reversal of light-dark illumination is in keeping with results on food intake obtained by Jakubczak (1975). He found that the pattern of food intake of 785-day-old rats was as adaptable to reversed light-dark illumination as food intake patterns of 220-day-old rats. It is known that water and food intake in the rat follows the same pattern (Siegel and Stuckey, 1947), although under certain experimental conditions, illumination may affect fluid intake and food intake independently (Rusak and Zucker, 1974).

Under the non-reinforced conditions of the present experiment, the daily number of drink responses of old rats was significantly greater than that of young and adult rats. The increased number of responses of the old animals is most likely due to what might be called "behavioral negligence." In fact, the shavings around the watertubes in the cages of the old rats were usually soaked with spilled water. Observations suggest that this spillage of water is the result of briefly sucking the water tube, thereby triggering the peristaltic pump and then turning away before the 5-second period of water delivery had ended.

It should be noted that all animals including the old rats, could easily fulfil their daily need of water within a period of 30 minutes, i.e., only a fraction of the day had to be spent on drinking. Therefore, it is noteworthy (see Figure 5) that in contrast to the young and adult rats, drinking patterns of the old rats, under the normal lighting conditions of the first 6 days, did not show a prolonged daily period of low or zero drinking activity as was observed in 3 and 12-month-old rats. This suggests that rest periods or sleep-wake cycles in these aged rats are altered. Changes in sleep patterns with age are well known in humans

Figure 5. The changes in drinking activity, sampled per 3 hours, of the animals before, during and after reversed day-night illumination. The drinking activity of the old (30-month) rats between the peaks does not return to low or zero responses in contrast to the responses in young (3-month) and adult (12-month) animals. This suggests that the old animals have much shorter rest or sleep periods. For further details see Figure 4.

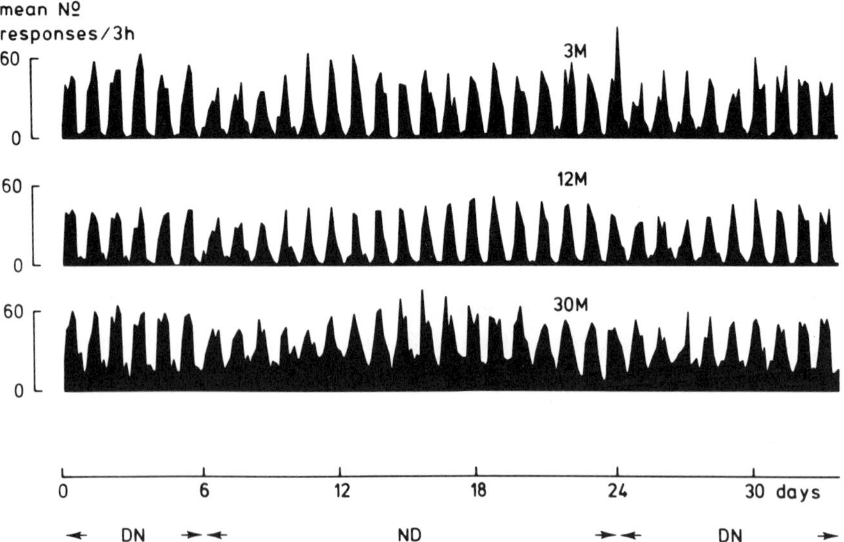

(Timiras, 1972). In rats it has been observed that animals of advanced age have a reduced sleeptime and shortened sleep bouts (Zepelin et al., 1972). Our observations are in agreement with these findings and suggest that the old animals take frequent brief naps and take short sucks at the watertube in between sleep periods.

It is possible that the performance deficits in the "drinktest," seen in 30-month-old rats are, when compared with younger rats, attributable to secondary factors, such as differences in motor activity or differences in sensitivity to footshock. Therefore, the spontaneous motor activity of animals of 3, 12 and 30 months old was measured by means of a capacitance device (Wolthuis et al., 1976) before the start of the training in the "drinktest." The device determines the magnitude of the animals' movements quantitatively and categorizes them according to amplitude. Computer processing results in six graphs which represent the changes in the number of rearings as a function of time, the percentage of time spent in an upright position, and the number of "horizontal" movements of four categories of increasing amplitudes. "Horizontal" movements of amplitude 1 consist largely of breathing, while those of amplitude 4 predominantly represent locomotion. Figure 6 shows that in several time segments, the 3-month-old rats show a significantly greater activity than the 12 and 30-month-old rats, primarily in the larger "horizontal" movements of amplitudes 2–4. The activity of the 12-month-old rats did not differ significantly from that of the old rats, except in "rearing time" during the first 16 minutes. These results are in agreement with those of Hofecker et al. (1974), who found no differences in motor activity with singly held animals of 12 and 24 months old.

Looking at the data of the acquisition and motor activity tests it can be seen 1. that spontaneous motor activity does, and acquisition does *not,* differ in 3 and 12-month-old rats, 2. that 12 and 30-month-old rats hardly differ in their spontaneous motor activity whilst their ultimately reached performance levels differ grossly and 3. that initial acquisition in the three age groups is very similar (notwithstanding differences in spontaneous motor activity). It seems reasonable to conclude at this stage that acquisition of the three age groups and their initial activity levels are not related.

Rats of 3 and 30 months old were also compared in an automated system for testing open field behavior. In principle the method consists of a video-scan of a black field, against which the albino animal is detected. The camera output signals voltages proportional to the X- and Y-coordinates of the animal (Tanger et al., 1978). As can be seen in Figure 7, the values of all parameters measured are decreased in 30-month-old rats, compared with 3-month-old animals. This finding of decreased exploratory activity supports our earlier findings of decreased motor activity in the old rats.

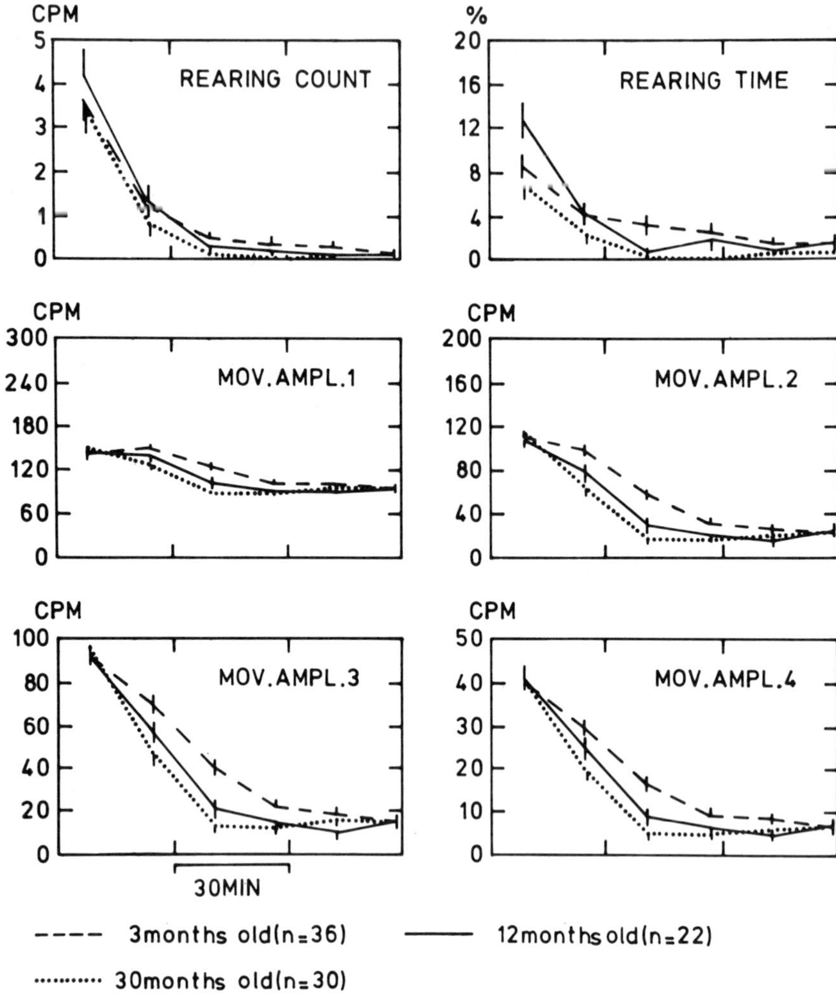

Figure 6. Spontaneous motor activity of 3, 12 and 30-month-old rats. The top left graph shows the number of rearings per min. (cpm) averaged over 16-minute periods, and the top right graph the time spent in an upright position, expressed as a percentage of those 16-minute periods. The lower graphs represent horizontal movements of increasing amplitudes, movement amplitude 4 being the largest. The graphs show that motor activity of 12-month and 30-month-old rats are very similar; while activity of 3-month-old rats, especially of horizontal movements 2–4 is significantly greater ($p < 0.05$). Mean values ± S.E.M.

Another factor which could contribute to the age-related differences in performance, might be a difference in sensitivity to footshock, e.g., by callous thickening of the food pads of the aged animals. In most experiments, animals trained in the "drinktest" were punished by electric footshocks. A decreased sensitivity to footshock would lead to a reduction in punishment level resulting in a decreased motivation. It is not very likely that a difference in footshock sensitivity can be held responsible for the decrements observed, because similar decrements are found when no footshock is used (Figure 1b), and also because performance during the first week was comparable for all age groups, and differences

Figure 7. The results of measurements of open field behavior during 60 minutes of 3 and 30-month-old rats with the automated video-scan system. The top left graph shows the cumulative distance run in meters as a measure of motor activity; the middle one of the upper 3 graphs shows the cumulative number of changes in corners as a measure of exploratory behavior; the top right and the bottom left graphs show the number of entries into the inner field and the time spent there respectively as parameters of emotionality; and the middle and right graphs of the bottom line show the cumulative time that movements of the indicated speed classes were detected. The open field parameters of the 30-month-old rats were decreased when compared with those of the 3-month-old rats. Movements of the latter animals tended to occur at higher speeds.

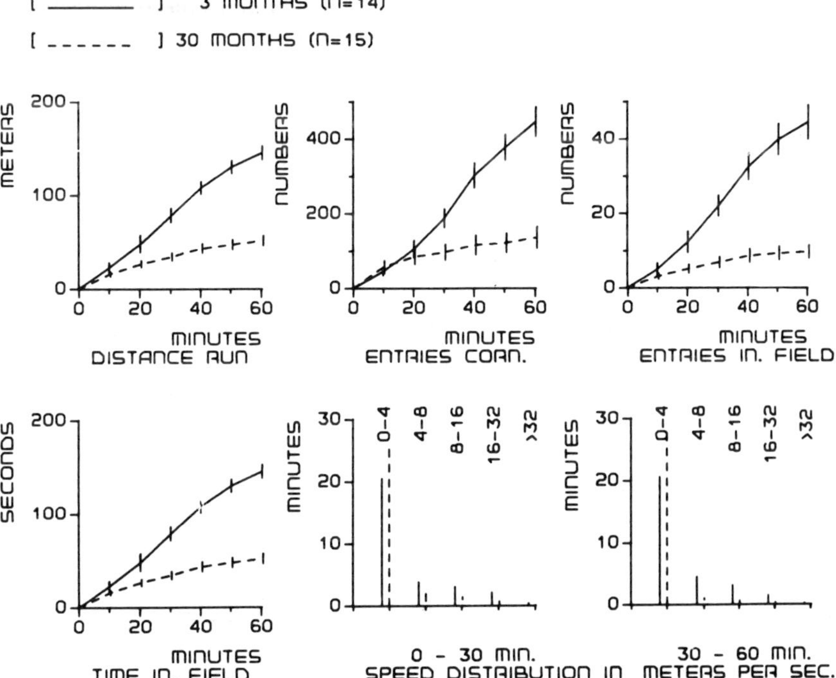

began to appear only several days after day 4, when maximum footshock levels had been reached. Furthermore, when the shock level was increased on day 14, this had no noticeable effect on performance. Nevertheless, it was decided to measure footshock sensitivity directly in rats of the 3 age groups by determining, with the successive approximation method (Wolthuis, 1971), the lowest footshock current at which the animals showed a flinch reaction. A flinch reaction is defined as a quick withdrawal of the paw in reaction to a painful stimulus. The results are shown in Table 1; no significant differences in flinch thresholds were found between the 3, 12 and 30-month-old rats. In addition, it was found that the thickness of the corneous tissue of the skin of the paws was approximately the same in the 3 and 30-month-old rats. Apparently the rats used in these experiments do not develop thickened layers of the stratum corneum on the paws, which may be related to the type of shavings or cage floors used in the animal rooms. It thus appears that a decreased footshock sensitivity cannot explain the acquisition deficits of the 30-month-old rats.

Biochemical Assays

In the course of these experiments, the question arose whether the acquisition deficits might be the consequence of gross overall metabolic changes in the brain during aging. Since it was impossible to investigate brain metabolism in its entirety, we attempted to select a representative section. From a biochemical and practical point of view, a study of glutamic acid turnover would offer some insight in the overall metabolic state of the brain. A number of reasons speak in favor of such a choice and suggest that glutamate occupies a key position in cerebral metabolism. Glutamate is a neurotransmitter (Johnson, 1972), it is a precursor for gamma-aminobutyrate (GABA) (Berl et al., 1961; Berl et al., 1970 a, b; Seiler and Wagner, 1976) and it is important for cerebral energy metabolism via α-ketoglutarate and the tricarboxylic acid cycle (Van den Berg et al., 1966). Moreover, the glutamate-glutamine system regulates the ammonia levels in the brain (Berl et al., 1962; Weil-Malherbe, 1962) and last, but not least, glutamate is incorporated into proteins (Blomstrand and Hamberger, 1970) and peptides (Reichelt and Kvamme, 1967).

The choice of studying the glutamate turnover was encouraged by results of other investigators suggesting that age-related changes in glutamate metabolism may occur. Not only a marked decrease of glutamic acid and glutamine content was found in aged rat brains (Himwich, 1973); but also the activity of glutamate dehydrogenase appears to be low in the brains of aged rats (Kanungo and Kaur, 1969). Furthermore, Fonda et al. (1973) found a lower activity of glutamate decarboxylase and a higher activity of GABA transaminase in the brains

Table 1. Footshock Thresholds of Female Small Wistar (WAG) Rats

Age	3 months (n = 10)	12 months (n = 10)	30 months (n = 10)
"Flinch" thresholds in μA ($\overline{X} \pm$ SEM)	62.0 ± 5.1	56.9 ± 6.3	61.2 ± 3.8

of aging mice and concluded that there is an age-related change in the glutamate system in mouse brain (Kirzinger and Fonda, 1978). For all these reasons, a study of overall brain glutamate metabolism was carried out to investigate whether age-related changes in turnover of glutamic acid in rat brain take place.

Evidence is available that glutamate metabolism in the brains is compartmentalized in at least two pools (Berl et al., 1961; Berl et al., 1962; Berl et al., 1970 a + b; Van den Berg et al., 1969; Van den Berg, 1970; Van den Berg and Ronda, 1976 a + b). One of these is a "small" compartment of which acetate is a precursor. When radioactive acetate is injected, the specific activity of glutamine is higher than that of glutamate (O'Neal and Koeppe, 1966; Van den Berg et al., 1966). The other compartment is "large" and glucose can be used as a precursor for this compartment, although it is also a "minor" precursor for the small one. The large compartment differs from the small one in that, when labelled glucose is injected, the specific activity of glutamate is higher than that of glutamine (Gaitonde et al., 1965; O'Neal and Koeppe, 1966). The kinetics of the small and the large compartments in young, adult and aged rat brains were studied by following the labelling of glutamate, glutamine and aspartate after injection of labelled acetate and glucose.

Female, small Wistar rats of 3, 12 and 30 months of age were injected intraperitoneally with a mixture of 300 μCi [^{3}H]-acetate and 30 μCi d-[2-^{14}C]-glucose. The levels of glutamate, aspartate and glutamine were determined and the incorporation of the radioactivity into these amino acids was measured according to methods described by Cheng and Waelsch (1963) and Van den Berg et al. (1969).

It was found that the brain levels of glutamate and aspartate were decreased in 30-month-old rats when compared with those of 3 and 12-month-old rats. No significant age-related differences were found, however, in glutamine levels. These results are in accord with data from literature (Davis and Himwich, 1975; Himwich, 1973; Timiras et al., 1973). Neither the protein levels nor the incorporation of the radioactivity into brain proteins (see Table 2) differed among the three age groups, suggesting that there are no general, age-related differences in protein synthesis. This conclusion is supported by the results of Menzies and Gold (1971), who found no changes in the turnover rates of mitochondrial proteins in rat brains with age.

Table 2. Radioactivity of the Protein Fraction in Brain

Incorporation of:	Time in min	Age 3 months (n)	12 months (n)	30 months (n)
^3H	10	0.24 ± 0.01 (7)	0.30 ± 0.02 (7)	0.29 ± 0.02 (8)
	20	0.29 ± 0.01 (7)	0.33 ± 0.04 (8)	0.32 ± 0.02 (7)
^{14}C	10	0.10 ± 0.01 (7)	0.10 ± 0.00 (7)	0.10 ± 0.01 (8)
	20	0.17 ± 0.01 (7)	0.19 ± 0.01 (8)	0.17 ± 0.01 (7)

Radioactivity of the protein fraction in brain, 10 and 20 minutes after injection of 300 μCi [^{3}H]-acetate and 30 μCi d-[2-^{14}C]-glucose (dpm/g frozen brain tissue x 10^{-5}). Determined protein levels were not different between the age groups; they were 6.99 ± 0.17, 7.04 ± 0.36 and 6.97 ± 0.18 (mean ± SEM) mg per 100 mg frozen brain tissue in rats of 3, 12 and 30 months, respectively. Between the three age groups no differences were found in the incorporation of the radioactivity into the brain proteins.

The incorporation of d-[2-^{14}C]-glucose into aspartate and glutamine (Figure 8) expressed as the respective relative specific activities (R.S.A.: specific activity of amino acid/specific activity of glutamate) did not show significant age-related changes. Since glucose is a precursor of the large glutamate pool in the brain, it can be concluded that no age-related changes occur in the metabolism of glutamate in the large compartment.

The incorporation of [^{3}H]-acetate into aspartate, also expressed as the R.S.A., did not differ among the three age groups. The R.S.A. of ^{3}H-labelled glutamine in brains of 30-month-old rats, however, was significantly decreased 10 minutes after injection of the precursor mixture when compared with 3-month-old rats (Figure 9). This difference had disappeared 20 minutes after injection. These results may indicate that the incorporation of [^{3}H]-acetate into glutamine is delayed in 30-month-old rats; therefore, it is suggested that, in contrast to the large compartment, the metabolism of glutamate in the small compartment is altered in the brains of aged rats.

Since glutamate turnover remains unchanged in the large compartment and since it has been suggested that the large glutamate compartment is associated with neuronal structures and the small compartment with glial cells (Balázs et al., 1973; Quastel, 1975), it would be tempting to suggest that metabolism of transmitter glutamate remains unchanged at old age. However, in our opinion the present evidence is too scanty for such a conclusion.

The incorporation of the radioactivity in aspartate does not change with age. Aspartate is formed from oxalo-acetate, an intermediate of the tricarboxylic acid cycle. The degree of labelling of aspartate, therefore, can be considered as a parameter for the turnover rate of the tricarboxylic acid cycle. Since no differences in aspartate labelling were found among the three age groups, it can be concluded that the turnover rate of the tricarboxylic acid cycle is unaffected by age. Because the tricarboxylic acid cycle is directly related to energy production, it is likely that large age-related changes in energy metabolism in rat brains do not occur. This conclusion is contrary to that reached by Patel (1977), who found a reduction in the oxidation of labelled glucose in cortex slices from senescent rats, which pointed to a decreased energy metabolism.

There appears to be a direct relation between ammonia levels and glutamine synthesis. It is, for example, well documented that an increased brain ammonia level or administration of high doses of ammonia leads to increased synthesis of glutamine in brains of animals (Hindfelt et al., 1977). The findings that neither the levels nor the incorporation of the radioactivity into glutamine are increased may indicate that, in rats, the brain ammonia levels do not increase with age. These results are in

Figure 8. The mean (± S.E.M.) relative specific activities (R.S.A) of ^{14}C-glutamine (specific activities of ^{14}C-glutamine/specific activities of ^{14}C-glutamate) 10 and 20 minutes after injection of the precursor mixture of [^{3}H]-acetate and d-[2-^{14}C]-glucose in 3, 12 and 30-month-old rats. The R.S.A. of ^{14}C-glutamine did not show significant age-related changes.

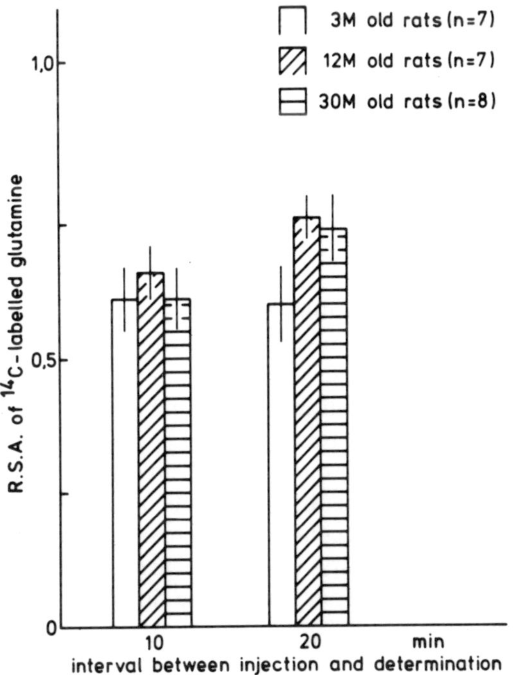

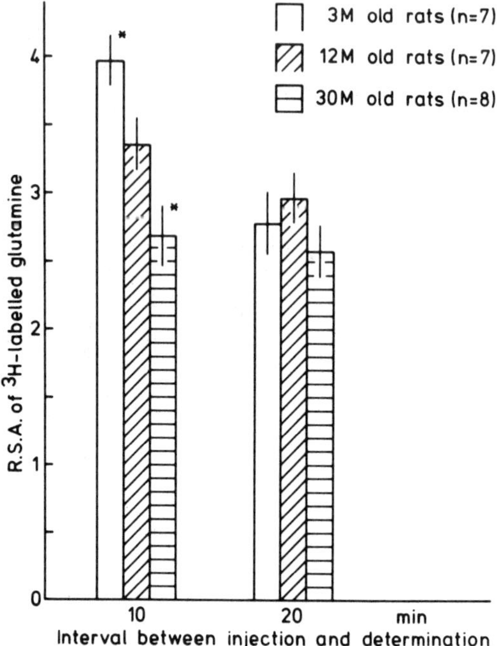

Figure 9. The mean (± S.E.M.) relative specific activities (R.S.A. of ^{3}H-glutamine (specific activity of ^{3}H-glutamine/specific activities of ^{3}H-glutamate) 10 and 20 minutes after injection of the precursor mixture of [^{3}H]-acetate and d-[2-^{14}C]-glucose in 3, 12 and 30-month-old rats. The R.S.A. of ^{3}H-glutamine was significantly ($* = p_2 < 0.05$) decreased in the 30-month-old rats 10 minutes after injection, when compared with the values of the 3-month-old rats; 20 minutes after injection this difference had disappeared.

contrast with those of Kirzinger and Fonda (1978), who found an increased ammonia level in the brains of senescent mice.

Summarizing, data reported in the literature as well as in our own experiments show that glutamate brain levels are lowered in aged animals. This might suggest that disturbances in glutamate metabolism occur with age. The present turnover studies of glutamate and some additional findings show, however, that age-related, overall gross changes in glutamate metabolism do not occur, albeit that metabolism of glutamate is somewhat delayed in the small compartment. The defects in acquisition of old rats, therefore, cannot be simply explained by gross changes in cerebral metabolism. There is a possibility that there are deficits in metabolism in certain small parts of the brain, which are not detectable with the methods we used.

Lipofuscin Assays

Although clear indications of gross age-related metabolic changes were not found, the possibility remains that neuronal function in aged rats is impaired by the accumulation of indisposable metabolities. Therefore, we decided to investigate the "age pigment" lipofuscin because it seems to be generally accepted that such a product is considered as intracellularly deposited "garbage" (Björkerud, 1964). The increasing intraneuronal accumulation of the age pigment lipofuscin is one of the consistent cytological changes correlated with aging of mammals (Bondareff, 1957; Brizzee et al., 1969; Brizzee et al., 1974; Brody 1960). In a quantitative microscopical study, Reichel et al. (1968), demonstrated that in rodent brain the average volume occupied by lipofuscin was largest (about 5%) in the hippocampus. Although the hippocampus is the most heavily pigmented area in terms of percentage of section volume, the purkinje cell layer, because of the relative scarcity of cells, is the area of maximum pigmentation per cell (about 17.5% of the cell volume—Reichel et al., 1968). Because of the large volume occupied by lipofuscin, it is conceivable that neuronal function is disturbed and this may, in turn, lead to acquisition deficits.

First, the question has to be answered whether induction or reduction of lipofuscin in the brain is paralleled by changes in learning and memory processes. To gain an insight in the quantitative changes of lipofuscin in the central nervous system microscopic measurements seem to be inadequate. A quantitative determination method described earlier by Csallany and Ayaz (1976) was first tried and appeared not to be sufficiently quantitative and reproducible. The extraction method was improved and is schematically represented in Figure 10. The improved method is sensitive enough to determine lipofuscin in substructures of the central nervous system; such as the hippocampus, the cerebellum and the cortex. In fact, these three structures were selected for further study; the hippocampus mainly for its role in learning and especially short-term memory processes (Isaacson, 1975), the cerebellum because of its involvement in motor coordination and the brain cortex for its integrative function.

Experiments have been started which attempted to measure lipofuscin chemically, in addition to "blind" microscopical estimates of lipofuscin accumulation in these brain structures. The preliminary results are shown in Table 3. It will be clear that such microscopic estimates are, at best, semiquantitative due to selective accumulation of lipofuscin in certain cell types. In the cerebellum, for example, the score is given as 0.9. If, however, only the purkinje cells were scored, this figure would be 1.7. The microscopic technique followed so far, estimates the size and tissue homogenized in chloroform : methanol (2 : 1)

↓

homogenate stirred 1 hour at 50° with water (two times)

↓

combined water layers stirred 1 hour at 50° with chloroform : methanol (2 : 1) (four times)

↓

solvent of combined organic layers removed on rotary evaporator to ca. 2 ml and then evaporated to dryness under nitrogen

↓

extracts taken up in chloroform : methanol (1 : 9)

↓

extracts chromatographied on Sephadex LH20 column

↓

fluorescence of fractions measured against a quinine sulfate solution (1 μg/ml 0.1 NH_2 SO_4)

Figure 10. Schematical representation of the improved procedure for extraction of lipofuscin from rat brain.

frequency of the lipofuscin accumulations. The whole structure is serially examined in 6 μ slices and the relative area taken in by cell bodies and neural tracts in each microscopic field were taken into account. Since hardly any lipofuscin was detectable in these structures of brains of 3-month-old rats and since the brains of 12-month-old rats have not yet been examined, Table 3 only shows the lipofuscin accumulation in these three structures of 30-month-old rats. In accordance with the results of Reichel et al. (1968), we also find the highest accumulation of lipofuscin in the hippocampus. Chemically, the data on lipofuscin are expressed as the relative fluorescence due to lipofuscin in relation to the fluorescence of a quinine sulfate solution (1 μg/ml 0.1 NH_2SO_4).

The data obtained so far show considerable variation. Nevertheless, they suggest that there may be a reasonable correlation between the microscopic estimates and the quantitative chemical determinations. With the improved lipofuscin determination method, we attempted to determine whether meclofenoxate-induced changes in the lipofuscin content of these brain structures of aged rats are accompanied by behavioral changes of the animals.

Table 3. Lipofuscin Accumulation in Different Brain Regions

Determination method	Hippocampus	Cortex	Cerebellum
Microscopical (n = 3)	1,6	1,1	0,9
Chemical (n = 4)	457.6 ± 99.0	235,1 ± 79,7	222,7 ± 89,6

Conclusions

Summarizing the data so far, there does not appear to be a single factor or group of factors which can be held responsible for the acquisition deficits found in our aging rats. In fact, it is surprising that so few disturbances have been found in the aged rats tested. A few comments on the results, however, may be in order.

One of the puzzling questions is why the acquisition curves of 3 and 30-month-old rats are so similar during the first week, whereas in the later stages of acquisition they start to diverge and even seem to reach a plateau in the case of the 30-month-old rats. This can be seen in Figure 1a for the small Wistar rats and in Figure 3 for the BN/BI rats. The answer to this question is not clear. The animals constantly remain in the test apparatus and are not intentionally deprived of water. The number of correct, i.e., water-rewarded responses is fairly stable and simply represents the animals' daily requirement of water, whereas the number of incorrect responses decreases when acquisition progresses. Since in the "drinktest" each correct response is equivalent to 0.25 ml water, and since the number of correct responses per day in young and aged animals is roughly the same, it seems reasonable to assume that the need for water and the motivational levels in this respect are approximately equal. Another factor which may contribute to the age-differences in acquisition, i.e., differences in the degree of punishment was excluded since footshock sensitivity did not change with age. In addition, if motivational factors were involved, one has to assume that the motivational levels change in the second half of the training period during which the acquisition curves start to diverge. Taken together, all these points can be taken to indicate that the age differences in acquisition are not due to age-dependent differences in motivation. They do not, however, completely exclude that such differences exist, since the motivational factors that can be measured are rather basic, i.e., the need of water and the sensitivity to footshock. Higher motivational levels might exist and differences therein might account for the difference we found.

The finding of age differences in the speed of extinction (see Figure 1b) is not surprising. Extinction of acquired behavior in the "drinktest" occurs rapidly; consequently differences in extinction speed are hard to detect. Perhaps the rapid extinction is due to the large amounts of responses required to meet the daily need of water. In future work, we will attempt to analyze the first 50 responses of the extinction phase separately. Even then, and apart from the interpretation of the extinction phenomenon as such, the difficulty remains that the performance levels at the start of extinction differ in young and old animals. When attempts were made to start extinction at the same performance level, it would generally take the aged animals more trials than the young ones to reach that level, which would render both groups incomparable.

The fact that the data obtained so far do not point at a single factor or a group of factors which can be held responsible for the acquisition deficits found in the aged rats, is perhaps not surprising. The combination of considerable changes in behavior with relatively minor biological changes in the brain becomes more acceptable when it is realized that the young and old rats do not only differ in age, but also differ vastly in behavioral experience; whereas, biologically speaking, we are testing a selected population of the fittest survivors with most of their adaptive and compensatory mechanisms still intact. Whatever the case, it is clear that research, which attempts to correlate changed behavior with biological changes, is still in the relatively primitive stage where inventories are taken. The present study should be regarded as such.

ACKNOWLEDGMENTS

We would like to thank Prof. Dr. C. Hollander who made most of the aged animals available and Dr. W.J.C. Bogaerts, Dr. R.A. Oosterbaan, Dr. C.J. van den Berg, Dr. W.C. Nijenmanting and Dr. E. Meeter who never ceased to show active interest and willingness to supply us with critical comments.

References

Balázs R, Patel AJ, Richter D: Metabolic compartments in the brain; their properties and relation to morphological structures. In Balázs R, Cremer JE (eds.) *Metabolic Compartmentation in the Brain*. London, Macmillan, 1973.

Berl S, Clarke DD, Nicklas WJ: Compartmentation of citric acid cycle metabolism in brain: effect of amino-oxiacetic acid, ouabain and Ca^{++} on the labelling of glutamate, glutamine, aspartate and GABA by [1-^{14}C]-acetate, [U-^{14}C]-glutamate, and [U-^{14}C]-aspartate. *J Neurochemistry* 17:999–1007, 1970a.

Berl S, Lajtha A, Waelsch H: Amino acid and protein metabolism. VI. cerebral compartments of glutamic acid metabolism. *J Neurochemistry* 7:186–197, 1961.

Berl S, Nicklas WJ, Clarke DD: Compartmentation of citric acid cycle metabolism in brain: labelling of glutamate, glutamine, aspartate, and GABA by several radioactive metabolites. *J Neurochemistry* 17:1009–1015, 1970b.

Berl S, Takagaki G, Clarke DD, Waelsch H: Metabolic compartments *in vivo*. Ammonia and glutamic acid metabolism in brain and liver. *Biological Chemistry* 237:2562–2569, 1962.

Birren JE: Age differences in learning a two choice water maze by rats. *Gerontology* 17:207–213, 1962.

Birren JE, Riegel KF, Morrison DF: Age differences in response speed as function of controlled variations of stimulus conditions: evidence of a general speed factor. *Gerontologia* Basel 6:1–18, 1962.

Björkerud S: Isolated lipofuscin granules. A survey of a new field. *Advances in Gerontological Research* 1:257–288, 1964.

Blomstrand C, Hamberger A: Amino acid incorporation *in vitro* into proteins of neuronal and glial cell-enriched fractions. *Neurochemistry* 17:1187–1195, 1970.

Bondareff W: Genesis of intracellular pigment in the spinal ganglia of senile rats. An electron microscope study. *Gerontology* 12:364–369, 1957.

Botwinick J, Brinley JF, Robbin JS: Learning a position discrimination and position reversals by Sprague-Dawley rats of different ages. *Gerontology* 17:315–319, 1962.

Botwinick J, Brinley JF, Robbin JS: Learning and reversing a four-choice multiple Y-maze by rats of three ages. *Gerontology* 18:279–282, 1963.

Brizzee KR, Cancilla PA, Sherwood N, Timiras PS: The amount and distribution of pigments in neurons and glia of the cerebral cortex. Autofluorescent and ultrastructural studies. *Gerontology* 24:127–135, 1969.

Brizzee KR, Ordy JM, Kaack B: Early appearance and regional differences in intraneuronal and extraneuronal lipofuscin accumulation with age in the brain of a nonhuman primate. *Gerontology* 29:366–381, 1974.

Brody H: The deposition of aging pigment in the human cerebral cortex. *Gerontology* 15:258–261, 1960.

Bunning E: *The Physiological Clock.* Revised second edition. New York, Springer Verlag, 1967.

Cheng SC, Waelsch H: Some quantitative aspects of the fixation of carbondioxide by the lobster nerve. *Biochemische Zeitschrift* 338:643–653, 1963.

Csallany AS, Ayaz KL: Quantitative determination of organic solvent soluble lipofuscin pigments in tissues. *Lipids* 11:412–417, 1976.

Davis J, Himwich WA: Meurochemistry of the developing and aging mammalian brain. In Ordy JM, Brizzee KR (eds.) *Advances in Behavioral Biology: Vol 16. Neurobiology of Aging.* New York, Plenum Press, 1975.

Doty BA: Age differences in avoidance conditioning as a function of distribution of trials and task difficulty. *Genetic Psychology* 109:249–254, 1966.

Dye CJ: Effects of interruption of initial learning upon retention in young, mature and old rats. *Gerontology* 24:12–17, 1969.

Fonda ML, Acree DW, Auerbach SB: The relationship of γ-amino-butyrate levels and its metabolism to age in brains of mice. *Archives of Biochemistry and Biophysics* 159:622–628, 1973.

Gaitonde MK, Dahl DR, Elliott KAC: Entry of glucose carbon into amino acids of rat brain and liver *in vivo* after injection of uniformy ^{14}C-labelled glucose. *Biochemical Journal* 94:345–352, 1965.

Goodrick CL: Learning by mature-young and aged Wistar albino rats as a function of test complexity. *Gerontology* 27:353–357, 1972.

Himwich WA: Neurochemical patterns in the developing and aging brain. In Rockstein M (ed.) *Development and Aging in the Nervous System.* New York, Academic Press, 1973.

Hindfelt B, Plum F, Duffy TE: Effect of acute ammonia intoxication on cerebral metabolism in rats with portacaval shunts. *Clinical Investigations* 59:386–396, 1977.

Hofecker G, Kment A, Niedermüller H, Said H: Assessment of activity patterns of one- and two-year-old rats by electronic recording. *Experimental Gerontology* 9:109–114, 1974.

Isaacson RL: Memory processes and the hippocampus. In Isaacson RL, Pribram KH (eds.) *The Hippocampus, Vol 2, Physiology and Behavior.* New York, Plenum Press, 1975.

Jakubczak LF: Re-entrainment of food intake of mature and old rats to the light-dark cycle. *Bull Psychonomic Society* 6:491–493, 1975.

Johnson JL: Glutamic acid as a synaptic transmitter in the nervous system. A review. *Brain Research* 13:1–19, 1972.

Kanungo MS, Kaur G: *Regulatory Changes in Enzymes as a Function of Age of the Rat.* In Proceedings of the 8th International Congress of Gerontology, Vol I, 1969.

Kay H, Sime ME: Discrimination learning with old and young rats. *Gerontology* 17:75–80, 1962.

Kirzinger SS, Fonda ML: Glutamine and ammonia metabolism in the brains of senescent mice. *Experimental Gerontology* 13:255–261, 1978.

McNamara MC, Benignus G, Benignus VA, Miller Jr AT: Active and passive avoidance learning in rats as a function of age. *Experimental Aging Research* 3:3–16, 1977.

Menzies RA, Gold PH: The turnover of mitochondria in a variety of tissues of young, adult and aged rats. *Biological Chemistry* 246:2425–2429, 1971.

Michel ME, Klein AW: Performance differences in a complex maze between young and aged rats. *Age* 1:13–16, 1978.

Miller Jr RG: *Simultaneous Statistical Interference.* New York, McGraw-Hill, 1966.

O'Neal RM, Koeppe RE: Precursors *in vivo* of glutamate, aspartate and their derivatives of rat brain. *Neurochemistry* 13:835–847, 1966.

Patel MS: Age-dependent changes in the oxidative metabolism in rat brain. *Gerontology* 32:643–646, 1977.

Quastel JH: Metabolic compartmentation in the brain and effects of metabolic inhibitors. In Berl S, Clarke DD, Schneider D (eds.) *Metabolic Compartmentation and Neurotransmission.* New York, Plenum Press, 1975.

Reichel W, Hollander J, Clarke JH, Strehler BL: Lipofuscin pigment accumulation as a function of age and distribution in rodent brain. *Gerontology* 23:71–78, 1968.

Reichelt KL, Kvamme E: Acetylated and peptide bound glutamate and aspartate in brain. *Neurochemistry* 14:987–996, 1967.

Rusak B, Zucker I: Fluid intake of rats in constant light and during feeding restricted to the light or dark position of the illumination cycle. *Physiology and Behavior* 13:91–100, 1974.

Seiler N, Wagner G: NAD^+-dependent formation of γ-aminobutyrate (GABA) from glutamate. *Neurochemical Research* 1:113–131, 1976.

Siegel PS, Stuckey HL: The diurnal course of water and food intake in the normal mature rat. *Comparative and Physiological Psychology* 40:365–370, 1947.

Tanger HJ, Vanwersch RAP, Wolthuis OL: Automated TV-based system for open field studies: effects of methamphetamine. *Pharmacology Biochemistry and Behavior* 9:555–557, 1978.

Timiras PS: *Developmental Physiology and Aging.* New York, MacMillan, 1972.

Timiras PS, Hudson DB, Oklund S: Changes in central nervous system free amino acids with development and aging. In Ford DH (ed.) *Neurobiological Aspects of Maturation and Aging.* Amsterdam, London, New York, Elsevier Scientific Pub, 1973.

Van den Berg CJ: Compartmentation of glutamate metabolism in the developing brain; experiments with labelled glucose, acetate, phenylalanine, tyrosine and proline. *Neurochemistry* 17:973–983, 1970.

Van den Berg CJ, Kržalić LJ, Mela P, Waelsch H: Compartmentation of glutamate metabolism in brain. Evidence for the existence of two different tricarboxylic acid cycles in brain. *Biochemical Journal* 113:281–290, 1969.

Van den Berg CJ, Mela P, Waelsch H: On the contribution of the tricarboxylic acid cycle to the synthesis of glutamate, glutamine and aspartate in brain. *Biochemical and Biophysical Research Communications* 23:479–484, 1966.

Van den Berg CJ, Ronda G: The incorporation of double labelled acetate into glutamate and related amino acids from adult mouse brain: compartmentation of amino acid metabolism in brain. *Neurochemistry* 27:1443–1448, 1976a.

Van den Berg CJ, Ronda G: Metabolism of glutamate and related amino acids in the 10-day-old mouse brain; experiments with labelled acetate and β-hydroxybutyrate. *Neurochemistry* 27:1449–1453, 1976b.

Verzar F: *Experimentelle Gerontologie*. Stuttgart, Ferdinand Enke Verlag, 1965.

Weil-Malherbe H: Ammonia metabolism in the brain. In Elliott KAC, Page JH, Quastel JH (eds.) *Meurochemistry—The Chemistry of Brain and Nerve*. Springfield, Illinois, Thomas, 1962.

Welch BL: The generalization of "Student's" problem when several different population variances are involved. *Biometrika* 34:28–35, 1947.

Wolthuis OL: Experiments with UCB 6215, a drug which enhances acquisition in rats: its effects compared with those of metamphetamine. *European J Pharmacology* 16:283–297, 1971.

Wolthuis OL, Knook DL, Nickolson VJ: Age-related acquisition deficits and activity in rats. *Neuroscience Letters* 2:343–348, 1976.

Zepelin H, Whitehead WE, Rechtschaffen A: Aging and sleep in the albino rat. *Behavioral Biology* 7:65–74, 1972.

Stein, ed. The Psychobiology of Aging: Problems and Perspectives

Animal Models of Aging: Sensory-motor and Cognitive Function in the Aged Rat

Byron A. Campbell, E. Evan Krauter[a], and Julia E. Wallace[b]

Department of Psychology, Princeton University, Princeton, New Jersey.

Introduction

Declining sensory, motor and cognitive abilities are often thought to be widespread, if not universal characteristics of aged people. As this volume attests, there is reason to believe that a closer, more systematic analysis of this assumption is warranted. For example, in terms of cognitive capacity, we know that the elderly do not show a generalized decline in all phases of learning and memory, rather the deficits appear to be task or process specific. Declines in performance are observed when attention is divided on short-term memory tasks, but not simpler tests of memory; in long-term memory age-related declines are noted in recall but not in recognition tasks (Schoenfield and Robertson, 1966).

Decreases in sensory and motor capacities are equally variable. For example, some senses such as pain (Kenshalo, 1977) are relatively unaffected by age, while others like vision and hearing decline predictably for most individuals (cf. Birren and Schaie, 1977).

Our rationale for this research was to describe the normal changes over age that occur in sensory, motor and cognitive function. We think that the availability of such data would be helpful to those studying the effects of various treatments and procedures that alleviate some of the more unfortunate consequences of aging. For animal research, in particular, there is always the possibility of confounding sensory and motor deficits with changes in cognitive performance. Behavioral tests of learning and memory always require some degree of sensory-motor skill,

[a]*Present address: University of South Carolina, Spartanburg, South Carolina.*
[b]*Present address: University of Northern Iowa, Cedar Falls, Iowa.*

making it essential to know the extent of sensory-motor decline and the impact of that decline on other aspects of behavior.

In developing an animal model of aging, we attempted to categorize, systematically, tasks in terms of their sensory, cognitive and motor requirements. In order to create the various classification schemes, we have made use of a number of existing principles to aid us in our selection of behavioral tasks. The first guideline was based on earlier formulations by Ribot (1882) and Jackson (cf. Taylor, 1931) who suggested that declines in behavioral functions follow a sequence inversely related to the order of behavioral development, the so-called "first-in last-out" principle. Their hypothesis led us to assess age-related changes in motor behavior by using those behavioral tasks already available for the evaluation of behavioral development (e.g., Altman and Sudarshan, 1975).

For the classification of cognitive tasks, we have chosen the information processing model of memory, outlined by Craik (1977) and adapted from Murdock (1967) and Waugh and Norman (1965). This model divided memory into three systems: sensory memory, primary memory, and secondary memory. These systems are typically differentiated by the types of perceptual and cognitive processing that goes on within each, a distinction not easily assessed in infrahuman species. For this reason, we divided our tasks into those measuring sensory memory, short-term memory and long-term memory. These distinctions are intended to be analogous to sensory, primary, and secondary information processing respectively, but are empirically differentiated by the relative retention intervals bridged by the various tasks.

General Methodology

The subjects in all of the following studies were Fischer 344 rats received from a colony maintained at Charles River Breeding Laboratories through the auspices of the National Institute of Aging. The animals were delivered to our laboratory at 3, 6, 12 or 24 months of age. A record of weight (weekly), disease and death was maintained for all rats. Life expectancies of the 24-month-old rats received in our laboratory proved to be quite comparable to those exhibited in other laboratories (e.g., Coleman, Barthold, Osbaldiston, Foster, and Jonas, 1977). This survival curve, portrayed in Figure 1, shows an increase in the probability of death for succeeding months, with a 50% survival expectancy at approximately 30 months and maximal longevity of 34 months. Weight data collected from all naive, non-deprived rats were similar to that reported by Chesky and Rockstein (1976) for Fischer rats. These data are shown in Figure 2.

Observations of the 24-month Fischer rat reveal only subtle physical differences when compared to the 6-month-old rat. In general, the fur of the older rat has a slightly yellowish pigmentation which, along with the

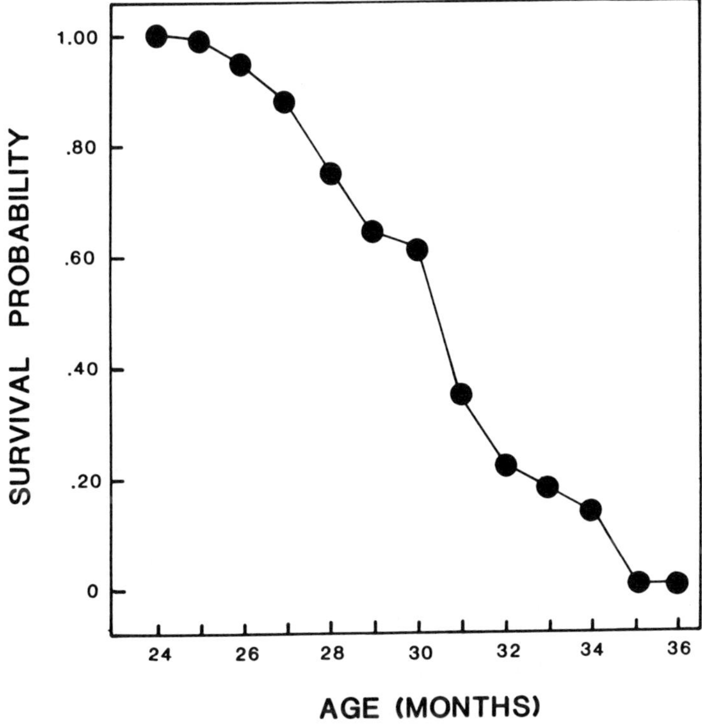

Figure 1. Probability of survival of Fischer-344 rats obtained at 24 months of age.

tail, appears to be less well groomed. The prevalance of observable tumors increases with age beyond 24 months and appears to correspond with the incidence reported by Coleman et al., (1977). When older animals are allowed to explore a flat surface, their gait and posture appear as coordinated as rats of younger ages. Tremors or other aberrant motor behaviors such as seizures were not observed.

Posture and Postural Adjustments

The first series of investigations examined several age groups of rats on a battery of tasks designed to measure simple motor and reflexive skills. The tasks for measuring the reflexive skills have been described by Brooks (1933) and Altman and Sudarshan (1975) and consisted of hopping and placing reactions, mid-air and surface righting responses, and geotactic reactions. The performance of old rats (26–27 months) in these tasks was identical to that of younger rats (6–15 months) indicating that our aged animals did not show evidence of gross neurological impairments.

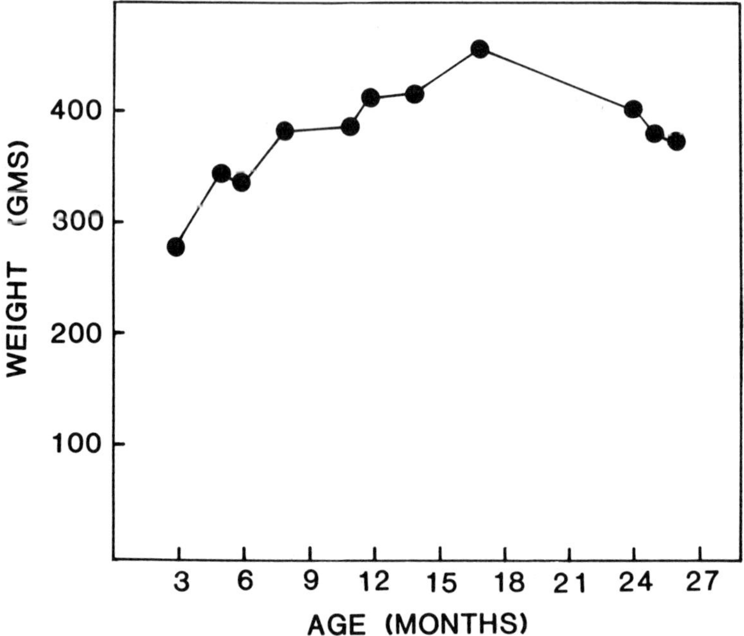

Figure 2. Weight of Fischer-344 rats as a function of age.

Locomotor Skills

In the next four tasks the response requirements were made more demanding and, in general, tapped motor skills that emerged later in development than the previously described postural adjustments. The following tasks required the rat to either climb, descend or walk under somewhat difficult circumstances. Performance levels for all age groups are shown in Figure 3.

In the first task subjects were suspended from a horizontal wire. All rats grasped the wire with their forepaws when lightly touched to the wire and remained suspended for at least a few moments when released. Mature rats (8 months) hung on for some time, but, unlike juvenile rats (Altman and Sudarshan, 1975), rarely attempted to climb up and support themselves with their hind feet. In contrast, aged rats (26 months) rapidly released their grip and fell. Latency to fall proved to be the simplest measure of this behavior and is recorded for all age groups in the top left panel of Figure 3.

Latency to descend a wire mesh pole was the next task. There were notable distinctions between the mature adults and oldest groups. Mature animals (5.5 and 8.5 months) clung to the pole and descended gradually, frequently turning head down before continuing the descent. The oldest rats often fell, sometimes slid, but never descended in a coordinated systematic manner, resulting in a much more rapid descent time (Figure 3, upper right panel).

In the elevated platform task, the rats were tested on three consecutive days for their ability to remain on a narrow elevated wooden bridge during a single 3-minute trial. The younger rats (5.5 or 8.5 months) typically moved quickly to one of the safe end platforms. The aged rats, however, almost always fell on each trial. The crucial determinant of falls appeared to be the older rats' inability to recover slips of their hind limbs from the elevated path.

In the final task of this series, the rats were trained to traverse a rod to reach an enclosed platform, first while the rod was stationary and later while the rod was slowly rotating. Following this training the rats received four sessions during which a method of limits was used to

Figure 3. Effects of age on four motor behaviors requiring sensory-motor coordination and/muscle strength.

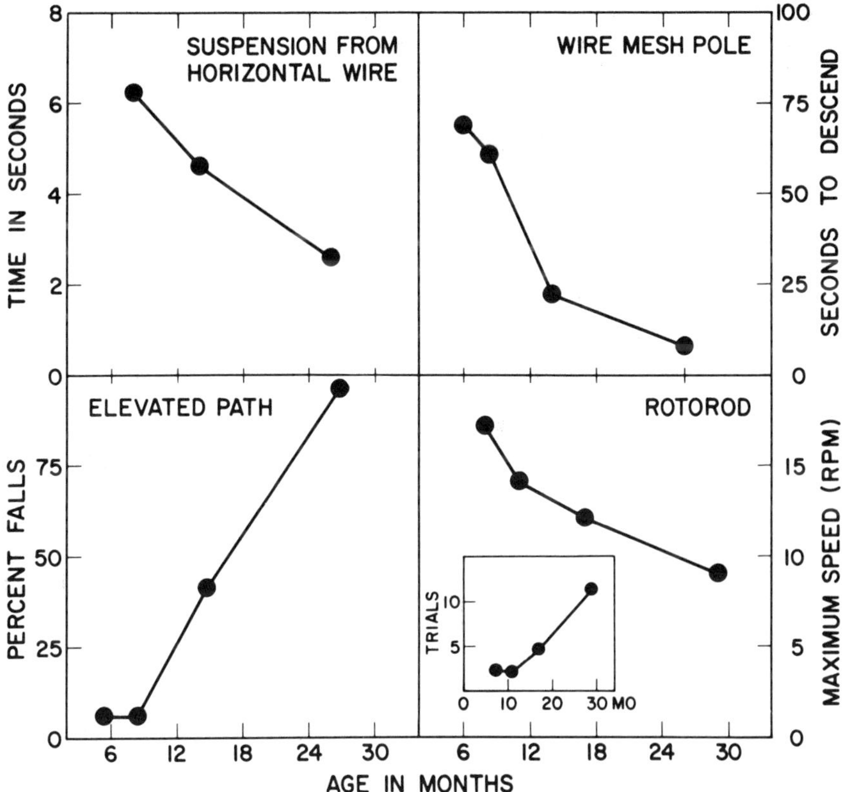

determine the rotation speed at which each rat could no longer successfully perform the response. As is shown in the bottom right panel of Figure 3, maximum successful speed decreased steadily with age. The insert shows the number of trials required to reach criterion on the stationary rod phase of this task. These data also suggest that motor performance of the aged rat can be enhanced considerably with repeated practice.

Sensory Capabilities and Sensory Reactivity

The goal of this phase of the research was to develop one or more measures of sensory-motor function which could be easily and rapidly administered and which did not require the debilitating effects of food or water deprivation. These requirements were met by utilizing the rat's startle reaction to either a punctate auditory stimulus or to electrical shock to the paws. In each instance, the startle response was recorded using a device similar to one used by Hoffman and his associates (e.g. Hoffman and Wible, 1970). Briefly, the apparatus consisted of a small animal chamber constructed of plexiglas and stainless steel rods which was held firmly between rubber cylinders in a rigid aluminum superstructure. The entire unit was housed in a sound-attenuating chamber. Movements of the chamber were converted to electrical current by a magnet and coil arrangement; the current amplified and displayed on a storage oscilliscope and recorded on a Grass polygraph. This configuration results in a system which is most sensitive to sharp, sudden movements such as startle reaction.

The first step in our research was to determine startle response thresholds and measure the magnitude of the startle response elicited by a range of stimulus intensities in adult and aged rats. Here, our purpose was to assess the sensitivity and reactivity of aging rats to intense stimuli.

In our first experiment, we used the method of constant stimuli to measure startle response thresholds to weak electric shock in rats of different ages. Single, 33 msec pulses of constant current, AC shock were delivered to the grid floor of the startle chamber at 30 sec intervals. The major findings are shown in Figure 4. Here it can be seen that the stimulus necessary to produce a 2 mm criterion startle response varied only slightly as a function of age (right panel), but response vigor was markedly less for the oldest group of animals at the higher shock intensities (left panel). Defining threshold as occurring halfway between the base level of responding for the 0 MA group and 100% responding, (cf. Masterson and Campbell, 1969) startle response thresholds were found to approximate those obtained in preweanling rats (Stehouwer and Campbell, 1978) for all age groups. The decline in the magnitude of the startle response elicited by shock (left panel) corresponds to the decline

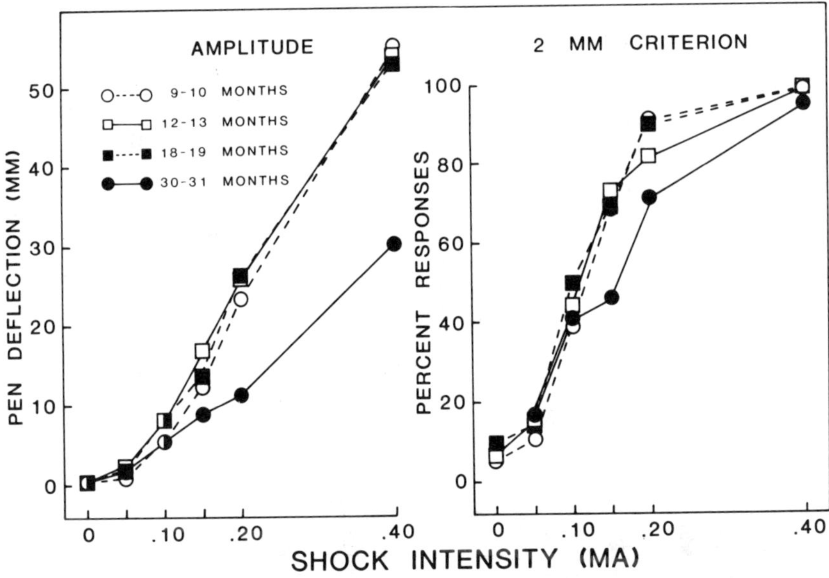

Figure 4. Mean amplitude of shock-elicited responses *(left panel)* and percent of shock-elicited responses 2 or more mm in amplitude *(right panel)* as a function of shock intensity for rats of different ages.

in muscle strength and the ability to make rapid movements that has been observed in man. At a later age this finding also parallels the decline in strength and coordination of the Fischer 344 rat seen in the preceding studies.

We used a white noise stimulus with a rectangular power spectrum, 800–8,000 Hz, to investigate auditory startle thresholds in rats. The stimulus was 20 msec in duration with a 1 msec rise and decay time and was delivered against a constant background of 70 db white noise. The results of these tests, shown in Figure 5, may be taken to indicate that there is a pronounced decrease in auditory startle reactivity with increasing age. The auditory startle response threshold was less than 90 db for the 9-13-month-old rats, about 90 db for the 18-19-month-old rats and 115 db for the 30-31-month-old rats (right panel). Differences in startle amplitude across noise intensity were even more striking (left panel). At the highest intensities, differences in response amplitude were found even between 9-10-month animals and 12-13-month animals.

Although these data reflect a sharp decline in auditory reactivity, they do not necessarily reflect a comparable change in auditory thresholds. In the case of electric shock, for example, reactivity declined with age but thresholds did not. In our next experiments auditory sensitivity was again measured but here we used the prestimulus inhibition technique

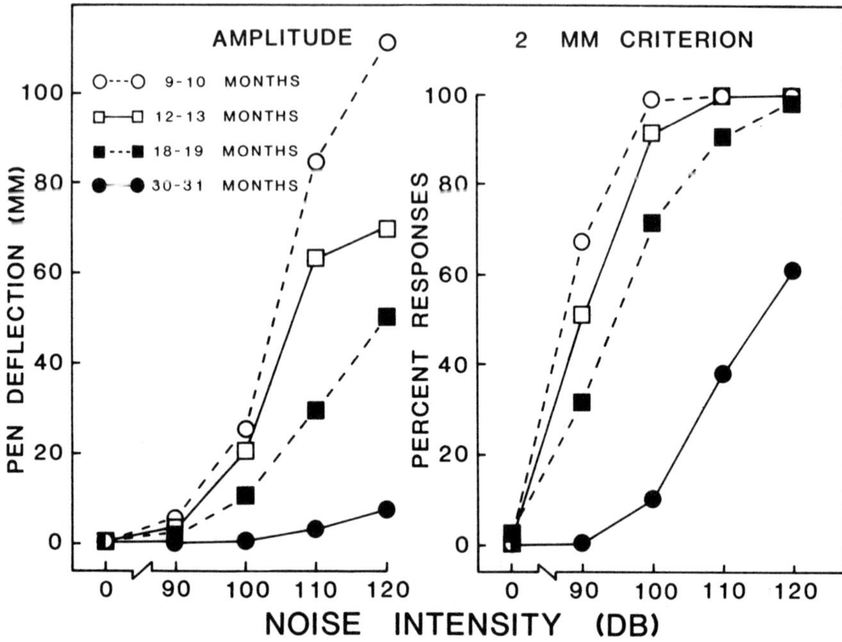

Figure 5. Mean amplitude *(left)* of the acoustic startle reaction and percent of startle reactions 2 or more mm in amplitude *(right)* as a function of age and intensity of the auditory stimulus.

described by Hoffman (Hoffman and Wible, 1970) and Ison (Ison and Hammond, 1971) as an index of sensory function. Using this procedure a weak stimulus is introduced just prior to the startle stimulus. At short prestimulus intervals (e.g., 50–100 msec) the startle response is severely attentuated (inhibited) in both animals and people. Prestimulus inhibition of startle is unlearned, highly consistent, proportional to stimulus intensity, and can be used as an index of sensory sensitivity.

Figure 6 shows the results of two experiments in which the prestimulus inhibition method was used. On prepulse trials the white noise was 25 msec in duration and preceded the tone startle stimulus by 60 msec. As can be seen in the first experiment, the noise prestimulus was effective at very low stimulus intensities, much lower than the intensities necessary to elicit a startle reaction.

The most important point to be made in these experiments is that the intensity necessary to inhibit the startle reaction changes relatively little during the first 2 years of life but drops during the succeeding months. In contrast, as shown in the inserts, there is a steady and reliable decline in startle amplitude on the control trials with increasing age. The amplitude data are consistent with the results from the last experiment and are interpreted to suggest that the processes involved in auditory stimulus detection decline relatively slowly during aging, while those mediating auditory reactivity decline much more rapidly.

Visual sensitivity was measured using the same prestimulus method. A light pulse of adjustable intensity was produced by a bank of silent high intensity light-emitting diodes located atop the startle chamber. On prestimulus trials the onset of a 20 msec light was followed 60 msec later by a 125 db tone startle stimulus. A schematic of the trial types is shown in the insert of Figure 7. The results of two experiments using this method are shown in Figure 7 with the x-axis showing light prestimulus intensity and the y-axis showing percent inhibition on prestimulus trials relative to control trials. The dramatic decrease in sensitivity to light as a function of age is clear in both experiments. In younger rats, the light prestimulus depressed the startle reaction at much lower intensities than in older rats.

Another way of looking at these same results is to select an arbitrary

Figure 6. Effects of a noise prestimulus on the auditory startle reaction in rats of different ages. The left and right panels are separate replications using rats of slightly different ages.

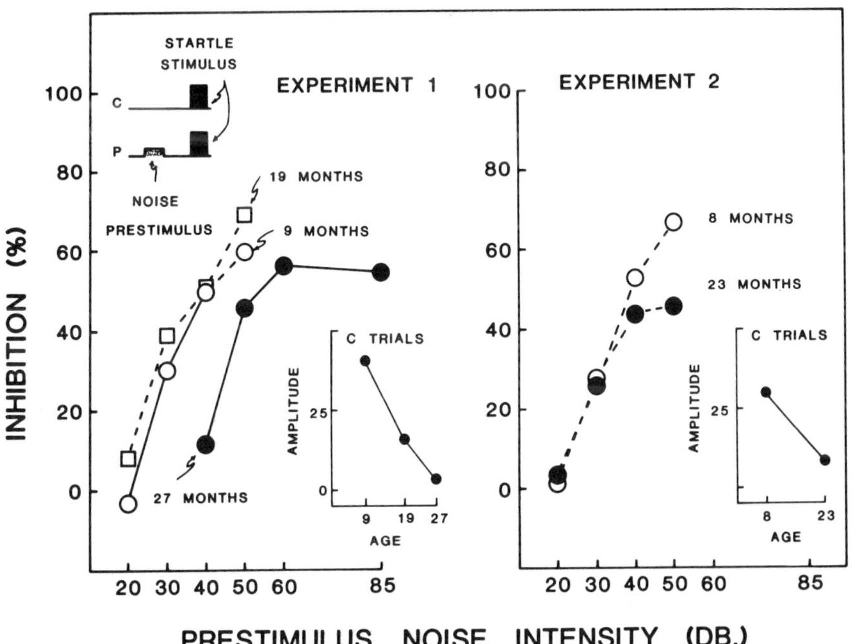

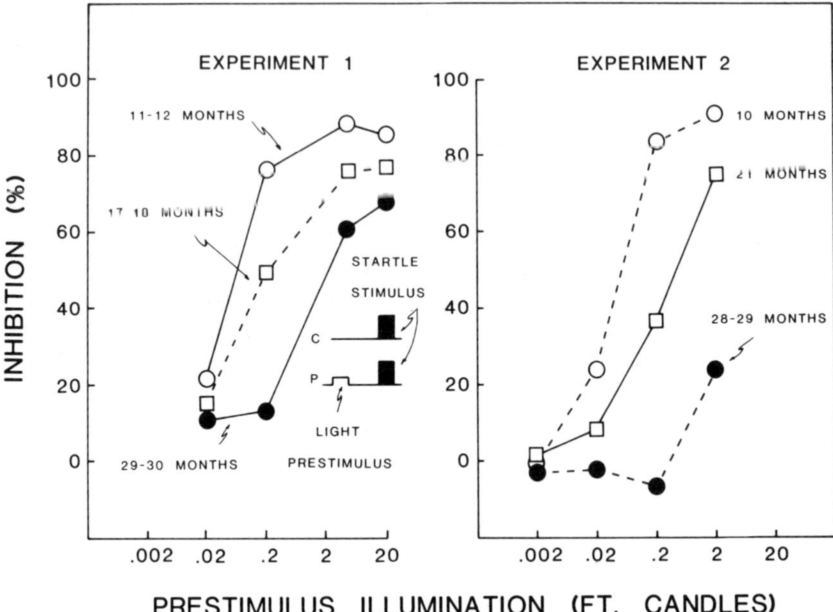

Figure 7. Effects of a light prestimulus on the auditory startle reaction in rats of different ages. The left and right panels are separate replications using rats of slightly different ages.

criterion of inhibition, such as 50%, and then plot the light intensity necessary to produce this criterion as a function of age. This analysis is shown in Figure 8. This figure shows even more strikingly the marked decrease in visual sensitivity that occurs as Fischer rats increase in age.

Summary

The behavioral profile that emerges from this battery of tests is of considerable interest in that it shows that aging is a selective process in lower animals just as it is in humans. Many simple reflexive behaviors, even some requiring some physical agility, such as the air-righting response, are virtually unchanged with age, while other behaviors requiring sensory motor coordination and some physical strength are severely degraded. Similarly, there are great differences in the effects of age on sensory systems. Cutaneous sensitivity, as measured by reactivity to painful stimuli, appears to be virtually unchanged in the aged animal. In contrast, both visual and auditory responsivity change markedly with age; the former being the most seriously affected.

We have summarized these data schematically in Figure 9 to illustrate graphically the selectivity of the aging process. This free-hand illustration was loosely based on the percent decline shown in the overall battery of motor tasks and in log unit changes for the sensory systems. Another way of depicting these life span developmental changes is to incorporate them with the data obtained by Altman and others describing early behavioral maturation. These trends are shown in Figure 10. In the rat, sensitivity to electric shock, posture and postural adjustment skills develop early and remain intact into old age.

The auditory startle reaction, first elicited at 12 days of age, increases in amplitude and decreases in latency until about day 30, a pattern which begins its reversal at about 12 months of age. In a similar fashion, many locomotor skills also develop relatively late and begin declining as early as 6–8 months of age. What is of particular note is the general tendency of these behaviors to follow a first-in, last-out sequence. While this is not surprising when we consider the overall pattern of human development and aging, it is reassuring to see the same trends appear in the rat when we apply a simple array of tests to these animals.

Figure 8. Prestimulus illumination levels necessary to produce 50% inhibition of the startle response as a function of age.

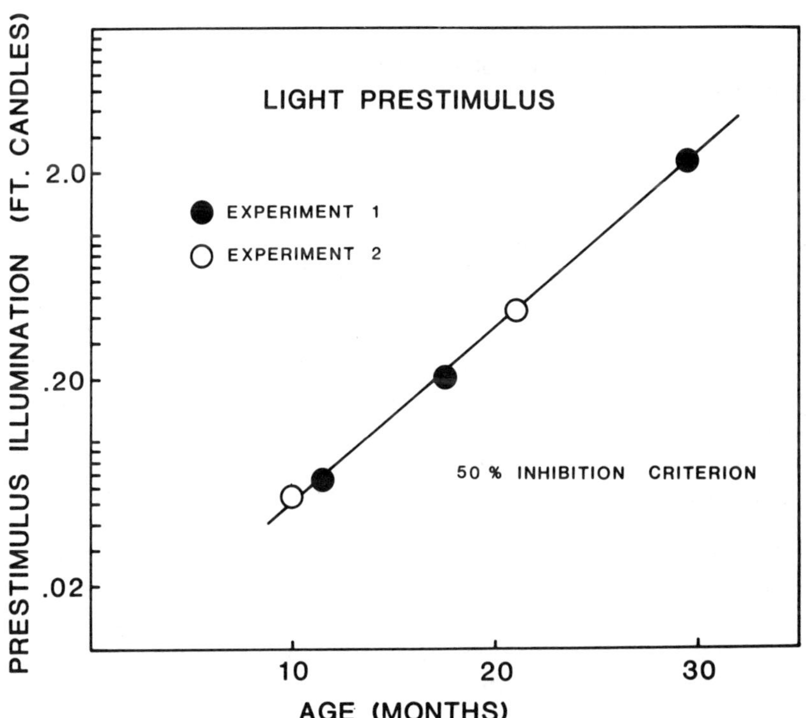

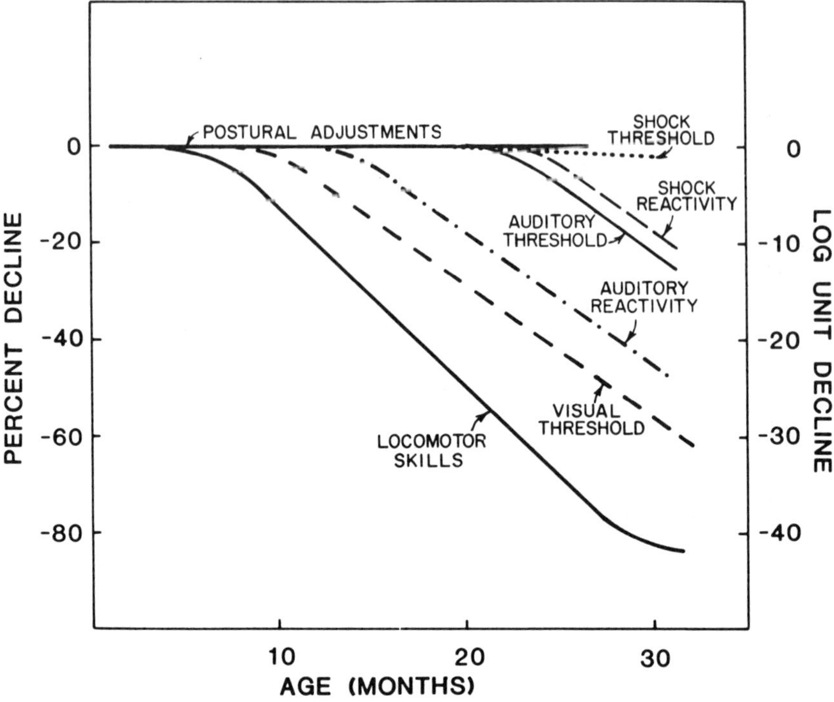

Figure 9. Schematic description of the effects of age on reflexive behaviors, postural adjustments, sensory reactivity, and locomotor skills.

Cognitive Function

Declining memory is often thought to be a widespread, if not universal, characteristic of aged humans. Recent research, however, has begun to challenge this assumption in a variety of ways. First, as normative data have been collected the extent of individual differences in general cognitive competence have been found to be enormous, ranging from the total dissolution of function seen in senile dementia to the persisting wit of octogenerians like George Bernard Shaw. Secondly, and more important are the recent findings from human cognitive psychology which show that the stages of the memory storage and retrieval process are differentially affected by age.

Craik (1977) has recently reviewed how information processing in humans is affected by aging. The changes observed are varied and complex. For example, sensory memory, the first stage in information storage, is relatively unaffected by aging unless the task requires divided attention. Also relatively unaffected by age in humans is simple short-term memory. Deficits appear only when the incoming information has to be reorganized or, as in sensory memory, when divided attention is required. Long-term memory and particularly retrieval from long-term memory, is the aspect of information processing most seriously affected by aging. Even here, however, some aspects of long-term memory are much more vulnerable than others. Age decrements are greatest in free recall where no retrieval cues are provided, and least when only simple recognition of previously learned material is required. Similarly, transformation of simple information into long-term memory is minimally impaired, whereas marked age-dependent differences emerge when elaborate encoding and conceptual reorganization of complex material are necessary.

This constellation of findings showing selective impairment of the information processing sequence in human subjects led us to suspect that comparable changes may be taking place in infrahuman animals such as the rat. Few changes in simple learned behaviors have been observed in rats of different ages. For example, aged animals are not inferior on a variety of simple tasks such as bar pressing (Goodrick, 1965), discrimination learning (Goodrick, 1972), water maze (Birren, 1962), or active avoidance (Doty, 1966). Only on "complex" learning measures such as the 14 unit T-maze used by Goodrick (1972) and Olton and Samuelson's (1976) recently developed spatial memory test (Barnes, 1979) have shown

Figure 10. Maturation and decline of selected reflexive, sensory, and psychomotor behaviors.

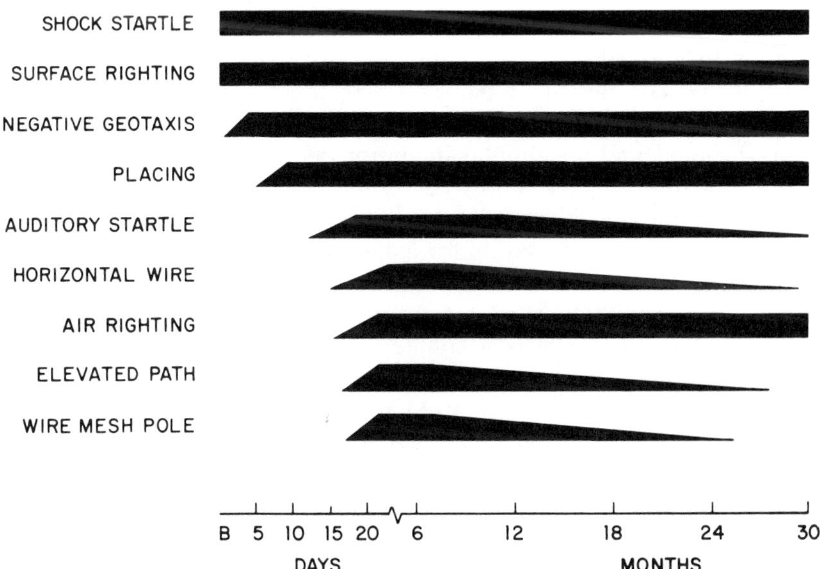

consistent differences in acquisition between mature and aged rats. This pattern of results suggests that aged rats, like aged people, have difficulty with tasks requiring elaborate encoding of the information to be stored in long-term memory.

Unfortunately there are no studies of sensory and short-term memory in the rat comparable to those reported for aged humans. One reason for the lack of comparable data is the vast difference in the conceptual models used by animal and cognitive psychologists to study the learning and retention process. For the most part, animal studies of aging have been categorized empirically by task rather than an inferred underlying process, while the latter approach is taken by those studying human memory. Since this approach has been relatively unsuccessful in identifying the nature of the deficits induced by aging in animals, we adopted the three stage information processing model as the conceptual framework for our research. In the work to be reported, we studied the effects of age on sensory memory, short-term memory, and long-term memory. The measures of long-term memory ranged from simple to complex and included tests designed to both measure recall and recognition-like processes.

Sensory Memory

No techniques have been established for studying sensory memory in animals, and it is difficult to conceive of precise analogues to the ingenious retrospective scanning techniques developed by Sperling (1960) that would be suitable for animal research. As an alternative to studying sensory memory, it is possible to study the temporal decay of prestimulus inhibition of startle. As we documented earlier, a brief stimulus presented just prior to a startle-inducing stimulus greatly inhibits the startle response. If one assumes that a perseverating central representation of the prestimulus is responsible for inhibition of startle, the similarities between sensory memory and prestimulus inhibition become apparent. The major difference in the two procedures lies in the behavioral measure used to read the central representation. In one instance the subject scans a decaying sensory representation for a specific stimulus, and in the other the decaying representation inhibits (competes with) elicitation of the startle response. Whether or not the underlying mechanisms are the same, inhibition of startle is a simple and reliable means of assessing speed of sensory information processing in animals of different ages.

The prestimulation paradigm used to determine sensory thresholds was also used in this portion of our research. Instead of varying stimulus intensity, we varied the interval between the prestimulus and the startle stimulus. In this instance, however, the prestimulus was also a startle stimulus (120 db, 20 ms) but the measure remained the same; percent of inhibition of startle. The procedure of using one startle stimulus to inhibit the startle response to a second stimulus was adapted to assure that stimulus was perceived by animals of all ages. As such, this prepulse inhibition procedure involved much more than just sensory memory since the first stimulus evoked sensory, central, and motor reactions which, in sum, acted to inhibit startle to the second stimulus. Thus, while the paradigm might be a clear measure of sensory information processing time at lower stimulus intensities, at this intensity it is possible to determine which components of the response inhibition process are altered by age.

The results of this experiment are shown in Figure 11. As can be seen the effectiveness of the prestimulus decreased linearly between 7 sec and 10 sec, and there was complete overlap between the various age groups. This suggests that the sensory, central, and motor systems necessary to respond to this type of stimulation are all relatively unaffected by age. Our work still in progress also suggests that lower prestimulus intensities are equally effective inhibitors of startle in rats of all ages.

Short-term Memory

Two measures of short-term memory were investigated. For the first, we used the eight arm radial maze described by Olton and Samuelson (1976). This is a particularly intriguing paradigm because of two independent sets of results. In the first, several researchers have noted that the

Figure 11. Percent inhibition of startle as a function of time between the prestimulus and startle stimulus.

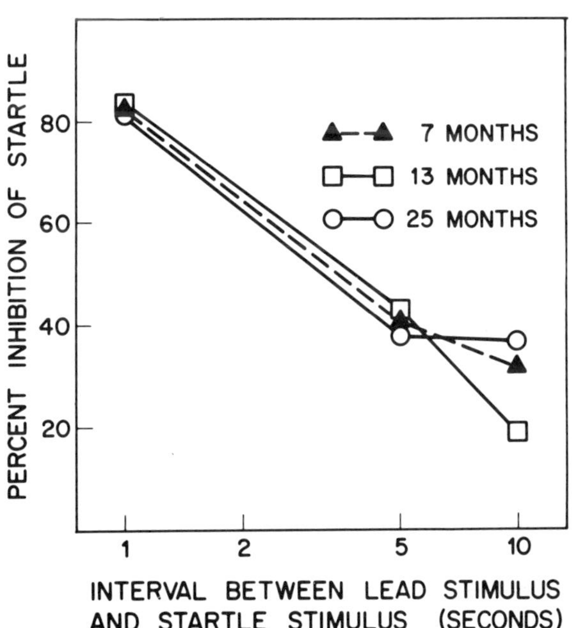

hippocampus shows marked neurohistological changes in both the aged human (Scheibel and Scheibel, 1977) and the aged rat (Hasan and Glees, 1973; Landfield, Rose, Sandles, Wholstadter, and Lynch, 1977). Secondly, Olton and his collaborators (Olton, Walker and Gage, 1978) have shown that rats with lesions disrupting the major fiber connections to the hippocampus are inferior in spatial maze performance when compared to intact controls. These data have been interpreted to suggest that the task might be a particularly sensitive measure of age-related deficits in learning and memory. In addition, Barnes (1979 and this volume) has also shown correlations between age, spatial memory and extracellularly recorded synaptic responses.

Rats were placed in the center of the maze and allowed to choose any of 8 baited arms radiating outward. Olton and Samuelson (1976) reported that in a consecutive series of eight choices, adult rats typically chose over seven different arms. The performance of four age groups of rats is shown in Figure 12 for the first and last five days of training. This figure shows that performance in the spatial maze is considerably worse in the older age groups even after extensive training.

Older rats in general, however, take longer to traverse this maze than younger rats, making it necessary for the older rats to remember their initial alley choices much longer than the younger rats. In order to

Figure 12. Number of different arms chosen in the radial maze as a function of age.

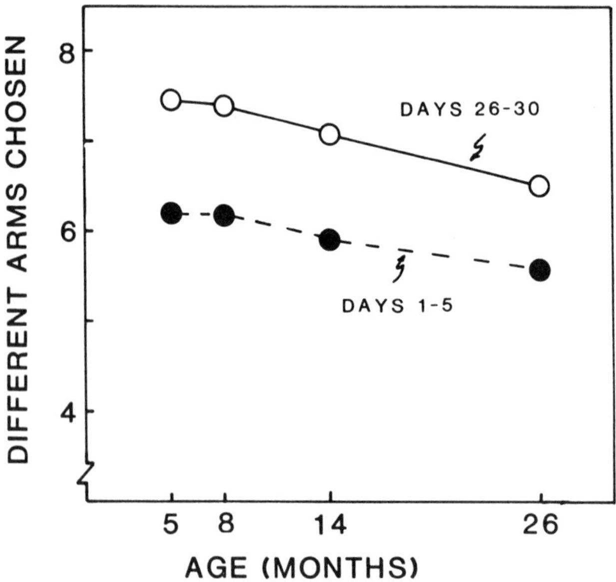

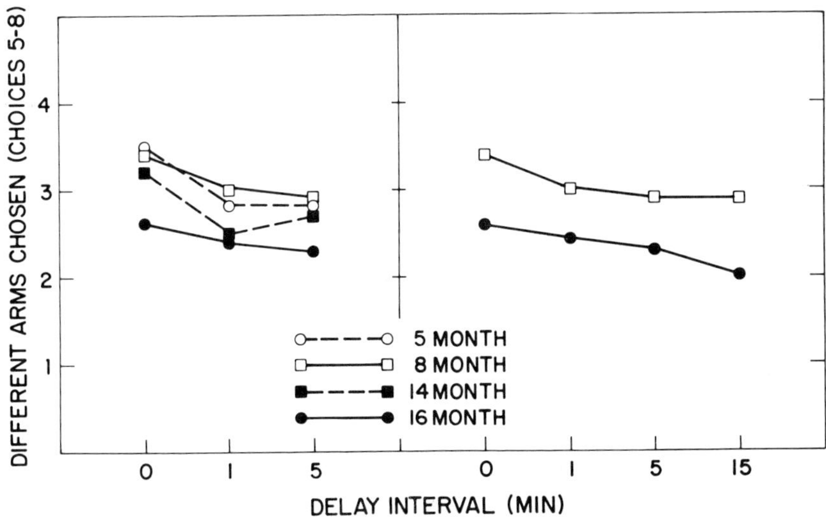

Figure 13. Number of different arms chosen in the radial maze as a function of age and delay interval between fourth and fifth choice. Only the 8-month- and 26-month-old rats were given the longest delay *(right panel)*.

provide a more accurate measure of short-term retention, each rat was removed from the maze following the fourth choice, retained in a holding cage for a specified retention interval, and then returned to the maze to complete the trial. The results of this procedure are shown in Figure 13. Performance levels for all age groups declined by an equivalent degree suggesting that there are no differential short-term retention capabilities in rats ranging from 8 to 26 months of age.

Our second measure of short-term memory involved a modification of a procedure developed by Konorski (1959). The paradigm consists of training rats to bar press on a CRF schedule in an operant chamber. The rats are then presented with two stimuli in a sequential manner. The stimuli were 5-sec auditory or visual signals. If both stimuli were of the same modality, a bar press during the second stimulus produced a food reward; if the stimuli were different, no reward was delivered. The paradigm allows for a delay to be inserted between the offset of the first stimulus and the onset of the second. When a delay occurs, the animal is required to remember whether the first stimulus was auditory or visual in order to compare it with the second. Figure 14 shows the performance of 6- and 23-month-old rats across three delay intervals. The discrimination index represents the probability of a correct response divided by the probability of a response on both correct and incorrect trials. What is evident in this figure and reminiscent of the findings obtained with the spatial maze, is that although there was a slight deficit in performance of

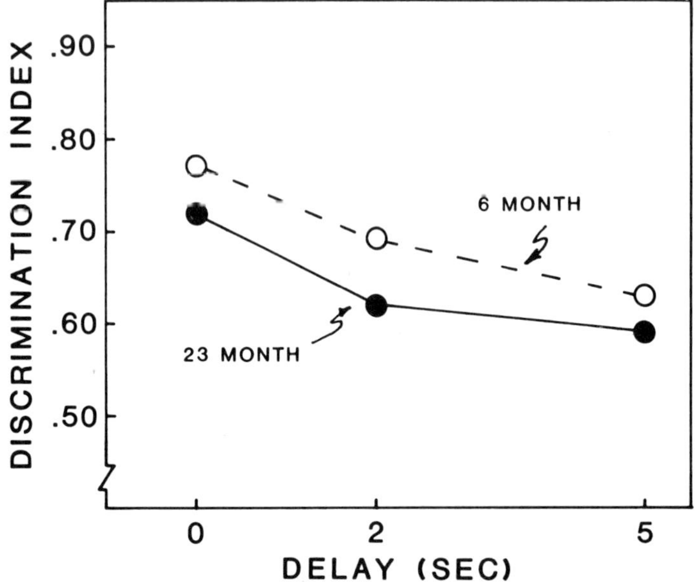

Figure 14. Discrimination performance at three delay intervals for two age groups in the Konorski paradigm.

the older rats on this task, this deficit was not exacerbated by increasing the delay interval.

To summarize, we have used two independent paradigms, both aimed at measuring the ability of the Fischer rat to retain events over short delay intervals. In both tasks asymptotic performance levels were lower in the aged rats, but rate of forgetting over short intervals was the same for both age groups. This suggests that sensory-motor function, motivational state or some other non-memorial process was degraded by age, but that short-term memory was unimpaired.

Long-term Memory

As noted previously, the major age-related deficits in man appear to be associated with the storage and retrieval of long-term memory. In many ways this is the easiest stage of information processing to study in laboratory animals since many established procedures are available. Less clear is the identification of classes of responses likely to be forgotten more rapidly in the aged animal. One possibility, as already mentioned, is that recall is more adversely affected by aging than recognition. As might be anticipated, this distinction is not easily made in animal research. We propose, however, that learned behaviors utilizing distinctive cues and simple go-no-go responses are more analogous to recognition memory than behavioral measures relying on internally generated cues such as those utilized in conjunction with various schedules of operant responding.

We could also classify learned behaviors by the order in which they emerge during ontogeny. Here, following Ribot's law we would predict that the earliest forms of learning would be more resistant to aging than later developing behaviors. This is the previously mentioned "first in, last out" principle.

The following experiments studied acquisition and retention of a late developing learned behavior that is also distinctively cued (passive avoidance), an earlier developing specifically signalled behavior (conditioned emotional response (CER) and a behavior utilizing internally generated cues (fixed interval responding) in mature and aged rats.

Passive Avoidance

The apparatus used for this experiment consisted of a standard step-through passive avoidance apparatus made up of a large white chamber attached to a smaller black chamber. During acquisition the rats were placed in the large, illuminated white chamber and allowed to enter the small black compartment. If the rats entered within a 60-second period, they immediately received a .2mA, .4 sec constant current AC shock applied to their feet through a grid floor. The intertrial interval was 30-sec (a previous study had shown that acquisition to a criterion of three consecutive 60-sec latencies was equivalent across age groups with a 30 sec ITI). The rats were tested for retention either 1- or 6-weeks later. Our results are shown in Figure 15.

As can be seen from the left portion of the figure, acquisition took several trials, and there were no differences in rate of learning among the various age groups. These results are unlike those seen early in development, where the younger animals typically require many more trials to acquire this response. After the 1- and 6-week retention interval animals of all age groups showed some "forgetting" on the first trial of the retention test, but returned to their previous long latencies of responding on the second test trial. These data are not the inverse of development where preweanling animals, trained to the same asymptote as post-weanling animals, show much more rapid forgetting than their older counterparts.

These data are also contrary to those reported by Gold and McGaugh (1975) who found that aged animals, given one passive avoidance training trial, showed much more rapid forgetting than mature adults. This finding considered in the context of the present study, suggests that older animals may suffer from a consolidation deficit when given only one trial. However, this deficit may be overcome with repeated trials and over-training.

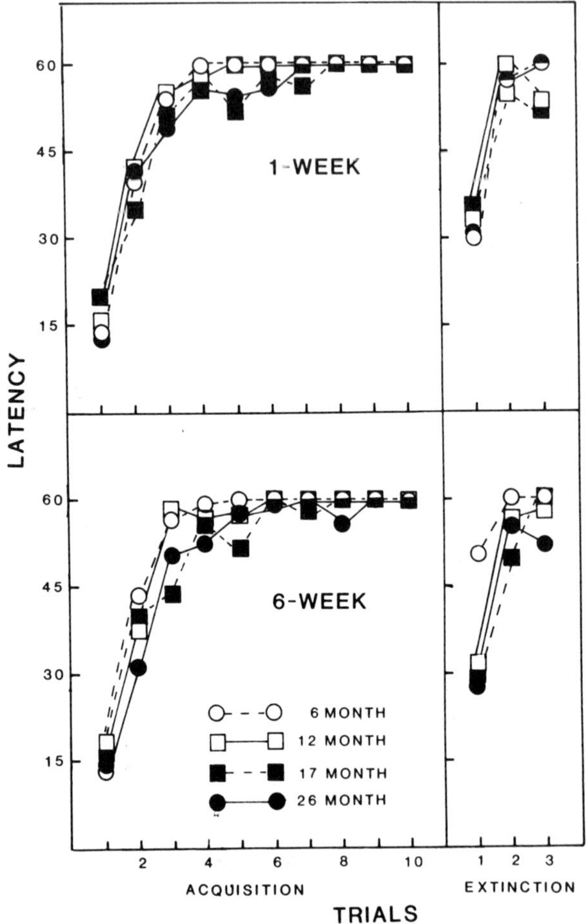

Figure 15. Acquisition and retention of a passive avoidance response in rats as a function of age.

Conditioned Emotional Responses (CER)

This task was selected as specifically-signalled, go-no-go type of task unlikely to show an age-related decline. As a learning task the CER has several advantages. First, conditioning takes place against a background of steady responding on a variable interval schedule. This provides a continuous measure of health and motivational state, and allows us to reduce individual differences by using the ratio of responding before and during the CS as the measure of conditioning.

In a preliminary series of experiments, we determined that acquisition levels could be easily equated across age groups if we used a compound noise-light CS and administered only one CS-US pairing per daily training session. Using these procedures we administered five conditioning trials to three age groups of rats on 5 consecutive days. Retention was measured after a 1- or 6-week retention interval, and consisted of daily extinction trials given on 7 consecutive days. As Figure 16 shows, acquisition levels were equivalent across age groups.

A finding consistent with our previous passive avoidance data was that there were no age-related differences during the first few days of extinction at either retention interval. The only age-dependent difference to emerge was the rapid extinction shown by the 24-month-old rats on the 6th and 7th days of extinction: a difference we viewed as either artifactual or motivational in nature.

The present studies showing no age-related retention losses over long retention intervals are generally consistent with findings from human subjects, provided that a differentiation is made between recognition and recall tasks. The only requirement of both the passive avoidance and CER tasks is that the rats recognize a previously feared stimulus and either respond or do not respond. To this extent the results are identical to reports for elderly individuals who show relatively little loss of recognition memory in the laboratory.

Figure 16. Acquisition and retention of a conditioned emotional response (CER) in rats as a function of age.

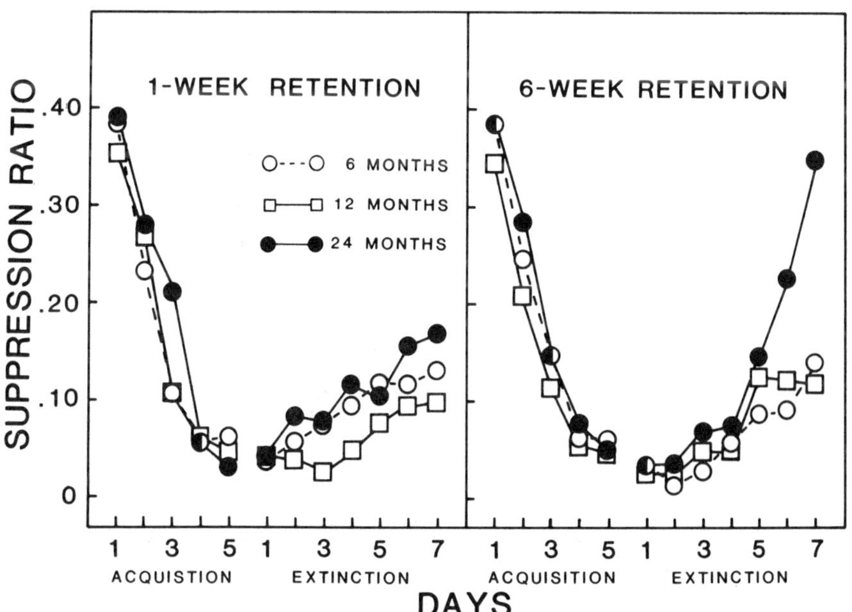

Fixed Internal Responding

On recall tasks, as noted earlier, the aged typically show substantial losses relative to those shown by mature adults. As with the other levels of information processing we analyzed, there are no accepted measures of recall memory in infrahuman species. There are, however, a variety of behavioral tasks in which the cues are internally generated rather than externally presented. Moreover, at least some of these, including fixed internal responding, are much more vulnerable to forgetting than stimulus-specific behaviors (Gleitman, 1971). For this reason we used conventional operant procedures to study acquisition and retention of fixed interval responding in mature and aged rats. After 8 days of training, all age groups showed the typical temporal scallop in which responding increases as the moment of food delivery nears. When tested for retention of this internally generated behavior after a 10-day interval, the older animals show substantial loss of the scallop while the younger group showed almost no change (Figure 17).

Theoretical Overview and Conclusions

In the first section of this report, we described the effects of aging on sensory, reflexive and sensory-motor behavior. The pattern of changes occurring during aging were far from uniform, and it is clear that the

Figure 17. Acquisition and retention of responding on a 60-second fixed interval schedule in 6, 12, and 26-month-old rats.

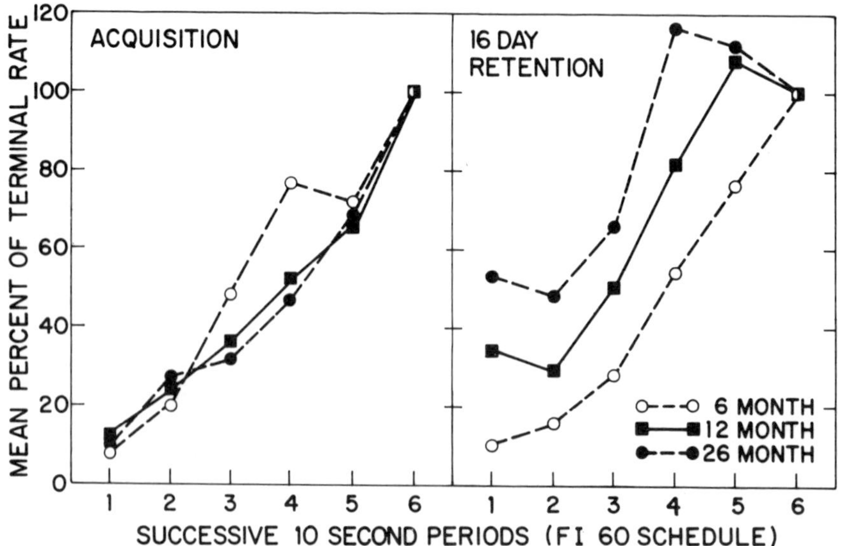

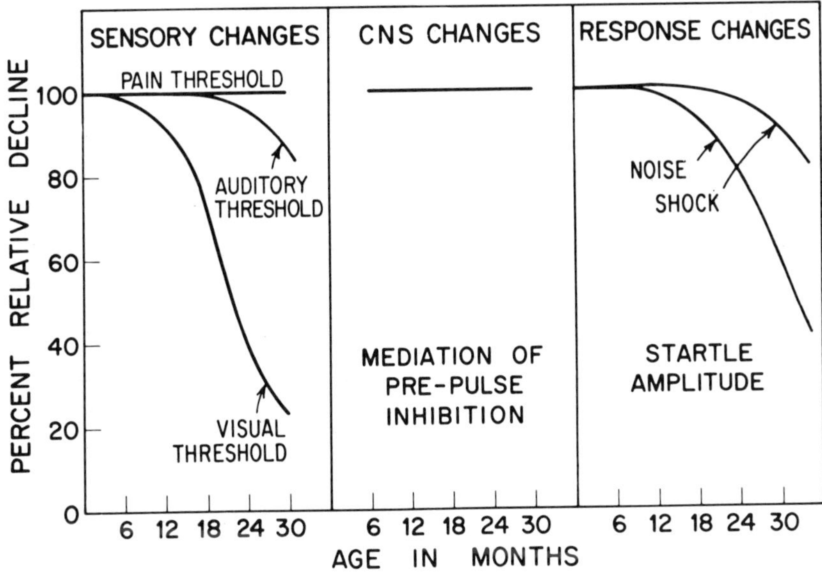

Figure 18. Schematic representation of the effects of age on sensory sensitivity, central nervous system function, and reactivity to startle stimuli.

pace of aging varies enormously from system to system and organ to organ. To help summarize some of these changes we have prepared another schematic representation. The left panel of Figure 18 shows that the decline in sensory function varies substantially from one modality to another. Sensory responsivity to pain is the least affected in the rat and visual sensitivity the most. The center panel depicts hypothesized changes in the neural mechanisms mediating sensory-motor function in the rat; a subject not previously discussed but one of considerable importance. Of all our research reported, our sensory memory experiment has direct bearing on this question. From this experiment we can infer that the time required for sensory information to reach the central nervous system and influence behavior elicited by another stimulus does not decrease with advancing age. To the extent that speed of interneuronal conduction is an index of normal nervous system function, these data may be taken to indicate that age has not impaired brain capability at the level mediating prepulse inhibition of startle.

The right-hand panel illustrates the relative decline of reflexive, startle and coordinated motor behaviors. Again there are differences in the rate of decline depending upon the response class involved.

When these three panels are considered together, one obvious conclusion is that peripheral sensory and motor systems decline much more rapidly during aging than do the parts of the central nervous system mediating simple sensory-motor behaviors. This is probably a basic principle of aging, one that is implicitly recognized but not often commented upon—the principle being that the brain is defended against the aging process relative to other organ systems. This is not an unlikely principle since the brain is also vigorously defended against most metabolic disturbances and is relatively unsusceptible to disease. The brain, for example, is the last organ affected by starvation, in terms of weight and energy utilization. In the aged it is not uncommon to encounter individuals who perform at the highest levels of cognitive function, but one never encounters an 80-year-old decathalon Olympic champion. This general rule undoubtedly applies to all mammals, including the rat.

The final figure (19) in this chapter illustrates the changes that take place in cognitive function of the rat during aging. When we consider the basic stages of information processing, sensory memory, short-term memory, and long-term memory, it is evident that the effects of aging, at least in the rat, are selectively related to the level of information processing required. Although these conclusions are based on relatively little evidence, it seems highly likely that sensory memory is the least affected by aging and long-term memory the most in the rat, just as it is in humans.

Figure 19. Schematic representation of the effects of age on sensory memory, short-term memory, and long-term memory.

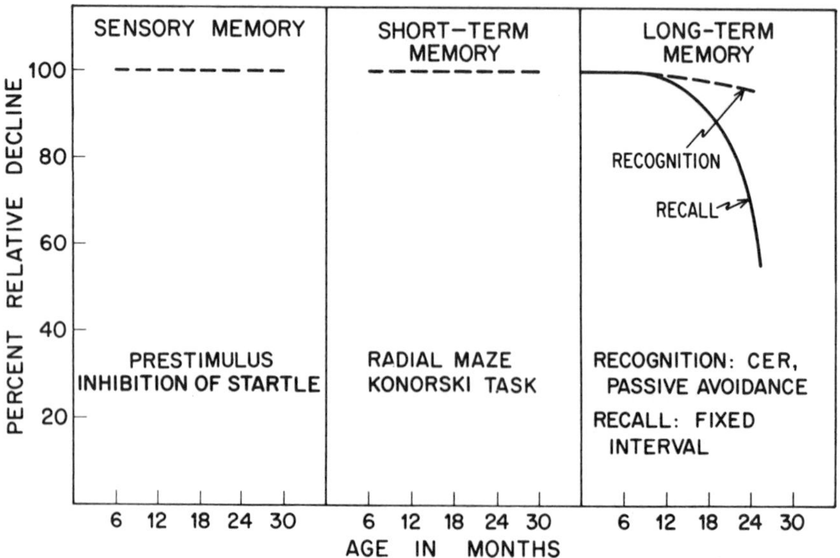

References

Altman J, Sudarshan K: Postnatal development of locomotion in the laboratory rat. *Animal Behavior* 23:896–920, 1975.

Barnes CA: Memory deficits associated with senescence: a neurophysiological and behavioral study in the rat. *J Comparative and Physiological Psychology* 93:74–104, 1979.

Birren JE: Age differences in learning a two-choice water maze by rats. *J. Gerontology* 17:207–213, 1962.

Birren JE, Schaie WK: *Handbook of the Psychology of Aging*. New York, Van Nostrand Reinhold, 1977.

Brooks CM: Studies on the cerebral cortex. II. Localized representation of hopping and placing reaction in the rat. *Am J Physiology* 105:162–171, 1933.

Campbell BA, Masterson FA: Psychophysics of punishment. In Campbell BA, Church RM (eds.) *Punishment and Aversive Behavior.* New York, Appleton-Century-Crofts, 1969.

Chesky JA, Rockstein M: Life span characteristics in the male Fischer rat. *Experimental Aging Research* 2:399–407, 1976.

Coleman GL, Barthold SW, Osbaldiston GW, Foster SJ, Jonas AM: Pathological changes during aging in barrier-reared Fischer 344 male rats. *J Gerontology* 32:258–278, 1977.

Craik FIM: Age differences in human memory. In Birren JE, Schaie KW (eds.) *Handbook of the Psychology of Aging*. New York, Van Nostrand Reinhold, 1977.

Doty BA: Age and avoidance conditioning in rats. *J Gerontology* 21:287–290, 1966.

Gleitman H: Forgetting of long-term memories in animals. In Honig WK, James RHR (eds.) *Animal Memory.* New York, Academic Press, 1971.

Gold PE, McGaugh JL: Changes in learning and memory during aging. In Ordy JM, Brizzee KR (eds.) *Neurobiology of Aging*. New York, Plenum Press, 1975.

Goodrick CL: Learning by mature-young and aged Wistar albino rats as a function of test complexity. *J Gerontology* 27:353–357, 1972.

Goodrick CL: Operant level and light-contingent bar presses as a function of age and deprivation. *Psychological Reports* 17:283–288, 1965.

Hasan M, Glees P: Ultrastructural age changes in hippocampal neurons, synapses and neuroglici. *Experimental Gerontology* 8: 75–83, 1973.

Hoffman HS, Wible BL: Role of weak signals in acoustic startle. *J Acoustical Society America* 47:489–497, 1970.

Ison JR, Hammond GR: Modification of the startle reflex in the rat by changes in auditory and visual environments. *J Comparative and Physiological Psychology* 75:435–452, 1971.

Kenshalo DR: Age changes in touch, vibration, temperature, kinesthesis and pain sensitivity. In Birren JE, Schaie KW (eds.) *Handbook of the Psychology of Aging*. New York, Van Nostrand Reinhold, 1977.

Konorski J: A new method of physiological investigation of recent memory in animals. *Bulletin de L'Academie Polonaise des Sciences,* 7:115–117, 1959.

Landfield PW, Rose G, Sandles L, Wohlstadter TC, Lynch G: Patterns of astroglial hypertrophy and neuronal degeneration in the hippocampus of aged memory-deficient rats. *J Gerontology* 32:3–12, 1977.

Murdock BB Jr: Recent developments in short-term memory. *Brit J Psychology* 58:421–433, 1967.

Olton DS, Samuelson RJ: Remembrance of places past: spatial memory in rats. *J Experimental Psychology: Animal Behavior Processes* 2:97–116, 1976.

Olton DS, Walker JA, Gage FH: Hippocampal connections and spatial discrimination. *Brain Research* 139:295–308, 1978.

Ribot TA: *The Diseases of Memory.* New York, Appleton and Co., 1882.

Scheibel ME, Scheibel AB: Differential changes with aging in old and new cortices. In Nandy K, Sherwin I (eds.) *The Aging Brain and Senile Dementia.* New York, Plenum Press, 1977.

Schonfield D, Robertson BA: Memory storage and aging. *Canadian J Psychology* 20:287–290, 1966.

Sperling G: The information available in brief visual presentations. *Psychological Monographs* 74:11, Whole No. 498, 1960.

Stehouwer DJ, Campbell BA: Habituation of the fore limb withdrawal response in neonatal rats. *J Experimental Psychology: Animal Behavior Processes* 4:104–119, 1978.

Taylor J: (ed.) *Selected Writings of John Hughling Jackson. Vol. 2. Evolution and Dissolution of the Nervous System.* London, Hodder and Stoughton, 1931.

Waugh NC, Norman DA: Primary memory. *Psychological Review* 72:89–104, 1965.

Stein, ed. The Psychobiology of Aging: Problems and Perspectives

Correlative Studies of Brain Neurophysiology and Behavior During Aging

Philip W. Landfield, Ph.D.

Department of Physiology and Pharmacology, Bowman Gray School of Medicine, Winston-Salem, North Carolina.

Introduction

Aging is a fundamental and complex biological process which appears to affect all higher vertebrates, and which proceeds throughout a large proportion of the life span (Strehler, 1962). Judging from physiological evidence (Shock, 1974), in fact, human aging phenomena began well before the midpoint of the life span. Despite the ubiquitous nature of the aging process, however, and despite its extensive biological and medical implications, almost nothing is known about its causes or underlying mechanisms.

In recent years, however, evidence has accumulated to indicate that aging of the brain, due to altered regulation of endocrine and autonomic systems, may play a central role in the general mammalian physiological aging process (Finch, 1976; Sacher, 1959; Shock, 1974; Meites, Huang and Simpkins, 1978). This evidence, however, does not address the initial causes of brain aging itself, or the nature of the dynamic changes in brain function which accompany it. Again, little is known with any certainty about these problems, although increasing research is being focussed on mechanisms of brain aging.

This increased attention is reflected in an improved understanding of the morphological concomitants of brain aging, and in a wider use of quantitative approaches and/or metallic impregnation and electron microscopic techniques in the study of age-related brain anatomical change (e.g., Brizzee, 1975; Brody, 1973, 1976; Feldman, 1976; Geinisman,

Bondareff and Dodge, 1978; Landfield, 1978; Lindsey, Landfield and Lynch, 1979; Scheibel and Scheibel, 1975; Tomlinson and Henderson, 1976; Vaughan and Peters, 1974; Wisniewski and Terry, 1973, 1976).

Additionally, the application of recent neurochemical approaches to the study of brain aging has provided important data on neurotransmitter metabolism, receptor binding, and second messengers (Carlsson, 1978; Finch, 1976, 1978; Joseph, Berger, Engel and Roth, 1978; Meites et al., 1978; McGeer and McGeer, 1976; Riegle and Meites, 1976; Schmidt and Thornberry, 1978; Simpkins, Mueller, Huang and Meites, 1977).

The value of these basic studies is obvious. Nevertheless, in themselves they seem unlikely to be able to provide a comprehensive picture of brain aging without some input from one of the major neurobiological disciplines; i.e., without some contribution from neurophysiology. Although there have been some EEG and evoked potential studies, the few experiments in defined monosynaptic or fiber systems have largely been confined to peripheral or spinal nervous systems (e.g., Birren and Wall, 1956; Vyskocil and Gutmann, 1972; Wayner and Emmers, 1958).

Without microelectrode studies to specify which dynamic mechanisms are most affected by age (e.g., EPSPs, action potentials, membrane polarization, inhibition, etc.), or which cellular loci exhibit signs of impairment (e.g., pre- or postsynaptic, dendritic, axonal, somal, etc.), it seems that it will be very difficult to determine which of the many morphological-chemical correlates of brain aging are in fact relevant to declining neuronal function. Thus, the availability of basic neurophysiological information will, I believe, substantially facilitate both the search for molecular-structural mechanisms, and the development of pharmacological agents capable of specifically manipulating brain aging phenomena. The latter, of course, might have therapeutic as well as experimental applications.

In addition to the study of dynamic neurophysiological brain changes during aging, the study of correlated *functional* (e.g., behavioral) alterations in the whole organism can provide significant theoretical insights; that is, finding a consistent correlation between basic neurophysiological variables and a component of behavior can importantly reduce (but of course not eliminate) the chances of focussing upon incidental, secondary neurophysiological age changes which have no functional relevance to the survival, reproductive success, or homeostatic regulation of the animal.

It also seems probable that our understanding of *normal* neurophysiological mechanisms, and their interactions with behavior, will be advanced by correlative studies in aging animals. Current data indicate that the aging brain can, in a sense, be viewed as an experimental preparation in which a few selective neurophysiological or other neurobiological mechanisms have been altered. Determining how these changes interact with other brain mechanisms, and determining which behavioral components are concomitantly altered, seems likely to substantially increase our insight into the nature of these relationships in the non-aged brain, as well as in the aged.

With the goal of resolving some of these issues, my associates and I undertook basic neurophysiological studies of a mammalian (rat) brain structure (hippocampus) several years ago, in conjunction with behavioral experiments. Below are summarized results from what is apparently the first series of microelectrode studies on a defined monosynaptic system in the aging mammalian brain, along with data from our attempts to relate these neurophysiological analyses to behavior (Landfield, McGaugh and Lynch, 1976, 1978b; Landfield and Lynch, 1977; Landfield, 1979). Before describing our findings, however, I will briefly consider a number of interpretative and control problems which seem to me to be highly relevant to neurophysiological-behavioral studies in aging mammals. Some of these problems are analogous to those found in similar studies of young animals, while others are specific to studies in aging animals.

Interpretative, Methodological and Control Issues

It is certainly well-known that evidence of within-group correlation does not imply causation; nonetheless, it is perhaps also useful to emphasize that correlation does at least fulfill one critical prediction arising from any hypothesis of causation (i.e., that 2 causally-related variables will co-vary). Further, the failure to find a predicted correlation between 2 variables allows for definitive rejection of an hypothesis of causation (assuming, of course, that the experiment is carefully performed).

A second major prediction arising from a causal hypothesis is that when one variable is experimentally manipulated, the dependent variable will co-vary. Spontaneous correlative analyses do not of course address this latter prediction. Nevertheless, correlative studies can strongly suggest which variables are the most appropriate candidates for subsequent manipulation studies. My associates and I have utilized this sequence of correlation and manipulation procedures in several instances, with what appear, to me at least, to be interesting results (e.g., Landfield, McGaugh and Tusa, 1972; Landfield, 1977; Landfield, Waymire and Lynch, 1978; Landfield, Lindsey and Lynch, 1978).

Nevertheless, correlative studies of this kind also contain a number of potential interpretative pitfalls; generally, these are fairly obvious and will only be briefly noted here. Included among these is the danger of making a Type I statistical error when comparing a number of variables and performing multiple tests for significant correlations (i.e., the probability of finding a significant correlation by chance alone is increased). This factor will of course affect interpretation of the significance level of an observed correlation. Additionally, a correlation of behavioral change with a (neurophysiological) change in a specific synaptic system does not of course necessarily imply a possible relationship of the behavior to that system, but only to the physiological change—which may be present in many synaptic systems within a structure, or even throughout the brain.

A second general point relevant not to correlative studies, but to most aging experiments aimed at the investigation of "primary" aging changes—as opposed to secondary consequences of diseases, or of widespread cellular or physiological deterioration—is that aging changes which *precede* others are more likely to be of primary origin (given that the terms "primary" and "secondary" are highly relative in this context). Clearly, the earlier in life at which an aging correlate appears, the more likely it is that the correlate is associated with causative aging phenomena. While this point may in some ways appear obvious, there have been few studies aimed at finding the earliest detectable change within a group of related variables.

Along similar lines, there is increasing recognition of the importance of protecting aging animals from infectious disease, if basic aging phenomena are to be separable from secondary degenerative changes arising from disease in the highly susceptible aging animals (e.g., see the NIA Volume edited by Gibson, Adelman and Finch, 1979; and the National Academy of Sciences report on Animal Models of Aging, 1980).

There are, moreover, a number of general methodological problems associated specifically with *neurophysiological* studies of aging animals. These include:

1. Age differences in temperature regulation.
2. Age differences in susceptibility to anesthesia or other preparative treatments.
3. Age differences in the extracellular environment (e.g., oxygen, ionic concentrations, etc.).
4. Age differences in electrode localization.

It is well established that temperature regulation is reduced (Finch, 1976), and that drug metabolism is altered (Goldberg and Roberts, 1976) with age. Thus, these factors, both of which can affect neuronal excitability, must be controlled for in neurophysiological studies. Many of the problems noted above can be avoided somewhat by the use of *in vitro* or chronic neurophysiological preparations, as opposed to the more conventional anesthetized or paralyzed preparations. If anesthetized preparations are used, temperature can be regulated, although the anesthesia remains a problem. An *in vitro,* but not a chronic, preparation can also control for gross extracellular changes due to altered endocrine, kidney, respiratory or liver function. However, intracellular cytoplasmic changes brought about by prolonged peripheral alterations may of course not be compensated for by *in vitro* procedures. Further, changes in extracellular space (Bondareff and Narotzky, 1972; Landfield, Rose, Sandles, Wohlstadter and Lynch, 1977) can alter the availability of substances even in the *in vitro* preparation. Finally, since the hippocampus (Diamond, Johnson and Ingham, 1975) and olfactory bulb (Hinds and McNelly, 1977), and perhaps other regions, continue to grow in rats with age, and the skull thickens and may increase in size, some physiological criteria of electrode placement seem necessary to complement stereotaxic methods in intact animal preparations. Electrode movement due to brain or skull growth may also be a problem in extended, chronic studies of rats.

Neurophysiological Studies of Brain Aging

Our neurophysiological experiments have to date been carried out primarily using the Schaffer collateral-commissural monosynaptic projection to the apical dendrites of hippocampal CAl pyramidal cells; and measuring the population spike response elicited in CAl cells by stimulation of these afferents (see Figure 1 legend) (Landfield et al., 1976, 1978b; Landfield and Lynch, 1977; Landfield, 1979). In these studies we chose to investigate the hippocampus for a number of reasons, among which was that the hippocampus is one of the structures affected earliest and most severely by morphological age changes, in essentially all mammalian species yet examined (Tomlinson and Henderson, 1976; Wisniewski and Terry, 1976). Therefore, if the above suggestion on the significance of studying early changes is reasonable, the hippocampus appears to be a highly appropriate structure for age-related investigations. Fortunately, the hippocampus also appears, along with cerebellum and olfactory bulb, to be a particularly good model system for studies of brain neurophysiology (Andersen, 1975; Kandel and Spencer, 1961; Lynch, Smith, Browning and Deadwyler, 1975; Prince, 1978). Further, studies of behavioral-neurophysiological relations during aging, using hippocampus, are facilitated by a large literature on correlations between behavior and hippocampal lesions or hippocampal electrical activity (Isaacson, 1974; O'Keefe and Nadel, 1978; Isaacson and Pribram, 1975).

An early concern, however, was that the brains of the aged animals would be so deteriorated that we would be unable to determine which neurophysiological changes occurred earliest or which physiological changes were correlated with behavior. This, however, proved not to be the case, and only a very limited number of variables have been found to be changed with age. In fact, our most recent studies (Landfield, 1979; Landfield, Lindsey and Lynch, in preparation) indicate that only one major neurophysiological variable is clearly affected by age; further, the degree of decline in this process is also closely correlated with the degree of decline in one of the few behavioral variables which we found to be impaired using our task (see below).

This somewhat remarkable specificity of neurophysiological impairment appears to owe something to the housing conditions in which these animals were maintained. That is, our subjects were specific-pathogen-free, Caesarian-derived Fischer 344 rats which are barrier-reared and maintained under sterile conditions (see Gibson et al., 1979 for a description of the colony). Our aged subjects were therefore free of all overt pathology or respiratory infections, and any animal that developed pathology during the course of these studies was removed from the data analysis. Additionally, the aged animals we used were below the mean longevity age for this colony (e.g., 24–25 months vs mean life span of 29 months).

Our studies have employed both the intact, urethane-anesthetized rat preparation (Landfield et al., 1978b; and in preparation) and the *in vitro* hippocampal slice preparation (Landfield and Lynch, 1977). The latter is gaining wide popularity as a model brain system. Its advantages have been demonstrated in some detail by a number of investigators (Deadwyler, Dudek, Cotman and Lynch, 1975; Lynch et al., 1975; Schwartzkroin and Prince, 1978; Skrede and Westgaard, 1971; Yamamoto, 1972) and will not be further elaborated here. It may simply be noted that most of the transverse, lamellar hippocampal pathways, including the Schaffer collaterals, appear to function normally in the transverse hippocampal slice.

Figure 1 shows schematic examples of the two preparations employed, along with patterns of population spike potentiation. This spike is the primary response measured in our studies and appears to be a summated extracellular "envelope" of synchronously discharged action potentials (Andersen, 1975; see legend for further descriptions).

The rodent or lagomorph hippocampus, both *in vivo* and *in vitro,* is widely noted for its particularly robust forms of frequency and posttetanic potentiation of excitatory potentials (Andersen, 1975; Bliss and Lomo, 1973; Figure 1). Hippocampal posttetanic potentiation (increased response amplitude following a stimulation train) is in fact so persistent (being reported to last from hours-to-weeks—Bliss and Lomo, 1973; Douglas and Goddard, 1975) that it is now generally termed "long-term" (LTP), or "long-lasting" (LLP), potentiation (Andersen, 1975; Douglas and Goddard, 1975; Lynch et al., 1975; Teyler, Bradley, Bergman and

Livingston, 1977). There are of course temporal analogies between memory and posttetanic potentiation which have long been recognized (e.g., Eccles, 1953). With hippocampal LTP, this temporal analogy is even more pronounced, and therefore has inevitably led to speculation, by many investigators in the field, that hippocampal long-term potentiation may be a physiological correlate of some aspects of memory.

Frequency potentiation, or the growth of responses *during* repetitive stimulation, has not been the subject of as much interest with regard to mechanisms of behavioral plasticity. However, as noted in further detail below, it is primarily the mechanisms of frequency potentiation, or at least of the ability to *sustain* frequency potentiated excitatory responses *during* repetitive stimulation, which are most impaired in the hippocampus of aging animals. Conversely, our most recent studies (Landfield, 1979; and in preparation) show that long-term potentiation of spike discharge is *not* at all impaired with age in our animals, according to current definitions and methods of measurement. This conclusion differs somewhat from our earlier findings (Landfield and Lynch, 1977; Landfield et al., 1978b), but the discrepancy likely appears to be due to differences in the sequences of stimulation procedures used (described below).

We have conducted analogous hippocampal experiments in both the intact, anesthetized, temperature-maintained preparation and the *in vitro* hippocampal slice in order to control for some of the problems noted earlier. Although, to date, the intact preparation has been used more extensively, very similar patterns have been seen in both preparations. This observation suggests that anesthesia or the *gross* extracellular environment are not major factors in observed age differences (i.e., animals are not anesthetized prior to slice preparation and the slice is maintained in a medium of constant glucose and ionic concentrations, constant temperature, and a continuous supply of O_2 gas). However, in the slice we have not yet conducted the prolonged (e.g., >60 sec) repetitive stimulation paradigms which were conducted in the intact animals. As is noted subsequently, alterations in the later phases of frequency potentiation are among the most consistent correlates of age and of behavioral change which we have yet found *in vivo*. Thus, an important future goal is to determine if similar age-related failures of later frequency potentiation also occur in the slice preparation. Nevertheless, it should be noted that age-related failure of *early* frequency potentiation is similar in both the intact and the *in vitro* preparations. Additionally, there were no systematic signs that the aged animals reacted differently to urethane anesthesia, judging from the dose needed for maintained anesthesia, from spontaneous unit activity, or from the percentage of animals exhibiting seizure discharges during repetitive stimulation (all of the latter were discarded from analysis). Further, body

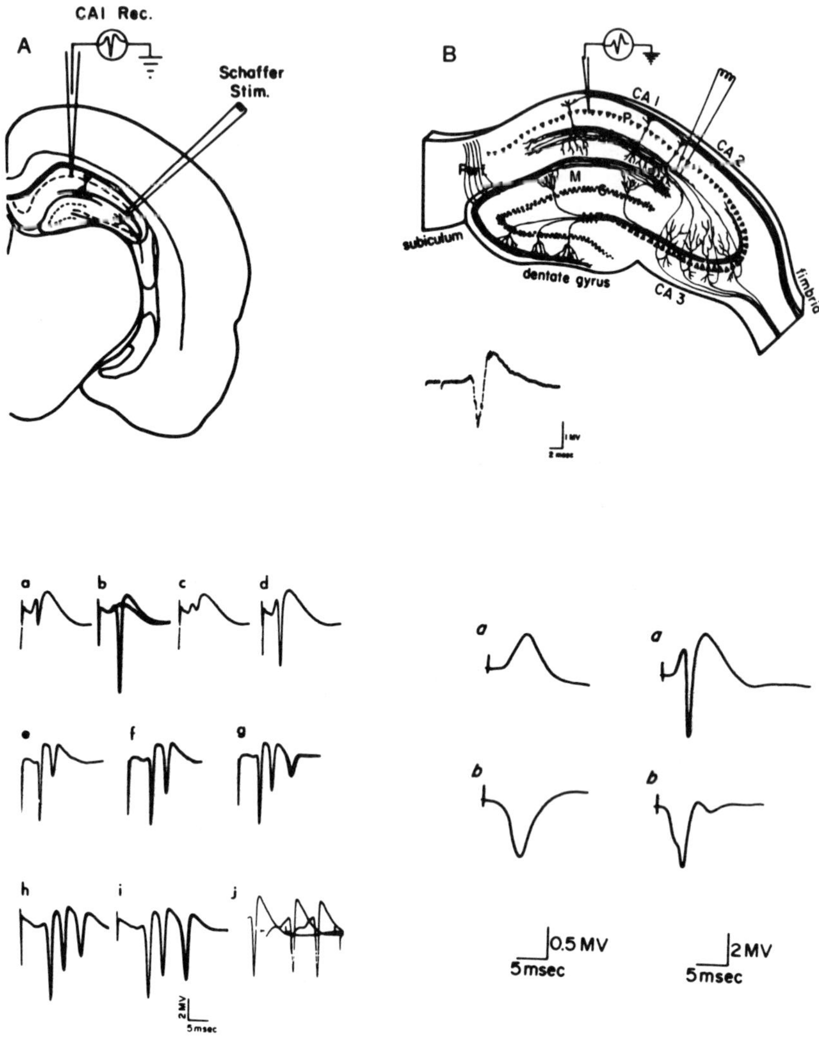

temperature was rectally monitored and continuously maintained by a heating pad at 35°C in aged and young animals. Thus, it seems unlikely that age differences in the response to anesthesia are a major factor in the age differences in neurophysiology, although this will be further examined in the next series of *in vitro* studies.

Data from studies in intact anesthetized animals (Landfield et al., 1978b) are shown in Figure 2. The graphs plot the population spike or

Figure 1. Schematic representations of the two preparations employed in these studies, and illustrations of the typical electrical responses observed. **A:** Intact preparation with stimulation electrode inserted into the Schaffer collateral path by stereotaxic and physiological localization; **B:** Representation of an *in vitro* slice preparation in which the Schaffer-commissural system to CA1 was also studied; *Lower left:* Population spike responses recorded in CA1 during or after repetitive stimulation. *a-d:* Long-term potentiation, as assessed wth 0.4 Hz stimulation *a:* Control; *b:* Superimposed responses 10 sec after a brief 100 Hz train, showing large potentiation, then rapid depression of the spike on the next 0.4 Hz pulse; *c:* Response at 30-sec post-tetanization; *d:* Response at 3 min post-tetanization; long-term potentiation is seen; *e–g:* Frequency potentiation of secondary and tertiary population spikes (first spike is already potentiated) during 9 Hz stimulation; *e, f, and g* are separated by 10-sec intervals. Multiple spikes are often elicited by each pulse during a brief train. *h–i:* Similar sequence showing growth of the 3rd spike. *j:* Stability of LT-potentiated spikes during 0.4 Hz stimulation at 5-min intervals (superimposed) following 100 Hz tetanization. *Lower right:* Reversal of polarity of the field EPSP potential, as a pipette situated in the CA1 somata *(a,a)* is lowered 200μ into the apical dendrites *(b,b)*; stimulation below *(left)*, and above *(right)*, population spike threshold. This polarity reversal is one of the primary criteria for establishing that the Schaffer collaterals are being activated.

SOURCE: *Landfield et al., 1978b, Brain Research; Landfield and Lynch, 1977, Journal of Gerontology; in preparation.*

field EPSP changes as percent of control, during a sequential series of 4 experiments carried out in each aged and young animal. In Figure 2a are shown results from the paired-pulse facilitation series (in which a second pulse is given at varying intervals following a conditioning pulse, leading in many synaptic systems to enhancement of the 2nd response at some intervals). No clear age differences were seen in the time course or percentage of facilitation of the "field EPSP" (other studies in this series measure the population spike). Further, no clear differences were observed prior to repetitive stimulation procedures in spontaneous unit activity, or in population spike thresholds, latencies or amplitudes, or in temporal patterns of field responses. Barnes (1979) did find reduced monosynaptic field EPSP control amplitudes in the dentate gyrus of 28-34-month-old rats; some of those results are also described elsewhere in this volume. However, it should be noted that there were notable differences between the two studies in age of the aged animals, in rat strain, in structure investigated, and in animal husbandry. In any case, it is possible that more detailed analyses will reveal subtle age differences in some of these variables in our animals as well, or that these changes may also become more pronounced in Fischer rats by 28-34 months. At present, however, it appears that if such age changes exist in specific-

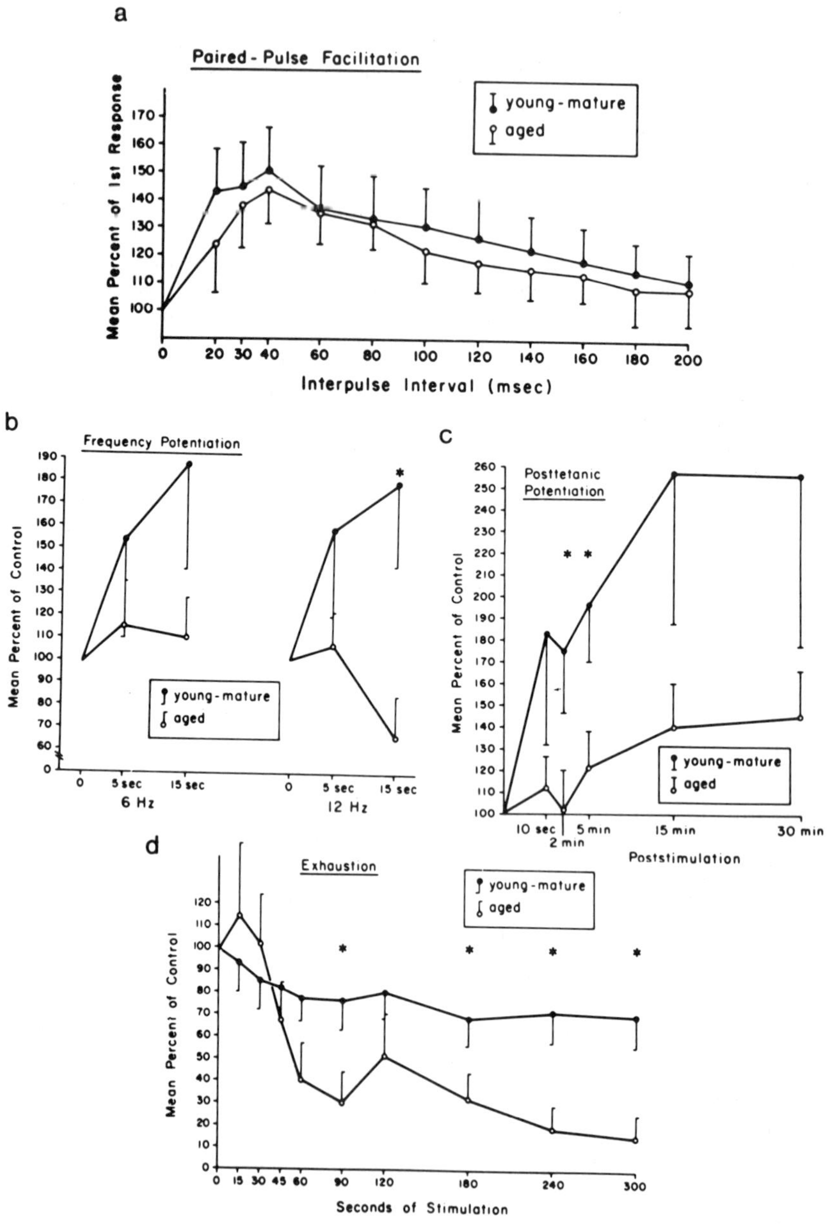

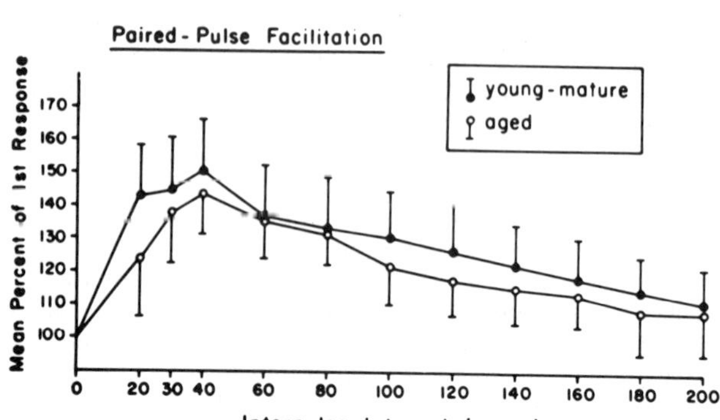
a
Paired - Pulse Facilitation
young - mature
aged
Mean Percent of 1st Response
100 110 120 130 140 150 160 170
0 20 30 40 60 80 100 120 140 160 180 200
Interpulse Interval (msec)

b
Frequency Potentiation
Mean Percent of Control
0 60 70 80 90 100 110 120 130 140 150 160 170 180 190
young - mature
aged
0 5 sec 15 sec
6 Hz
0 5 sec 15 sec
12 Hz
*

c
Posttetanic Potentiation
Mean Percent of Control
100 110 120 130 140 150 160 170 180 190 200 210 220 230 240 250 260
* *
young - mature
aged
10 sec 2 min 5 min 15 min 30 min
Poststimulation

d
Exhaustion
young - mature
aged
Mean Percent of Control
0 10 20 30 40 50 60 70 80 90 100 110 120
* * * *
0 15 30 45 60 90 120 180 240 300
Seconds of Stimulation

Figure 2. Series of repetitive stimulation studies conducted sequentially in each intact animal. Except for in **a**, all values reflect the percent change in the prestimulation control population spike. **a:** No major age differences are seen in amplitude facilitation of the 2nd "field EPSP" response elicited by the 2nd of a pair of stimulation pulses, at various interstimulus intervals; **b:** Frequency potentiation of the population spike is impaired with age, particularly at higher frequencies (12 Hz) and longer durations (15-sec) of stimulation; **c:** Long-term (or post-tetanic) potentiation only shows evidence of an age difference shortly after a brief train of 100 Hz stimulation, suggesting possible differences in susceptibility to depression, rather than in long-term potentiation *per se;* **d:** Using a prolonged repetitive stimulation ("exhaustion") paradigm (4 Hz), the potentiation of the population spike can be seen to be "biphasic" over time, with the second phase failing substantially in aged hippocampus (this biphasic pattern is somewhat obscured in the young group by plotting of means, but was present in most individual animals). Asterisks represent significantly different points.

SOURCE: *Landfield et al., 1978b; Brain Research.*

pathogen-free Fischer rats by 24-25 months, they are relatively minor.

In contrast to the relatively well-maintained neural responses to single-pulse, or control 0.3 Hz, stimulation, major age differences were found *during* 15 seconds of repetitive stimulation. Further, these age differences in frequency potentiation were increased by increasing frequency (e.g., from 6 to 12 Hz) or duration (from 5 to 15 sec) of stimulation (Figure 2b). As noted, a highly similar early failure of frequency potentiation was seen in aged hippocampal slices during 10 seconds of 15 Hz stimulation, primarily toward the end of the stimulation train. The inability of aged hippocampus to sustain frequency potentiation of the population spike during repetitive stimulation, then, appears to develop at an age when few other neurophysiological changes are detectable—at least by these methods.

Following the frequency potentiation series, a 5 second train of 100 Hz was administered and long-term potentiation (LTP) of the Schaffer collateral population spike was assessed by administering essentially single-pulse (0.3 Hz) test probes at several intervals during the 30 minutes following the train (Figure 2c). A significant delay in the development of LTP was seen in aged animals, although LTP in the aged hippocampus did attain levels by 15 minutes after the 100 Hz train which were not significantly different from those of the LTP in young animals. A similar delay of LTP development was also seen in hippocampal slices from aged animals (Landfield and Lynch, 1977).

Because normal levels of LTP were eventually attained, however, and because initial levels of frequency potentiation were normal, in aged hippocampus, these data might indicate that potentiation mechanisms *per se* are relatively normal in aged rat hippocampus, but that the hippocampus of aged rats could be more susceptible to the depressive effects of repetitive stimulation (Landfield and Lynch, 1977; Landfield et al., 1978b). Of course, failed potentiation and increased depression are difficult to untangle experimentally, and may exhibit considerable overlap at cellular levels.

Figure 2d shows the paradigm which in some ways appears of most interest in these aging studies. In this experiment 4 Hz stimulation was given continuously for 5 minutes, following the 30-minute LTP assessment period (robust frequency potentiation is not seen because this procedure was initiated after responses had already been potentiated by the 100 Hz train).

A distinct *biphasic* pattern of frequency potentiation of the population spike over time was seen in most animals (potentiation, relative depression, renewed potentiation). In Figure 2d this is largely obscured in the mean values for the young animals, since the depression occurred at somewhat different times in individual animals. However, this biphasic pattern is clearly seen in the mean values for the aged animals. Further, it may be noted that it is in the development of the 2nd phase of spike potentiation that the aged animals appear to be most deficient. This 2nd phase fails completely in many aged animals during the 5 minute train.

As is described subsequently (Figure 3) it is now clear that the 2nd phase of frequency potentiation would not have been so stable in young animals at 4 Hz, if it had not been preceded by the LTP-inducing 100 Hz train. That is, the 2nd phase of frequency potentiation can itself apparently undergo LTP.

The mechanisms underlying the depression phase in this biphasic pattern are far from clear (as of course are the mechanisms underlying potentiation), but could conceivably involve potentiation of inhibitory neurons, temporary depletion of transmitter, Na^+ spike inactivation, membrane conductance changes, receptor desensitization, etc., among other mechanisms.

A key observation in both the *in vivo* and the *in vitro* studies, however, has been that the *antidromic* population spike is well-maintained for extended periods in aged hippocampus, at stimulation frequencies above 15 Hz. Further, no biphasic pattern is seen. This finding of orthodromic specificity seems to indicate that the locus implicated in the age deficits is either synaptic (pre- or post-) or involves the nonsynaptic apical dendritic membrane. The latter has recently been shown to contain unique excitatory and inhibitory mechanisms (Prince, 1978; Schwartzkroin and Prince, 1978; Wong and Prince, 1979).

Behavioral-Neurophysiological Correlations During Aging

As mentioned earlier, the study of behavioral factors as correlates of neurophysiological variables during aging can make at least two important contributions: it can aid in determining whether an observed physiological change may be relevant to *functional* brain decline; and it can clarify the relationship of brain neurophysiology to behavior in both non-aged, and aged animals. In this regard, within-group analyses generally provide more sensitive tests of a correlative relationship than do between-group analyses. However, our initial attempts to correlate behavior and neurophysiology during aging (Landfield et al., 1976; 1978a; Landfield and Lynch, 1977) did not utilize the within-group paradigm, since our neurophysiological studies were conducted over extended periods and not all animals could be behaviorally assessed under the same circumstances. Instead, we randomly examined aged animals from groups which had been found to exhibit passive avoidance deficits (e.g., Gold and McGaugh, 1975). Such group paradigms are not, however, convincing with regard to correlation, and we noted that detailed within-group analyses were needed before it could be determined whether or not consistent neurophysiological-behavioral correlations obtained in the aging animals (Landfield and Lynch, 1977). As described below, we have subsequently carried out a within-group analysis examining behavior and neurophysiology in the same aging animals (Landfield, 1979; and in preparation; see Barnes, 1979; also, this volume for studies from another laboratory using a somewhat similar paradigm). To date, our findings are highly consistent with the initial working hypothesis that the specific neurophysiological deficit we observed in hippocampus may be closely correlated with age-related behavioral deficits.

In our earlier studies we termed our aging animals "retention-deficient" and "memory-deficient" (Landfield et al., 1976; 1978b; Landfield and Lynch, 1977). This was based on our interpretation of studies by Gold and McGaugh (1975) showing that in aged Fischer rats retention performance on a passive avoidance task decayed over time somewhat analogously to the decay in retention performance with time in aging humans (e.g., Botwinick, 1970). However, my interpretation of these behavioral deficits has since been modified in part by results from the task we subsequently employed to investigate specific behavior-neurophysiological correlations within the same animals. This task was a 1-way active avoidance, 2-choice, spatial discrimination (e.g., an avoidance Y-maze). The aged animals learned, *and retained,* the spatial discrimination and the escape very nearly as well as did young animals. Further, the aged animals ran as quickly to escape foot shock as did the young animals, suggesting that there were at least no major age-related deficits in running abilities or in pain perception. However, the aged animals exhibited dramatic impairments in the ability to actively *avoid* the foot shock, even though animals were allowed up to 120 seconds in which to do so (vs the 5-10 sec usually allowed in active avoidance tasks) (Landfield, 1979; and in preparation). Thus, while it remains possible that these aged animals are "memory-deficient," such deficiencies are only apparent in *some* tasks. Until we understand how a major deficiency in 1-way active avoidance, in the absence of measurable deficiencies in 1-way active escape, or in 2-choice spatial discrimination learning, is relevant to memory impairment, it is perhaps more appropriate to describe the behavioral deficiencies in these aged animals more empirically, in terms of the specific tasks in which they are clearly deficient. Thus, the aging Fischer rat should perhaps be termed "avoidance deficient."

It is widely recognized that an analogous situation obtains for hippocampally-lesioned rats as well. That is, such lesioned rats do not appear to exhibit the same global memory deficits found in hippocampally-lesioned humans, but rather are specifically impaired only in some tasks. In fact, a substantial number of aspects of the hippocampal lesion behavioral syndrome, including impairments in 1-way avoidance, in passive avoidance, in reversal and extinction, and in complex maze tasks (e.g., Isaacson, 1974) are also seen in aging animals (Elias and Elias, 1976). In both conditions, moreover, simple learning and escape behaviors seem relatively normal.

Additionally, the human hippocampal-lesion and the human aging syndromes are quite similar in pattern (although the patterns differ from those of rats). In humans, hippocampal lesions impair performance on a wide range of "recent memory" tasks and are associated with emotional apathy and reduced arousal. Older memories and I.Q., however, are relatively intact (Milner, 1970). While there is controversy on whether this recent memory deficit depends upon an inability to inhibit competing information, or is an actual impairment of storage or retrieval functions (Weiskrantz and Warrington, 1975), a deficit of global recent memory *performance* is readily apparent by current operational definitions. By these same criteria, selective recent memory deficits and reduced arousal also accompany human aging (Shakow, Dolkert, and Goldman, 1941; Botwinick, 1970).

It seems conceivable that the strong similarities between the respective hippocampal-lesion syndromes and the aging behavioral syndromes within the two species are related to findings indicating that in humans (Tomlinson and Henderson, 1976), and in rats (Geinisman et al., 1978; Landfield et al., 1977; Lindsey et al., 1979), the hippocampus exhibits some of the earliest and most severe neuropathological changes during aging. If early hippocampal pathology is a factor in age-dependent behavioral impairment, which seems to be a reasonable possibility, then seemingly the chances of finding hippocampal neurophysiological correlates of behavioral age changes are increased. This possibility was examined in the study outlined below.

Following behavioral assessment on the active avoidance task, we conducted neurophysiological studies on the same animals. Several animals (of an original 22 aged rats) developed pathology during behavioral testing and were removed from the study; data from others were discarded, due to failure to obtain a clearly-defined monosynaptic Schaffer collateral response, or because a seizure developed during repetitive stimulation. Thus, concomitant neurophysiological and behavioral data were obtained from a final group of eleven aged animals (24-25 months). The young control group (4-6 months) consisted of 8 animals. A mid-aged group (15 months) was also included, but was not assessed behaviorally.

Nearly all young animals rapidly learned the avoidance task following an acquisition series of 4 foot-shock, escape trials. Only approximately half of the aged group avoided at least once in 3 avoidance tests over 10 days (which were interspersed with 3 additional foot-shock escape trials). Even those aged animals which did avoid, exhibited considerably higher latencies to actively avoid than did the young animals (despite no age differences in escape latencies or correct Y-maze choices during escape). This result did not appear to be due to increased freezing in aged animals, judging from an earlier open field test, and from overt indicants (or lack thereof) of fear.

Figure 3 plots the results of the subsequent neurophysiological studies, in which a sequential series of 4 experiments employing repetitive stimulation was carried out in each animal (e.g., 4.5 Hz for 180 sec; 9 Hz for 90 sec; 100 Hz for 5 sec; and again, 4.5 Hz for 180 sec; 5-min intervals separated each procedure, except for 100 Hz, which was followed by a 30-min interval). The graphs plot percent change of the population spike in the young group, in those aged animals which avoided at least once (Aged-Avoid), and in those aged rats that did not make a single avoidance response in 3 chances (Aged-No Avoid). (The data from the mid-aged group are not plotted here, but in several aspects their values fell between the aged and the young groups, suggesting that some of these neurophysiological changes are detectable as early as 15 months of age).

The group data replicated most of our prior findings for intact animals; that is, frequency potentiation of the spike was found to be biphasic (or multiphasic) and the aged animals were found to be primarily deficient in the development of the 2nd phase (Figures 3A and 3B).

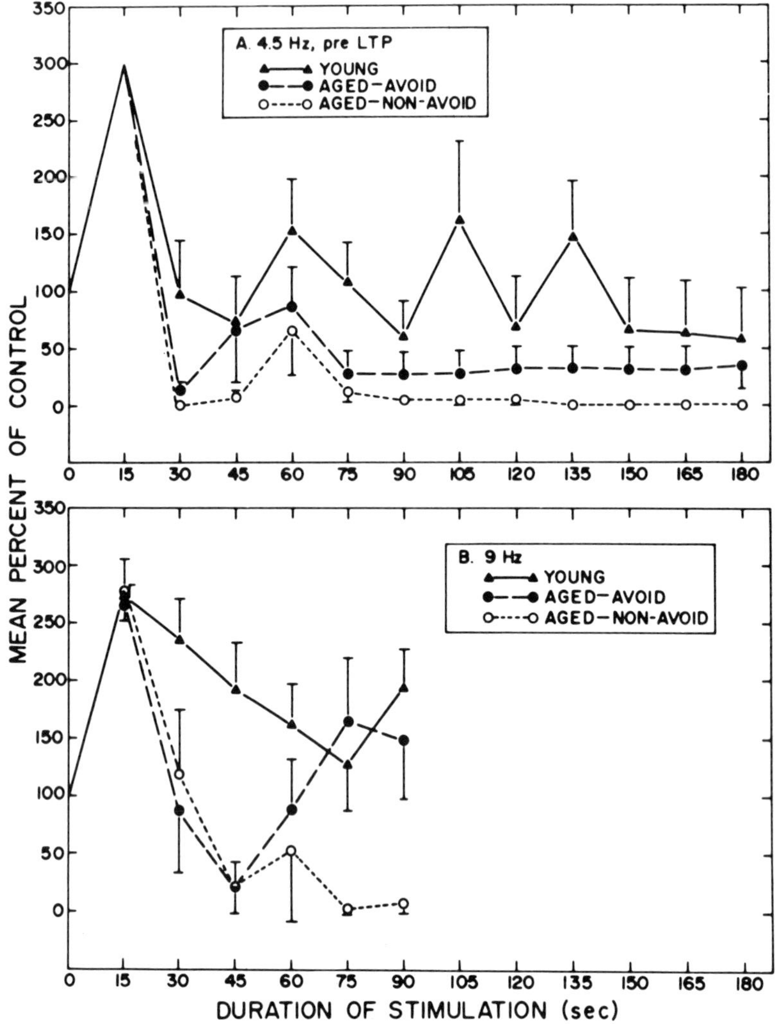

Figure 3. Measures of CA1 population spike potentiation obtained during and after sequential orthodromic repetitive stimulation paradigms, from the same animals studied behaviorally. (The amplitude of the potentiated first population spike at 15-sec post-onset of stimulation in A was taken as the basic reference value; the prestimulation control spike was assumed to be 33% of this for all groups. This reference was used here, instead of the prestimulation control spike, because the spikes at 15-sec post-onset when they are generally maximally potentiated (by about 300% exhibited surprisingly similar *absolute* values (9–10 mv) across age groups, and were substantially less variable than were prestimulation spike values. (1–4 mv) obtained at 125% of threshold. **A:** Effects of 4.5 Hz stimulation for 3 min; aged animals are significantly impaired but the 2nd phase of potentiation is only weakly developed, even in young animals. **B:** Effects of 9 Hz stimulation for 90 sec. The biphasic potentiation pattern is more

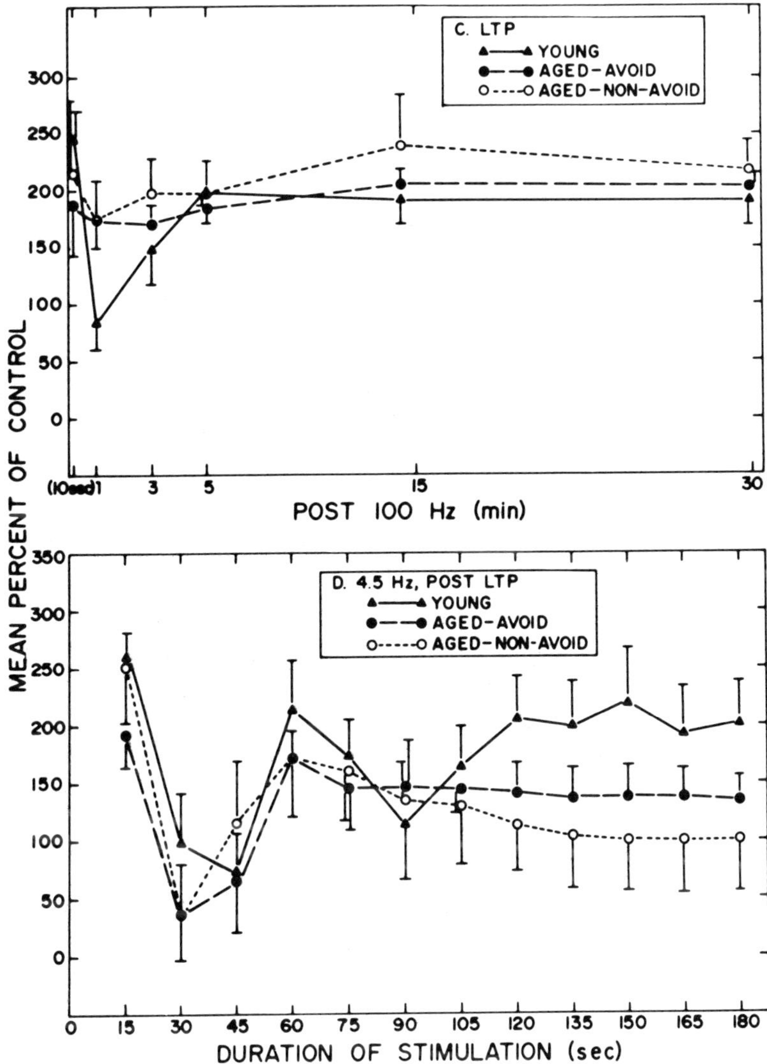

clearly seen. **C:** LTP of the spike as assessed by responses to 0.4 Hz stimulation following a 100 Hz, 5-sec train. In this study, the aged animals did not exhibit greater post-tetanization depression as they had in earlier studies (see text). **D:** Following the LTP study, 4.5 Hz stimulation induces a considerably stronger 2nd phase of frequency potentiation than it did prior to 100 Hz, in all age groups. The spike in aged animals, however, is still significantly reduced during the 2nd phase. In all figures, the aged group has been divided and plotted according to whether or not an animal had made at least one avoidance in the 3 prior avoidance tests. Strength of the 2nd phase of potentiation at 9 Hz significantly separated aged "avoiders" from "nonavoiders," although a similar tendency can also be seen at 4.5 Hz.

SOURCE: *Landfield et al., in preparation.*

The delayed development of LTP in aged animals following a 5 sec 100 Hz train was not however seen in this study. Instead, it was the young animals in this study that showed a brief post-100 Hz depression (Figure 3C). This discrepancy seems to be due to major differences between the 2 studies in the repetitive stimulation procedures which preceded the 100 Hz, LTP-inducing train. In the first study, repetitive stimulation was given for a total of 30 seconds prior to the 100 Hz train (Figure 2), while in the 2nd experiment it was administered for 270 sec, during which the population spike was able to follow in young animals, but was depressed in aged animals (Figure 3). This prolonged 270-second period of repetitive neuronal discharge in young animals apparently led to an increased depression following the 100 Hz train.

In any case, it seems clear that, with these procedures there was no age deficit in LTP according to standard methods of assessment (Figure 3C).

As in the earlier studies, the age deficit in frequency potentiation was more pronounced at higher stimulation frequencies (e.g., 9 Hz vs 4.5 Hz, Figure 3B vs 3A).

Two additional findings were noted in this study, however. First, the 2nd phase of potentiation was elicited much more vigorously, even in young animals, by 9 Hz, as compared to 4.5 Hz, stimulation. It seems conceivable that this effect is of some mechanistic significance since 9 Hz falls within the theta rhythm frequency range in rats, while 4.5 Hz does not (see Conclusions).

Second, following the 100 Hz (LTP) procedure (Figure 3C), the 2nd phase of frequency potentiation was more stable and robust during 4.5 Hz stimulation that it was prior to 100 Hz, in both young and aged animals (Figure 3D vs 3A). This suggests that *the 2nd phase of frequency potentiation can itself undergo long-term potentiation.*

Analyses of variance showed that, of all neurophysiological variables investigated, only the persistence of the 2nd phase of frequency potentiation significantly separated aged animals that had avoided from those that had not. This correlative effect, moreover, was most pronounced at 9 Hz (Figure 3B), but a similar trend was also seen during the post-LTP 4.5 Hz stimulation.

When aged animals were rank-ordered for numbers of avoidances (ties broken by latencies, and some data from escape performance), correlative analyses showed that highly significant within-group correlations obtained between the capacity of the hippocampus to sustain the population spike during 9 Hz stimulation, and active avoidance performance ($r_s = + .75$ in aged; $r_s = + .85$ with young and aged combined).

This highly significant correlation suggests that the neurophysiological age changes in sustained frequency potentiation may be functionally relevant.

Conclusions and Summary

Clearly, it is much too early to attempt to draw inferences regarding the underlying bases of the neurophysiological age deficit. The range of possible mechanisms which could account for the age-related failure of the orthodromic population spike during repetitive stimulation is exceedingly large, and includes impaired transmitter recycling or mobilization, reduced postsynaptic enzymatic inactivation of transmitter, receptor desensitization, exhaustion of apical dendritic membrane gating mechanisms, lower concentrations of available transmitter substrate, exhaustion of various biochemical or Ca^{++} mechanisms involved in potentiation processes, the potentiation of inhibitory interneurons, or increased dendritic hyperpolarization (e.g., by increased K^{+} conductance), to name only a few.

The range of possibilities is somewhat reduced, however, by the undiminished capacity of the population spike to follow repetitive *antidromic* stimulation in hippocampus of aged rats. Thus, if a nonsynaptic factor underlies this aging phenomenon, it would apparently have to be localized in dendritic (as opposed to somal) regions. The apical dendritic *nonsynaptic* membrane has, as noted, been shown to exhibit substantially different properties from somatic membrane (Prince, 1978). Of the several *synaptic* region (either pre- or post-) mechanisms which could be involved, however, impaired transmitter functions clearly represents an important possibility, judging from numerous studies in peripheral systems.

As a first step toward analyzing possible underlying mechanisms, therefore, we recently quantified synaptic vesicles in hippocampus of aging and young animals; in some animals this was done following prolonged 4 Hz repetitive stimulation and concomitant measurement of the population spike (Landfield, Wurtz, and Lindsey, 1979). Reduced vesicles were found with aging (Figure 4), and initial data raised the possibility of a relationship of this reduction to neurophysiological variables. It must be emphasized, however, that this latter finding on the relations of vesicle populations to the neurophysiological deficit is highly preliminary.

A basic, mechanistic analysis of the nature of the aging changes will also require systematic intracellular studies. However, while such studies are likely to be facilitated by use of the *in vitro* hippocampal slice preparation, a detailed understanding of these mechanisms still appears to be some time away. Nonetheless, several useful results have, in my view, been obtained during these initial neurophysiological-behavioral studies. These are summarized below:

1. A consistent and specific neurophysiological correlate of brain aging has been described in a defined, monosynaptic system.

2. This correlate appears to be present in disease-free animals at an age when few other neurophysiological changes are apparent.
3. The neurophysiological change is in turn highly correlated with a specific behavioral deficit (active avoidance); the latter is also present at an age when few other behavioral changes are evident (e.g., escape and 2-choice spatial discrimination learning or retention, and runway speed, are nearly normal). Of course, the assessment of this correlation will require additional studies to determine its extent, detailed nature, and reliability.
4. A number of hippocampal potentiation phenomena, previously unreported for young or aged animals, were noted in these studies, including the *biphasic* (or multiphasic) nature of population spike frequency potentiation during prolonged repetitive stimulation; the capacity of the 2nd phase of spike frequency potentiation to itself undergo long-term potentiation; and the particular sensitivity of this 2nd potentiation phase to induction by stimulation within theta rhythm frequencies.

Finally, I wish to consider briefly an hypothesis which is suggested by the present data on the sensitivity of 2nd phase of potentiation to theta range stimulation, and by earlier findings (Landfield, 1977). This hypothesis is that *the hippocampal theta rhythm may be an endogenous*

Figure 4. Mean vesicles per terminal and per sq μ of terminal in the Schaffer-commissural zone of aged (A) animals (24–28 months) in comparison to micrographs from young-mature (Y) group. A correction for small swelling, or shrinkage differences, using mitochondrial cross diameters, did not affect results ("corrected").

SOURCE: *Landfield et al., 1979; Brain Research Bulletin.*

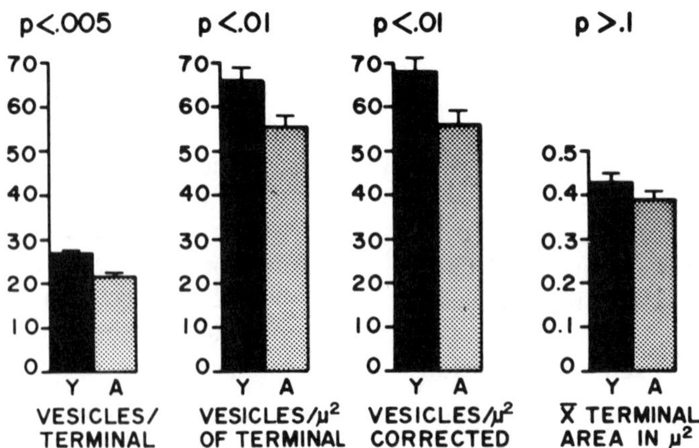

mechanism for inducing frequency potentiation. Theta rhythms, and in fact all hypersynchronous EEG rhythms, bear close similarities to repetitive electrical stimulation at cellular levels; that is, each rhythmic wave, and each stimulation pulse, elicits highly synchronous action potential discharges within a large population of underlying cells or fibers (Andersen and Anderson, 1968; Ranck, 1975; Verzeano, 1970; Landfield, 1976). In the case of theta rhythms in rats, synchronous neuronal discharges (Ranck, 1975) occur at the approximate rate of 5-12 Hz and are correlated with *overt* behaviors which seem to involve orienting, attention and some movements (Issaacson and Pribram, 1975; Landfield, 1976). This overlap between the spontaneous theta frequency range and the effective frequency range for eliciting the 2nd phase of frequency potentiation, then, along with the apparent similarity of stimulation and synchronous EEG waves at cellular levels, seems to raise the possibility that normal activation of theta rhythms at 5-10 Hz, during alertness, could induce frequency potentiation in the underlying neural elements (and thereby, perhaps, induce an "amplification" of the processing of biologically meaningful information).

I have suggested this possibility earlier, in simpler form (e.g., Landfield, 1977), based upon observations that electrical stimulation of septal regions at 7.7 Hz (which is classically viewed as a means of "mimicking" hippocampal theta rhythms) also induced a large frequency potentiation of an undefined, multisynaptic positive slow wave in the hippocampal somal layer (Landfield, 1977). It is perhaps also of interest in the present context that 7.7 Hz septal stimulation facilitated 1-way active avoidance (Landfield, 1976, 1977) in tasks similar to those in which the aged animals are impaired.

The possibility of a link between theta, frequency potentiation and active avoidance of course remains very speculative at this point. Nevertheless, if future experimental tests should support this view, then this relationship could have important implications for our understanding of the nature of the brain aging deficit, of the nature of some aspects of brain information processing, and of the functional significance of some synchronous EEG rhythms.

At present, however, all that can be said is that a consistent, frequency-specific neurophysiological correlate of brain aging has been described in healthy, aging rats below the age of mean longevity. Further, this physiological change appears to be correlated with a specific behavioral change. Clearly, we do not yet understand the mechanisms underlying the neurophysiological deficit, or its full behavioral implications; nevertheless, the procedural and temporal specificity of this age change seems likely, in my view, to greatly facilitate both the search for more basic chemical and physiological mechanisms, and the development of pharmacological agents aimed at manipulating these brain aging phenomena.

ACKNOWLEDGMENTS
Research discussed here was supported by NIH grants AG 01737 (formerly AG 00341) to P. Landfield and AG 00538 to G. Lynch and J. McGaugh.

Important contributions to this research were made by my collaborators Dr. G. Lynch, J. Lindsey, C. Wurtz and Dr. J. McGaugh. I also wish to acknowledge major technical contributions made to the behavioral research by Matthew Maxwell and Lyndon Braun, and to the E.M. analyses by Dr. Kevin Lee. I also thank Ms. Stephanie Burgoyne and Ms. Terrie McNutt for valuable clerical assistance.

References

Andersen P: Organization of hippocampal neurons and their interconnections. In Isaacson RL, Pribram KH (eds.) *The Hippocampus*. New York, Plenum Press, 1975.

Andersen P, Andersson SA: *Physiological Basis of the Alpha Rhythm*. Appleton-Century-Crofts, New York, 1968.

Barnes CA: Memory deficits associated with senescence: a neurophysiological and behavioral study in the rat. *J Comparative Physiology and Psychology* 93:74–104, 1979.

Birren JE, Wall PD: Age changes in conduction velocity, refractory period, number of fibers, connective tissue space and blood vessels in sciatic nerve of rats. *J Comparative Neurology* 104:1–16, 1956.

Bliss T, Lomo T: Long-lasting potentiation of synaptic transmission in the dentate area of the anesthetized rabbit following stimulation of the perforant path. *J Physiology* 232:289–297, 1973.

Bondareff W, Narotzky R: Age changes in the neuronal environment. *Science* 176:1135–1136, 1972.

Botwinick J: Geropsychology. *Annual Review of Psychology* 21:239–272, 1970.

Brizzee KR: Gross morphometric analyses and quantitative histology of the aging brain. In Ordy JM, Brizzee KR (eds.) *Neurobiology of Aging*. New York, Plenum Press, 1975.

Brody H: Aging of the vertebrate brain. In Rockstein M, Sussman M (eds.) *Development and Aging in the Central Nervous System*. New York, Academic Press, 1973, pp. 121–133.

Brody H: An examination of cerebral cortex and brain stem aging. In Terry RD, Gershon S (eds.) *Neurobiology of Aging*. New York, Raven Press, 1976, pp. 171–181.

Carlsson A: Age-dependent changes in brain monoamines. In Finch C, Potter D, Kenny A (eds.) *Parkinson's Disease II. Aging and Neuroendocrine Relationships*. New York, Plenum Press, 1978.

Creutzfeldt, OD, Watanabe S, Lux HD: Relations between EEG phenomena and potentials of single cortical cells. II. Spontaneous and convulsoid activity. *Electroencephalography Clinical Neurophysiology* 20:19–37, 1966.

Deadwyler SA, Dudek FE, Cotman CW, Lynch GS: Intracellular response of rat dentate granule cells *in vitro*: posttetanic potentiation to perforant path stimulation. *Brain Research* 88:80–85, 1975.

Diamond MC, Johnson RE, Ingham C: The development, adult and aging patterns of the cerebral cortex, hippocampus and diencephalon. *Behavioral Biology* 14:163–174, 1975.

Douglas R, Goddard G: Long-term potentiation of the perforant path-granule cell synapse in the rat hippocampus. *Brain Research* 86:205–215, 1975.

Eccles JC: *The Neurophysiological Basis of Mind*. Oxford, Clarendon Press, 1953.

Elias PK, Elias MF: Effects of age on learning ability: contributions from the animal literature. *Experimental Aging Research* 2:165–186, 1976.

Feldman ML: Aging changes in the morphology of cortical dendrites. In Terry RD, Gershon S (eds.) *Neurobiology of Aging*. New York, Raven Press, 1976.

Finch CE: The regulation of physiological changes during mammalian aging. *Quarterly Review of Biology* 51:49–83, 1976.

Finch CE: Age-related changes in brain catecholamines: a synopsis of findings in C57BL–J mice and other rodent models. In Finch CE, Potter DE, Kenny AD (eds.) *Parkinson's Disease II: Aging and Neuroendocrine Relationships*. New York, Plenum Press, 1978.

Geinisman Y, Bondareff W, Dodge JT: Dendritic atrophy in the dentate gyrus of the senescent rat. *Am J Anatomy* 152:321–330, 1978.

Gibson DC, Adelman R, Finch C (eds.): *Development of the Rodent as a Model System of Aging - Book II*. Department of Health, Education, and Welfare, Publ. No. 79–161, 1979.

Gold PE, McGaugh JL: Changes in learning and memory during aging. In Ordy JM, Brizzee KR (eds.): *Neurobiology of Aging*. New York, Plenum Press, 1975.

Goldberg PB, Roberts J: Influences of age on the pharmacology and physiology of the cardiovascular system. In Elias MF, Eleftheriou BF, Elias PK (eds.): *Experimental Aging Research. Progress in Biology.* 1976, pp. 71–103.

Hinds JW, McNelly NA: Aging of the rat olfactory bulb: growth and atrophy of constituent layers and changes in size and number of mitral cells. *J Comparative Neurology* 171:345–368, 1977.

Isaacson RL: *The Limbic System*. New York, Plenum Press, 1974.

Isaacson RL, Pribram KH (eds.): *The Hippocampus*. New York, Plenum Press, 1975.

Joseph JA, Berger RE, Engel BT, Roth GS: Age-related changes in the nigrostriatum: a behavioral and biochemical analysis. *J Gerontology* 33:643–649, 1978.

Kandel ER, Spencer, WA: Electrophysiological properties of an archicortical neuron. *Annals of the NY Academy of Sciences* 94:570–603, 1961.

Landfield PW: Synchronous EEG rhythms: their nature and their possible functions in memory, information transmission, and behavior. In Gispen WH (ed.): *Molecular and Functional Neurobiology.* Amsterdam, Elsevier, 1976.

Landfield PW: Different effects of posttrial driving or blocking of the theta rhythm on avoidance learning in rats. *Physiology and Behavior* 18:439–445, 1977.

Landfield PW: An endocrine hypothesis of brain aging and studies of brain-endocrine correlations and monosynaptic neurophysiology during aging. In Finch C, Potter D, Kenny A (eds.): *Parkinson's Disease II. Aging and Neuroendocrine Relationships*. New York, Plenum Press, 1978.

Landfield PW: Neurobiological changes in hippocampus of aging rats: quantitative correlations with behavioral deficits and with endocrine mechanisms. In *Proceedings of the XIth International Congress of Gerontology, Tokyo, 1978,* Excerpta Medica, Amsterdam, 1979.

Landfield PW, Lindsey JD, Lynch G: Correlations between monosynaptic hippocampal neurophysiology and avoidance behavior in aging and young rats (in preparation).

Landfield PW, McGaugh JL, Tusa RJ: Theta rhythm: a temporal correlate of memory storage processes in the rat. *Science* 175:87–89, 1972.

Landfield PW, McGaugh JL, Lynch G: Impaired synaptic potentiation in the hippocampus of aged, retention-deficient rats. *Society for Neuroscience, Abstracts* II:312, 1976.

Landfield PW, Rose G, Sandles L, Wohlstadter TC, Lynch G: Patterns of astroglial hypertrophy and neuronal degeneration in the hippocampus of aged, memory-deficient rats. *J Gerontology* 32:3–12, 1977.

Landfield PW, Lynch G: Impaired monosynaptic potentiation in *in vitro* hippocampal slices from aged, memory-deficient rats. *J Gerontology* 32:523–533, 1977.

Landfield PW, Lindsey JD, Lynch G: Apparent acceleration of brain aging pathology by prolonged administration of glucocorticoids. *Soc Neuroscience Abstracts* IV:350, 1978a.

Landfield PW, McGaugh JL, Lynch G: Impaired synaptic potentiation processes in the hippocampus of aged, memory-deficient rats. *Brain Research* 150:85–101, 1978b.

Landfield PW, Waymire JC, Lynch G: Hippocampal aging and adrenocorticoids: quantitative correlations. *Science* 202:1098–1102, 1978c.

Landfield PW, Wurtz C, Lindsey JD: Quantification of synaptic vesicles in hippocampus of aging rats and initial studies of possible relations to neurophysiology. *Brain Research Bulletin* 4, 1979.

Lindsey JD, Landfield PW, Lynch G: Early onset and topographical distribution of hypertrophied astrocytes in hippocampus of aging rats: a quantitative study. *J Gerontology* 5:661–671, 1979.

Lynch G, Smith RL, Browning M, Deadwyler SA: Evidence for bidirectional dendritic transport of horseradish peroxidase. In Kreutzberg G (ed.) *Physiology and Pathology of Dendrities*. New York, Raven Press, 1975.

McGeer W, McGeer PL: Neurotransmitter metabolism in the aging brain. In Terry RD, Gershon S (eds.) *Neurobiology of Aging*. New York, Raven Press, 1976.

Meites J, Huang HH, Simpkins JW: Recent studies on neuroendocrine control of reproductive senescence in rats. In Schneider EL (ed.) *The Aging Reproductive System*. New York, Raven Press, 1978.

Milner B: Memory and the medial temporal regions of the brain. In Pribram KH, Broadbent DE (eds.) *Biology of Memory*. New York, Academic Press, 1970.

O'Keefe J, Nadel L: *The Hippocampus as a Cognitive Map*. New York, Clarendon (Oxford University Press) 1978.

Prince DA: Neurophysiology of epilepsy. *Annual Review of Neuroscience* 1:395–415, 1978.

Ranck JB Jr: Behavioral correlates and firing repertoires of neurons in the dorsal hippocampal formation and septum of unrestrained rats. In Isaacson RL, Pribram KH (eds.): *The Hippocampus*. New York, Plenum Press, 1975.

Riegle GD, Meites J: Effects of aging on LH and prolactin after LHRH, L-dopa, methyldopa, and stress in male rats. *Proceedings of Society for Experimental Biology and Medicine* 151:507–511, 1976.

Sacher GA: Relation of life span to brain weight and body weight in mammals. In Wolstenholme GE, O'Connor M (eds.) *Ciba Foundation Colloquia on Aging. The Life Span of Animals*. London, Churchill, 1959.

Schmidt MJ, Thornberry JF: Cyclic AMP and cyclic GMP accumulation *in vitro* in brain regions of young, old and aged rats. *Brain Research* 139:169–177, 1978.

Scheibel ME, Scheibel AB: Structural changes in the aging brain. In Brody H, Harmon D, Ordy JM (eds.) *Aging I*. New York, Raven Press, 1975.

Schwartzkroin PA, Prince DA: Cellular and field potential properties of epileptogenic hippocampal slices. *Brain Research* 147:117–130, 1978.

Shakow D, Dolkert MB, Goldman R: The memory function in psychoses in the aged. *Diseases of the Nervous System* 2:43–48, 1941.

Shock NW: Physiological theories of aging. In Rockstein M (ed.) *Theoretical Aspects of Aging*. New York, Academic Press, 1974.

Simpkins JW, Mueller GP, Huang HH, Meites J: Evidence for depressed catecholamine and enhanced serotonin metabolism in aging male rats: possible relation to gonadotropin secretion. *Endocrinology* 100:1672–1678, 1977.

Skrede KK, Westgaard RH: The transverse hippocampal slice: a well defined cortical structure maintained *in vitro*. *Brain Research* 35:589–593, 1971.

Strehler BL: *Time, Cells, and Aging*. Academic Press, New York, 1962.

Teyler TJ, Bradley EA, Bergman T, Livingston K: A comparison of long-term potentiation in the *in vitro* and *in vivo* hippocampal preparations. *Behavioral Biology* 19:24–34, 1977.

Tomlinson BE, Henderson G: Some quantitative cerebral findings in normal and demented old people. In Terry RD, Gershon S (eds.) *Neurobiology of Aging*. New York, Raven Press, 1976.

Vaughan DW, Peters A: Neuroglial cells in the cerebral cortex of rats from young adulthood to old age: an electron microscope study. *J Neurocytology* 3:239–405, 1974.

Verzeano M: Evoked responses and network dynamics. In Whalen RE, Thompson RF, Verzeano M, Weinberger NM (eds.) *The Neural Control of Behavior*. New York, Academic Press, 1970, pp. 27–54.

Vyskocil F, Gutmann, E: Spontaneous transmitter release from nerve endings and contractile properties in the soleus and diaphragm muscles of senile rats. *Experientia* 28:280–281, 1972.

Wayner MJ, Emmers R: Spinal synaptic delay in young and aged rats. *Am J Physiology* 194:403–405, 1958.

Weiskrantz L, Warrington EK: The problem of the amnesic syndrome in man and animals. In Isaacson RL, Pribram KH (eds.) *The Hippocampus*. New York, Plenum Press, 1975.

Wisniewski HM, Terry RD: Morphology of the aging brain, human and animal. In Ford DM (ed.) *Progress in Brain Research, Volume 40*. Amsterdam, Elsevier, 1973.

Wisniewski HM, Terry RD: Neuropathology of the aging brain. In Terry RD, Gershon S (eds.) *Neurobiology of Aging*. New York, Raven Press, 1976.

Wong RKS, Prince DA: Dendritic mechanisms underlying penicillin-induced epileptiform activity. *Science* 204:1228–1231, 1979.

Yamamoto C: Activation of hippocampal neurons by mossy fiber stimulation in thin brain sections *in vitro*. *Experimental Brain Research* 14:423–435, 1972.

Stein, ed. The Psychobiology of Aging: Problems and Perspectives

Spatial Memory and Hippocampal Synaptic Plasticity in Senescent and Middle-aged Rats[a]

C. A. Barnes and B. L. McNaughton

Department of Psychology, Dalhousie University, Halifax, N.S., Canada, B3H 4J1.

Anecdotal and experimental evidence from both humans and animals indicates that the ability to learn new material declines towards the end of the normal life span of the organism (e.g., Goodrick, 1972; Gordon and Clark, 1974; Medin, O'Neil, Smeltz, and Davis, 1973; Birren and Schaie, 1977). Since the locus of this deficit is not well understood or agreed upon in terms of psychological processes (i.e., acquisition, retention, recall, strategy, sensory processing, etc.) a search for the underlying physiological mechanism may seem somewhat premature at best. This is particularly so as it seems highly unlikely that a behavioral deficit with aging will show a unitary mechanism, in view of the number of physiological, anatomical, and biochemical variables which are known to change with age. Nevertheless, there exists in the brain a physiological process which, in the light of recent evidence, makes a rather good candidate for the fundamental physical change involved in memory formation. Thus it is of interest to see whether this specific physiological process changes with age in a manner which correlates with the change in memory capability. Such a demonstration would then open the way for more critical experiments to determine whether the two are causally related.

[a]This work was supported by grant no. A0365 from the National Research Council of Canada, and grant no. S76-0967 from the Canada Council, both to G. V. Goddard. Portions of the data analysis and the preparation of this chapter were completed while the first author was supported by N.I.H. postdoctoral fellowship F32 AG05170-01, and the second author by a National Research Council of Canada postdoctoral fellowship.

We shall begin then by outlining our working hypothesis and the evidence which has thus far accumulated in its favor. The emergence of the neuron doctrine has led to general (although not complete) agreement that learning must, at the very least, involve some change in the input-output characteristics of some population of neurons. Given this as an axiom, the most logical place to begin looking is the interface between neuronal elements, the synapse.

In 1949, Hebb proposed that learning takes place through the strengthening of those synapses involved in the learned stimulus-response sequence. Lacking experimental data, Hebb nevertheless made several bold assumptions concerning the physiology of synapses in the brain from which he derived a workable "cell assembly" theory of learning. First, most synapses should be rather weak to begin with. That is, they should only be able to elicit output from the post-synaptic neuron when acting in concert with other synapses on the same cell. Second, the synapse should undergo a sustained strengthening following intense activity, but only if such activity was correlated with the discharge of the post-synaptic neuron (i.e., if several inputs were coactive). Thus, a neuron would form elementary associations among input events, since a previous output could be subsequently elicited by a subset of the original input. This, after all, can be taken as a definition of associative learning. Since Hebb's original proposal, a number of more detailed models for associative memory in neural systems have appeared (Brindly, 1969; Eccles, 1977; Gardner-Medwin, 1976; Gilbert, 1974; Little and Shaw, 1974; Longuet-Higgins, Willshaw, and Buneman, 1970; Marr, 1971; Uttley, 1976). Almost unanimously, these models make use of Hebb's fundamental postulates.

It now appears that Hebb's boldness has been vindicated, at least with respect to the existence in the brain of the fundamental mechanism he postulated. Prior to 1973, the only form of activity-dependent synaptic alterations known were all far too transient to fulfill the requirements for a long-term storage device. Furthermore, those changes which had been studied were solely dependent on the pattern of activity of the single afferent fiber in which they occurred. Thus they did not fulfill the requirement of cooperativity necessary for a mechanism of association. In 1973, however, Bliss and Lømo, and Bliss and Gardner-Medwin showed that when synapses of the so-called perforant pathway were subjected to reasonably mild episodes of high-frequency activity, their efficiency in activating the granule cells of the fascia dentata was significantly increased. Moreover, this increased synaptic efficacy persisted for at least several weeks in some animals. Douglas (1977) showed that this long-lasting growth, which we shall refer to specifically as "enhancement," could be elicited by imposed temporal patterns of activity which were similar to those frequently seen in cortical neurons, namely short bursts of activity consisting of a few impulses (5-10) at high frequency (200-400 Hz). McNaughton and Barnes (1977), and Andersen, Sundberg, and Sveen (1977) independently showed that lasting enhancement was restricted to those synapses on a given neuron which were involved in the high frequency input event. Finally, McNaughton, Douglas, and Goddard (1978) showed that, although the discharge of the post-synaptic neuron is not involved in the generation of enhancement as Hebb postulated, the process is dependent on the cooperative, high frequency activity of a considerable number of afferent fibers. This has the same logical consequence as Hebb's mechanism in that it has the potential for recording the association of events.

Since we were seeking a correspondence between changes in the enhancement process and changes in memory function, it was necessary to select a behavioral task which was likely to involve information storage in the hippocampus. Unfortunately, there has been a great deal of dispute as to the exact role of this structure in behavior. Recently, however, O'Keefe and Nadel (1978) have proposed an entirely new theory which appears to resolve many of the apparent conflicts which arise when the voluminous literature on the subject is viewed from the standpoint of previous hypotheses. They propose that the hippocampus forms associations about the relations of objects to one another and thus is the physical locus of a cognitive, spatial map. This is not the forum for a critique of the O'Keefe-Nadel hypothesis, and it might be pointed out that the scientific community is not in complete agreement as to its acceptability. We simply raise it as the reason for our choice of experimental paradigm, since in our view it appears to account very well for the behavioral effects of hippocampal lesions in animals as well as the amnestic syndrome found in humans with hippocampal damage, which is something no previous hypotheses have done satisfactorily. As our results will show, this choice turned out to be a favorable one, although it remains possible that other non-spatial tasks may be correlated with hippocampal physiology as well.

The data to be presented derive from two separate sets of experiments[1] using two different populations of senescent and control animals. In both studies the behavioral tests were carried out first and then the animals underwent surgery for implantation of extracellular stimulating and recording electrodes. The young and old animals were male Long Evans rats tested at the age of approximately 12 and 30 months respectively. We shall describe the behavioral data from both experiments first.

[1]The details of experiment 1 have been published previously (Barnes, 1979). The circular platform data from experiment 2 is one of several tasks reported in Barnes, Nadel and Honig, 1980. The physiology from experiment 2 has been presented in abstract form (Barnes and McNaughton, 1979).

Behavior

Procedure

The same circular maze was used in both studies in two spatially different environments. The maze consisted of a circular platform around the perimeter of which were located 18 equally spaced holes. Beneath the maze surface was a dark chamber which we will refer to as the goal tunnel. The maze surface and the goal tunnel could be rotated independently of one another allowing the goal to be positioned in a specific location in space while the surface could be rotated randomly from trial to trial to eliminate the use of surface cues. In both studies the maze environment was brightly illuminated. It is a common observation that rats will attempt to remove themselves from a brightly lit environment if there is a dark enclosure available to them. To this end, an adaptation period was given to each rat during which the animal was simply placed into the goal tunnel and allowed to remain undisturbed for four minutes. Subsequent trials began with the rat being placed in random orientation inside an opaque cylinder that rested at the center of the maze surface. After 30 seconds, the cylinder was quickly raised well above the maze surface so that the animal was free to move (see Figure 1).

In the first study the animals' behavior was monitored on a television screen on which was superimposed (through the use of a video mixer) a bright spot (see Figure 1). This could be used to manually track the animal by means of a potentiometer-coupled joy stick. The x and y coordinates of the animals' positions in space were continually recorded and subsequently analyzed by digital computer. In addition the animals' errors were noted by the experimenter. An error consisted of a nose-head-neck deflection into any of the 17 incorrect holes. Due to the pattern of the results obtained in the first experiment, it was sufficient to record only the number and location of the errors made by each animal in the second experiment.

The essential difference between the two studies involved the extra-maze environment, and the way in which the goal tunnel and external cues were manipulated. In the first study, the maze was located in a large room with distant uneven surfaces (drapery and partition screens) with no imposing cues (see Figure 1). The maze area was illuminated by two flood lights that were directed towards the maze surface. In the second study the maze was placed inside a curtained, circular enclosure that had a specific set of cues that remained in a fixed relation to one another and to the goal tunnel throughout the experiment (see Figure 2). In the first experiment the location of the tunnel was held constant for seven trials. On Trial 8, it was shifted 135° to a new position and was held constant for the remaining trials. In the second experiment, the position of the tunnel remained fixed throughout; however, Trials 13 and

Figure 1. A pictorial representation of the circular maze and data collection system as employed in experiment 1. The platform was located in a brightly illuminated studio in which the extra maze visual cues were predominantly general gradients of intensity and texture (see text). The animals' behavior was monitored via a television camera suspended well above the maze surface. A second television camera was focussed on the beam of an oscilliscope whose *xy* coordinates were controlled by a potentiometer-coupled joy stick. The two television signals were mixed so that they appeared superimposed on the animals head. Thus a continuous record of the animals' position coordinates could be obtained.

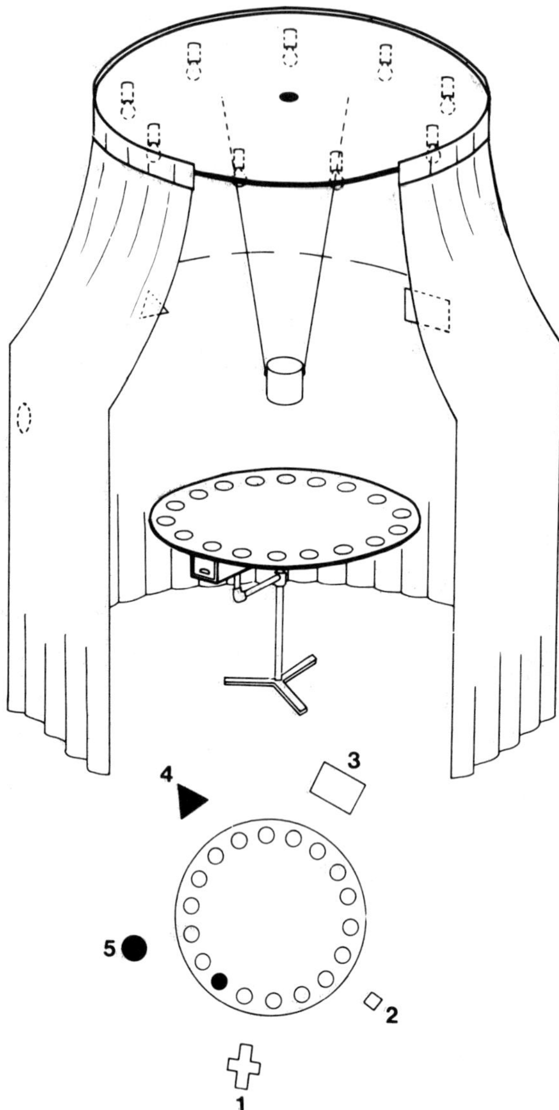

Figure 2. Schematic drawing of circular platform, startbox, and curtained room, as employed in experiment 2. The objects placed on the curtain were arranged around the platform as shown in the lower part of this figure. The darkened hole indicates the position of the goal tunnel.

14 involved manipulations of the visual cues. These manipulations are described in more detail below.

Results

In general, the animals showed a definite pattern of improvement from trial to trial. In early trials animals tended to make many center crossings and to investigate the peripheral holes in a somewhat random fashion. With more experience there was a shift in strategy to a sequential hole-to-hole search. Finally many rats learned to go directly from the center of the maze to the goal tunnel without error. These general patterns are illustrated by the examples of the video-tracking plots from experiment 1 shown in Figure 3. A qualitative impression of the differences in group performance can be obtained from Figure 4 in which the pooled moment-to-moment positions of all of the animals from each group are represented by dots. A clear difference in overall group performance becomes apparent by Trial 4. This difference tended to increase up to Trial 7, after which the location of the goal tunnel was changed. Note that on Trial 8 the animals tended to cluster near the previously correct goal hole, and that the behavior of the two groups does not appear to differ. This indicates that spatial cues, rather than some uncontrolled cues involving the goal tunnel itself, were being employed by the rats to solve this problem. The remaining trials, however, show that the young rats were again more accurate in locating the correct goal tunnel position.

These qualitative results are corroborated by a quantitative analysis of the number of errors per trial shown in Figure 5A. In addition to the number of errors, the total distance that the animals covered on the maze surface before finding the goal was monitored. The general result was that, after the first several trials, the old animals spent more time on the maze surface, covered a greater distance, and made more errors.

In experiment 2 the asymptotic number of errors per trial was again statistically different between age groups. Furthermore, in spite of the difference in the spatial environment between the two studies, the final level of performance was virtually identical to the results obtained in experiment 1 (see Table 1). One of the defining features of a cognitive map is that no specific environmental cue should be a critical determinant of the animals' performance. Rather, it is the overall cue configuration, i.e., the relationship among the parts, which is of paramount importance. A cognitive map is thus highly resistant to removal of its parts provided that the relationship among the remaining parts remains constant. To test whether the animals were using such a cognitive map, two of the five cues on the curtains were removed on Trial 13 (numbers 1 and 5 in Figure 2). This had no discernible effect on the performance of rats in either age group (i.e., the performance was not significantly worse in either age group). When all the cues were removed, however, the

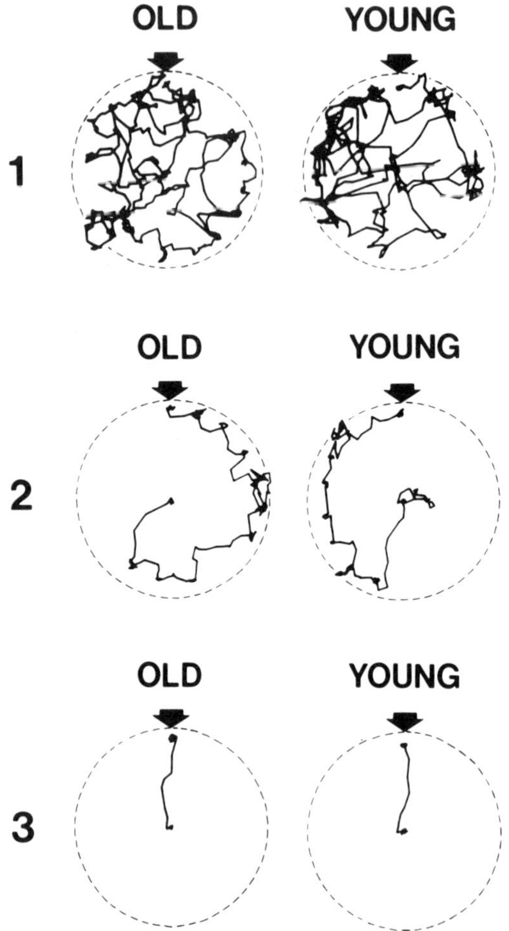

Figure 3. Representative examples showing the general progression of behavior on the circular maze. Early trials were characterized by a random search pattern with frequent center crossings. With experience this strategy was abandoned for a sequential hole to hole search pattern which finally evolved into a direct approach to the goal tunnel. (Arrow indicates goal tunnel location).

SOURCE: *Barnes, 1979.*

performance in both groups was severely disrupted. These data indicate that the animals were indeed using a cognitive map involving the relationship among the specific cue objects. When all the cues were replaced on Trials 15 and 16, the previous levels of performance were reinstated. The rats' ability to remember the location of the goal tunnel after a one-week test-free interval was examined on Trial 17. The young animals showed no decrease in level of performance whereas the number of errors made by the old animals increased by about 20% (a statistically significant increase).

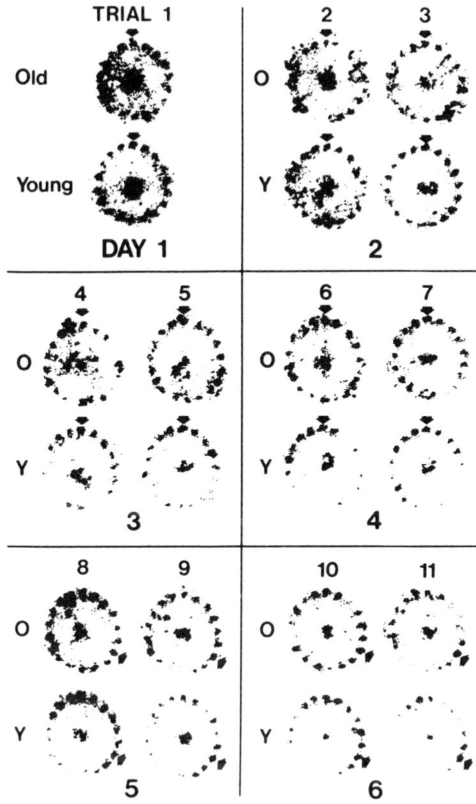

Figure 4. Cumulative plots of the pattern of exploration on the circular maze in experiment 1. These plots were constructed by superimposing the data from all animals within each group for each trial. The arrow indicates the location of the goal tunnel. Notice that the position of the goal tunnel is changed on Trial 8.

Discussion

A possible objection to the conclusion that the performance deficit shown here was due to impaired spatial memory in the senescent animals might be that the visual ability in the two populations would be expected to differ. There are two possible ways in which visual impairment might account for the observed results. First, the old animals might be less highly motivated to escape from a brightly lit maze surface if their sensitivity were impaired. This explanation is improbable, however, since in both studies, and in both age groups, the proportion of animals which did not enter the tunnel immediately upon finding it was less than three percent. Furthermore, in no case did the animal leave the tunnel

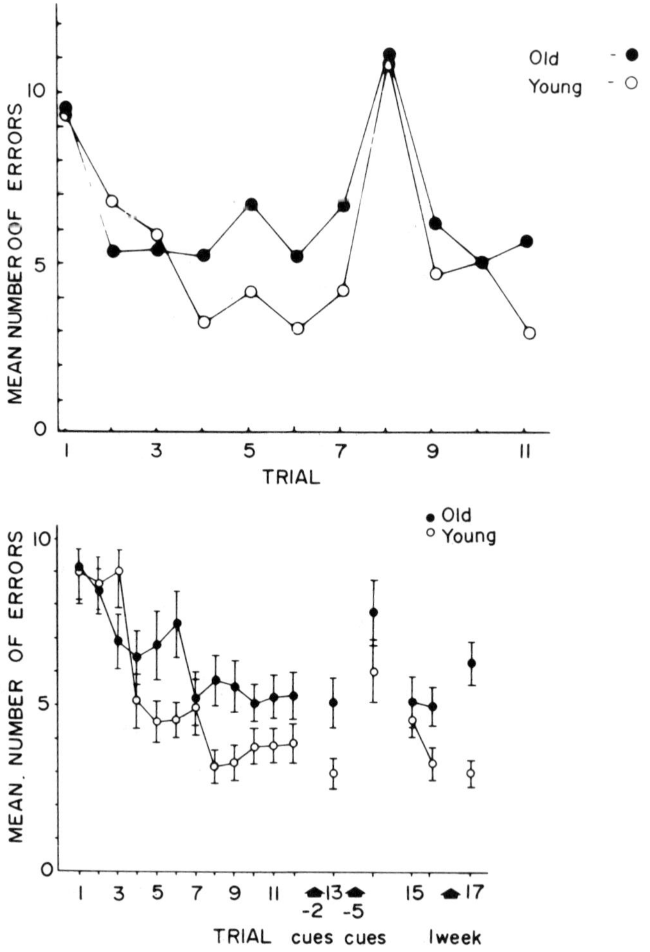

Figure 5. A. Mean number of errors for each age group, across all trials, in experiment 1. The young rats made statistically fewer errors on Trials 4, 5, 6, 7, 9, and 11. Note that the position of the goal tunnel was changed on Trial 8.

SOURCE: *Barnes, 1979.*

B. Mean (± 1 S.E.M.) number of errors for each age group, across all trials, in experiment 2. The young rats made statistically fewer errors than the old rats on Trials 5, 6, 8–13, 16, and 17. Note removal of two and five cues from the curtains on Trials 13 and 14 respectively. All cues were replaced on Trial 15.

SOURCE: *Barnes et al., 1980.*

Table 1. Mean Number of Errors on Circular Maze in Experiment 1 and Experiment 2

	1	2	Difference
Young	3.5	3.8	−8%
Old	5.8	5.3	+9%

after entering it. This indicates that both groups of animals were comparably and highly motivated to escape from the maze surface.

The second argument relates to the possible loss in visual acuity with advanced age. While such loss undoubtedly occurs, it is unlikely to have been a critical determinant in the present experiments. This conclusion derives from the observation that the asymptotic values of the mean error scores within each age group were almost identical between the two studies, even though they were carried out in two drastically different visual environments. In the first study, there were no prominent discrete visual cues. Only broad visual gradients were available. In the second experiment, the visual environment was characterized by a number of prominent visual cues on a uniform background. The fact that performance was consistent between studies, despite the large differences in visual information available, strongly implies that the solution used by the animals did not depend on the quality of available information, over a rather wide range. This is consistent with the notion that the deficit in the old animals could lie in a failure to relate specific places to an integrated cognitive map of the environment.

Physiology

Procedure

Following behavioral testing, recording and stimulating electrodes were surgically implanted in the hilus of the fascia dentata and in the angular bundle respectively (see Figure 6).[2] These were secured in place with dental acrylic, and connected to a miniature socket which permitted the awake animals to be easily coupled to the stimulating and recording system. The angular bundle is the optimal stimulation site for activating the perforant path fibers which cluster in this region in their trajectory from the entorhinal cortex to the granule cells of the fascia dentata (Lømo, 1971; McNaughton and Barnes, 1977). The granule cells themselves are organized in a curved sheet with their dendrites projecting radially from the center of curvature in the hilus.

[2]The detailed procedures for surgery and extracellular recording are given in Barnes (1979).

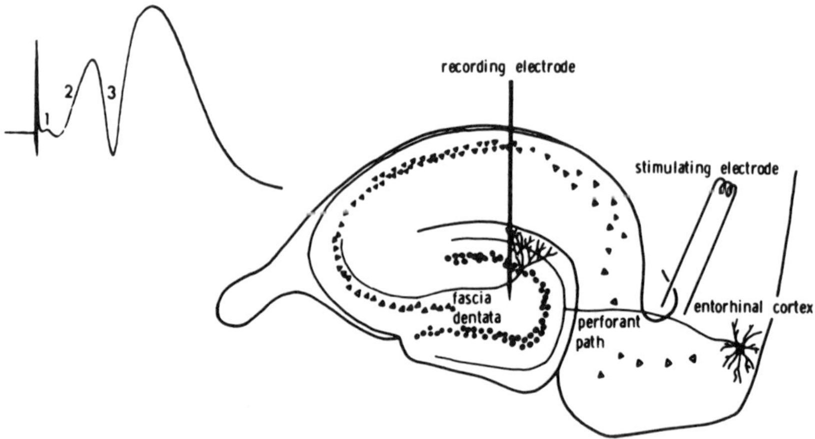

Figure 6. Schematic illustration of the perforant path projection to the fascia dentata and the configuration of the stimulating and recording electrodes. The fascia dentata is horseshoe-shaped in cross section with the dendrites of its principal neurons, the granule cells, oriented radially. The perforant path makes synaptic contact in the outer ⅔ of the dendritic tree. When the perforant path is activated with a sufficiently strong electrical stimulus, an electrode located in the central region of the horseshoe, or hilus, records an evoked response such as shown at the upper left. Following the stimulus artifact a small deflection (1) is seen, and is due to the electrical activity of the afferent fibers. After this a diphasic field potential is observed, consisting of a positive-going wave (2) due to the flow of excitatory synaptic current, on which is superimposed a sharp negative going "population spike" (3) representing the summed discharge of the granule cells.

Following activation of a sufficient number of perforant path fibers, an electrode located in the hilus records a diphasic field potential which is very nearly proportional to the average membrane current density at the granule cell bodies (Barnes and McNaughton, 1979). The initial positive-going phase of this field potential reflects the membrane current due to synaptic activation in the granule cell dendrites (component 2, Figure 6). This positive-going component is termed the population EPSP (excitatory post-synaptic potential; Lømo, 1971). Superimposed on this positive waveform is a fast negative-going wave called the population spike (Andersen, Bliss, and Skrede, 1971), which provides a relative measure of the number of granule cells which have reached their discharge threshold (component 3, Figure 6). For the enhancement experiments, the stimulus current was set at a level just sufficient to elicit a measurable population spike and was held constant throughout the remainder of the experiment. The baseline amplitudes of the EPSPs and population spikes were determined on several consecutive days by measuring the average response to stimuli delivered at low frequency (1/5 Hz). This low frequency testing has no effect on the subsequent magnitude of the synaptic response. The average of the amplitudes of the population EPSPs and spikes from each animal obtained during this baseline test period were used as the reference level, against which the evoked responses were compared after high frequency stimulation. After the baseline tests, the animals were subjected to several sessions in which the perforant path was activated by repeated short bursts of high frequency stimulation (20 msec of 400 Hz). The number and interval between high frequency stimulation sessions were varied between the two experiments as described below.

Results

In the first phase of experiment 1, a single session of high frequency stimulation was followed by seven days during which only low frequency test stimuli were delivered. The response to the latter were used as a measure of the change in synaptic efficacy induced by the high frequency stimuli. In the second phase of this experiment, beginning on the eighth day, high frequency stimulation was given at 24-hour intervals for three consecutive days. The result was monitored by low frequency testing for a further two weeks. An example of the way in which the evoked potential changed over the course of the experiment can be seen in Figure 7.

Following high frequency stimulation, the amplitude of the population EPSP was significantly increased above baseline level, and returned to baseline approximately exponentially thereafter. Neither the magnitude nor the decay time constant of this synaptic enhancement was significantly different between age groups (see Figure 8). By the eighth day following the first high frequency stimulation session, synaptic enhancement had decayed to negligible levels.

Differences between the age groups began to appear following the second repetition. Twenty-four hours after this episode the enhancement of the synaptic response was significantly higher at all subsequent observation times. These differences are best understood with reference to Figure 8 which shows the exponential curves fit by least squares analysis.[3] It will be seen that the three repetitions of the high frequency stimulation significantly affected neither the initial magnitude nor the decay time course in the old group, when compared to the effects of a single high frequency session. A strikingly different result was observed in the young group. With repeated high frequency stimulation, enhancement decayed more and more slowly so that the total enhancement tended to accumulate. This is revealed by the exponential analysis in

[3]The coefficients for the fits to the curves measured after one and after three repetitions were: old r^2 = .86 and .75 respectively; and young r^2 = .93 and .81 respectively.

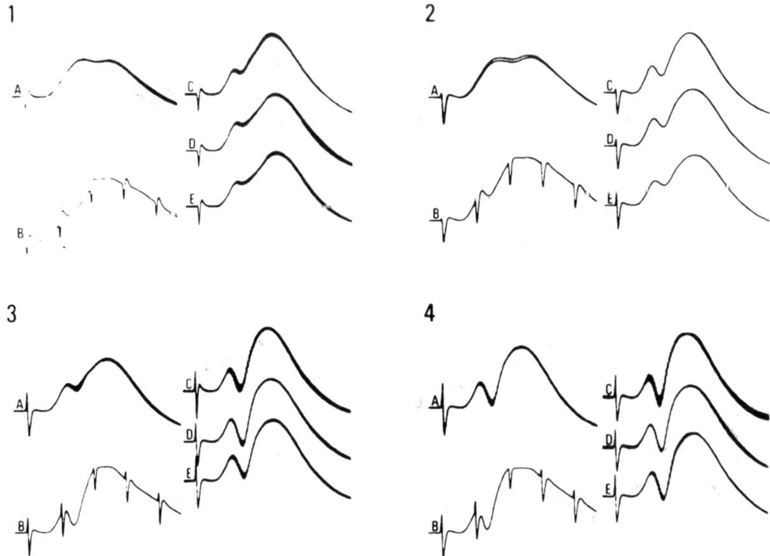

Figure 7. Examples of averaged evoked responses (with 95% confidence limits) collected from one young rat over the course of experiment 1: T1 to T4 refer to the first through fourth sessions of high-frequency stimulation.
1) The average response collected immediately before T1 is seen as "A," the high-frequency stimulation (T1) as "B" (with the mean only), two minutes after as "C," 10 minutes after as "D," and one hour after as "E." The points "C," "D," and "E" below are as presented here.
2) The means and standard errors of the responses for the day 7 and 8 time points after T1 are shown overlapped in "A." The high-frequency stimulation (T2) is shown as "B."
3) The average response collected 24 hours after T2 is shown as "A," and the high-frequency stimulation (T3) as "B."
4) The average response collected 24 hours after T3 is shown as "A," and the high-frequency stimulation (T4) as "B."
Calibration: 2mV, 2msec.

Figure 8 which shows that increases in both the initial magnitude and in the decay time constant resulted from repeated high frequency stimulation in the young animals.[4] The population spike, although considerably more variable, showed a similar effect.

The object of the second study was to determine whether senescent animals would show a similar increase in decay time constant given a sufficient number of repetitions. In this experiment, two baseline days of low frequency testing were followed by 12 high frequency stimulation

[4]The decay time constant after the first high frequency stimulation in experiment 1 was four days in both age groups. After three repetitions of the enhancing stimulus the time constant was extended to 29 days in the young group.

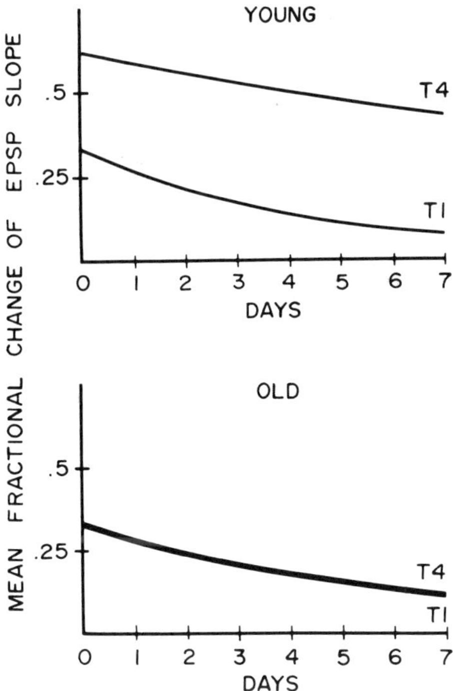

Figure 8. Exponential curves fit to the data for the decay of synaptic enhancement obtained from experiment 1. Following a single (T1) and three (T4) high-frequency stimulation sessions, the exponential fits gave r^2 values ranging from .75 and .93. While the two curves are virtually indistinguishable in the old group of rats, repeated high-frequency stimulation significantly prolonged the decay of enhancement in the young rats.

SOURCE: *Barnes, 1979.*

sessions given at 24-hour intervals. The effect of this stimulation was then followed daily for an additional three weeks. The results for the population EPSP are shown in Figure 9. The magnitude of enhancement grew toward an asymptote with daily repetitions in both age groups, however, the young group approached this asymptote more quickly than the old group. This may be seen more clearly with reference to Figure 10. This figure shows that the rate of growth of the decay time constant was a decreasing function of the number of high frequency stimulus trials. The young group reaches its maximum value on Trial 5, whereas the old group does not reach its maximum value until Trial 10.[5]

Although the final decay time constant for the old group in this study

[5]There is a discrepancy in the magnitude of the time constants shown in Figure 10 and the final time constant following the last high frequency stimulation (Figure 9). This results from the fact that the decay of enhancement is only approximately exponential. The decay is more rapid early in the time course (McNaughton, 1978). Thus decay rates determined on a day-to-day basis will appear more rapid then decay rates determined over the course of several weeks.

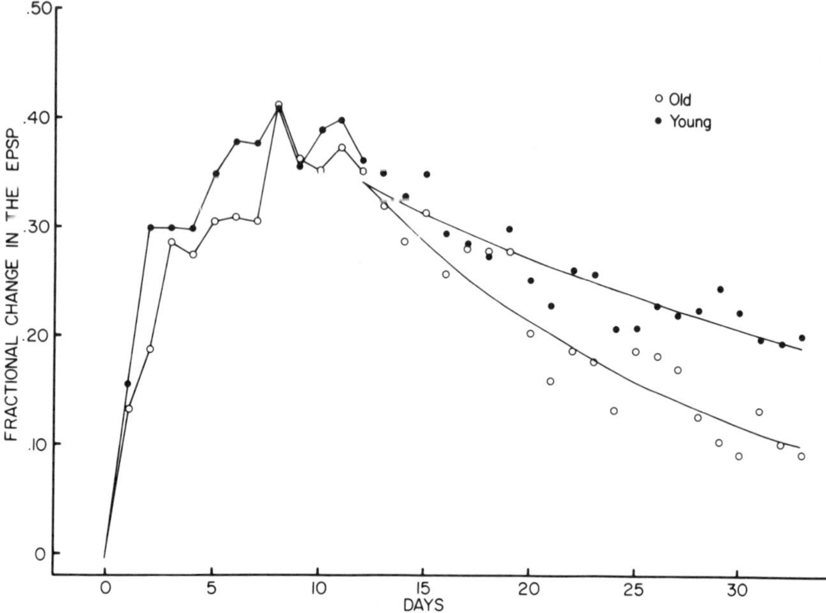

Figure 9. The magnitude of synaptic enhancement in the young and old age groups from experiment 2. The first 12 data points represent the magnitude of enhancement 24 hours following each of the 12 high frequency stimulus sessions. The remaining data points were taken at subsequent 24-hour intervals. After 12 repetitions of the high frequency stimulus, both groups had reached approximately the same asymptotic level of enhancement. However, it is clear that this value was approached more quickly in the young animals. The two curves drawn through the data points following the last high-frequency stimulation session are exponential functions fit by the method of least squares. While these curves support the conclusion that the magnitude of enhancement was the same between age groups following the last high frequency session, the decay of enhancement was significantly faster in the old population. Nevertheless, twelve repetitions of the enhancing stimulus did produce a larger decay time constant than the three repetitions in experiment 1.

(17 days) was considerably increased over the corresponding value following three daily repetitions (4 days in experiment 1), it was nevertheless significantly below the value attained by the young population (37 days; see Figure 9).

Discussion

We conclude from these data that the decay time constant of synaptic enhancement in the fascia dentata is considerably prolonged in both age groups by daily repetition of the enhancing stimulus. The process underlying the increase in the decay time constant, however, is deficient in these senescent animals. Although synaptic enhancement reached an

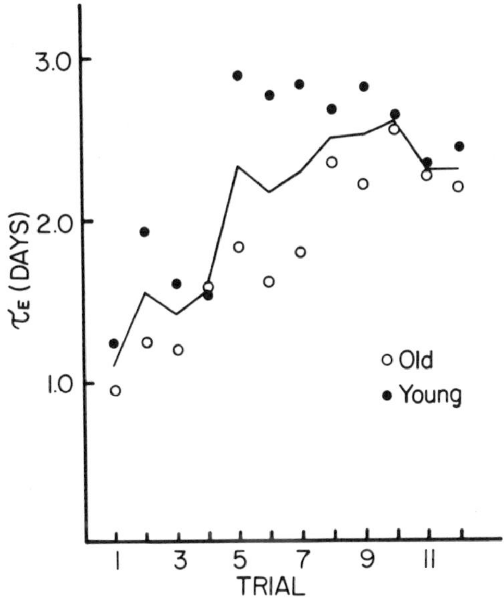

Figure 10. Increase in the time constant of enhancement following repeated trials of high frequency stimulation for the two age groups. These data points represent the decay of enhancement over the 24-hour period following each high frequency stimulation. The solid line represents the mean data for the young and old groups combined. Note that the maximum value in the young groups was reached earlier than the maximum value in the old group.

asymptotic value of approximately 40% in both age groups in experiment 2, it appears that no reasonable amount of stimulus repetition will induce this change to become as persistent in the old as in the young animals.

The results of the experiments presented here should not be confused with those of Landfield and Lynch (1977) and Landfield, McGaugh, and Lynch (1978), who found significant differences between age groups in the initial values of "frequency potentiation" and "post-tetanic potentiation" in the Schaeffer collateral synapses on the hippocampal pyramidal cells. In experiments 1 and 2 (discussed above), there were no differences between age groups found in the initial magnitude of enhancement following bursts of high frequency stimulation. McNaughton (1977) and McNaughton et al. (1978) have demonstrated that the short-lasting processes (5 to 10 minutes maximal) represent different physical phenomena from enhancement. Frequency and post-tetanic potentiation are not sufficiently long-lasting, nor do they exhibit the cooperative characteristics logically required for a mechanism of lasting associative memory. Nevertheless, it is possible that there is some causal relation between the magnitude of post-tetanic potentiation and the persistence of enhancement, and this possibility deserves further study.

Summary and Conclusions

We have demonstrated an inverse correspondence between the decay rate of post-tetanic synaptic enhancement and the asymptotic level of performance on a spatial memory task. That is, the old animals as a group showed poorer performance and less persistent enhancement than the young animals.

A necessary condition for the hypothesis that enhancement and memory are causally related is that there be a correlation between the physiology and behavior within groups as well as between groups. This condition was met in the first experiment. Statistically significant within group correlations ranging from −.43 to −.64 were found between the asymptotic performance on the circular maze and the residual level of enhancement at corresponding time points. In other words, those young animals that showed the poorest performance also tended to show the least persistent enhancement in their age group. Similarly for the old animals, the poorest performance was correlated with the least persistent enhancement.

While these correlations are not logically *sufficient* to demonstrate a causal relationship, they nevertheless support the hypothesis that the deficit in performance of a task requiring spatial memory is at least in part attributable to deficient retention of hippocampal synaptic enhancement. This hypothesis leads to at least two testable predictions. The first is that the locus of the behavioral deficit should be primarily in retention. In fact the one-week retention data from the second study using the circular platform are in agreement with this prediction. A rigorous demonstration, however, will require a detailed study of the rates of forgetting in different age groups. A second prediction is that any experimental intervention which affects the decay rate of hippocampal synaptic enhancement should correspondingly affect retention of the spatial memory. Presumably, in the case of the older animals, we should be looking to prolong this decay.

References

Andersen P, Bliss T, Skrede K: Lammellar organization of hippocampal excitatory pathways. *Experimental Brain Research* 13:222-238, 1971.

Andersen P, Sundberg SH, Sveen O: Specific long-lasting potentiation of synaptic transmission in hippocampal slices. *Nature (London)* 266:737, 1977.

Barnes CA: Memory deficits associated with senescence: a neurophysiological and behavioral study in the rat. *J Comparative and Physiological Psychology* 93:74-104, 1979.

Barnes CA, Nadel L, Honig WK: Spatial memory deficit in senescent rats. *Canadian J Psychology,* 34:29–39, 1980.

Barnes CA, McNaughton BL: Neurophysiological comparison of dendritic cable properties in adolescent, middle-aged, and senescent rats. *Experimental Aging Research* 5:195-206, 1979.

Barnes CA, McNaughton BL: Daily high-frequency stimulation differentially prolongs synaptic enhancement in middle-aged and senescent rat hippocampus. Paper presented at meeting of the *Society for Neuroscience,* Atlanta, Georgia, Nov., 1979.

Birren JE, Schaie KW: (eds.) *Handbook of the Psychology of Aging.* New York, Nostrand Reinhold, 1977.

Bliss T, Gardner-Medwin A: Long-lasting potentiation of synaptic transmission in the dentate area of unanesthetized rabbit following stimulation of the perforant path. *J Physiology (London)* 232:357-374, 1973.

Bliss T, Lømo T: Long-lasting potentiation of synaptic transmission in the dentate area of the anesthetized rabbit following stimulation of the perforant path. *J Physiology (London)* 232:331-356, 1973.

Brindley G: Nerve net models of plausible size that perform many simple learning tasks. *Proceedings of the Royal Society* B 184:173-191, 1969.

Douglas RM: Long-lasting synaptic potentiation in the rat dentate gyrus following brief high-frequency stimulation. *Brain Research* 126:361-365, 1977.

Eccles JC: An instruction-selection theory of learning in the cerebellar cortex. *Brain Research* 127:327-352, 1977.

Gardner-Medwin AR: The recall of events through the learning of associations between their parts. *Proceedings of the Royal Society* B 194:375-402, 1976.

Gilbert PFC: A theory of memory that explains the function and structure of the cerebellum. *Brain Research* 70:1-18, 1974.

Goodrick CL: Learning by mature-young and aged Wistar albino rats as a function of test complexity. *J Gerontology* 27:353-357, 1972.

Gordon SK, Clark WC: Application of signal detection theory to prose recall and recognition in elderly and young adults. *J Gerontology* 29:64-72, 1974.

Hebb DO: *The Organization of Behavior.* New York, Wiley, 1949.

Landfield PW, Lynch G: Impaired monosynaptic potentiation in *in vitro* hippocampal slices from aged, memory-deficient rats. *J Gerontology* 32:523-533, 1977.

Landfield PW, McGaugh JL, Lynch G: Impaired synaptic potentiation processes in the hippocampus of aged, memory-deficient rats. *Brain Research* 150:85-101, 1978.

Little W, Shaw G: Statistical theory of short- and long-term memory. *Behavioral Biology* 14:115-133, 1974.

Longuet-Higgins HC, Willshaw DJ, Buneman OP: Theories of associative recall. *Quarterly Review of Biophysics* 3:223-244, 1970.

Lømo T: Patterns of activation in a monosynaptic cortical pathway: the perforant path input to the dentate area of the hippocampal formation. *Experimental Brain Research* 12:18-45, 1971.

Marr D: Simple memory: a theory for archicortex. *Proceedings of the Royal Society* B 262:23-81, 1971.

McNaughton BL: Dissociation of short- and long-lasting modification of synaptic efficacy at the terminals of the perforant path. Seventh Annual Meeting of the *Society for Neuroscience.* Anaheim, California, 1977, Abstract.

McNaughton BL, Barnes CA: Phsyiological identification and analysis of dentate granule cell responses to stimulation of the medial and lateral perforant pathways in the rat. *J Comparative Neurology* 175:439-454, 1977.

McNaughton BL: The dynamics of synaptic modulation in the medial and lateral components of the perforant pathway to the fascia dentata in the rat. Unpublished doctoral dissertation, Dalhousie University, Halifax, Canada, 1978.

McNaughton BL, Douglas RM, Goddard GV: Synaptic enhancement in fascia dentata: Cooperativity among co-active afferents. *Brain Research* 157:277-293, 1978.

Medin DL, O'Neil P, Smeltz E, Davis RT: Age differences in retention of concurrent discrimination problems in monkeys. *J Gerontology* 28:63-67, 1973.

O'Keefe J, Nadel L: *The Hippocampus as a Cognitive Map*. London, Oxford University Press, 1978.

Uttley AM: A two-pathway informon theory of conditioning and adaptive pattern recognition. *Brain Research* 102:23-35, 1976.

Stein, ed. The Psychobiology of Aging: Problems and Perspectives

Aging and Senescence in Selected Motor Systems of Man

Arnold B. Scheibel

Depts. of Anatomy and Psychiatry, and Brain Research Institute, UCLA Center for the Health Sciences, Los Angeles, California.

With increasing age, the entire central nervous system begins to reflect, inexorably, a series of changes which appear both characteristic and generalized. Such changes have been described in a rich neuropathological literature over the past century (Critchley, 1942). More recently, the application of both quantitative techniques (Brody, 1955) and special methods for visualization of neuropil elements (Scheibel and Scheibel, 1975) have added a considerable body of new information. These approaches emphasize the nervous system as an information processing organ, whose capacity degrades as a result of loss of synaptic connections. This loss is, in turn, a function of decreasing amounts of dendrite surface membrane and of available synaptic surface as the dendrite domains regress during the process of senescence (Scheibel, 1978).

Although a number of general features common to the aging process have been identified in the nervous system, the process appears to advance at its own rate and with its own idiosyncratic pathology in each neural area. Most of these age and area-specific characteristics are presently being delineated, and the chrome silver methods of Golgi provide a powerful tool in identifying early senescent changes in axon systems and dendrite domains (Scheibel, 1978; Scheibel and Scheibel, 1975; Scheibel, Tomiyasu, and Scheibel, 1977). In this paper, we will review a group of changes which develop in two of the motor systems of the human central nervous system: the giant pyramidal cells of Betz of the motor strip area, and the motoneurons of the anterior horn of the spinal cord. In each case, some possible functional consequences of the neuropathology (or better yet, "gerohistology") will be deduced which may be relevant to symptomatology experienced by the aged patient.

Betz Cells of the Motor Strip

Most studies of aging human cerebral cortex to date have emphasized the association areas, especially the prefrontal and temporal (superior and middle temporal gyri) cortices, as showing the earliest signs of senescent change (Brody, 1955). The giant pyramidal cells of Betz seem to constitute a powerful exception to this category, appearing to be among the most aging-sensitive of all neurons (Scheibel, Tomiyasu, and Scheibel, 1977). Quite apart from their great size and elaborate dendritic domains, they are of particular interest because of their very limited number, i.e., 35,000 to 40,000 per motor strip (Lassek, 1954). Appreciable loss among so limited a complement of cells is particularly likely to result in identifiable clinical signs or symptoms, thereby providing an unusual opportunity for structure-function correlations. In addition, Betz neurons have been shown to have a highly specific distribution, 85% or more being localized to areas of the motor strip supplying large extensor muscles of the lower extremity and the axial muscles of the back (Lassek, 1954).

The giant pyramidal cells of Betz are characterized by their size (50–100μ in cell body diameter) and an enormous circumferential array of basilar dendritic shafts, some of which may extend for several millimeters or more from the cell body and, in fact, exceed the length of the apical dendrite (Scheibel and Scheibel, 1978). These basilar dendrite shafts show a good deal of variation in pattern, but most seem to be involved in the formation of dense and complex dendrite bundles with other shafts of both Betz and non-Betz pyramids. The possible significance of such bundles in programming neuronal ensembles has been discussed elsewhere (Scheibel and Scheibel, 1973).

Senescent changes in Betz cells resemble those we have seen at other sites in the human cortex and include 1. patchy loss of spines which spreads to include increasing amounts of dendritic surface; 2. nodulation of dendrite shafts followed by areas of constriction and fragmentation; 3. preferential and eventually total loss of the basilar (circumferential) dendritic array; 4. envelopment of the cell body with fibrous astroglia, culminating in 5. shrinkage and loss of the apical shaft and cell body (Figures 1, 2).

Using the methods of Golgi to follow the pattern of soma-dendritic change, and cresylechtviolet stains to allow quantification of cell loss, it can be determined that 70–80% of Betz cells are lost by the seventh or eighth decade of life (see graph, Figure 3). This enormous attrition in a very limited cell pool may be unique in the central nervous system and stimulates questions as to the functional sequellae of such massive cell loss.

Physiological experiments have shown that the largest contingent of

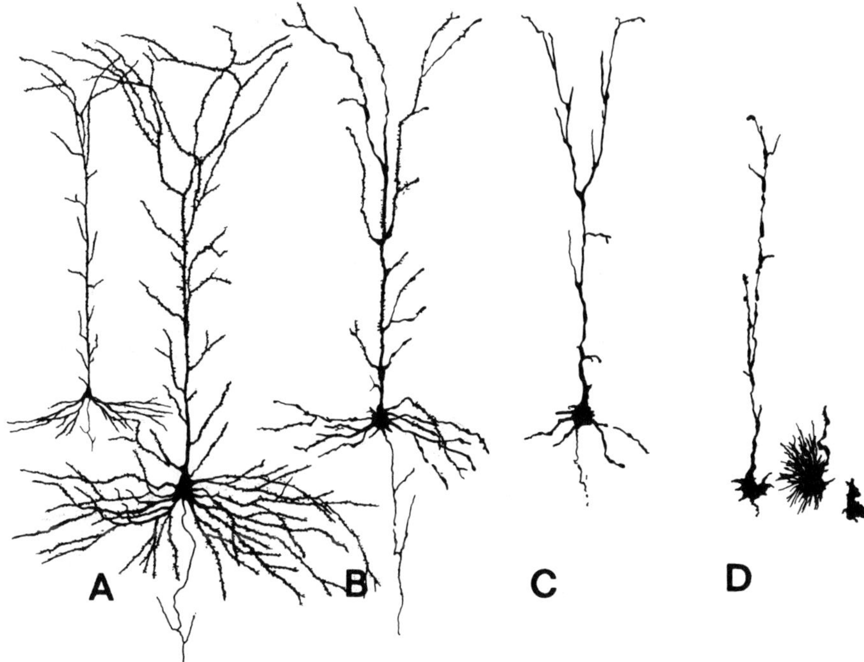

Figure 1. Sequence of changes occurring in human Betz cell with senescence, starting with the fully developed neuron in a young adult (A) and continuing through a series of degradative changes characteristic of the sixth to eighth decades of life (B and C), culminating in cell death (D). A smaller non-Betz pyramid is shown in A for comparison. Note the earlier loss of basilar (circumferential) dendrites (B and C) and the irregular swelling and nodulation of the apical shaft system. Drawn from the Golgi preparations at 200 ×.

cortico-spinal axons make up only about 1% of the total fiber ensemble, and these axons are undoubtedly the processes of the giant cells. Unlike the firing patterns generated by other cortical pyramids, the largest (Betz cell) axons have been found to deliver, characteristically, a phasic burst of spikes just before the onset of a patterned motor act, as measured by electromyographic electrodes recording from appropriate muscle pairs (Evarts, 1965,1967). The role of this brief episode of activity appears to be inhibition of extensor muscle activity (Lundberg and Voorhoeve, 1962) thereby decreasing anti-gravity tone and conditioning the weight-bearing musculature for the inception of the subsequent patterned motor act. With partial or complete lysis of antigravity tone, the programmed motor sequence, or at least the initial frame of action, can proceed with maximal efficiency, the extensor tone being immediately reinstituted at the end of the motor sequence. With increasing loss of the Betz cell

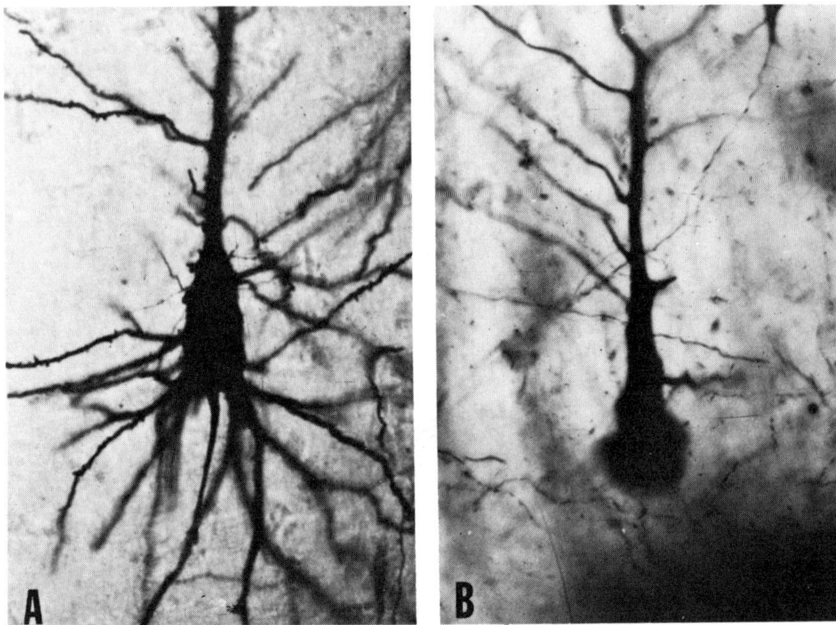

Figure 2. Photographs of human Betz cells from a 40-year-old patient (A) and from a 79-year-old patient (B). Massive changes in the basilar (circumferential) dendrite system and swelling of the cell body are obvious. Original photographs on Kodachrome 35mm film from rapid Golgi variant × 200.

ensemble, lysis of anti-gravity tone becomes increasingly ineffective. The patterned act can be generated but must be superimposed on extensor muscle systems under increased residual tone. The expected results might include slowing of activity and stiffening across joints and, especially after a few hours of work, exercise or walking, sensations of stiffness and muscle pains in the legs and lower back. These symptoms are common in the aged and become increasingly a part of all motor activity in the senescent period of life. It is true that some of the "slowing down," "stiffening," and "aching" of age relate to changes in connective tissue, in the neuromuscular unit (see below) and undoubtedly in the nigro-striatal-basal ganglionar system. Nonetheless, the structural changes we have described in the giant cells of Betz probably add another significant component to the familiar clinical picture.

Motoneuron Systems of the Spinal Cord

The pool of spinal motoneurons making up the final common pathway and the gamma (spindle biasing) mechanism constitute a neuronal ensemble which is also highly and differentiably responsive to aging and

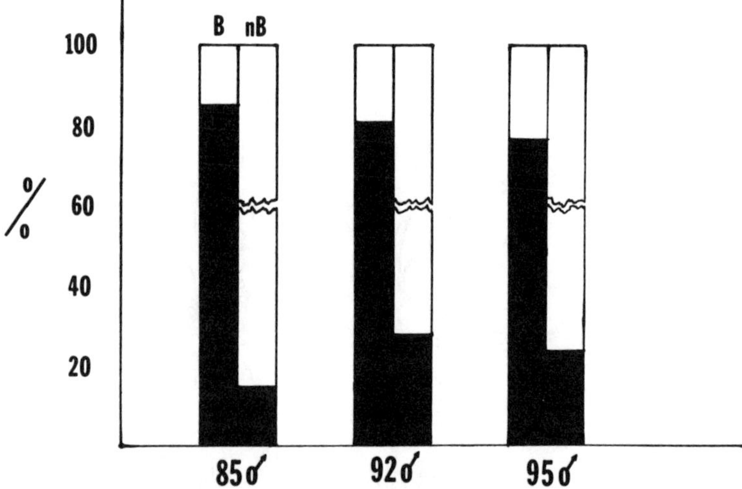

Figure 3. Bar graph based on preliminary data showing the very large proportion of damaged Betz cells (B) in three aged patients compared to the very much smaller proportion of changed non-Betz (nB) cells in the motor strip area. Broken bars indicate that the total number of non-Betz pyramids is very much greater than that of Betz cells. These estimates are based on a study of both Golgi and Nissl stained sections.

senescence. Golgi studies show the loss of dendritic branches and destruction of the great longitudinal dendrite bundle systems first described in the cat (Scheibel and Scheibel, 1970) and so much more prominent in primates and man (Scheibel, unpublished observations). The possible relationship of such bundles to motor output programs has been discussed elsewhere (Scheibel and Scheibel, 1973; Figures 4,5).

The most obvious changes shown by these neurons viewed with standard histological stains under the light microscope include swelling of the cell body, eccentricity of the nucleus, fragmentation of Nissl substance and engorgement of the cell body with lipofuscin granules. In several patients aged 75 to 91, initial quantitative studies indicate that 60–90% of the neurons contain concentrations of these yellow-green refractile bodies sufficient to compress the nucleus against one wall of the cyton. Although lipofuscin is also seen in the motoneurons of patients in their fifties and sixties, the amounts are always very much smaller, and the central position of the nucleus seldom appears compromised.

These initial studies have also revealed a pattern of differential or idiosyncratic aging which may be of significant import. As motoneurons progress through the final sequences of complete dendrite destruction and cell body loss, the small and medium sized elements appear more vulnerable and are lost in larger quantities. An initial series of differential

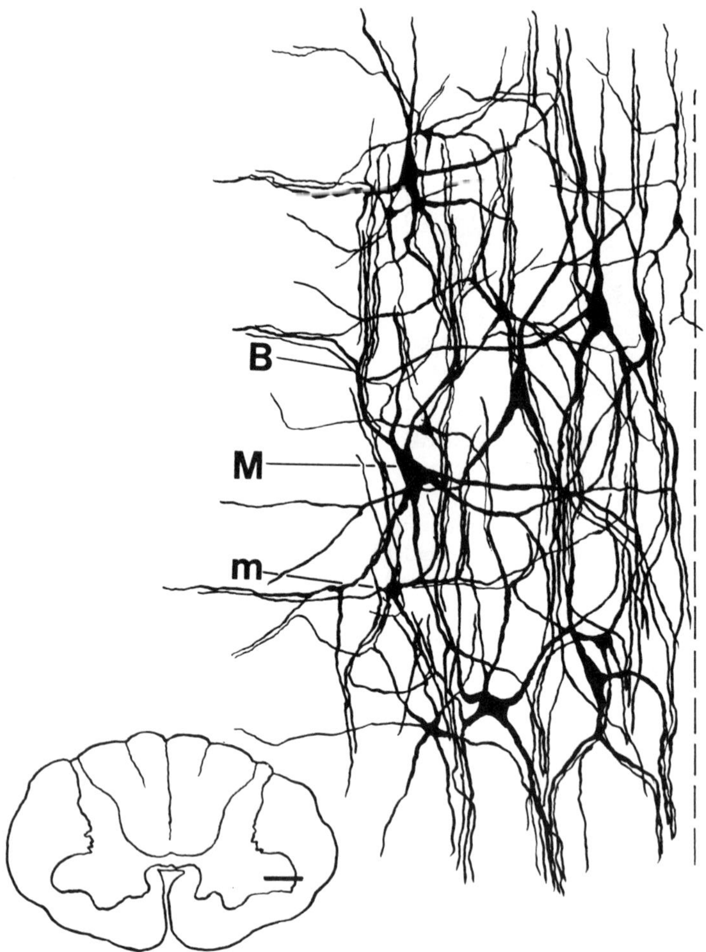

Figure 4. Drawing of horizontal section through the ventral horn of a human spinal cord, age 40. Note the many cell sizes, the elaborate dendrite systems arranged in the sagittal plane, and the dendrite bundles produced by these dendrite shafts. Drawn from a Golgi stained section at L4-5, 200 ×.

counts made in 2 middle-aged patients, compared with 3 patients in their eighties, suggests that small cells of the motoneuronal pool ($< 15\mu$) disappear in largest numbers, with medium size (15–40μ) cells next most sensitive to the deteriorative process. Neurons over 40μ also may carry considerable amounts of lipofuscin but, presumably because of their greater cell body volume, are able to contain larger amounts of pigment without suffering such major deterioration of nuclear and intracytoplasmic functions.

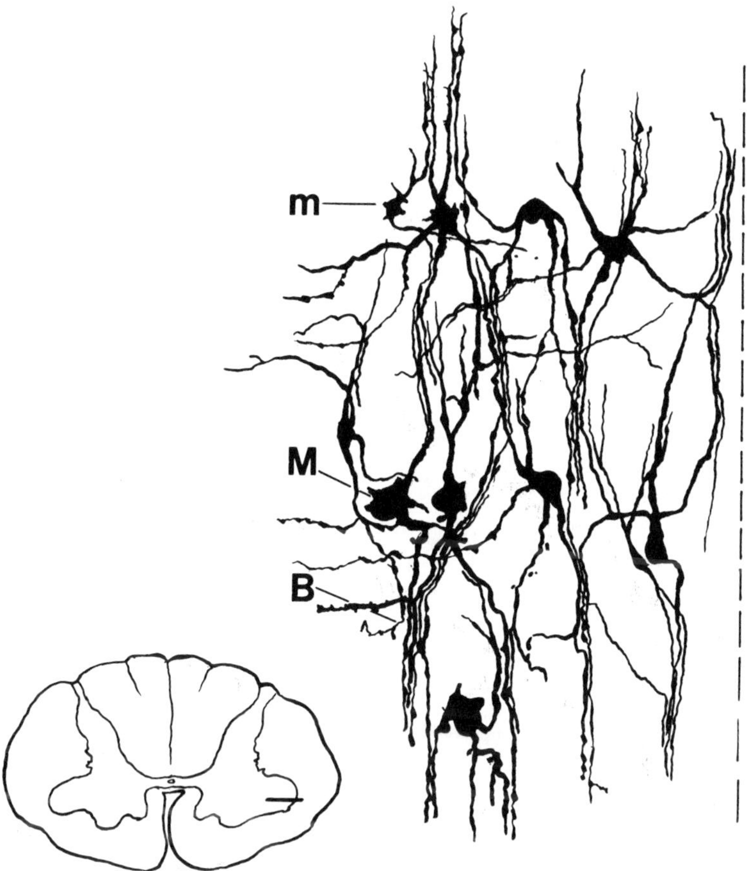

Figure 5. Drawing of horizontal section through the ventral horn of a human spinal cord, age 89. Note that predominantly larger cells remain, and the dendrite systems are less elaborate, the individual shafts appearing nodulated and often shortened. Drawn from a Golgi stained section at L4-5, 200 ×.

Just as the selective loss of an initially limited population of Betz cells in motor cortex appears to have specific functional consequences, so, we believe, does the idiosyncratic loss of smaller elements of the motoneuronal pool produce identifiable clinical effects. The smallest motoneurons (exclusive of interneurons which are also found here and which can be identified in fortunate Golgi impregnations by their axonal trajectories) are the gamma, and small alpha cells. The former bias spindle firing patterns and thereby guarantee continuously reporting muscle receptors, whether the muscle belly is relaxed or under stretch. With loss of the gamma efferent system, spindles become silent when they are unloaded by shortening of the muscle belly. The resultant partial loss of proprioceptive feedback from the muscle mass, while not in itself catastrophic, impairs speed and precision of neuromuscular activity. It might be noted in passing that the incomplete and continuously interrupted flow of sensory data characterizing this situation essentially repeats the pattern present in the early months of life of the infant when the gamma apparatus is not yet mature (Skoglund, 1960).

The preferential loss of small alpha motoneurons may have an appreciable effect on motor performance. A recently discovered mechanism of motoneuron activity, the size principle (Henneman, Somjen, and Carpenter, 1965), suggests that there is a regular sequence of entrainment of motoneurons to an imposed stimulus, the smallest being activated earliest; the largest coming on line at longest interval, and with the highest threshold, following the stimulus. In addition, it is well known that smaller motoneurons generally innervate red muscle fibers while large neurons supply white muscle fibers. Aside from the obvious difference in color which is attributed to differing concentrations of myoglobin, the major functional difference between the two categories of muscle fibers lies in the fact that white fibers are phasic in operation and are capable of a high degree of power and speed in contraction, but fatigue easily. Red fibers, by contrast, are tonic and resistant to fatigue and are well adapted for sustained work. However, they lack the power and speed of contraction which marks the white muscle fiber.

On the basis of the apparently increased degree of vulnerability of the smaller motoneurons to senescent change, deterioration, and death, it would appear that the tonic fatigue-resistant, red muscle fibers are the peripheral elements most likely to lose innervation. The large phasic fibers would maintain their capability as a function of the increased resistance of the large alpha motoneurons to senescent changes. Overall decrement in motor performance would be reflected in somewhat later onset of muscle activity and rapid fatigability along with some degree of wasting of the total muscle mass due to trophic effects of small motoneuron loss. It is worth noting that such changes are common in the elderly. One other facet of the clinical picture of aging should also be remarked. In man, as in most animals, the tonic muscles are usually the antigravity extensor components which are capable of prolonged contraction. Age-linked attrition in these muscle fiber systems is bound to result in a predominance of flexor muscle activity. The increasing "stoop" or flexor cast of all but the most doughty aged is regrettably familiar.

In looking backward at the presumed effects of progressive Betz cell loss on extensor muscle systems already discussed, and pairing such functional *sequellae* with those that may be expected to follow the preferential loss of small, tonic muscle fiber-innervating, motoneurons, it becomes clear that the extensor, antigravity muscle systems are those which most accurately reflect the status of the central neuronal pool.

Overview

In earlier communications (Scheibel, 1978; Scheibel and Scheibel, 1975: Scheibel, Tomiyasu, and Scheibel, 1977), we have stressed the wide variation in response patterns of cortical neurons to the aging process. Clearly, on the basis of neuronal structure and psychophysiological patterns, some patients are old at 65 while others remain young at 90. Such variability also obtains at the level of the spinal motoneuron. The structural changes we describe, and their putative functional consequences must be considered models of fully developed gerohistology rather than the expected picture in every aging human spinal cord and cerebral cortex. It is probably safe to say that the pattern and trend are the same for every aging individual. The time table alone is idiosyncratic, depending in part, undoubtedly, on genetic factors, nutrition, the amount of challenge presented to the nervous system, and the possible presence of a host of hypotheticated noxious agents, inorganic and organic, about which we can only speculate at present.

Within this very broad framework of reference, we must assume from our own observations and from those of others that, with the progression of the aging process, sequences of changes occur in many neural systems which may appreciably affect the sensorimotor, perceptive, and cognitive performance level of every individual. Here we have considered changes in three systems related to motor output: the giant pyramidal cells of Betz of the motor strip area, the alpha and gamma motoneurons of the ventral horn of the spinal cord, and the muscle systems to which they project. Further studies are under way to provide quantitative support for these essentially qualitative descriptions and to examine ultrastructural aspects of the changes already seen.

References

Brody H: Organization of the cerebral cortex. III. A study of aging in the human cerebral cortex. *J Comp Neurol* 102:511–556, 1955.

Critchley M: Aging of the nervous system, Chapter 19. In Cowdrey E (ed.) *Problems of Aging* (2nd ed.). Williams and Wilkins Co., Baltimore, 1942.

Evarts E: Relation of discharge frequency to conduction velocity in pyramidal tract neurons. *J Neurophysiol* 28:216–228, 1965.

Evarts E: Representation of movements and muscles by pyramidal tract neurons of the precentral motor cortex. In Yahr D, Purpura DP (eds.) *Neurophysiological Basis of Normal and Abnormal Motor Activities*. New York, Raven Press, 1967, pp. 215–253.

Henneman F, Somjen G, Carpenter D: Functional significance of cell size in spinal motoneurons. *J Neurophysiol* 28:560–580, 1965.

Lassek AM: *The Pyramidal Tract.* Charles C Thomas, Springfield, 1954.

Lundberg A, Voorhoeva P: Effects from the pyramidal tract on spinal reflex arcs. *Acta Physiol Scand* 56:201–219, 1962.

Scheibel AB: Structural aspects of the aging brain: spine systems and the dendritic arbor. In Katzman R, Terry R, Brik K (eds.) *Alzheimar's Disease: Senile Dementia and Related Disorders.* New York, Raven Press, 1978, pp. 353–374.

Scheibel ME, Scheibel AB: Organization of spinal motoneuron dendrites in bundles. *Exp Neurol* 28:106–112, 1970.

Scheibel ME, Scheibel AB: Dendrite bundles as sites for central programs: an hypothesis. *Internat J Neurosci* 6:195–202, 1973.

Scheibel ME, Scheibel AB: Structural changes in the aging brain. In Brody H, Harman D, Ordy J (eds.) *Aging, Vol. I.* New York, Raven Press, 1975, pp. 11–37.

Scheibel ME, Scheibel AB: The dendritic structure of the human Betz cell. In Brazier M, Petsche H (eds.) *Architectonics of the Cerebral Cortex.* New York, Raven Press, 1978, pp. 43–57.

Scheibel ME, Tomiyasu U, Scheibel AB: The aging human Betz cell. *Exp Neurol* 56:598–609, 1977.

Skoglund S: The activity of muscle receptors in the kitten. *Acta Physiol Scand* 50:203–221, 1960.

Stein, ed. The Psychobiology of Aging: Problems and Perspectives

Individual Differences in Dendritic Growth in Human Aging and Senile Dementia

S. J. Buell[a] and P. D. Coleman

Department of Anatomy, University of Rochester, School of Medicine and Dentistry, Rochester, New York.

Introduction

Traditionally the process of aging in the cerebral cortex has been viewed as a relentless deterioration characterized by loss of neurons (Brody, 1955,1970) and regression of dendrities (Scheibel et al., 1975, 1976). However, recent studies in the rodent brain indicate that these involutional changes may be accompanied by compensatory growth of dendrites (Hinds and McNelly, 1977) and perhaps also of axons (Scheff, Bernardo and Cotman, 1978). We present here data showing that in human brain, dendrites continue to grow throughout the life span in normal aging and that senile dementia represents a net regression or a failure of dendritic growth.

The data described in this report were obtained from parahippocampal gyrus of the brain. This region has been considered a part of the Papez circuit (Shipley, 1974) in morphological studies of rodents CNS. In rats other portions of the Papez circuit have been shown to undergo changes in long-term potentiation properties with age and may be associated with spatial memory alterations (Barnes, this volume). After studying neuropathological material McLardy (1970) suggested that the lesions most frequently associated with memory deficits in humans are in the parahippocampal gyrus.

[a]Present address: Department of Neurology, Laboratory of Neurovirology, Johns Hopkins School of Medicine, Baltimore, Maryland.

Materials and Methods

At autopsy, samples of parahippocampal gyrus were taken from fifty brains. Summary information on each subject used in this study is presented in Table 1. Subjects were divided into three groups: normal adult (mean age 51.2 years), normal elderly (mean age 79.6) and senile dementia (SD) (mean age 76.0) on the basis of reported behavior and pathological criteria. There were five cases in each group. Behavioral information was obtained from interviews with patients' physicians or nurses or from hospital charts. A list of behaviors characterizing SD was established with the aid of psychiatric consultation.[a] The list included: memory impairment, confusion, speech disturbance (e.g., perseveration), impaired judgment, sexual exposure, deterioration in eating and/or dress habits, hoarding, hallucinations, etc.

All subjects classified as SD exhibited over half of these characteristics. None of the non-senile aged or adult cases were reported to have exhibited any of these characteristics. Cases were rejected from the study for any of the following reasons: history of severe head trauma, severe seizure disorder, severe cerebro-vascular accident, chronic alcohol abuse, documented psychiatric disorder (other than SD), intellectual deterioration without a diagnosis of frank dementia, and insufficient information to judge mental and neurological status. In addition, cases were excluded from the SD group if examination of Bodian (1936) silver-stained sections gave no evidence of extensive senile plaques and neurofibrillary tangles. None of the cases used showed evidence of infarct, hemorrhage or spongiform changes.

A block of parahippocampal gyrus was removed from between the level of the apex of the uncus and a cut two centimeters caudal to the first cut. Tissue from the right hemisphere was placed in Golgi-Cox fixative (Van der Loos, 1956). Alternate sections were cut at 200 μm and 40 μm. The 200 μm sections were processed through ammonia and fixer to give a standard Golgi-Cox appearance. The 40 μm sections were counterstained with cresyl violet and were used for cytoarchitectonic orientation. A corresponding tissue block from the left hemisphere was immersed in 10% formalin for later Bodian (1936) silver proteinate, Nissl, haemotoxylin and eosin, and Congo Red staining.

The 200 μm thick Golgi-Cox stained material was used to collect quantitative information on dendritic parameters. This information was obtained with a semi-automatic dendrite tracking computer-microscope system (Coleman et al., 1977). All slides used for tracking were coded, so all tracking was done without knowing from which brains the sections

[a]We wish to thank Dr. John Romano, distinguished university professor of psychiatry, for aid in this aspect of the study.

Table 1. Summary of Clinical and Pathological Data for Each Case

	Case No.	Age (yr)	Sex	PMD[a] (hr)	Race	Plaques/ NFD	History	Cause of Death
Adult	10	44	F	19.00	Cauc.	No	CA cervix, widespread metastasis, small squamous CA in cerebellum, none in cerebrum, mental and neurological status normal.	Pneumonia, respiratory arrest, bowel obstruction secondary to tumor.
	12	53	F	7.25	Cauc.	No	CA, with skin as possible primary site, metastasis to lung, liver. Mental and neurological status normal other than preterminal confusion and lethargy due to pain and medication.	Cardiac arrest secondary to terminal CA.
	15	54	M	11.25	Cauc.	No	Angina, asthma, 2 MI's. Mental and neurological status normal.	Probable MI, arrhythmia, drop in blood pressure.
	21	50	F	15.60	Cauc.	No	CA breast. No metastasis to brain. Mental and neurological status normal.	Pneumonia.
	27	55	M	21.50	Cauc.	Slight	Excellent health. Mental and neurological status normal. Atherosclerosis of coronary blood vessels apparent at autopsy.	Acute coronary insufficiency during strenuous exercise resulting in sudden death.
$\bar{X}$		51.2		14.92				
Aged	9	75	M	4.50	Cauc.	Moderate	Previous MI, systemic atherosclerosis. Otherwise good health. Active as stock broker/consultant until shortly before death. Mental and neurological status normal.	Respiratory arrest 6 days after 2nd MI, cardiogenic shock.
	11	68	M	11.00	Cauc.	Moderate to heavy	Myeloid metaplasia, α-Thallesemia, mental and neurological status normal other than bilateral neural hearing loss.	Pneumonia.

Table 1. *(continued)*

	Case No.	Age (yr)	Sex	PMD[a] (hr)	Race	Plaques/ NFD	History	Cause of Death
	31	92	F	19.80	Cauc.	Slight to Moderate	Good health. Well oriented, independent, took pride in appearance. Some occasional mild confusion. Mental and neurological status normal other than preterminal near-comatose state (2 days).	Cardiac arrest three days after coronary thrombosis.
	33	76	F	2.25	Cauc.	Very slight	Good health other than systemic atherosclerosis. Alert, independent, gave music lessions until shortly before death. Mental and neurological status normal.	Coronary thrombosis.
	48	87	F	15.00	Cauc.	Very slight	Good health other than systemic atherosclerosis. Alert, well oriented, independent. Mental and neurological status normal except for occasional confusion and delusions.	Cardiac failure lasting a few minutes, secondary to a 10-year history of coronary atherosclerosis.
$\overline{X}$		79.6		10.51				
SD	29	81	M	5.75	Negro	Heavy	Angina, hypertension, history of mild alcoholism but no alcohol consumption during last several years of life. Diagnosis of severe senile dementia of "long duration". Confused, wandering, incontinent, required total care except feeding. No other neurological abnormalities.	Massive pulmonary embolism less than one hour before death.
	38	80	F	8.50	Cauc.	Heavy	Generally good health other than decubitus ulcers. Diagnosis of severe senile dementia. Disoriented, severe memory impairment, speech incoherent. Patient became mute, belligerent, anti-social. Mild seizure disorder.	Acute bilateral bronchopneumonia.

40	70	M	15.75	Cauc.	Heavy	Good health other than systemic atherosclerosis and hemorrhagic cystitis. 10 to 15-year history of severe progressive senile dementia. Confused, disoriented, violent, paranoid, disturbances in speech, sleep, continence, gait.	Septicemia of 1-day duration due to bronchopneumonia.
43	70	M	15.50	Cauc.	Heavy	Osteoarthritis, systemic atherosclerosis. Diagnosis of severe senile dementia of at least 3½ years duration. Disturbance in memory, speech, gait, sleep, strength. Possible superimposition of mild Parkinsonism.	Congestive heart failure.
47	79	M	17.75	Cauc.	Moderate	CA prostate, abnormality in fibula. Diagnosis of severe senile dementia of more than 4-years duration. Complete disorientation regarding person, place, and time. Possible small CVA in right parietal cortex 3 days before death. No other neurological abnormalities.	Bronchopneumonia after 2 days of semi-comatose state.
$\bar{X}$	76.0		12.65				

[a] PMD - Post mortem delay before fixation; Cauc. - Caucasian; Plaques/NFD - Results of subjective evaluation of degree of involvement of hippocampus and parahippocampal gyrus with senile plaques and neurofibrillary degeneration (NFD).

were taken. Cells that satisfied the following criteria were considered to form a sample that was available for tracking: 1. cell body at or near the center of the section thickness, 2. no dendrites obscured by glia, blood vessels, etc., and 3. no dendrites trailing off as a series of dots (incomplete impregnation). Beginning at the parahippocampal sulcus and moving toward the apex of the gyrus, a random subset of this sample was chosen for tracking by the throw of a die. Three cells were tracked on each of five slides from each brain to give a total of 15 cells per brain, 75 cells per group and 225 cells total. Tracking was done under a long working distance 100× oil immersion objective.

Results

Qualitative Golgi

Within every section from each of the fifteen cases there was a wide variation in the appearance of individual neurons. Neurons ranged from those with rich dendritic arborizations extending over great distances to those with grossly atrophied dendritic arborizations sometimes consisting of only a single segment. These two extremes could frequently be found in close proximity. There were no consistent differences among the adult, aged and SD groups with regard to the qualitative appearance of these cells or the apparent number of cells which were grossly atrophied.

Quantitative Golgi

Effect of Post-mortem Time (PMT) Before Fixation on Dendritic Parameters

The time between death and immersion of tissue in fixative ranged from 2.5 to 21.5 hours for our cases and did not differ significantly among the three groups ($p > 0.30$). A regression analysis of total dendritic length of basal and of apical dendrites as a function of PMT showed non-significant ($p > 0.30$ and $p > 0.20$ respectively) negative slopes. These negative slopes decreased at the rate of approximately 1.4% per hour.

Group Data

Computer counts of numbers of intersections of dendrites with successive computer-constructed concentric spheres centered on the cell body of individual cells show that the normal elderly group had more extensive dendritic trees than either the adult or the SD groups and that the SD group had less extensive dendritic trees than either the adult or aged groups. Figures 1A and 1B present these data for the apical and basal tree respectively. It is clear that the differences among groups are smaller, though still significant, in the basilar system than in the apical system. Note too that differences among groups are less at distances close to the cell body (20–40 μm) than at distances further away from the cell body.

Differences among groups were also found when dendrite length and numbers were examined in a centrifugal ordering scheme. All differences in these analyses were significant at least at the $P < 0.05$ level (Buell and Coleman, 1979). The similarity of the shapes of these curves (Figure 1; Buell and Coleman, 1979) for the adult and aged groups indicates that the dendritic growth in the aged cases was similar in nature to that of the normal development which led to the adult form. Thus, this growth appears to be distinct from previous reports of occasional aberrant sprouting in neurons in aged dogs (Lafora, 1914; Mervis, 1978) and in presenile dementia in humans (Scheibel and Tomiyasu, 1978).

Having established the statistical significance of differences among groups, the examination of dendritic trees in a centripetal ordering scheme indicates the portion of the dendritic tree that gives rise to these differences. Lengths and numbers of dendrities as a function of order in a centripetal ordering scheme are present in Figures 2A–C (apical dendrites) and 2D–F (basal dendrites). In this ordering scheme, segments which ended without giving rise to further branching are called terminal segments. The segments that gave rise to these terminal segments are called next-to-terminal (NTT) segments. All remaining segments are grouped together. These graphs show that the terminal segments constitute a large proportion of the total length of the dendritic tree: 61–65% for the apical trees and 68–70% for the basal trees. NTT segments account for 23–30% of the total dendritic tree.

Figures 2A and 2D show that the greater complexity of dendritic trees in aged cases and the decreased complexity in SD cases shown in Figure 1 by the concentric spheres analysis are due largely to changes in the terminal segments. NTT segments contribute to the differences among groups to a lesser extent. In the basal tree NTT segments show no differences among groups. Figures 2B and 2C show that in apical dendrites these differences in the terminal segments are related to both the number and average length of segments. Figures 2E and 2F show that the differences among groups seen in basal dendrites (Figure 2D) are due entirely to differences in average segment length of terminal dendrites with no differences among groups in the number of terminal dendritic segments.

Individual Data

In view of the importance of terminal dendrites to the differences among groups it is useful to examine this portion of the dendritic tree in individual cases. Such data are presented in Figures 3 and 4 which show the total length of terminal dendrites in apical and basal regions of the dendritic tree, respectively. The most striking information presented in

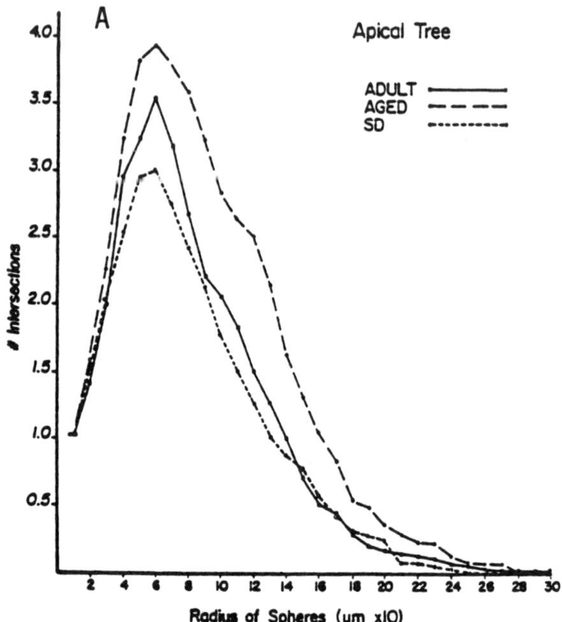
NUMBER OF INTERSECTIONS/SPHERE/CELL
A
Apical Tree
ADULT
AGED
SD
Intersections
4.0
3.5
3.0
2.5
2.0
1.5
1.0
0.5
2 4 6 8 10 12 14 16 18 20 22 24 26 28 30
Radius of Spheres (μm x10)

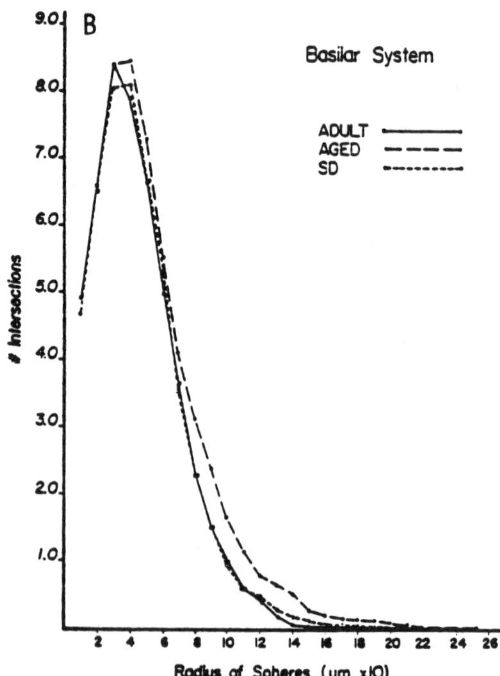
NUMBER OF INTERSECTIONS / SPHERE / CELL
B
Basilar System
ADULT
AGED
SD
Intersections
9.0
8.0
7.0
6.0
5.0
4.0
3.0
2.0
1.0
2 4 6 8 10 12 14 16 18 20 22 24 26
Radius of Spheres (μm x10)

these graphs is the considerable variability within each group and the overlap among cases in the three groups. Case 27, an active healthy 55-year-old male in the adult control group who died suddenly during strenuous exercise, had less extensive terminal dendrites than any of the other subjects, including the SD group. Case 27 was deficient in almost all other measures of the dendritic tree. Cases 29, 38, 43 and 47 in the SD group had terminal dendrites (indeed, all dendrites) that were more extensive than those of a few cases in the adult and in the aged samples in the apical and/or basal dendritic trees.

Discussion

These data establish that in the adult human, one cell type in one brain region has a dendritic tree which is growing. Cells with shrunken dendritic trees as described by others (Scheibel et al., 1975, 1976; Mervis, 1978) were also seen by us in all of our cases. However, our data clearly indicate that growing dendritic trees predominate over regressing trees. This conclusion is supported by the elegant stereological electron microscopic study of Hinds and McNelly (1977) which showed growth of mitral cell dendrites in olfactory bulb of aging rats.

Ours is the first Golgi study to describe normal growth of dendrites in aging. The differences, between our data and the data obtained previously by others, are probably due to differences in methodology, although we cannot at this time rule out regional or species variations as possible factors. The advantages of a blind study in which quantitative methods are applied to randomly sampled neurons are obvious. In addition, our sections were thicker than the sections used in other aging studies. Examination of these thicker sections under a high power objective was made possible by a long working distance $100\times$ oil objective. Cut ends (6% of all terminal segments in our data), created by the sectioning of the tissue, were not used by us as a criterion for selection of trees to be

---

Figure 1. Number of intersections per cell of apical (A) and basal (B) dendrites with concentric spheres centered around the cell body and spaced 10 μm apart. Points represent averages taken across the 75 cells in each group. The three groups are similar at the two tails of the curves but in the region between the tails the adult group is intermediate between the aged and SD.

	p (sign test)	
	Apical	*Basal*
Adult vs Aged	<0.001	<0.001
Aged vs SD	<0.001	<0.001
Adult vs SD	<0.05	<0.05

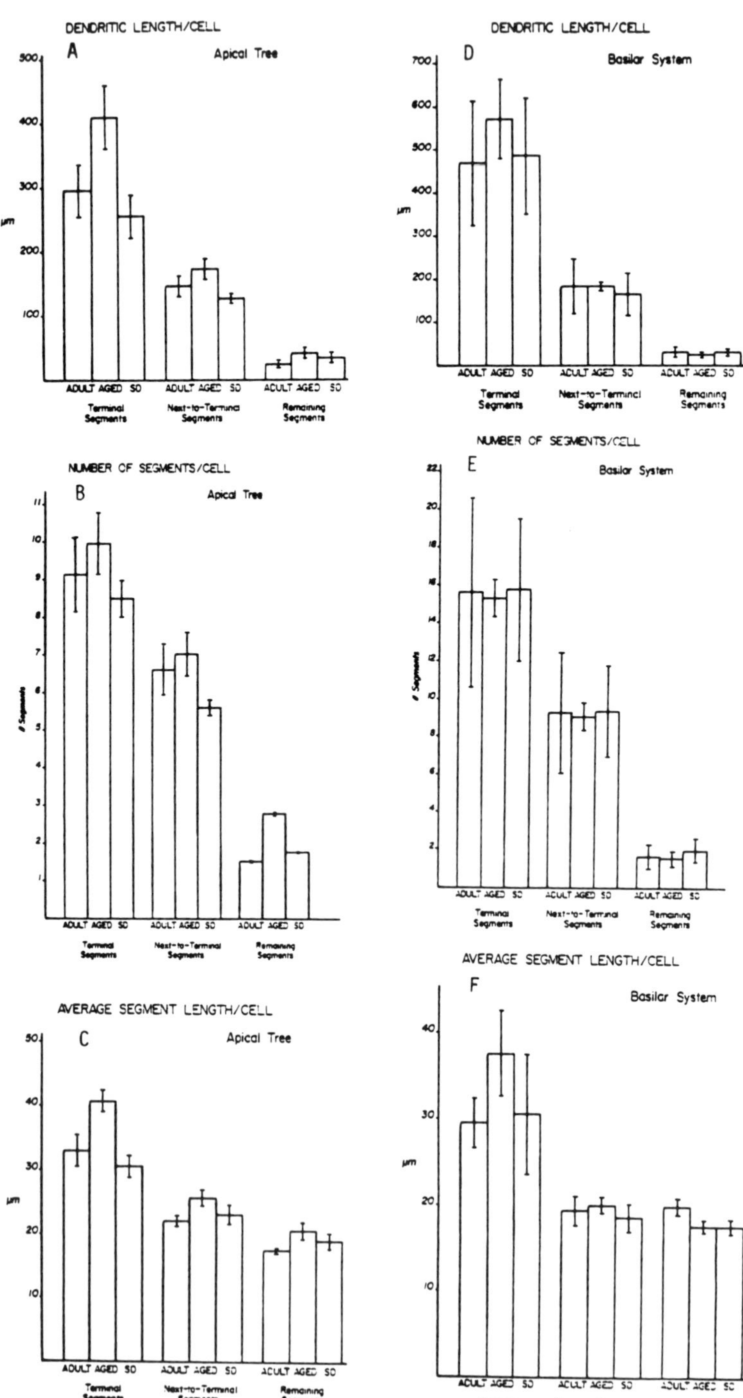
DENDRITIC LENGTH/CELL
A
Apical Tree
µm
ADULT AGED SD
Terminal Segments
Next-to-Terminal Segments
Remaining Segments
DENDRITIC LENGTH/CELL
D
Basilar System
NUMBER OF SEGMENTS/CELL
B
Apical Tree
Segments
NUMBER OF SEGMENTS/CELL
E
Basilar System
AVERAGE SEGMENT LENGTH/CELL
C
Apical Tree
AVERAGE SEGMENT LENGTH/CELL
F
Basilar System

quantified. It is apparent that rejecting cells on the basis of cut ends in thinner sections (125 μm) could bias a sample toward smaller, perhaps regressing, dendritic trees (Feldman, 1976; Vaughan, 1977). The possibility that our results were caused not by a growth of dendrites with age, but by a differential loss of neurons with smaller dendritic trees is unlikely because measurement of cell body sizes showed no difference among the three groups.

Our data can be taken to suggest that the growth of apical dendritic trees in aging is largely a process of lengthening and branching of terminal segments of the dendritic tree. The net effect of advancing age on the terminal segments of the basilar dendritic tree is only growth; there does not appear to be sufficient branching to show a net increase in numbers of terminal basal dendrites. Although the increase in average segment length of terminal dendrites is practically the same in both apical and basal dendrites (aged/adult is 124% and 125% respectively) the failure to branch seems to be the cause of the differentially lesser growth of the total basal tree in aging. This is also the reason that NTT basal segments do not differ among groups.

The presence of cells with regressed dendritic trees in conjunction with a net growth of dendritic trees in aging suggests a model in which there are two populations of neurons in the aging cortex. One is regressing and dying. The other is surviving and growing. In normal aging, it is the surviving and growing population which predominates. With the passage of time there must be a shift of neurons from the surviving, growing population to the regressing, dying population. The extent to which this may represent an adaptive process is not known. The age at which growth may cease to predominate in normal aging is also not currently known: our oldest case to date (92 years) was among those with the largest, most extensive dendritic trees.

The rate of growth with age suggested by our data is an underestimate of the rate of growth of the surviving, growing neurons because our average data include neurons from the regressing, dying population. These two groups are confounded in our analyses because all the distributions of dendritic parameters of individual cells failed to show any break point that would allow us to distinguish the two groups.

Figure 2. Apical and basal systems ordered in a centripetal direction.

A. Total length of segments per tree. **B.** Average number of segments per tree. **C.** Average length of segments per tree. **D–F.** Basilar system ordered in a centripetal direction. **D.** Total length of segments per tree. **E.** Average number of segments per tree. **F.** Average length of segments per tree. Points represent means ± SEM taken across the 75 cells in each of the three groups.

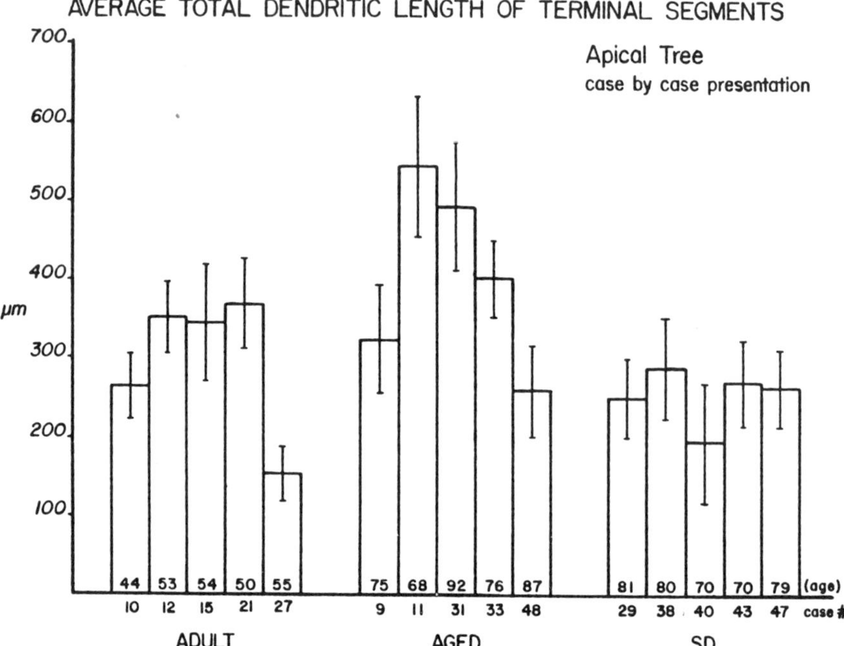

Figure 3. Total dendritic length per cell of the terminal segments of the apical system for each case. Means ± SEM.

Figure 4. Total dendritic length per cell of the terminal segments of the basilar system in each case. Means ± SEM.

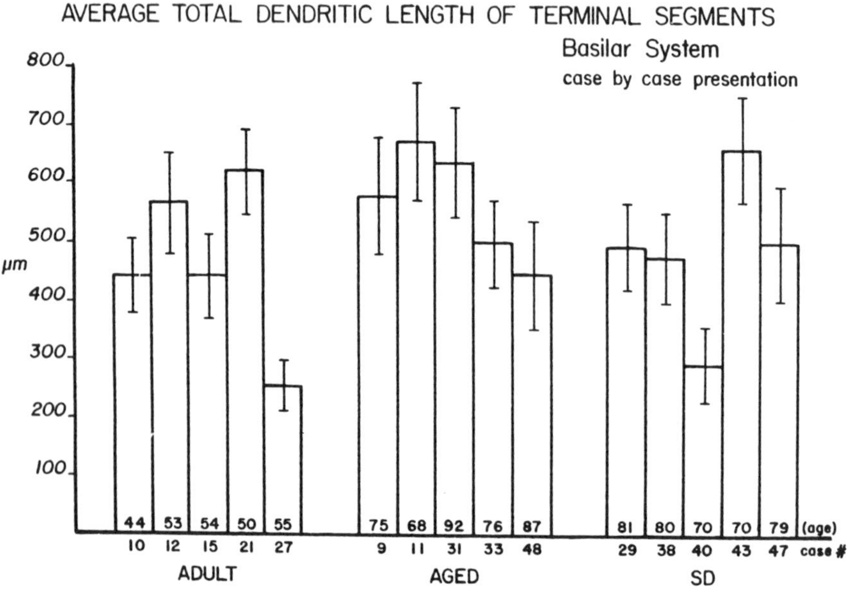

Although some cells could clearly be identified as having regressed dendritic trees, and others as having flourishing dendritic trees there was a middle ground, containing the majority of the cells, in which such easy distinctions were not possible. Consequently, we chose to err on the conservative side by including all cells in every analysis.

The data from individual cases serve to place the role of dendrite growth in some perspective. Although the SD group means are generally less than means of either the adult or aged groups, the finding that some frankly demented subjects have more extensive dendritic trees than some normally functioning, active adults or elderly cases suggests that, either the particular region of brain we studied is not related to ability to function, or that there are factors other than dendrites which are also important to functioning. The position of the cortex we studied in the entorhinal cortex → perforant path → dentate gyrus → hippocampus system favors the latter possibility. Other factors important to functioning include cell numbers, synapse numbers, integrity of transmitter systems, and neuronal metabolism; many of which are discussed in other chapters in this volume. Thus, although the statistics of group data indicate a significant relation between dendritic parameters and dementia, other aspects of our data lead us to believe that we must moderate the importance of this relationship. There was considerable overlap in dendrite data from demented and non-demented cases, and relatively small dendritic differences (rarely exceeding 15%) between the non-demented adult group and the SD group. In view of this, the enormous differences in behavior between our demented and non-demented cases cause us to question whether lengths and numbers of dendrites of individual neurons are a major factor in the dementia of Alzheimer's disease. Our current data on individual neurons can not reveal whether total dendritic extent in the neutrophil relates more closely to the dementia of Alzheimer's disease.

It is unlikely that these individual differences were a consequence of variability in PMT since, for example, case 27 and case 31 with comparable PMT (21.5 and 19.8 hours, respectively) had dendritic trees which were the smallest and among the most extensive, respectively, found in this study. Within the SD group the length of basilar terminal segments in cases 40 and 43 differ by almost 100% despite nearly identical PMT.

Duration of SD may be a factor in dendritic extent. Those cases with a shorter history of SD tended to have the more extensive dendritic trees (cases 43 and 47) while the case with the least extensive dendritic trees (case 40) had the longest history of SD.

Although our finding of growth of dendrites in normal human aging is clear, the factor(s) causing this growth are not known. Possibilities include: 1. the growth seen is a continuation of a life-long process of dendritic growth, 2. the growth is a compensatory phenomenon in response to loss of neighboring cells and/or afferent axons, and 3. the growth may be a response to the environmental stimulation provided by an active life. Certainly these possibilities are not mutually exclusive.

References

Bodian D: A new method for staining nerve fibers and nerve endings in mounted paraffin sections. *Anat Rec* 65:89–97, 1936.

Brody H: Organization of the cerebral cortex. III. A study of aging in the human cerebral cortex. *J Comp Neurol* 102:511–556, 1955.

Brody H: Structural changes in the aging nervous system. *Interdiscipl Topics Geront* 7:9–21, 1970.

Buell SJ, Coleman PD: Dendritic growth in aged human brain and failure of growth in senile dementia. *Science* 206:854–856, 1979.

Coleman PD, Garvey CF, Young JH, Simon W: Semi-automatic tracking of neuronal processes. In Lindsay RD (ed.) *Computer Analysis of Neuronal Structures*. New York, Plenum Press, 1977, pp. 91–110.

Feldman M: Aging changes in the morphology of cortical dendrites. In *Aging,* Vol. 3. New York, Raven Press, 1976, pp. 211–227.

Hinds JW, McNelly NA: Aging of the rat olfactory bulb: growth and atrophy of constituent layers and changes in size and number of mitral cells. *J Comp Neurol* 171:345–368, 1977.

Lafora GR: Neuronal dendritic neoformations and neuroglial alterations in the senile dog. *Trab Lab Invest Biol de la Univ Madrid* 12:39–53, 1914. Translated by del Cerro M, Amaral DG, Kelly P, *Behav Biol* 24:123–140, 1978.

McLardy T: Memory function in hippocampal gyri, but not in hippocampus. *Internat J Neurosci* 1:113–118, 1970.

Mervis R: Structural alterations in neurons of aged canine neocortex: a Golgi study. *Exp Neurol* 62:417–432, 1978.

Scheff SW, Bernardo LS, Cotman CW: Decrease in adrenergic axon sprouting in the senescent rat. *Science* 202:775–778, 1978.

Scheibel ME, Lindsay RD, Tomiyasu U, Scheibel AB: Progressive dendritic changes in aging human cortex. *Exp Neurol* 47:392–403, 1975.

Scheibel ME, Lindsay RD, Tomiyasu U, Scheibel AB: Progressive dendritic changes in the aging human limbic system. *Exp Neurol* 53:420–430, 1976.

Scheibel AB, Tomiyasu U: Dendritic sprouting in Alzheimer's presenile dementia. *Exp Neurol* 60:1–8, 1978.

Shipley MT: Presubiculum afferents to the entorhinal area and the Papez circuit. *Brain Research* 67:162–168, 1974.

Van der Loos H: Une combination de deux vieilles methodes histologiques pour le system nerveux central. *Mschr Psychiat Neurol* 132:330–334, 1956.

Vaughan DW: Age-related deterioration of pyramidal cell basal dendrites in rat auditory cortex. *J Comp Neurol* 171:501–516, 1977.

Stein, ed. The Psychobiology of Aging: Problems and Perspectives

Effect of Age on Morphological and Biochemical Parameters of the Human Brain

W. Meier-Ruge, O. Hunziker, P. Iwangoff, K. Reichlmeier and U. Schultz

Institute of Basic Medical Research, Lichtstrasse 35, CH-4002 Basel, Switzerland.

Introduction

Currently limited knowledge of normal brain aging interested us in studying the morphological and neurochemical characteristics of the aging process. The fundamentals for pharmacological intervention in the aging brain require knowledge of age-dependent functional alteration in CNS-anatomy and neurochemistry. In a morphometric investigation the capillary network in the cerebral cortex of 65–74-year-old individuals showed an increase of capillary diameter, volume and total length per unit cortex volume. These findings tend to indicate that decreased cerebral blood flow in the elderly is possibly the result of changed morphometric parameters of the capillary network. The morphometrically determined capillary parameters in patients older than 75 years were similar to those 19–64 years old. These findings stimulate the speculation of the existence of two age groups with a different genetically programmed life expectance.

Neurochemical investigations of glycolytic enzymes of the aging brain demonstrate a change in soluble hexokinase activity which decreases with age. The alteration in these key enzymes is considered to limit turnover capacity of the glycolytic pathway and ATP-formation.

In brain tissue of patients with senile dementia of the Alzheimer type far more enzymes of the glycolytic pathway are significantly decreased, demonstrating that this disease is possibly more a primary degenerative disease than a form of accelerated aging. Carbonic anhydrase decreases significantly in the normal aging brain. Further, an age-induced decrease in cAMP-stimulated protein kinase was observed.

Age-dependent decrease of glycolytic turnover is discussed in connection with a decline of cognitive function. This discussion is based on the facts that the synthetic processes of cholinergic transmitter for 90% of the nerve cells in the brain of fundamental importance, are highly dependent on glycolytic energy transformation. The serious inhibition of glycolytic turnover capacity in senile dementia supports this conception.

Aging is an insidious and progressive process, characterized by the organism becoming susceptible to an increasing number of diseases. However, with reference to the aging brain, it is surprising how low the incidence of age-related brain disease is. For example, Slater and Roth (1977) estimated the following prevalence rates of mental disorders in the elderly (aged 65 years or over, living at home or permanently in a hospital):

Unspecific severe brain syndromes	1.05%
Manic-depressive disorders and paraphrenia	2.44%
Senile dementia (incl. arteriosclerotic dementia)	4.56%
Psychosis, all forms mentioned above	8.05%
Character disorders, including paranoid states	3.61%
Mild forms of organic brain syndrome	5.71%
Neurosis and allied disorders	8.93%
All disorders	26.30%

This table shows that psychiatrically diagnosed diseases in aging are present in 26.3% of the population over 65 years. Consequently a group of 73.7% remains, in which we are likely to find "minor symptoms of senility." Many of these mental aging diseases, in particular senile dementia, senile psychosis and manic depressive disorders seem to be linked to hereditary factors. Broe et al. (1976) calculated the following rate of neurological disorders in a normal population of the elderly (aged 65 years or more) in Glasgow (Scotland):

Essential tremor (M. Huntington)	1.7%
Parkinson's disease	1.6%
Stroke	7.3%
Senile dementia	5.8%
Other diagnosis	4.0%
All disorders	20.4%

This table again shows that a large proportion of the complaints afflicting the elderly are due to minor symptoms of aging (about 80% which have, however, a number of serious consequences in the daily life of the aging individual: as aging reduces the functional redundancy of the different organs, in particular the brain, the kidney, skeletal muscle etc., it becomes more and more difficult for the different organs to adapt adequately to adverse environmental stimuli. In other words, aging is characterized by an increasing danger of an exhaustion of energy-dependent metabolic regulation processes. In the past years a number of interesting observations have made it obvious that the normal aging process of the brain is compatible with a diminished reserve capacity of the functional steady state of the brain (Ordy, 1972; McGeer and McGeer, 1976; Stein and Firl, 1976; Samorajski, 1976; McNamara et al., 1978; Sylvia and Rosenthal, 1978). To examine this concept and to obtain more insight into the aging process, our group has performed a series of morphological and neurochemical investigations of the aging human brain.

The Morphology of the Aging Brain

Today it is a well accepted fact that in the course of aging, a 10 to 15% loss in brain weight (Roessle and Roulet, 1932; Hempel, 1968; Peress et al., 1973; Treff, 1974) cannot be correlated with declining mental activity. Also, the suggestion that a progressive nerve cell loss is linked to a declining cognitive function, accepted for many years as a reasonable theory according to Brody (1955), is no longer plausible. With introduction of new stereological techniques, recent investigations demonstrated either no changes in cell number of specific brain areas, or only a moderate overall loss of neuronal cells in the range of 15–25%. (Shefer, 1973; Brody, 1976; Tomlinson and Henderson, 1976).

Our morphometric investigation of the human inferior olivary nucleus showed that the number of neurons decreases significantly between the ages of 20 and 80 years in a linear regression reaching a decline of nerve cells of −19.7% at the age of 80 years (Sandoz and Meier-Ruge, 1977; Meier-Ruge et al., 1978). In addition to nerve cell loss, a 10 to 15% decrease of cerebral blood flow was considered to be of importance for the decline in mental capacity of the elderly. To determine the significance of the age-dependent reduction of cerebral blood flow, we studied the stereological characteristics of the capillary network in the aging human brain cortex. Until recently, no data was available concerning the significance of stereological changes of the capillary network on cerebral microcirculation.

The second question which particularly interested us was the alteration of the shape of the nerve cells during aging: all investigations that report loss of dendrites in the process of aging (Bondareff and Geinisman, 1976; Scheibel and Scheibel, 1977) are not always in agreement concerning the question of the degree of change seen in the elderly. This question is hard to answer because of the methodological problems of the Golgi-stain which selectively affects only a very limited number of nerve cells (~ at a 1% level). Therefore we performed a systematic analysis of changes in the shape of nerve cells and attempted to correlate these stereologic changes with age-dependent loss of dendrites. Before providing the details of these investigations, a short paragraph on our stereological methods may be helpful.

Morphometric Analysis of Capillaries

Thirty-eight human brains from post-mortem autopsies were investigated (Figure 1). All brains were free of metabolic, neurologic and psychiatric diseases. The post-mortem time up to withdrawing and deepfreezing the tissue blocks varied between 4 and 24 hours.

In all cortical regions, the capillaries were selectively demonstrated in 14-μm thick, untreated sections of fresh tissue with an alkaline phosphatase reaction (Meier-Ruge et al., 1978). The selectivity of capillary staining was studied by three-dimensional reconstruction of the capillary network (Wiederhold et al., 1976). The effect of post-mortem delay on morphometric parameters of the brain cortex capillaries was investigated experimentally by Hunziker and Schweizer, (1977). The capillaries were measured with an optical-electronic image-analysis system "Leitz-Classimat" (Hunziker et al., 1974). The optical input system of the Classimat is a microscope combined with a black-and-white television camera and a data processing unit. The stereological parameters measured were capillary diameter (D_i; μm), capillary distances $\triangle_{AB}$ (μm) and specific capillary surface-to-volume ratio ($S_i/V_i \mu m^{-1}$).

Values of different stereological parameters per capillary fragment were used to calculate size classes of diameter and virtual length (L_i = individual length per capillary fragment) with reference to their frequency distribution (Figure 1.) The data of volume and total length originated from values per measuring field. Of each cortex region, containing a series of 20 sections, nine sections were randomly selected and measured in random sequence. The data determined with the Leitz-Classimat were evaluated statistically by computer to yield the overall average values of morpbometric parameters. Student's t tests were used to determine statistical significance. An analysis of variance preceded each t test.

Morphometric Analysis of Neurons

Quantitative investigations of neuronal cells in the cortex involve numerous problems due to extension of the cortex, as well as the variety of shapes (Gihr, 1963) and sizes (Haug, 1967) of the nerve cells. The Leitz Texture Analyser (TAS) as an instrument of optic electronic image-analysis (Serra and Müller, 1973) considerably facilitates quantitative, histological studies on the nervous system.

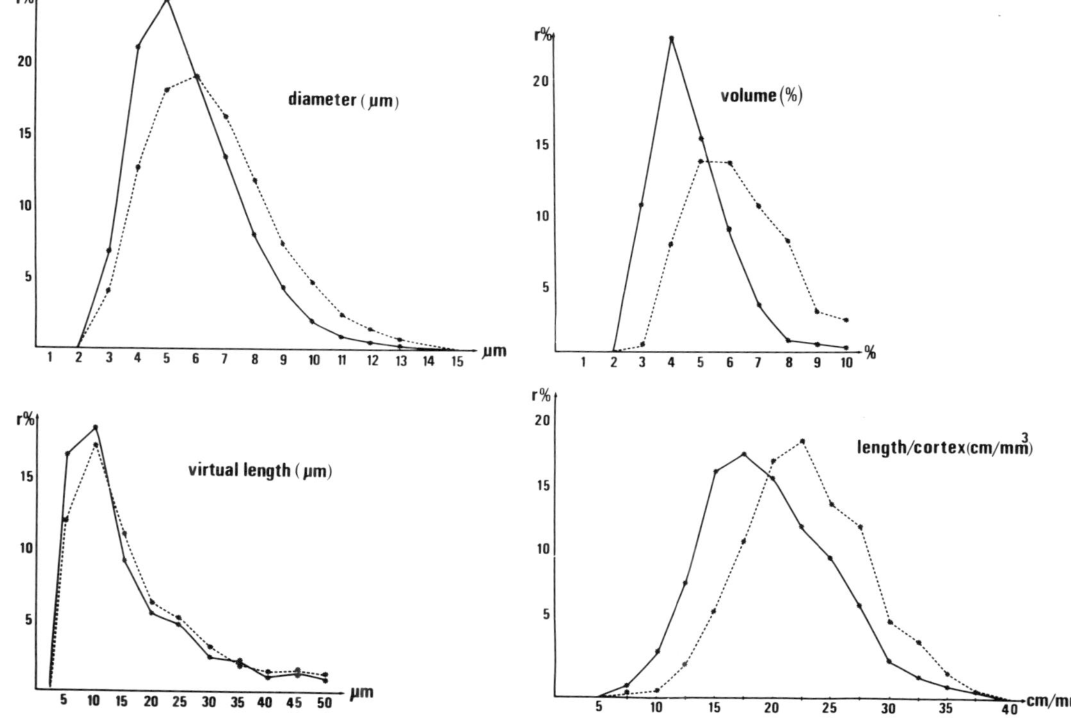

Figure 1. Relative frequency distribution (r ¾ brain cortex capillaries in man. Young cases (19–54 years; n = 6); . . . . old cases (65–74 years; n = 6). There is an increase in capillary diameter, capillary volume and length per unit brain cortex volume.

SOURCE: *Hunziker et al., 1977.*

In stereotaxically defined areas from the precentral gyrus of the human brain, 10 serial frozen sections of 14 μm thickness were randomly selected. In each section, 3 measuring directions were localized (the directions were identical for all sections). For each direction, the scanning stage of the TAS was preprogrammed to start from the pial surface and to reach the white matter by steps of 50 μm (magnif. factor of the objective: 40×). Using an electronically set measuring field (mask) of the TAS, each neuron of which the nucleolus was visible in the section (Haug, 1972) was measured.

The theoretical background involved in the TAS is mathematical morphology and the hit or miss transformation (Matheron, 1975). For our studies we used the concept of isotropic openings (Matheron, 1975; Hunziker et al., 1976). In this way, changes of nerve cell shape (area and perimeter) can be determined exactly: the total area of a neuron is measured by the number of scanning points within the nerve cell. For the perimeter or shape of a neuron, the number of interception points between the structure and the TV-lines are determined by the use of a hexagon opening procedure. In the TAS the increasing size and form of a hexagon which is enlarged step by step, is electronically compared with the neuron investigated. Most important for statistical treatment of the hexagon opening values of a nerve cell is the fact that a shape is characterized by a function and not by a finite number of parameters. As the received results are independent from the size classes selected, the data were evaluated by the correspondence analysis theory of Benzecri (Benzecri, 1973; Lebart and Fénelon, 1974).

Changes of the Capillary Network in Old Age

Our investigations revealed increased capillary diameter, volume and total length per unit cortex volume (Hunziker et al., 1978), in subjects between 65 and 74 years. In the same study, a decreased distance between capillaries in the cortex was observed. These results argue against the widespread assumption of a decreased blood supply in the brain during old age. In fact, the ratio of capillary vessels to brain tissue shifts in favor of the blood-supplying capillary network, characterized by a higher capillary volume fraction (Figure 1). Therefore, the decrease of microcirculation in the aging brain is more a symptom of adaptation to changed stereologic parameters than a result of a disturbed blood supply.

A corresponding change in stereological parameters was observed in the six other cortical areas of the brain. In addition, there was no correlation of the capillary parameters with the heart weights of the particular subjects (Hunziker et al., 1979). Also no correlation between hypertension and the capillary values, within the same age-group of

65–74 years, was established. The fact that the capillary parameters, such as diameter, volume-fraction, specific surface area, mean intercapillary distances and total length per unit cortex volume in patients older than 75 years were similar to those in young individuals, could support the assumption that genetic differences are the reason for the different values of the capillary parameters between the 65–74 years old group and the very old one being 86–94 years of age (Table 1).

The changed stereological parameters could reflect the result of accelerated aging of the vascular wall, representing an additional life limiting factor. The elucidation of this interesting finding could be the subject of further quantitative-morphological and biochemical studies.

Nerve Cell Changes in the Aging Brain

Our measurements of the nerve cell areas and perimeters in the human brain cortex demonstrated that neuronal perikaryon size and shape do not change significantly up to an age of about 75 years (Schulz et al., 1980) and is consistent with previous reports (Treff, 1974; Hall et al., 1975). It is remarkable that age-dependent changes of perikaryal size and shape only become obvious at an age of 85–94 years (Figure 2). The studies of our group show that the mean perikaryal values per measured brain cortex layer decrease in perimeter and area. Stereological data, obtained by the Leitz Texture Analyzer System, were calculated according to a correspondence analysis and finally evaluated in a multi-variate statistical procedure (Hunziker et al., 1976; Schulz et al., 1978). The measured perikaryal size differences between young and old aged subjects were attributed to senile atrophy. The most pronounced decrease of the perikaryal area was observed in the external pyramidal layer (Figure 2; see number 2, 3 and 4 of rhombuses and stars), which in normal life has the highest glucose turnover in the brain cortex (Kennedy et al., 1975; Sokoloff, 1977). This study shows that loss of dentritic spines and dendrites in the process of brain aging (Bondareff and Geinisman, 1976; Feldman, 1976; Scheibel and Scheibel, 1977) reaches a mean level of atrophy expressed in an altered nerve cell shape very late in life. It is interesting to note that these alterations of the nerve cells are correlated with changes of the surface/volume ratio of the capillary network in the brain cortex.

None of the findings mentioned in this chapter explain the many abnormal symptoms such as disturbed memory, changed sleeping behavior, decreased alertness and disturbed cognitive function seen in the elderly. This was the reason why we also became interested in the neurochemistry of the aging brain, hoping to get a better understanding of the aging process and to receive a better insight into the metabolic performance of the aging brain.

Table 1.

AGE GROUPS \ STEREOLOGICAL PARAMETERS		$\bar{V}_{Vi}$ %	$\bar{S}_i/\bar{V}_i$ μM^{-1}	$\bar{\Delta}_{AB}$ μM	$\bar{L}_{Vi}$ CM/MM^3	$\bar{D}_i$ μM
I 19-44 YEARS N = 6		2.23 ±0.46	0.494 ±0.024	55.85 ± 4.25	21.58 ± 4.35	6.35 ± 0.45
II 45-54 YEARS N = 4		2.41 ±0.30	0.485 ±0.011	60.52 ± 2.42	22.29 ± 2.70	6.41 ± 0.22
III 55-64 YEARS N = 5		2.61 ±0.42	0.489 ±0.023	57.45 ± 1.81	24.13 ± 4.25	6.10 ± 0.44
IV 65-74 YEARS	IV_N N = 6	3.09 ±0.59	0.438 ±0.016	57.38 ± 2.73	26.06 ± 3.06	7.16 ± 0.33
	IV_H N = 4	3.06 ±0.53	0.462 ±0.006	54.90 ± 2.64	25.35 ± 3.60	6.96 ± 0.15
V 75-84 YEARS N = 6		2.24 ±0.58	0.507 ±0.026	59.60 ± 5.73	18.85 ± 5.14	5.94 ± 0.35
VI 85-94 YEARS N = 7		2.26 ±0.46	0.487 ±0.012	56.20 ± 3.32	21.10 ± 3.82	6.55 ± 0.24
STUDENT t-TEST $P \leq 0.05$ = LIMIT OF SIGNIFICANCE.						
STUDENT t-TEST limit of significance: $P \leq 0.05^*$ $P \leq 0.005^{**}$		$I < IV_N^*$ $II < IV_N^*$ $V < IV_N^*$ $VI < IV_N^*$	$I > IV_N^{**}$ $II > IV_N^{**}$ $III > IV_N^{**}$ $V > IV_N^{**}$ $VI > IV_N^{**}$ $IV_H > IV_N^*$ $V > VI^*$	$I < II^*$ $II > III^*$ $II > IV_N^*$ $II > VI^*$	$I < IV_N^*$ $II < IV_N^*$ $V < IV_N^*$ $VI < IV_N^*$ $III > V^*$	$I < IV_N^{**}$ $II < IV_N^{**}$ $III < IV_N^{**}$ $V < IV_N^{**}$ $VI < IV_N^{**}$ $I > V^*$ $II > V^*$ $III < VI^*$ $V < VI^{**}$

The stereological parameters of capillaries in the precentral gyrus of the human cerebral cortex. Mean values of six age-groups (± S.D.). It is obvious that group IV (65-74 years) has significantly higher capillary diameters (D_i), an increased capillary length (L_{Vi}) and a higher volume fraction (V_{Vi} %).

Abbreviations: V_{Vi} = volume fraction; S_i/V_i = specific surface area; Δ_{AB} = minimal intercapillary distances; L_{Vi} = total capillary length per unit cortex volume; D_i = diameter; i = index of capillaries; (Hunziker et al., 1979).

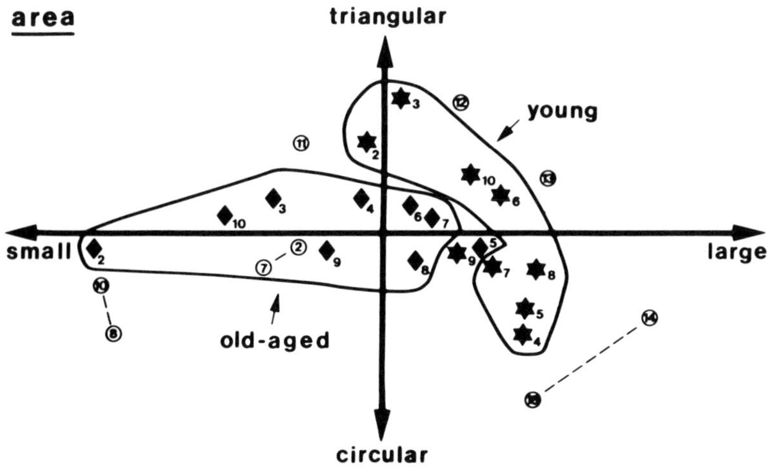

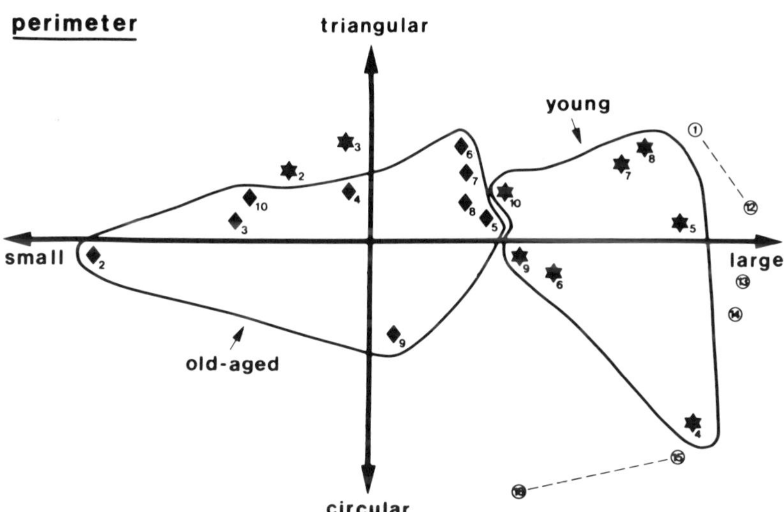

Figure 2. Age-induced change of nerve cell area and perimeter towards smaller values. Neurons with larger perimeters of the young group (stars) are clearly separated from neurons with smaller perimeters of the very old group (rhombuses). The figure demonstrates the result of a multivariate analysis of mean neuronal cell values per measured cortex layer (numbered rhombuses and stars refer to the layer). The results are obtained from the precentral gyrus of the human brain. Stars = young group of 19–44 years, rhombuses = aged group of 85–94 years.

Neurochemistry of the Aging Human Brain

Some investigations have demonstrated that transmitter enzymes such as DOPA-decarboxylase, glutamic acid decarboxylase and tyrosine hydroxylase decrease in the aging brain (McGeer and McGeer, 1976, McGeer et al., 1977). These observations support our working hypothesis that the disturbance of metabolic parameters is more relevant to the aging process than morphological changes, although the etiology of these changes is at present unknown. Considering that the brain uses glucose as its main, or even only source of energy, it can be supposed that changes in glycolytic turnover have serious consequences in the energy requiring synthetic process, particularly neurotransmitter synthesis and transport (Siesjö and Plum, 1973; Kennedy et al., 1975; Sokoloff, 1977; Siesjö and Rehncrona, 1979).

One of our main interests, therefore, was to study the influence of aging on glycolytic enzymes of the human brain. In this connection, carbonic anhydrase was also of importance to us, because of the CO_2 resulting from glucose decomposition, has to be eliminated from brain tissue. In addition, the cAMP-protein kinase system was included as an indicator of cell response to neurohormonal stimuli.

The Glycolytic Energy Supply of the Aging Brain

Thirteen different glycolytic enzymes were studied in the frontal cortex and putamen of 50 subjects between 19 and 92 years of age. All the cases investigated were free of neurologic and psychiatric diseases. The effect of post-mortem delay and the influence of the duration of the patient's agony on the activity of these enzymes was examined extensively by Iwangoff et al. (1978; 1979a).

Most of the glycolytic enzymes remained unaltered or changed only slightly with age (Table 2). Fructose-6-phosphate kinase (F6PK), hexokinase (HK) and glucose-6-phosphate dehydrogenase (G6PDH) are significantly changed (Meier-Ruge et al., 1978; Iwangoff et al., 1979a). The activity of glucose-6-phosphate dehydrogenase and soluble hexokinase increases with age. The increase of soluble hexokinase activity is most likely the result of an increased release from mitochondrial membranes.

Fructose-6-phosphate kinase decreases significantly with age. In a refined study which contained only cases with sudden death (Iwangoff et al., 1979a) a more significant negative correlation of fructose-6-phosphate kinase with age was observed (Figure 3). These findings of age-induced changes of the rate-limiting enzymes of the glycolytic pathway—hexokinase and fructose-6-phosphate kinase—may decrease glucose turnover capacity.

In contrast to the limitation of a glycolytic ATP-formation with increasing age, no changes appear to occur in ATPase activity (Figure 4). The unlimited capacity to break down ATP led us to suggest that the provision

Table 2. Glycolytic Enzymes in Human Brain Cortex

Enzyme[a]	Age in years		
	I:19-50	II:51-70	III:71-92
HK	1.24 ±0.10[b]	0.88 ±0.10	1.81 ±0.20
PGI	78.8 ±5.4	77.2 ±3.6	71.5 ±6.7
F6PK	2.51 ±0.70	2.94 ±0.57	1.09 ±0.39
ALD	4.70 ±0.32	4.55 ±0.22	3.78 ±0.34
TIM	1351.6 ±65.1	1191.9 ±65.5	1260.7 ±84.4
GAPDH	89.1 ±3.9	86.1 ±3.7	96.6 ±3.5
PGK	76.6 ±3.2	74.8 ±3.2	77.1 ±3.1
PGM	61.9 ±5.9	57.6 ±3.7	45.9 ±5.7
EN	41.0 ±1.7	37.8 ±2.8	39.2 ±1.4
PK	71.9 ±4.2	76.1 ±4.8	79.6 ±2.5
LDH	78.8 ±2.6	74.3 ±2.4	79.2 ±2.6
G6PDH	0.78 ±0.06	0.77 ±0.05	0.75 ±0.04
GDH	1.29 ±0.08	1.36 ±0.08	1.13 ±0.05

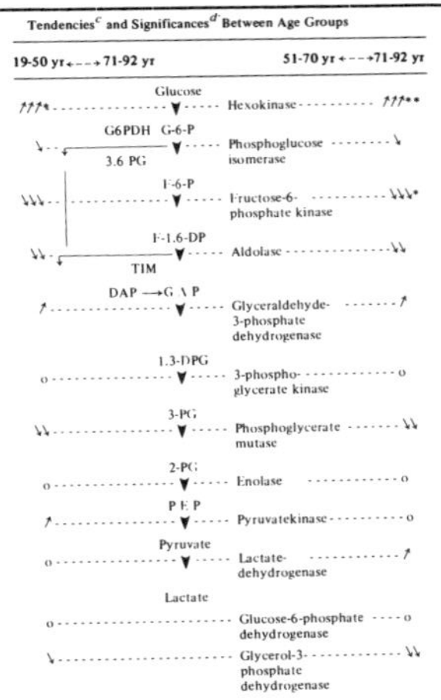

Tendencies[c] and Significances[d] Between Age Groups

19-50 yr ←→ 71-92 yr	Metabolite	Enzyme	51-70 yr ←→ 71-92 yr
↗↗↗*	Glucose	Hexokinase	↗↗↗**
↘	G6PDH G-6-P 3.6 PG	Phosphoglucose isomerase	↘
↘↘↘	F-6-P	Fructose-6-phosphate kinase	↘↘↘*
↘↘	F-1.6-DP TIM	Aldolase	↘↘
↗	DAP → GAP	Glyceraldehyde-3-phosphate dehydrogenase	↗
0	1.3-DPG	3-phosphoglycerate kinase	0
↘↘	3-PG	Phosphoglycerate mutase	↘↘
0	2-PG	Enolase	0
↗	PEP	Pyruvatekinase	0
0	Pyruvate	Lactate-dehydrogenase	↗
	Lactate		
0		Glucose-6-phosphate dehydrogenase	0
↘		Glycerol-3-phosphate dehydrogenase	↘↘

Age-dependent changes in glycolytic enzymes of the human brain cortex (n = 32) in different age groups.

[a] Abbreviations: HK = hexokinase; PGI = phosphoglucose isomerase; F6PK = fructose-6-phosphate kinase; ALD = aldolase; TIM = triosephosphate isomerase; GAPDH = glyceraldehyde-3-phosphate dehydrogenase; PGK = 3-phosphoglycerate kinase; PGM = phosphoglycerate mutase; EN = enolase; PK = pyruvate kinase; LDH = lactate dehydrogenase; G6PDH = glucose-6-phosphate dehydrogenase; GDH = glycerol-3-phosphate dehydrogenase.

[b] Mean values are expressed as μmoles/min x g (wet tissue) turnover of substrate ± SEM.

[c] Tendencies:
- 0- 5% 0
- 5-15% ↗ ↘
- 15-30% ↗↗ ↘↘
- >30% ↗↗↗ ↘↘↘

[d] Significance:
- * 2P < 0.05
- ** 2P < 0.01

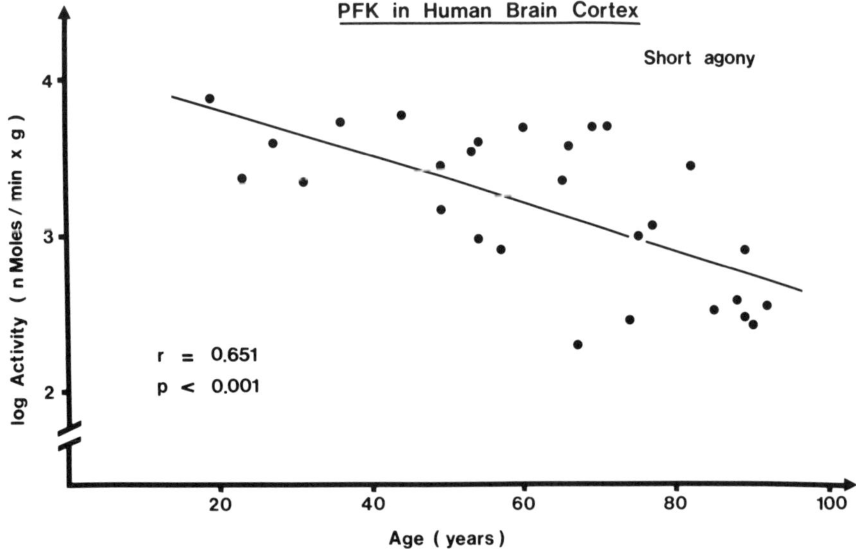

Figure 3. Age-induced decrease of phosphfructokinase (PFK = fructose-6-phosphate kinase) activity in human brain cortex (n = 28) from cases with sudden death.

SOURCE: *Iwangoff et al., 1979a.*

of energy under conditions of increased energy demand may constitute a critical situation for the aging brain.

McNamara et al. (1978) observed, that after electroconvulsive shock in old rat brains there is a reduced recovery of ATP and creatine phosphate. Also Sylvia and Rosenthal (1978) described impaired cytochrome response in aged rat brains after stress.

The Regulation of the pO_2/pCO_2 Ratio in Old Age

Carbonic anhydrase was of interest to us, because the CO_2 is the end product of glucose decomposition and directly linked to its degrading enzyme. We observed that carbonic anhydrase activity decreases between an age of 20 and 92 years in a range of 30% (Figure 5); Reichlmeier et al., 1977; Meier-Ruge et al., 1978).

This finding may be relevant to a decreased CO_2 production due to a decreased glycolytic turnover, because carbonic anhydrase activity is regulated by the actual CO_2 production. The effect of carbonic anhydrase on the acid-base equilibrium (Severinghaus et al., 1969; Annau, 1977) affects tissue pH and ionic transport processes. Its decline may therefore be of influence in ionic transport processes and thus in polarization processes at nerve cell membranes (Schindler et al., 1971, 1972; Garg and Mathur, 1975; Bourke et al., 1976; Kimelberg et al., 1978).

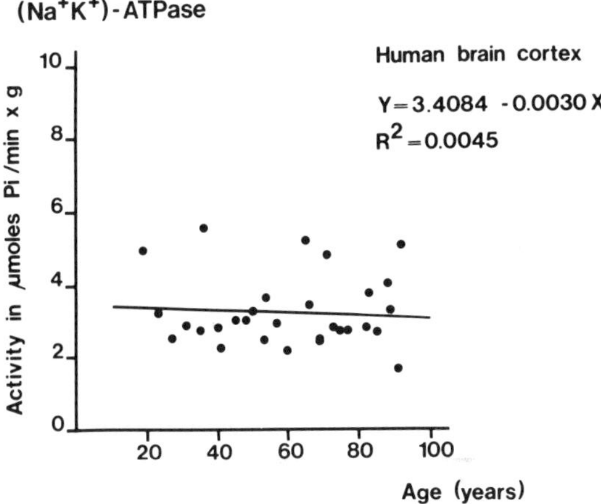

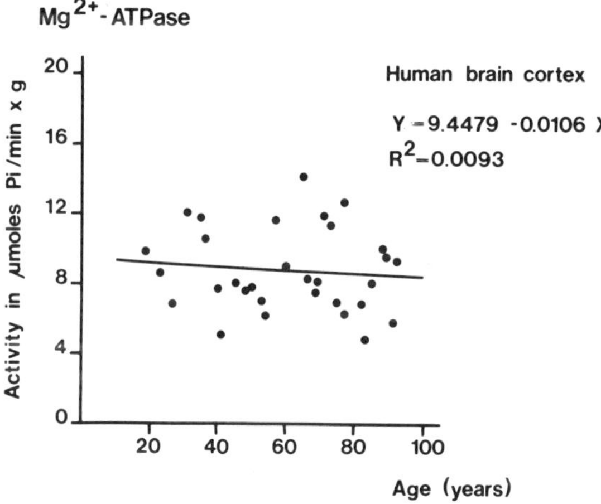

Figure 4. Unchanged ATPase activity in human brain cortex with reference to chronologic age (n = 30).

Age-Dependent Decrease of cAMP-Stimulation of Protein Kinase in Human Brain

Studies on cAMP-protein kinase were performed because this enzyme is a dynamic indicator of nerve cell response to transmitter or neurohormonal activity. In the human brain, protein kinase shows a progressive decline of its cAMP-dependent activity with increasing age (Reichlmeier et al., 1977, 1978a,b). Our more recent results show that with increasing age, the greatest loss in total protein kinase activity is found in the human frontal brain cortex and thalamus, followed by hippocampus,

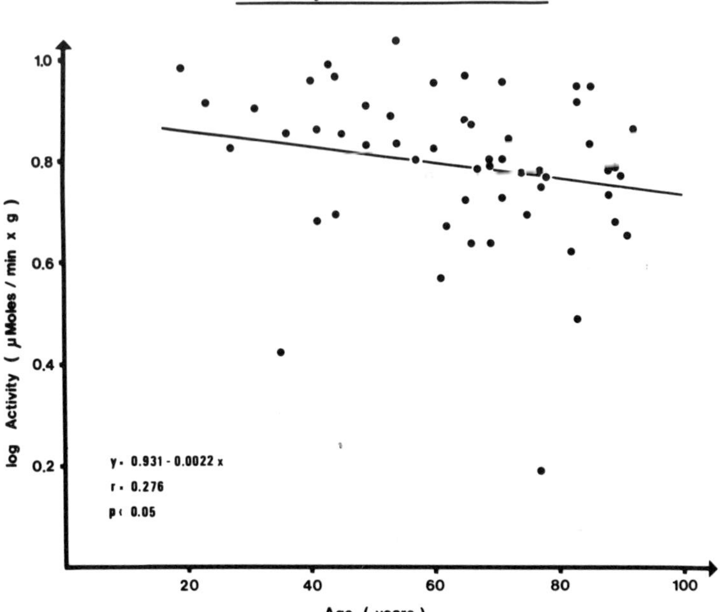

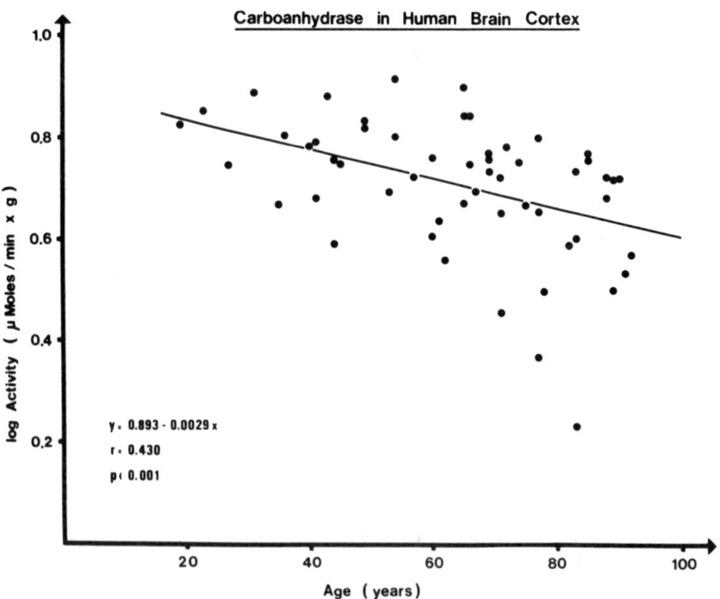

Figure 5. Influence of age on the decline in carbonic anhydrase in human brain cortex and putamen (n = 55).

SOURCE: *Iwangoff et al., 1979a.*

amygdala and globus pallidus (Figure 6). In subcellular brain cortex fractions, the age-dependent decrease of protein kinase activity was found to be associated with the membrane-bound enzyme (Reichlmeier et al., 1978b).

Protein kinase intracellularly mediates information carried by second messengers (Nimmo and Cohen, 1977). The kinase catalyze the transfer of phosphate groups from ATP to different proteins in the cell, such as membrane proteins (Routtenberg and Ehrlich, 1975; Greengard, 1976,-1978; Ueda and Greengard, 1977), nuclear proteins (Johnson, 1977) or enzymes which are altered in their activity state by phosphorylation (Morgenroth et al., 1975; Goldstein et al., 1976). The real physiological or functional relevance of the changed protein kinase is difficult to assess at the moment. Further studies have to elucidate the significance of age-related protein kinase activity changes and their consequences for neuronal function.

Figure 6. Cyclic cAMP-dependent protein kinase activity in the brain cortex of four age groups (Group I: mean age = 35.9 yr; n = 11; Group II: mean age = 60.3 yr; n = 12; Group III: mean age = 73.3 yr; n = 11; Group IV: mean age = 86.7 yr; n = 10).

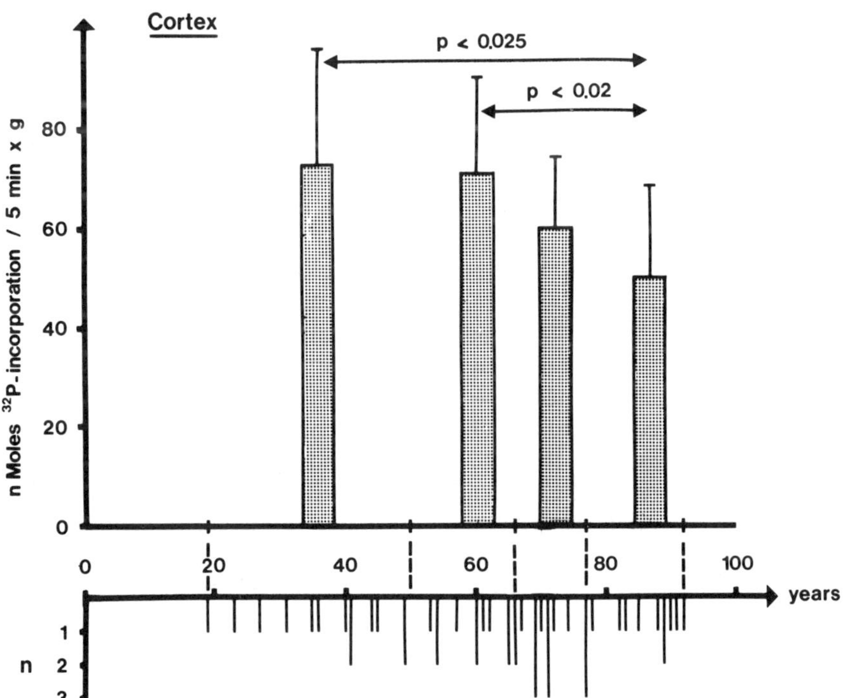

Neurochemical Changes in Dementia of the Alzheimer Type

In a collaborative study with David M. Bowen and Alan N. Davison we investigated cases with senile dementia of the Alzheimer type and compared the results with normal aging brains (Bowen et al., 1979; Iwangoff et al., 1979b).

We observed an aggravation of the changes found in normal aging brain described earlier in this paper. In addition, other glycolytic enzymes, which are not subject to age-dependent changes, are significantly decreased in senile dementia; in particular, phosphoglucose isomerase, aldolase, triosephosphate isomerase and lactate dehydrogenase (Figure 7).

The reinforced decrease in fructose-6-phosphate kinase is less characteristic in senile dementia than the changes are in the other glycolytic enzymes, because fructose-6-phosphate kinase is known to be considerably decreased by bronchopneumonia (Bird et al., 1977), which is usually the ultimate cause of death in dementia.

Discussion and Conclusions

Currently, we are neither able to correlate morphometrically described age-dependent changes with a decline of cognitive function, nor a decrease of cerebral blood flow with functional consequences in the aging brain.

If one considers that glucose is the main energy source of the brain (Krebs and Kornberg, 1957; Lehninger, 1965; Siesjö and Plum, 1973), it has to be expected that a serious decrease in the glycolytic turnover of the brain (Bowen et al., 1979; Iwangoff et al., 1979b) may cause dramatic functional defects in the CNS (Gibson and Blass, 1976), especially in the extremely energy-dependent cholinergic system (Siesjö and Rehncrona, 1979; Blass, 1979).

The conception of an age-dependent glycolytic energy deprivation of the brain is supported by the findings in senile dementia. In the first place, there is a serious disturbance of glycolytic energy metabolism in senile dementia accompanied by a decline of choline acetyl transferase activity and a moderate decrease in acetylcholine esterase activity. These decreases produce a deficit in cholinergic transmitter synthesis which is characteristic of senile dementia (Davies and Maloney, 1976; Perry et al., 1978; Haubrich and Chippendale, 1977; Bowen and Davison, 1978). The decrease in choline acetyl transferase activity is accompanied by an increase of senile plaques (Perry et al., 1978). The fact that about 90% of the nerve cells of the brain are cholinergic and that the function of this cholinergic system is extremely energy dependent (Siesjö and Rehncrona, 1979; Blass, 1979) supports the hypothesis that there may be a direct link between cognitive function and glycolytic energy transformation.

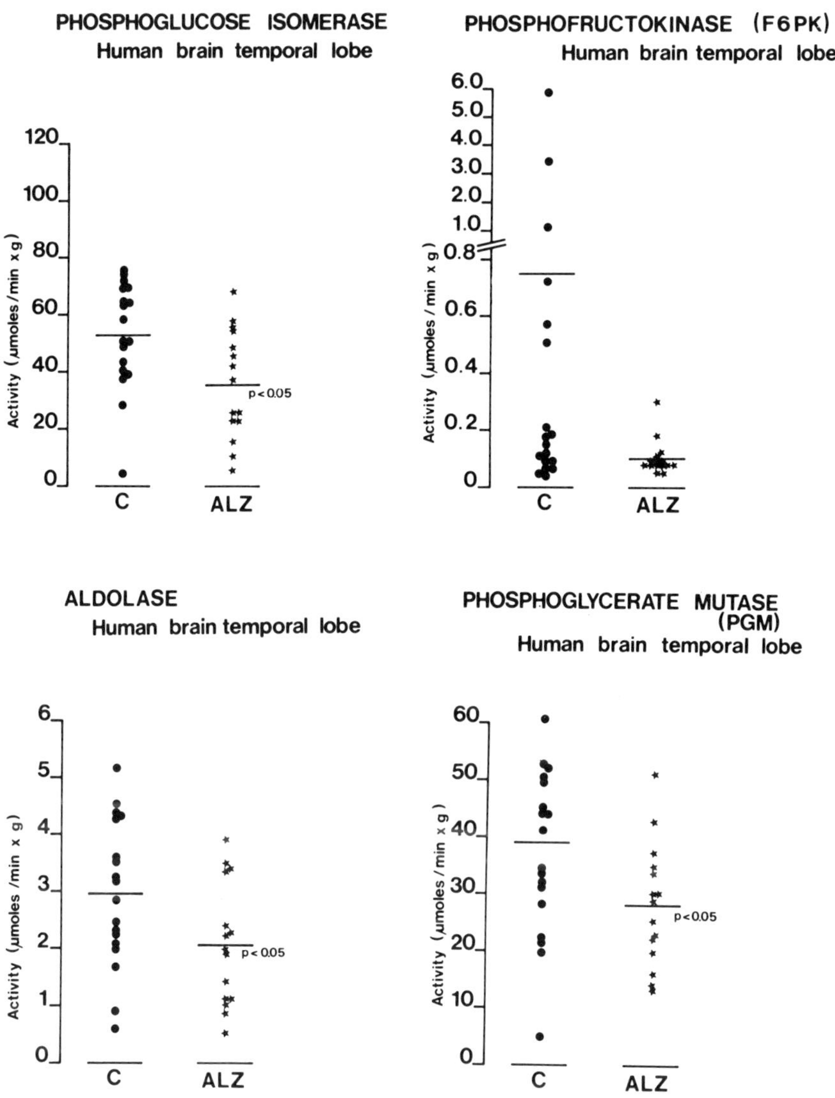

Figure 7. Changes of glycolytic enzymes in senile dementia of the Alzheimer type (ALZ) (n = 15) which, in comparison to the controls (n = 18), are significantly decreased. The age of all cases varies between 74 and 86 years.

In the second place, Gibson and Blass (1976) demonstrated that hypoxia and an associated decrease of the glycolytic energy metabolism can impair acetylcholine synthesis. This offers a plausible explanation for the functional consequences of the changes we found in senile dementia. Recent observations of the normal regional distribution of muscarinic receptors in the brains of persons with senile dementia would also fit into this concept. It was impossible to show any statistically significant difference in the concentration of muscarinic receptors (Perry et al., 1977; White et al., 1977; Davies and Verth, 1978), suggesting that senile dementia mainly damages the energy dependent, transmitter synthesis and transport and not the receptor side.

Finally, in the absence of brain disease, choline acetyltransferase activity and cholinergic function also decreases progressively in old age (Drachman and Leavitt, 1974; Davies, 1978). Further studies are necessary to correlate the decline of cognitive function with the decrease of glycolytic energy transformation.

References

Annau Z: The effect of carbonic anhydrase inhibition on electrical self stimulation of the brain during hypoxia. *Life Science* 20:1043–1050, 1977.

Benzecri JP: *L'analyse des Données*. Tome II. *L'analyse des Correspondances*. Paris, Dunod Editeur, 1973.

Bird ED, Gale JS, Spokes EG: Huntington's chorea. Post-mortem activity of enzymes involved in cerebral glucose metabolism. *J Neurochem* 29:539–545, 1977.

Blass JP: Effects of impaired cerebral carbohydrate metabolism: relevance to dementia. In Roberts PJ (ed.) *Biochemistry of Dementia*. Chichester, England, John Wiley and Sons Ltd., 1979, (in press).

Bondareff W, Geinisman Y: Loss of synapses in the dentate gyrus of the senscent rat. *Am J Anat* 145:129–136, 1976.

Bourke RS, Kimelberg HK, Nelson LR: The effect of temperature and inhibitors on HCO_3-stimulated swelling and ion uptake of monkey cerebral cortex. *Brain Res* 105:309–323, 1976.

Bowen DM, Davison AN: Biochemical changes in the normal aging brain and in dementia. In Issacs B (ed.) *Recent Advances in Geriatric Medicine*. Churchill-Livingstone, 1978, pp. 41–59.

Bowen DM, White P, Spillane JA, Goodhardt MJ, Curzon G, Iwangoff P, Meier-Ruge W, Davison AN: Accelerated aging or selective neuronal loss as an important cause of dementia? *Lancet* I:11–14, 1979.

Brody H: Organization of the cerebral cortex. III. A study of aging in the human cerebral cortex. *J Comp Neurol* 102:511–556, 1955.

Brody H: An examination of cerebral cortex and brain stem aging. In Terry RD, Gershon S (eds.) *Neurobiology of Aging. Aging,* 1976, 3:177–181. Raven Press, New York.

Broe GA, Akhtar J, Andrews GR, Caird FI, Anne JJ, Gilmore J, McLennan WJ: Neurological disorders in the elderly at home. *J Neurology, Neurosurgery and Psychiatry* 39:362–366, 1976.

Davies P: Loss of choline acetyltransferase activity in normal aging and in senile dementia. *Adv Exper Med Biol* 113:251–256, 1978.

Davies P, Maloney AJF: Selective loss of central cholinergic neurons in Alzheimer's disease. *Lancet* II: 1403, 1976.

Davies P, Verth AH: Regional distribution of muscarinic acetylcholine receptor in normal and Alzheimer's-type dementia brains. *Brain Res* 138:385–392, 1978.

Drachman DA, Leavitt J: Human memory and the cholinergic system. *Arch Neurol* 30:113–121, 1974.

Feldman ML: Aging changes in the morphology of cortical dendrites. In Terry Rd, Gershon S (eds.) *Neurobiology of Aging. Aging,* 1976, 3:211–227. Raven Press, New York.

Garg LC, Mathur PP: Effect of ouabain on cerebrospinal fluid formation after carbonic anhydrase inhibition. *Arch Int Pharmacodyn* 213:190–194, 1975.

Gibson G, Blass JP: Impaired synthesis of acetylcholine in brain accompanying mild hypoxia and hypoglycemia. *J Neurochem* 27:31–42, 1976.

Gihr M: Rekonstruktion von Neuronenzellen. *Int Congr Stereology* 18:01–37, 1963.

Goldstein M, Bronaugh RL, Ebstein B, Roberge C: Stimulation of tyrosine hydroxylase activity by cyclic AMP in synaptosomes and in soluble striatal enzyme preparations. *Brain Res* 109:563–574, 1976.

Greengard P: Possible role for cyclic nucleotides and phosphorylated membrane proteins in post-synaptic actions of neurotransmitters. *Nature* 260:101–108, 1976.

Greengard P: Phosphorylated proteins as physiological effectors. *Science* 199:146–152, 1978.

Hall TC, Miller AKH, Corsellis JAN: Variations in the human Purkinje cell population according to age and sex. *Neuropath Appl Neurobiol* 1:267–292, 1975.

Haug H: Probleme und Methoden der Strukturzählung in Schnittpräparaten. In Weibel E (ed.), *Quantitative Methods in Morphology.* Berlin-Heidelberg, Springer, 1967, pp. 57–78.

Haug H: Stereological methods in the analysis of neuronal parameters in the central nervous system. *J Microscopy* 95:165–180, 1972.

Hempel KJ: Quantitative und topische Probleme der Altersvorgänge im Gehirn. *Verh Dtsch Ges Path* 52:179–202, 1968.

Hunziker O, Abdel'Al S, Frey H, Veteau M-J, Meier-Ruge W: Quantitative studies in the cerebral cortex of aging humans. *Gerontology* 24:27–31, 1978.

Hunziker O, Abdel'Al S, Schultz U: The aging human cerebral cortex: a stereological characterization of changes in the capillary net. *J Gerontol* 34:345–350, 1979.

Hunziker O, Frey H, Schulz U: Morphometric investigations of capillaries in the brain cortex of the cat. *Brain Res* 65:01–11, 1974.

Hunziker O, Schulz U, Walliser CHR, Serra J: Morphometric analysis of neurons in different depths of the cat's brain cortex after hypoxia. *Nat Bureau of Standards* (NBS), Spec. Publ., 431:203–206, 1976.

Hunziker O, Schweizer A: Post-mortem changes in stereological parameters of cerebral capillaries. *Beitr Path* 161:244–255, 1977.

Iwangoff P, Armbruster R, Enz A, Sandoz P: Influence of aging, post-mortem delay and agonal state on phosphofructokinase (PFK) in human brain tissue obtained at autopsy. *IRCS Medical Science* 6:83, 1978.

Iwangoff P, Reichlmeier K, Enz A, Meier-Ruge W: Neurochemical findings in physiological aging of the brain. In Meier-Ruge W (ed.) *CNS Aging and Its Neuropharmacology. Interdiscipl Topics Geront,* 1979a, 15:13–33. S. Karger, Basel-New York.

Iwangoff P, Armbruster R, Enz A, Meier-Ruge W, Sandoz P: Glycolytic enzymes from human autoptic brain cortex: normally aged and demented cases. In Roberts PJ (ed.) *Biochemistry of Dementia.* Chichester, England, John Wiley and Sons Ltd., 1979b, pp. 258–262.

Johnson EM: Cyclic AMP-dependent protein kinase and its nuclear substrate proteins. *Adv Cyclic Nucleotide Res* 8:267–309, 1977.

Kennedy C, Des Rosiers MH, Jehle JW, Reivich M, Sharpe F, Sokoloff L: Mapping of functional neural pathways by radiographic survey of local metabolic rate with (^{14}C) deoxyglucose. *Science* 187:850–853, 1975.

Kimelberg HK, Biddlecome S, Narumi S, Bourke RS: ATPase and carbonic anhydrase activities of bulk-isolated neuron, glia and synaptosome fractions from rat brain. *Brain Res* 141:305–323, 1978.

Krebs HA, Kornberg HL: A survey of the energy transformations in living matter. *Ergeb Physiol Biol Chem Pharmacol* 49:212–298, 1957.

Lebart L, Fénelon JP: *Statistique et Informatique Appliquées.* Deuxième Edition, Dunod Editeurs, Paris, 1974.

Lehmenkühler A, Caspers H, Speckman E-J: Actions of CO_2 on cortical spreading depression. *Pflügers Arch Ges Physiol* 336:R83, 1973.

Lehninger AL: *Bioenergetics: the Molecular Basis of Biological Energy Transformation.* New York-Amsterdam, W.A. Benjamin Inc., 1965.

Matheron G: *Random Sets and Integral Geometry.* New York, Winley Intersciences, 1975.

McGeer PL, McGeer EG: Enzymes associated with the metabolism of catecholamines, acetylcholine and GABA in human controls and patients with Parkinson's disease and Huntington's chorea. *J Neurochem* 26:65–76, 1976.

McGeer PL, McGeer EG, Suzuki JS: Aging and extrapyramidal function. *Arch Neurol* 34:33–35, 1977.

McNamara MC, Miller Jr AT, Shen AL, Wood JJ: Restitution of ATP and creatine phosphate after experimental depletion in young, adult and old rats. *Gerontology* 24:95–103, 1978.

Meier-Ruge W, Hunziker O, Iwangoff P, Reichlmeier K, Sandoz P: Alterations of morphological and neurochemical parameters of the brain due to normal aging. In Nandy K (ed.) *Dementia: A Biomedical Approach. Developments in Neuroscience,* 1978, 3:33–44. Elsevier/North-Holland, Biomed. Press, New York-Amsterdam.

Morgenroth VH, Hegstrad LR, Roth RH, Greengard P: Evidence for involvement of protein kinase in the activation by adenosine 3′:5′-monophosphate of brain tyrosine-3-monooxygenase. *J Biol Chem* 250:1946–1948, 1975.

Nimmo HG, Cohen PH: Hormonal control of protein phosphorylation. *Adv Cyclic Nucleotide Res* 8:145–266, 1977.

Ordy JM: Neurochemistry of Aging. In Gaitz CM (ed.) *Aging in the Brain.* New York-London, Plenum Press, 1972, pp. 41–61.

Peress NS, Kane WC, Aronson SM: Central nervous system findings in a tenth decade autopsy population. *Progr Brain Res* 40:473–483, 1973.

Perry EK, Perry RH, Blessed G, Tomlinson BE: Necropsy evidence of central cholinergic deficits in senile dementia. *Lancet* I:189, 1977.

Perry EK, Tomlinson BE, Blessed G, Bergmann K, Gibson PH, Perry RH: Correlation of cholinergic abnormalities with senile plaques and mental test scores in senile dementia. *Brit Med J* II:1457–1459, 1978.

Reichlmeier K, Citherlet K, Ermini M: Some aspects of the protein kinase system in the aging human brain cortex. *Z. Physiol Chem* 359:308–309, 1978a.

Reichlmeier K, Enz A, Iwangoff P, Meier-Ruge W: Age-related changes in human brain enzyme activities: a basis for pharmacological intervention. In Roberts J, Adelman RC, Cristofalo VJ (eds.) *Pharmacological Intervention in the Aging Process. Advanc Exper Med Biol* 1978b, 97:251–252. Plenum Press, New York-London.

Reichlmeier K, Schlecht HP, Iwangoff P: Enzyme activity changes in the aging human brain. *Experientia* 33:R798, 1977.

Roessle R, Roulet F: *Mass und Zahl in der Pathologie.* Berlin-Wien, J. Springer, 1932.

Routtenberg A, Ehrlich YH: Endogenous phosphorylation of four cerebral cortical membrane proteins: role of cyclic nucleotides, ATP and divalent cations. *Brain Res* 92:415–430, 1975.

Samorajski T: How the human responds to aging. *J Amer Geriatr Soc* 24:04–11, 1976.

Sandoz P, Meier-Ruge W: Age-related loss of nerve cells from the human inferior olive, and unchanged volume of its gray matter. *IRCS Medical Science* 5:376, 1977.

Scheibel ME, Scheibel AB: Differential changes with aging in old and new cortices. *Adv in Behavioral Biol* 1977, 23:39–58. Plenum Press, New York-London.

Schindler U, Betz E, Pfeiffer H, Strohm M: Cortical metabolites during constant high CO_2 concentrations and their changes during pH variation. *Europ Neurol* 6:83–87, 1971/72, pt.1.

Schulz U, Hunziker P, Frey H: The stereology of neurons in the cerebral cortex of aging individuals. In Chermant JL (ed.) *Quantitative Analyses of Microstructures in Material, Science, Biology and Medicine*. Dr. Riederer-Verlag, Stuttgart, 1978, pp. 359–366.

Schulz U, Hunziker O, Frey H, Schweizer A: Post-mortem changes in stereological parameters of cerebral neurons. *Path. Res. Pract.,* 166:260–270, 1980.

Serra J, Müller W: The Leitz TAS. *Leitz Mitt Wiss Techn Suppl* 1, 1973.

Severinghaus JW, Hamilton FN, Coter S: Carbonic acid production and the role of carbonic anhydrase in decarboxylation in brain. *Biochem J* 114:703–705, 1969.

Shefer VF: Absolute number of neurons and thickness of cerebral cortex during aging, senile and vascular dementia, in Pick's and Alzheimer's disease. *Neurosci Behav Physiol* 6:319–324, 1973.

Siesjö BK, Plum F: Pathophysiology of anoxic brain damage. In Gaull G (ed.) *Biology of Brain Dysfunction*. New York, Plenum Press, 1973, pp. 319–372.

Siesjö BK, Rehncrona S: Adverse factors affecting neuronal metabolism. Relevance to the dementias. In Roberts PJ (ed.) *Biochemistry of Dementia*. Chichester, England, John Wiley and Sons, Ltd., 1979, in press.

Slater E, Roth M: Aging and the mental diseases of the aged. In Slater E, Roth M (eds.) *Clinical Psychiatry*. London, Baillière Tindall, 1977, pp. 533–629.

Sokoloff L: Relation between physiological function and energy metabolism in the central nervous system. *J Neurochemistry* 29:13–26, 1977.

Speckman E-J, Caspers H: Comparative study on cortical DC shifts associated with changes of the pCO_2 in rats and cats. *Pflügers Arch Ges Physiol* 336:R83, 1973.

Stein DG, Firl AC: Brain damage and reorganization of function in old age. *Exp Neurol* 52:157–167, 1976.

Sylvia AL, Rosenthal M: The effect of age and lung pathology on cytochrome a,a_3 redox levels in rat cerebral cortex. *Brain Res* 146:109–122, 1978.

Tomlinson BE, Henderson G: Some quantitative cerebral findings in normal and demented old people. In Terry RD, Gershon S (eds.) *Neurobiology of Aging. Aging,* 1976, 3:183–204. Raven Press, New York.

Treff WM: Das Involutionsmuster des Nucleus dentatus cerebelli. Eine morphologische Analyse. In Platt D (ed.) *Altern*. Stuttgart-New York, F.K. Schattauer, 1974, pp. 37–54.

Ueda T, Greengard P: Adenosine 3′:3′-monophosphate-regulated phosphoprotein system of neuronal membranes. *J Biol Chem* 252:5155–5163, 1977.

Wiederhold K-H, Bielser W Jr, Schulz U, Veteau M-J, Hunziker O: Three-dimensional reconstruction of brain capillaries from frozen serial sections. *Microvascular Res* 11:175–180, 1976.

White P, Goodhardt MJ, Keet JP, Hiley CR, Carasco LH, Williams IEI: Neocortical cholinergic neurons in elderly people. *Lancet* I:668–671, 1977.

Stein, ed. The Psychobiology of Aging: Problems and Perspectives

Uptake and Release of Amino Acids in the Senile Brain

W. J. Dekoninck, J. Jacquy, Ph. Jocquet, A. Gerebtzoff, and G. Noel

Geriatrie Clinique, Le Rayon de Soleil, Rue de Gozee 706, 6110 Montignies-le-Tilleul, Belgium.

Introduction

When the brain is examined in its entirety, it appears that cerebral blood flow and metabolism of this organ do not decrease with age *provided* that rigorous health criteria are used to select the aged subjects (Sokoloff, 1978). However, in senile chronic brain syndrome, cerebral blood flow and metabolism decrease significantly, in comparison to young adults and healthy old subjects. Some authors (Ingvar et al., 1968; Ingvar and Gustafson, 1970; Simard et al., 1971) have demonstrated that the fall in cerebral blood flow is proportional to the extent of mental alteration but others (Dekoninck et al., 1976, 1977; Sokoloff, 1978) question a strict parallelism between clinical manifestations and cerebral, hemodynamic and metabolic parameters measured in old people stricken with senile cerebral signs. In fact, Sokoloff argues that the change in cerebral blood flow and metabolism observed in the asymptomatic old person is of equal magnitude to that noted in the senile patient of the same age (Sokoloff, 1978). In addition, it appears that patients with senile dementias of the multi-infarct type present a more pronounced cerebral blood flow reduction than patients of the same age with other senile dementias and with the same psychological impairments (Hachinski et al., 1975; Dekoninck et al., 1977).

Other workers present experimental evidence which can be taken to suggest the greater importance and increased frequency of cerebral metabolic abnormalities as a cause of dementia. For example, Hoyer and coworkers found that in some demented patients between 40 and 83 years of age (no etiological separation made), cerebral blood flow and metabolic rates for oxygen ($CMRO_2$) were decreased in the presence of normal, high or low cerebral metabolic rates for glucose (CMRgl). In other demented subjects, the cerebral blood flow was normal or high with normal, high or low $CMRO_2$ values (Hoyer and Becker, 1966; Quadbeck and Hoyer, 1972; Hoyer et al., 1975). Hoyer and his colleagues have described the passage (influx and/or efflux) of certain amino acids across the blood-brain barrier in old demented patients. The uptake of amino acid appeared to correlate with modifications in the cerebral uptake of glucose (Hoyer, 1969).

The purpose of our study was to determine whether the observed decreases in $CMRO_2$ and CMRgl were significantly related to cerebral amino acid flux (input or release) in a group of senile demented patients that were compared to younger adults and asymptomatic subjects of the same age.

Materials and Methods

Choice of Patients

Twenty-nine senile demented patients aged 70 to 88 years who were hospitalized for at least one year in our Geriatric Unit were chosen for this study. They all presented a well stabilized equivalent dementia syndrome characterized by: 1. spatio-temporal disorientation with periods of aggressivity and agitated psychomotor behaviour (requiring neuroleptic drugs), 2. important mnesic disabilities, ideo-motor apraxia, and 3. inability to perform basic self-care gestures (dressing, washing, feeding of oneself), incontinence, repeated fugues. We tried to quantify the severity of the dementia syndrome by using two behavior rating scales so that we could obtain patients with approximately equal psychomotor disabilities (Dekoninck et al., 1977; Gottfries et al., 1969). One scale, the Gottfries Behavior Scale is composed of a series of 30 questions which are based upon the motor and emotional behavior of the subject. The number of negative responses obtained is taken as an indication of the extent of psychomotor alteration.

The General Behavior Scale is composed of 27 items each of which is scored from 0 to 9 depending upon the degree and the frequency of the observed alteration: the higher the score, the greater the alteration observed in the behavior.

All old patients were given tests to separate the Alzheimer senile dementias (ASD) from the multi-infarct dementias (MISD) and to exclude cases of acute or chronic diseases thought to alter blood flow and metabolic activity of the brain, for example, cardiac failure, cardiac arrhythmia, diabetes, liver and kidney abnormalities, cancer, anemia, neurosyphyllis, brain trauma, or normal pressure hydrocephalus. Examining the history of the gradual mental alterations and the analysis of results of the complementary investigations, such as examination of mean arterial pressure (MAP), electroencephalogram (EEG), fundus oculi (FO) and cerebral tomography (CT Scan), permitted us to make a clinical distinction among the degenerative and vascular types of senile dementia. This distinction was completed by the use of the Meyer-Gross et al. (1969) ischemic scale—the higher the score, the greater the probability of ischemic dementia. Normal non-hospitalized adults (A) and old patients equal in age to the senile dementia group, but without clinical evidence of cerebral disease (cerebral asymptomatic elderly or CAE), were used as control groups.

Using these criteria, we observed a high frequency of slight to moderate CT Scan abnormalities in the CAE group as well as a greater number of patients with hypertension, with fundic vascular alterations and with cerebral softenings in the MISD group. Serial EEG studies revealed that in both groups of demented patients there was a severe slowing of the background, a prominent admixture of bifrontal delta episodes mainly in ASD patients, and slight differences in the focal features in cases of MISD.

The MISD group obtained higher scores on the Meyer-Gross test but on all other measures they performed the same as patients with other forms of dementia.

Cerebral Metabolism

The blood concentrations in oxygen (in % ml) were performed by a polarographic method (apparatus CORNING 175, Massachusetts, USA) while the glucose (in % mg) was measured by a colorimetric method using the glucose oxidase-peroxidase reaction (Perid Boehringer).

Free serum amino acid levels were determined automatically in a Technicon amino acid analyzer (TSM, New York). In brief, the technique consists of liquid chromatography using ion exchange columns, and is similar to the procedures developed by Stein and Moore (1954) and later modified by Efron (1965). Proteins are precipitated from one ml of serum with the addition of 40 mg of sulfalocylic acid (solid). After high-speed centrifugation (4000 rpm), the supernatant is subjected to analysis. Just prior to colorimetry, the eluents containing the amino acids are placed in solutions of ninhydrine and hydrazine sulfate. Readings for amino acids are taken at 570 nanometers, while readings for proline and hydroxyproline are taken at 440 nanometers. The precise location of the serum amino acids can be seen in the chromatogram drawn in Figure 1.

The concentration of amino acids was expressed in micromoles per 100 ml and was determined by planimetry, by comparison to a "standard" for amino acids provided by Technicon and by a known standard of norleucine. Thus, it is possible using serial chromatography, to isolate and calculate the concentration of 17 amino acids in the same sample at

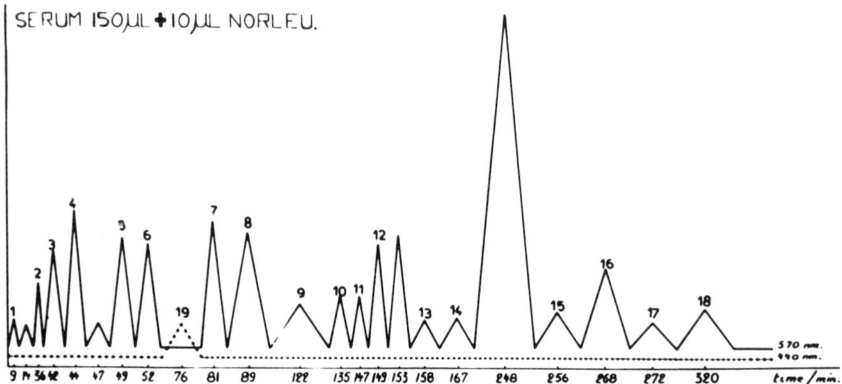

Figure 1. Diagram of a serum chromatogram. Numbers indicate the places of the different aminoacids (see text). Peaks for phosphoetanolamine, urea, asparagine (between 1 and 5), alpha and gamma-aminoisobutyric acids, etanolamine and ammonia (between 12 and 15) are not numbered. The standard norleucine is figured in dotted line.

three different times. The amino acids examined and the percent variation of the samples are noted as follows: taurine (11); aspartic acid (8); threonine (6); serine (3.7); glumatic acid (6.5); glutamine (36); glycine (4); alanine (11); valine (8); cystine (9.5); isoleucine (9); leucine (5.5); tyrosine (7); phenylanine (6.5); ornithine (4); lysine (4.5); histidine (7); arginine (13.5) and proline (5.5).

Because of weak ninhydrin detection, citrulline, asparagine and methionine were not assayed while the high percentage of error in the dosage of glutamine negated the study of this amino acid.

The cerebral extraction ratios (CER) for oxygen (O_2), glucose (gl), some free amino acids (aa) and the cerebral release ratios (CRR) for some other amino acids, were calculated by using the arteriovenous differences and applying the following formula:

$$\text{CER or CRR} = \frac{a - v}{a} \times 100$$

depending on whether a-v is positive (extraction) or negative (release). Arterial blood was obtained from the femoral artery and venous blood from the puncture of the bulb of the internal jugular vein as it exits the skull (Myerson et al., 1927).

The cerebral metabolic rates (CMR) of the parameters being studied were calculated by multiplying the cerebral blood flow by the arterio-venous differences. Hemispheric cerebral blood flow was obtained by the rheoencephalography method which gives, with a good approximation, the blood flow in the cerebral grey matter (Jacquy et al., 1974).

Statistics

In order to compare the means values of the metabolic parameters from two different clinical groups, we used one factor analysis of variance and found significant differences between the two groups of demented patients. Because of the difficulty in calculating a correlation coefficient for two distinct groups being compared, we used a discriminant function analysis or the Hotelling's T^2-Test (Snedecor and Cochran, 1972). The Hotelling test permits us to determine if clusters of points (each cluster represents a mixture of two variables from one clinical group) were significantly distant from each other. For example, it becomes possible to determine if the extraction or release ratios of one amino acid in two different groups are statistically in relationship with a modification of the oxygen or the glucose ratios obtained in the same two groups.

Results

Table 1 presents the mean values for cerebral oxygen and glucose data in the senile demented patients (and in the two subgroups) as compared with Adults (A) and with Cerebral Asymptomatic Elderly (CAE). There was a progressive decrease in the glucose-oxidative metabolism (expressed by the oxygen and glucose ratios and rates) from group A to group CAE and to group SD. However, the MISD subgroup revealed a significant reduction of the oxidative parameters when compared to those observed in the other groups. This cerebral metabolic decrease also appears in the ratios in which blood flow does not play a role. Considering all the amino acids together, we did not observe any differences in ratios or rates, but studying each amino acid from one clinical group to another, we observed a significant difference (uptake or release) for some amino acids. Table 2 lists the names of these amino acids with their mean ratios (a) and their mean rates (b) found in the three main groups and in the two subgroups of senile demented subjects. There exists a significant cerebral uptake of taurine, serine, glutamic acid and histidine in the CAE group compared to the A group (Table 2). There is also an uptake of taurine, glutamic acid, lysine and histidine in the SD group compared to the A group and only of phenyalanine and histidine for the comparison with the CAE group (Table 2). Comparing the two subgroups of SD (ASD and MISD), we observe a cerebral uptake of glutamic acid, glycine, tyrosine, phenyalanine, ornithine and lysine in the ASD group compared to the MISD group. For the comparison ASD versus A we also observe an uptake of taurine, serine, glutamic acid, glycine and lysine in the ASD group.

1. *In the CAE group* (compared to A group), we noted an increase of the ratios for taurine, serine and histidine with a significant F rela-

Table 1. Mean Metabolic Values ± SD

Metabolic Parameters	Adults (A)	Cerebral Asymptomatic Elderly (CAE)	Senile Dementia: Alzheimer (ASD)	Senile Dementia: Multi-infarct (MISD)	Senile Dementia: Both (SD)
Cerebral extraction ratio for oxygen ($CERO_2$)	$.32 \pm .04$	$.29 \pm .06$	$.3 \pm .07$	$.25 \pm .08$ $p < .05^{a}$	$.27 \pm .08$
Cerebral metabolic rate for oxygen ($CMRO_2$ in ml/100 g/min)	$6.23 \pm .56$	4.21 ± 1.04 $p < .001^{a}$	3.81 ± 1.49 $p < .01^{a}$	$2.16 \pm .87$ $p < .001^{b}$ $p < .01^{c}$	2.84 ± 1.4 $p < .01^{b}$
Cerebral extraction ratio for glucose (CERgl)	$.11 \pm .03$	$.09 \pm .02$ $p < .05^{a}$	$.11 \pm .02$ $p < .05^{b}$	$.09 \pm .02$ $p < .05^{c}$	$.1 \pm .02$
Cerebral metabolic rate for glucose (CMRgl in mg/100g/min)	9.5 ± 11	7.4 ± 1.2 $p < .01^{a}$	8.7 ± 3	4.8 ± 1.2 $p < .001^{b}$ $p < .001^{c}$	6.4 ± 2.8 $p < .01^{a}$
Cerebral ratios (extraction or release) for total amino acids	-69 ± 99	29 ± 151	101.5 ± 261	-46.2 ± 264	14.9 ± 268
Cerebral metabolic rates (consumption or production in μm/100g/min) for total amino acids	-3.22 ± 12	3.6 ± 15.5	15.5 ± 27	1.7 ± 15.8	7.4 ± 22

[a] Significant difference with A.
[b] Significant difference with CAE.
[c] Significant difference with ASD.

Table 2. Mean Ratios (a) and Rates (b) in $\mu M/100g/min \pm SEM$ of Amino Acids with Significant Differences

Amino acids		Adults (A)	Cerebral Asymptomatic Elderly (CAE)	Alzheimer (ASD)	Multi-infarct (MISD)	Both (SD)
Taurine	a	-43 ± 17	-1.5 ± 9 $p < .05^a$	-1.5 ± 14 $p < .05^a$	-13 ± 23	-8.4 ± 15
	b	$-3 \pm 1.$	$-.03 \pm .3$ $p < .01^a$	$.7 \pm .6$	$.4 \pm .3$ $p < .001^a$	$.5 \pm .3$ $p < .001^a$
Serine	a	-7.9 ± 8	8.1 ± 3 $p < .02^a$	7.3 ± 4.5 $p < .05^a$	2.2 ± 5	4.3 ± 3.4
	b	$-.5 \pm 1.3$	$.8 \pm .4$	$.66 \pm .5$	$.4 \pm .4$	$.5 \pm .3$
Glutamic acid	a	-12.5 ± 4.3	$-.8 \pm 5.2$	10.5 ± 6.5 $p < .02^a$	-4.8 ± 6	1.5 ± 4.6
	b	$-1.4 \pm .4$	$.36 \pm .5$ $p < .05^a$	1.6 ± 1 $p < .02^a$	$-.01 \pm .3$ $p < .05^c$	$.7 \pm .5$ $p < .05^a$
Glycine	a	1.2 ± 5	1.4 ± 3	10 ± 3.7 $p < .05^a$ $p < .05^b$	-1.9 ± 3.5 $p < .02^c$	3 ± 2.7
	b	$.9 \pm 1.6$	$.3 \pm .6$	2.6 ± 9	$-.15 \pm .5$ $p < .01^c$	$1 \pm .5$
Tyrosine	a	4.4 ± 3	1.6 ± 4.4	12.2 ± 5.6	-2.3 ± 3.6 $p < .05^c$	3.7 ± 3.4
	b	$.24 \pm .2$	$.34 \pm .4$	$.77 \pm .37$	$-.04 \pm .15$ $p < .05^c$	$.29 \pm .2$
Phenyl-alanine	a	1.8 ± 7.2	$.95 \pm 2.8$	9.5 ± 5.9	-3.9 ± 4.7	1.6 ± 3.8
	b	$.4 \pm .5$	-1.2 ± 1.4	$.7 \pm .3$	$.02 \pm .1$ $p < .05^c$	$.3 \pm .17$ $p < .05^b$
Ornithine	a	-6.1 ± 10	6.8 ± 4.5	7.9 ± 5.9	-10.9 ± 5.8 $p < .05^c$ $p < .05^b$	-3.3 ± 4.5
	b	$-.5 \pm 1.7$	$.7 \pm .4$	$1 \pm .5$	$-.46 \pm .33$ $p < .02^c$	$.12 \pm .33$
Lysine	a	-13.6 ± 6	$.6 \pm 5.7$	3.8 ± 4.7	-9.5 ± 6 $p < .05^c$	-4 ± 4.1
	b	-2.4 ± 1.1	$-.4 \pm .9$	$.7 \pm .6$ $p < .01^a$	$-.3 \pm .5$	$.1 \pm 4$ $p < .01^a$
Histidine	a	-24.2 ± 20	11.8 ± 6.4 $p < .05^a$	$-.46 \pm 9.9$	-15.6 ± 8.7 $p < .05^b$	-9.1 ± 6.6 $p < .05^b$
	b	-1.6 ± 1.1	$1 \pm .5$ $p < .05^a$	$.04 \pm .5$	$-.33 \pm .2$ $p < .05^b$	$-.2 \pm .2$ $p < .05^a$ $p < .02^b$

[a] Significant difference with A.

[b] Significant difference with CAE.

[c] Significant difference with ASD.

tionship for a decrease of the glucose extraction ratios ($P <$ from .05 to .02). The increase of the cerebral consumption (expressed by the rates) of taurine, glutamic acid and histidine reveals a significant relationship for a decrease of both $CMRO_2$ and CMRgl ($P < .001$ for taurine; $P < .01$ for glutamic acid and histidine).

2. *In the SD group* (compared to CAE group), we observed an uptake of phenylalanine (increase of the cerebral rate) in relation to a significant decrease of $CMRO_2$ ($P < .01$) and CMRgl ($P < .001$). However, there is also a cerebral release of histidine (negative ratio and rate) correlated with a reduction of ratio and rate for oxygen ($P < .01$) and in relation to a decrease of ratio and rate for glucose ($P < .001$). Comparing the SD group to the A group, we observed, in the SD group, a significant increase of the CMR for taurine, glutamic acid, lysine and histidine and a reduction for $CMRO_2$ ($P < .01$) and CMRgl ($P < .001$). The amount of amino acid uptake is not proportional to the degree of the oxidative metabolism reduction.
3. *In the ASD subgroup* (compared to the MISD subgroup), there is an increase of cerebral uptake (expressed in ratio and/or rate) of glutamic acid, glycine, tyrosine, phenylalanine, ornithine and lysine in relationship to an increase of glucose ratios ($P < .02$) and rates ($P < .001$). The correlation between an increase of the ratios and rates for these amino acids and an increase of the oxygen ratio and rate also exists but it is not as significant as that for the glucose.
4. *In the SD group (compared to A and CAE),* we observed a significant increase of taurine, glutamic acid, histidine metabolic rates with a concomitant decrease of $CMRO_2$ and CMRgl.

Discussion

We know that the brain contains a reserve of free amino acids and proteins (about 40% of brain dry weight) and that the cerebral pool of amino acids is supported by glucose derived synthesis and by passage of blood amino acids across the brain-blood barrier. This barrier seems to be permeable to most of the circulating amino acids but this permeability depends upon complicated mechanisms of selective and competitive inhibition transport. The passage of amino acids across the brain-blood barrier is also influenced by the chemical structure and rates of each substrate on both sides of the barrier (Lajtha and Toth, 1961). It has been shown that the blood concentrations of amino acids are not stable in man because of a number of factors—general metabolism and hormones, alimentation and physical effort, and daily influence of amino acid levels in blood.

Though the human cerebral arteriovenous differences of amino acids are small, Hoyer (1969) has demonstrated that glucose forming, or glucose-derived, amino acids, have either a cerebral input or output. In line with this view, other authors (Barkulis et al., 1960; Sacks, 1965) have shown that 70 percent of the cerebral glucose uptake is transformed into amino acids, whereas only 30% is utilized to produce carbon dioxide and water through aerobic glycolysis.

Since the cerebral asymptomatic elderly (CAE) we studied had cerebral arterial alterations demonstrated by the abnormalities of paraclinical examinations, it is not surprising that there was a decrease of both the oxygen and glucose metabolic rates compared to adults (A)—32% and 21% respectively.

In fact, we were more surprised not to have found any observable clinical signs accompanying this decrease of cerebral metabolism. But in this type of "normal" elderly subject, we noted a cerebral amino acid uptake that suggested that the cerebral amino acid pool was not saturated. Perhaps the decreased cerebral glucose uptake contributes to the desaturation of the amino acid pool by a reduction in amino acid synthesis. One might therefore postulate that cerebral amino acid captation in the CAE diminishes the influence of a cerebral glucose deficit observed in these subjects. It seems hazardous, however, to assume that the brain is able to utilize amino acids instead of glucose in order to obtain energy for better cerebral function. Indeed, it has been proven that in some pathological circumstances (hypoglycemic crisis, liver failure, Wilson's disease) the cerebral consumption of amino acids does not pass $\pm$ 4 μM/100 g/min. which constitutes 3% of the normal cerebral glucose consumption (Knauf et al., 1964).

Concerning subjects with senile dementia, Hoyer (1969) has described a cerebral amino acid output especially in patients in which the role of oxygen depression is important compared to other types of senile dementia where the metabolic rates are not so depressed. We also observed in some cases of senile dementia (MISD), a cerebral release of amino acids when the cerebral uptake of oxygen and glucose were low. This cerebral output of amino acids could be explained either by an increase in the cellular catabolism or by an excess of intracerebral amino acid formation from the non-oxidized glucose.

In contrast, the cerebral uptake of amino acids observed in the Alzheimer's type of senile dementia could be explained either by a possible desaturation of the cerebral amino acid pool or by an attempt to produce cerebral glucose which will probably not produce energy because of the lack of oxygen (vicious circle).

In conclusion, our data can be taken to suggest that there is a significant relationship between amino-acid flux in both directions through the blood-brain barrier and the cerebral input of both oxygen and glucose.

References

Barkulis SS, Geiger A, Kawakita Y, Aguilar V: A study of the incorporation of ^{14}C derived from glucose into the free aminoacids of the brain cortex. *J Neurochem* 5:339–348, 1960.

Dekoninck WJ, Jacquy J, Jocquet PH, Noel G: Cerebral blood flow and metabolism in senile dementia. *Proceedings of the 8th International Salzburg Conference on Cerebral Vascular Disease, Excerpta Medica,* Amsterdam-Oxford, 1976, pp. 29–32.

Dekoninck WJ, Calay R, Hongne JC: Cerebral blood flow in elderly with chronic cerebral involvement. *Acta Neurol Scandin* Supt 64 56:412–413, 1977.

Efron ML: Quantitative estimation of aminoacids in physiological fluids using a Technicon aminoacid analyzer. In *Automation in Analytical Chemistry,* Technicon Symposium, New York, 1965, pp. 637–642.

Gottfries CG, Gottfries I, Roos BE: The investigation of homo-vanillic acid in the human brain and its correlation to senile dementia. *Brit J Psychiat* 115:563–574, 1969.

Hackinski VC, Iliff D, Zilhka E, DuBoulay GH, McAllister VL, Marschall J, Rossrussel RW, Symon N: Cerebral blood flow in dementia. *Arch Neurol (Chic)* 32:632–637, 1975.

Hoyer S, Becker K: Hirndurchblutung und Hirnstoffwechselbefunde bei neuropsychiatrisch Kranken. *Nervenarzt* 37:322–324, 1966.

Hoyer S: Cerebral blood flow and metabolism in senile dementia. In Brock N, Fieschi C, Ingvar DH, Lassen NA, Schürmann K (eds.) *Cerebral Blood Flow.* Berlin-Heidelberg-New York, Springer, 1969, pp. 235–236.

Hoyer S: Der Aminosäuren—Stoffwechsel des normalen menschlichen Gerhirn. *Klin Wochenschr* 48:1239–1243, 1970.

Hoyer S, Oesterreich K, Weinhardt F, Kruger G: Veränderungen von Durchblutung und oxydativen Stoffwechsel des Gehirns bei Patienten mit einer Demenz. *J Neurol* 210:227–237, 1975.

Ingvar DH, Obrist W, Chivian E, Cronqvist S, Risberg J, Gustafson N, Hagendal M, Wittbom-Cigen: General and regional abnormalities of cerebral blood flow in senile and presenile dementia. In International Symposium on CSF-CBF, Lund and Copenhagen, May 9–11, 1968, *Scand J Clin Invest,* 1968, (supt 102) XII:B.

Ingvar DH, Gustafson L: Regional cerebral blood flow in organic dementia with early onset. *Acta Neurol Scand* supt 43 46:42–73, 1970.

Jacquy J, Dekoninck WJ, Piraux A, Calay R, Bacq J, Levy D, Noel G: Cerebral blood flow and quantitative rheoencephalography. *Electroencephal and Cl Neurophysiol* 37:507–511, 1974.

Knauff HG, Gottstein U, Miller B: Untersuchungen über den Austausch von freien Aminosäuren und Harnstoff zwischen Blut und Zentralnervensystem. *Klin Wschr* 42:27–39, 1964.

Lajtha A, Toth J: The brain barrier system-II. Uptake and transport of aminoacids by the brain. *J Neurochem* 8:216–225, 1961.

Mayer-Gross W, Slater E, Roth M: In *Clinical Psychiatry,* Ed. 3. London, Baillière, Tindall and Carssell, 1969.

Myerson A, Halloran RD, Hirsch HL: Technic for obtaining blood from the internal jugular vein and internal carotid artery. *Arch Neurol Psychiat* 17:807–808, 1927.

Quadbeck G, Moyer S: Cerebral blood flow and metabolism disorders of the brain. In Meyer JS, Reivich H, Lechner H, Eichorn O (eds.) *Research on the Cerebral Circulation.* Springfield, Thomas, 1972, p. 196.

Sacks W: Cerebral metabolism of doubly labelled glucose in humans *in vivo. J Appl Physiol* 20:117–130, 1965.

Simard D, Olesen J, Paulson OB, Lassen NA, Skinhøj E: Regional cerebral blood flow and its regulation in dementia. *Brain* 94:273–288, 1971.

Snedecor GW, Cochran WG: Multiple regression, numerical example of the discriminant function. In *Statistical Methods,* (VI Edition). The Iowa State University Press, Ames, Iowa, U.S.A., 1972, pp. 416–418.

Sokoloff L: Cerebral blood flow and metabolism in the differentiation of dementias: general considerations. In Katzman R, Terry RD, Bick KL (eds.) *Alzheimer's Disease: Senile Dementia and Related Disorders. Aging,* (Vol. 7), New York: Raven Press, 1978, pp. 197–202.

Stein WH, Moore S: The free aminoacids of human blood plasma. *J Biol Chem* 211:915–922, 1954.

Stein, ed. The Psychobiology of Aging: Problems and Perspectives

Neurotransmitter and Neurophysiological Changes in Relation to Pathology in Senile Dementia or Alzheimer's Disease

David M. Bowen and Alan N. Davison

Department of Neurochemistry, Institute of Neurology, University of London, Queen Square, London, England.

Introduction

Partial brain failure includes a wide range of conditions affecting behavior of the elderly. The commonest is dementia which is usually defined as a global diffuse deterioration in mental function, primarily in thought and memory, and secondly in feeling and conduct. In the western world both the percentage and actual numbers of the people susceptible to dementia are increasing, making the condition an important human problem. In the United States in 1950 about 8 percent of the persons, about 12 million, were older than 65 years. By 1978 the susceptible population exceeded 22 million, a number projected to increase to over 51 million by the year 2030 (Plum, 1979). About 10% of the population over 65 years old have organic dementia—half severe and about one fifth require hospitalization (Wang, 1977). It has been estimated (Pearce and Miller, 1973) that about 14% of cases may be treatable. The disease is not due to a single cause. It may be the result of inflammatory, vascular, toxic, neoplastic, traumatic, malnutritional, infectious or degenerative processes—some of which causes are extracerebral (Tables 1 and 2). An example is the demonstration of "slow virus" in biopsy material from patients with Jakob-Creutzfeldt disease or the transmissible agent producing spongioform encephalopathy in non-human primates found in 2 familial out of 35 cases with dementia of the Alzheimer's type (Traub, Gajdusek and Gibbs, 1977). In these cases, the resulting biochemical changes may themselves be secondary to viral disease or the transmissible agent may occur as a secondary pathogen in an already diseased brain.

Table 1. Diseases Producing Presenile Dementia[a]

Disease	Relative Incidence
Cerebral atrophy of unknown cause	57
Tumors	10
Arteriosclerotic dementia	10
Alcoholic dementia	7
Normal pressure hydrocephalus	6
Creutzfeldt-Jakob disease	4
Huntington's chorea	4
Others	4

[a] Adapted from Marsden and Harrison (1972).

The primary dementias are those in which dementia is the only or dominant symptomatology. Most cases of presenile dementia associated with cerebral atrophy of unknown cause (Table 1) have a slowly progressive course with probably most being cases of Alzheimer's disease. "Senile dementia of Alzheimer's type," which does not differ in pathology from the presenile form (Corsellis, 1976), accounts for at least 50% of all dementia in old age (Tomlinson, 1977). The disease is characterized histologically by intense senile plaque formation and neurofibrillary degeneration in the cortex.

Neurophysiology

In patients described as having "chronic brain syndrome and psychosis," the early studies of Kety demonstrated significant reduction in cerebral

Table 2. Pathological Classification of Dementia in Old Age[a]

Disease	Relative Incidence
Senile dementia of Alzheimer's type	50
Arteriosclerotic dementia	
definite cases	12
probable cases	16
Mixed senile and arteriosclerotic dementia	
definite cases	8
probable cases	10
Unclassified	6
Other specific causes	4
No morphological changes	4

[a] Adapted from Tomlinson (1977).

oxygen and glucose consumption. Measurement of cerebral blood flow (CBF) by the intracarotid radioactive xenon technique (Hachinski, Iliff, Zilkha, du Bouley, McAllister, Marshall, Ross-Russell and Symon, 1975) showed significant loss of the fast-clearing tissues (largely grey matter) in multi-infarct and Alzheimer's dementias. In later stages of senile dementia there is a substantial reduction in cerebral flow changes, presumably related to brain atrophy (Ingvar and Gustafson, 1970). However, reduction of regional CBF to mean values of 43 ml/100g/min in pre-senile cases (39–53 yrs) and 35 ml/100g/min in senile cases (62–79) have been found by Melamed, Lavy, Siew, Bentin and Cooper (1978) not to correlate with ventricular enlargement or widening of cortical sulcii. It was therefore suggested that loss of brain substance is not an important factor in reduction of CBF in dementia.

Grubb, Raichle, Gado, Eichling and Hughes (1977) have reported a 37% reduction in CBF in patients with cerebral atrophy and a 42% lowering in patients with normal pressure hydrocephalus. There is a comparable loss of utilization of oxygen by the brain (Table 3). It is assumed that CBF is reduced as a consequence of the decreased neuronal metabolism in these patients, probably mediated by reduced hydrogen ion concentration and lower pCO_2. Vasoconstriction occurs, leading to increased cerebrovascular resistance and a fall in CBF. Cerebral oxygen utilization, but not blood flow, is reduced in Parkinson's disease (Lenzi, Jones, Reid and Moss, 1979). Thus the reduction in CBF in dementia may be a key change.

Unfortunately, the examination of blood or other techniques such as estimation of ventricular size by air encephalography or by computerized axial tomography are not reliable in differentiating normal pressure hydrocephalus from other forms of dementia. Changes in CBF after acute decrease in the intracranial pressure were also not helpful in distinguishing patients with normal pressure hydrocephalus from those with cerebral atrophy (Grubb et al., 1977). Interestingly, there is evidence that in the later stages of hydrocephalus the intensity of granulovacuolar

Table 3. Blood Flow and Oxygen Uptake in Brain Atrophy[a]

	Normal (N = 7)	Cerebral Atrophy (N = 19)
Cerebral blood flow (ml/100g/min)	54 ±9	34 ±6[b]
Cerebral oxygen utilization (ml/100g/min)	3.6 ±0.5	2.4 ±0.4[b]

[a] Adapted from Grubb et al. (1977).

[b] Significantly reduced ($p < 0.001$). The diagnosis of Alzheimer's disease was made in 13 out of the 19 cases, 2 had Creutzfeld-Jakob disease and one Huntington's chorea. 7 patients with cerebral atrophy had the diagnosis confirmed by a brain biopsy.

degeneration advances to a degree as severe as seen in classical Alzheimer's disease. At this stage of pathogenesis, treatment by shunting with intraventricular catheters is of little benefit (Ball and Vis, 1978).

Cases of Alzheimer's disease have been found to have EEG abnormalities (Johannesson, Brun, Gustafson and Ingvar, 1977) which progress slowly. Patients with Pick's disease had normal EEG even when dementia was marked. A positive correlation between regional CBF in postcentral areas in which there was neuronal loss correlated with increasing EEG abnormality. When degenerative changes occurred in the frontal and anterior-temporal cortical regions with concomitant flow reduction, the alpha rhythm appeared to be undisturbed. It is of interest that results of a neurological, neuroradiological and psychological study of patients with presenile dementia by Kaszniak, Fox, Gandell, Garron, Huckman and Ramsey (1978) suggests that the degree of functional brain impairment and subtle metabolic abnormalities rather than cerebral atrophy, influences mortality.

Pathology

Nerve Cell Loss

Multi-infarct dementia due to cerebrovascular disease occurs with unevenly distributed brain damage with scattered micro- and macroinfarcts. In non-vascular senile dementia there is more generalized atrophy; the brain weight may drop from the expected level of 1,200–1,350 grams to 1,000 or less. The frontal and temporal regions are especially affected, and frequently ventricles are enlarged. Since identification and counting of the 20,000 million nerve cells in the brain is a difficult problem, there is some debate as to whether or not such losses reflect cell loss or shrinkage. Using biochemical indices, Bowen, Smith, White, Flack, Carrasco, Gedye and Davison (1977) and Bowen, White, Spillane, Goodhardt, Curzon, Iwangoff, Meier-Ruge and Davison (1979) have analyzed whole temporal lobes from normal elderly and matched demented subjects. This work indicates that between 26–36% of nerve cell components are lost from the temporal lobe at the end point in the pathological process. If these losses are not due to shrinkage of the perikaryon, they may reflect reduction in the nerve cell population, and this is consistent with Colon (1973) who, using histological methods, reported a 57% loss of neocortical neurons in Alzheimer's disease. Ball (1978) has demonstrated an exponential correlation between the density of cortical neurons in the hippocampus and both the number of nerve cells with neurofibrillary degeneration and the number with granulovacuolar degeneration. Thus, where there is nerve cell loss, as in the posterior half of the hippocampus of the brain of senile dementia patients, there is a greater concentration of tangles and granulovacuoles. The posterior portion of the hippocampus may therefore be considerably more susceptible to degenerative nerve cell changes prominent in dementia of the Alzheimer type than other regions of the brain. The hippocampus is the portion of the limbic system most often associated with the process of learning and memory (e.g., Penfield's findings indicate that a profound memory disorder results from bilateral damage to the human hippocampus, Leaton, 1971).

Nerve cell changes are usually thought to be restricted to neocortex and hippocampus. However, there is evidence that both the perikaryon and dendritic processes of Purkinje cells are affected in senile dementia (Table 4; Mehraein, Yamada and Tarnowski-Dzikusyko, 1975). The reduction in RNA and the volume of the nucleolus (Table 4) was taken to indicate a decline in protein synthesis. Suzuki, Korey and Terry (1964), however, report that protein synthesis is normal in a crude microsomal preparation. Further studies need to be carried out on neuron specific synthesis.

Nerve cell loss may be the result of a primary defect in neuronal glucose metabolism. There is very little available information on the oxidative activity of biopsy material. Suzuki, Katzman and Korey (1965), who studied a biopsy from a 62-year-old Alzheimer patient, concluded that respiratory rate and lactic acid production were within normal limits. Studies on post-mortem samples suggest that all glycolytic enzymes involved in hexosephosphate metabolism are reduced, although an effect of terminal state on glycolytic enzymes has not been eliminated (Bowen et al., 1979).

Glia

Astrocytes have been implicated in the pathogenesis of the metabolic dementia, hepatic encephalopathy (Plum, 1978). It is often assumed that

Table 4. Lipofuscin and RNA Contents and Nucleolar Volumes in "Senile dementia of Alzheimer's type"[a]

Variable	Nerve Cell Type	
	Hippocampus	Purkinje
Lipofuscin content (change in dementia, %)	0	0
RNA content (change in dementia, %)	33[b]	28[b]
Nucleolar volume (change in dementia, %)	25[b]	23[b]

[a] Adapted from Mann and Sinclair (1978).

[b] Significant ($p < 0.001$) loss, compared with age-matched controls.

astrocytes increase in number in areas of brain undergoing degenerative change. Data for the striatum from choreic brain suggest, however, that the absolute number of astrocytes is not increased (Lange, Thorner, Hopf and Schröder, 1976). Based on the β-glucuronidase and carbonic anhydrase activities of temporal lobe preliminary data suggest that twice as many "macroglia" (astrocytes and oligodendrocytes) than neurons survive in the Alzheimer brain (Bowen et al., 1977). Comparison of changes in carbonic anhydrase activity and nerve cell markers indicate that structural changes in nerve cells precede the change in the glial marker (Bowen et al., 1979). Cathepsin A, a potential marker of microglia, is high in senile brain (Bowen et al., 1977), which conforms with the established view that an increase in cells of this type occurs in Alzheimer brain.

Senile Plaques

One of the most striking histopathological changes in Alzheimer's disease is the presence, frequently close to blood vessels, of argyrophilic or senile plaques. They consist of aggregations of granular or filamentous fragments and some have a central amyloid type B core. IgG has been identified in the amyloid (Ishii and Haga, 1976), suggesting that the core consists largely of antigen-antibody complex. However, the data on antineuronal antibody immunoreactivity (ANIR) in serum is confusing. Mayer, Chughtai and Cape (1976), who studied both female and male senile dementia cases, report an excess of ANIR in only females. Nandy (1978), however, who examined only males, finds that ANIR is reduced.

Degenerating mitochrondria and dense lysosomal bodies are found around the rim of the plaques. Electron microscopic examination (Gonatas and Gambetti, 1970) suggests that the plaques are derived from presynaptic terminals and degenerating neurites. Shrinkage of the apical dendritic tree and a decreased density of its spines shown in Ammon's horn neurons of some cases of Alzheimer's disease have been described (Mehraein et al., 1975) Scheibel and Tomiyasu, (1978) have also used the Golgi technique and found progressive deteriorative changes in cortical neurons from senile dementia cases of the Alzheimer's type. There is loss of dendritic spines, irregular swelling of cell body and dendrites, and progressive loss of the dendritic domain, culminating in cell death.

Neurofibrillary Degeneration (NFD)

In the electron microscope, NFD appears as helically paired twisted filaments (Kidd, 1963). The paired helical filaments are about 22 nm in width, periodically reduced to about half (10 nm) every 80 nm from the lesions in Alzheimer's disease and other dementias. Iqbal, Wisniewski, Grundke-Iqbal and Terry (1977) found an abnormal protein in neurons isolated from the post-mortem brain of patients with senile dementia.

The protein appeared to be related to the neurofilaments and neurotubules of the nerve axon. Recent work (Grundke-Iqbal, Johnson, Wisniewski, Terry and Iqbal, 1979) with antisera indicates cross-reaction between antibodies to tubulin, paired helical filaments and neurofibrillary tangles. Antibody to paired helical filamentary protein does not cross react with neurofilaments. Possibly such changes in filamentous proteins might be induced by a virus (De Boni and Crapper, 1978) or by a toxic substance such as lead (Niklowitz, 1975) or aluminum. Increased aluminum found in senile dementia brain speciments is also found in age-matched controls (McDermott, Smith, Iqbal and Wisniewski, 1977). Certainly dementia is an established clinical entity in dialysis encephalopathy in which there is raised brain aluminum concentration. It is of interest that significant loss of choline acetyltransferases (CAT) activity has recently been reported in the brain of one strain of mice infected with a particular type of scrapie agent (Table 5).

Lipofuscin

A well described feature of the aging brain is the lipofuscin insoluble pigment granules which accumulate within cells. The pigment appears to be derived from lysosomes which fail to digest certain cellular lipids. Lipfuscin deposition, however, does not appear to be exacerbated in senile dementia (Mann and Sinclair, 1978; Table 4).

Neurotransmitters

Uemura and Hartmann (1978) were able to isolate a normal population of neocortical neuronal perikarya from Alzheimer brain, suggesting that there are normal as well as diseased neurons. Senile plaques are often associated with capillaries (Mirjakawa, Sumiyashi, Murayama and Deshimaru, 1974), perhaps showing that neurons which are selectively

Table 5. Choline Acetyltransferase Activity in Scrapie and Control Mouse Brain[a]

Mice Injected With:		CAT Activity (μmols/h/g protein ± S.E.M.) Forebrain	Cerebellum
Control	(10)	21.4 ± 2.2	4.1 ± 0.7
Semliki Forest Virus	(7)	21.1 ± 1.8	4.6 ± 0.4
Scrapie 79A	(5)	5.7 ± 2.0[b]	1.6 ± 0.4[c]
22C	(5)	17.3 ± 3.5	3.4 ± 0.3

[a] Adapted from McDermott et al., 1978.
[b] $p < 0.01$.
[c] $p < 0.05$.

affected may be vulnerable because of their being in close proximity to an extra-neural toxic factor (e.g., lead, aluminum or an antibody). Oxygen deprivation, already implicated in the rarer dementia Huntington's chorea (Bowen, Goodhardt, Strong, Smith, White, Branston, Symon and Davison, 1976b), may be another factor, for the pattern of hippocampal damage is similar in hypoxic and Alzheimer brain (Ball, 1978). Organo-tin compounds, which inhibit glucose oxidation (Lock, 1976), cause selective damage in hippocampus (Brown, Aldridge and Street, 1978). However, since the Sommer sector is spared, the foci of damage do not correspond to that seen in Alzheimer's disease. Plum (1978) points out that there is little evidence to support the view that chronic hypoxia underlies the brain changes of Alzheimer's disease. There are other reasons for believing that vascular anatomy may not be directly involved, for the selectivity may be due to loss of a specific type of neuron.

α-aminobutyrate (GABA)

In cases of senile dementia apparent loss of glutamate decarboxylase (GAD; a marker of GABA-containing neurons) in the neocortex can be related to a combination of terminal bronchopneumonia and reduced cerebral blood flow (Bowen, Smith, White and Davison, 1976a). Although Perry, Gibson, Blessed, Perry and Tomlinson (1977) believe that there may be some reduction in glutamate decarboxylase activity other than that due to the terminal state of the patient, this reduction may be related to alterations in cerebral function of a more general nature. Preliminary results show GAD activity to be within the normal range in biopsy samples of Alzheimer's disease, yet autopsy data suggests that GABA receptors are reduced (Table 6).

Acetylcholine

In the frontal cortex Bowen et al. (1976a) found a marked reduction in CAT activity (a marker of cholinergic neurons) which was related to the

Table 6. Markers of Neocortical GABA Transmitter Pathways in Dementia

Variable	Control	Dementia Due to Alzheimer's Disease	Dementia Not Due to Alzheimer's Disease
GAD (nmol/100 mg protein/min, ± S.D.)[a]	7.86 ± 2.68 (9)	8.99, 7.85	6.53, 7.43
GABA binding (nmol/g protein, ± S.E.M.)[b]	1800 ± 79 (3)	913 ± 86[c] (4)	n.d.

[a] Spillane (1978) and [b] Reisine et al. (1978), both presenile and senile age range cases were examined.

[c] Significantly lower than control ($p < 0.05$).

degree of pathological damage (Table 7) and hence possibly to the dementia (Figure 1). GAD activity does not appear to be related to either the intensity of senile degeneration or mental test score. CAT is particularly reduced in the hippocampus but the caudate nucleus is relatively spared (Bowen et al., 1976a, Perry et al., 1977). In addition to the reduction in cholinergic marker from the neocortex in post-mortem samples, there was a significant reduction in enzyme activity in biopsy specimens from Alzheimer patients (Figure 2). Davies and Maloney (1976) also found a reduction in acetylcholinesterase activity in the brain of demented patients. However, no significant difference in post-synaptic muscarinic cholinergic receptor concentration was apparent in the brain of age-matched control subjects and those with senile dementia (White, Hiley, Goodhardt, Carrasco, Keet, Williams and Bowen, 1977), except in the hippocampus in one study (Reisine, Yamamura, Bird, Spokes and Enna, 1978), but not another (Davies and Verth, 1978).

Monoamine Neurotransmitters

Other transmitter systems appear also to be affected but to a lesser extent. Serotonergic markers are reduced (Bowen et al., 1979) and catecholamine metabolism may be diminished. Dopamine and noradrenaline concentrations have been found to be lower in different areas of post-mortem brain from Alzheimer's patients (Winblad, Adolfsson, Gottfries, Oreland and Roos, 1978) and some years ago Gottfries, Gottfries and Roos (1969) demonstrated a significant reduction in the dopamine metabolite, homovanillic acid, in Alzheimer's cases compared to controls. Histochemical results (Berger, Escourolle and Mayne, 1976) also suggest that noradrenergic and dopaminergic cells are affected and L-

Table 7. CAT and Senile Degeneration in Neocortex in "Senile Dementia of Alzheimer's Type" (SDAT)[a]

Diagnosis	CAT Activity (nmol/g Tissue/min)	Senile Degeneration[b] (Rel. Score)
Control	5.40 ± 1.23 (7)	–
SDAT		
Patient 1	3.87	1.0
Patient 2	3.57	1.5
Patient 3	2.78	1.5
Patient 4	2.22	3.0
Patient 5	2.05	1.8
Patient 6	2.03	3.0

[a] Adapted from Bowen et al. (1976).

[b] Mean of relative scores for senile plaque formation and NFD. Scored on a scale 0 - 3 (none to severe).

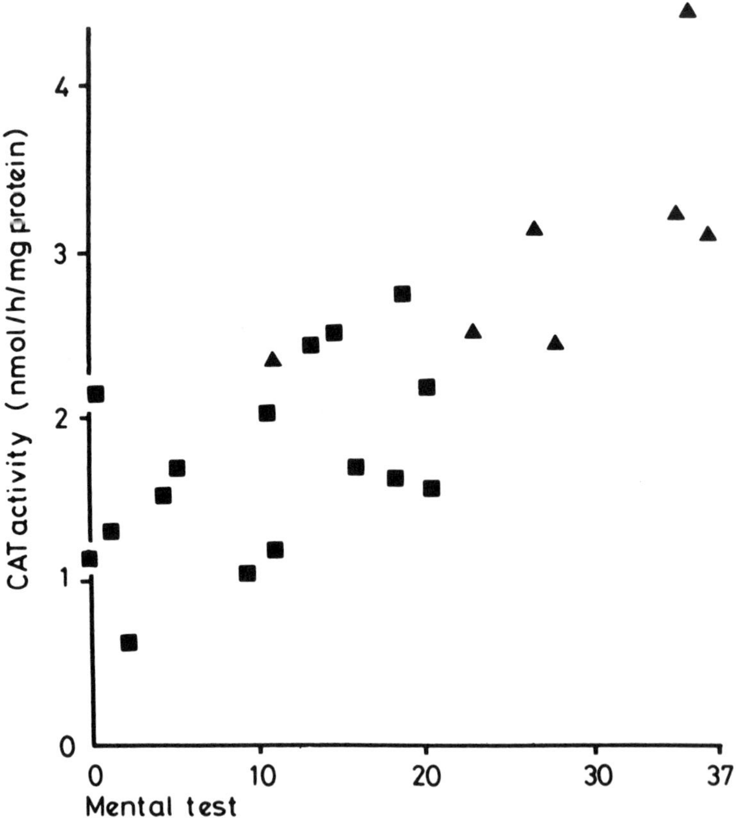

Figure 1. Relationship between neocortical CAT activity and mental test score ($r = 0.81$, $p < 0.001$) in "Senile dementia of Alzheimer's type" (■) and depressed patients (▲).

ADAPTED FROM: *Perry, Tomlinson, Blessed, Bergman, Gibson and Perry (1978).*

dopa therapy is reported to be of benefit (Lewis, Ballinger and Presly, 1978). Davies and Malone (1976), however, comment that tyrosine hydroxylase activity, the rate limiting enzyme in catecholamine synthesis, is not reduced.

Further work is needed on markers of catecholamine-containing neurons in *histologically* assessed Alzheimer brain tissue. An additional impetus for such studies is that there are some indications that serum biopterin may be strikingly low in demented patients (Leeming, Blair and Malikian, 1979). Tetrahydrobiopterin (TH_4) is the essential co-factor donating hydrogen for the rate-limiting enzymes tyrosine and tryptophan hydroxylases. Dihydropteridine reductase, which catalyzes the formation of TH_4 is inhibited by aluminum (Leeming and Blair, 1979). The relevance of reduced serum biopterin to the brain disease is difficult to assess for

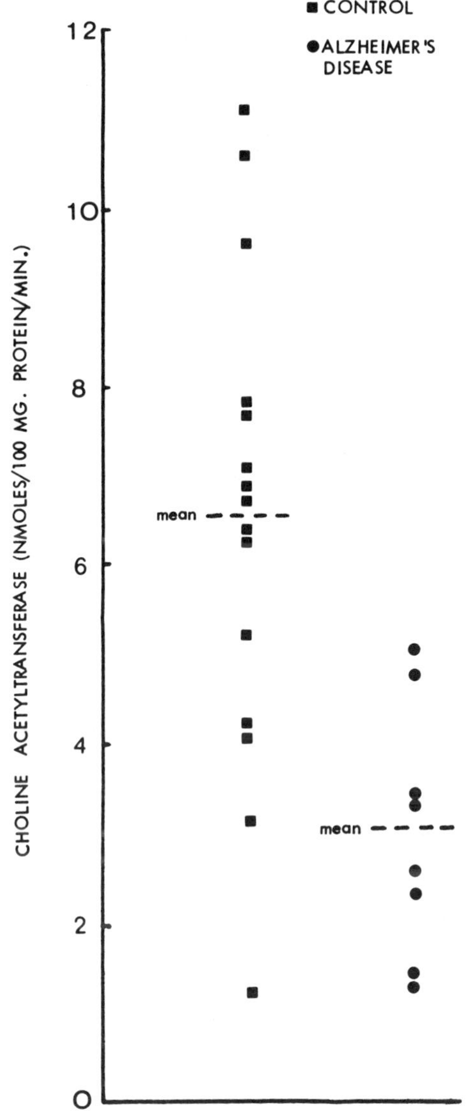

Figure 2. CAT activities in neocortex from cortical biopsies. Mean values differ significantly. ($p < 0.01$).

ADAPTED FROM: *Bowen et al., (1979).*

TH_4 can probably be synthesized by the brain (Gal, Bybee and Sherman, 1979).

The high affinity binding of dihydroaloprenolol (Bowen et al., 1979) is not reduced in Alzheimer brain, suggesting that β-adrenergic receptors are spared.

Other Neurotransmitters

Apart from GABA no other putative amino acid transmitter has been investigated in senile dementia. Few of the 15 or so neuropeptides that may be considered candidates for a modulator or transmitter role in the brain have been investigated. Opiate receptors appear not to be reduced in the temporal lobe. Angiotensin converting enzyme is age-dependent in Alzheimer cases but not in controls of similar age (Bowen et al., 1979). Immunoreactivity to vasoactive intestinal peptide, which is concentrated in the cortex, is reduced in cerebrospinal fluid (CSF) from cases with cerebral atrophy (Fahrenkrug, Schaffalitzky de Muckadell and Fahrenkrug, 1977). Vasopressin should perhaps be studied for it acts on selected brain regions, including the hippocampus, facilitating the consolidation of memory (Wimersma-Greidanus and de Weid, 1977) and may be of use in human memory disorders (Legros, Gilot, Seron, Claessars, Adams, Moeglen, Audibert and Berchier, 1978; Oliveros, Jandali, Trinsit-Berthier, Nemy, Benghezal, Audibert and Moeglen, 1978).

Summary and Conclusions

Neurophysiological studies, such as cerebral blood flow measurements, suggest that in Alzheimer's disease, neuronal metabolism is altered. The findings of Ingvar and Lassen (1976) are particularly interesting, for in the demented, the augmentation of flow during attempted activation by reading and psychological tests was less than normal, and in some cases the blow flow was even diminished. The question remains as to whether Alzheimer's disease is similar to normal aging, for changes during the latter appear to alter the capacity of the brain to respond to increasing energy demands (Sylvia and Rosenthal, 1979).

The cholinergic system appears to be affected at an early stage in the pathogenesis of Alzheimer's disease, for CAT activity is reduced in both biopsy specimens and in post-mortem material from less severely impaired patients (Bowen et al., 1979). These observations, taken with the correspondance between CAT activity, senile degeneration and mental state, suggest that the depletion in activity is of clinical significance. Although controversial (Butler, Drachman and Goldberg, 1978), there is evidence that CAT activity is altered by changes in nerve impulse activity (Bowen, 1979). The enzyme may not be critical in regulating acetylcholine synthesis, for studies on animal brain indicate it is present in excess. It appears that acetylcholine synthesis is primarily regulated by choline transport through a sodium-dependent high affinity uptake system. This process is energy-dependent, being reduced by metabolic inhibitors and enhanced by dextrose (Kuhar and Murrin, 1978). It is of interest, too, that the choline uptake system, like cerebral blood flow, appears to be coupled to neuronal activity. There is a decrease in choline uptake following administration of anesthetics and drugs known to reduce acetylcholine synthesis. Where drugs increase acetylcholine turnover there is an increase in choline uptake. For these reasons treatment with choline (Levy, 1978), choline agonists or with centrally acting anticholinesterases (Smith and Swash, 1979) may only be partially successful. There are some discrepancies in experimental studies on choline utilization, for although Flentge and Van den Berg (1979) found increased choline in the brain of rats given choline intraperitoneally, there was no increase in acetylcholine concentration in the brain. Moreover, there is a decrease in the synthesis of acetylcholine following mild hypoxia (Gibson, Blass and Jenden, 1978). It would, therefore, seem possible that drugs stimulating neuronal metabolism would enhance acetylcholine synthesis, providing sufficient choline were available (even though choline acetyltransferase activity was reduced). This interesting possibility remains to be investigated, particularly in cases of Alzheimer's disease in which the deficiency in CAT has been demonstrated at biopsy and where the diagnosis has been confirmed histologically.

Although GAD and tyrosine hydroxylase activities may be spared, there is evidence that serotonin and GABA receptors are reduced indicating that transmitter pathways, other than the cholinergic system, are involved in pathogenesis. Evidence for interaction between the cholinergic and serotonergic systems has recently been reported (MacDermot, Higashida, Wilson, Mutsuzawa, Minna and Nirenberg, 1979).

References

Ball MJ: Neuronal loss, neurofibrillary tangles and granulovacuolar degeneration in the hippocampus with aging and dementia. *Acta Neuropathology (Berlin)* 37:111–118, 1978.

Ball MJ: Topographic distribution of neurofibrillary tangles and granulovacuolar degeneration in hippocampal cortex of aging and demented patients. A quantitative study. *Acta Neuropathology (Berlin)* 42:73–80, 1978.

Ball MJ, Vis CL: Relationship of granulovacuolar degeneration in hippocampal neurons to aging and to dementia in normal pressure hydrocephalics. *J Gerontology* 33–41, 1978.

Berger B, Escourolle R, Moyne MA: Axones, caticholaminergues du cortex cérébral humain. *Rev Neurologie (Paris)* 136:183, 1976.

Bowen DM, Smith CB, White P, Davison AN: Neurotransmitter-related enzymes and indices of hypoxia in senile dementia and other abiotrophies. *Brain* 99:459–496, 1976a.

Bowen DM, Goodhardt MJ, Strong AJ, Smith CB, White P, Branston NM, Symon L, Davison AN: Biochemical indices of brain structure, function and "hypoxia" in cortex from baboons with middle cerebral artery occlusion. *Brain Research* 117:503–507, 1976b.

Bowen DM, Smith CB, White P, Flack RHA, Carrasco L, Gedye JL, Davison AN: Chemical pathology of the organic dementias. II. Quantitative estimation of cellular changes in post-mortem brains. *Brain* 100:427–453, 1977.

Bowen DM, White P, Spillane JA, Goodhardt MJ, Curzon G, Iwangoff P, Meier-Ruge W, Davison AN: Accelerated aging or selective neuronal loss as an important cause of dementia? *Lancet* i:5, 1979.

Bowen DM: Biochemistry of Alzheimer's Disease. In Curzon G (ed.) *The Biochemistry of Psychiatric Disturbances*. John Wiley, 1979, in press.

Brown AW, Aldridge WN, Street BW: Selective neuronal destruction in rat brain following intoxication with trimethyltin chloride. *Neuropathology and Applied Neurobiology* 5:83, 1979.

Butler IJ, Drachman DB, Goldberg AM: The effect of disuse of cholinergic enzymes. *J Physiology* 274:593–600, 1978.

Cohen EL, Wurtman RJ: Brain acetylcholine; increase after systemic choline administration. *Life Sciences* 16:1095–1102, 1975.

Colon EJ; The cerebral cortex in pre-senile dementia. *Acta Neuropathology (Berlin)* 23:281–290, 1973.

Corsellis JAN: Aging and the dementias. In Blackwood W, Corsellis JAN (eds.) *Greenfield's Neuropathology*. London, Edward Arnold, 1976, pp. 796–848.

Davies P, Maloney AJF: Selective loss of central cholinergic neurons in Alzheimer's disease. *Lancet* ii:1403, 1976.

Davies P, Verth AH: Regional distribution of muscarinic acetylcholine receptor in normal and Alzheimer's-type dementia brains. *Brain Research* 138:385–392, 1978.

De Boni N, Crapper DR: Paired helical filaments of the Alzheimer-type in cultured neurons. *Nature* 271:566–568, 1978.

Fahrenkrug J, Schaffalitzky de Muckadell OB, Fahrenkrug A: Vasoactive intestinal peptide (V.I.P.) in human cerebrospinal fluid. *Brain Research* 124:581–584, 1977.

Flentge F, Van den Berg CJ: Choline administration and acetylcholine in brains. *J Neurochemistry* 32:1331–1333, 1978.

Gal EM, Bybee JA, Sherman AD: De novo synthesis of dihydrobiopterin: evidence for its quinoid structure and lack of dependence of its reduction to tetrahydrobiopterin by dihydrofolate reductase. *J Neurochemistry* 32:179–186, 1979.

Gibson GE, Blass JP, Jenden DJ: Measurement of acetylcholine turnover with glucose used as precursor: evidence for compartmentation of glucose metabolism in brain. *J Neurochemistry* 30:71–76, 1978.

Gonatas NK, Gambetti P: The pathology of the synapse in Alzheimer's disease. In Wolstenholme GEW, O'Connor M (eds.) *Alzheimer's Disease and Related Conditions*. London, Churchill, 1970, pp. 169–183.

Gottfries CG, Gottfries I, Roos BE: The investigations of homovanillic acid in the human brain and its correlation to senile dementia. *Brit J Psychiatry* 115:563–574, 1969.

Grubb RL, Raichle ME, Gado MH, Eichling JO, Hughes CP: Cerebral blood flow, oxygen utilization and blood volume in dementia. *Neurology* 27:905–910, 1977.

Grundke-Iqbal I, Johnson AB, Wisniewski HM, Terry RD, Iqbal K: Evidence that Alzheimer neurofibrillary tangles originate from neurotubules. *Lancet* i:578–580, 1979.

Hachinski VC, Iliff M, Zilkha E, duBouley GH, McAllister VL, Marshall J, Ross Russell RW, Syman L: Cerebral blood flow in dementia. *Arch Neurology* 32:632–637, 1975.

Ingvar DH, Gustafson L: Regional blood flow in organic dementia with early onset. *Acta Neurology, Scandinavia* Suppl 46, 1970.

Ingvar DH, Lassen NA: Regulation of cerebral blood flow. In Himwich HE (ed.) *Brain Metabolism and Cerebral Disorders*. New York, Spectrum Publications, 1976, pp. 181–206.

Iqbal K, Wisniewski HM, Grundke-Iqbal I, Terry RD: Neurofibrillary pathology: an update. In Nandy K, Sherwin I (eds.) *The Aging Brain and Senile Dementia*. New York, Plenum Press, 1977, pp. 209–227.

Ishii T, Haga S: Immuno-electron microscopic localization of immunoglobulins in amyloid fibril of senile plaques. *Acta Neuropathology (Berlin)* 36:243–250, 1976.

Johannesson G, Brun A, Gustafson I, Ingvar DH: EEG in presenile dementia related to cerebral blood flow and autopsy findings. *Acta Neurology, Scandinavia* 56:89–103, 1977.

Kazniak AW, Fox J, Gandell DL, Garron DC, Huckman MS, Ramsey RG: Predictors of mortality in presenile and senile dementia. *Annals of Neurology* 3:246–252, 1978.

Kidd M: Paired helical filaments in electron microscopy in Alzheimer's disease. *Nature* 197:192–193, 1963.

Kuhar MJ, Murrin LC: Sodium-dependent high affinity choline uptake. *J Neurochemistry* 30:15–21, 1978.

Lange H, Thorner G, Hopf A, Schröder KF: Morpometric studies of the neuropathological changes in choreatic diseases. *J Neurological Sciences* 28:401–425, 1976.

Leaton RN: The limbic system and its pharmacological aspects. In Rech RH, Moore KE (eds.) *An Introduction to Psychopharmacology.* New York, Raven Press, 1971, pp. 137–174.

Leeming RJ, Blair JA, Melikan V: Biopterin derivatives in senile dementia. *Lancet* i:215, 1979.

Leeming RJ, Blair JA: Dialysis dementia, aluminum and tetrahydrobiopterin metabolism. *Lancet* i:556, 1979.

Legros JJ, Gilot P, Seron X, Claessens J, Adam A, Moeglen JM, Audibert A, Berchier P: Influence of vasopressin on learning and memory. *Lancet* i:41–42, 1978.

Levy R: Choline in Alzheimer's disease. *Lancet* ii:944–945, 1978.

Lewis C, Ballinger BR, Presley AS: Trial of levodopa in senile dementia. *Br Medical J* 1:550, 1978.

Lock EA: The action of triethyltin on the respiration of rat brain cortex slices. *J Neurochemistry* 26:887–892, 1976.

MacDermot J, Higashida H, Wilson SP, Matsuzawa H, Minna J, Nirenberg M: Adenylate cyclase and acetylcholine release regulated by separate serotonin receptors of somatic cell lines. *Proc. National Academy of Science, USA* 76:1135–1139, 1979.

Mann DMA, Sinclair KGA: The quantitative assessment of lipofuscin pigment, cytoplasmic RNA and nucleolar volume in senile dementia. *Neuropathology and Applied Neurobiology* 4:129–135, 1978.

Marsden CG, Harrison MJG: Outcome of investigation of patients with presenile dementia. *Brit Med J* 2:249–254, 1972.

Mayer PP, Chugtai MA, Cape RDT: An immunological approach to dementia in the elderly. *Age and Aging* 5:164–170, 1976.

McDermott JR, Smith AI, Iqbal K, Wisniewski HM: Alzheimer's disease and brain aluminum level. *Lancet* ii:701–711, 1977.

McDermott JR, Fraser H, Dickinson AG: Reduced choline acetyltransferase activity in scrapie mouse brain. *Lancet* ii:318–319, 1978.

Mehraein P, Yamada M, Tarnowski-Dzidusyko E: Quantitative studies on dendrites and dendritic spines in Alzheimer's disease and senile dementia. In Kreutzberg GW (ed.) *Advances in Neurology* Vol. 12: The Physiology and Pathology of Dendrites. New York, Raven Press, 1975, pp. 453–458.

Melamed E, Lavy S, Siew F, Bentin S, Cooper G: Correlation between regional cerebral blood flow and brain atrophy in dementia. Combined study with ^{133}xenon inhalation and computerized tomography. *J Neurology, Neurosurgery and Psychiatry* 41:894–899, 1978.

Mirjakawa T, Sumiyashi S, Murayama E: Capillary plaque-like degeneration in senile dementia. *Acta Neuropathology (Berlin)* 29:229–236, 1974.

Nandy K: Brain-reactive antibodies in aging and senile dementia. In Katzman R, Terry RD, Bick KL (eds.) *Alzheimer's Disease: Senile Dementia and Related Disorders*. New York, Raven Press, 1978, pp. 503–512.

Niklowitz WJ: Neurofibrillary changes after acute experimental lead poisoning. *Neurology* 25:927–934, 1975.

Oliveros JC, Jandali MK, Timsit-Berthier M, Remy R, Benghesal A, Audibert A, Moeglen JM: Vasopressin in amnesia. *Lancet* i:42, 1978.

Pearce J, Miller E: *Clinical Aspects of Dementia*. Baltimore, Williams and Wilkins, 1973.

Perry EK, Perry RH, Blessed G, Tomlinson BE: Neurotransmitter enzyme abnormalities in senile dementia—choline acetyltransferase and glutamic acid decarboxylase in necropsy brain tissue. *J Neurological Science* 34:247–265, 1977.

Perry EK, Tomlinson BE, Blessed G, Bergmann K, Gibson PH, Perry RH: Correlation of cholinergic abnormalities with senile plaques and mental test scores in senile dementia. *Brit Medical J* 2:1457–1459, 1978.

Plum F: Metabolic dementias. In Katzman R, Terry RD, Bick KL (eds.) *Alzheimer's Disease: Senile and Related Disorders*. New York, Raven Press, 1978, pp. 135–139.

Plum F: Dementia: an approaching epidemic. *Nature* 279:372–373, 1979.

Reisine TD, Yamamura H, Bird ED, Spokes E, Enna SJ: Pre- and post-synaptic neurochemical alterations in Alzheimer's disease. *Brain Research* 159:477–482, 1978.

Scheibel AB, Tomlinson U: Dendritic sprouting in Alzheimer's senile presenile dementia. *Experimental Neurology* 60:1–8, 1978.

Smith CM, Swash M: Physostigmine in Alzheimer's disease. *Lancet* i:42, 1979.

Spillane JA: Alzheimer's disease: a state of cholinergic deficiency. M.D. Thesis, University of London, 1978.

Suzuki K, Korey SR, Terry RD: Studies on protein synthesis in brain microsound system. *J Neurochemistry* 11:403–412, 1964.

Suzuki K, Katzman R, Korey SR: Chemical studies on Alzheimer's disease. *J Neuropathology and Experimental Neurology* 24:211–223, 1965.

Sylvia AL, Rosenthal M: Effects of age on brain oxidative metabolism *in vivo*. *Brain Research* 165:235–248, 1979.

Tomlinson BE: Morphological changes and dementia in old age. In Smith WL, Kinsbourne M (eds.) *Aging and Dementia*. New York, Spectrum, 1977, pp. 25–56.

Traub R, Gajdusek DC, Gibbs Jr CJ: Transmission virus dementia: the relation of transmissible spongiform encephalopathy to Creutzfeld-Jakob disease. In Smith WL, Kinsbourne M (eds.) *Aging and Dementia*. New York, Spectrum, 1977, pp. 91–169.

Uemura E, Hartmann HA: RNA content and volume of nerve cell bodies in human brain. 1. Prefrontal cortex in aging normal and demented patients. *J Neuropath Expt Neurol* 37:487–496, 1978.

Wang HS: Dementia in old. In Wells CE (ed.) *Dementia* 2nd edition. Philadelphia, F.A. Davis, 1977, pp. 15–26.

White P, Hiley CR, Goodhardt MJ, Carrasco HL, Keet JP, Williams IEI, Bowen DM: Neocortical cholinergic neurons in elderly people. *Lancet* i:668–670, 1977.

Wimersma-Greidanus TJB, de Weid D: The physiology of the neurohypophysical system and its relation to memory processes. In Davison AN (ed.) *Biochemical Correlates of Brain Structure and Function*. London, Academic Press, 1977, pp. 215–248.

Winblad B, Adolfsson R, Gottfries CG, Oreland L, Roos BE: Brain monoamines, monoamine metabolites and enzymes in physiological aging and senile dementia. In Frigerio A (ed.) *Recent Developments in Mass Spectrometry in Biochemistry and Medicine*. New York, Plenum Press, 1978, pp. 253–267.

Stein, ed. The Psychobiology of Aging: Problems and Perspectives

Memory, Aging, and Pharmacosystems

David A. Drachman and B. J. Sahakian

Department of Neurology, University of Massachusetts Medical Center, Worcester, Massachusetts

The Psychobiology of Aging

Approaches to the Study of Memory

For most neuroscientists an understanding of the neurobiology of memory has been elusive. Two major obstacles have impeded a clear grasp of the subject: first, the difficult in agreeing upon the definition of what is meant by "memory" (Richter, 1966); and second, the fact that the study of memory must be conducted simultaneously at several different levels of scientific investigation. Divergent disciplines are involved whose differing vocabularies are an obstacle to easy communication. To illustrate these points, consider how one can encompass both the *memory* loss of an elderly patient in a nursing home, and the *memory* resulting from training of the dorsal ganglion of a cockroach, within a single coherent scheme. What is the connection between the psychological observations in the human and the biochemical and physiological observations in the insect ganglion? And finally, how should basic neuroscientists approach the complex disorders of human memory, or neurologists utilize the fundamental findings in simple arrays of nerve cells?

To deal with these questions, it is necessary: 1. to define what is meant by "memory"; and 2. to distinguish the levels at which memory, as a psychological function, can be related to the brain, as a physical organ.

In 1892, William James observed that "Memory proper . . . is the knowledge of a former state of mind after it has already dropped from consciousness . . .". Memory is thus concerned with the fact that experience alters subsequent behavior and, therefore, that *some change must have occurred within the brain*. It can be further defined to include the *operations* or *processes* by which both *incorporation of information*, and *access to that information*, takes place. Both *psychological* and *physical* processes are involved. By definition memory must also include the *contents* of information—the "software," or "memories" which have been stored as a result of prior experience.

Having defined memory in this manner, it is important to consider the levels of neural functioning at which these memory operations and contents may be related to the brain (Table 1). The most fundamental approach has been the study of the *ultimate basis of memory*, or of "plasticity" (neural changes resulting from behavioral experience) within the brain. Here the molecular, synaptic, and physiological bases of producing an enduring record have been studied (Eccles, 1965; Kosower, 1972); the brain has been regarded as a *tissue*, much like the liver, containing innumerable repeating cellular or molecular components, each capable of undergoing lasting change as the result of experience. At the next level the *gross substrate of memory* is considered. Here the brain is regarded as an *ensemble of organs*, or anatomically definable structures, some of which perform particular operations that result in the storage of information (Barbizet, 1970; Kinsbourne, 1971). A third approach has been the search for the representation of information in the brain, or the "*nature of the engram*." Engrams are presumed to consist of *large arrays of neurons* in whose terminals changes have taken place, to facilitate neurotransmission. Collectively, these changes result in patterns of neural activity that are the physical or physiological counterparts of stored information, and learned behaviors. Finally, a complete comprehension of brain/memory relationships must include an awareness of the mechanisms by which a variety of disease processes produce *memory disruption*. Classically, disorders of the nervous system that impair human memory have provided invaluable insights into the normal memory and cognitive functions of the brain (Barbizet, 1970; Richter, 1966).

In a brief overview, it is impossible to do more than touch upon the knowledge regarding the nature of memory that has been accumulated at each of these levels of neurobiological investigation. However, it is worth pointing out that most investigators believe that changes in

Table 1. Memory and the Brain: Levels of Neural Function

1. The ultimate basis of memory; the brain as a uniform tissue.
2. The gross substrate of memory; the brain as an ensemble of organs.
3. The nature of the engram; patterns of neuronal arrays.
4. Disorders of memory; natural diseases of the human brain.

synaptic connectivity are the ultimate substrate for plasticity in the nervous system (Mark, 1974; Roberts, 1965). Anatomical, biochemical, physiological and pharmacological changes in the synapse have all been considered in this context. At the gross anatomical level, the limbic system, and particularly the hippocampal complexes, as well as the "temporal stem" (Horel, 1978) and certain thalamic nuclei (Barbizet, 1963, 1970; Brierley, 1966; see Drachman and Arbit, 1966; Penfield and Milner, 1958; Victor et al., 1961), have been noted to play special roles in the storage of information. The site of information storage has included, at the least, much of the "association cortex" of the cerebral hemispheres, with regional and lateralized specialization. The nature of the engram is still poorly understood, although it is now widely accepted that memories are not stored as specific coded macromolecules. Rather, these "complex perceptual and cognitive processes involve dynamic integration of vast regions of the brain," as described by John and Schwartz (1978). In our view, sequenced patterns of neural activity are the most likely basis for information storage in the brain. These patterns, once stored by multiple synaptic facilitation, remain ready to be played, like magnetic tape recordings, in response to the appropriate stimulus.

A complete understanding of the neurobiology of memory requires comprehension not only of the nature of the behavioral or psychological aspects of memory processes, but also of the neural processes that underlie such behavior, from the molecular to the clinical neurological level.

Clinical Disorders of Memory

A number of neurological disorders have been noted to produce memory impairment; brain tumors, cerebrovascular accidents, head injuries, herpes simplex encephalitis, Wernicke-Korsakoff's psychosis, and dementia, to name a few (Haase, 1977). Most notably, patients with bilateral lesions of the hippocampal complexes due to a variety of etiologies, have provided especially valuable insights into brain/memory relationships (Drachman and Arbit, 1966; Penfield and Milner, 1958; Victor et al, 1961). This is so because relatively circumscribed brain lesions have produced quite isolated abnormalities involving a single phase of memory, leaving other aspects of cognitive functioning strikingly intact. In many ways, anatomical/psychological correlation has provided the cornerstone for establishing the biological basis of certain memory functions (Drachman and Arbit, 1966).

The relationship between lesions of the hippocampal complexes are marked; isolated memory impairment was first recognized by Scoville and Milner (1957). These authors noted impairment of learning in patients who had undergone bilateral surgical resections of the temporal lobes as a treatment for intractible epilepsy. Drachman and Adams (1962) later observed similar memory defects in patients who had recovered from herpes simplex encephalitis, a necrotizing infectious process which produces severe damage of the hippocampal complexes. These patients and those of Scoville and Milner had normal IQs, and appeared neurologically intact except for their inability to learn new information. Drachman and Ommaya (1964) then studied rhesus monkeys who had undergone bilateral resections of the hippocampal complex. The monkeys were also impaired in their ability to learn new information, but had normal immediate memory (i.e., ability to respond to cues after a delay). Returning to the study of human subjects with hippocampal lesions, Drachman and Arbit (1966) designed a battery of tests to distinguish between immediate memory and storage, as well as other non-memory cognitive functions. They demonstrated that immediate memory, as determined by digit spans and spans of paired light-sequences, was unimpaired in patients with hippocampal lesions. Such patients, however, were completely unable to store information that *exceeded* their memory spans even after unlimited repetitions. Furthermore, these patients showed no impairment in other intellectual functions as determined by the standard Wechsler Adult Intelligence Scale (WAIS) and its subtests (Wechsler, 1955) (Figure 1).

These studies as well as those of other authors, established the fact that the hippocampal complexes are crucial to the storage of new information (Brierley, 1966; Scoville and Milner, 1957; Victor et al., 1961). Further, they supported the position that memory must consist of at least three separate components—immediate memory, storage, and old memory stores; and that only memory storage (acquisition) was dependent on the hippocampal complexes. These investigations gave biological validity to the concept that memory functions are a property of brain, depending on specific neural structures; and they aided in defining the limits of each phase of memory.

Other studies have demonstrated the relation of additional neural structures, including the dorsomedian nuclei of the thalamus, the mammillary bodies, the pulvinar and the corpus callosum, to memory functions (Adams, 1969; Brion, 1969; Sperry, 1975). However, the totality of structure/function relationships that involve the brain and memory fail to explain more than a small fraction of the clinically evident disorders of memory. Lesions of the hippocampal complexes are rare; thalamic and mammillary lesions are only marginally more common. Overall, the recognition that damage to certain anatomically defined brain structures may impair memory functions has not provided an understanding of the overwhelmingly common memory disorders—those that occur with *normal aging,* and in the *dementias*.

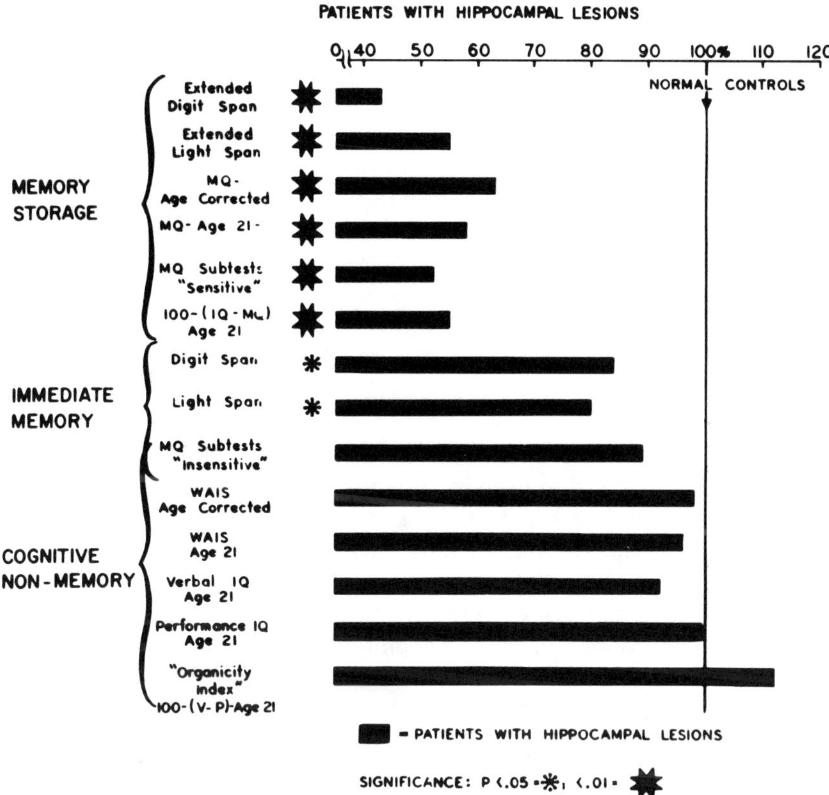

Figure 1. Psychometric test battery, HC patients compared with controls. HC patients show marked impairment of memory storage, contrasting with only slight impairment of immediate memory and normal cognitive nonmemory performance.

Aging and the Dementias

The complaint of impairment of memory is common in a large proportion of normal aged individuals, and many studies have documented the differences in the ability of young and elderly subjects to learn new information. In addition, it is known that temporal electroencephalographic (EEG) abnormalities, with both slow and sharp activity, are frequently found in aged individuals (Busse and Obrist, 1963; Kooi et al, 1964; Obrist, 1954; Obrist and Busse, 1965).

To test the hypothesis that lesions of the hippocampal complexes might account for both the memory impairment and the temporal EEG changes of the aged, and to characterize the nature of the cognitive deficit, we studied the M/C performances of normal aged adults (59-89 years of age) and correlated them with electroencephalographic recordings (Drachman and Hughes, 1971). A test battery similar to that first used in patients with hippocampal lesions was used. The battery included tests of immediate memory span; storage of supraspan lists of digits and words; retrieval of information from old store (e.g., animals, girls' names, etc.); and the WAIS. Scores derived from the WAIS (including the Verbal IQ and Performance IQ scores) were corrected to a base age of 21 to permit direct comparison of the aged group with the young group. In addition, an "Organicity Index" was calculated (OI = 100 − (V − P)) to indicate the difference between the Verbal (V) and Performance (P) IQ of each subject, a score of 100 indicating that Verbal and Performance scores were equal.

From Figure 2 it is clear that aged subjects show a different pattern of M/C impairment from that seen in patients with HC lesions. Impairment of memory storage is evident, as is seen in the HC patients; but *un*like the HC patients, the storage impairment is not as severe, and Performance IQ, Full-scale IQ and Organicity Index all show significant impairment as well. The pattern of cognitive function in the aged subjects is, therefore, one of more widespread cognitive impairment, rather than the isolated memory storage deficit of the HC patients. And, when EEG abnormalities of the temporal region are compared with cognitive changes in the elderly, they fail to correlate with memory impairment. Rather, they show a striking relationship to impairments on the Organicity Index (Drachman and Hughes, 1971). This indicates that the M/C deficit of the elderly, and the corresponding electroencephalographic changes, do not reflect underlying lesions of the hippocampal complexes, but rather suggest a more widespread and diffuse cerebral impairment.

In addition to the *normal impairment of cognitive* function that takes place with aging, *dementing disorders* may occur in the elderly and produce even greater disruption of memory and intellectual function, resulting in a significant degree of disability. It is estimated that almost 5% of the surviving population over age 65 will be totally disabled by dementia, while another 11% are partially dependent because of their loss of intellectual abilities (Katzman, 1976; Wang, 1977). Of these patients, at least half owe the major cause of their cognitive impairment to Alzheimer's Disease. It is still debatable whether this most common cause of dementia is a specific disease process or merely an accelerated example of normal neuronal attrition; i.e., whether it is qualitatively or quantitatively different from normal aging (Katzman, 1976; Tomlinson and Henderson, 1976; Wang, 1977). The pathology is well-recognized, however, and has been described with care from the gross to the

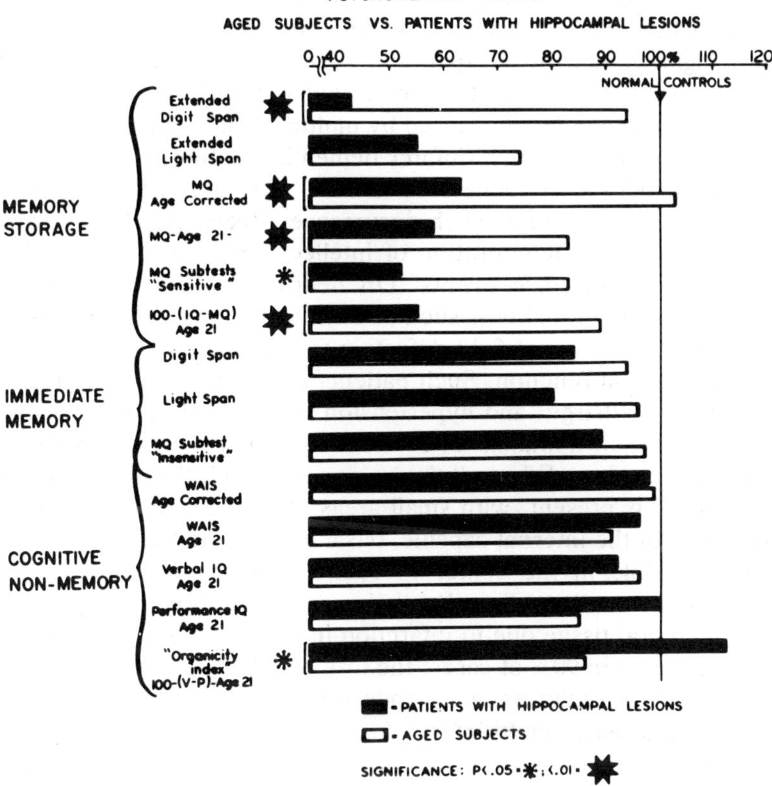

Figure 2. Psychometric test battery, HC patients compared with aged subjects. HC patients perform far worse on tests of memory storage and slightly better than aged subjects on nonmemory tests.

ultrastructural level (Corsellis, 1976; Terry and Wisniewski, 1975, 1977; Tomlinson, 1977; Tomlinson and Henderson, 1976). Briefly, it is characterized by the occurrence of neurofibrillary tangles in neurons, particularly in the hippocampal regions; cortical senile plaques, consisting of an amyloid core surrounded by degenerating neurites (dendritic and axonal processes); granulovacuolar degeneration of hippocampal neurons; and perhaps loss of dendritic spines. Surprisingly, although there is considerable loss of neurons with aging, there is little if any increase in neuronal loss in Alzheimer's Disease (Katzman, Terry, and Bick, 1978, see Discussion, pp. 396–399).

Clinically, Alzheimer's disease often begins as a "lucid dementia," with impaired cognitive functions, but no change in the sensorium or state of consciousness. Subtle changes in judgment, decisiveness and memory are often the earliest symptoms of this condition. Loss of interest and energy occur as well, overlapping with the symptoms of depression, which may accompany the patient's awareness of his failing intellect. Cognitive decline is rapid, and within two or three years most patients are unable to care for themselves independently.

Dementia is also commonly caused by multiple small cerebral infarcts. Clinically, the picture of multi-infarct dementia is often ushered in by short-lived episodes of weakness of a limb, difficulty with speech or dizziness. After two or three such occurrences, there may be a steady downhill course, with deterioration of intellect in the absence of additional clear cut neurologic events. On neurological examination the stigmata of focal abnormalities, such as asymmetry of reflex responses, mild hemiparesis, or visual field defects may accompany the finding of impaired intellectual function. Such patients often show some degree of bradyphrenia or lethargy; and hypertension is commonly present. Pathologically, the classical findings of cerebral infarctions—usually multiple and small—are evident. When all the lesions are small, the picture of the "lacunar state" is present, with small areas of cerebral softening found predominantly in the internal capsule, basal ganglia and thalamus, and a thickened arteriole in the center of each lesion. Tomlinson and his coworkers have found in clinical/pathological correlations that the loss of 50cc of cerebral tissue due to infarction in patients over the age of 65 results in dementia in 90% of cases; the loss of 100cc produces dementia in virtually 100% (Tomlinson and Henderson, 1976).

Alzheimer's Disease, multi-infarct dementia, or a combination of the two account for almost 85% of all dementias. The other causes, too numerous to discuss in detail here, include a variety of etiologies such as mass lesions compressing the brain (subdural hematomas, brain tumors); "normal pressure" hydrocephalus; metabolic disorders (B12 deficiency, remote carcinomas, renal failure); degenerative diseases (Pick's disease); infections (Jakob-Creutzfeld disease; cryptococcosis); etc. (Haase, 1977).

Both in normal aging and in Alzheimer's Disease it seems clear that focal lesions of specific neural structures are unlikely to account for the diffuse impairment of memory and cognitive function seen in most cases. Several years ago we began to speculate that the M/C impairment in both conditions might be due, in part, to impaired synaptic plasticity. The potential for widespread interference with normal neuronal plasticity due to a biochemical disorder within one or more pharmacosystems seemed intriguing, and suggested a possible mechanism for these M/C deficits.

The Cholinergic System in Aging and Dementia

The cholinergic pharmacosystem includes those neurons situated throughout the brain that interact by means of cholinergic synapses. It is by no means an anatomically contiguous structure, and efforts to map it have revealed only a few recognizable structures or pathways that have major cholinergic dependence (Shute and Lewis, 1967). Although it was believed until recently that the cerebral cortex had few cholinergic neurons, recent studies with the muscarinic receptor ligand, ^{3}H-quinuclidinyl benzilate (QNB) have shown that many cortical areas contain large numbers of cells capable of responding to acetylcholine.

There is evidence in man and animals that cholinergic drugs have profound effects on learning and memory. Many studies have documented the fact that cholinergic antagonists disrupt M/C functioning. The findings regarding cholinergic agonists are more ambiguous; although it appears that under certain conditions, they enhance learning and memory performance.

Cholinergic Antagonists

Most of the studies dealing with the role of the cholinergic system in human memory utilize atropine or scopolamine as experimental agents (Drachman and Sahakian, 1979a). These drugs, which block muscarinic acetylcholine (ACh) receptors, act centrally as well as peripherally, since they are tertiary amines that can cross the blood-brain barrier. In general, the cholinergic antagonists can be shown to impair certain aspects of human memory and cognitive function in a highly consistent manner. Ostfeld and Aruguete (1962), for example, examined normal subjects given 0.8 mg of scopolamine subcutaneously (s.c.). These subjects were impaired in their ability to recall lists of ten common objects or to repeat paragraphs, although span was not disrupted. Ostfeld and his colleagues, using considerably larger doses of atropine, had previously shown a similar effect (Ostfeld, Machne, and Unna, 1960). Safer and Allen (1971) found that a moderate dose of scopolamine interfered with the ability of normal subjects to retain a series of digits after a 20 second delay. Information that had been learned before drug administration was unaffected during the period of drug effect, however. The theory that scopolamine interferes with the acquisition of new information is further supported by the studies of Crow and Grove-White (1971, 1973). In addition, a number of experiments with anti-cholinergic agents have been carried out by Hrbek, Soukupova, and their colleagues in Czechoslovakia during the last decade (Hrbek et al. 1971, 1974; Soukupova, Vojtechovsky and Safratova, 1970). In general, their work supports the concept that scopolamine impairs learning of visual and verbal materials.

To define more precisely the nature of the scopolamine-induced deficit in M/C functioning, we studied the effects of cholinergically active drugs on the performance of young normal subjects. Groups of 20 either: 1. served as normal controls; 2. were given 1.0 mg of scopolamine subcutaneously (s.c.); or 3. were treated with methscopolamine, a quaternary scopolamine analogue that has only peripheral anticholinergic efforts, since it cannot cross the blood-brain barrier. Our tests (previously described) evaluated the effects of these drugs on 3 phases of memory and other cognitive functions.

Cholinergic blockade with scopolamine proved to have a highly significant effect on M/C function (Figure 3). Although, immediate memory span was spared, scopolamine markedly interfered with the ability of subjects to store new information (both in serial order of digits, and in free recall of words) as compared with non-treated subjects. Furthermore, retrieval from old memory store was mildly but significantly impaired. No retrograde amnesia was noted for the period preceding drug administration. Strikingly, the Verbal IQ was unaffected, but Performance IQ was markedly reduced by scopolamine, as was the OI. Treatment with methscopolamine produced no differences from normal performance, indicating that the effects observed with scopolamine were due to a central (rather than a peripheral) action of the drug.

The pattern of alteration of M/C functions produced by cholinergic blockade with scopolamine appeared highly reminiscent of the pattern we had seen in aged normal subjects. *A comparison* of the two groups was made, and we found that normal aged subjects showed an identical

Figure 3. Memory and cognitive performance of scopolamine-treated subjects versus controls. Normal controls' performances are shown as a straight line at 100% with scopolamine group's performance represented proportionately.

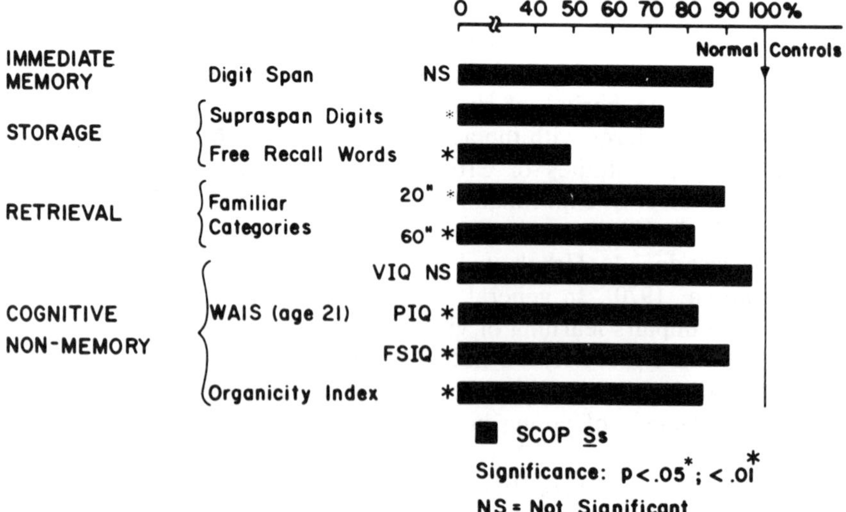

pattern of impaired and preserved M/C functions (Figure 4). This led us to hypothesize that impairment of cholinergic function might be a cause of the intellectual deficits found in normal aged individuals and in patients with dementia.

To test this hypothesis, we compared the performance of young subjects given scopolamine with aged subjects, using an additional testing format. We chose the dichotic listening task—a test of the ability of subjects to perceive and remember two different memoranda simultaneously presented to the two ears. Signals presented in this manner are believed to ascend to the opposite cerebral hemisphere and then be interpreted in the dominant hemisphere (Milner, Taylor, and Sperry, 1968; Studdert-Kennedy and Shankweiler, 1970). There is strong evidence that the dichotic listening test involves the functions of auditory

Figure 4. Normal (undrugged) elderly subjects compared with young subjects who have received scopolamine. Note that the pattern of M/C performances are closely similar in the two groups.

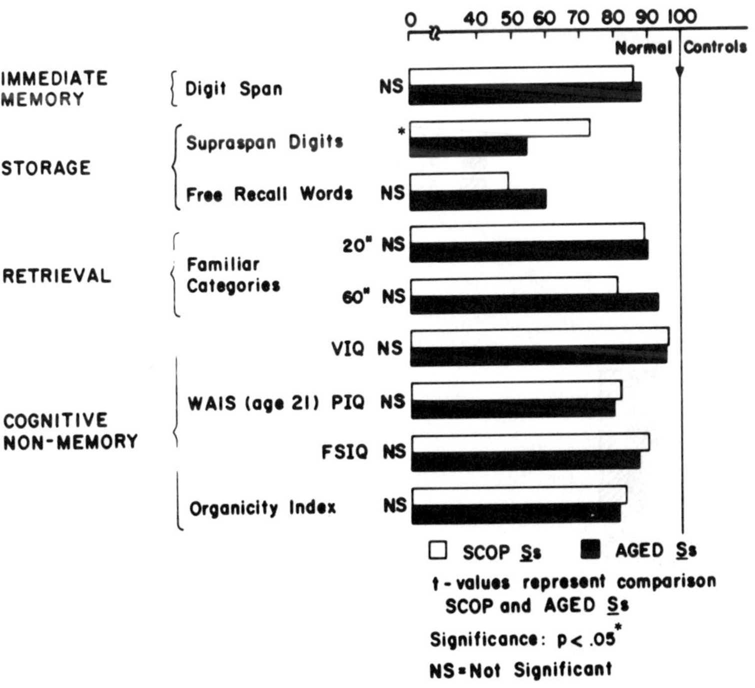

and association cortex, since there is striking impairment of left ear (nondominant) messages that occurs when the corpus callosum is sectioned, interrupting the cortical-cortical crossover of information (Milner et al., 1968). Six young normal subjects were found to have entirely normal dichotic listening performances in the control (undrugged) condition (Drachman et al., 1979). When they were given .8 to 1.0 mg scopolamine s.c., a definite impairment of their ability to handle simultaneous messages was demonstrated. "Double simultaneous correct" responses to the signals presented to both ears were most profoundly affected, falling from 35% in the undrugged condition to 19% after administration of scopolamine (Figure 5).

This finding was compared with the performance of 20 normal aged (age 65 to 85 yr) subjects, and once again showed a striking similarity. The results of this comparison of aged normal subjects, and young scopolamine subjects, corroborated the view that cholinergic blockade reproduced many of the M/C phenomena seen with aging.

Figure 5. The performance of young subjects, both undrugged and while treated with scopolamine, is compared with that of normal aged subjects on the dichotic listening test. See text for details.

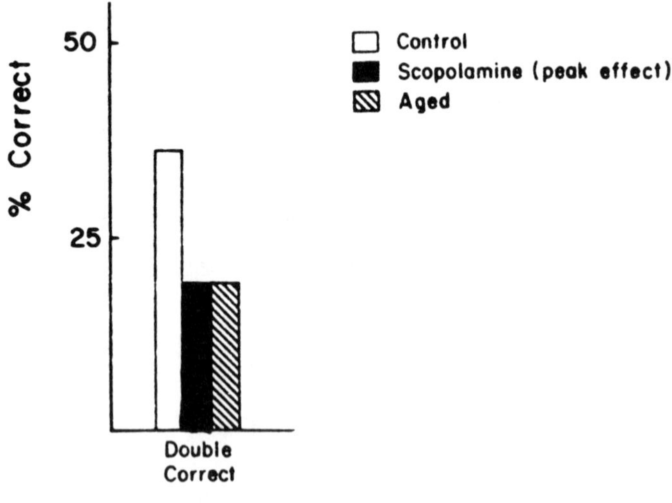

Biochemical Studies

Subsequently, a number of biochemical studies of the brains of elderly and demented patients have supported the hypothesis that memory disorders associated with these conditions might be due to "a relatively specific dysfunction of cholinergic transmitter function (e.g., impaired synthesis, release, or receptor uptake of acetylcholine). . . . " (Drachman and Leavitt, 1974). White et al (1977) have demonstrated that muscarinic ACh receptor-binding sites, as measured by the ^{3}H-QNB ligand method, are diminished in frontal cortex with advancing years, and are also diminished in the temporal lobes in cases of Pick's disease. Using this same ^{3}H-QNB ligand method, Reisine, Yamamura, and their colleagues recently reported a decrease in receptor binding in the hippocampus of patients with Alzheimer's disease compared to controls (Reisine et al., 1978). It has also been demonstrated that choline acetyltransferase (CAT) (an enzyme necessary for the synthesis of ACh) and acetylcholinesterase (an enzyme involved in the normal hydrolysis of released ACh) are decreased markedly in the cerebral cortex and hippocampal regions of patients with Alzheimer's disease (Carlsson, 1979; Davies and Maloney, 1976; White et al., 1977). Interestingly, enzymes necessary for the synthesis of other neurotransmitters [i.e., dopamine-β-hydroxylase (DBH), glutamic acid decarboxylase (GAD), tyrosine hydroxylase (TH), and aromatic aminoacid decarboxylase (AAD)] are *not* depleted in these conditions. The exact interpretation of these findings is not yet entirely clear. They may indicate a specific loss of the biochemical machinery necessary for cholinergic synaptic function; or a nonspecific loss of cholinergic neurites (i.e., axons and dendrites) as part of a general destructive process.

Cholinergic Agonists

If disordered function of the cholinergic system is responsible for the memory deficits of the aged and demented, it is logical to consider the therapeutic use of agents that would facilitate the function of cholinergic neurons. Precursors of acetylcholine, drugs preventing the hydrolysis of ACh, and muscarinic receptor agonists are all appropriate candidates, since they are capable of increasing central cholinergic function.

We first examined the effectiveness and specificity of physostigmine, an anticholinesterase agent, in reversing the pharmacologic dementia produced by scopolamine. Young normal subjects received either scopolamine alone (1.0 mg, s.c.) or scopolamine followed by physostigmine (4.0 mg, s.c.). As discussed earlier, scopolamine alone produced impairment of performance on the M/C test battery (Figure 3). Treatment with physostigmine largely reversed many features of the scopolamine-induced dementia. A comparison of the cognitive performance with scopolamine alone and scopolamine combined with physostigmine is shown in Figure 6. The most dramatic improvement was in memory storage, where free recall of words was improved by more than 60%. Significant improvement was also found in tests of cognitive nonmemory functions, including the WAIS Performance IQ, Full Scale IQ, and the Organicity Index. The results of this study clearly showed that physostigmine was able to produce a significant improvement in scopolamine-induced dementia, particularly when compared to an analeptic agent that effects the catecholamine system (amphetamine) (Figure 6).

These results, as well as other findings, have stimulated an interest in the use of cholinergic agonists for the improvement of cognitive function, particularly in the treatment of M/C disorders associated with aging. At present, however, there are still relatively few studies on the effects of cholinergic agonists on human memory. The drugs that have been tried in studies of human M/C function include physostigmine (an anticholines-

Figure 6. Physostigmine (PHYSO) Or d-amphetamine (D-AMPHET) are administered to young subjects with scopolamine-induced dementia (SCOP). Physostigmine treatment markedly improves memory storage performance and full-scale IQ; amphetamine produces significant worsening in memory storage and no improvement in other functions. See text for details.

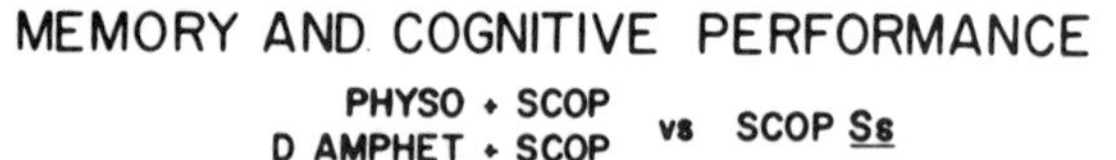

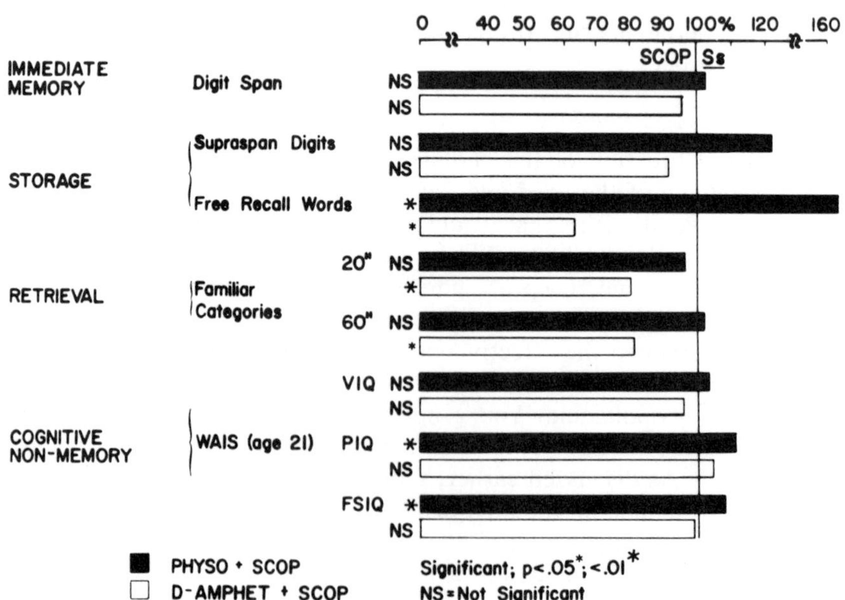

terase agent), arecoline (a cholinergic muscarinic agonist), and only recently, choline (Ch) (a precursor of ACh) (Drachman and Sahakian, 1979a; Drachman and Leavitt, 1974; Drachman, 1977; Davis et al., 1976, 1978; Sitaram, Weingartner and Gillin, 1978; Boyd et al., 1977; Etienne et al., 1978; Smith et al., 1978; Smith and Swash, 1979; Signoret, Whiteley and Lhermitte, 1978; Iversen and Iversen, 1975).

Although there are inconsistencies among the results of cholinergic agonists on human learning and memory, there is evidence that these agents may improve M/C function under certain circumstances. In young subjects, in particular, minor improvements in cognitive behavior have been noted with small doses of cholinergic agonists; larger doses produced a decrement of performance. Thus, Drachman and Leavitt (1974) found that when young normal subjects were given 1.0 mg of physostigmine s.c., their performance on all tests of M/C function showed a trend towards improvement that did not quite reach statistical significance, the largest increment being in supraspan digit storage (112% of normal). When they were given 2.0 mg of physostigmine, they showed a trend towards impairment in all memory and cognitive tests, which again did not quite reach the level of significance. These findings suggest that, in normal subjects, cholinergic function may be near optimal levels, a small dose of physostigmine producing slight improvement in M/C function, while larger doses interfere with performance.

In another study Drachman and Sahakian (1979b) observed the effects of 1.0 mg physostigmine in a small group of 13 aged subjects compared with 20 age-matched controls (Figure 7). The treated subjects showed a strong trend towards M/C improvement, particularly in memory storage and Performance IQ ($p = 0.06$), although sample sizes were relatively small and subjects did not serve as their own controls, producing relatively large variances between subjects.

Recently, Davis and his associates have carried out further tests of the effectiveness of physostigmine in improving memory in young normal subjects. Using a slow intravenous infusion of 1.0 mg of physostigmine, they demonstrated a slight improvement in free recall of previously learned word lists, and a more distinct improvement in the ability to store new lists of words using Buschke's selective reminding test (Davis et al., 1978). Only subjects with a low baseline level of performance were used in the drug study, to avoid the problem of a ceiling level of performance. These authors had previously studied subjects given 3.0 mg of physostigmine and found no improvement in memory function, with some worsening of digit span (Davis et al., 1976). This again points to a critical and small dose of physostigmine that may improve memory functions, with impairment at higher doses.

Sitaram et al. (1978) have demonstrated enhanced learning following treatment with either arecoline or choline chloride; however, Davis et al.

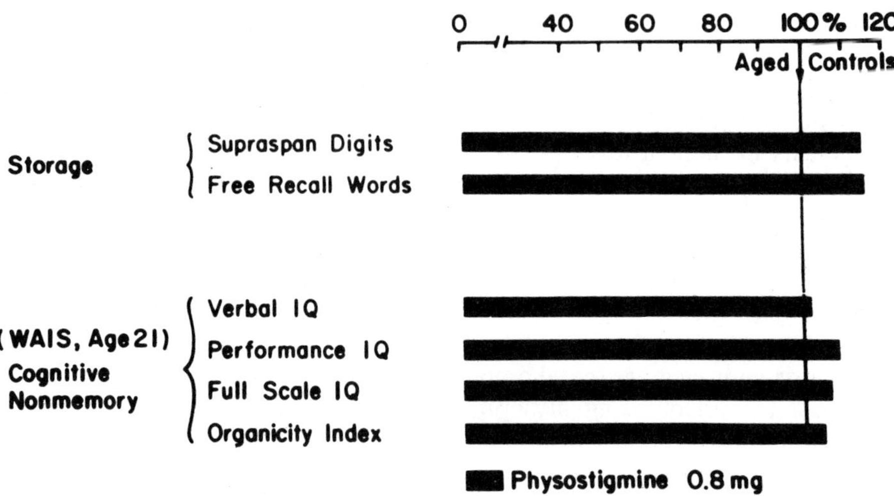

Figure 7. Administration of physostigmine to normal aged subjects compared with undrugged aged controls. There is a trend suggesting improvement in M/C functions following treatment with physostigmine. See text for details.

(in press) found no effect of choline chloride on learning and memory. Hence the question of effectiveness of cholinergic agonists in improving M/C function in normal young subjects is suggestive, but not entirely resolved.

Currently in our laboratory we are treating M/C disorders in aged and demented individuals with combinations of lecithin and physostigmine. The rationale for this combination of treatment is based on both supplementation of basal levels of ACh available, and selectivity of enhancement of ACh function at synapses that are appropriately active. A demonstrable improvement in M/C function following treatment may be clearer in these subjects where a greater increase in the activity of cholinergic synapses may be necessary in order to reach optimal levels.

Pharmacosystem Interactions

It is clear then that the cholinergic pharmacosystem plays a primary role in the mediation of learning and memory. It is outside the scope of this chapter to attempt a thorough discussion of the various regulatory mechanisms by which different pharmacosystems may interact. It is highly likely, however, that neurons of other pharmacosystems are involved in the modulation of M/C functions, either directly or indirectly through their effects on arousal, attention, reward, or other mechanisms.

The dopaminergic and noradrenergic systems, in particular, seem to be of critical importance in the learning process. It appears that the underlying mechanisms involved in the mediation of motivation and reward—processes essential for learning—are to a large extent catecholaminergic (Sahakian and Koob, 1978; Snyder, 1974; Van Dyke and Byck, 1977). Thus while cholinergic agents may be able to modify learning and memory *directly,* catecholaminergic agents may be able to do so *indirectly* through their actions on arousal, attention, motivation, conation, and reward (Foote and Bloom, 1979; Lyon and Robbins, 1975; Sahakian and Koob, 1978; Sahakian and Robbins, 1977; Snyder, 1974). More effective treatment of clinical cognitive impairment may require accurate knowledge of the functional state of deficiency.

How Do Cholinergically-Active Drugs Affect Memory?

Approaches and Strategies to Treatment

Cholinergic agonists and antagonists most likely alter synaptic excitability throughout much of the central cholinergic pharmacosystem (Karczmar, 1977). It is important to consider how such widespread cholinergic modification might exert any selective action among the innumerable stored neural patterns and the memories they represent. How can storage, retention, or retrieval of *specific* information be affected by raising or lowering cholinergic excitability as a *whole?*

During the phase of acquisition, or storage, of new information, two cholinergic mechanisms may be involved. Since synaptic transmission is presumably the first step that eventually leads to plastic synaptic change, blockage of initial transmission would prevent the subsequent storage and consolidation of memories; facilitation of transmission should favor their occurrence. Second, interference with hippocampal function during acquisition should impair memory storage by means of a different mechanism that has yet to be clearly established. Drugs with cholinergic activity most consistently affect memory processes at the initial (acquisition) phase, regardless of which mechanism—or both—accounts for the observations.

Another way in which modification of the cholinergic pharmacosystem may alter memory is through increasing or decreasing the gain in information-containing neural systems. Several investigators have proposed that memories may be stored both by increasing sensitivity in certain synapses and decreasing it in others (Drachman, 1977). The recognizability of information may depend on the difference in sensitivity between these synapses and alternate pathways—the *"signal-to-noise ratio*." Drugs that modify the gain in the cholinergic system might, therefore, be able to optimize recall of stored information by helping to achieve maximal separation of signal and noise (as occurs on the linear portion of the curve, Figure 8). Depending on the original signal strength, either an increase or a decrease in the gain might improve recall.

In the case of aged or demented patients, where diminished cholinergic receptors (elderly and Pick's dementia) or ACh synthesis (Alzheimer's disease) are found, it may be necessary to amplify the signal. However, in the treatment of Alzheimer's dementia, where ACh synthesis is diminished, anticholinesterase agents *alone* may be ineffectual, since the baseline ACh secretion levels may be extremely low. A reasonable strategy might require both supplementation of the ACh stores with precursors, and facilitation of active synapses (with anticholinesterases) in order to achieve an improvement in cholinergic transmission. Finally, it should be added that in certain instances where, for example, conation may be low—as in "extrapyramidal dementia"—treatment with a dopaminergic agonist such as levodopa can produce intellectual and motor improvement (Drachman and Stahl, 1975).

Clearly, our understanding of the neural basis of learning and memory remains largely obscure, and it is evident that the cholinergic system is involved only in limited aspects of M/C functioning. Dendritic distributions, energy metabolism of neurons, and protein synthesis required for establishing neural connectivity are undoubtedly also important in mem-

Figure 8. A hypothetical signal detection curve is shown for information stored in the brain, possibly in the cholinergic system. Signal and noise are most easily discriminated on the linear portion of the curve. S denotes signal; N, noise. See text for details.

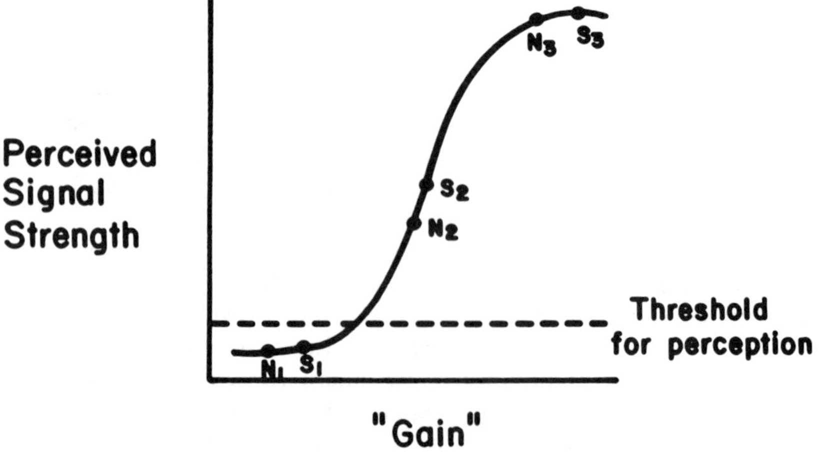

ory formation. However, the use of pharmacologic agents, such as cholinergic agonists which appear to affect M/C functioning, provide an appropriate approach to treatment of the decline in intellectual functioning associated with aging and Alzheimer's disease. And perhaps several years from now statements like:

> "Unfortunately we have at present no drugs that are known to reliably prevent or reduce the disabilities of normal aging—even less the ravages of arteriosclerosis or senile dementia. Research effort should be aimed at developing pharmacologic aids that will be capable of preventing the disabilities of old age." (Lehmann, 1977, p. 130)

will have become obsolete.

ACKNOWLEDGMENTS
The authors are indebted to Ms. Janet Leavitt who performed some of the psychological tests and statistical analyses reported here. This research was supported in part by the Sterling Morton Research Fund and NIH Research Grant No. RR48.

References

Adams RD: The anatomy of memory mechanism in the human brain. In Talland GA, Waugh NC (eds.) *The Pathology of Memory* New York, Academic Press, 1969.

Barbizet J: Defect of memorizing of hippocampal-mammillary origin: a review. *J Neurol Neurosurg Psychiat* 26:127–135, 1963.

Barbizet J: *Human Memory and Its Pathology.* San Francisco, W.H. Freeman and Co., 1970.

Boyd W, Graham-White J, Blackwood G, Glen I, McQueen J: Clinical effects of choline in Alzheimer senile dementia. *Lancet* ii:711, 1977.

Brierley J: The neuropathology of amnesic states. In Whitty CWM, Zangwill OL (eds.) *Amnesia.* New York, Appleton-Century-Crofts, 1966.

Brion S: Korsakoff's Syndrome: clinico-anatomical and physiological considerations. In Talland GA, Waugh NC (eds.) *The Pathology of Memory.* New York, Academic Press, 1969.

Busse E, Obrist W: Significance of focal electroencephalographic changes in the elderly. *Postgrad Med* 34:179–182, 1963.

Carlsson A: The impact of catecholamine research on medical science and practice. In Usdin E, Kopin I, Barchas J (eds.) *Catecholamines: Basic and Clinical Frontiers* New York, Pergamon, 1979.

Corsellis J: Aging and dementias. In Blackwood W, Corsellis J (eds.) *Greenfield's Neuropathology (3rd ed.)* Chicago, Year Book Medical Publishers, 1976.

Crow T, Grove-White I: Differential effect of atropine and hyoscine on human learning capacity. *Brit J Pharmacology* 43:464P, 1971.

Crow T, Grove-White I: An analysis of the learning deficit following hyoscine administration to man. *Brit J Pharmacology* 49:322–327, 1973.

Davies P, Maloney A: Selective loss of central cholinergic neurons in Alzheimer's Disease. *Lancet* ii:1403, 1976.

Davis K, Hollister L, Overall J, Johnson A, Train K: Physostigmine: effects on cognition and affect in normal subjects. *Psychopharmacology* 51:23–27, 1976.

Davis K, Mohs R, Tinklenberg J, Hollister L, Pfefferbaum A, Kopell B: Cholinomimetics and memory. *Arch Neurol,* (In press).

Davis K, Mohs R, Tinklenberg J, Pfefferbaum A, Hollister L, Kopell B: Physostigmine: improvement of long-term memory processes in normal humans. *Science* 201:272–274, 1978.

Deutsch J: The cholinergic synapse and the site of memory. *Science* 174:788–794, 1971.

Drachman DA: Memory and cognitive function in man: does the cholinergic system have a specific role? *Neurology* 27:783–790, 1977.

Drachman DA, Adams RD: Herpes simplex and acute inclusion body encephalitis. *Arch Neurol* 7:45–63, 1962.

Drachman DA, Arbit J: Memory and the hippocampal complex. II. Is memory a multiple process? *Archives of Neurology* 15:52–61, 1966.

Drachman DA, Hughes JR: Memory and the hippocampal complexes. III. Aging and temporal EEG abnormalities. *Neurology* 21:1–14, 1971.

Drachman DA, Leavitt J: Human memory and the cholinergic system: a relationship to aging? *Arch Neurol* 30:113–121, 1974.

Drachman DA, Noffsinger D, Sahakian BJ, Kurdziel S, Fleming P: Aging, memory, and the cholinergic system: a study of dichotic listening. Paper to be presented at the 104th Annual Meeting of the American Neurological Association (St. Louis, October, 1979).

Drachman DA, Ommaya AK: Memory and the hippocampal complex. *Arch Neurol* 10:411–425, 1964.

Drachman DA, Sahakian BJ: The effects of cholinergic drugs on human learning and memory. In Barbeau A, Growdon J, Wurtman RJ (eds.) *Nutrition and the Brain (Vol. 5).* New York, Raven Press, 1979a.

Drachman DA, Sahakian BJ: Memory and cognitive function in the elderly: preliminary trial of physostigmine, 1979b.

Drachman DA, Stahl S: Extrapyramidal dementia and levodopa. *Lancet*:809, 1975.

Eccles JC: Possible ways in which synaptic mechanisms participate in learning, remembering, and forgetting. In Kimble DP (ed.) *The Anatomy of Memory.* California, Science and Behavior Books, Inc., 1965.

Etienne P, Gauthier S, Johnson G, Collier B, Mendis T, Doster D, Cole M, Muller H: Clinical effects of choline in Alzheimer's Disease. *Lancet* i:508–509, 1978.

Foote SL, Bloom FE: Activity of norepinephrine-containing locus coeruleus neurons in the unanesthetized squirrel monkey. In Usdin E, Kopin I, Barchas J (eds.) *Catecholamines: Basic and Clinical Frontiers.* New York, Pergamon, 1979.

Haase GR: Diseases presenting as dementia. In Wells CE (ed.) *Dementia, Edition 2.* Philadelphia, F.A. Davis Co., 1977.

Horel JA: The neuroanatomy of amnesia: a critique of the hippocampal memory hypothesis. *Brain* 101:403–446, 1978.

Hrbek J, Komenda S, Macakova J, Siroka A, Navratil J, Medek A: The effect of scopolamine (0.6 mg) and physostigmine (1.0 mg) on higher nervous activity in man, followed-up during five hours after application. *Activ Nerv Sup* (Praha) 16:213–215, 1974.

Hrbek J, Komenda S, Siroka A, Macakova J: On the interaction of scopolamine and physostigmine in man. *Activ Nerv Sup* (Praha) 13:200–201, 1971.

Iversen S, Iversen L: *Behavioral Pharmacology.* Oxford, Oxford University Press, 1975.

James W: *Psychology.* New York, Henry Holt and Company, 1892, p. 287.

John ER, Schwartz EL: The neurophysiology of information processing and cognition. *Ann Rev Psychol* 29:1–29, 1978.

Karczmar A: Exploitable aspects of central cholinergic functions, particularly with respect to the EEG, motor, analgesic and mental functions. Cholinergic mechanisms and psychopathology. *Advances in Behav Biol* 24:679–708, 1977.

Katzman R: The prevalence and malignancy of Alzheimer's Disease. *Arch Neurol* 33:217–218, 1976.

Katzman R, Terry R, Bick K: *Alzheimer's Disease: Senile Dementia and Related Disorders*. New York, Raven Press, 1978.

Kinsbourne M: Cognitive deficit: experimental analysis. In McGaugh J (ed.) *Psychobiology Behavior from a Biological Perspective*. New York, Academic Press, 1971.

Kooi K, Güvener A, Tupper C, Bagchi B: Electroencephalographic patterns of the temporal region in normal adults. *Neurology* 14:1029–1035, 1964.

Kosower EM: A molecular basis for learning and memory. *Proc Nat Acad Sci USA* 69:3292–3296, 1972.

Lehmann HE: The use of medication to prevent custodial care. In Eisdorfer C, Friedel R (eds.) *Cognitive and Emotional Disturbances in the Elderly*. Chicago, Year Book Medical Publishers, Inc., 1977.

Lyon M, Robbins T: The action of central nervous system stimulant drugs: a general theory concerning amphetamine effects. In Essman W, Valzelli L (eds.) *Current Developments in Psychopharmacology, Vol. 2*. New York, Spectrum, 1975.

Mark R: *Memory and Nerve Cell Connections*. Oxford, Claredon Press, 1974.

Milner B, Taylor S, Sperry R: Lateralized suppression of dichotically presented digits after commissural section in man. *Science* 161:184–185, 1968.

Obrist W: The electroencephalogram of normal aged adults. *Electroenceph Clin Neurophysiol* 6:235–244, 1954.

Obrist W, Busse E: The electroencephalogram in old age. In Wilson W (ed.) *Applications of Electroencephalography in Psychiatry*. Durham, Duke University Press, 1965.

Ostfeld AM, Aruguete A: Central nervous sytem effects of hyoscine in man. *J Pharmac Exper Therap* 137:133–139, 1962.

Ostfeld AM, Machne X, Unna K: The effects of atropine on the electroencephalogram and behavior in man. *J Pharmacol Exp Therap* 128:265–272, 1960.

Penfield W, Milner B: Memory deficit produced by bilateral lesions in the hippocampal zone. *Arch Neurol Psychiat* 79:475–497, 1958.

Reisine TD, Yamamura HI, Bird ED, Spokes E, Enna SJ: Pre- and postsynaptic neurochemical alterations in Alzheimer's Disease. *Brain Research* 159:477–481, 1978.

Richter D (ed.) *Aspects of Learning and Memory*. 1966.

Roberts E: Summation. In Kimble DP (ed.) *The Anatomy of Memory*. California, Science and Behavior Books, Inc., 1965.

Safer D, Allen R: The central effects of scopolamine in man. *Biological Psychiatry* 3:347–355, 1971.

Sahakian BJ, Koob GF: The relationship between pipradrol-induced responding for electrical brain stimulation, stereotyped behavior and locomotor activity. *Neuropharmacology* 17:363–366, 1978.

Sahakian BJ, Robbins T: Are the effects of psychomotor stimulant drugs on hyperactive children really paradoxical? *Medical Hypotheses* 3:154–158, 1977.

Scoville WB, Milner B: Loss of recent memory after bilateral hippocampal lesions. *J Neurol Neurosurg Psychiat* 20:11–21, 1957.

Shute C, Lewis P: The ascending cholinergic reticular systems: neocortical, olfactory, and subcortical projections. *Brain* 90:487–520, 1967.

Signoret J, Whiteley A, Lhermitte F: Influence of choline on amnesia in early Alzheimer's Disease. *Lancet* ii:837, 1978.

Sitaram N, Weingartner H, Gillin J: Human serial learning: enhancement with arecholine and choline and impairment with scopolamine. *Science* 201:274–276, 1978.

Smith C, Swash M: Physostigmine in Alzheimer's Disease. *Lancet* I:42, 1979.

Smith C, Swash M, Exton-Smith A, Phillips M, Overstall P, Piper M, Bailey M: Choline therapy in Alzheimer's Disease, *Lancet* ii:318, 1978.

Snyder SH: *Madness and the Brain*. New York, McGraw-Hill, 1974.

Soukupova B, Vojtechovsky M, Safratova V: Drugs influencing the cholinergic system and the process of learning and memory in man. *Activ Nerv Sup* 12:91–93, 1970.

Sperry RW: Lateral specialization in the surgically separated hemispheres. In Milner B (ed.) *Hemispheric Specialization and Interaction*. Cambridge, Massachusetts, M. I. T. Press, 1975.

Studdert-Kennedy M, Shankweiler D: Hemispheric specialization for speech perception. *J Acoust Soc Am* 48:579–594, 1970.

Terry RD, Wisniewsky HM: Structural and chemical changes of the aged human brain. In Gershon S, Raskin A (eds.) *Aging (Vol. 2)*. New York, Raven Press, 1975.

Terry RD, Wisniewski HM: Structural aspects of aging of the brain. In Eisdorfer C, Friedel R (eds.) *Cognitive and Emotional Disturbances in the Elderly*. Chicago, Year Book Medical Publishers, Inc., 1977.

Tomlinson BE: Morphological changes and dementia in old age. In Smith W, Kinsbourne M (eds.) *Aging and Dementia*. New York, Spectrum, 1977.

Tomlinson BD, Henderson G: Some quantitative cerebral findings in normal and demented old people. In Terry RD, Gershon S (eds.) *Aging (Vol. 3)*. New York, Raven Press, 1976.

Van Dyke C, Byck R: Cocaine: 1884–1974. In Ellinwood EH Jr, Kilbey MM (eds.) *Cocaine and Other Stimulants*. New York, Plenum Press, 1977.

Victor M, Angevine J, Mancall E, Fisher C: Memory loss with lesions of hippocampal formation. *Archives of Neurology* 5:244–263, 1961.

Wang HS: Dementia in old age. In Wells CE (ed.) *Dementia*. Philadelpia, F.A. Davis Company, 1977.

Weschsler D: *Manual for the Wechsler Adult Intelligence Scale*. New York, Psychological Corporation, 1955.

White P, Hiley C, Goodhardt M, Carrasco L, Keet J, Williams I, Bowen D: Neocortical cholinergic neurons in elderly people. *Lancet* 668–670, 1977.

Stein, ed. The Psychobiology of Aging: Problems and Perspectives

The Relationship of Hypertension to Cognitive Functioning[a]

Merrill F. Elias, Ph.D.

Department of Psychology, University of Maine at Orono, Orono, Maine.

Introduction

There has been a long-standing debate among those who study the aging process as to whether "normal aging" can be distinquished from pathological aging. One extreme represents researchers who view aging as a normal process that can be studied separately from disease. The other argues that aging represents the accumulation of diseases and that the life span can be expanded appreciably by finding cures for the major diseases. It is doubtful that this issue will be resolved in the near future or that arguments as to the correct view will cease.

Most gerontological researchers do agree that the incidence of many diseases is positively correlated with advancing age and that performance trends, particularly in cross-sectional studies, are different for healthy aging samples as opposed to samples with disproportionately greater numbers of ill persons in one or more age cohort(s). Two questions which have not been answered are : 1. which specific diseases have a deleterious effect on cognitive performance; and 2. do these diseases have a disproportionate effect for different age cohorts, i.e., for groups of individuals who are of different ages by virtue of birth at different periods of time. These questions have stimulated a series of research studies in our laboratory in which we have examined the influence of coronary

[a]Research reported from "our laboratory" and the research of K. C. Light and W. E. Watson was supported, in part, by research grants from the National Institute on Aging (NIH), and AG00868 to Merrill F. Elias. Many thanks to Joan E. B. Cooper for her assistance in preparing this chapter.

heart disease and uncomplicated essential hypertension on the cognitive performance of different age cohorts. Our studies of heart disease and behavior have not reached a point which would allow a comprehensive review; however, we do report on a series of studies of essential hypertensive patients. We chose hypertension as a beginning point in our studies *because* it represents a subtle form of vascular disease. By definition, no grossly apparent signs of central or peripheral nervous system pathology are present, and yet the literature indicates that essential hypertensives (as a group) perform less well than normotensives. Space does not allow a review of all the relevant literature (see Elias, 1978; Elias, in press a, b for reviews), but we can summarize major studies that relate, in an important way, to our data. (The reader may find the glossary of terms in Table 1 of value).

Slowing of Response

Speed and Reaction-Time

The studies which indicate a slowing of response with advancing age are legion (Elias, Elias, and Elias, 1977). Birren (1965) was one of the first investigators to call attention to two possible factors contributing to this phenomenon:

> "a primary age factor of subcortical basis reflected in all or most processes mediated by the central nervous system, and a factor of cortical integrity influenced by disease, particularly those resulting in local cell loss and interference with circulation and ischemia." (p. 199)

The emphasis on diseases of circulation was very likely influenced by Birren, Butler, Greenhouse, Sokoloff, and Yarrow's (1963) finding that a group of men (65 +) suffering from atherosclerosis performed less well on serial reaction time tasks than a group of very healthy older men (65+).

One of the first studies providing clear evidence that hypertensive disease may be related to response slowing was performed by Spieth (1964, 1965). Spieth's subjects were men (age range 35 to 59 years) drawn from a population of military and civil airplane pilots, air traffic controllers, and volunteers. All the subjects exceeded the average in terms of general intelligence and socioeconomic level. Subjects were divided into groups depending on their specific diagnosis, e.g., arteriosclerosis, hypertension, hypertension with arteriosclerosis, and whether or not they were taking medication at the time of testing. Scores from these tests, WAIS Digit-Symbol Substitution Test (Wechsler, 1955), the Trail Making Test (Reitan, 1958), and a ten-choice serial reaction time task adapted from the Psychomet Test (Birren et al., 1963), were combined into a composite speed score.

Table 1. A Glossary of Terms Used in this Chapter[a]

Arteriosclerosis is a group of vascular diseases which are characterized by hardening, thickening, and loss of elasticity of the vessel walls.

Atherosclerosis is an occlusive disease that influences the nutrient vessels of the brain, heart, and kidneys by a progressive choking of the flow of blood. It is almost inevitably associated with advancing age, but may not be clinically significant if it does not interfere with blood flow in a significant manner.

Blood pressure (arterial blood pressure) is determined by the amount of blood that is pumped by the heart per unit of time and the diameter of the blood vessels.

Cerebrovascular accident is the technical name of a stroke. An ischemic stroke is defined as an interruption in cerebral blood flow which results in one or several neurological symptoms lasting for more than one day.

Diastolic blood pressure is the minimum pressure occurring during the relaxation phase of the cardiac cycle.

Essential hypertension is hypertension with no immediately identifiable pathology. It is very likely a common symptom of a number of disease processes.

Mean arterial pressure is 1/3 pulse pressure + diastolic pressure.

Normal blood pressure (Normotensive) has never been precisely specified as it depends in part on statistical averages and clinical judgment as to what is not normal. A commonly accepted set of values is 120 systolic and 80 diastolic, although 140/90 mm Hg, 145/90 mm Hg, and 150/95 mm Hg have been considered the upper limits of normal depending on an individual's age. Within the normal range of blood pressure, a sudden upward rise might be considered abnormal for a given individual.

Plasma Renin Activity (PRA) "High PRA is typical of subjects whose hypertension is either caused by or results in kidney damage. The majority of persons with essential hypertension have normal PRA while approximately 25 percent have suppressed PRA. This last group of subjects shows no response when blood pressure falls to a level where renin secretion normally is stimulated. Secretion of renin does occur but only when the fall in pressure becomes more extreme." (See Light, 1975.)

Pulse Pressure is the difference between systolic and diastolic blood pressure.

Renin "is a substance normally produced by the kidney when a fall in blood pressure occurs and threatens the kidney's perfusion. It has no pressor properties in itself, but one of its products, angiotensin, acts on arteriolar smooth muscle to produce contraction. This contraction increases vascular resistance and thus raises blood pressure so that adequate blood flow through the kidney and other vital organs is maintained." (See Light, 1975.)

Secondary hypertension is hypertension caused by a known disease process such as heart disease or renal insufficiency.

Systolic blood pressure is the maximum pressure occurring during the systolic (contraction) phase of the cardiac cycle.

Transient ischemic attack is a term reserved for ischemic stroke with symptoms that clear up after a day or seconds and may be associated with cell death.

[a] Adapted from Elias (in press) by permission.

Results indicated that arteriosclerotic subjects performed more poorly than healthy subjects. The findings for hypertensive subjects were less clear because certification stress (stress over consequences of possible revocation of medical certification to fly or control air traffic) was confounded with medication for hypertension, i.e., subjects who were potentially more stressed and were not taking medication, exhibited slower time scores than both the normotensive controls and the medicated subjects who were presumably less stressed. This study is frequently cited as indicating that blood pressure control via medication improves cognitive functioning.

Recently, Light (1975) elaborated on Spieth's (1964, 1965) study by using larger samples of hypertensive and normotensive subjects (age range 18 to 59 years). Her hypertensive subjects (> 140/90 mm Hg) and 24 of 43 normotensive subjects (< 140/90 mm Hg) were carefully screened for hypertension-related pathology in connection with a hypertension clinic at Upstate Medical Center, Syracuse, New York (Streeten, Anderson, Freiberg and Delakos, 1975). In addition to examining the relationships among blood pressure, age, and discrimination-serial reaction time tasks, Light (1978) investigated the effects of various levels of plasma renin activity (PRA) on the reaction time performance of medicated and unmedicated hypertensive patients. PRA was chosen as a classificatory variable because there is evidence that it has prognostic significance for essential hypertensives. Hypersecretion of renin occurs when hypertension is caused by, or results in, damage to the kidney (non-benign hypertension). Approximately 16% of hypertensives examined have low PRA levels and 57% have normal PRA levels (Marx, 1976). In one longitudinal study, 11% of normal PRA and 14% of high PRA hypertensive subjects developed either cardiovascular or cerebrovascular disease over a period of 4.5 years, although none of the subjects with low PRA levels experienced infarction during this time period (Brunner, Laragh, Baer, Newton, Goodwin, Krakoff, Bard and Buhler, 1972). Light reasoned that because PRA level is prognostically important, it should be related to early changes in performance, e.g., slowing in response speed, that may precede clinically recognizable pathological changes in the nervous system. Light's subjects were formed into three groups: 18 to 31 years, 32 to 45 years, and 46 to 59 years; hypertensive subjects were classified by PRA levels.

Results indicated that discrimination-serial reaction time increased with age, particularly for the complex discrimination tasks, but there was no age by blood pressure interaction. In contradiction to Spieth's finding, "medicated" hypertensive subjects exhibited slower reaction times than the hypertensive subjects, and did not differ significantly from normotensives. However, Spieth's study and Light's study differed in a number of respects, including the fact that Light's medicated subjects had discontinued medication from 3 to 21 days prior to testing and were tested under the influence of a potent diuretic [foresemide (Lasix R)] which lowered blood pressure values to normal or near-normal levels.

The only untreated hypertensive subjects in Light's study who showed slowing in response (relative to normotensive controls) were those with high PRA levels, while slowing was observed at all PRA levels for medicated subjects. Medicated subjects performed more poorly than non-medicated subjects for the low and normal PRA group, but not for the high PRA group. Light suggested that the chronic use of anti-hypertensive drugs may have produced behavioral side effects resulting from impaired autoregulatory abilities in the medicated subjects whose vasculature had adapted to sustained hypertension. However, there was no direct evidence in support of this hypothesis, and Light (1978) has pointed out that slowing for the medicated hypertensives might be related to unknown personality differences between those who seek treatment early and those who do not, to a direct diuretic side effect, or to an artifact of testing conditions. It should be pointed out, however, that no specific class of drugs appeared to influence performance more than any other and duration of hypertension did not appear to account for differences between medicated and non-medicated subjects. While the PRA effect is interesting and potentially important, it was not replicated in a second study (Light, 1978). It may have been a statistical artifact in the first study as there were very few untreated high PRA subjects (N = 4) in relationship to normal (N = 28) and low (N = 10) PRA subjects.

Light (1978) replicated her original study with respect to medicated versus non-medicated subjects. In so doing she compared hypertensives with subjects classified with regard to several vascular diseases: normotensive, untreated hypertensive, medicated hypertensive, coronary artery disease, transient ischemic attack (TIA), and stroke. All the TIA patients were neurologically normal at the time of testing. Hypertension was defined as systolic and diastolic blood pressure in excesss of 140/90 mm Hg for the 18 to 36-year-old subjects (younger group) and 150/90 mm Hg for the 56 to 77-year-old subjects. As in the first study, testing was accomplished in the hypertension screening clinic at Upstate Medical Center while hypertensive patients and normotensive controls were under the influence of a potent diuretic (furosemide).

Table 2 shows the findings for each diagnostic group with a composite reaction time score averaged over age. There was no age by disease interaction, but older subjects performed more poorly. As in Light's original study (1975), no differences in serial reaction time were observed between healthy normotensive controls and non-medicated hypertensives, although, medicated hypertensives differed from controls. Patients with coronary heart disease did not differ significantly from normotensive controls, but the two groups with cerebrovascular disorders (stroke and TIA) differed significantly from the normotensive controls and the three

Table 2. Results of K. C. Light's Study of Performance on a Serial-Discrimination Reaction Time Task[a, b]

Class	N	Total RT
Normotensive	52	347.1 23.3
Untreated hypertensive	47	352.7 25.7
Treated hypertensive	130	358.7 26.5
Coronary heart disease	13	357.0 30.1
Transient ischemic attack	10	403.7 46.6
Stroke	19	382.4 44.1

[a] Data from Light (1978) by permission.
[b] All timed measures are given in seconds.

groups of patients with cardiovascular disorders. TIA and stroke patients did not differ significantly for each other. As may be seen in Table 3, there were no significant differences in serial reaction time for subjects on different classes of medication, although too few persons were using tranquilizers alone to make a comparison of this drug class with other drug classes. Of course, differences among subjects in doses and drug histories could have obscured the results. Often there is little the clinical investigator can do to control these variables. The possibility also exists that hypertensive persons on medication had difficulty in adjusting to withdrawal from the medication prior to clinic testing on the RT task or, alternatively, that some unknown sample characteristics, e.g., trait or state anxiety, depression, contributed to the performance differences between medicated and unmedicated subjects. In short, we have to rely on speculation with regard to the reasons for the differences in reaction time between medicated and non-medicated hypertensives because control over dosage, history, and appropriateness of previous drug treatment was not possible and because the duration of hypertensive symptoms could not be determined precisely.

It is important to note that neither Spieth (1964, 1965) nor Light (1978) could assess the age by blood pressure interaction without combining diagnostic categories. When the disease categories were combined, neither investigator found evidence which suggested that serial reaction time performance was more adversely affected by vascular disease for

Table 3. Relationship of General Category of Drug for the Treatment of Hypertension and Performance[a, b]

	N		Total RT
Sympathetic inhibitor plus other drug	72	M	357.0
		SD	23.3
Sympathetic inhibitor alone	17	M	362.0
		SD	24.8
Diuretic and vasodilator or tranquilizer	13	M	351.5
		SD	30.4
Diuretic or vasodilator alone	26	M	365.6
		SD	33.5
Tranquilizer alone	2	M	358.9
		SD	11.1

[a] All timed measures are given in sec.
[b] Taken from Light (1978) by permission.

older than for younger samples within the age range studied. Both investigators found that older subjects performed less well than younger subjects.

Discrete RT Tasks

In a study employing the same patients that had participated in Light's serial reaction time study at Upstate Medical Center, Watson (1976) employed an information processing paradigm in which subjects were asked to match two stimuli on the basis of a defined set of rules. For this paradigm, it is presumed that as time (SOA interval) between the two stimuli decreases, subjects have less time to encode the stimuli. There were no statistically significant differences between hypertensive and normotensive groups and the time required to encode the stimuli (slope of the lines) was essentially no greater for the young and middle-aged normotensives than for the middle-aged hypertensive group. Time scores for each SOA were greater for the older than for the younger subjects.

In comparison to Light, Watson used fewer subjects, practiced for much longer, a discrete rather than serial reaction response, and subjects who were not under the influence of a diuretic at the time of testing. Any one of these factors could have explained Watson's failure to replicate the findings of Light with a different kind of reaction time task. However, recent studies in our laboratory (Watson et al., unpublished) with a larger number of very highly practiced subjects and a different kind of information processing paradigm, again involving a discrete reaction time response, revealed no differences between hypertensive and normotensive subjects. As for Light, Spieth, and Watson's studies, reaction was slower for older subjects, but no age by blood pressure interaction was obtained.

Cognitive Functioning

Light's positive findings stimulated studies in our laboratory with the same population of subjects used by Light, i.e., patients and controls from the Upstate Medical Center and Syracuse area. We elected to use the WAIS and selected tests from the Halstead-Reitan neuropsychological test battery because we were concerned with the practical significance of Light's studies in terms of commonly used measures of cognitive functioning. We performed the WAIS study under conditions identical to those employed by Light, i.e., subjects were carefully screened medically and were tested under the influence of a potent diuretic which lowered blood pressure to normal, or near normal, levels at the time of testing. Neuropsychological testing was too time consuming to be undertaken at the diagnostic clinic (Upstate Medical Center) and thus it was performed in our laboratory under circumstances in which subjects had either been returned to medication or had not yet received treatment. Otherwise, conditions were similar to those which characterized Light's study.

Results of WAIS Study

For the WAIS study (Schultz, Dineen, Elias, Pentz, and Wood, 1979) subjects in essential hypertensive and normotensive groups were divided into two age groups (Table 4). In addition to medically examined normotensive controls, a group of normotensive subjects (non-examined controls) were tested under circumstances in which no diuretic was given. The non-examined and examined normotensives did not differ with respect to any of the WAIS scores. Similarly, previous medicated and non-medicated subjects did not differ significantly, and there were no differences between subjects classified into high, low, and normal PRA groups. Thus, in this chapter the data are presented with these groups combined.

There was a significant age by blood pressure interaction for the Verbal scaled scores. Significant differences between hypertensives and normotensives were observed for the younger, but not for the older group of subjects (Table 5). In an initial analysis, no age by blood pressure group or blood pressure main effect was observed for Performance scaled scores. However, when subjects were matched on Verbal scaled scores, a blood pressure group by age interaction was observed for the Performance WAIS scores. Performance scores were significantly lower for the hypertensives in both age groups but this effect was more pronounced

Table 4. Means and Standard Deviations for Age (yr), Education (yr), and Blood Pressure Values (mm Hg)[a, b]

	Controls		Hypertensives	
	Younger	Older	Younger	Older
N	23	19	31	37
Age	27 (5.0)	56 (7.2)	15 (5.3)	14 (5.3)
Education	16 (2.0)	16 (1.45)	15 (2.80)	14 (2.60)
Systolic	115 (13.7)	122 (14.2)	150 (13.3)	160 (16.9)
Diastolic	71 (6.7)	72 (9.2)	98 (10.4)	103 (9.8)

[a] Adapted from Schultz, Dineen, Elias, Pentz, and Wood (1979) by permission.
[b] Means are rounded to the nearest whole number to reflect accuracy of measurement.

for the younger than for the older subjects. The younger subjects performed less well than the older subjects but only in the normotensive control group. Space does not permit a summary of detailed results for the subtests of the WAIS individually. These data can be found in Schultz et al., (1979).

Thé finding of inferior WAIS performance for the hypertensive subjects was not unexpected. Wilkie and Eisdorfer (1971) have reported inferior WAIS performance for hypertensives. These investigators studied two

Table 5. Means and Standard Deviations of Scaled Scores for the WAIS[a]

	Controls		Hypertensives	
	Younger	Older	Younger	Older
Verbal	87.1 (7.0)	78.9 (9.3)	74.1 (10.3)	74.3 (10.9)
Performance[b]	63.9 (9.1)	55.2 (9.6)	59.1 (8.6)	54.6 (9.8)
Performance[c]	69.9 (4.7)	61.8 (7.7)	55.5 (9.2)	55.9 (5.1)

[a] From Shultz, Dineen, Elias, Pentz, and Wood (1979) by permission.
[b] Verbal scaled scores not matched.
[c] Groups matched for verbal scaled scores.

age groups of elderly subjects over a ten-year period and reported data on change scores (Test 1 versus Test 2). One group was 60 to 69 years of age at the beginning of the experiment and the other ranged from 70–79 years of age. Hypertension (diastolic = 105+ mm Hg) was associated with a significant change from T_1 to T_2 for the younger group. Surprisingly, borderline hypertension was actually associated with an increase in performance scores over the ten-year period. For the older group, no hypertensive subjects were surviving at T_2, and the borderline hypertensives (90–105 mm Hg) and normotensives (66–95 mm Hg) now showed a significant decline in performance. The decline was slightly larger for the borderline hypertensives. The hypertensives that did not return for T_2 had the lowest initial WAIS scores, and this was true for both age groups. Wilkie and Eisdorfer (1971) suggested that the moderate increase in blood pressure for the borderline hypertensive subjects may have helped to support cerebral perfusion. This notion has a modest indirect grounding in the literature (e.g., Obrist, 1964), but the Wilkie-Eisdorfer study did not provide a direct test of this hypothesis.

For Wilkie and Eisdorfer's older groups of subjects, low significant correlations between initial WAIS scores and blood pressure values were observed for all the WAIS subtests except for vocabulary and picture arrangement ($r = -0.22, -0.30$). For the younger group, no significant correlations between initial verbal scores and blood pressure values were obtained. In general, then, the Wilkie-Eisdorfer study indicated that the older group of elderly subjects was more adversely affected by hypertension than the younger group of elderly subjects. In the present experiment, a difference between hypertensives and normotensives for the Verbal scaled scores was observed for the younger subjects but not for the older subjects; for the Performance scaled scores, differences between hypertensives and normotensives were more exaggerated for the younger subjects. The studies are not contradictory. The Wilkie and Eisdorfer study involved many methodological differences from ours: 1. they used much older subjects, 2. their subjects were *not* taking a diuretic at the time of testing, 3. many of their hypertensives displayed hypertension-associated-pathologies and 4. they employed a longitudinal design. We are planning a longitudinal follow-up (5-year) study with our young and middle-aged hypertensives. One major question is whether our findings of more exaggerated performance differences for younger subjects is an artifact of our cross-sectional design or truly reflective of an interaction between age and hypertension.

Neuropsychological Test Results

Subjects participating in neuropsychological testing represented a subsample of subjects who were employed in the WAIS study. They were subjects who volunteered to come to the laboratory for more extensive testing on selected tests from the Halstead-Reitan Battery: 1. the Category Test, the Tactual Performance Tests (Time, Memory, and Localization Portions); 2. the Finger Tapping Test; and 3. Parts A and B of the Trail Making Test. Each of these tests has been particularly useful in discriminating between brain-damaged and normal subjects (Reitan 1955; 1958), and the particular tests chosen included a very difficult test of learning set ability (Category Test), a simple psychomotor response test (Tapping), and a tactual discrimination task (Tactual Performance Test) which includes two quick tests of memory (memory for forms and memory for the location of forms).

The design of the neuropsychological test study and the WAIS study differed in two respects: 1. subjects were not tested while blood pressure values were lowered to normal by a diuretic; 2. subjects in the medicated hypertensive group were actually taking medication at the time of testing. As for the WAIS study, subjects were assigned to the hypertensive group if blood pressure values exceeded 140/90 mm Hg, if the physicians' diagnosis of hypertension (essential) was confirmed at the hypertension clinic, and if they met the medical diagnostic criteria summarized earlier in this chapter. Normotensive subjects had no history of hypertension and blood pressure values less than 140/85 mm Hg. There were no differences among or between: PRA levels, medicated versus unmedicated subjects, and examined versus non-medically examined normotensives. Thus, the final design involved four groups: younger and middle-aged hypertensive and normotensive subjects.

Generally, older subjects performed less well on the tests involving timed serial response (TPT-Time and Trail Making). The range of scores on TPT-Memory and Finger Tapping were so restricted that they have little practical meaning. (An age by blood pressure interaction was observed for both with more exaggerated differences for the younger hypertensives).

An important trend was observed for the Category scores (Table 6). *A priori* comparisons indicated a significant difference between hypertensives and normotensives for the younger group, but the difference was not significant for the older subjects. Normotensive younger subjects performed significantly better than normotensive older subjects, but young and old hypertensive subjects did not differ. Standardized discriminant coefficients indicated that the Categories Test was by far the most discriminating of the tests employed with regard to differences between the blood pressure groups. Poorer performance on the Categories Test by hypertensives was predicted on the basis of Goldman, Kleinman, Snow, Bidus, and Korol's (1974) finding of a positive correlation between diastolic blood pressure and errors on the Category Test ($r = 0.52$, $df = 12$) for a group of poorly educated VA hospital patients who varied widely in IQ and education. (When scores were adjusted statistically for

Table 6. Means and Standard Deviations[a] for Errors on the Category Test[b]

	Younger	Older
Normotensive	22 (18.1) N = 16	40 (27.3) N = 21
Hypertensive	49 (27.4) N = 11	48 (19.3) N = 14

[a] In parenthesis.

[b] Abstracted from data presented by Pentz, Elias, Wood, Schultz, and Dineen (1979) by permission.

IQ and age, the correlations were $r = 0.48$ and $r = 0.57$ respectively). For the hypertensive subjects in the present experiment, a significant positive correlation was obtained between errors on the Category Test and diastolic blood pressure values ($r = 0.452$, N = 25). Neither the Goldman et al. study nor our study indicated a significant correlation between systolic blood pressure values and errors for the hypertensive subjects.

A correlational analysis which included all normotensive subjects and hypertensive subjects referred to our laboratory (N = 65) regardless of blood pressure values or age, indicated a correlation of $r = 0.263$ between diastolic blood pressure values and errors on the Category Test. Age was positively correlated with TPT-Timed scores and performance on the Trail Making Tests (timed tests), range 0.287–0.370. The correlational analyses support findings for the study in which subjects were classified into discrete blood pressure and age groups, but r^2s for these correlations are low. These low r^2s indicate that prediction of age and blood pressure status from these tests is poor. We reached the same general conclusion when ω^2 analyses (measures of strength of association) were applied to our analyses of variance data, and when we attempted to classify patients as hypertensive or normotensive on the basis of test scores, but without knowledge of their diagnostic category. Using both approaches, the prediction of hypertensive status from Category scores (or age from time scores) was very poor. This is not surprising as the variability among subjects within groups was quite high, particularly for the Category scores (see Table 5).

In summary, our data indicated that hypertensives as a group appear to perform less well on the Category Test than normotensives, yet there is no evidence that essential hypertensives, as individuals, can be characterized as cognitively inferior or brain-damaged. Similarly, there is no evidence that well educated hypertensives are inferior performers in an absolute sense. While hypertensives performed less well than normotensives on the WAIS, performance for hypertensive subjects was well above the average for the population as a whole. Examination of Light's data for the serial reaction time study with a very large number of subjects (n = 203) indicates very small differences in serial reaction time, i.e., normotensive ($\overline{X}$= 335.29 sec), non-medicated hypertensive ($\overline{X}$= 341.26 sec), medicated hypertensive ($\overline{X}$= 355.84 sec); range SD = 16.25–25.29 sec. In fact, Light reported a correlation of $r = 0.34$ between mean arterial pressure and performance and a correlation of $r = 0.54$ between age and performance. Age accounted for a larger portion of the variance in serial reaction time scores, but neither age nor mean arterial pressure accounted for *large* portions of variance in a clinical-predictive sense. Just as one finds that not all older persons perform more poorly than all young persons, one also finds that not all essential hypertensive subjects perform more poorly than all normotensive subjects. While it may seem inappropriate to emphasize such an obvious point, the reader has only to review studies of neuropsychological test performance and hypertension to find that essential hypertensives are often characterized as suffering from cognitive dysfunction (e.g., Goldman et al., 1974). Generally, studies suggesting cognitive impairment in hypertensives have either not employed subjects who are, strictly speaking, essential hypertensives or they have not used carefully medically examined *normotensive* control groups who have been matched with respect to age and education (see Elias, in press for a review). When these controls are employed, the prediction of hypertensive status from cognitive performance is poor. This comes as no surprise. It is recognized that essential hypertension reflects multiple disease entities (Page and McCubbin, 1978; Simonson and Brozek, 1959; Marx, 1976).

Summary and Conclusions

Future Studies

Investigations of hypertension and cognitive performance in humans are often constrained to existing treatment and diagnostic programs (e.g., Spieth, 1965; Light, 1975, 1978; Pentz et al., 1979; Schultz et al., 1979). Under these circumstances, the investigator must fit the research paradigm to the existing treatment or diagnostic program. The result is that methodologies vary from study to study and it is, consequently, difficult to resolve conflicting findings. This is revealed in the literature on hypertension, age, and cognitive performance. Spieth (1965) found no differences between medicated and normotensive subjects; Light (1975, 1978) found that the latter performed better than the former and that, contrary to Spieth's findings, untreated hypertensives did not perform more poorly than normotensives on a composite speed score (serial reaction time tasks). The two studies differed in a number of significant respects including: 1. the possibility of different stress levels for Spieth's three groups of subjects; 2. the fact that Light's subjects were tested under the influence of a potent diuretic; 3. the fact that subjects in Light's experiment had been removed from medication from 3 to 21 days prior to testing. In a study in which subjects were tested under the same conditions as Light's subjects, we (Schultz et al., 1979) found no differences between medicated and non-medicated hypertensives; both groups performed more poorly than controls, but we used a test of general intelligence, the WAIS, rather than a test of serial reaction time. Further, our studies of neuropsychological test performance (Pentz et al., 1979) did not indicate significant differences between hypertensives that were, and were not, medicated at the time of testing. The medicated group performed more poorly than the non-medicated group, but the differences were not statistically significant. The differences decreased further when the subjects were equated for blood pressure values obtained at a time when the patients were free from medication for purposes of medical examination. We might postulate that serial reaction time tasks are more sensitive to direct side effects of drugs than are more general cognitive tasks, but we found no differences between medicated and non-medicated subjects on any of the subtests of the WAIS involving timed serial performance (Schultz et al., 1979). Furthermore, Light (1979) did not find that any general class of medications for hypertension was associated with poorer performance than any other. The question of effects of medication on performance will not be resolved easily. It is difficult, if not impossible, to control types and dosages of medications for hypertension. It is a common practice for physicians to alter these parameters in order to satisfactorily reduce blood pressure levels, and different combinations of drugs are often used. Light found that the estimated duration of hypertension was not associated with performance, but it is most difficult to estimate duration of hypertension adequately, particularly for older subjects who matured at a time when the emphasis on early diagnosis and treatment of hypertension was less than it is today. To determine adequately the relationship of duration of hypertension to cognitive behavior, it may be necessary to perform longitudinal studies with "at risk" individuals. (We use the term "at risk" to refer to individuals who have a higher than average probability developing hypertension at some time of their life as indicated by one or more predictors, e.g., children who are not hypertensive but are "at risk" in view of a family history of hypertension.) Alternatively, animal studies may contribute some insight into the effects of medication on the performance of hypertensives (Elias, 1978, in press, a).

Our studies did not indicate a difference among subjects classified into high, normal, and low plasma renin activity groups; but, as was true for

Light's studies, the number of subjects who could be classified as falling in the high renin groups was very small relative to normal and low renin subjects and in an absolute sense. Thus, we cannot conclude, the PRA has no influence on performance. PRA has not been adequately examined as a factor, but it is an important variable for further study because it provides a prognostic index. Data will have to be collected for a very large number of subjects in order to obtain enough high PRA patients to adequately test the PRA hypothesis.

The Issue of Age Bias

Age bias, introduced by the deleterious effects of disease on cognitive functioning, can result in two ways: 1. there is an abnormally high incidence of disease in one or more age groups; 2. the disease has a more pronounced influence on the behavior of specific age groups, e.g., the elderly person. Previous research (Wilkie and Eisdorfer, 1971) indicates that for *elderly* individuals with severe pathologic hypertension, the cognitive functioning of older elderly groups is more seriously affected by the disease than the cognitive performance of younger elderly groups.

The question we raised in our experiments was whether uncomplicated essential hypertensive subjects would show decrements on the WAIS and some commonly used neuropsychological tests, and whether the effects would be more pronounced for the middle-aged subjects. Surprisingly, there has been a consistent finding (in our studies) of more exaggerated differences between hypertensives and normotensives for the young as opposed to the middle-aged groups on those tests for which a blood pressure by age interaction has been obtained, i.e., the WAIS, the Category Test, the TPT-Memory Test, and the Finger Tapping Test. On these tests, hypertensives performed more poorly than normotensives; performance differences between hypertensives and normotensives were greater for the younger hypertensives; and, younger subjects performed better than older subjects, but only for the normotensive groups.

It is not an understatement to say that there is considerable uncertainty as to which factors may be contributing to this unexpected phenomenon. We used cross-sectional sampling procedures and thus our differences may be related to some unknown artifact of sampling. Studies such as ours depend on volunteers and we do not know what factors may influence differentially the characteristics of younger and middle-aged normotensive and hypertensive volunteers. We have examined the possibility that anxiety and depression may be contributing to the poor performance of hypertensives, particularly younger hypertensives. Wood, Elias, Schultz, Pentz, and Dineen, (1979) found that hypertensives (young and middle-aged) were more depressed and exhibited higher state anxiety scores than normotensives, but correlations between these anxiety and depression tests and performance (Zung, 1965; Spielberger, Gorsuch, and Lushene, 1970) measures were low and non-significant (Pentz et al., 1979). Of course, correlations with these few tests do not rule out the possible influence of personality variables and other "performance-extraneous variables" that may be influencing the age by blood pressure interaction. However, there are some data that indicate that this interaction may, indeed, represent a developmental trend. Hertzog, Schaie, and Gribbin (1978) found performance *increments* on several subtests of the Primary Mental Abilities Test when 56-year-old essential hypertensives were retested after seven years. Normotensives exhibited performance *decrements* on the same longitudinal comparisons. We do not really have enough information about the essential hypertensives in this sample to advance hypotheses as to why this trend was obtained, but these authors (Personal Communication, Hertzog and Shaie, 1979) plan to provide the results of a more in-depth examination of these data in the near future. One might advance the hypothesis that differences are less between the middle-aged hypertensive and normotensives than the younger normotensives and hypertensives because the latter hypertensives are survivors. This is unlikely as these are not severely hypertensive patients but rather essential hypertensives. It is possible that the poorer performing young essential hypertensives develop pathology prior to middle age and are, therefore, not included in the middle-aged samples (hypertensives with hypertension-associated pathology are excluded). A longitudinal follow-up of our subjects from the Upstate Medical Center Clinic is absolutely essential to test this hypothesis and to determine whether the poor performance of young adult hypertensives represents an artifact of our cross-sectional designs. A follow-up would also allow us to determine which of the younger essential hypertensives develop hypertension-associated pathology during the follow-up period, and to compare their performance during the initial testing when they were diagnosed as essential hypertensives.

An Epilogue

A discussion of mechanisms underlying the poorer performance of groups of hypertensive subjects is absent from this chapter by design. There is no *direct* evidence that positive associations between uncomplicated essential hypertension and performance are related to cerebral perfusion or difficulties in auto-regulation as some investigators have hypothesized, e.g., Light, 1975, 1978; Spieth, 1965; Wilkie and Eisdorfer, 1971. While the hypothesis has some merit with respect to the elderly pathogenic hypertensive in the Wilkie and Eisdorfer study, it is premature with respect to studies of younger and middle-aged hypertensives. There are simply too many other possibilities, including artifacts of design and selection, that have not been fully explored. Moreover, Elias, (1978, in press, a) has shown that positive assocation between hypertension are often non-causal in nature. Human studies, including ours, have been purely descriptive in nature, and thus, do not speak directly to the issue of causal associations between essential hypertension and performance.

References

Birren JE: Age changes in speed of behavior: its central nature and physiological correlates. In Welford AT, Birren JE (eds.) *Behavior, Aging, and the Nervous System.* Springield, Ill., Charles C Thomas, 1965.

Birren JE, Bulter RN, Greenhouse SW, Sokoloff L, Yarrow MR: Interdisciplinary relationships: Interrelations of physiological, psychological, and psychiatric findings in healthy elderly men. In Birren JE, Butler RN, Greenhouse SW, Sokoloff L, Yarrow M (eds.) *Human Aging: A Biological and Behavioral Study.* (National Institute of Mental Health, U.S. Public Health Service Publication No. 986). Washington, U. S. Government Printing Office, 1963.

Birren JE, Spieth WJ: Age, response speed and cardiovascular functions. *J Gerontology* 17:390–391, 1962.

Brunner HR, Laragh JH, Baer L, Newton ME, Goodwin FT, Krakoff LR, Bard RH, Buhler FR: Essential hypertension: renin and aldosterone, heart attack and stroke. *New Eng J Medicine* 286:441–449, 1972.

Elias MF: Animal models for the study of age, hypertension and behavior: testing the non-causality hypothesis. In Sprott RL (ed.) *Aging and Intelligence.* New York, Van Vostrand-Reinhold, in press, a.

Elias MF: Relationships between hypertension and performance: causal or coincidental. In Sprott RL (ed.), *Aging and Intelligence.* New York, Van Nostrand-Reinhold, in press, b.

Elias, MF: Some contributions of genetic selection to the study of hypertension and behavior over the life span. In Bergsma D, Harrison DE (eds.) *Genetic Effects on Aging.* The National Foundation March of Dimes Birth Defects: Original Article Series. New York, Alan R. Liss, Inc., Vol. XIV, 1, 1978, pp. 121–156.

Elias MF, Elias PK, Elias JW: *Basic Processes in Adult Developmental Psychology.* St. Louis, Missouri, C. V. Mosby, 1977, pp. 221–254.

Goldman H, Kleinman KM, Snow MY, Bidus DR, Korol B: Correlation of diastolic blood pressure and signs of cognitive dysfunction in essential hypertension. *Diseases of the Nervous System* 35:571–572, 1974.

Hertzog C and Schaie KW are planning to prepare a chapter which will provide expanded information on the hypertension data (Personal Communication, June, 1979).

Hertzog C, Schaie KW, Gribbin K: Cardiovascular diseases and changes in intellectual functioning from middle to old age. *J Gerontology* 33:872–883, 1978.

Light KC: Effects of mild cardiovascular and cerebrovascular disorders on serial reaction time performance. *Experimental Aging Research* 4:3–22, 1978.

Light KC: Slowing of response time in young and middle-aged hypertensive patients. *Experimental Aging Research* 1:209–227, 1975.

Marx JL: Hypertension: a complex disease with complex causes. *Science* 194:821–825, 1976.

Obrist WD: Cerebral ischemia and the senescent electroencephalogram. In Simonson E, McGavack TH (eds.) *Cerebral Ischemia*. Springfield, Ill., Charles C Thomas Publishing Co., 1964.

Page IH, McCubbin JW: *Renal Hypertension*. Chicago, Year Book Medical, 1968.

Pentz, CA, Elias, MF, Wood WG, Schultz NA, Dineen J: Relationship of age and hypertension to neuropsychological test performance. *Experimental Aging Research* 5:351–372, 1979.

Reitan RM: The validity of the Trail Making Test as an indicator of organic brain damage. *Perceptual and Motor Skills* 8:271–276, 1958.

Reitan RM: An investigation of the validity of Halstead's measures of biological intelligence. *Archives of Neurological Psychiatry* 73:28–55, 1955.

Schultz NR Jr, Dineen JT, Elias MF, Pentz CA, Wood WG: WAIS Performance for different age groups of hypertensive and control subjects during the administration of a diuretic. *J Gerontology* 34:246–253, 1979.

Simonson E, Brozek J: Russian research in arterial hypertension. *Annals of Internal Medicine* 50:129–193, 1959.

Spielberger CD, Gorsuch RL, Lushene RE: *STAI Manual for the State-Trait Anxiety Inventory*. Palo Alto, California, Consulting Psychologists Press, Inc., 1970.

Spieth, W: Slowness of task performance and cardiovascular diseases. In Welford AT, Birren JE (eds.) *Behavior, Aging, and the Nervous System*. Springield, Ill., Charles C Thomas, 1965.

Spieth W: Cardiovascular health status, age, and psychological performance. *J Gerontology* 19:277–284, 1964.

Streeten DHP, Anderson GH, Freiberg JM, Dalakos TG: The use of angiotensin II antagonist (saralasin) in the recognition of (angiotensinogenic) hypertension. *New Engl J Medicine* 292:647–662, 1975.

Wang HS, Busse EW: Heart disease and brain impairment among aged persons. In Plamore E (ed.) *Normal Aging II*. Durham, N.C., Duke University Press, 1974.

Watson WE: *Components of reaction time slowing with aging and with hypertension*. Unpublished master's thesis, Syracuse University, Syracuse NY, 1976.

Watson WE, Dineen J, Elias MF, Pentz CA, Wood WG: A comparison of hypertensives and mormotensives with an information processing task. An unpublished study. Sponsored by the National Institute on Aging (AG 00868).

Wechsler D: *Manual for the Wechsler Adult Intelligence Scale*. New York, The Psychological Corporation, 1955.

Wechsler D: A standardized memory scale for clinical use. *J Psychology* 19:87–95, 1945.

Wilkie FL, Eisdorfer C: Intelligence and blood pressure in the aged. *Science* 172:959–962, 1971.

Wilkie FL, Eisdorfer C, Nowlin JB: Memory and blood pressure in the aged. *Experimental Aging Research* 2:3–16, 1976.

Wood WG, Elias MF, Schultz NR, Pentz CA: Anxiety and depression in young and middle-aged hypertensive and normotensive subjects. *Experimental Aging Research* 5:15–30, 1979.

Zung WWK: A self-rating depression scale. *Archives of General Psychiatry* 12:63–70, 1965.

Stein, ed. The Psychobiology of Aging: Problems and Perspectives

Aging of the Somatosensory System in Man*

John E. Desmedt and Guy Cheron

Brain Research Unit, University of Brussels, 115 Bd de Waterloo, B1000 Brussels Belgium.

There are only few quantitative data to document the current belief that the aging decrement of physiological capabilities may not involve to the same extent, nor at the same rate, the various parts of the human nervous system. Histological studies reporting extensive loss of neurons in the cerebral cortex have been questioned on several grounds (bias in neuron counting, smallness of samples, etc.) but they appear to suggest that the loss may be less severe in some areas such as the postcentral gyrus (Brody, 1970; Hanley, 1974; Corsellis, 1976). The electronic averaging of somatosensory evoked potentials (SEP) elicited by well-defined exteroceptive stimuli offers a noninvasive method for testing the electrical responses of neurons at different levels of the afferent pathway. For example, the recording of sensory nerve action potentials (SNAP) along the peripheral nerve (Gilliatt and Sears, 1958) permits the peripheral conduction velocity (CV) to be estimated; the averaged SEPs recorded at the level of the neck provides data about the time of entry of the afferent volley in the spinal cord, while the cerebral SEP recorded from the contralateral scalp identifies the arrival of the corticipetal volley and the subsequent cortical responses (Desmedt, 1971; Desmedt, Noël, Debecker and Namèche, 1973; Halliday, 1978; Desmedt and Cheron, 1978, 1980; Small, Beauchamp and Matthews, 1980; Desmedt and Brunko, 1980).

•The research reported has been supported by grants from the Fonds de la Recherche Scientifique Médicale and the Fondation Interuniversitaire pour l'Etude Scientifique des Processus de Vieillissement (Belgium), and by the Muscular Dystrophy Association of America.

SEPs are rather specific neural activities time-locked to a sensory event and their consistent features can be used to document possible changes with age of the response sizes and of the transit times along the somatosensory pathway. We tested two well-defined groups of subjects: normal young adults between 20 and 25 years (mean 22 years) and healthy people between 80 and 90 years (mean 82.3 years). The latter were persons without evidence of any specific (cardiovascular, pulmonary, mental or neurological) disease or diabetes and who were maintaining an active community life (Desmedt and Cheron, 1980b). In view of the selection inevitably exercised by mortality, these octogenarians seemed to offer a fair opportunity for discovering how well the SEP features can be maintained and which are the ones to deteriorate first in normal aging. They were carefully chosen in an attempt to evaluate only the aging changes in the absence of complicating disease factors.

Methods

Twenty five, normal young adults and 19 octogenarians who had been medically screened were studied in detail. The subjects rested on a comfortable couch in a sound-proofed, electrically shielded room. They were asked to remain relaxed and avoid contraction of the cephalic muscles. In conformity with the Helsinki declaration the subjects had given explicit consent for the recording procedures which they subsequently described as mild and acceptable.

The stimuli were electrical pulses delivered to the fingers II and III through silver ring electrodes. The stimulus intensities were monitored by a current probe and maintained at about 3 times subjective threshold. The limbs were warmed by infrared illumination before the session and the tissue temperature was 36–37°C in all subjects. The afferent volley was recorded with stainless steel sterile needles inserted close to the median nerve at different levels and averaged. SEPs were recorded from the neck (level of sixth cervical vertebra) and from the contralateral parietal scalp focus, with an earlobe reference. The bandpass of the amplifier extended from 2.5 kHz to 0.15 Hz (Desmedt, Brunko, Debecker and Carmeliet, 1974). A Nicolet digital computer model 1074 was used with bin width of 80 μs and 1,024 trials uncontaminated by artifacts were as a rule averaged. The traces were written out by a X-Y plotter. Details of the procedures can be found elsewhere (Desmedt, 1977; Desmedt and Cheron, 1980a,b).

The SEP components are labelled by considering their positive (P) or negative (N) polarity and their peak latency, thus following recent recommendations of an international committee (Donchin et al., 1977).

Results

The electrical stimulation of fingers does not involve any muscle contraction and elicits a well-defined volley in skin and joint afferents without any group I fibers. The SNAPs recorded along the median nerve are reduced in peak voltage in the octogenarians. Their onset latency represents a conduction time which is linearly related to the distance between the finger cathodes and the recording site (Figure 1). The neck SEP presents a clear negative component (Figure 2A,C) which is thought to represent activities generated in the dorsal horn (Desmedt and Cheron,

Figure 1. Graph relating the onset latency of various evoked potentials (abscissa) to the distance between the stimulating cathode on the finger and the level of the recording electrode (ordinate). The onset latencies of the sensory nerve action potentials recorded from wrist to axilla indicate a peripheral conduction velocity of 61 m/s. This fits in with the onset latency of the neck SEP recorded at the sixth cervical vertebra (C6). The onset of the N22 SEP component is indicated along the abscissa by an arrow and it represents the arrival time of the afferent volley at the cortex. The dotted line corresponds to a maximum central conduction velocity of 49 m/s in this male subject of 81 years. While the peripheral CV is slowed, the central CV is within the normal adult range.

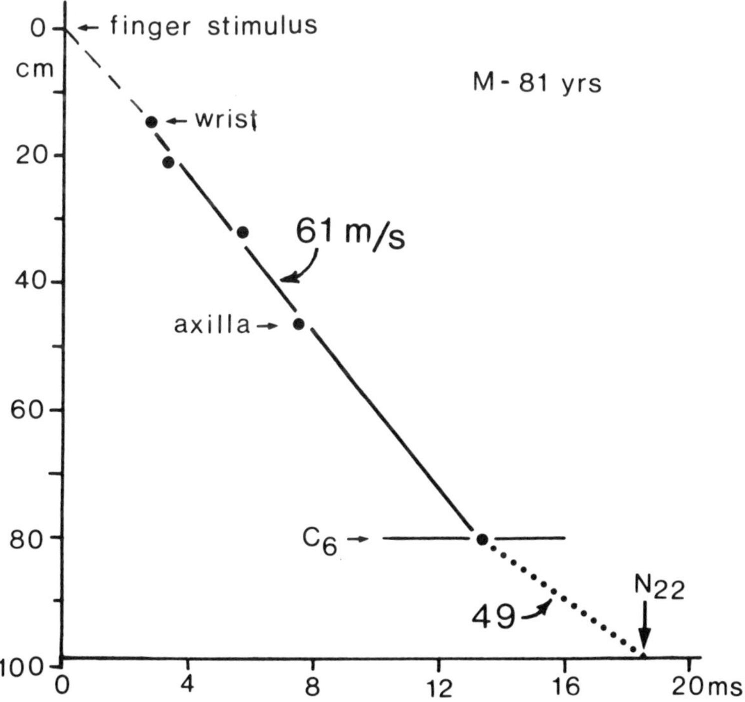

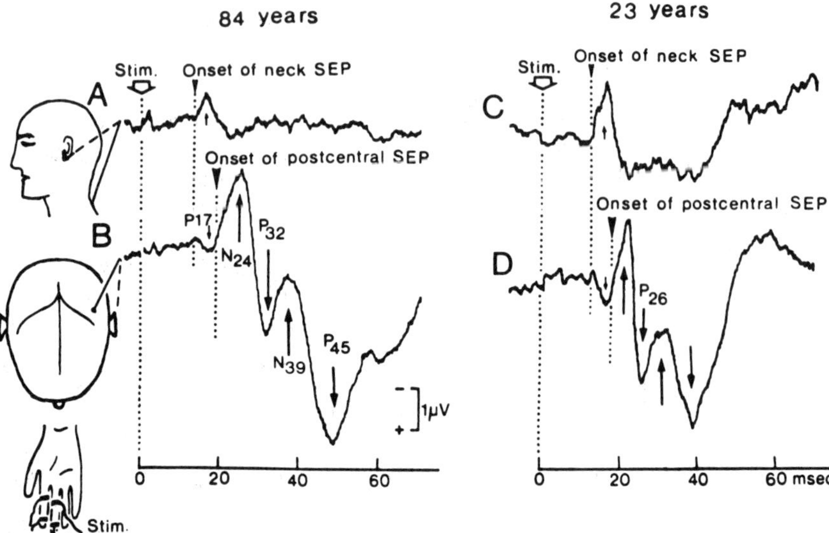

Figure 2. Averaged somatosensory evoked potentials elicited by electrical stimulation of fingers II and III of the right hand in healthy subjects of 84 years (left) and of 23 years (right). The recording conditions and the calibration of the traces are identical for the two subjects. A and C, neck SEP recorded at the level of the sixth cervical vertebra with an earlobe reference. B and D, SEPs recorded at the contralateral parietal scalp focus for the hand. The SEP components are indicated by an arrow and labelled (see text). Negativity of the recording electrode drives the trace upwards. The vertical rows of dots indicate respectively, the time of delivery of the finger stimuli, the onset of the neck SEP corresponding to signal cord entry of the afferent volley, and the onset of the postcentral negative N24 component corresponding to arrival of the volley at the cortex.

1980c). Its onset latency fits in remarkably well with the extrapolated afferent CV calculated between wrist and axilla (Figure 1). The mean peripheral afferent CV is 71.1 m/s in the young adults and 61.2 m/s in the old subjects ($p < 0.001$). This results in a mean delay of about 2 ms for the arrival of the volley at the spinal cord in the octogenarians.

The peak voltage of the neck SEP is significantly reduced in the old subjects, 0.4 ± 0.1 μV, as compared to the young adults, 0.9 ± 0.3 μV ($p < 0.001$). This must be related at least in part to afferent axon loss, as documented by a reduction to about 25% of the antidromic action potentials recorded from digital nerves (Desmedt and Cheron, 1978). The electrophysiological test for axonal loss is more reliably made by the antidromic action potentials which are recorded under more reproducible conditions (DiBenedetto, 1972).

The SEP recorded from the contralateral scalp focus for the hand presents a typical sequence of components. After the diffuse far-field P17 (representing volume-conducted subcortical activities in the corticipetal pathway) a clear negative component N24 is recorded which is restricted to the contralateral parietal region (Figure 2B,D). The N24 is characteristic of the SEP in man and it is also a prominent feature in the human newborn and child (Desmedt and Manil, 1970; cf Desmedt, Brunko and Debecker, 1980 for a recent discussion). This negative early component is not recorded in mammals and primates in whom the cortical SEP starts with a surface-positive component (Woolsey, 1958; Desmedt, 1971).

The onset of N24 provides direct evidence for the time of arrival of the volley at the receiving areas of postcentral cortex. When taking into account individual variations in head size, the transit times between the onsets of the neck SEP and the N24 present no significant difference between the two groups studied ($p < 0.005$). The maximum central CV along the lemniscal pathway can be calculated from these transit times after allowing for 4 synaptic delays ($0.3 \times 4 = 1.2$ ms) (see Desmedt, 1971; Desmedt et al., 1973): the mean values of central CV of 45.4 m/s in the young adults and 44.4 m/s in the octogenarians are not significantly different ($p > 0.7$) (Desmedt and Cheron, 1970, 1980b).

The profile of SEP shows a definite trend towards larger components with increased transit times between their onsets in the octogenarians (Figure 2). For example the mean N24 peak amplitude is significantly larger in the old, 1.1 μV than in the young adults, 0.7 μV ($p < 0.01$). The duration of N24 is also significantly increased as illustrated by typical traces in Figure 2.

Discussion

These electrophysiological observations with a non-invasive method, document rather striking quantitative changes during normal aging of the brain. The alterations of the sensory potentials are quite definite, yet of moderate severity. The findings on the whole, do not suggest any general rundown of the system with chronological age since some of the functional measures are decreased while others are maintained within normal limits, or can even be increased (Figure 2).

The reduction in sensory nerve potential amplitude must be related to an increased incidence with age of various histological anomalies. These may be due to cumulative mechanical damage in addition to the atrophy and loss of sensory neurons (Dyck, 1975). The mean slowing of the maximum afferent CV, namely -9.6 m/s over the 60 years separating the two groups, corresponds to a mean reduction of only -0.23% per year, if it is assumed that the decrease is linearly distributed over that age span. In any case, the time of entry into the spinal cord (indexed by the neck SEP onset) undergoes a mean delay of only about 2 ms in the octogenarians. This would appear unlikely to affect, by itself, the perceptual functions.

An unexpected feature is the lack of any significant reduction of the transit time from cord to cortex, and of the maximum central CV. The central axons are of course not directly exposed to mechanical trauma as are peripheral axons. In addition, they are much shorter which should make them less susceptible to axonal atrophy (Onishi, O'Brien, Okazaki and Dyck, 1976) when metabolic support capabilities undergo an age decrement. The question of whether the rates of aging decrement might be slower for the relay neurons in dorsal column nuclei and in ventrobasal thalamic nuclei is also a possiblity. Indirect evidence along that line is the histological constancy of neuron content in other discrete brain stem nuclei (Konigsmark and Murphy, 1972; Monagle and Brody, 1974; Hanley, 1974).

The increased amplitude of the early components of the cortical SEP is at first surprising, in view of the loss of neurons mentioned by histologists (Brody, 1970). However, it is important to consider as background the patterns of aging changes in dendrites, dendritic spines and intracortical connections. Aging pyramidal neurons in neocortex appear to show a greater reduction of their basal dendrites than of their apical dendrites (Scheibel and Scheibel, 1975). Buell and Coleman (1979) recently indicated that the main feature in normal aging cortex is rather the hypertrophy of the apical dendritic tree. Thus, the two groups concur, at least for pointing towards a relative increase of the apical dendritic system of pyramids in aging human neocortex. This may have some relation to our finding of increased parietal N24, in view of the maturation story, since prominent N24 SEP components with increased duration have also been documented in the normal human newborn (Desmedt and Manil, 1970) and anatomical studies indicate a later maturation of the basal dendritic system (as compared to apical) in immature mammals (Molliver and Vanderloos, 1970; Desmedt et al., 1980). Thus it could be considered that the enhancement of the early cortical negative component would be somehow related to a relative functional increase of apical connections in pyramids both in the human newborn and infant, and in the aged (Desmedt and Cheron, 1980a,b). In any case, the enhancement of the early cortical negativity in the octogenarians is an important finding that suggests the occurrence of major reorganization at the neuronal level within the cortex of the parietal region.

References

Brody H: Structural changes in the aging nervous system. Interdisciplinary Topics. *Gerontology, Karger (Basel)* 7:9–21, 1970.

Buell SJ, Coleman PD: Dendritic growth in the aged human brain and failure of growth in senile dementia. *Science* 206:854–856, 1979.

Corsellis JAN: Some observations on the Purkinje cell population and on brain volume in human aging. In Terry RD, Gershon S (eds.) *Neurobiology of Aging* Vol. 3. New York, Raven Press, 1976, pp. 205–210.

Desmedt JE: Somatosensory cerebral evoked potentials in man. In Rémond A (ed.) *Handbook of Electroencephalography and Clinical Neurophysiology,* Vol. 9. Amsterdam, Elsevier, 1971, pp. 55–82.

Desmedt JE: Some observations on the methodology of cerebral evoked potentials in man. In Desmedt JE (ed.) *Attention, Voluntary Contraction and Event-related Cerebral Potentials. Progress in Clinical Neurophysiology.* 1977, Basel, Karger, vol. 1;, 1977, pp. 12–29.

Desmedt JE, Brunko E: Functional organization of far-field and cortical components of somatosensory evoked potentials in normal adults. In Desmedt JE (ed.) *Progress in Clinical Neurophysiology, Vol. 7.* Basel, Karger, 1980, pp. 27–50.

Desmedt JE, Brunko E, Debecker J: Maturation and sleep correlates of the somatosensory evoked potentials. In Desmedt JE (ed.) *Clinical Uses of Cerebral, Brain Stem and Spinal Somatosensory Evoked Potentials. Progress in Clinical Neurophysiology,* Vol. 7. Basel, Karger, 1980, pp. 146–161.

Desmedt JE, Brunko E, Debecker J, Carmeliet J: The system bandpass required to avoid distortion of early components when averaging somatosensory evoked potentials. *Electroencephalography and Clinical Neurophysiology* 37:407–410, 1974.

Desmedt JE, Cheron G: Aging, cerebral evoked potentials, and the somatosensory pathway. *Neurology* 28:347, 1978.

Desmedt JE, Cheron G: Somatosensory pathway and evoked potentials in normal human aging. In Desmedt JE (ed.) *Clinical Uses of Cerebral, Brain Stem, and Spinal Somatosensory Evoked Potentials. Progress in Clinical Neurophysiology,* Vol. 7. 1980, Basel, Karger, 1980a, pp. 162–169.

Desmedt JE, Cheron G: Somatosensory evoked potentials to finger stimulation in healthy octogenarians and in young adults: wave forms and central transit times of parietal and frontal components. *Electroencephalography and Clinical Neurophysiology* 1980b, vol. 49.

Desmedt JE, Cheron G: Central somatosensory conduction in man: neural generators and interpeak latencies of the far-field components recorded from neck and right or left scalp and earlobes. *Electroencephalography and Clinical Neurophysiology* 1980c, Vol. 49 (in press).

Desmedt JE, Manil J: Somatosensory evoked potentials of the normal human neonate in REM sleep, in slow wave sleep and in waking. *Electroencephalography and Clinical Neurophysiology* 29:113–126, 1970.

Desmedt JE, Noël P, Debecker J, Namèche J: Maturation of afferent conduction velocity as studied by sensory nerve potentials and by cerebral evoked potentials. In Desmedt JE (ed.) *New Developments in Electromyography and Clinical Neurophysiology,* Vol. 2. Basel, Karger, 1973, pp. 52–63.

DiBenedetto M: Evoked sensory potentials in peripheral neuropathy. *Archives of Physical Medicine and Rehabilitation* 53:126–132, 1972.

Donchin E, Callaway E, Cooper R, Desmedt JE, Goff WR, Hillyard SA, Sutton S: Publication criteria for studies of evoked potentials: report of a committee. In Desmedt JE (ed.) *Attention, Voluntary Contraction and Event-related Cerebral Potentials. Progress in Clinical Neurophysiology,* Vol. 1. Basel, Karger, 1977, pp. 1–11.

Dyck PJ: Pathologic alterations of the peripheral nervous system of man. In Dyck PJ, Thomas PK, Lambert EH (eds.) *Peripheral Neuropathy.* Philadelphia, W.B. Saunders, 1975, pp. 296–336.

Halliday AM: Clinical applications of evoked potentials. In Matthews WB, Glaser GH (eds.) *Recent Advances in Clinical Neurology,* Vol. 2. Edinburgh, Churchill Livingstone, 1978, pp. 47–73.

Hanley T: Neuronal fall-out in the aging brain: a critical review of the quantitative data. *Age and Aging* 3:133–151, 1974.

Gilliatt RW, Sears TA: Sensory nerve action potentials in patients with peripheral nerve lesions. *J Neurology, Neurosurgery and Psychiatry* 21:109–118, 1958.

Konigsmark, Bruce W, Murphy EA: Volume of the ventral cochlear nucleus in man its relationship to neuronal population and age. *J Neuropathology and Experimental Neurology* 31:304–316, 1972.

Molliver ME, Vanderloos H: The ontogenesis of cortical circuity: the spatial distribution of synapses in somaesthetic cortex of newborn dog. *Ergebnisse der Anatomie und Entwicklungs Geschichte* 42:1–54, 1970.

Monagle RD, Brody H: The effect of age upon the main nucleus of the inferior olive in the human. *J Comparative Neurology* 155:61–66, 1974.

Onishi A, O'Brien PC, Okazaki H, Dyck PJ: Morphometry of myelinated fiber of fasciculus gracilis of man. *J Neurological Sciences* 27:163–172, 1976.

Scheibel ME, Scheibel AB: Structural changes in the aging brain. In Brody H, Harman D, Ordy JM (eds.) *Aging,* Vol. 1. New York, Raven Press, 1975, pp. 11–37.

Small DG, Beauchamp M, Matthews WB: Subcortical somatosensory evoked potentials in normal man and in patients with central nervous system lesions. In Desmedt JE (ed.) *Clinical Uses of Cerebral, Brain Stem and Spinal Somatosensory Evoked Potentials. Progress in Clinical Neurophysiology,* Vol. 7. Basel, Karger, 1980 pp. 190–204.

Woolsey CN: Organization of somatic sensory and motor areas of the cerebral cortex. In Harlow HF, Woolsey CN (eds.) *Biological and Biochemical Bases of Behavior.* Madison, University of Wisconsin Press, 1958, pp. 63–81.

Stein, ed. The Psychobiology of Aging: Problems and Perspectives

Psychophysiological Studies of Aging Effects on Cognitive Processes[a]

Gail R. Marsh and Wayne E. Watson

Center for the Study of Aging and Human Development and Department of Psychiatry, Duke University Medical Center, Durham, North Carolina.

Introduction

One of the major reserach efforts in psychophysiology is to discover how physiological variables are related to mental processes. Once such relationships are established, then the physiological variables can be used as indices of mental processes. Typically such indices are measurements at some peripheral body site, such as the electrical activity from the heart, skin or brain recorded from the chest, palm or scalp, respectively. Such peripheral sites are important since brain physiology cannot be directly observed in the human as it can in animals. These indices achieve meaning only when an experiment has established a high correlation with a proposed mental process. Since mental processes are inferred from observable behavior via a theoretical model, when correlations are low it could be due, among other things, to use of a poor theoretical model, or to collection of inappropriate physiological data through poor recording techniques.

In the study of mental processes via physiological indices it is not assumed that a causal link exists between the two phenomena. Thus a psychophysiologist may be quite content to use physiological indices that are epiphenomena as long as those measures allow tracking of mental events. The term "transfer function" is often used to describe the relationship between a physiological variable and an observable behavior

[a] We acknowledge financial support from Training Grant AG-00029 and Research Grant AG-00364 from the National Institutes of Health.

that is thought to be related to a mental process. Thus, for example, one may wish to plot an observable behavior such as how fast a response key is pressed in relation to the physiological index, heart rate. The postulated relationship is that the faster key press is demonstrative of faster decision making due to greater attention or arousal.

One of the difficulties in exploring age effects on behavior and physiology is that the transfer functions for a number of the indices of mental functions may be changed by the process of aging. If the heart, skin, or the brain itself are changed by age (which they certainly are), then different transfer functions will have to be worked out for each age grouping. The outlines of such age-related changes will be described below along with some of the constraints within which such work must take place.

Autonomically Controlled Systems

The aging nervous system is known to undergo several physiological and anatomical changes. It is also confronted by a body that is undergoing a multitude of changes. The problem of control of body function is thereby compounded by the changes in the various body systems, in addition to the changes internal to the nervous system. This is nowhere better seen than in the autonomic nervous system and the systems that it controls. Two such systems have received the lion's share of attention: the cardiovascular system and the sudomotor system of the skin.

Cardiovascular Activity

The cardiovascular system changes in many ways with age. In an unstimulated state the heart beats more slowly, with a more prolonged contraction and with a weaker force. The heart muscle loses elasticity which constrains the volume to which the heart can fill. The aorta and arterial tree also lose elasticity, making the heart work into a network more analogous to iron plumbing than one composed of stretchable rubber walls. These alterations force compensatory changes such as a lesser volume of blood pumped out with each beat to help restrain the large pulse pressure induced by each beat. As the constraints on the system become tighter with age, both systolic and diastolic blood pressure slowly rise as the heart attempts to keep the necessary volume of blood flowing. With these compensatory changes already operating, it can be seen that additional stress via postural changes, exercise or emotion can rapidly push the older cardiovascular system to its limits.

Other aspects of cardiovascular control show equally great changes. The blood pressure reflex which depends on receptors in the carotid sinus and aorta and is coordinated in the brain stem, loses a great deal of sensitivity with age. Since this reflex normally works to control blood pressure, the system is less able to control blood pressure accurately as the reflex loses sensitivity.

Further, the heart and blood vessels lose some of their reactivity to norepinephrine, the sympathetic nervous system neurotransmitter, and to epinephrine. The action of these catecholamines on the cardiovascular system is to increase blood pressure, heart rate and the contractile force of the heart. However, age-related alteration of several aspects of the catecholamine-cardiovascular interaction has made interpretation of the data difficult. The threshold for effects of norepinephrine on the cardiovascular system drops with age (Frolkis, Bezrukov, Bobatskaya, Verkhratsky, Zomasttian, Shevtchuk and Shtchegoleva, 1970). This is not accompanied by an accentuation of response since the cardiovascular system in the elderly does not show as large an increase in cardiac contractility to norepinephrine as it does in young adults (Lakatta, Gerstenblith, Angell, Shock and Weisfeld, 1974). There is, additionally, a decreased contractility of the arteries in response to norepinephrine (Tuttle, 1966). Thus, while thresholds may be lower, reaction of the system within its normal working range is decreased with age. On the other hand, the response of the norepinephrine-releasing system to stress is much enhanced in the elderly (Palmer, Ziegler and Lake, 1978). Thus, while the cardiovascular system may be less responsive, other systems may be more effectively stimulated by the higher level of norepinephrine release.

It should be noted that, in a normal young adult, although one aspect of cardiovascular function may change, there are often compensatory changes in other aspects of the system to keep the output of the total system relatively constant. For example, while heart rate may fall, cardiac output often increases for each beat, thereby keeping blood flow constant. In the elderly the capacity for such compensation is reduced. The effect of this loss of compensation is that the range of variability of most cardiovascular measures is reduced in the elderly.

Psychophysiological data obtained in typical, low stress, reaction time tasks have substantiated what would be predicted from the above circumstances: that heart rate and blood pressure change very little during these tasks (Morris and Thompson, 1969; Thompson and Nowlin, 1973). Since psychophysiologists are recording physiological activity because they are interested in the relationships of those variables to mental activity, the decreases in reactivity have generally been interpreted in psychological, rather than physiological, terms. In fact, most often, the focus of the study will be on hypothesized mental processes such as arousal or attention. Comparison of such processes across age groups is based on the assumption that the same transfer function works for all groups. This assumption, however, is likely to be false.

For example, psychophysiologists have generally been interested in recording aspects of cardiovascular function, such as heart rate, because these variables were thought to be related to the amount of arousal or attention demanded by the task. One well-replicated finding (Lacey, 1967) is that the greater the slowing of heart rate just prior to acting in a reaction time task, the faster will be the response. Young adults show this pattern consistently; elderly adults do not (Morris and Thompson, 1969; Thompson and Nowlin, 1973). Figure 1 is a diagrammatic representation of this finding.

The results were interpreted to suggest that the elderly have a lower level of arousal, or decreased attentive powers. Other research (Lacey and Lacey, 1970) has shown that heart rate and brain potentials were strongly related, and both were correlated with reaction time. Since Thompson and Nowlin (1973) were unable to find a correlation between these two physiological variables in the elderly, it has been suggested that concordance between activity in the CNS and peripheral nervous system may deteriorate with age and could be an important aspect of behavior in reaction time tasks (Thompson and Marsh, 1973; Marsh and Thompson, 1977). However, Froehling (1974) did find a strong relationship between brain potentials, heart rate and reaction time in elderly

Figure 1. Young adults show increased slowing of heart rate during the preparatory period of a warned reaction time task. The elderly group, by comparison, shows little change.

SOURCE: *Morris and Thompson, 1969, by permission.*

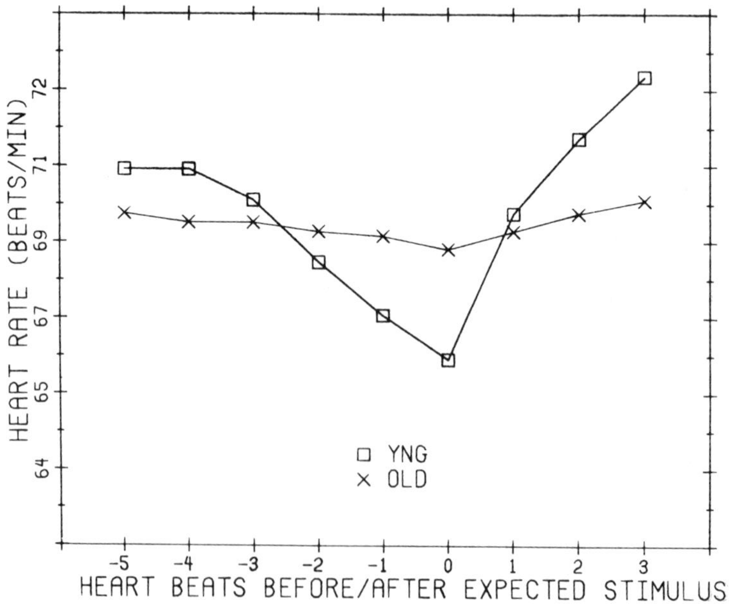

males. She noted that the persons used in her study were of above average health for their age group, which may account for the differences between that study and others.

The above studies found decreased variabiltiy in heart rate in the elderly in low stress reaction time studies. These studies interpreted these results in terms of psychological factors, such as decreased attentive capabilities. Such an interpretation seems to be based on a false assumption. Heart rate change with age may be largely determined by changes in cardiovascular physiology which have little impact on attentive abilities. To make psychological interpretations without establishing a new transfer function which incorporates the changed physiology, is to run the risk of forming false theoretical conclusions.

A recent study (Furchtgott and Busemeyer, 1979) has indicated that heart rate data gathered from older adults may have a further complexity. They found that the elderly often did not return to baseline levels before the start of the next trial. Thus, in addition to phasic changes in heart rate preceding and during a task, they suggest that it may also be necessary to monitor heart rate recovery during the intertrial interval.

Vigilance tasks have also been used to examine the performance of the elderly. The underlying general hypotheses have been that the elderly were less aroused and that physiological and behavioral measures obtained over a prolonged task period would demonstrate such decrements. The typical pattern in such tasks is for few targets to be missed during the early portion of the monitoring task, but for omission error rate to increase late in the task. In long-term monitoring tasks, the increased errors have generally been attributed to a decrease in arousal. These studies show that during time spent "on task," older persons decline no more than younger persons (Davies, 1968). Thus there is no reason to invoke concepts of lowered arousal in the elderly. Only one study has produced evidence of lower arousal in a vigilance task. Surwillo (1966) showed palmar skin temperature to rise for the elderly, while it fell for the young during an hour of monitoring a Mackworth clock. Such skin temperature increases are typical of a drowsy person. However, other measures (changes in heart rate and electrodermal activity) showed no difference in rate of decline between old and young. Furthermore, while Surwillo (1966) did show a lower level of performance for the elderly for the last 15 min of monitoring, most studies using other types of vigilance tasks have shown no difference between old and young (Davies, 1968). Thus, there seems to be little evidence for loss of arousal with age.

Electrodermal Activity

Electrodermal activity in the elderly has been observed to be of lower amplitude and frequency than in younger persons. Thus, the elderly produce fewer spontaneous electrodermal responses per minute (Surwillo and Quilter, 1965). Since such skin activity is taken as an indication of emotional arousal, a straightforward interpretation would be that older persons are less emotionally aroused (especially less anxious). It is also the case that the basal level of electrodermal activity is lower in older persons and that electrodermal activity elicited by specific stimuli is lower in amplitude (Shmavonian, Yarmat and Cohen, 1965). Such lowered levels of reactivity in younger persons would be interpreted as lowered levels of cognitive engagement in the tasks. However, the findings for the elderly otherwise seem to parallel those for the young. For instance, those words eliciting the largest electrodermal responses are those that are best recalled (Shmavonian and Busse, 1963; Zelinski, Walsh and Thompson, 1978).

Here again, the anatomy and physiology of the older person must be examined as a possible determinant of many of these effects. Two similar models of electrodermal effects have been proposed (Edelberg, 1972; Fowles and Rosenberry, 1973; Fowles and Venables, 1970). Both models propose the sweat glands and the epidermis itself as separate generators of electrical potential acting in parallel. To the extent that sweat gland activity was reduced, that the sweat gland population was reduced, or that some alteration in the resistive qualities of the epidermis took place with age, then reduced electrodermal activity would be recorded. Several studies have shown a reduction in the population of sweat glands with age (MacKinnon, 1954; Ferreira and Winter, 1965). This change alone could affect other skin parameters, such as dryness. That these and possibly other skin alterations do affect electrodermal recording has been established (Garwood, Engel and Quilter, 1979). It may be possible that, in the young, one type of generator (the sweat gland) may predominate while in the elderly the other generator (the epidermis) may predominate under some conditions.

Again, conclusions drawn about psychological states based on physiological data may be incorrect, until better understanding is achieved of how the physiological systems and their characteristics have changed since young adulthood. Only with such knowledge will it be possible to make proper interpretations from the physiological to the psychological state.

One of the issues studied with regard to aging changes is whether the older person is, in some sense, less aroused. The studies of age changes in arousal have all fallen short of showing a specified change in arousal level. They all appeal to the inverted U concept of Yerkes and Dodson (1908) on how arousal and performance are related. That is, performance is poor at a low arousal level and improves with increasing arousal until some critical point is passed, whereupon further increases in arousal bring about loss in performance level. None of the studies have tested at least three different levels of arousal, which is the minimum needed to establish a curvilinear relationship between performance and arousal level as the latter is increased by task demands. Thus, there are no substantial data to support the notion of either over- or under-arousal on the part of the elderly. (For a review of the evidence in detail, see Marsh and Thompson, 1977.)

One aspect of the Yerkes-Dodson relationship between arousal and performance that seems to be largely overlooked (for an exception see Kahneman, 1973) is that the arousal-performance relationship is altered by the complexity of the task. Performance on simple tasks improves with increasing arousal until very high levels of arousal are attained, at which point performance drops. Complex tasks peak much earlier and show decreases in performance when only moderately high levels of arousal are reached. Before one can test for arousal level differences between groups, there is the additional necessity of verifying whether the task is equally complex for both groups. Obtaining that assurance seems about as easy as obtaining agreement among investigators as to whether the elderly are over- or under-aroused.

Direct CNS Measures

Psychophysiological measures of CNS function, such as EEG and event-related potentials, have provided evidence for slowing of cognitive and sensory functions. The EEG spectrum shows an increase of low frequencies after 75 years of age (Obrist and Busse, 1965). The more often studied alpha rhythm shows a decrease in frequency after 60 years of age (Otomo, 1966). Reactivity of the EEG to events in the environment is also altered by age. Wilson (1962) showed that alpha blocking to a bright light habituated more rapidly in the elderly than in a young group. Health status, while not studied directly, does affect the EEG spectrum. Hospitalized elderly show greater slowing, which is spread more diffusely over the entire scalp, than do persons who are still active (Marsh and Thompson, 1977). Fewer changes in the EEG spectrum were noted in a longitudinal study of healthy persons still active in community affairs, then would have been predicted from earlier cross-sectional studies (Wang, Obrist and Busse, 1970).

The event-related potential (ERP) has been shown to reflect age-related differences. The ERP is the electrical event recorded from the scalp just following the delivery of a stimulus to a person. A steady decline in amplitude is found from age 40 onward, for the somatosensory and visual ERP recorded from a person who has been instructed to merely remain relaxed and alert (Schenkenberg, 1970; Dustman, Schenkenberg and Beck, 1976). Such a decline was not found for the auditory ERP. Some of the early peaks in the visual and somatosensory ERP have shown amplitude increases with age (Straumanis, Shagass and Schwartz, 1965;

Luders, 1970; Dustman and Beck, 1969). These early components of the ERP (occurring before a latency of 80 msec) are generally regarded as reflecting stimulus parameters (e.g., brightness, number of edges).

When the stimuli are given in a context in which they must be cognitively processed by the subject (as opposed to the above passive conditions), the later components (occurring later than 80–100 msec after the stimulus) become important. These later components are believed to reflect the cognitive aspects of the stimulus. For instance, if stimuli are paired such that the first (S1) is always followed by the second (S2) at a constant interval (such as 1.2 sec), and the person must respond in some manner to S2, then a continuing negative wave (the contingent negative variation, or CNV) will begin about 500 msec after S1 and continue until S2. Simple stimuli, such as clicks or flashes are often used. CNV amplitude has been related to expectancy and is found primarily over frontal and central midline areas of the scalp. The modality of the stimuli is not related to CNV amplitude, rather it is the expectancy set of the person that is important.

Loveless and Sanford (1974) could find no difference in CNV amplitude between old and young groups at several different test intervals between S1 and S2, ranging from 0.5 to 15 sec. However, they did find a difference in the form of the CNV. The young subjects showed an abrupt increase in amplitude just before S2, while the elderly did not. This could be interpreted as the young showing some superior ability to "expect" the stimulus or estimate the interval. However, since S2 signaled a key press, it is likely that the increase was the premotor potential that has been related to preparedness for a key press (Deeke, Becker, Grozinger, Scheid and Kornhuber, 1973). This seems even more plausible when the differences in response time (RT) latency and variability between old and young are taken into account: the old were slower and more variable, thus delaying premotor potential onset. Further, Deeke (Deeke, Englitz and Schmitt, 1978) has shown that premotor potentials are much reduced in amplitude with age.

In a study of CNV amplitude (Marsh and Thompson, 1973) S1 was a standard tone and S2 was a tone to be judged as above, below or the same as the standard in pitch. The CNV amplitude was found to be smaller in old males compared to young adult males. However, young adult females were also lower in amplitude than the young males. The CNV amplitudes were inversely related to the ability to perform the auditory discrimination.

Two other aspects of the ERP have received specific attention in aging studies: N100 (or N1) and P300 (or P3 or late positive component—LPC). These potentials are especially intriguing since they seem to be related to mental processes that have been extensively investigated by psychologists interested in cognitive processes. A number of experiments by Hillyard and colleagues (Hillyard, Hink, Schwent and Picton, 1973; Schwent, Snyder and Hillyard, 1976; Van Voorhis and Hillyard, 1977) have related N1 to "stimulus set" selection, and LPC to "response set" selection as these concepts of selective attention have been set forth by Broadbent (1970, 1971). Essentially, stimulus set allows a person to selectively attend to specific stimuli, if these stimuli can be segregated from other stimuli by some easily identifiable physical feature, such as intensity or pitch for an auditory stimulus, or color or location for a visual stimulus. Response set is involved when the person must use higher level stimulus attributes (such as the meaning of a word, digit or letter) in order to select among stimuli. N1 has been shown to be enhanced by stimuli that were selected under stimulus set, and the LPC has been reported to be enhanced by stimuli that were selected while under response set conditions. When old and young were compared in an auditory experiment of this type, the amplitude and latency of N1, under stimulus set conditions, was not different (Ford, Hink, Hopkins, Roth, Pfefferbaun and Kopell, 1979). Further the changes in N1 amplitude due to stimulus set selection were equivalent in young and old. LPC amplitude was larger in response to the targets than nontargets (response set selection) and the difference was similar for both young and old. The LPC was longer in latency in the older group under all conditions. Thus, in this selective attention task, young and old were not differentiated by their ERPs except by the overall effect of the elderly having an unchanging longer LPC latency.

An important aspect of cognitive processes is how long they take. One process, that of scanning through short-term memory, has been studied extensively using a procedure introduced by Sternberg (1969). In this procedure, a person holds several single digits in memory as a list and a probe digit is presented on a screen. The person must respond as quickly as possible as to whether the probe matches any of the digits held in memory. As the memorized list is made longer, search time is lengthened. The task has been divided into several components: encoding the stimuli, comparison of the probe with each digit in the list, decision ("yes" or "no" to having found a match), and response execution (usually a key press). With persons in their mid-fifties, the comparison process has been shown to be slowed (Anders, Fozard and Lillyquist, 1972). Further, persons in their late sixties show an increased amount of time spent in other components of the process, such as the encoding and response execution states. The LPC seems to be related to the comparison or decision stage for, as the memorized list is lengthened, the LPC latency also increased (Marsh, 1975). This same study also found older persons had a strong, but non-significant tendency ($p = .06$), for a longer overall latency LPC than younger persons (i.e., 630 msec vs 550 msec).

Watson (1977) partially replicated the Marsh (1975) study and found the LPC latency difference between young and old to be significant. This study also found that the amplitude of the LPC decreased with increasing list length, and the effect was stronger for older than for younger persons. In both studies, the parietal region of the head showed the largest amplitude LPC and the most statistically significant effects. In a second experiment, Watson (1977) showed that irrelevant digits flanking the probe digit slowed the decision response as well as the LPC. However, both young and old were slowed to an equal extent. This was interpreted as indicating that the elderly were equally capable of using selective attention mechanisms to eliminate interference from non-relevant stimuli. Earlier work by Rabbitt (1965) had shown that irrelevant stimuli on cards in a card-sorting task slowed older persons more than young. In the Watson study, the subjects knew in which location relevent stimuli would appear, while in the Rabbitt study, the subjects did not. Presumably in the Rabbitt study subjects had to examine each item on a card, while in the Watson study, items in irrelevant locations could be ignored.

In some studies, the ability of the selective attention merchanism to use warning cues to help in the processing of information has been found to decrease with age. However, the use of such advance information cues may depend on the complexity of the rules for its use. Rabbitt (1964) instructed each person to hold a list of four digits and four letters in memory. On each trial, a single number or digit was presented which required a response with either the right or left hand. Letters were assigned to one hand and digits to the other for responding. Of the four letters (numbers) two were assigned to one finger and two to a second finger on the same hand. The advance information consisted of telling the person whether a digit or a letter would be presented on that trial. The elderly did not benefit from the advance information, even when given up to 1500 msec to interpret it.

However, a similar experiment by Marsh and Linnoila (1979) produced a contrary result. In this experiment, when one of eight keys (four to each side of a central starting position) was illuminated, it was to be pressed as quickly as possible. The elderly benefited from advance information that predicted whether one of the right or left four keys would be illuminated. The difference between Rabbitt's study and Marsh and Linnoila's may have been in the ease of use of the advance information. Information which requires a great deal of processing may be of little use, while information which requires only a little processing may be very useful.

A further test of this hypothesis was carried out by Watson and Marsh (in preparation). A visual display of four letters (placed at the corners of an imaginary square) was presented to each person on each trial. A memorized list of three letters was maintained by each person. If any one of those three letters appeared in the display, the "yes" key was pressed (right hand) as quickly as possible, otherwise a "no" key was pressed (left hand). Advance information consisted of arrows. In an easy condition, either one or three arrows pointed radially outward, from a central fixation point, to one or three of the display locations. The difficult condition was identical, except that instead of presenting the arrows in a radial fashion from the fixation point, they were presented linearly in a row across the screen, just above the fixation point. Thus, the person had to perform a mental reorientation to extract the meaning of the arrow or arrows.

As expected, RT for an older group of males (aged 59–72) was slower overall than for a younger group (aged 20–29). RT was faster in the one-arrow than the three-arrow condition, indicating that the arrows were effective as cues for limiting the search of the display. However, no difference in RT was found between the radial arrow (easy) and linear arrow (difficult) conditions for either group, which suggests that our attempt to manipulate processing difficulty failed.

A second method for assessing the effectiveness of the arrows as search-limiting cues produced an intriguing finding. For the trials on which three arrows were presented, four letters were presented half of the time, and for the remaining half, letters were presented only at the three indicated locations; the remaining location was blank. Since visual search time is determined by the number of letters searched, if the advance information was totally effective, then the RT for three arrows should be the same, no matter if three letters are displayed or four. The results showed that for "yes" responses the advance information was totally effective and equally so for young and old. However, for "no" responses, the three-letter displays were searched faster than the four-letter displays for both young and old. In effect, to some extent it would appear that both groups went on to check the remaining fourth, uncued location when they failed to find a match in the cued locations.

ERPs elicited by the arrow stimuli were recorded from frontal (Fz) and central (Cz) and from midparietal (P3 and P4) locations on left and right hemispheres, all referenced to linked mastoids. The N1 component was larger for young than for old, at both Fz and Cz. The responses at Cz were larger and are illustrated in Figure 2.

It can be seen that the old group had only a barely discernable N1 component. No component corresponding to N1 was observed for any subject at the parietal locations. For the LPC at all four scalp locations, the amplitude was larger and the latency was longer for one arrow than for three arrows. Perhaps this should be considered in conjunction with the notion that one arrow carries more information than three arrows. (That is, one arrow reduces the number of locations to be searched from four to one, while three arrows only reduce the number of locations from four to three.) Older persons had longer latency LPCs than did younger

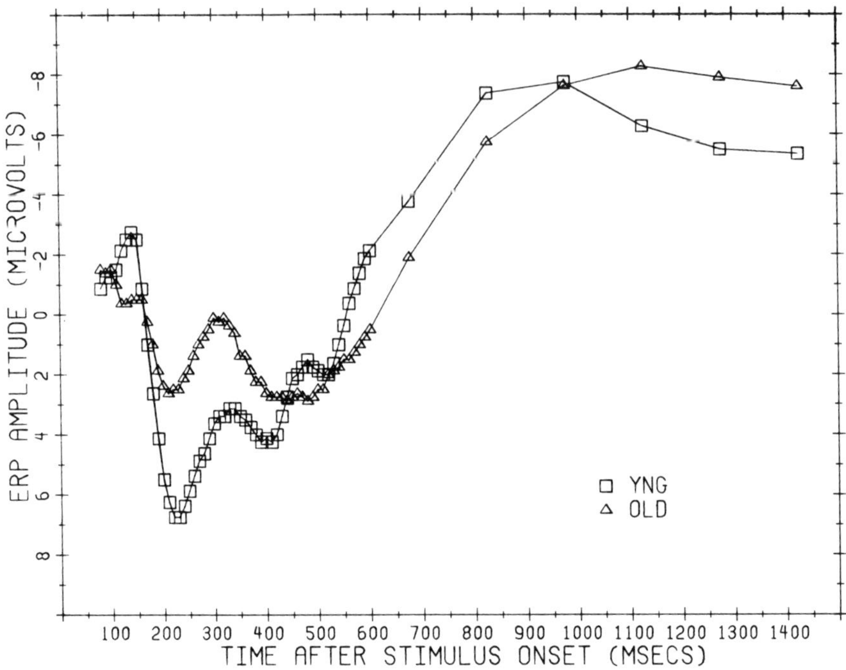

Figure 2. The reduced amplitude of the ERP for the elderly group over the latency period of 100–600 msec is easily seen. The later plateau of the CNV for the elderly can also be noted. These ERP were elicited by the warning cue (both one- and three-arrow cues have been averaged together for this illustration). These recordings were made at Cz with reference at the linked mastoids.

persons. Overall, the amplitude of ERP components in the older group was about 60% of those found in the younger group.

The CNV peaked and declined at about 900 msec at Fz and Cz in the young, but not until about 1100 msec in the old. At P3 and P4, the CNV waveform did not peak, but maintained its amplitude. The largest CNV was seen at Cz and the smallest at Fz. For all locations the largest CNV amplitudes were seen to one-arrow cues. CNVs for young and old are illustrated in Figure 2.

General Discussion

In summary, older persons are as competent as young adults in selecting among stimuli using simple stimulus attributes [e.g., pitch and intensity in the Ford et al. (1979) study and the arrows in the present study]. However, the longer latency LPCs in the elderly suggest that decisions about the target stimuli do take longer. RTs for the elderly support this interpretation.

Several models of how the LPC relates to brain function have been suggested. One model (Donchin, Kubovy, Kutas, Johnston and Herning, 1974) proposes that the LPC reflects the operation of a "generalized cortical processor." LPC latency is linked to the latency of the initiation of the processor. An alternative model has been proposed (Squires, Hillyard and Lindsay, 1973) in which the LPC reflects the output of a template match mechanism. LPC amplitude is proportional to the degree to which two items match. This model is directly applicable to an interpretation of the list length manipulation of the memory search tasks. For memory search, the first model would predict latency shifts, if there was any delay in initiating the general processor, while the second would predict amplitude differences dependent on the proportion of matches to mismatches. There is support for both models, since as lists get longer the initiation of the generalized processor could be delayed and the number of matches to mismatches obviously declines.

Returning to the issue of transfer functions, there is a need to determine if the task-related differences in ERPs are different for different age groups. It is possible that both young and old respond mentally in exactly the same way to task manipulations, but that age-induced alterations in peripheral physiology make it appear as though changes had occurred in mental processes. However the common view would be the opposite, that mental processes are changed by aging just as physiological processes are. The evidence from the studies examined here would support the notion that age and task separately affect the ERP. However the exact nature of these changes is still obscure. In general, the psychophysiologist studying age effects must establish how the physiological responses being measured are related to behavior in each age group, before investigation can begin on how age and task may affect mental processes.

For linguistics Chomsky (1965) has said that a theory that cannot account for the development of language lacks explanatory adequacy. Aging studies can contribute toward explanatory adequacy in any field, by providing data to falsify models that can only account for results in a limited age range and by developing models which encompass findings from the whole of the life span.

References

Anders TR, Fozard JL, Lillyquist TD: The effects of age upon retrieval from short-term memory. *Developmental Psychology* 6:214–217, 1972.

Broadbent DE: Stimulus set and response set: two kinds of selective attention. In Mostofsky DI (ed.) *Attention: Contempory Theory and Analysis*. New York, Appleton-Century-Crofts, 1970.

Broadbent DE: *Decision and Stress*. New York, Academic Press, 1971.

Chomsky N: *Aspects of the Theory of Syntax*. Cambridge, Ma., MIT Press, 1965.

Davies DR: Age Differences in Paced Inspection Tasks. In Talland GA (ed.) *Human Aging and Behavior.* New York, Academic Press, 1968.

Deeke L, Becker W, Grozinger B, Scheid P, Kornhuber HH: Human brain potentials preceding voluntary limb movements. *Electroencephalography & Clinical Neurophysiology* Suppl. 33:87–94, 1973.

Deeke L, Englitz H-G, Schmitt G: Age-dependence of the Bereitschaftspotential. In Otto D (ed.) *Multidisciplinary Perspectives in Event-related Brain Potential Research.* EPA 600/9 77 043, 1978.

Donchin E, Kubovy M, Kutas M, Johnston R, Herning RI: Graded changes in evoked response amplitude as a function of cognitive activity. *Perception & Psychophysics,* 14:319–324, 1974.

Dustman RE, Beck EC: The effects of maturation and aging on the wave form of visually evoked potentials. *Electroencephalography & Clinical Neurophysiology* 26:2–11, 1969.

Dustman RE, Schenkenberg T, Beck EC: The development of the evoked response as a diagnostic and evaluative procedure. In Karrer R (ed.) *Developmental Psychophysiology of Mental Retardation: Concepts and Studies.* Springfield, Ill., Charles C Thomas, 1976.

Edelberg R. Electrical activity of the skin: its measurement and uses in psychophysiology. In Greenfield NA, Sternback RA (eds.) *Handbook of Psychophysiology.* New York, Holt, Rinehart and Winston, 1972.

Ferreira A, Winter W: Age and sex differences in the palmar sweat print. *Psychosomatic Medicine* 27:207–211, 1965.

Ford JM, Hink RF, Hopkins WF, Roth WT, Pfefferbaum A, Kopell BS: Age effects on event-related potentials in a selective attention task. *J Gerontology* 34:388–395, 1979.

Fowles D, Rosenberry R: Effects of epidermal hydration on skin potential responses and levels. *Psychophysiology* 10:601–611, 1973.

Fowles D, Venables P: The reduction of palmar skin potential by epidermal hydration. *Psychophysiology* 7: 254–261, 1970.

Froehling SD: Assessment of Behavioral and Physiological Functioning In Elderly Males. Unpublished doctoral dissertation, University of Miami, 1974.

Frolkis VV, Bezrukov VV, Bogatskaya LN, Verkhratsky NS, Zomasttian VP, Shevtchuk VG, Shtchegoleva IV: Catecholamines in the metabolism and functions regulation in aging. *Gerontologia* 16:129–140, 1970.

Furchgott E, Busemeyer JK: Heart rate and skin conductance during cognitive processes as a function of age. *J Gerontology* 34:183–190, 1979.

Garwood MK, Engel BT, Quilter RE: Age differences in the effect of epidermal hydration on electrodermal activity. *Psychophysiology* 16:311–317, 1979.

Hillyard SA, Hink RF, Schwent VL, Picton TW: Electrical signs of selective attention in the human brain. *Science* 182:177–180, 1973.

Kahneman D: *Attention and Effort.* Englewood Cliffs, N.J., Prentice-Hall, 1973.

Lacey JI: Somatic response patterning and stress: some revisions of activation theory. In Appley MH, Trumbull R (eds.) *Psychological Stress: Issues and Research.* New York, Appleton-Century-Crofts, 1967.

Lacey JI, Lacey B: Some autonomic-central nervous system inter-relationships. In Black P (ed.) *Physiological Correlates of Emotion.* New York, Academic Press, 1970.

Lakatta EG, Gerstenblith G, Angell CS, Shock NW, Weisfeld ML: Diminished inotropic response of aged myocardium to catecholamines. *Circulation Research* 36:262–269, 1974.

Loveless NE, Sanford AJ: Effects of age on the contingent negative variation and preparatory set in a reaction-time task. *J Gerontology* 29:52–63, 1974.

Luders H: The effects of aging on the wave form of the somatosensory cortical evoked potential. *Electroencephalography & Clinical Neurophysiology* 29:450–460, 1970.

MacKinnon P: Variations with age in the number of active palmar digital sweat glands. *J Neurological & Neurosurgical Psychiatry* 17:124–126, 1954.

Marsh GR: Age differences in evoked potential correlates of a memory scanning process. *Experimental Aging Research* 1:3–16, 1975.

Marsh GR, Linnoila M: The effects of Deanol on cognitive performance and electrophysiology in elderly humans. *Psychopharmacology* 66:99–104, 1979.

Marsh GR, Thompson LW: Psychophysiology of aging. In Birren JE, Schaie KW (eds.) *Handbook of the Psychology of Aging*. New York, Van Nostrand-Reinhold, 1977.

Marsh GR, Thompson LW: Effects of age on the contingent negative variation in a pitch discrimination task. *J Gerontology* 28:56–62, 1973.

Morris JD, Thompson LW: Heart rate changes in a reaction time experiment with young and aged subjects. *J Gerontology* 24:269–275, 1969.

Obrist WD, Busse EW: The electroencephalogram in old age. In Wilson WP (ed.) *Application of Electroencephalography in Psychiatry.* Durham, N.C., Duke University Press, 1965.

Otomo E: Electroencephalography in old age: dominant alpha pattern. *Electroencephalography & Clinical Neurophysiology* 21:489–491, 1966.

Palmer GJ, Ziegler MG, Lake CR: Response of norephinephrine and blood pressure to stress increases with age. *J Gerontology* 33:482–487, 1978.

Rabbitt PMA: Set and age in a choice-response task. *J Gerontology* 19:301–306, 1964.

Rabbitt PMA: An age decrement in the ability to ignore irrelevant information. *J Gerontology* 20:233–238, 1965.

Schenkenberg T; Visual, auditory and somatosensory evoked responses of normal subjects from childhood to senescence. Unpublished doctoral dissertation, University of Utah, 1970.

Schwent VL, Snyder E, Hillyard SA: Auditory evoked potentials during multichannel selective listening: role of pitch and localization cues. *J Experimental Psychology: Human Perception & Performance* 2:313–325, 1976.

Shmavonian BM, Busse EW: Psychophysiological techniques in the study of the aged. In Williams RH, Tibbetts C, Donahue W (eds.) *Processes of Aging. Vol. I.* New York, Atherton Press, 1963.

Shmavonian BM, Yarmat AJ, Cohen SI: Relationships between the ANS and CNS in age differences in behavior. In Welford AT, Birren JE (eds.) *Behavior, Aging and the Nervous system.* Springfield, Ill, Charles C Thomas, 1965.

Squires KC, Hillyard SA, Lindsay PH: Cortical potentials evoked by confirming and disconfirming feedback following and auditory discrimination. *Perception & Psychophysics* 13:25–31, 1973.

Sternberg S: Memory-scanning: mental processes revealed by reaction-time experiments. *American Scientist* 57:421–457, 1969.

Straumanis JJ, Shagass C, Schwarts M: Visually evoked cerebral response changes associated with chronic brain syndrome and aging. *J Gerontology* 20:498–506, 1965.

Surwillo WW: The relation of autonomic activity to age differences in vigilance. *J Gerontology* 21:257–260, 1966.

Surwillo WW, Quilter RE: The relation of frequency of spontaneous skin potential responses to vigilance and to age. *Psychophysiology* 1:272–276, 1965.

Thompson LW, Marsh EG: Psychophysiological studies of aging. In Eisdorfer C, Powell Lawton M (eds.) *The Psychology of Adult Development and Aging*. Washington, D.C., American Psychological Association, 1973.

Thompson LW, Nowlin JB: Relation of increased attention to central and autonomic nervous system states. In Jarvick LF, Eisdorfer C, Blum JE (eds.) *Intellectual Functioning in Adults*. New York, Springer Publishing Co., 1973.

Tuttle RS: Age-related changes in the sensitivity of rat aortic strips to norepinephrine and associated chemical and structural alterations. *J Gerontology* 21:510–516, 1966.

Van Voorhis S, Hillyard SA: Visual evoked potentials and selective attention to points in space. *Perception & Psychophysics* 22:54–62, 1977.

Wang HS, Obrist WD, Busse EW: Neurophysiological correlates of the intellectual function of elderly persons living in the community. *Am J Psychiatry* 126:1205–1212, 1970.

Watson WE: Response competition, memory search, and aging: the processing of irrelevant information. Unpublished doctoral dissertation, Syracuse University, 1977.

Watson WE, Marsh GR: Memory search and the effectiveness of search-limiting cues. Manuscript in preparation.

Wilson S: Electrocortical reactivity in young and aged adults. Unpublished doctoral dissertation, George Peabody College for Teachers, 1962.

Yerkes RM, Dodson JD: The relation of strength of stimulus to rapidity of habit-formation. *J Comparative Neurology of Psychology* 18:459–482, 1908.

Zelinski EM, Walsh DA, Thompson LW: Orienting task effects on EDR and free recall in three age groups. *J Gerontology* 33:239–245, 1978.

Stein, ed. The Psychobiology of Aging: Problems and Perspectives

Influence of Age on the Human Cerebral Potentials Associated with Voluntary Movements

L. Deecke

Abteilung Neurologie, Universität Ulm, D 7900 Ulm, West Germany.

Introduction

The normal characteristics of movement-associated potentials in man have been widely investigated (Kornhuber and Deecke, 1964, 1965; Vaughan et al., 1968; Deecke et al., 1969, 1973, 1976; Figure 1). Premovement cortical activity starts as early as 1 to 1.5 sec or longer prior to the onset of the voluntary movement (mean 0.8 sec). This slow cortical negativity has been called the *Bereitschaftspotential* (BP) or readiness potential and, even in the case of unilateral movement, is bilaterally distributed. Only later, about 0.5 sec prior to the onset of movement, a contralateral preponderance of the precentral negativity occurs in many subjects, whereas bilateral symmetry is maintained over parietal leads. The BP is widely distributed over the precentral and parietal cortex with normal amplitudes of 5 to 6 μV, when measured at the contralateral precentral region or at the vertex. It is believed that the BP represents an early preparatory process facilitating synaptic events in apical dendrites of upper cortical layers of those areas that will become active with the intended movement (Deecke et al., 1976).

A second brain potential occurs about 90 to 80 msec prior to the onset of movement. This has been termed the pre-motion positivity (PMP). It consists of a positive potential of 1 to 2 μV that is also widely distributed over the parietal and precentral regions of both hemispheres. It is seen in all monopolar leads of Figure 1. The PMP may represent a motor command released by the parietal cortex and conveyed to subcortical movement generators such as the cerebellum or basal ganglia (Kornhuber, 1974).

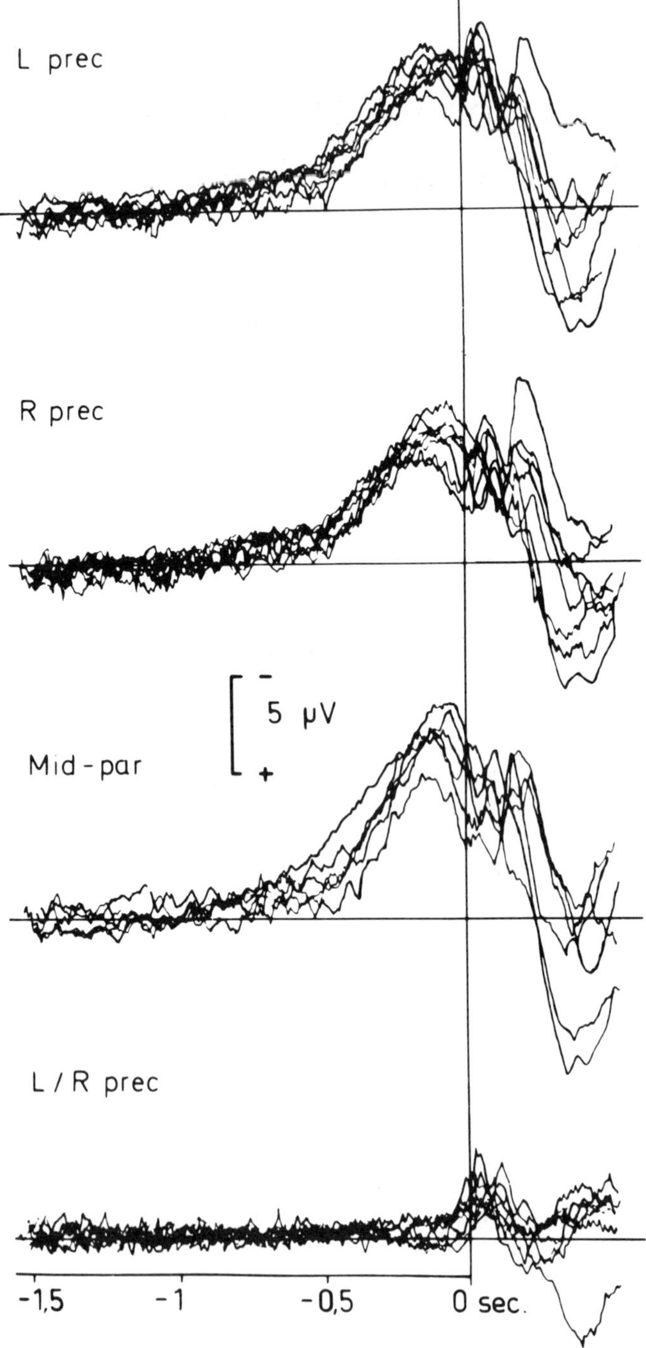
L prec
R prec
5 μV
Mid-par
L / R prec
-1,5
-1
-0,5
0 sec.

Only the third potential occurring prior to movement onset, the motor potential (MP) is unilaterally distributed. It is seen in the lower trace of Figure 1 as an additional negativity of 1 to 1.5 μV occurring on the average 60 to 50 msec prior to the first muscle action potential in the agonist. The MP is restricted to the motor cortex contralateral to the movement. It is thought to reflect activity of motor cortex cells generating the efferent volley, which finally travels down the pyramidal tract, etc.

Since the experimental subjects in all these studies were young university students, changes in movement-related potentials over the normal life span were unknown until recently (Deecke et al., 1978). When investigating patients with Parkinson's disease, a gross diminution of the BP was found (Deecke et al., 1977, 1978; Deecke and Kornhuber, 1978). For comparison age-matched controls were needed which led to the investigation of normal subjects of older age groups.

Methods

Group I (17–29 years) consisted of the data taken from 34 normal subjects of previous experiments. Group II (30–39 years), III (40–49 years), IV (50–59 years) and V (60–69 years) each contained 6 subjects, usually three females and three males. Three subjects performed right-sided and three left-sided voluntary index finger flexions by pulling the

---

Figure 1. Cerebral potentials preceding voluntary movement in a normal young adult subject. Rapid volar flexions of the right index finger. Superposition of the traces of 8 different experiments performed on different days of the same subject, each trace representing the average of 600–800 trials. The upper three groups of records represent recordings from left precentral (L prec) right precentral (R prec) or mid parietal (Mid-par) against linked ears reference (negative up). Bipolar recording between the left (negative upwards) and the right precentral leads (L/R) at the bottom. Zero time (vertical line) indicates the onset of the earliest EMG activity in flexor indicis muscle. The records disclose a high consistency and allow the identification of three different potentials:

1. The negative *Bereitschaftspotential* (BP) or readiness potential starting about 0.8 sec bilaterally over parietal and precentral regions.
2. The pre-motion positivity (PMP), a positive kinking of the waveform 90–80 msec prior to first EMG activity, also bilateral over parietal and precentral regions.
3. The negative motor potential (MP), onset time 60–50 msec, unilateral, restricted to contralateral motor cortex, best seen in bipolar left versus right precentral recording (bottom).

SOURCE: *Deecke et al., 1976, Figure 1.*

trigger of a modified pistol. These subjects were neurological clinic patients with non-cerebral diseases (ruptured intervertebral disks etc.) All were right-handed. As stated above, movement onset was defined as the very first EMG activity detected in the agonist muscle (M. flexor digitorum communis, pars indicis). The EMG, recorded through bipolar surface electrodes, was rectified and averaged. The index finger was rapidly moved, held in position, and returned only after analysis time. Four to five hundred finger movements at irregular intervals of 4–9 sec were averaged per experiment. The subjects fixed their gaze on a target during the trials and avoided eye blinking. In addition, oculomotor and other artifacts were eliminated by on-line editing. Cranial electrode positions included C_3, C_4, C_z, P_3, P_4 and P_z (10/20 system) referred to linked ear lobes. Monopolar recordings and two bipolar derivations C_3/C_4 and C_3/C_z were stored on tape and reverse-averaged off-line. BP amplitude was calculated as the arithmetic mean of the six monopolar leads (five leads in group I because there was no vertex recording). Two points of measurement were selected: BP_{150} equal to the amplitude (with respect to a pre-potential base-line), 150 msec before movement onset, and BP_0 at movement onset. Statistical analysis included an analysis of variance and tests of correlation.

Results and Discussion

The results show that a BP can be recorded in all subjects including the elderly. Representative original recordings are shown in Figure 2 for a 31-year-old subject of group II (left) and a 67-year-old subject of group V (right). A marked reduction of the negative BP is seen in the older subject. This finding of a gradual decline of the negative BP with age was confirmed by comparing the group means, as was done in Figure 3. The hatched columns represent BP_{150} measurements, white columns, BP_0 amplitudes. Both amplitudes showed gradual decline with age. Statistically, the reduction of BP_0 with age (analysis of variance over groups II to V) was significant ($p < 0.01$). The reduction of BP_{150} was just short of significance ($p = 0.06$). Group I was not included in the analysis of variance since the 34 subjects of this group belonged to a previous set of experiments. Furthermore, electrode placements of this series did not include the vertex with its generally large potential. The slightly larger amplitude in group II as compared to I can thus be explained. BP_0 of group II averaged -5.48 μV with the vertex and only -5.3 μV without the vertex, a figure, that compares exactly to the BP_0 of group I. It can be concluded, therefore, that the average BP amplitude is rather constant until the end of the fourth decade of life and then gradually declines. This could also be shown by using correlation tests. The average coefficient of correlation (r) across the 6 leads was 0.58 for BP_{150} ($2p <$

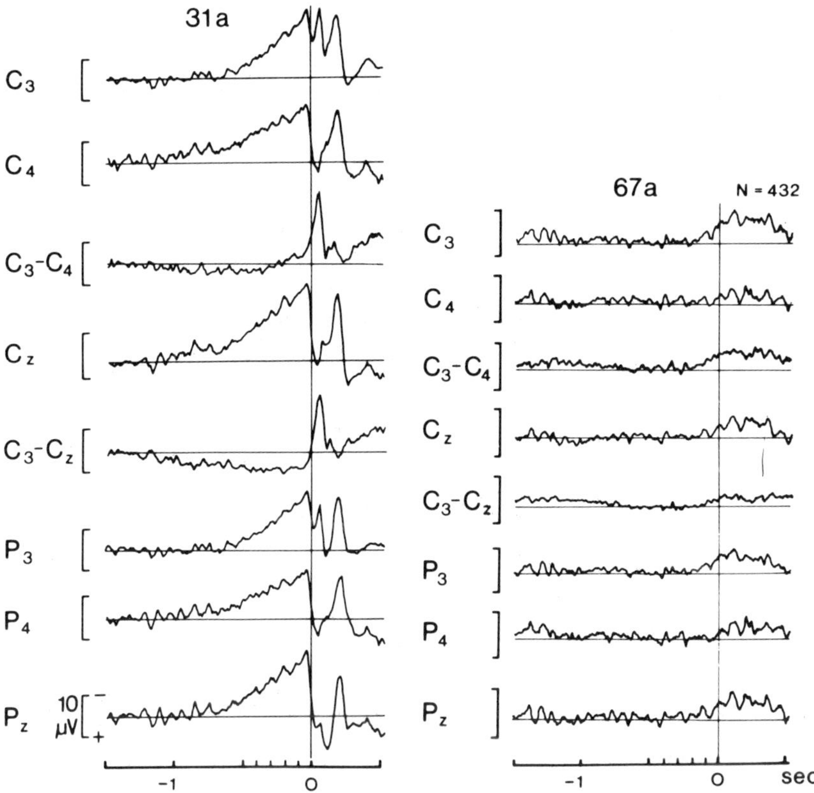

Figure 2. Typical recordings of cerebral potentials preceding voluntary right index finger flexions at different ages. In the left set of records from a subject of 31 years (a) the 3 different potentials BP, PMP and MP as described in Figure 1 are clearly discernable. In particular, a large BP with maximum at the vertex (C_z) and left-precentrally (C_3) is noted. In the right set of records from an older subject of 67 years, BP amplitude is grossly reduced. Electrode placements according to the 10/20 system, N = number of trials after editing.

0.01) and 0.66 for BP_0 ($2p < 0.001$). In Figure 4, the BP_{150} (stippled) and BP_0 (solid) single regression lines for the 6 leads are plotted. All correlations were significant on the basis of the two-tailed hypothesis except for BP_{150} at P_3 which was significant only in the one-tailed test.

Unlike the BP, the motor potential (MP) showed no significant reduction with age (double line in Figure 4, coefficient of determination r^2 = 0.066). The MP was measured as the potential difference BP_0 minus BP_{150} in the bipolar recording C_3/C_4 (Deecke et al., 1969, 1976). This finding indicates that the motor potential which reflects the activity in the contralateral motor cortex immediately prior to the onset of EMG activity, is relatively constant with age.

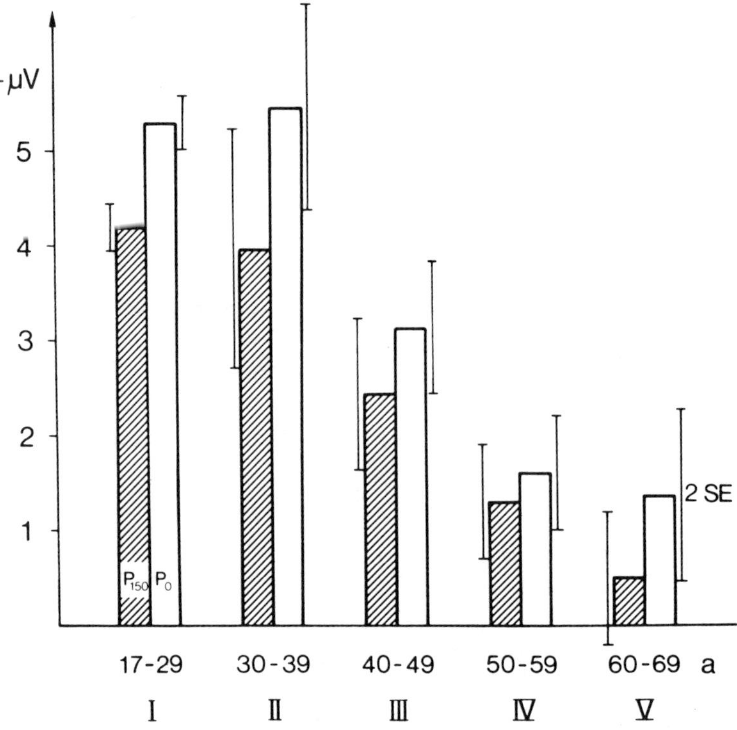

Figure 3. Mean *Bereitschaftspotential* in different age groups. Hatched columns, BP amplitude measured 150 msec prior to first EMG activity (P_{150}), blank columns, BP at first EMG activity (P_0). Group I (17–29 years) taken from 34 previous experiments (therefor smaller standard error, SE, than in groups II to V). Groups II to V consisted of 6 subjects each, on average 3 female, 3 male, 3 performing right, 3 left index finger flexions. Columns represent the mean amplitude per group. Mean BP per experiment was calculated from the 6 monopolar leads (C_3, C_4, C_z and P_3, P_4, P_z), in group I only 5, vertex (C_z) with maximum amplitudes not recorded (therefore, slightly smaller P_0 than in group II).

One finding deserves special attention. As is seen in Figure 4, the BP regression lines cross zero in the higher age groups beyond 65. This means that positive BPs occurred. An example for a positive BP in all monopolar leads in a 65-year-old subject is shown in Figure 5. In our younger subjects, positive BPs usually occur in the lateral frontal leads only (F_3 and F_4 not at F_z) but never in precentral or parietal leads (Figure 6). However, in two of our normal elderly subjects a global positivity in all monopolar recordings was observed. Positive BPs occurred in our cases of bilateral Parkinson's disease to the extent that the mean BP across all patients was slightly positive. We were surprised to note that

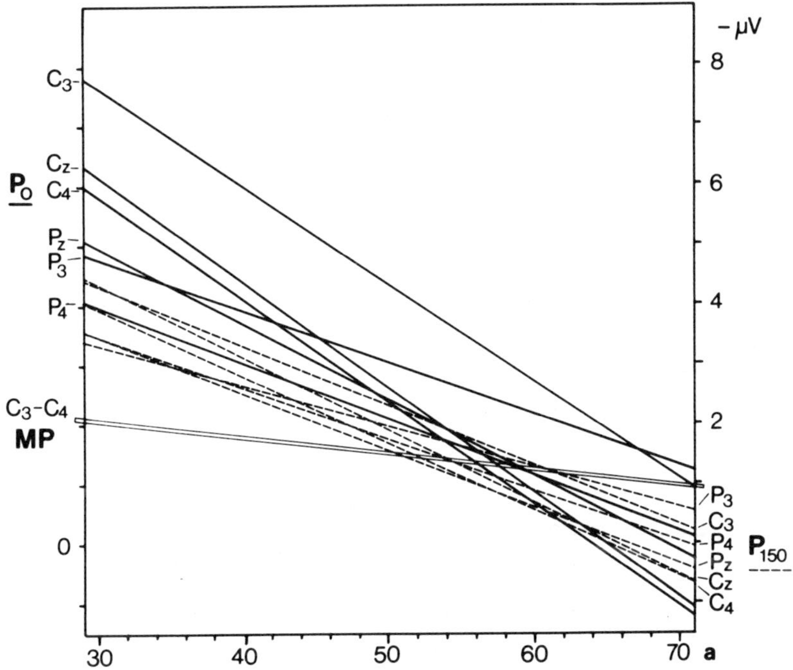

Figure 4. Regression lines of the *Bereitschaftspotential* (ordinate) versus age (abscissa) at the different recording locations. Solid lines for P_0 (amplitude at first EMG activity) with electrode position indicated on the left; dotted lines for P_{150} (amplitude 150 msec prior to first EMG activity) with electrode location on the right. For simplicity, subscript 3 stands for contralateral, subscript 4 for ipsilateral locations for left-sided movements as well as for right-sided movements. Double line for the motor potential (MP), measured as the difference $P_0 - P_{150}$ in the bipolar recording contralateral versus ipsilateral precentral ($C_3 - C_4$). All BP regressions were significant. Some cross the zero line at higher age above 65 which means that positive BPs were observed. The MP is more stable with age (correlation of determination, $r^2 = 0.066$).

an all-possitive BP could also occur in clinically healthy elderly subjects. It should be remembered that positivity is relative and can only be interpreted as less negativity over the cranial convexity than at the reference.

In view of similar positivities in cerebral disease (Parkinsonism), we were first inclined to attribute an all-positive BP to subclinical grades of cerebral atrophy or arteriosclerosis. However, we were able to test this notion with the advent of computerized tomography. Thus, 4 years after our experimental series, CT scans of the same subjects with positive BPs were performed. Figure 7 gives the computerized tomogram of the experimental subject of Figure 5, who was now 70 years old. Even at

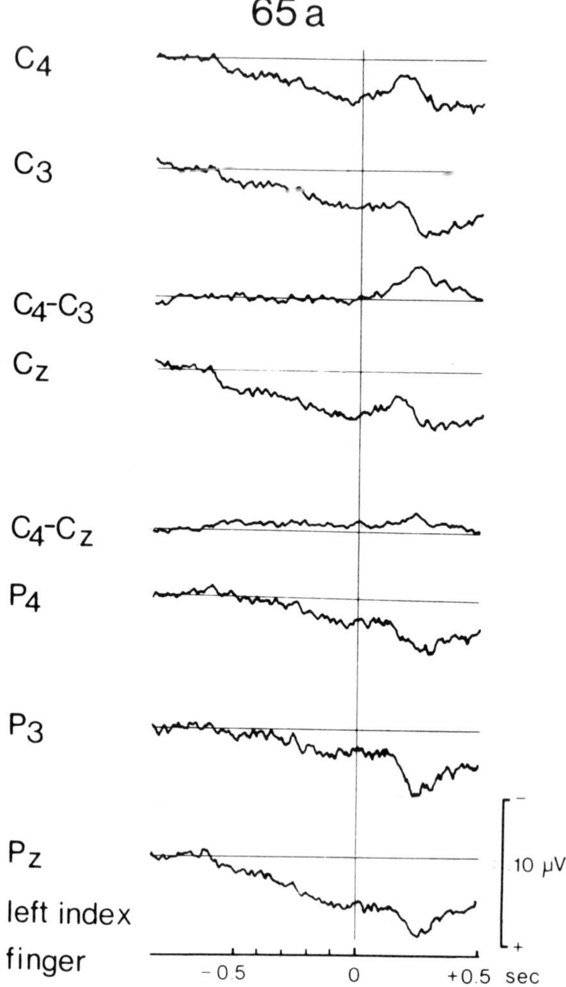

Figure 5. Positive *Bereitschaftspotential* in a 65-year-old subject. C_4, C_3, C_z and P_4, P_3, P_z were referred to linked earlobes. The subject performed 425 left-sided finger movements, but positivity occurred also with right-sided movements. The subject was a neurological in-patient just recovered from a lumbar slipped disc with radicular symptoms L 5 left. Her central neurological and mental state were normal and she had no brain atrophy as shown in the CT scan 4 years later (Figure 7).

this age, the person did not show the slightest sign of ventricular widening or enlargement of cortical sulci. The other subjects also showed no external or internal brain atrophy.

In conclusion, a gradual decrease of the average *Bereitschaftspotential* (BP) or readiness potential was found with age. This decline appears

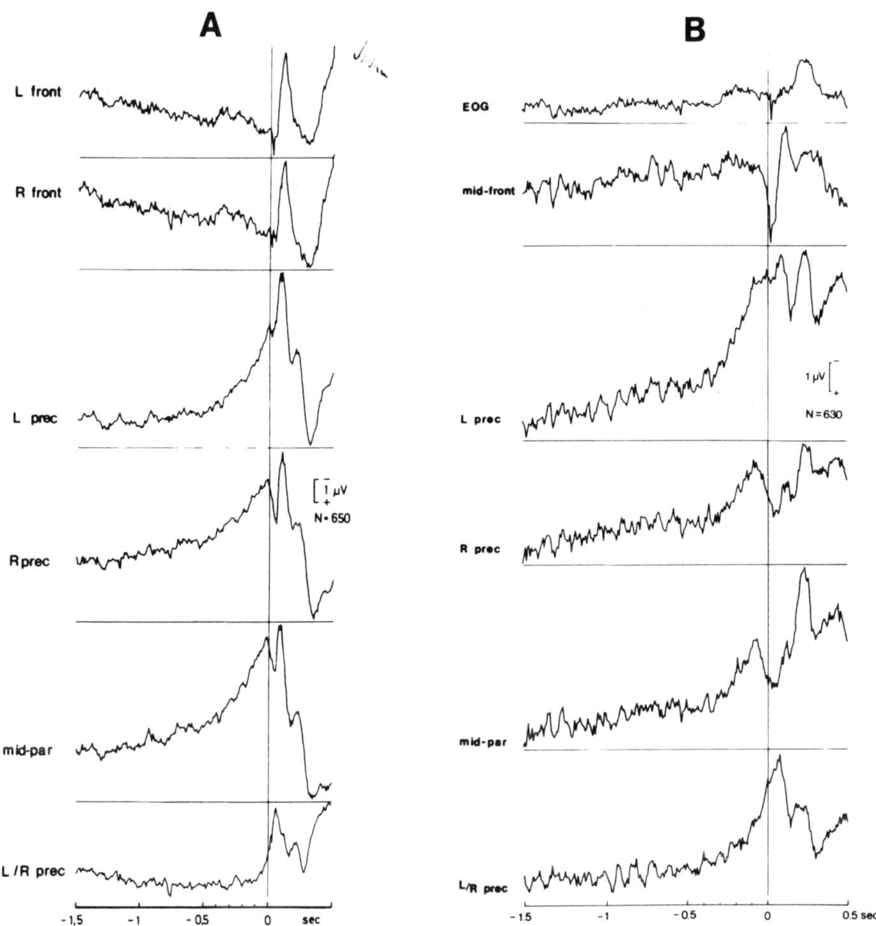

Figure 6. *Bereitschaftspotential* recordings in two young adult subjects including frontal electrode locations. In normal young subjects positive BPs occur only in the lateral frontal leads (A) but never in precentral or parietal leads. Also mid-frontally (B) a negative BP is found, which is due to the activity of the mesial supplementary motor cortex prior to voluntary movement (cf. Deecke and Kornhuber, 1978). Subject A performed 650, subject B 630 quick volar movements of the right index finger.

SOURCE: *Deecke et al., 1976, Figures 4 and 6.*

after the fourth decade of life. The reduction of BP as a result of aging is probably a true diminution of this cortical potential, which may be interpreted as a negative shift of the cortical DC-potential during preparation for movement. It seems unlikely that the reduction is solely caused by an increase in skull thickness or in the amount of cerebro-spinal fluid between the cortical surface and the skull. Such factors would affect

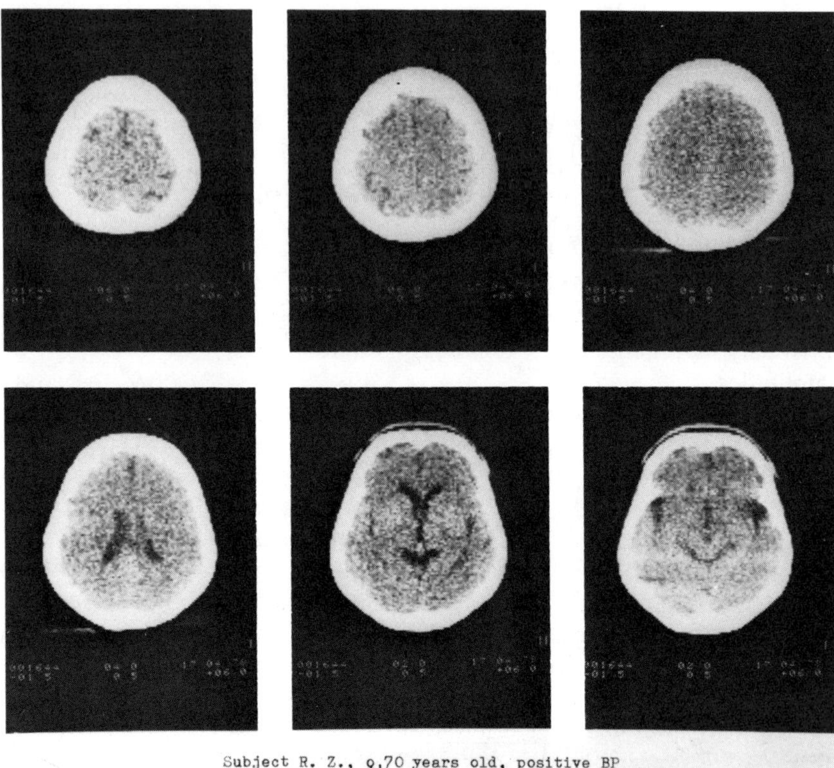

Figure 7. Representative sections of computerized cranial tomogram of subject R.Z., who had an all-positive *Bereitschaftspotential* as shown in Figure 5. CT scan was performed 4 years after the experiment and exhibited still no signs of cerebral atrophy neither externally (no enlargement of sulci, upper sections) nor internally (no widening of ventricles, lower sections). Thus an all-positive BP is not related to brain atrophy.

other potentials as well, and the amplitude of the alpha-rhythm, for instance, is not markedly reduced with age. Also, the fact that the motor potential was also not significantly affected by aging (Figure 4) is evidence against a general reduction of all cortical potentials with age. Late components of averaged evoked responses and the CNV have been reported by some authors to be reduced with age (Goodin et al., 1978) while others found little or no reduction in amplitude, if a certain level of motivation was maintained (Marsh, 1975; Lüders, 1970; Loveless and Sanford, 1974).

The factors responsible for the age-dependent reduction of the BP are unknown. Is it related to disappearance of certain functional elements of the cortex (neurons, synapses, etc.) with age? Two findings would argue against this assumption: 1. our normal subjects with all-positive BPs showed no brain atrophy in their computerized tomograms. 2. In contrast, in senile dementia patients who generally exhibit a global brain atrophy and thus a gross decrease in cortical elements, the late components of the visual evoked response III and IV were not diminished but actually enhanced in amplitude as compared to normal controls (Visser et al., 1976). It is true that normal aging causes a diffuse and progressive reduction of gray matter blood flow as shown by the Xenon inhalation technique (Naritomi et al., 1979). In addition, nerve cell loss with aging undoubtedly occurs in cortex, basal ganglia and brain stem (Brody, 1976; Bugiani et al., 1978; Monagle and Brody, 1974), but such reduction is obviously not necessarily related to a diminution of brain potential amplitudes.

The observation of occasional positive BPs in group V (60–69 years) deserves some comment. In young adults, positive BPs occur only in lateral frontal leads referred to linked ears or mastoids (e.g., F_3, F_4, Fp_1, Fp_2 but not at F_z due to the activity of the supplementary motor cortex prior to voluntary movement; Figure 6; Deecke et al., 1976; Deecke and Kornhuber, 1978). In patients with bilateral Parkinsonism, an all-positive BP is not unusual. There was a general slight positive BP when averaging over 10 cases (Deecke et al., 1977). It is surprising that occasional all-positive BPs can also occur in healthy elderly subjects. Positive BPs were observed in mentally retarded children (Karrer et al., 1978). With the use of ear or mastoid references in all the above cited studies, it remains unclear whether the observed positivity results from an absolute positivity over the skull convexity or from relatively stronger negativity at the reference electrodes which reflect activity from temporo-basal cortex or brain stem. A relation of BP positivity with cortical atrophy was excluded by CT.

Is there decreasing level of motivation, then, in the elderly that causes the progressive BP reduction? In young adults it has been shown that the BP amplitude is strongly dependent on intentional engagement or motivation (Kornhuber and Deecke, 1965; McAdam and Seales, 1969). Still, in view of numerous other possibilities, it is not feasible at present to prove *per exclusionem* lack of motivation to be a critical factor. Loveless (1979) testing evoked potential, contingent negative variation, and voluntary movement paradigms reported that the BP was not significantly reduced with age. But he used only 6 trials and our averages over 400–500 trials (after editing) are more reliable. To the extent that BP and late CNV reflect similar brain activity, the recent findings by Tecce et al. (1980) may be relevant. They found a selective diminution of CNV rebound recorded in frontal and central brain areas of old individuals that they attributed to a lack of attention rather than of motivation. Further studies are needed to clarify which is the major etiologic factor for the observed amplitude reductions or potential reversals in elderly subjects.

References

Brody H: An examination of cerebral cortex and brain stem aging. In Terry and Gershon (eds.) *Neurobiology of Aging. Aging, Vol. 3.* New York, Raven Press, 1976, pp. 177–181.

Bugiani O, Salvarani S, Perdelli F, Mancardi GL, Leonardi A: Nerve cell loss with aging in the putamen. *Europ Neurol* 17:286–291, 1978.

Deecke L, Scheid P, Kornhuber HH: Distribution of readiness potential, pre-motion positivity, and motor potential of the human cerebral cortex preceding voluntary finger movements. *Exp Brain Res* 7:158–168, 1969.

Deecke L, Becker W, Grözinger B, Scheid P, Kornhuber HH: Human brain potentials preceding voluntary limb movements. *Electroenceph Clin Neurophysiol* 33:(Suppl.)87–94, 1973.

Deecke L, Grözinger B, Kornhuber HH: Voluntary finger movement in man: cerebral potentials and theory. *Biol Cybern* 23:99–119, 1976.

Deecke L, Englitz H-G, Kornhuber HH, Schmitt G: Cerebral potentials preceding voluntary movement in patients with bilateral or unilateral parkinson akinesia. In Desmedt JE (ed.) *Attention, Voluntary Contraction and Event-related Cerebral Potentials. Prog Clin Neurophysiol Vol. 1.* Basel, Karger, 1977, pp. 151–163.

Deecke L, Kornhuber HH: An electrical sign of participation of the mesial "supplementary" motor cortex in human voluntary finger movement. *Brain Res* 159:473–476, 1978.

Deecke L, Englitz H-G, Schmitt G: Age-dependence of the Bereitschaftspotential. In Otto DA (ed.) *Multidisciplinary Perspectives in Event-related Brain Potential Research.* Washington, U.S. Government Printing Office, 1978, pp. 330–332.

Goodin DS, Squires KC, Henderson BH, Starr A: Age-related variations in evoked potentials to auditory stimuli in normal human subjects. *Electroenceph Clin Neurophysiol* 44:447–458, 1978.

Karrer R, Warren C, Ruth R: Slow potentials of the brain preceding cued and non-cued movement: effects of the development and mental retardation. In Otto DA (ed.) *Multidisciplinary Perspectives in Event-related Brain Potential Research.* Washington, U.S. Government Printing Office, 1978, pp. 322–329.

Kornhuber HH: Cerebral cortex, cerebellum and basal ganglia: an introduction to their motor functions. In Schmitt FO (ed.) *The Neurosciences III.* Study Program Cambridge-London MIT Press, 1974, pp. 267–280, III.

Kornhuber HH, Deecke L: Hirnpotentialänderungen beim Menschen vor und nach Willkürbewegungen, dargestellt mit Magnetbandspeicherung und Rückwärtsanalyse. *Pflügers Arch* 281:52, 1964.

Kornhuber HH, Deecke L: Hirnpotentialänderungen bei Willkürbewegungen und passiven bewegungen des menschen: bereitschaftspotential und reafferente potentiale. *Pflügers Arch* 248:1–17, 1965.

Lüders H: The effects of aging on the waveform of the somatosensory cortical evoked potential. *Electroenceph Clin Neurophysiol* 29:450–460, 1970.

Loveless NE, Sanford AJ: Effects of age on the contingent negative variation and preparatory set in a reaction time task. *J Geront* 29:52–63, 1974.

Loveless NE: Aging effects in simple RT and voluntary movement paradigms. In Kornhuber HH, Deecke L (eds.) *Motivation, Motor and Sensory Processes of the Brain. Electrical Potentials, Behaviour and Clinical Use. Prog Brain Res*, 54 (1980) in press.

Marsh GR: Age differences in evoked potential correlates of a memory scanning process. *Exp Aging Res* 1:3–16, 1975.

McAdam DW, Seales DM: Bereitschaftspotential enhancement with increased level of motivation. *Electroenceph Clin Neurophysiol* 27:73–75, 1969.

Monagle RD, Brody H: The effects of age upon the main nucleus of the inferior olive in humans. *J Comp Neurol* 155:61–66, 1974.

Naritomi H, Meyer JS, Sakai F, Yamaguchi F, Shaw T: Effects of advancing age on regional cerebral blood flow. *Arch Neurol* 36:410–416, 1979.

Tecce JJ, Savignano-Bowman J, Kahle JB: Effects of visual distraction on contingent negative variation and type A and B CNV shapes. In Otto DA (ed.): *Multidisciplinary Perspectives in Event-related Brain Potential Research*, Washington, U.S. Government Printing Office, 1978, pp. 358–363.

Tecce JJ, Yrchik DA, Meinbresse D, Dessonville CL, Cole JO: Age-related diminution of CNV rebound. I. Attention Functions. In Kornhuber HH, Deecke L (eds.): *Motivation, Motor and Sensory Processes of the Brain: Electrical Potentials, Behaviour and Clinical Use*, *Prog Brain Res* 54 (1980) in press.

Vaughan Jr HG, Costa LD, Ritter W: Topography of the human motor potential. *Electroenceph Clin Neurophysiol* 25:1–10, 1968.

Visser SL, Stam FC, van Tilburg W, op den Velde W, Blom JL, de Rijke W: Visual evoked responses in senile and presenile dementia. *Electroenceph Clin Neurophysiol* 40:385–392, 1976.

Stein, ed. The Psychobiology of Aging: Problems and Persepctives

A Fresh Look at Changes in Reaction Times in Old Age

P.M.A. Rabbitt

Department of Experimental Psychology, University of Oxford, South Parks Road, Oxford

Introduction

As people grow old the most striking change in their everyday competence is that they become slower. In psychological laboratories this change has been measured by the use of Choice Reaction Time tasks (C.RT tasks). In such tasks any one of a set of N different signals may occur on any trial and a subject has to make the appropriate one of N corresponding responses to it as fast and accurately as possible. The next signal then appears and the next response is made. This process continues until the experimenter is satisfied that there is enough data, until the subject grows mutinous or until other constraints terminate the experiment. Usually, but not invariably, young and elderly subjects have been compared at more than one level of task difficulty. Variations in difficulty are typically achieved by varying the number of different signals to each of which a different response is required. Results from very large number of such studies can be taken to suggest that changes in C.RT are more sensitive indices of changes in the CNS function accompanying old age than are any other measures yet available to human experimental psychologists (Birren, 1955, 1979; Birren, Riegel and Morrison, 1962; Botwinnick, Robbin and Brinley, 1960; Welford, 1958, 1965, 1977). This makes it all the more surprising that we still have no good theory as to what particular changes in CNS function these well-documented increases in C.RT may represent. It is also sad to observe that the data presently available are so inadequate that no model based upon them can be taken seriously.

Such hypotheses as have been put forward have centered around a single feature of C.RT data. People of all ages take longer to respond as the number of signals and responses between which they must choose (N) increases. Indeed this early finding by Merkel (1885) was replicated by Hick (1952) and extended to differences in signal probability by Hyman (1953). Hick formally expressed the relationship between C.RT and the number of signal and response alternatives (N) as a simple equation:

$$C.RT = a + b\,(\log_2 N + 1)$$

now known as "Hick's Law." The terms *a* and *b* represent empirically derived constants determining, respectively, the intercept and the slope of a linear relationship.

As Birren (1955, 1979) has often pointed out, the results of his own and many other studies all suggest that as people grow old the same relationship between C.RT and N persists, but *both* empirically derived constants, *a* and *b*, increase with age. In other words, both the slope and the intercept of the function illustrating the increase in C.RT with N grow larger as people get older; so that observed differences between the C.RTs of elderly and young subjects increase with task difficulty (N). Figure 1 plots data from an experiment by Rabbitt and Vyas (unpublished) to illustrate these relationships. Note that these data were obtained from subjects who were given very little practice (500 trials on each of 4 conditions).

Hick (1952) and Hyman (1953) suggested, and most subsequent research workers have adopted the idea, that the slope of the C.RT/$\log_2$N function can be used as an index of the maximum rate at which people can process information. Human beings were regarded as limited capacity single channel information processing systems which can process any amount of information up to, but not more than, some limiting value of X bits of information in unit time. The linearity of the C.RT/$\log_2$N function was held to be strong evidence for this finite information channel capacity (Hick, 1952; Fitts, 1954; Alluisi, Muller and Fitts, 1957; Garner, 1962). If we follow the same assumptions, we may say that information channel capacity reduces in old age. This is a useful general statement but we need to go beyond use of the information theory metric to inquire *why* this is so, or what happens to the aging CNS to produce this particular reduction in efficiency.

Birren (1979) reviews the question in a more practical way, pointing out that comparisons, such as that illustrated in Figure 1, can also be summarized by a statement that, as task efficiency increases, so does the *difference* between C.RTs of old and young subjects. This interesting way of looking at the data allows us to begin to formulate simple hypotheses based on the arithmetic of reaction times and neuronal function. For example, practiced young subjects in Simple RT tasks (one signal, one response) may attain mean RTs of 160–180 msecs. We can safely estimate that about 10 msecs of this time is necessary for processes in their peripheral sense organs [e.g., sensory integration time for light flashes at the retina (Pirenne, 1968)] and perhaps 20 msecs or more can be allowed for such factors as mechanical lag in the muscles and joints. This leaves 130 msecs to 150 msecs to be accounted for in terms of CNS events. Since we know that individual neurons cannot fire more often than once every millisecond, we must conclude that not more than 130 to 150 neuronal events, in series, can occur to bridge the gap between signal and response. Of course we need not take this to mean that *only* a chain of 150 neurons or 150 synapses intervene between eye and hand in such a transaction. Many parallel processes may, of course, be simultaneously carried on, but it is evident that no single one of these processes can involve more than 130 to 150 synaptic crossings.

As C.RT tasks become more difficult—for example, as the N of signals and responses increases—so C.RT rises. On the simple assumptions which we have adopted we may interpret this as happening because, as N increases, increasingly complex computations involving increasingly large numbers of different neurons become necessary. This gives us a simple functional hypothesis to explain why increases in C.RT with N become more marked in old age. Let us suppose that every CNS microevent (e.g., conduction across a synapse or transmission of a spike over a finite distance) is lagged by some constant, K msecs, in old people relative to the young. We may further suppose that K increases with age. Then a simple task, which requires only M such microevents, will be lagged by M × K msecs in an elderly population. Since we have already assumed that N increases with task difficulty, we must suppose that the age lag, M × K, increases proportionately. From these simple assumptions, we can predict both the rise with age in the slope constant, *b* for Hick's (1952) information transmission equation and the general increase in C.RT as a multiplicative function of age and task difficulty (for all sources of task difficulty, both increases in N and others) to which Birren (1979) has drawn our attention.

This would be a simple and satisfying story and it is a pity that there is no reason to believe that it is true. On the contrary, it faces problems at four different levels of explanation. First, on the straightforward question of empirical evidence, the data reviewed by Birren and others are certainly not general. In particular, these data were obtained from subjects who were given very little practice. When old and young subjects are given even moderate amounts of practice, the interaction between age and task difficulty disappears. A second problem is methodological. All the studies reviewed by Birren (1955, 1979), Botwinnick (1973), and Welford (1958, 1965, 1977), and indeed all studies in the

A

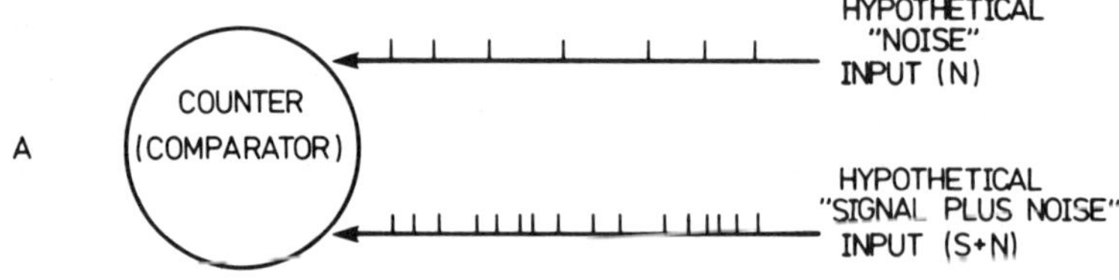

B

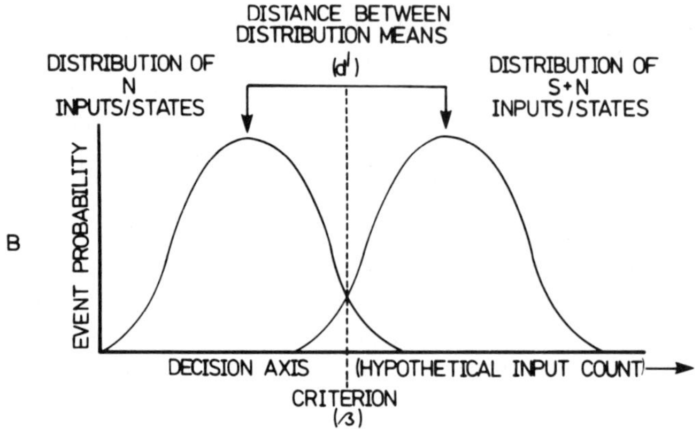

C

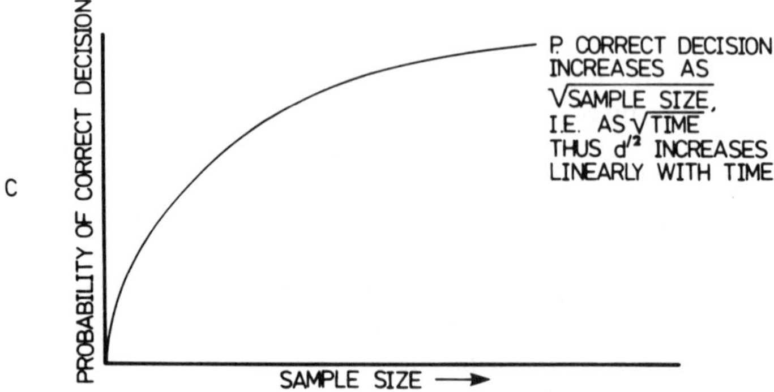

Figure 1. Decision criteria for a hypothetical comparator resolving noise from signal plus noise input. The conventional signal detection theory diagram for such a comparator is given under B. In C the relationship between sample size and accuracy derived from elementary sampling theory is illustrated. Part D shows the hypothetical movement of noise and signal plus noise distributions along the decision access as samples of events, and so implicitly reaction times increase in size.

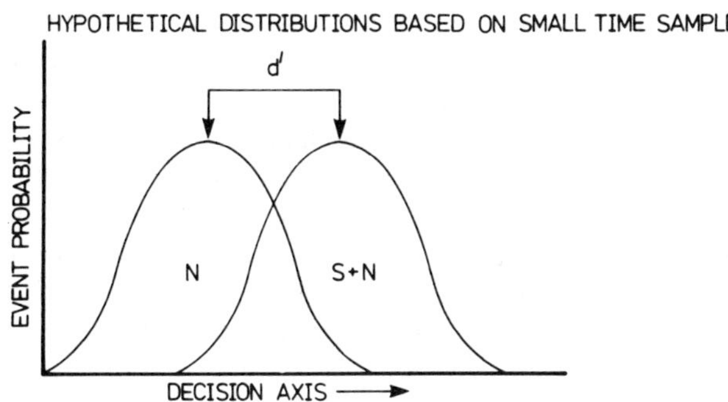

D

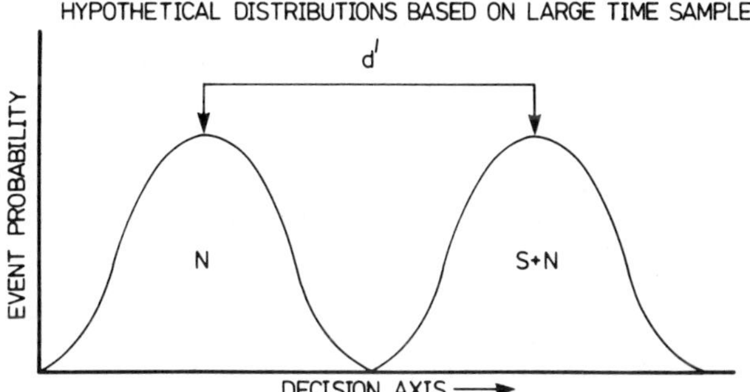

gerontological C.RT literature, without exception to date, have taken as performance indices only overall mean or median correct C.RTs and percentage error scores. They have sometimes also presented simple estimates of C.RT variance, but never *within* and always *between* subjects. Only sometimes have they equated error rates when comparing the C.RTs of old and young subjects.

Many recent investigations of C.RT tasks show that these simple indices are quite inadequate to assess differences in performance, whether between tasks or between individual subjects performing them (Olsen, 1977; Pacella and Pew, 1968; Pew, 1969; Rabbitt, 1979; Rabbitt and Vyas, 1970, 1979; Schouten and Bekker, 1967).

A third, associated, point is both methodological and theoretical. It is now generally known that we cannot regard human performance, even at apparently trivial C.RT tasks, as being a matter of the passive registration of a signal and the consequent reflex activation of a simple chain of neurons (which can be described as a Markov sequence of events with an overt response as the last event in the chain). We now realize that subjects continuously and actively control their performance from trial to trial in serial C.RT tasks. They discover both their own internal performance limitations and the limitations imposed on them by the task conditions and adapt their performance to optimize efficiency in regard to both (Rabbitt, 1979). They also actively make, and implement from moment to moment, complex cognitive decisions such as whether to strive for speed or accuracy and which of several different possible *kinds* of errors to allow themselves. In order to follow how subjects make these complex shifts in the parameters of active control we have to simultaneously measure, or derive, a large number of independent performance indices so that we can see how some of these indices relate to others.

Finally, a simple conceptualization of reaction time as the sum of delays involved in the completion of each of a linear string of successive neuronal events does not answer to our current best guesses about the way in which neuronal decision processes operate. These current assumptions give us a wide variety of predictions for the mutual relationships between C.RT task difficulty and advancing age, most of which are quite different from those which Birren (1979) and others seem to deduce from their reviews of the literature.

Let us consider in turn each of these four kinds of problems with current interpretations of age changes in C.RT, and see how the results and models now available guide us.

Recent Experimental Evidence: The Effects of Practice on Performance at Serial C.RT Tasks

Prolonged Practice and Serial C.RT Performance of Normal Young Adults

As we have seen, C.RT was found to increase with the binary logarithm of the number of signal and response states between which a subject must select [e.g., C.RT = a + b ($\log_2 N$ + 1); (Hick, 1952)]. It was soon recognized that this relationship only holds true relatively early in practice. Mobray and Rhoades (1959) found that one, highly practiced subject ceased to show any increase in C.RT between 2-choice, 4-choice and 8-choice C.RT tasks. Most investigators who have worked with C.RTs have, by now, satisfied themselves formally or informally of the reality of this effect. It is now known that, at least from 2-choice to 10-choice keyboard tasks, the slope of C.RT upon N for normal young adults reduces with practice until it becomes 0. The slope of C.RT on N for elderly subjects also steadily reduces with practice. Adequate data are not yet available so that it remains an open question whether, if old subjects practice long enough, they also may cease to show effects of N on C.RT over this range. If this turns out to be the case we will, of course, have to conclude that differences in the slope functions of C.RT upon N for old and young subjects do not vary over this range of task difficulty. In this case we would either find that after sufficient practice all differences in C.RT between old and young groups disappear, or more likely we would find that the C.RTs of the elderly are lagged, relative to those of the young, by an increase in a, the intercept constant of Hick's (1952) equation.

Work with other, more complex, tasks also involving RT measures suggests that these findings may be quite general. For example, memory search tasks examine variations in C.RT with the size of a target set of signals which a subject must identify, and briefly remember, in order to decide whether a subsequent probe signal is a target set member or not (e.g., Sternberg, 1966, 1975). In these tasks C.RT is found to increase linearly (rather than logarithmically) as the size of the target set is increased. In such tasks old subjects show increased slopes and intercepts for the linear functions relating C.RT to target set size, relative to young controls (Anders, Fozard and Lillyquist, 1972).

Once again recent work has shown that after extended practice young people cease to show any change in C.RT with target set size, and even cease to show negative transfer, when they are abruptly switched to discriminations involving unfamiliar target sets (Kristoffersen, 1976). Thus it is again an open question whether differences between young and old subjects would survive extended practice.

Finally Rabbitt (1962, 1965, 1967) found that when people scan displays to find target items embedded among background items, their scanning times increase with the number of different targets for which they have to search. Rabbitt (1965) reported that this increase in scanning time was more marked for old than for young subjects. Rabbitt, Cumming and Vyas (1979) have since observed that, after 30 days' practice, subjects take no longer to find one of 8 than one of 2 possible targets. Again this raises the question as to whether the interaction of age with task difficulty (number of targets) will survive extended practice.

The effects of Practice on Differences in C.RT Between Young and Old Subjects

1. *One-to-one signal to response mapping tasks.* Rabbitt and Vyas (unpublished) tested matched groups of 50 young (17 to 23 years) and 50 old (68 to 83 years) subjects on a computerized replication of Hick's (1952) Experiment using 2-choice, 4-choice and 8-choice conditons. Error rates did not differ significantly between age-groups at any stage in practice. Mean C.RTs for each task during the first and last 500 of 6,000 successive responses are given in Table 1.

   A 3-way Analysis of Variance gave significant main effects for differences between age groups ($F = 36.4$; df 1:98; $p < 0.01$), between tasks ($F = 42.1$; df 2:194; $p < 0.01$) and between trials early and late in practice ($F = 34.2$; df 1:98; $p < 0.01$). All interactions, i.e., those between age and practice, age and task difficulty, task difficulty and practice and age × task difficulty × practice were significant ($p < 0.01$ in each case). Table 1 shows that RTs were slower for the old than for the young throughout the task, that both groups improved with practice, and that the old improved with practice more than did the young. This improvement with practice was most marked in the difficult conditions. As practice continued, task difficulty had less effect on C.RT as we would predict from Mowbray and Rhoades (1959). For the present discussion, the salient point is that early-in-practice differences between C.RTs of old and young subjects become larger as task difficulty increases. Later-in-practice old people's C.RTs seem to be lagged by a constant relative to those of the young subjects at all levels of task difficulty.

2. *Practice and differences due to variations in signal set discriminability.* Jordan, Rabbitt and Vyas (1977) have described the results of 3 experiments in which C.RTs of both old and young subjects increased as discriminations between multidimensional displays became more difficult. Early-in-practice differences between C.RTs of old and young subjects increased as tasks became more difficult. Later-in-practice C.RTs for both groups still increased with task difficulty, but at all levels of task difficulty C.RTs of old subjects were lagged by a constant relative to those of the young.
3. *Practice and differences due to variations in response complexity.* Rabbitt, Fearnley and Vyas (1975) described a task in which young subjects responded to light signals by pressing keys with patterns of 1, 2, 3 or 4 simultaneous finger movements ("chords"). As expected, C.RT increased with chord complexity. Rabbitt, Jordan and Vyas (in press) repeated this experiment to compare groups of old and young subjects. In both groups C.RT increased with chord complexity. Early-in-practice differences between C.RTs of old and young subjects increased as chords became more complex. Later in practice, at all levels of chord complexity, C.RTs of old subjects were lagged by a constant relative to those of the young.

Table 1. Means of Mean RTs for 50 Young (Aged 17 to 30) and 50 Elderly (Aged 60 to 78) Subjects Early and Late in Practice at 2-choice, 4-choice and 8-choice Serial Self-paced Choice Tasks

	Responses 1 - 500			Responses 5501 - 6000		
	2-choice	4-choice	8-choice	2-choice	4-choice	8-choice
Young	430 $\sigma = 92$	720 $\sigma = 123$	830 $\sigma = 150$	260 $\sigma = 34$	418 $\sigma = 36$	509 $\sigma = 42$
Old	560 $\sigma = 141$	892 $\sigma = 214$	1104 $\sigma = 398$	356 $\sigma = 42$	518 $\sigma = 48$	582 $\sigma = 48$

The experiments we have reviewed cast doubt on the generality of the conclusion that age differences in C.RT increase with task difficulty. This is certainly true very early in practice, as in all the experiments reviewed by Birren, 1955, 1979; Botwinnick, 1973; Welford, 1958, 1965, 1977; and others. After very little practice, however, quite a different picture appears and it is possible that we shall find that in most tasks C.RTs of the old are lagged by a constant relative to those of the young across all levels of task difficulty.

Overall Mean C.RTs or Median C.RTs With Inter-subject Variance and Percentage Error Rates are Inadequate Indices on Which to Base Theories of Performance Changes in Old Age

It is now well known that in any C.RT task as subjects respond faster and faster they eventually reach a lower limit to RT at which further increases in speed lead to diminished accuracy (Olsen, 1977; Pacella and Pew, 1968; Pew 1969; Rabbitt and Vyas, 1970; Schouten and Bekker, 1967). Rabbitt and Vyas (1970) pointed out that this fact poses a problem of control. Experimenters usually give their subjects the vague exhortation "Respond as fast as you can and make as few errors as possible." Obviously subjects cannot know, in a novel task, just how fast they can respond before errors begin to become intolerably frequent. Thus they can only fulfill these instructions by responding faster and faster until errors occur, detecting the occurrence of these errors, and then "tracking" their response rate to stay within the fast optimum RT band which maximizes speed while maintaining accuracy. In other words they first discover, and then observe, the Speed Error Trade Off Limit (SETOL) at which gain in response speed begins to cost errors.

A simple graphical technique for computing Speed Error Trade Off Limits (SETOLs) for any subject in any task is given in Figure 2, which also illustrates how a subject must first discover his SETOL by making at least one error and then adjust the entire distribution of responses he emits in order to maximize speed while maintaining accuracy.

We see from Figure 2 that before we can usefully comment on a person's performance at any C.RT task, we need much more information than merely his overall mean correct C.RT or median C.RT with some indication of RT variance and percentage of errors he commits. We must know, at least:

1. How accurately he can detect any errors which he makes.
2. Whether all the errors he makes are of the same kind (and so can be related to the same RT distribution) or whether some errors which he makes occur for different reasons than others, so that we must relate sub-groups of errors to different error RT distributions (Rabbitt, 1979).

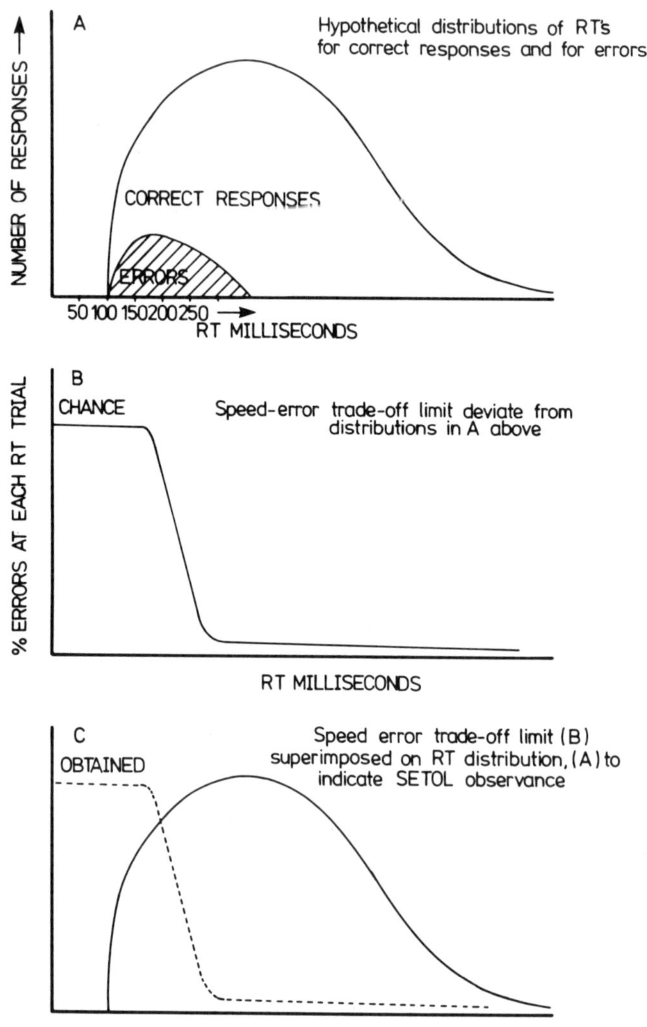

Figure 2. Speed-error trade-off limits calculated from distributions of reaction times for correct responses and errors.

3. We need to know the entire distribution of all his correct responses and also, separately, the entire distribution of all his incorrect responses. From these we may compute his SETOL for that particular task.
4. We must further relate the distributions of correct and incorrect responses which he actually emits to his obtained SETOL to see whether he has chosen to respond riskily, making many fast responses and sacrificing accuracy for speed, or whether he rather responds

cautiously, maintaining accuracy, but responding unnecessarily slowly. Unless we can obtain all these indices we cannot make useful comparisons between different groups of people or even between the same people on different occasions. This is because overall mean C.RT is extremely sensitive to very slight shifts in the skew of overall RT distributions. A shift in the skew of a C.RT distribution which results in only a fractional increase or decline in error rate (as a function of the number of fast, "risky" responses emitted) can show up as a shift of more than 150 msecs in computed overall mean C.RT. Moreover, since such shifts are shifts in *skew* they need not be signalled by large changes in the computed standard deviation of C.RT about a derived mean. Note that a shift of 150 msecs in overall mean RT represents a shift of 25% or more in measured mean RT relative to a (rather high) baseline of 600 msecs (in most published experiments ranges of measured C.RTs range from 250 msecs to 700 msecs). Note that differences in mean C.RTs between old and young subjects are very seldom as large as 25% of the young subjects' overall mean correct C.RT. Thus differences of 150 msecs or less between C.RTs of old and young subjects simply cannot be interpreted unless SETOLS and associated indices are computable. Such differences may mean any one of a number of things: for example, they may simply mean that the old people behave more cautiously than the young and control their C.RTs to avoid SETOLs by a very wide margin. Alternatively, they may also mean that old people have less fine control over their C.RTs from trial-to-trial. We cannot conclude from such data, without further evidence, that the old are simply *slower.*

Rabbitt (1979) tried to test this last notion, by comparing old and young subjects practiced on 2-choice serial C.RT task. He found that old people detected any errors which they made quite as efficiently as did the young. As usual, overall mean C.RTs were much slower for the old. However, surprisingly, mean C.RTs for *errors* were as fast for the old as for the young. It seemed that old and young had different SETOLs so that the old began to make errors in RT bands within which the young were still very accurate. But it also seemed that the old people regularly transgressed their SETOLs by a greater margin than did the young, and made relatively fast errors.

One possible, but highly counter-intuitive, hypothesis was that old people behave less cautiously than the young and brashly respond too fast trying to gain speed at the expense of accuracy. A closer examination of the data suggested that this was not so and that the result came about because the old subjects simply could not control their response speed from trial to trial as delicately as the young. When old subjects tried to respond just a little faster in order to track their SETOLs they instead made coarse, large reductions in C.RT which resulted in substantial transgressions of their SETOLs and in fast errors. When they tried to go a little slower in order to improve accuracy they again could only make coarse adjustments to their RTs which resulted in unnecessarily slow responses. Thus the characteristic of age changes in performance in this task seemed to be more a loss of fine control of timing of responses than either a marked increase in caution, or a progressive failure to monitor performance because of poor error-detection, or a very large shift in SETOL. In fact, the observed shifts in SETOLs from these data were 50 msecs or less, while the observed changes in overall mean C.RT were much higher. In other words, overall mean C.RT changed with age by significantly more than the critical, absolute limit to fast accurate performance.

This again emphasizes that the data currently available on age changes in C.RT are quite inadequate. This is as true of recent studies by the present author as it is of the vast number of earlier experiments reviewed by Birren, Botwinnick, Welford and others. A second, less immediate, methodological point is that, because subjects carrying out easy serial C.RT tasks rarely make more than 2% to 3% of errors we require many thousands of responses from them before we can obtain adequate correct RT and error RT distributions and compute SETOLs and indices of SETOL observance. This is yet another reason why data from unpracticed subjects is of little interest. These subjects are unpracticed precisely because they have had no chance to locate and to track their SETOLs. To do this they *must* make, and detect, many errors and so have a chance to make many hundreds of responses in aggregate. If we sample only 50 to 100 responses from individual subjects, we can examine only their performance over a period during which they had no idea where their SETOL for that task was located or how they might best distribute their RTs to maximize speed and accuracy. In other words, we test a performance which they can only have based on some general experience with quite different tasks. In the case of our elderly subjects this experience may not be either recent or vividly remembered. It would hardly be surprising if they needed more practice than the young to adjust to tasks so novel to them.

Some Alternative Assumptions in Terms of Which Models For Age-changes in C.RT May Be Formulated

If differences in C.RT between old and young people increased with task difficulty (and we have seen that we have no reason to believe that they do except in certain circumstances), a very simple functional explanation would be possible. We could suppose that in any given task detection of a signal and production of a response to it require at least M successive neuronal events, and that M increases as tasks become more difficult. We could further suppose that as people grow older each neuronal event is lagged by a constant, L. The total observed neuronal lag would then be M × L, and so would increase as tasks become harder. As we have seen, things are certainly not as simple as this. A first point is that we do not yet know what recent results by Rabbitt and Vyas (above), Jordan and Rabbitt (1976) or Rabbitt, Jordan and Vyas (1980) mean, because they again compare old and young subjects only in terms of their overall C.RTs and percentages of errors. Thus, the stable age-lags over a range of task difficulty observed in these experiments may mask significant changes in the relative positions of old and young people's SETOLs as task difficulty increases, may mask changes in the ways in which old and young subjects choose to observe their SETOLs in these different tasks, or may mask changes in the kinds of errors which old and young subjects commit and in the relative efficiency with which they detect these errors (Rabbitt and Vyas, 1970; Rabbitt, Cumming and Vyas, 1979). Until we have more data, we do not know how the old and the young modify adaptive control over their performance as tasks become more difficult, or even whether they exercise such active control to the same ends (i.e., do they differ in caution or impulsivity?). Thus, prior to considerations of models which are based on assumptions of particular changes in neuronal function with age, we need enough data to describe age-changes in terms of control system theory.

While admitting the lack of an adequate account at this intermediate level of explanation, we can already safely say that any model based on the assumption of a simple age-lag on all neuronal events is not likely to be correct on either empirical, theoretical or even logical grounds. First there is no good evidence that, in humans, speed of nerve conduction declines or synaptic delay increases in old age. Second, models for CNS processes which envisage simple chains or successive neuronal events are implausible. Neurons cannot simply act as passive transmitters and receivers of trains of pulses. Rather they must act as statistical decision-taking mechanisms, distinguishing between random inputs (Noise, N) and inputs provoked by real events (Signal plus Noise, S + N). Any particular neuronal center which must act as a comparator device to "decide" whether a particular signal has occurred must assess whether activity on the input lines which it monitors represents only random background Noise (N), or whether it rather represents Signal plus Noise (S + N). (See, for example, discussions of the psychophysics of signal detection by Green and Swets, 1966.) To make such a decision, the neural comparator must sample activity in the input line which it monitors for some finite period of time (see Figure 1a). Neural events—spikes for example—which occur during this sample must be counted in some way. A decision that a particular time sample of neural events contains N or S + N can only be made by reference to some *a priori* knowledge of the event probability density distributions which correspond to these two states (see Figure 1b). The longer the temporal sample of activity taken, the more accurate the discrimination between N and S + N states will be, since we know from elementary statistical sampling theory that the reliability of a statistical comparison increases as the square root of the size of sample upon which it is based (see Figure 1c). It follows that the longer subjects take to make a discrimination, the more likely they are to get it right. Conversely, the less time they take, the greater the probability of an error becomes. In other words we can deduce the necessity for a speed-error trade-off limit (SETOL) from these first principles.

It follows from the same assumptions that the more difficult N/S + N discriminations become, the longer time sample of activity will have to be taken to make them correctly, and so the longer C.RT we will observe. We can be more precise than this because, since the reliability of the N/S + N discrimination will increase as the square root of the time sample of events taken to make it, accuracy must increase as the square root of RT but RT must also, but the same argument, increase exponentially as discriminations become more difficult (for a similar argument applied to vigilance tasks see Taylor, 1967).

It is at once apparent that models based on these or similar assumptions [e.g., the "random walk" model proposed by Laming (1969) or the "accumulator" model proposed by Audley (1962), and further developed by Vickers, (1970, 1979)] offer a very wide variety of plausible hypotheses for the nature of processes which produce age changes in C.RT. One obvious hypothesis is that the level of random background noise in the CNs increases in old age. This idea was first put forward before signal detection theory, or similar metrics, were available to allow its full development (Crossman and Szafran, 1956).

In terms of a simple "comparator" model such as we have described, an increase in the *mean* level of CNS noise would result in a shift of the N probability-density function as illustrated in Figure 1d. All N/S + N discriminations would become more difficult, because although the S + N probability density distribution would also be moved to the right along the decision axis, the ratio of S events to N events would reduce, and the distance between the means of the hypothetical N and S + N distributions (i.e., d′ in signal detection theory notation) would diminish. Since all discriminations will thus become more difficult, longer time samples would have to be taken in order to make them correctly. Old people with "noisy" CNSs would thus take longer than young people to reach correct decisions. But a moment's thought shows that the precise *nature* of the *relative* changes in sample times required by old and young people as discriminations become more difficult cannot be derived immediately from these simple premises alone. If only the mean of the probability density distribution of N states increases with age, the difference Old RT—Young RT will probably increase exponentially as discriminations become more difficult (because discrimination difficulty is overcome in proportion to $\sqrt{RT}$). However, if both the mean and the variance of the N distribution changes with age, and if the mean and variance of the S + N distribution also changes, but in a different way, predictions are much less clear and a variety of special cases can be formulated depending on the particular assumptions made. Among a range of possible predictions is one that over a particular range of discrimination difficulty the sample times (RTs) necessary for old people will appear to be lagged by a constant relative to those necessary for the young—when the rather coarse limits of experimental accuracy are taken into consideration.

This simple model raises other interesting lines for speculation. It assumes that decision reliability increases as the square root of decision time; that is, as the square root of the time sample of neural events on which the decision is based. Clearly, accuracy cannot indefinitely increase as samples become indefinitely large. This is not just because the square root law assumes diminishing returns of accuracy for increases in sample size. There are also functional considerations since a running count or "tally" of events, accumulated during a long time sample, obviously cannot be stored anywhere except in a noisy neuronal system. It follows that indefinitely large sample sizes will be impractical, since the running tally of events sampled will be progressively made more inaccurate by random noise as sample durations increase. This suggests the interesting idea of a "delay-error trade-off" which may result in decisions becoming increasingly inaccurate as the samples of events on which they are based increase beyond a maximum duration. On such a model very slow RTs might be more inaccurate than others. Again, if this is so, and if CNS noise increases with age, the maximum useful sample size will also reduce with age. Thus the optimum band of RTs within which decisions could be made would be narrower as age increases. In everyday terms, if a young man takes longer than X msecs to make a decision he may become progressively more likely to get it wrong, but if an old man does not make a decision even faster, i.e., within X–Y msecs, he should not hope to get it right.

If our old subjects also face this limitation, the efforts which they make to adjust their decision criteria to their failing capacity will also determine the sample sizes on which they operate. On the one hand, as decisions become more difficult, RT differences between young and old subjects could again be affected in a variety of complex ways. The point need not be further labored that any model based only on shifts in overall correct C.RT, whether these appear as "constant lags" or "age × task difficulty interactions" gives us no real insight into the nature of CNS changes accompanying advancing age. On the other hand, the theoretical apparatus developed from signal detection theory is now powerful enough to generate very specific, testable predictions for subtle changes in several performance parameters simultaneously.

Conclusion

One of the most striking changes in performance with advancing age is the concomitant slowing of choice reation time (C.RT). This has been investigated in scores of laboratory experiments but we must conclude that we still know very little about it. Most experiments which have compared the C.RTs of old and young people have found that as task difficulty increases the C.RTs of the old rise more sharply than those of the young.

This conclusion applies only for subjects in the very earliest stages of practice. If subjects are extensively practiced, C.RT may be invariant over a wide range of task difficulties. Moreover when old and young subjects are given only a moderate amount of practice on the same experiments, the C.RTs of the old appear to be lagged by a constant relative to those of the young. Even these recent data are of very limited interest. If we are to compare the performance of old and young subjects, we need to examine the entire RT distributions of their correct and incorrect responses to determine what speed-error trade-off-limits restrict their performance in each group. In addition it is important to examine how subjects within each group adjust their RT distributions to observe their own limitations. Without such data age-changes in overall mean C.RT are not interpretable.

An important first step is to gather enough data so that we can have reasonable descriptions of age-changes in performance in terms of control system models. When such data are available, and when we have selected among the alternative control system descriptions of age-changes, we may profitably begin to speculate further and try to fit our data to models based on various possible assumptions about the nature of changes in CNS function and neuronal function in old age. Until we can do this, it is probably a waste of time to adopt prematurely any oversimplified working hypothesis such that: "as people grow older the time required for any individual neuronal event increases." This is because the little we know about decision processes in the CNS suggests that it is naive to regard such processes as mediated by passively activated chains of successive events. Rather we must regard transactions between neurons as statistical decision processes by means of which "the system" decides whether only random background neural activity (Noise) or an actual event (Signal plus Noise) has occurred during a particular period of time.

As a simple exercise, it can be shown that if we suppose that the level of random neural activity (Noise) in the CNS increases with age, we can generate a large variety of predictions from elementary signal detection theory which will fit many different possible patterns of interaction between age, task difficulty and C.RT. The provision of reliable data to guide us would represent an extremely useful advance.

References

Alluisi EA, Muller PF Jr, Fitts PM: An information analysis of verbal and motor responses in a forced-paced serial task. *J Experimental Psychology 53:*153–158, 1957.

Anders TR, Fozard JL, Lillyquist TD: Effects of age upon retrieval from short-term memory. *Developmental Psychology* 6:214–217, 1972.

Audley RJ: A stochastic model for the act of choice. In Nagel E, Suppes P, Tarski A (eds.) *Logic, Methodology and Philosophy of Science: Proceedings of the 1960 International Congress*. Stanford University Press, 1962.

Birren JE: Age changes in speed of simple responses and perception and their significance for complex behavior in old age in the Modern World. *Report of the 3rd Congress of the International Association for Gerontology, London, 1954*. Edinburgh, Livingstone, 1955, pp. 235–247.

Birren JE: Tutorial review of changes in choice reaction time with advancing age. In Baumeister H (ed.) *Bayer Symposium No. 6*. Bonn, Springer Verlag, 1979.

Birren JE, Riegel KF, Morrison DF: Age differences in response speed as a function of controlled variations in stimulus conditions. Evidence of a general speed factor. *Gerontologia* 6:1–18, 1962.

Botwinnick J: Aging and Behavior. New York, Springer Publishing Co. Inc., 1973.

Botwinnick J, Robbin JS, Brinley JF: Age differences in card sorting performance in relation to task difficulty, task set and practice. *J Experimental Psychology* 59:10–18, 1960.

Crossman ERFW, Szafran J: Changes with age in the speed of information intake and discrimination. *Experientia Supplimentum* 4:128–135, 1956.

Fitts PM: The information capacity of the human motor system in controlling the amplitude of movement. *J Experimental Psychology* 47:381–391, 1954.

Green DM, Swets JA: Signal Detection Theory and Psychophysics. New York, John Wiley, 1966.

Garner WR: Uncertainty and Structure as Psychological Concepts. New York, Academic Press, 1962.

Hick WE: On the rate of gain of information. *Quarterly J Experimental Psychology* 4:11–26, 1952.

Jordon TC, Rabbitt PMA: Response times to stimuli of increasing complexity as a function of aging. *Brit J Psychology* 68:189–201, 1977.

Merkel J von: Die zeitlichen Verhaltness der Willensthatigheit. *Philosophische Studien* 2:73–127, 1885.

Mowbray GH, Rhoades MV: On the reduction of choice reaction time with practice. *Quarterly J Experimental Psychology* 11:16–23, 1959.

Olsen R: Three kinds of speed-error trade-off. In Dornic S (ed.) *Attention and Performance VI.* Hillsadale, New Jersey, Lawrence Erlbaum Associates, 1977.

Pacella RE, Pew R: Speed-accuracy trade-off in reaction times: effect of discrete criterion times. *J Experimental Psychology* 76:19–24, 1968.

Pew RW: The speed-accuracy operating characteristic. In Korter WE (ed.) *Attention and Performance II. Acta Psychologica* 30:16–26, 1969.

Pirenne I: *The Eye,* 4th edition. Oxford University Press, 1968.

Rabbitt PMA: An age decrement in the ability to ignore irrelevant information. *J Gerontology* 20:233–238, 1965.

Rabbitt PMA: Age and discrimination between complex stimuli. In Welford AT, Birren JE (eds) *Behavior, Aging and the Nervous System.* Springfield, ILL., Charles C Thomas, 1965.

Rabbitt PMA: Chapter in Holden, 2 (ed.) *Motor Skill,* 1980. In press.

Rabbitt PMA: Current paradigms and models in human information processing. Ch. 4. In Hamilton V, Warburton D (eds.) *Human Stress.* John Wiley, 1979.

Rabbitt PMA: How old and young subjects monitor and control responses for accuracy and speed. *Brit J Psychology* 70:305–311, 1979.

Rabbitt PMA, Cumming G, Vyas SM: Improvement, learning and retention of skill at visual search. *Quarterly J Experimental Psychology* 31:441–459, 1979.

Rabbitt PMA, Jordan TC, Vyas SM: Effects of response complexity in old age. Submitted to J Gerontology, 1980.

Rabbitt PMA, Vyas SM: An elementary preliminary taxonomy for some errors in laboratory choice RT tasks. *Acta Psychologica* 33:56–76, 1970.

Rabbitt PMA, Vyas SM: Response times to stimuli of increasing complexity as a function of aging. Submitted to J of Gerontology, 1980.

Rabbitt PMA, Vyas SM, Fearnley S: Programming sequences of complex responses. In Rabbitt PMA, Dornic S (eds.) *Attention and Performance V.* London & New York, Academic Press, 1975.

Schouten JF, Bekker JAM: Reaction time and accuracy. In Sanders AF (ed.) *Attention and Performance.* Amsterdam, The Netherlands, North Holland Publishing Company, 1967.

Sternberg S: High speed scanning in human memory. *Science* 153:652–654, 1966.

Sternberg S: Memory scanning. New findings and current controversies. *Quarterly J Experimental Psychology* 27:1–32, 1975.

Vickers D: Evidence for an accumulator model of psychophysical discrimination. *Ergonomics* 13:37–48, 1970.

Vickers D: Decision processes in visual perception. John Wiley, 1979.

Welford AT: Aging and Human Skill. Oxford, England, Oxford University Press for the Nuffield Foundation, 1958.

Welford AT: Performance, biological mechanisms and age: a theoretical sketch. In Welford AT, Birren JE (eds.) *Behavior, Aging and the Nervous System.* Springfield, Ill. Charles C Thomas, 1965.

Welford AT: Serial reaction times, continuity of task, single channel effects and age. In Dornic S (ed.) *Attention and Performance VI.* Hillsdale, New Jersey, Lawrence Erlbaum Associates, 1977.

Index